T0311616

INSTITUTIONAL ECONOMICS

VOLUME ONE

INSTITUTIONAL ECONOMICS

Its Place in Political Economy

VOLUME ONE

John R. Commons

with a New Introduction by
Malcolm Rutherford

Routledge
Taylor & Francis Group

LONDON AND NEW YORK

Originally published in 1934 by the Macmillan Company

Published 1990 by Transaction Publishers

Published 2017 by Routledge
4 Park Square, Milton Park, Abingdon, Oxon OX14 4RN
605 Third Avenue, New York, NY 10017

Routledge is an imprint of the Taylor & Francis Group, an informa business

New material this edition copyright © 1990 by Taylor & Francis.

Library of Congress Catalog Number: 89-32259

Library of Congress Cataloging-in-Publication Data

Commons, John Rogers, 1862-1945.
    Institutional economics : its place in political economy / John R. Commons; with a new introduction by Malcolm Rutherford.
        p. cm.
    Reprint. Originally published: New York: Macmillan, 1934.
    Bibliography: p.
    Includes index.
    ISBN 0-88738-797-7
        1. Institutional economics. I. Title.

HB99.5.C65   1986   89-32259
330—dc20   CIP

ISBN: 978-0-88738-797-5 (pbk)(v.1)
ISBN: 978-0-88738-831-6 (v.2)
ISBN: 978-0-88738-832-3 (2 vol. set)

TABLE OF CONTENTS

CHARTS

TABLES

INTRODUCTION TO THE TRANSACTION EDITION

This reissue of J. R. Commons' major work, *Institutional Economics: Its Place in Political Economy,* is particularly timely as interest in Commons' work has never been greater. At least fifteen substantial articles dealing exclusively or largely with Commons' ideas have been published in the last six years alone, and many more are either forthcoming or currently in preparation.[1] In contrast, the secondary literature on Commons prior to this was both relatively sparse and episodic in character. Even as recently as the period between 1970 and 1980, when the secondary literature began to grow, a single special issue of the *Journal of Economic Issues* accounted for almost half of the significant output.[2] It is also noticeable that whereas virtually all of the secondary literature used to be produced by institutionalists for institutionalists, the more recent work on Commons includes papers written by noninstitutionalists and directed at noninstitutionalist audiences (see particularly Endres 1985; M. Perlman 1986; and Vanberg 1988).

This growing and broadening interest in Commons is undoubtedly due to the general revival of concern with the role of institutions in economics, and, more particularly, to the rapid growth in the attention being given to issues such as the importance of property rights, the behavior of courts and the evolution of common law, the behavior of legislatures and the determination of statute law, the evolution of organizational forms, and the use of the transaction as a basic unit of analysis. All these issues were among Commons' central concerns but did not figure largely in the work of the other leading early institutionalists. Commons is quite alone among the major writers in the American institutionalist tradition in the extent of his interest in law and organizations and their evolution, and it is exactly this that gives Commons' work its considerable contemporary relevance.

The fuller recognition of Commons' work and its present-day importance is, however, hindered by a number of widely held beliefs. It is accepted by many that Commons, like some other institutionalists of his time, produced work that was almost entirely descriptive and lacking in theoretical content. Commons has also been accused of taking a "naive," "collectivist" approach to institutions, conceptualizing them entirely as the intended outcomes of processes of deliberative collective decision making (Seckler 1966; 1975), and this claim has often been repeated (Schotter 1981; Langlois 1986). As more and deeper readings of Commons' work have appeared these two conceptions have been repeatedly challenged. Commons' work does contain a conceptual and theoretical framework (although not one that lends itself to making exact predictions), and his approach to institutions, although emphasizing the collective processes through which conflicts are resolved and particular rules enforced, is neither "naive" nor inconsistent with the idea that social customs and common practices can arise in an unplanned and spontaneous fashion (see Rutherford 1983; Chasse 1986; Vanberg 1988; Biddle 1988A).

Perhaps more serious, because it is not as possible to refute, is the view of Commons' writings, and particularly of *Institutional Economics*, as difficult, obscure, full of unfamiliar terminology, and requiring great effort to understand. Right from the very first appearance of *Institutional Economics* the book was assailed as "ponderous," "curiously disorganized, and filled with vagueness, clumsy terminology, rambling digressions and tedious repetition" (Bye 1935, pp. 201–2). Its length, organization, and style make it quite daunting, and most of its potential readership, particularly among more orthodox economists, have probably never even opened its pages, being dissuaded by its awful reputation alone. Yet, as Frank Knight argued in his 1935 review, "if they will take it in the right spirit, minds trained in orthodox economic theory and devoted to clarity, definiteness and 'system' are the very ones to read it with great profit" (Knight 1935, p. 805).

This introduction attempts both to underline the continuing relevance of the ideas contained within *Institutional Economics* and to increase their accessability. Some analysis of the place and organization of the book will be provided first, to be followed by a discussion of some of the major themes in the book and their role in Commons' overall conceptual framework. Introductions such as this usually devote considerable space to biographical information, but this will not be done here. The relevant details of Commons' life are already well known and easily available elsewhere (Commons 1934B; S. Perlman 1945; Harter 1962).

THE PLACE OF *INSTITUTIONAL ECONOMICS*

In order to fully understand *Institutional Economics* it is important to comprehend its place in Commons' work in relation both to Commons' other theoretical writings and to his many empirical investigations and vast practical experience. Commons is often regarded as a simple empiricist, deriving his more theoretical ideas directly from his own experience. Commons himself encouraged this view, opening *Institutional Economics* with the words: "My point of view is based on my participation in collective activities, from which I here derive a theory of the part played by collective action in control of individual action" (p. 1). This is a little misleading. From the very beginning of his career Commons was concerned with the development of conceptual and theoretical ideas, and one can trace an intellectual evolution in Commons' work that operated through the *testing* and subsequent modifying of his ideas in the light of his practical experiences. This evolution begins with *The Distribution of Wealth* (1893), and proceeds through *Proportional Representation* (1896), *A Sociological View of Sovereignty* (1899–1900), to *The Legal Foundations of Capitalism* (1924), *Institutional Economics* (1934A) and, finally, to *The Economics of Collective Action* (1950) published five years after Commons' death.

Commons' first major book, *The Distribution of Wealth*, attempts to combine marginalist notions concerning value and distribution with historicist ideas and reformist concerns. It reveals the pervasive influence of R. T. Ely in its emphasis on property rights and institutionalized monopoly advantages and privileges. It is clear that the attempt to expand economic theory to include extensive consideration of the role of property rights was a goal that Commons adopted from the outset and never abandoned. In *The Distribution of Wealth* he argues that "the place of law in Political Economy is a subject which has received from English economists no attention at all commensurate with its far-reaching importance." The "English economists have taken the laws of private property for granted, assuming that they are fixed and immutable," but such laws are "changeable," have a "profound influence upon the production and distribution of wealth," and are therefore in need of close examination (p. 59). It is in this broad sense that it is true that *The*

Distribution of Wealth "contains the foundations of Commons' economics" (Dorfman 1963, p. xv).

More specifically, Commons was concerned with the conflict between labor and capital and particularly with the position of labor, and this was a concern that persisted throughout Commons' career. Commons discussed the problems of low wages and unemployment and contrasted labor's position with the ability of businesses to generate and capitalize rents out of patents, copyrights, trade names, franchises, monopoly and "good-will." The issues of monopoly rents and good-will were developed later into his extensive discussions of intangible property, but his more immediate response to the problems faced by labor was to suggest the creation of a "right to employment" secured by government. At this point in his thinking Commons looked to direct government regulation and action to bring about institutional change although he believed that this was unlikely to occur given the then current form and composition of government. Commons, therefore, turned his attention to political reform, notably proportional representation, and to the development of a theory of the sociological basis of sovereignty.

In his essay *A Sociological View of Sovereignty* Commons analyses two historical processes. In the first, "the state gradually deprives other institutions of the right to use violence," while, in the second, "new groups force their way into the coalition controlling the state" (Chasse 1986, p. 761). The state is thus "an accumulated series of compromises between social classes, each seeking to secure for itself control over the coercive elements which exist implicitly in society with the institution of private property" (Commons 1899–1900, p. 45). These ideas are retained and developed in Commons' later works, but at this time proportional representation was the institutional adjustment that Commons thought would best continue the historic process of compromise between social classes. Commons' view was that territorial representation resulted in weak candidates who concentrated on not making enemies. What was required was a government consisting of individuals representing identifiable interests groups and who could argue and negotiate for those groups. Related to this was Commons' critique of traditional "log-rolling" activities among legislators and his concern that courts and commissions might be taking over legislative functions (Chasse 1986, pp. 762–63).

Between the turn of the century and the publication of his next major theoretical work in 1924, Commons was heavily involved in the empirical investigation of labour unions, in collective bargaining and mediation, in the work of bodies such as the U.S. Industrial Commission, the Industrial Relations Commission, the Wisconsin Industrial Commission, the Federal Trade Commission, and the National Monetary Association, and in the study of law and the basis of court decisions. These experiences deeply affected his earlier views — not on the importance in economics of property rights, nor the "fundamental vision" outlined in *A Sociological View of Sovereignty* (Chasse 1986, p. 762) — but on how particular institutions functioned and how the needed compromise between social classes could best be accomplished. His many "experiments in collective action," as he called them, gave him a very different view of legislatures, log-rolling, and the potential of courts and commissions. As Chasse has said: "From sweeping legislative changes, he turned to more flexible devices — commissions with insulated staffs, the courts, and independent outside interest groups affecting the state through 'the device of collective bargaining'" (Chasse 1986, p. 766).

Commons' mature views are presented in his three major books, *The Legal Foundations of Capitalism, Institutional Economics*, and *The Economics of Collective Action*, of which the second is by far the most important. It represents Commons' last major and most complete "research statement" (Parsons 1985). *The Legal Foundations* concentrates more narrowly on the history of court decisions and the concept of reasonableness as used by the courts. *Institutional Economics* both incorporates and refines this analysis and seeks to bring it together with a discussion of the evolution of economic ideas and the nature of a fully "rounded out" political economy. It is Commons' most complete attempt to incorporate legal institutions within economics. By contrast *The Economics of Collective Action* is a simplified exposition of his main ideas and not itself a major research treatise (Parsons 1950, p. 10). Thus, despite the later work, *Institutional Economics* stands as Commons' *magnum opus* (Coats 1983), the intellectual culmination of his extraordinary career as both theorist and practical experimentalist.

THE PURPOSE AND ORGANIZATION OF *INSTITUTIONAL ECONOMICS*

Institutional Economics is a difficult book in part because of its complexity of purpose and the way in which Commons organized his material. Commons' overall objective in the book was to give institutional economics — by which he meant the study of "collective action in control of individual action" or the "proprietary economics of rights, duties, liberties, and exposures" (pp. 1, 8) — its proper place in "the whole of a rounded-out theory of Political Economy" (p. 6). However, this involved neither a simple substitution of institutional for other types of economics, nor (as in his earlier *Distribution of Wealth*) a simple coupling of institutional concerns onto existing economic analysis. Existing types of economic analysis often masked the role of institutions within their basic conceptual frameworks. The problem was to reinterpret existing economic concepts, to tease out their hidden meanings and in this way to "include and give a proper place to all the economic theories since John Locke" (p. 6). Thus, in the preface to *Institutional Economics* Commons states that: "Each idea here incorporated is traced back to its originator, and then the successive modifications of that idea are developed and the earlier double or treble meanings of the idea are separated, until each, as a single meaning, is combined with the others in what I conceive to be the Science of Political Economy as it is developing since the last Great War" (p. v). Similarly, in the introduction, Commons writes that "institutional economics consists partly in going back through the court decisions of several hundred years" and also "in going back through the writings of economists from John Locke to the Twentieth Century, to discover wherein they have or have not introduced collective action" (p. 5).

An added complication is that *Institutional Economics* is a book that also deals at length with Commons' own experiences, his "years of experiment" (p. 9), so that the complete expression of his objective is found in his statement: "What I have tried to do is to work out a system of thought that shall give due weight to all economic theories, modified by my own experience" (p. 8). These experiences and their results sometimes take up lengthy sections of the book, for example thirty-three pages deal with his efforts in setting up unemployment and accident insurance programs (pp. 840–73), but throughout the book Commons is making references to his wide experience — from his involvement in the Pittsburgh-Plus case to his investigations of the Federal Reserve System.

Organizationally, *Institutional Economics* is deeply affected by the nature of Commons' objectives. On one level the book is organized around the central concepts of "Method," "Efficiency," "Scarcity," "Futurity," and "Reasonable Value." However, running through and around these themes is Commons' discussion of the history of economic thought. The chapter entitled "Method" starts with a discussion of Locke but then moves into a detailed outline of Commons' own views on transactions, his basic unit of analysis. The history of economic thought theme is picked up again in the next five chapters entitled respectively "Quesnay," "Hume and Peirce," "Adam Smith," "Bentham versus Blackstone," and "Malthus." These chapters deal with a variety of issues including matters of method, particularly Commons' pragmatism, the role of scarcity and conflict in economics as opposed to a presumed harmony of interest, and the importance of custom and common law as opposed to individual pleasures and pains. A more generalized treatment and elaboration of some of these issues is provided in the first six sections of the next chapter "Efficiency and Scarcity." The last four sections return to the history of thought with a more explicit discussion of the efficiency and scarcity theme in connection with Ricardo and Malthus, Marx and Proudhon, and Menger, Wieser, Fisher and Fetter. The next chapter on "Futurity" covers an astonishing two hundred and fifty-nine pages and deals with many and various aspects of incorporeal and intangible property and with Commons' profit margin theory of business depressions. The first part of the chapter contains a lengthy treatment of the work of Henry Dunning MacLeod. The writings of Sidgwick, Knapp, Hawtrey, Cassel, Wicksell, and Bohm-Bawerk are also discussed. The next chapter on "Reasonable Value" is almost as long and opens with a critical discussion of Veblen, particularly his treatment of intangible property. It then proceeds into a discussion of the behaviour of legislatures and courts in bringing about a reconciliation of conflicting interests and, notably, a limitation of the use of economic power to reasonable levels. The final chapter "Communism, Fascism, Capitalism" deals more briefly with Commons' views on how best to avoid totalitarian solutions to society's conflicts.

In overall terms, it is particularly important to understand the exact purpose of Commons' extensive discussions of the history of economic thought. In line with his philosophical pragmatism "Commons did not want to passively reflect the ideas of the past, but to engage in a dialogue with them — using them as raw material to be blended with his own experiential knowledge and shaped into tools for understanding and solving present-day problems" (Biddle 1988B, p. 6).

MAIN THEMES IN *INSTITUTIONAL ECONOMICS*

Institutional Economics is a book far too vast in scope to summarize adequately. Instead some of the major themes in the book will be outlined, concentrating on those points of greatest interest to modern economists concerned with institutional questions.

Method

Commons has often been regarded as following a holistic, as opposed to an individualistic, methodology (Gruchy 1947; Ramstad 1986). It is true that Commons was especially concerned with "whole-part" relationships, including the relationship between individuals and institutions, and that this relationship presents a problem that all of those concerned to deal with institutions in economics must face. Approaches to the problem have usually been divided into the individualistic and holistic. Individualistic approaches give primacy to the individual, emphasizing that individual actions create institutions and that institutions are to be analyzed as the intended or unintended outcomes of individual actions. In this, little attention is given to the role of institutions in shaping individual goals, preferences, and values. Individualism often entails a *reductive* or *psychologistic* approach that takes as its ultimate objective the explanation of social phenomena by theories of individual action alone, that is, without reference to other social phenomena as givens. By contrast, the holist gives primacy to the social and institutional and tends to stress the socialization of the individual. The individual is seen as having internalized the norms of the society he is born into and inhabits. This may be taken to the extreme of arguing in a way that suggests that collective or social phenomena are autonomous entities with distinct functions, purposes, or wills of their own. However, even if the argument is not taken to that extreme the holist would certainly reject the reductivist program of attempting to reduce all social phenomena to the outcome of the actions of noninstitutionalized individuals.

That Commons' approach emphasizes the role that institutions play in shaping individuals seems clear. Commons talks of the individual as an "Institutionalized Mind" and argues:

Individuals begin as babies. They learn the custom of language, of cooperation with other individuals, of working towards common ends, of negotiations to eliminate conflicts of interest, of subordination to the working rules of the many concerns of which they are members. They meet each other, not as physiological bodies moved by glands, nor as "globules of desire" moved by pain and pleasure, similar to the forces of physical and animal nature, but as prepared more or less by habit, induced by the pressure of custom, to engage in those highly artificial transactions created by the collective human will.... Instead of isolated individuals in a state of nature they are always participants in transactions, members of a concern in which they come and go, citizens of an institution that lived before them and will live after them (pp. 73–74).

Commons' reference here to the "collective human will" might suggest more than an emphasis on the institutional and the adoption of that extreme holism that runs in terms of autonomous social entities. This would be a mistaken interpretation. Commons repeatedly refers to the "collective will," but all he means by this is the overall outcome of individual and collective, governmental and judicial, decision-making processes. The collective will is simply what emerges from the decisions of individuals. This brings up the role of the individual in Commons' work. The individual may be an "Institutionalized Mind," but he is also an actor with his own intellect and volition. Choice may often be made on the basis of custom and habit, but choice may also be "rational or scientific" and "sagacious" (p. 306). Such choices occur most often when some novel situation or new problem is met with. Indeed, habit is presented by Commons as something that frees the mind for dealing with "what is unexpected." Habit looks after the routine, while "the intellectual activity is concerning itself with the limiting factors or strategic transactions" (p. 698).

There is a clear link between the notion of a "strategic transaction" and Commons' discussion of institutional change. An existing rule or practice, or, for that matter, the lack of an established rule or practice, may become a key constraint, a limiting factor, to use Commons' terminology. This leads individuals or organized groups to attempt to establish some new rule or practice, a strategic transaction. This effort may take place on a variety of levels. The rule or practice in question may apply just to some particular group or organization. Such new practices or rules may spread to become common practices and social customs. Alternatively, the courts may be involved in litigation over some existing rule or common practice or in deciding a conflict over alternative rules or practices. Finally, the attempt to change social rules may involve political efforts, or attempts to exercise pressure on political parties, in order to affect legislation. Commons' analysis, thus, is quite consistent with the individualistic view that institutions emerge and change only through the actions of individual decision makers. Individuals, not autonomous social forces, determine the nature and evolution of institutions.

Commons' methodology, then, represents neither an extreme, reductive individualism, nor an extreme holism. In Commons' work it is quite clear that institutions deeply affect individuals, particularly in the form of their "habitual assumptions." Commons' notion of the institutionalized mind is *not*, however, inconsistent with an analysis of the evolution of institutions that runs in terms of the actions of individual decision makers. This combination of ideas has more recently been christened "institutional individualism" (Agassi 1975). It gives ultimacy neither to the social whole nor to the individual, but it instead conceptualizes institutions and individuals as involved in a continual process of mutual interaction.

Shortcomings of Existing Economics

For Commons, virtually all other writers in the history of economics (with the possible exceptions of MacLeod and Veblen) had failed to take adequate account of the institutional element. He offered a number of reasons for this widespread blindness to institutional questions, the most important of which were a tendency to focus on a natural abundance and harmony instead of scarcity and conflict and the resulting need to *create* a degree of harmony through institutional constraints; a tendency to substitute psychological propensities for custom and institutions; and, finally, a deep and broad confusion of concepts relating to material goods with concepts relating to ownership and property *rights*.

Commons' discussion of Locke, Quesnay, and Smith deals at some length with the first theme. Of most interest is his analysis of Smith. In Commons' view Smith's world was one of abundance, and in such a world the exercise of self-interest cannot injure others: "If there is abundance of nature's resources, no person can injure any other person by taking from him all he can get, if he does this by exchanging his own labour for that of the other" (p. 161). Each party has an "abundance of alternatives" and can freely choose without coercion. Also, any choice made will not negatively affect the alternatives available to others (p. 161). Self-interest here is constrained not by institutions but by a "sense of propriety," a "divine instinct of mutuality of interests" (pp. 161–62). This focus on abundance and divine beneficence diverted Smith's attention from the fact of mutuality as a "historic product of collective action in actually creating mutuality of interests out of conflict of interests." Had he concentrated on this actual historic process Smith would have seen not the "invisible hand" but the "visible hand of the common-law courts, taking over the customs of the time and place, in so far as deemed good, and enforcing these good customs on refractory individuals" (p. 162).

On the other hand, "the first of the economists to make conflict of interests universal in economics was David Hume in his theory of *scarcity*" (p. 6). In this Hume was followed by Malthus, and Malthus, in turn, provided the foundations for the evolutionary thinking of Darwin and Wallace (p. 246). The notion of scarcity leads to the idea of the prevalence of conflict and the need for institutional constraints. The acquisition of scarce things must be regulated by "the collective action which creates the rights and duties of property and liberty without which there would be anarchy" (p. 6).

Related to the above issue is the second problem mentioned by Commons, the tendency to substitute psychology for institutions. This can be seen in a wide variety of ways. In Locke and Smith individuals are divinely endowed with given psychological propensities that provide a substitute for an institutional analysis. Locke's state of nature, for example, is populated by "intellectual beings like himself." Locke "projected backward the practices, to which he was accustomed and which he wished to see perpetuated, into an eternal reason binding upon men henceforth without change" (p. 50). In Smith, the instinct of sympathy, truck and barter, and the sense of propriety "take the place of all collective action in economic affairs" (p. 166).

An even more complete substitution of psychology for institutions is found in Bentham. Bentham's individuals are noninstitutionalized, responding only to pleasure and pain. His concept of the community is a mere aggregation of individual atoms, not a concept of "membership, citizenship, or participation" or of "both individual and concerted action, governing and being governed" (p. 243). In addition, Bentham does not merely ignore the common law processes of resolving disputes but wishes to replace them with legislative acts based on the greatest good for the greatest number. Bentham's ethics are based on individual desires, and this completes the "dualism of individual and society" (p. 225).

In terms of the work of the "psychological economists from Jevons to Fetter" (p. 439), Commons argues that their psychology deals only with man's relationship to materials. The psychology of diminishing marginal utility, time preference, etc., may well be universal but it neglects and deflects attention from institutional issues of *ownership*. Its starting point is individual psychology where there are no social conflicts of interest. What is of more concern to institutional economics is the "social psychology of negotiations and transactions, arising out of conflicts," which requires "enforceable rights and duties" (p. 440).

This raises the last issue mentioned above, the conflation of materials with ownership that Commons found so pervasive in the history of economic thought. In classical and "hedonic" economics, property has a "corporeal" meaning only, and in this way property is made "equivalent to the material thing owned" (p. 5). The corporeal meaning given to property and the lack of any clear distinction between materials and ownership of materials gave rise, in Commons' view, to such numerous confusions as those between wealth and assets, output and income, efficiency and scarcity, use values and scarcity values. In each case there is a confusion of material output, of the augmentation of material wealth by greater output or efficiency, with income concepts related to ownership and the ability to withhold. Thus: "Output is a service rendered to other people regardless of the price; income is the price received by the owner, based on his right to withhold service from others in the proprietary process of bargaining or waiting until the others will pay a satisfactory price. *Income* is the proprietary acquisition of assets; *output* is the engineering augmentations of wealth" (p. 257).

To overcome these confusions, what is required is not the development of new concepts so much as a clear separation of the various double meanings of the older concepts (p. 424). The proprietary meaning associated with ownership and institutions must be distinguished from that of material goods. Such a distinction allows for the explicit recognition of the institution of property and its gradual evolution from a purely corporeal concept to incorporeal property (debts) and, most importantly, to intangible property (future profit). This, in turn, provides the basis for the development of a truly institutional economics:

> Not until it became vaguely felt by the heterodox economists in the middle of the Nineteenth Century — such as Marx, Proudhon, Carey, Bastiat, MacLeod — that ownership and materials were not the same thing, were the beginnings laid for institutional economics. These economists were vague in that they had the older idea of "corporeal" property (even yet retained by economists), which identifies ownership with the materials owned, or distinguishes only "corporeal property" from the "incorporeal property" which is contract or debt. Hence, it was not until the new idea of "intangible property" arose out of the customs and actual terminology of business magnates in the last quarter of the Nineteenth Century that it was possible for Veblen and the Supreme Court to make the new distinctions which clearly separate from each other not only the ownership of materials and the ownership of debts, but also the ownership of expected opportunities to make a profit

by withholding supply until the price is persuasively or coercively agreed upon. This ownership of expected opportunities is "intangible property" (p. 5).

The expansion of property from corporeal to incorporeal and intangible property also makes the dimension of time, or futurity, as Commons calls it, more explicit. Incorporeal property involves the right to a future payment. Intangible property involves the right to the future income obtained from a particular source or opportunity. Even an exchange involving corporeal property does not necessarily involve the immediate delivery of the physical objects involved. Property of all types involves the rights to the *future* ownership of physical objects.

Transactions and Working Rules

Commons' basic unit of analysis is the transaction. This notion is used by Commons to overcome the various problems outlined above. The transaction is a relationship *between* individuals, and what is transacted is the *right* to property of various kinds. The transaction highlights the conflicts of interest between the various transactors and the potential roles of negotiation, persuasion, coercion, and duress. The concept of a transaction directs attention to the institutional context of defined property rights and defined abilities to exercise legal and economic power. The institutional context within which transactions take place consists of what Commons calls the "working rules," including custom and law, that define what each party to the transaction can, cannot, must or must not, and may do. Transactions "are the alienation and acquisition, between individuals, of the *rights* of future ownership of physical things, as determined by the collective working rules of society" (p. 58).

As is well known, Commons distinguishes between rationing, managerial, and bargaining transactions. A bargaining transaction is between legal equals, while managerial and rationing transactions are between a legal superior and a legal inferior. In managerial transactions the superior is "an individual or a hierarchy of individuals, giving orders which the inferiors must obey." In the rationing transaction the superior is "a collective superior or its official spokesman," for example, a legislature, a court, an arbitration tribunal, or a corporation's board of directors (p. 59). Bargaining transactions *"transfer ownership* of wealth by voluntary agreement between legal equals," managerial transactions *"create wealth* by commands of legal superiors," rationing transactions "apportion the burdens and benefits of wealth creation by the *dictation* of legal superiors" (p. 68).

Examples of rationing transactions given by Commons include many of the activities of legislatures and courts: a legislature deciding on taxes or tariffs, or a judicial decision of an economic dispute. Also included are the decisions of a cartel concerning the output of its members (p. 68). Managerial transactions involve the relationship between "foreman and worker, sheriff and citizen, manager and managed, master and servant, owner and slave" (p. 64). It is within the sphere of managerial transactions that the problems of agency arise (p. 65). Both rationing and managerial transactions involve the use of legal authority, but such authority is not unconstrained by working rules. The rationing decisions of legislatures and courts are constrained by constitutional rules, precedent, and custom. Managerial transactions are constrained by "the law of command and obedience that has been created by the common-law method of making new law by deciding disputes that arise out of managerial transactions" (p. 66).

In contrast, bargaining transactions involve legal equality, but legal equality is not incompatible with the differential ability to exercise economic power. For Commons, economic power, or the lack of it, was determined by two main factors: the number of alternative opportunities available to the parties to the bargain and their respective abilities to withhold (bargaining power). The best available alternatives define what Commons calls the "limits of coercion" (p. 331), and the terms of the transaction will settle somewhere between these limits, exactly where depending on the bargaining power each party can bring to bear. Again, the working rules of society, particularly in the form of common law, affect the exercise of economic power, limiting it to levels considered reasonable by the courts. In this connection Commons discusses such issues as the evolution of common law on discrimination, unfair competition, inequality of bargaining power, and due process (pp. 62–63, see also pp. 331–48).

As one final point, it should be noted that working rules represent exactly that "collective action in control of individual action" that Commons defined as his subject. Working rules in the form of law and custom determine the nature of the transactions undertaken and the terms on which they will be undertaken. A change in working rules may shift a transaction from a rationing to a bargaining type or vice versa. It may allow greater or less managerial discretion. It may expand or restrict the ability to exercise economic power. Working rules, then, are more than just constraints. By controlling individual action, working rules may "expand" the "will of the individual" by enabling an individual to achieve goals that require the organization and direction of the actions of others. Similarly, working rules may "liberate" individuals from coercion or duress exercised by others.

Organizations and Going Concerns

Thus far, attention has been concentrated on the notion of working rules as general rules of conduct enforced by custom or by the sanctions imposed by the state. These rules can be seen as affecting the transactions undertaken by individuals and organizations. However, Commons was concerned to move beyond an analysis of individual actors, or organizations treated as individual actors, operating within collective controls in the form of general rules of conduct. In particular, he wanted to provide an analysis of "collective action" in a somewhat different sense, in the sense of the growth of collective organizations such as corporations, unions, political parties, and associations of various kinds. Such organized forms of collective action Commons called "going concerns," a going concern being a "joint expectation of beneficial bargaining, managerial, and rationing transactions, kept together by 'working rules' and by control of the changeable strategic or 'limiting' factors which are expected to control the others" (p. 58).

In this way the concept of working rules is applied by Commons to the internal rules and practices of particular organizations as well as to those more general rules of conduct discussed above. As Vanberg (1988) points out, there is much ambiguity in Commons' use of such terms as working rules and going concerns, with the result that the distinctions to be made between (i) the society and the general rules of social conduct, (ii) the state and the constitutional rules of the state, and (iii) private collective organizations and the internal rules and regulations of such organizations, are blurred. The lack of clear distinctions does create significant problems in Commons' work. On the other hand, and as will be seen below, Commons' system involves a considerable degree of interplay between these various levels of going concerns and working rules.

To return to the issue of particular organizations, there are two key points in Commons' argument. The first point is that "the working rules which determine for individuals" the limits of their "correlative and reciprocal economic relationships may be laid down and enforced by a corporation, or a cartel, or a holding company, or a cooperative association, or a trade union, or an employers' association, or a trade association, or a joint trade agreement of two associations, or a stock exchange or board of trade, or a political party" and that "these economic collective acts of private concerns are at times more powerful than the collective action of the political concern, the State" (p. 70). Individuals, then, are constrained not just by general social rules of conduct but also by the rules of those particular organizations of which they are members.

The second point of significance is that Commons argues that an organization should not be treated as if it were an individual but as a *coalition*, which depends for its continued existence on the continued "willingness of participants to make their respective contributions to the collective effort" (Vanberg 1988, p. 32). Organizations are created by individuals or groups to pursue particular objectives and operate in the expectation of joint benefit. Organizations come and go, rise and fall in the face of changing legal, technical, and social conditions, but while they exist their internal rules and procedures are shaped by the conflicts and disputes that arise within the organization. In the face of a dispute or conflict the "officers of an organized concern" must make a decision. Such decisions "by becoming precedents, become the working rules, for the time being, of the particular organized concern" (pp. 72–73). The evolution of an organization's own internal rules and practices, then, are deeply affected by the nature of the conflicts between the various groups that go to make up the coalition. This is a point that is insufficiently appreciated even in modern institutional economics.

Legislatures and Courts

The various levels of working rules outlined above represent different aspects of collective action in control of individual action. But Commons also saw the set of working rules evolving over time in what he called a process of "artificial selection." What is perhaps most interesting about Commons' discussion of institutional change is the interplay that exists between the practices of individuals and particular organizations, more general customary rules, and the common and statute law.

In Commons' view the state is a concern that has taken over the power to use physical sanctions. The state "consists in the enforcement, by physical sanctions, of what private parties might otherwise endeavour to enforce by private violence" (p. 751). Instead of private violence, a "form of concerted action, under the name Political Parties, has evolved" with the purpose of "selecting and getting control of the hierarchy of legislative, executive, and judicial personalities whose concerted action determines the legal rights, duties, liberties, and exposures involved in all economic transactions" (p. 751). Political parties "have become the economic concerns through which the sanctions of physical force are directed towards economic gain or loss" (p. 752). Other concerns also influence the political process through organized lobbying or pressure groups. Large organized groups can "employ lobbyists and politicians to control the legislatures and line up the voters" (pp. 889–90). Legislatures operate on the basis of vote-trading or "log-rolling." However, in *Institutional Economics* Commons does not "criminate" the process of log-rolling as he did in his earlier work. Rather, he presents the outcome of log-rolling "as nearly a reasonable reconciliation of all conflicting interests as representative democracy has been able to reach in parliamentary countries" (p. 755). Log-rolling "may be said to be the democratic process of agreeing upon the rationing of economic burdens and benefits" (p. 756). If the log-rolling process has problems they lie in the difficulties of attaining agreement and in the fact that not all interest groups are properly represented. Commons retains his argument in favour of proportional representation as the best method of ensuring representation of all major economic interest groups, but he is also uncomfortably aware that it can lead to many parties and deadlocked legislatures (pp. 898–900). Commons gives a hint of the argument he later develops in more detail in his statement that "in a sense the lobby is more representative than the legislature" (p. 898).

Commons' ideas on the operation of legislatures may be partly responsible for the notion that he conceptualizes working rules and changes in those rules as the intended outcome of political processes of decision making. However, Commons himself places much greater emphasis on the customs and common practices of individuals and concerns and the decisions of the common law courts in deciding disputes. What is noticeable here is that individuals and concerns will tend to develop new practices or rules over time in pursuit of their own objectives or out of the resolution of internal conflicts. Whenever an existing rule or practice becomes a limiting factor some effort will be made to develop a new rule or practice. New practices "arise out of existing customs, precedents, and statutes" (p. 707). Such practices may spread to become social customs. Customs arise out of "similarity of interests and similarity of transactions engaged in" (p. 699). This, of course, is quite consistent with the idea that customs arise spontaneously in an "invisible hand" fashion, but Commons was not willing to limit his analysis to such invisible hand processes. He was aware that many, if not most, social situations create conflicts over the rules to be followed. In Commons' work there is no presumption that the invisible hand will result in harmony over the rules to be followed, instead it is the court system that must decide disputes and *create* order, or a "workable mutuality," out of conflict.

When a dispute over some rule, practice, or custom reaches the court, the court will decide on the existing practices or customs. The court bases its decision on its own criteria of precedent, public purpose, and reasonableness, and approves what it considers to be "good" practices and eliminates what it considers to be "bad" practices. In this fashion a custom may be given legal sanction, or the practice of some particular concern may be generalized into a social rule: "A local practice becomes common law for the nation" (p. 712). This process of the courts taking over good practices and eliminating bad practices is one that Commons is constantly referring to. Commons talks of the development of labor law out of the conflicts brought about by union activity. For example, the 1842 decision holding that "a combination of workmen designed to benefit themselves...was not an unlawful conspiracy" (p. 770). Similarly, with the development and refinement of the concept of intangible property out of business practice, Commons traces the development of the court's distinction between a "reasonable" power to withhold (goodwill) from the unreasonable exercise of that power (privilege). Commons criticises Veblen's exploitation view of business as due to his "failure to trace out the evolution of business customs under the decisions of the courts" (p. 673). It is through this process of common-law decision making that collective action "takes over... the customs of business or labor, and enforces or restrains individual action, wherever it seems to the Court favourable or unfavourable to the public interest and private rights" (p. 5).

In *Institutional Economics* Commons expresses no concerns about the court system usurping the functions of the legislature, and it is quite clear that he regards the common law system of making law by deciding disputes as one of great strength and flexibility. Problems can arise if the "habitual assumptions" of judges are obsolete, and the judicial system is limited by only being able to decide disputes after the event, but Commons suggests that the common law method can be successfully extended to quasi-judicial bodies dealing with labor or commercial arbitration, and that judicial decision making can be supplemented by the experimental rule making of commissions.

In this fashion the legislature and the courts are engaged in the determination of the set of working rules that bear on the transactions undertaken by individuals and concerns. The courts are of particular significance as even the statute law has to be interpreted by the court: "The statute...enacted by Congress does not become a law until it is interpreted by the Court in a particular dispute" (p. 712). The overall process is one of the "evolutionary collective determination of what is reasonable in view of all the changing political, moral, and economic circumstances and the personalities that arise therefrom to the Supreme bench" (pp. 683–84). With the continuation and improvement of these political and judicial processes Commons saw a movement toward the resolution of the conflicts of labor and capital and the attainment of a "Reasonable Capitalism" (p. 891).

CONCLUSION

The foregoing makes it abundantly clear that throughout his career Commons was deeply concerned with the same broad set of theoretical and practical problems. For Commons, theory and practice should go hand in hand. His concern with how to alter economic theory so as to take proper account of the institutional factor and his practical concern with how to bring about a reasonable reconciliation of the conflicting interests of business and labor are simply different aspects of the same problem. *Institutional Economics* is a book that concentrates somewhat on the theoretical issues, but Commons' practical interests are never out of sight for long. That many of the particular practical issues discussed by Commons seem of less pressing importance today is in part the result of his many institutional reform efforts. In contrast, his theoretical concerns still remain.

There are many themes and ideas in *Institutional Economics* that have significance for any modern economist interested in institutional issues. Commons' methodology, his emphasis on transactions, his conceptualization of transactions as transfers of property *rights*, his concern with organizations as collective economic actors, his analysis of legislative decision making as log-rolling, the great attention he paid to the common law and the common law *method* of deciding disputes, and his overall emphasis on conflict of interest and the need for organized selection and enforcement of rules are all issues of considerable modern importance. *Institutional Economics* is a book that was intended to persuade economists to give these institutional issues greater attention. At the time of its original publication its impact on economics was limited, at least in part because of its style and organization, but with the benefit of hindsight many of Commons' arguments and concerns have become much more clear. His vision of an economics that gives the institutional element its proper place is one that has never lost its validity and one that has recently regained much of its former strength and vitality. Without doubt Commons ranks as "the most fascinating and, in the long run, the most obviously seminal of the great triumvirate of first generation American institutionalists" (Coats 1983, p. 149).

NOTES

[1] Published and forthcoming articles include Atkinson (1983; 1987), Biddle (1988A; 1988B), Carter (1985), Chasse (1986), Coats (1983), Endres (1985), Kanel (1985), McClintock (1987), Parsons (1985; 1986), M. Perlman (1986), Ramstad (1986; 1987; 1988), Rutherford (1983), Schweikhardt (1988), and Vanberg (1988). In addition, papers by Atkinson, Biddle, Richard Gonce, Ramstad, Rutherford, and Rick Tilman are due to be given at various conference sessions during 1989.

[2] It is not the intent here to give a full listing of the secondary literature on Commons. Prior to 1940 secondary work consisted primarily of commentaries by other institutionalists such as Mitchell (1924; 1935) and Copeland (1936). In the forties the main contributions came from Gruchy (1940; 1947) and Parsons (1942); in the fifties from Dorfman (1959), Harris (1952), and Hamilton (1953); and in the sixties from Harter (1962), Kennedy (1962), and Chamberlain (1963). The literature expanded substantially between 1970 and the early 1980s with major articles from Barbash (1976), Dugger (1979; 1980), Goldberg (1976), Gonce (1971; 1976), Isserman (1976), Liebhafsky (1976), Ostrom (1976), Randall (1978), and Zingler (1974). Of these articles, five were part of a symposium on "Commons and Clark on Law and Economics" in the December 1976 issue of the *Journal of Economic Issues*.

BIBLIOGRAPHY

Agassi, Joseph. 1975. Institutional Individualism. *British Journal of Sociology* 26 (June): 144–55.

Atkinson, Glen J. 1983. Political Economy: Public Choice or Collective Action. *Journal of Economic Issues* 17 (December): 1057–65.

———. 1987. Instrumentalism and Economic Policy: The Quest for Reasonable Value. *Journal of Economic Issues* 21 (March): 189–202.

Barbash, Jack. 1976. The Legal Foundations of Capitalism and the Labour Problem. *Journal of Economic Issues* 10 (December): 799–810.

Biddle, Jeff. 1988A. Purpose and Evolution in Commons's Institutionalism. Mimeo. Forthcoming in *History of Political Economy*.

———. 1988B. The Ideas of the Past as Tools for the Present: The Instrumental Presentism of John R. Commons. Mimeo. Forthcoming in JoAnne Brown and David van Keuren, eds., *The Estate of Social Knowledge*. Baltimore: Johns Hopkins University Press.

Bye, Raymond T. 1935. Review of *Institutional Economics* by John R. Commons. *Annals of the American Academy of Political and Social Science* 178 (March): 200–202.

Carter, Michael R. 1985. A Wisconsin Institutionalist Perspective on the Microeconomic Theory of Institutions: The Insufficiency of Pareto Efficiency. *Journal of Economic Issues* 19 (September): 797–813.

Chamberlain, Neil W. 1963. The Institutional Economics of John R. Commons. In *Institutional Economics: Veblen, Commons and Mitchell Reconsidered*. Berkeley: University of California Press, pp. 63–94.

Chasse, John Dennis. 1986. John R. Commons and the Democratic State. *Journal of Economic Issues* 20 (September): 759–84.

Coats, A. W. 1983. John R. Commons as a Historian of Economics: The Quest for the Antecedents of Collective Action. *Research in the History of Economic Thought and Methodology* 1: 147–61.

Commons, John R. [1893]. *The Distribution of Wealth*. New York: Augustus M. Kelley, 1963.

———. 1896. *Proportional Representation*. Boston and New York: Thomas Crowell.

———. [1899–1900]. *A Sociological View of Sovereignty*. New York: Augustus M. Kelley, 1967.

———. [1924]. *The Legal Foundations of Capitalism*. Madison: University of Wisconsin, 1968.

———. [1934A]. *Institutional Economics: Its Place in Political Economy*. Madison: University of Wisconsin, 1959.

———. [1934B]. *Myself*. Madison: University of Wisconsin, 1963.

———. 1950. *The Economics of Collective Action*. New York: Macmillan.

Copeland, Morris A. 1936. Commons's Institutionalism in Relation to Problems of Social Evolution and Economic Planning. *Quarterly Journal of Economics* 50 (February): 333–46.

Dorfman, Joseph. 1959. *The Economic Mind in American Civilization*, Vol. 4. New York: Viking.

———. 1963. The Foundations of Commons' Economics. Introduction to J. R. Commons, *The Distribution of Wealth*, New York: Augustus Kelley, pp. i–xv.

Dugger, William M. 1979. The Reform Method of John R. Commons. *Journal of Economic Issues* 13 (June): 369–81.

———. 1980. Property Rights, Law and John R. Commons. *Review of Social Economy* 38 (April): 41–54.

Endres, A. M. 1985. Veblen and Commons on Goodwill: A Case of Theoretical Divergence. *History of Political Economy* 17 (Winter): 637–49.

Goldberg, Victor P. 1976. Commons, Clark and the Emerging Post-Coasian Law and Economics. *Journal of Economic Issues* 10 (December): 877–93.

Gonce, Richard O. 1971. John R. Commons's Legal Economic Theory. *Journal of Economic Issues* 5 (September): 80–95.

————. 1976. The New Property Rights Approach and Commons's Legal Foundations of Capitalism. *Journal of Economic Issues* 10 (December): 765–97.

Gruchy, Allan G. 1940. John R. Commons' Concept of Twentieth-Century Economics. *Journal of Political Economy* 48 (December): 823–49.

————. 1947. *Modern Economic Thought: The American Contribution.* New York: Prentice-Hall.

Hamilton, David. 1953. Veblen and Commons: A Case of Theoretical Convergence. *Southwestern Social Science Quarterly* 34 (September): 43–50.

Harris, Abram. 1952. John R. Commons and the Welfare State. *Southern Economic Journal* 19 (October): 222–33.

Harter, Lafayette G. 1962. *John R. Commons: His Assault on Laissez-Faire.* Corvallis: Oregon State University.

Isserman, Maurice C. 1976. God Bless Our American Institutions: The Labour History of John R. Commons. *Labour History* 17 (Summer): 312–28.

Kanel, Don. 1985. Institutional Economics: Perspectives on Economy and Society. *Journal of Economic Issues* 19 (September): 815–28.

Kennedy, W. F. 1962. John R. Commons, Conservative Reformer. *Western Economic Journal* 1 (Fall): 29–42.

Knight, Frank H. 1935. Review of *Institutional Economics* by John R. Commons. *Columbia Law Review* 35 (May): 803–5.

Langlois, Richard N. 1986. The New Institutional Economics: An Introductory Essay. In Richard N. Langlois, ed., *Economic as a Process: Essays in the New Institutional Economics.* Cambridge: Cambridge University Press, pp. 1–25.

Liebhafsky, H. H. 1976. Commons and Clark on Law and Economics. *Journal of Economic Issues* 10 (December): 751–64.

McClintock, Brent. 1987. Institutional Transaction Analysis, *Journal of Economic Issues* 21 (June): 673–81.

Mitchell, Wesley C. 1924. Commons on the Legal Foundations of Capitalism. *American Economic Review* 14 (June): 240–53.

————. 1935. Commons on Institutional Economics. *American Economic Review* 25 (December): 635–52.

Ostrom, Vincent. 1976. John R. Commons's Foundations for Policy Analysis. *Journal of Economic Issues* 10 (December): 839–57.

Parsons, Kenneth H. 1942. John R. Commons' Point of View. Reprinted in John R. Commons, *The Economics of Collective Action.* New York: Macmillan, 1950, pp. 341–75.

_____. 1950. Introduction. In J. R. Commons, *The Economics of Collective Action*. New York: Macmillan, pp. 9–18.

_____. 1985. John R. Commons: His Relevance to Contemporary Economics. *Journal of Economic Issues* 19 (September): 755–78.

_____. 1986. The Relevance of the Ideas of John R. Commons for the Formulation of Agricultural Development Projects: Remarks upon Receipt of the Veblen–Commons Award. *Journal of Economic Issues* 20 (June): 281–95.

Perlman, Mark. 1986. Subjectivism and American Institutionalism. In Israel M. Kirzner, ed., *Subjectivism, Intelligibility and Economic Understanding*. New York: New York University Press, pp. 268–80.

Perlman, Selig. 1945. John Rogers Commons, 1862–1945. Reprinted in J. R. Commons, *The Economics of Collective Action*. New York: Macmillan, 1950, pp. 1–7.

Ramstad, Yngve. 1986. A Pragmatist's Quest for Holistic Knowledge: The Scientific Methodology of John R. Commons. *Journal of Economic Issues* 20 (December): 1067–1105.

_____. 1987. Institutional Existentialism: More on Why John R. Commons Has So Few Followers. *Journal of Economic Issues* 21 (June): 661–71.

_____. 1988. The Institutionalism of John R. Commons: Theoretical Foundations of a Volitional Economics. Mimeo. Forthcoming in *Research in the History of Economics Thought and Methodology*.

Randall, Alan. 1978. Property Institutions and Economic Behaviour. *Journal of Economic Issues* 12 (March): 1–21.

Rutherford, Malcolm. 1983. J. R. Commons's Institutional Economics. *Journal of Economic Issues* 17 (September): 721–44.

Schotter, Andrew. 1981. *The Economic Theory of Social Institutions*. Cambridge: Cambridge University Press.

Schweikhardt, David B. 1988. The Role of Values in Economic Theory and Policy: A Comparison of Frank Knight and John R. Commons. *Journal of Economic Issues* 22 (June): 407–14.

Seckler, David. 1966. The Naivete of John R. Commons. *Western Economic Journal* 4 (Summer): 261–65.

_____. 1975. *Thorstein Veblen and the Institutionalists*. Boulder: Colorado Associated University Press.

Vanberg, Viktor. 1988. Carl Menger's Evolutionary and John R. Commons' Collective Action Approach to Institutions: A Comparison. Mimeo. Forthcoming in *Review of Political Economy*.

Zingler, Ervin K. 1974. Veblen vs. Commons: A Comparative Evaluation. *Kyklos* 27 (No. 2): 322–44.

PREFACE

This book is modeled upon textbooks in the Natural Sciences. Each idea here incorporated is traced back to its originator, and then the successive modifications of that idea are developed and the earlier double or treble meanings of the idea are separated, until each, as a single meaning, is combined with the others in what I conceive to be the Science of Political Economy as it is developing since the last Great War. The originators of new ideas and theories have appeared before and after revolutionary wars, during what I call the War Cycle. Since I base my analysis on the Anglo-American common law, I begin with the English Revolution of 1689; then follows the World War of the French Revolution, 1789; then the American Revolution of 1861, an outcome of the suppressed European revolution of 1848; then the war of a dozen revolutions beginning 1914.

As I have explained elsewhere in my autobiography, I have been a part of two of these revolutionary cycles: the American, which abolished slavery, and the world revolutions of the past twenty years. My first book, *The Distribution of Wealth* (1893), was dominated by the theories prevailing during the last quarter of the Nineteenth Century; my *Legal Foundations of Capitalism* (1924) and this *Institutional Economics* (1934) are dominated by the theories emerging in the revolutionary cycle of which we now are a part.

Among the many students and assistants from whom I have derived much during the past twenty-five years, Mrs. Anna Campbell Davis has assisted me on legal and economic cases during seven years, and Mr. Reuben Sparkman on economic cases during four years. My colleagues in the Department of Economics have given me invaluable help, and other economists, including former and present students, to whom I have submitted manuscripts in my writing and rewriting, have picked out flaws and helped me over difficulties.

JOHN R. COMMONS

MADISON, WISCONSIN
August, 1934

INSTITUTIONAL ECONOMICS

CHAPTER I

THE POINT OF VIEW

My point of view is based on my participation in collective activities, from which I here derive a theory of the part played by collective action in control of individual action. The view may or may not fit other people's ideas of institutional economics. The comments and criticism by readers and students of both my *Legal Foundations of Capitalism* and the various mimeographed copies and revisions of this book on Institutional Economics, to the effect that they could not understand my theories nor what I was driving at, and that my theories were so personal to myself that perhaps nobody could understand them, leads me to set aside personal inhibitions and boldly to treat myself as an Objective Ego, participating, for fifty years, in many forms of collective action.

In this first chapter, and again in the section on accidents and unemployment,[1] I set forth a record of this participation. I hold that this book is not so much a theory personal to myself as it is a theory conforming to many experiments in collective action and requiring therefore a reconciliation with the individualistic and collectivistic theories of the past two hundred years.

My participation began with my membership, in 1883, in the local typographical union of Cleveland, Ohio. I came to the job with all the naïveté and curiosity of a "country printer" who had obtained the all-round training of seven years in a small newspaper and job office in a small village of rural Indiana. This new experience of working twelve hours a day, seven days a week for about $15 per week, and the efforts of the union to control both the employer and printers of a great daily newspaper, and then my travels as a tramp printer, prior to 1886, converted me from a vague idea of preparing myself for journalism into a plan of studying the whole problem of economics in every direction that I could.

My first reading in economic theory was Henry George's individualistic and theological *Progress and Poverty*, recommended to

[1] Below, p. 2.

1

me by a fellow-printer. I never was able to reach conclusions deductively, as George had done. I resented his condemnation of trade unions,[2] which, in my own case, I knew resulted in conditions of employment preferable to those existing in the open shop across the way.

My first introduction to the problem of the relation of law to economics was in the classes of Professor Ely[3] at Johns Hopkins University, 1888. In 1899 I investigated, for the United States Industrial Commission, the subject of Immigration, which took me to the headquarters of practically all the national trade unions. This led to a further investigation of restrictions of output by capitalistic and labor organizations. After 1901 I participated in labor arbitration with the National Civic Federation, representing "labor, employers, and the public," and, in 1906, with the same organization, in an investigation of municipal and private operations of public utilities.

In 1905 I drafted a civil service law and in 1907 a public utility law at the request of Governor Robert M. La Follette of Wisconsin. The public utility law was designed to ascertain and maintain reasonable values and reasonable practices by the local public utility corporations. In 1906 and 1907, I investigated with others, for the Russell Sage Foundation, labor conditions in the steel industry at Pittsburgh. During 1910 and 1911, when the Socialists were in control of the city of Milwaukee, I organized for them a Bureau of Economy and Efficiency. In 1911 I drafted, and then participated for two years in the administration of, an Industrial Commission law for the state of Wisconsin, with the purpose of ascertaining and enforcing reasonable rules and practices in the relations between employers and employees. From 1913 to 1915 I was a member of the Industrial Relations Commission appointed by President Wilson. In 1923 Professor Fetter, Professor Ripley, and I represented four Western states before the Federal Trade Commission on the Pittsburgh Plus case of discrimination practiced by the United States Steel Corporation.

In 1923 and 1924, as president of the National Monetary Association, I investigated the workings of the Federal Reserve system in New York and Washington. This was followed, in 1928, by aid given to Congressman Strong of Kansas on his price stabilization bill before the House Committee on money and currency.

---

[2] George, Henry, *Progress and Poverty* (1879). Reference to his *Complete Works* (1906–1911).

[3] Cf. Ely, Richard T., *Property and Contract in Their Relation to the Distribution of Wealth* (2 vols., 1914).

Meanwhile, between 1924 and 1926, I administered for two years, as chairman, a voluntary plan of unemployment insurance in the clothing industry of Chicago. This plan was similar to that which I had previously devised, in 1923, for legislation. The plan, with improvements, was finally enacted into law in Wisconsin in 1932.

In do not see how any one going through these fifty years of participation in experiments could fail to arrive at two conclusions: conflict of interests and collective action. Even the state and city turned out to be collective action of those who were in possession of sovereignty.[4]

Meanwhile, I was necessarily studying hundreds of decisions, mainly of the United States Supreme Court and of Labor and Commercial Arbitration tribunals, endeavoring to discover on what principles these tribunals decided disputes of conflicting interests—the Court acting under the clauses of the Constitution relating to due process of law, to the taking of property and liberty, and to equal protection of the laws. These decisions were discussed in my *Legal Foundations of Capitalism* (1924), to which the present volume is a related study of the theories of economists. I found that few of the economists had taken the point of view here developed, or had made contributions that would make it possible to fit legal institutions into economics or into this constitutional scheme of American judicial sovereignty.

The main thing which I noticed, while working with the lawyers in drafting a public utility law in 1907, was the change effected by the Supreme Court of the United States, after 1890, in the meaning of the word "property." The change added to the earlier meaning of "corporeal" property in the Slaughter House Cases, 1872, and the Munn Case, 1876, the new meaning of "intangible" property which the Court gave to the word property after 1890. The additional meaning was rounded out by several decisions between 1897 and 1904.

The meaning of intangible property, according to these decisions, and as I have further developed its meaning since the publication of my *Legal Foundations of Capitalism*, is: the right to fix prices by withholding from others what they need but do not own. Intangible property also includes the meaning of liberty, which previously was treated separately. All Court decisions since 1890 on reasonable value will be found to have turned on this meaning of intangible

[4] I am permitted by the editor of the *American Economic Review* to use an article in the June number, 1932, as the substance of what follows. See also the comments by Professor Joseph E. Shafer, in an earlier number of the same *Review*, which have led me to state this personal point of view.

property and the corresponding conflicts of interest coming before the courts.

Thorstein Veblen, to his great credit, was introducing the same idea of intangible property into economics during the period following 1900, and it was mainly on that ground that he became known as an "institutional" economist. But the difference was that Veblen obtained his case material from the testimony of financial magnates before the United States Industrial Commission of 1900, so that his notion of intangible property ended in the Marxian extortion and exploitation. But my sources were my participation in collective action, in drafting bills, and my necessary study, during these participations, of the decisions of the Supreme Court covering the period; so that my notion of intangible property ends in the common-law notion of reasonable value.

On analyzing this notion, not only in Supreme Court cases but also in collective bargaining, labor arbitration and commercial arbitration cases, I discovered that, of course, the decisions of these tribunals began with conflict of interests, then took into account the evident idea of dependence of conflicting interests on each other; then reached a decision by the highest authority, the Supreme Court or the labor and commercial arbitration courts, endeavoring to bring—not harmony of interests—but order out of the conflict of interests, known by the Court as "due process of law."

Meanwhile I was trying to find what could be the unit of investigation which would include these three constituents of conflict, dependence, and order. After many years I worked out the conclusion that they were found combined together only in the formula of a *transaction,* as against the older concepts of commodities, labor, desires, individuals, and exchange.

So I made the transaction the ultimate unit of economic investigation, a unit of transfer of legal control. This unit enabled me to classify all the economic decisions of the courts and arbitration tribunals under the variable economic factors involved in transactions as they actually are made. This classification permitted an historical development, showing how it was that the courts, as well as arbitration tribunals, ruled out what they deemed, at the time, to be coercive and unreasonable values arrived at in transactions, and approved what they deemed, under the circumstances, to be persuasive transactions and reasonable values.

Going back over the economists from John Locke to the orthodox school of the present day, I found that they held two conflicting meanings of wealth, namely: that wealth was a *material* thing, and again that it was the *ownership* of that thing. But ownership, at least in its modern meaning of intangible property, means power to *restrict* abundance in order to maintain prices; while the material things arise from power to *increase* the abundance of things by efficiency in production, even in overproduction. Hence, ownership becomes the foundation of institutional economics, but material things are the foundations of the classical and hedonic economics, whose "corporeal" meaning of property was equivalent to the material thing owned.

Not until it became vaguely felt by the heterodox economists in the middle of the Nineteenth Century—such as Marx, Proudhon, Carey, Bastiat, MacLeod—that ownership and materials were not the same thing, were the beginnings laid for institutional economics. These economists were vague in that they had the older idea of "corporeal" property (even yet retained by economists), which identifies ownership with the materials owned, or distinguishes only "corporeal property" from the "incorporeal property" which is contract, or debt. Hence, it was not until the new idea of "intangible property" arose out of the customs and actual terminology of business magnates in the last quarter of the Nineteenth Century that it was possible for Veblen and the Supreme Court to make the new distinctions which clearly separate from each other not only the ownership of materials and the ownership of debts, but also the ownership of expected opportunities to make a profit by withholding supply until the price is persuasively or coercively agreed upon. This ownership of expected opportunities is "intangible" property.

Thus, institutional economics consists partly in going back through the court decisions of several hundred years, wherein collective action, not only by legislation but also by common-law decisions interpreting the legislation (culminating in the common-law method of the Supreme Court of the United States), takes over, by means of these decisions, the customs of business or labor, and .enforces or restrains individual action, wherever it seems to the Court favorable or unfavorable to the public interest and private rights.

Such an interpretation also consists in going back through the writings of economists from John Locke to the Twentieth Century, to discover wherein they have or have not introduced collective action. Collective action, as well as individual action, has always been there; but from Smith to the Twentieth Century it has been excluded or ignored, except as attacks on trade unions or as postscripts on ethics or public policy. The problem now is not to create a different kind of economics—"institutional" economics—divorced from preceding schools, but how to give to collective action, in all its varieties, its due place throughout economic theory.

In my judgment this collective control of individual transactions is the contribution of institutional economics to the whole of a rounded-out theory of Political Economy, which shall include and give a proper place to all the economic theories since John Locke, who first laid the theoretical foundations for the labor theories of value and for modern capitalism.

The first of the economists to make conflict of interests universal in economics was David Hume in his theory of *scarcity,* rather than Locke and Smith in their theory of divine *abundance.* But Hume, followed by Malthus, also made scarcity the basis of coöperation, fellow feeling, justice, and property: If there were unlimited abundance of everything there would be no self-interest, no injustice, no property rights, no ethics.

It is only scarce things, actual or expected, that are wanted and desired. Since they are scarce, the acquisition of them is regulated by the collective action which creates the rights and duties of property and liberty without which there would be anarchy. Since this scarcity is a fact recognized by economists, they have already presupposed the institution of property in their very concepts of wants and desires. Institutional economics openly avows scarcity, instead of taking it for granted, and gives to collective action its proper place of deciding conflicts and maintaining order in a world of scarcity, private property, and the resulting conflicts.

I make conflict of interests predominant in transactions. But I conclude that this cannot be allowed to be the only principle, because there are also mutual dependence and the maintenance of order by collective action. I start, like economists, with scarcity, as universal for all economic theory. Then I proceed, as did Hume and Malthus, to show that out of scarcity derives not only conflict, but also the collective action that sets up order on account of mutual dependence.

Order, or what I call working rules of collective action, a special case of which is "due process of law," is itself quite changeable in the history of institutions; and I find this order concretely represented in the various rationing transactions, which would be needless in a world of abundance.

It is for this reason of scarcity that I make efficiency also a universal principle, because it overcomes scarcity by coöperation. But coöperation does not arise from a *presupposed* harmony of interests, as the older economists believed. It arises from the necessity of *creating a new harmony* of interests—or at least order, if harmony is impossible—out of the conflict of interests among the hoped-for coöperators. It is the negotiational psychology of persuasion, coercion, or duress. The greatest American piece of actual coöperation, latterly under ill repute, is the holding companies which suppress conflicts, if persuasion proves inadequate. A more universal coöperation, suppressing conflict in behalf of order, is proposed by Communism, Fascism, or Nazism. These have found their own way of submerging conflicts of interest. Hence, harmony is not a presupposition of economics—it is a consequence of collective action designed to maintain rules that shall govern the conflicts.

All that Communism, Fascism, or Nazism needs to abolish historic capitalism is to abolish bargaining transactions and to substitute for them the managing and rationing of a planned economy.

This is why I relegate the classical and communistic engineering economics and the Austrian home economics to the *future*, and develop a negotiational psychology as the present transfer of legal control to take effect in the future production, consumption, or labor process. Production and consumption cannot be carried on without first obtaining legal control. Possibly this changes the idea of causation. It places causation definitely in the future instead of in the past, where it was placed by the labor theories of Locke and the classical and communist economists; or instead of in the present sensations of pain and pleasure of production or consumption of the hedonic economists since the time of Bentham. It becomes a *volitional* theory of future consequences of present negotiations and transfers of legal control, determining whether production shall go on or slow down or stop, or determining the extent to which future consumption will be expanded or contracted or pauperized.

Perhaps the question turns on the *kind* of psychology implied in the terms, wants and desires. If I look at or participate with people actually engaged in transactions—as do the courts when they analyze or impute motives to disputants—I find futurity always there, not in production or consumption, but in the persuasions or coercions of bargaining transactions, the commands and obedience of managerial transactions, and the arguments and pleadings of rationing transactions, which will ultimately determine production and consumption. In these negotiations and decisions, which are of the essence of institutional economics, it is always *future* production and *future* consumption that are at stake, because the negotiations determine the legal control which must precede physical control.

If this negotiational psychology, as others have alleged, changes the whole problem of causation in economics and the whole of all the definitions of wants and desires, I can only say that it is what actually is there and should be incorporated as one of the multiple causations to be watched by economists. I think this is being done;

but when the older schools and their modern strict conformists worked out their theories they tried to select a single principle of causation, like labor or desire, whereas modern theories are certainly theories of multiple causation. Hence I do not think that "institutional causation" excludes other causations; but it is the volitional economics which operates in all kinds of transactions which always look forward to future consequences. Institutional economics takes its place as the proprietary economics of rights, duties, liberties, and exposures, which, as I shall endeavor to show throughout, give to collective action its due place in economic theorizing.

I do not see that there is anything new in this analysis. Everything herein can be found in the work of outstanding economists for two hundred years. It is only a somewhat different point of view. The things that have changed are the interpretations, the emphasis, the weights assigned to different ones of the thousands of factors which make up the world-wide economic process. All of these are traceable to the dominant political and economic problems by which economists were faced at the time and place in which they wrote, and to their different social philosophies in the changing conflicts of interest of two centuries.

What I have tried to do is to work out a system of thought that shall give due weight to all economic theories, modified by my own experience. This would have been impossible except for my past thirty years in this thrilling state of Wisconsin, with two such leaders as Robert M. La Follette, the individualist, and Victor Berger, the socialist, and with the generosity of its people in supporting this magnificent University. Wisconsin is a miniature of world-wide conflicts of interest and of efforts to obtain by investigation reasonable values and reasonable practices out of economic conflict. The effort would have been impracticable without the continuance of the early civil service law insisted on by Governor La Follette, which has recently been jeopardized by the incoming Democrats. The initiative of the state, however, has been restrained, partly by decisions of the Supreme Court of the United States, partly by national administrative bodies taking jurisdiction of state affairs, and recently by the unprecedented nationalistic experiments in which all of us are now participating.

I confess that this book is burdened by much repetition. But this I could not help, partly on account of unfamiliarity of students and readers with the novelty of the subject and partly because, in a theory that gives due weight to the many sources of multiple causation, a single concept or principle recurs at every point where one or the other many changeable causes infringe. If a preceding cause, which I thought had been expounded, is omitted or forgotten at this different angle of vision of the same thing, then the proper weight of the instant cause is distorted, and the reader or student calls it to my attention. For this reason I am compelled to repeat it anyhow. My point of view as an experimentalist is therefore quite the same as that of an arbitrator, a legislator, a court, an administrator—endeavoring to decide a dispute where many conflicting interests with conflicting principles, causes, or purposes, must be made to work together peaceably, if possible.

Earlier contemporary articles and books which I published during these years of experiment, especially after 1899, many of them in coöperation with my students or with actual participants, furnish most of the data for the theories of this volume. They are mainly as follows:

ARTICLES

"State Supervision for Cities," *Annals of the American Academy of Political and Social Sciences* (May 1895), 37–53.

"Taxation in Chicago and Philadelphia," *Journal of Political Economy* (September 1895), 434–460.

"A Comparison of Day Labor and Contract Systems on Municipal Works," *American Federationist*, III, IV (January 1897 to January 1898). Thirteen articles.

"The Right to Work," *The Arena*, XXI (1899), 132–141.

"Economic Theory and Political Morality," *Proceedings American Economic Association* (1899), 62–80.

"A Sociological View of Sovereignty," *American Journal of Sociology*, (1899–1900), V, 1–15, 155–171, 347–366, 544–552, 683–695, 814–825; VI, 67–89.

"A New Way of Settling Labor Disputes," *American Monthly Review of Reviews*, March 1901.

Report of the U. S. Industrial Commission, U. S. Government Report, Immigration and Education, XV (1901), 1–41; Final Report, XIX (1903), 977–1030, 1085–1113.

Regulation and Restriction of Output, Eleventh Special Report of the Commissioner of Labor (1904). H. R. Document No. 734, 58th Congress, 2d Session.

"The New York Building Trades," *Quarterly Journal of Economics*, XVIII (1904), 409–436.

"Labor Conditions in Meat Packing and the Recent Strike," *Quarterly Journal of Economics*, XIX (1904), 1–32.

"Types of American Labor Unions: The Teamsters of Chicago," *Quarterly Journal of Economics*, XIX (1905), 400–436.

"Types of American Labor Unions: The Longshoremen of the Great Lakes," *Quarterly Journal of Economics*, XX (1905), 59–85.

"Causes of the Union-Shop Policy," *Publications of American Economic Association*, Third Series, VI (1905), 140–159.

Commons, John R., and Frey, J. P., "Conciliation in the Stove Industry," U. S. Government Report, Department of Commerce and Labor (Bulletin of the Bureau of Labor, January 1906, No. 62, 124–196).

"Types of American Labor Unions: The Musicians of St. Louis and New York," *Quarterly Journal of Economics*, XX (1906), 419–442.

Report to the National Civic Federation Commission on Public Ownership and Operation (3 vols., 1907), "The Labor Report," I, 60–112.

"Is Class Conflict in America Growing and Is It Inevitable," *American Journal of Sociology*, XIII (May 1908).

"Wage Earners of Pittsburgh," *Charities and the Commons*, XXI (March 6, 1909), 1051–1064.

"American Shoemakers, 1648–1895: A Sketch of Industrial Evolution," *Quarterly Journal of Economics*, XXIV (1909), 39–83.

"Horace Greeley and the Working Class Origins of the Republican Party," *Political Science Quarterly*, XXIV (1909), 468–488.

"Eighteen Months' Work of the Milwaukee Bureau of Economy and Efficiency," Milwaukee Bureau of Economy and Efficiency (1912), *Bulletin 19*, 34 pp.

"The Industrial Commission of Wisconsin; Its Organization and Methods," published by the Wisconsin Industrial Commission, Madison, 1914.

U. S. Commission on Industrial Relations, *Final Report and Testimony Submitted to Congress* (11 vols.), I (1916), Section II, 169–230.

"Unemployment—Compensation and Prevention," *Survey*, XLVII (Oct. 1, 1921), 5–9.

"Tendencies in Trade Union Development in the United States," *International Labor Review*, V (1922), 855–887.

"A Progressive Tax on Bare Land Values," *Political Science Quarterly*, XXXVII (1922), 41–68.

Commons, John R., McCracken, H. L., Zeuch, W. E., "Secular Trend and Business Cycles: A Classification of Theories," *Review of Economic Statistics*, IV (1922), 244–263.

"Unemployment—Prevention and Insurance," *The Stabilization of Business* (ed. by Lionel T. Edie, Macmillan, 1923), 164–205.

"Wage Theories and Wage Policies," Papers and Proceedings of the Thirty-Fifth Annual Meeting of the American Economic Association, *American Economic Review Supplement*, XIII (1923), 110–117.

"The Delivered Price Practice in the Steel Market," *American Economic Review*, XIV (1924), 505–519.

"Law and Economics," *Yale Law Journal*, XXXIV (Feb. 1925), 371–382.

"The Passing of Samuel Gompers," *Current History Magazine* (Feb. 1925).

"The Stabilization of Prices and Business," *American Economic Review*, XV (1925), 43–52.

"The True Scope of Unemployment Insurance," *American Labor Legislation Review*, XV (Mar. 1925), 33–44.

"Marx Today: Capitalism and Socialism," *Atlantic Monthly*, CXXXVI (1925), 682–693.

"Karl Marx and Samuel Gompers," *Political Science Quarterly*, XLI (1926), 281–286.

Stabilization Hearings, House Committee on Banking and Currency, H. R. 7895 (1927), 1074–1121; H. R. 11806 (1928), 56–104, 423–444.

"Price Stabilization and the Federal Reserve System," *Annalist*, XXIX (April 1, 1927), 459–462.

"Reserve Bank Control of the General Price Level: A Rejoinder," *Annalist*, XXX (July 8, 1927), 43–44.

Commons, John R., and Morehouse, E. W., "Legal and Economic Job Analysis," *Yale Law Journal*, XXXVII (1927), 139–178.

"Farm Prices and the Value of Gold," *North American Review*, CCXXV (1928), 27–41, 196–211.

"Jurisdictional Disputes," in *Wertheim Lectures on Industrial Relations 1928*, Harvard University Press (1929), 93–123.

Unemployment in the United States, Hearings, Senate Committee on Education and Labor, Senate Report 219 (1929), 212–236.

"Institutional Economics," *American Economic Review*, XXI (1931), 648–657.

BOOKS

The Distribution of Wealth, The Macmillan Company, 1893.

Social Reform and the Church, Thomas W. Crowell, 1894.

Proportional Representation, Thomas W. Crowell, 1896; revised 1907, The Macmillan Company.

Commons, John R., in collaboration with others, "Regulation and Restriction of Output," United States Government Report, published as *Eleventh Special Report of the Commissioner of Labor,* H. R. Document No. 734, 58th Congress, 2d Session, 1904.

Trade Unionism and Labor Problems, Ginn and Company, 1905; Second Series 1921.

Races and Immigrants in America, The Macmillan Company, 1907.

Commons, John R., and associates, *A Documentary History of American Industrial Society,* The Arthur H. Clark Company, 1910, 10 vols.

Labor and Administration, The Macmillan Company, 1913.

Commons, John R., and Andrews, J. B., *Principles of Labor Legislation,* Harper & Brothers, 1916; revised 1920, 1927.

Commons, John R., and associates, *History of Labour in the United States,* The Macmillan Company, 1918, 2 vols.

Industrial Goodwill, McGraw-Hill Book Company, 1919.

Industrial Government, The Macmillan Company, 1921.

Legal Foundations of Capitalism, The Macmillan Company, 1924.

Commons, John R., Draper, E. G., Lescohier, D. D., and Lewisohn, S. A., *Can Business Prevent Unemployment?* Alfred A. Knopf, 1925.

CHAPTER II

METHOD

I. John Locke

John Locke was the outcome of the revolutionary Seventeenth Century of England. Maltreated in two revolutions by those whom he opposed and by those whom he approved, he published, anonymously, or for politicians to sign, or merely made copious notes, during thirty years. He did not publish openly in England until he was fifty-seven years of age, after the Revolution of 1689 which brought him home from exile and established modern Capitalism.

His range of experience was as wide and intense as the century afforded. Puritan by training and a life appointee at Oxford, he was silenced by the Puritans when they got control and removed by the King when he got control. His fortunes rose and fell with Shaftesbury, minister of state, in whose home he lived, for whom he wrote on religion, science, and politics, and whom he followed in exile. He saw the great and the small executed, imprisoned, their property confiscated, their opinions suppressed by Church, King, Puritan, and Judge Jeffries. He was a friend and associate of the new scientists, from Newton to Leeuwenhoek, a painstaking investigator in the "new learning" and a member of their new Royal Society for the Improvement of Knowledge by Experiment.[1]

The outcome, in the person of Locke, was skepticism in place of knowledge, probability in place of certainty, reason in place of authority, research in place of dogmatism, constitutional government in place of absolutism, independence of the judiciary for the sake of property, liberty, and toleration. In every branch of learning he epitomized the Seventeenth Century, dominated the Eighteenth, and controlled the institutional and psychological concepts of orthodox economists in the Nineteenth and Twentieth Centuries, after philosophers and psychologists had abandoned them.

His *Essay Concerning Human Understanding* provoked Berkeley to idealism, Hume to skepticism, the French to materialism, and

---

[1] Chartered by Charles II in 1662.

Kant to the *a priori* forms and categories of knowledge, but Locke himself intended it only for reasonableness in all things. His *Two Treatises on Civil Government* justified the Revolution of 1689 and led the American and the French Revolutions to the natural rights of man superior to law, custom, and monarchs, but Locke intended only to substitute the common-law rights of Englishmen in 1689 for the divine rights of Kings alleged to descend from Adam. The same treatise made Labor the foundation of both political science and economic science and set Adam Smith on a theory of labor-pain as a measure of natural value; Ricardo on a theory of labor-power as the measure of normal value; Marx on a theory of social labor-power as the measure of robbery. But Locke's idea of labor was private property in the products of one's own labor, and he intended only an argument against taking property by the King without a hearing and decision by an independent judiciary. His *Letters on Toleration* were the conclusions drawn from his doubts respecting the limits of human understanding and the limits of government in restraining liberty of opinion, of speech, and of assembly. All of these papers he had been writing and rewriting or publishing in scraps anonymously or abroad for more than thirty years, but he published them openly at home within the twelve months that displaced an arbitrary monarch by a constitutional monarch.

1. *Ideas*

Locke's *Essay Concerning Human Understanding* was started with the practical purpose of finding how much the human mind could really know and not know. It grew out of the disputations and dogmatisms of the Seventeenth Century that were leading to confusion, intolerance, and civil war.

"... five or six friends," he says, "meeting at my chamber, and discoursing on a subject very remote from this, found themselves quickly at a stand, by the difficulties that rose on every side. After we had a while puzzled ourselves, without coming any nearer a resolution of those doubts which perplexed us, it came into my thoughts, that we took a wrong course; and that before we set ourselves upon inquiries of that nature, it was necessary to examine our own abilities, and see what objects our understandings were, or were not, fitted to deal with."[2]

[2] *The Works of John Locke*, "Epistle to the Reader" in *Essay Concerning Human Understanding* (11th ed., 1812, 10 vols.), I. All references to Locke are to this edition of his works.

This was Locke's "new way" of investigating our mental tools of research before investigating the output of the tools. It marks his creative genius and resulted in this essay on Ideas, Words, and Probability.

Ideas in the mind, said Locke, are the only objects that men really know, signified outwardly by words. The "received doctrine" had been that men have "native ideas, and original characters, stamped upon their minds, in their very first being." Locke disposed of this doctrine in detail and then proceeded: "Let us . . . suppose the mind to be, as we say, white paper, void of all characters, without any ideas; how comes it to be furnished? . . . To this I answer, in one word, from experience." [3]

Experience, said Locke, is both sensation and reflection. The five senses convey into the mind "corpuscles" which are reflected there as ideas of sensible qualities existing in external objects and these are expressed by signs, such as the words yellow, heat, hard. Reflection, like a mirror, is the "operations of our own mind within us, as it is employed about the ideas it has got"; yet accompanied by feelings of "satisfaction or uneasiness arising from any thought." These operations, "when the soul comes to reflect on and consider, do furnish the understanding with another set of ideas, which could not be had from things without," and are "wholly in himself." [4] They "might properly enough be called internal sense," and the ideas originating from this internal sense are "perception, retention, attention, repetition, discerning, comparing, compounding, and naming."

The foregoing sensations and their reflections are the two sources of "simple ideas," and the understanding does not have "the least glimmering of any ideas, which it doth not receive from one of these two." [5] These simple ideas, further reflected, are the ideas of Pleasure and Pain which afford "reason to prefer one thought or action to another"; the idea of Power, observing in ourselves that we move our bodies and that natural bodies are able to produce motions in other bodies; the idea of Existence, as when we consider ideas to be actually in the mind, or things actually outside us; the idea of Unity, as when we consider "one thing, whether a real being or an idea"; and the idea of Succession, "constantly offered to us by what passes in our own minds." [6]

Compounded from these simple ideas are complex ideas which are

[3] *Ibid.*, Vol. I, Bk. II, Ch. 1, Secs. 1, 2.
[4] *Ibid.*, Sec. 4.
[5] *Ibid.*, Ch. 1, Sec. 5.
[6] *Ibid.*, Ch. 7.

"collections" of simple ideas, namely "Substances," such as man or air; "Relations," such as husband and wife; and "Modes," such as space, time, good, evil, justice, murder, fear, etc. These simple and complex ideas are the only things we know. ". . . the mind, in all its thoughts and reasonings, hath no other immediate object but its own ideas, which it alone does or can contemplate . . . and Knowledge" is "nothing but the perception of the connexion and agreement, or disagreement and repugnancy, of any of our ideas." [7]

Thus Locke makes a complete separation of the mind within from the world without. The mind observes itself operating about certain ideas which it combines and recombines from simple ideas to the highly complex ideas of substance, cause, effect, morality, divine law, and civil law.

This separation of an internal mechanism, the mind, copying an external mechanism, the world, is characteristic of economic theory from Locke to the end of the Nineteenth Century. The concepts necessary to get away from this dualism and to substitute a functional relation between the mind within and the world without were not, for economic theory, constructed until Menger, in 1871,[8] under the name "diminishing utility," worked out the idea of a feeling of dependence upon external objects believed to be fitted to satisfy wants, a feeling which diminished in intensity with the increase in abundance of these objects; and not until Böhm-Bawerk, in 1888, constructed the idea of a present diminished value of future commodities. Thus it required the later concepts of Scarcity and Futurity to furnish the functional notion of changing degrees of dependence of the mind and body upon the present and future external world, instead of the separation, by Locke and his followers, of the mind within from the world without. Even so, these hedonic economists followed Locke's corpuscular theory of sensations and ideas.

Locke's mechanistic idea of the mind was that of a passive receptacle of ideas, in the form of Newton's corpuscles arriving from without, which then were reflected within. This too, was characteristic of the physical economists, culminating in Karl Marx, who reduced the individual consciousness to a mere copy of the production and acquisition of wealth. In order to unite, in the idea of an expected repetition of transactions, Locke's corpuscular sensations, reflections, and volitions, it required a still further notion of the mind as the whole body in action, instead of particular sensations

---

[7] *Ibid.*, Vol. II, Bk. IV, Ch. 1, Secs. 1, 2.

[8] Preceded by Gossen (1854), Jevons (1871), and followed, independently, by Walras (1874).

coming into the body, with this whole body as a *creative* agency looking towards the future and manipulating the external world and other people in view of expected consequences. This remained for the most recent psychology and economics to accomplish.[9]

Yet Locke prepared the way by his doctrine of Experience and by his demonstration that the origin of all our ideas is only the five senses which give us only a more or less imperfect picture, and not an innate or certain knowledge of the world. Modern psychology and economics require only the abandonment of his physical concept of the mind, derived as it was by analogy to the only sciences— physics, optics, and astronomy—then in vogue, and the substitution of concepts suitable for the same experimental method of studying psychology, history, and economics as that which he and his contemporaries employed in the physical sciences.

With this object in view, it appears that if we add the emotional term "meaning" to Locke's intellectual term "idea" we shall obtain what he had in mind, but without the mechanistic analogy of subjective corpuscles moving around in the mind, separated from the world without. The term "meaning," as here intended, signifies the emotional aspect of which ideas are the purely intellectual aspect. It implies both the subjective and objective sides of a volitional process of acting and reacting upon the changing world without and within.

This concept of "meaning" changes Locke's concept of "idea" from a merely passive copy in a looking glass to an active mental construction of ideas selected and transformed internally in order to investigate and understand the otherwise unmanageable complexity of external activities. The color red is supposed to consist of 400 million million vibrations per second and the color violet of 800 million million per second.[10] We see red, but that is only the meaning we give to certain repetitions in the world's mechanism, which are not red at all, and therefore not a copy. It may mean a murder or it may mean a rose. It is our inference of what has happened, or our expectation of something that will happen, based on experience, repetition, memory, and our interest in the happening. It is the diverse meanings we give to 400 million million vibrations per second. So it is with every object of nature, of human nature, and of our own subjective ideas and emotions. Our knowledge is not

[9] Pragmatism, Gestalt psychology, institutional economics. See also Reichenbach, Hans, in collaboration with Allen, E. S., *Atoms and Cosmos; the World of Modern Physics* (tr. and revised 1933), on recent attempts to combine corpuscular and wave theories of light. See also Whitehead, A. N., *Adventures of Ideas* (1933), especially Ch. XI, on "Objects and Subjects."

[10] Jeans. Sir James, *The Universe around Us* (1929), 108.

copies, but is, on the intellectual side, ideas actually created within; on the emotional side, meanings, which relate the ideas to the sensations. On the side of weighing alternatives these are valuings which, on the volitional side, are acting and transacting.

For, the term "meaning" is the name of an idea which we construct in order to carry the formula of a relation between the parts of experience and the whole of experience; hence it pictures something inseparable from feelings and emotions. The latter, when they reach the threshold of action, we name value, that is, the relative importance assigned objectively to external objects as shown actually and measurably by our dealings with the world of nature and other persons about us.

This signifies that "meaning" carries the idea of expectation. The word "meaning" signifies more than the so-called content of an idea—it signifies the expectations aroused by the idea. Locke's "ideas" were only internal copies of something going on without, worked over by a merely intellectual mind within, whereas the term "meaning" signifies the importance of those ideas for action immediately or later.

In this respect the term "meaning" signifies an inseparable aspect of valuing, choosing, and acting. Locke's word "value" meant solely an external quality, that is, use-value, existing in objects, but reflected as an internal "idea." But modern usage is converting the noun value into the verb "valuing" which consists of the meanings, or feelings of relative importance, aroused by immediate or expected events. Meaning and valuing are therefore inseparable from each other, the one being an internal emphasis, the other an external emphasis of the same volitional process of acting upon and reacting to the world about.

For, meaning and valuing are inseparable from choosing, which is the external evidence of the meanings assigned and values imputed. Locke's idea of Power gave him much trouble and was revised in the second edition.[11] The explanation is evident. His separation of the mind as a passive mechanism within from the world as an active mechanism without, could give him no volitional meaning of the word Power. He saw only a physical process of the mind within, moving things without, just as he saw other objects moving other things. Thus the Will became an analogy to optics, or heat, or chemical action, and left for him no room for the idea of choosing between alternatives. The latter is an idea which does not occur at all in physical science and has only within the past

---

[11] Locke, *Essay Concerning Human Understanding*, I. Ch. XXI on "Of Power"

thirty years become the foundation of a new economic theory. In fact, Locke's discussion of "Power" has not a single reference to the phenomenon of choice. Choice, for him, had to do only with ideas of pleasure and pain. Had he applied his experimental instead of the introspective method to psychology, as he and his contemporaries had applied it to physics, then, instead of following a physical analogy for his explanation of the will, he might have observed that the Will—his idea of Power—is a process of repeatedly choosing and acting upon the best alternative actually accessible at the time. These alternatives are also continually changing in their activity, their meanings, and their relative importance. Nothing like this occurs in physics, optics, or astronomy. Converted into terms of Will, his meaning of Power is a functional relation between the whole of the living body and the external world, wherein the Will is itself a process of choosing between different degrees of power over the world and other people, according to those meanings and valuings which are the relative importance attributed to the available alternatives.[12]

This functional concept of a choice involves, indeed, also a physical process, but one entirely different from that of the science of physics. It involves, in one and the same act, the threefold dimension of performance, avoidance, and forbearance: performance, the exertion of physical or economic power in one direction; avoidance, the rejection of the next best alternative performance; and forbearance, the choice of a lower as against a higher degree of power in the actual performance.

This threefold dimension of physical and economic power is unknown to physics. It is the dimensions of the will in its bodily action, upon which economic and legal theory is builded.[13] It is an active process of choosing, and since this is the characteristic of living behavior distinguished from inanimate behavior, we shall often employ the term "choosing" as the equivalent of such terms as "value," "behavior," "acting," "transacting," and as the proper meaning of Locke's "power." These three dimensions of a choice— performance, avoidance, forbearance—were unknown to Locke and can find no place in his physical analogy of the mind, either as a passive mechanism within copying a world mechanism without, or as a direct action on external things, like the analogies from physics.

Thus understood, however, as the physical and economic dimensions of human behavior, the four terms, Idea, Meaning, Valuing, and Acting, are the inseparable intellectual, emotional, and volitional

[12] Below, p. 301, Ability and Opportunity.
[13] Commons, John R., *Legal Foundations of Capitalism* (1924), 69 ff.

process of man's actions in dealing with the physical and human world, instead of Locke's separated mechanisms of an internal world and an external world. We shall, at a later point, distinguish physical power from economic and moral power.

Yet the term "meaning" retains the similar significance ascribed by Locke to his term "idea," for it indicates, not that certain knowledge which is nothing short of infinite, but that actual feeling based usually on illusory knowledge, upon which, however, human beings actually behave, actually induce others to act, and likewise change their habits of acting in process of time. We shall, therefore, use the term "idea" as a purely artificial intellectual "construct," created by man for purposes of investigation; and shall distinguish ideas from the *meanings* of ideas, which are emotional as well as intellectual.

Words, with Locke, are, of course, signs of mental copies. If properly used, a word, he says, should "excite in the hearer the same idea which it stands for in the mind of the speaker." [14] Yet this does not happen. Words excite different ideas, and—speaking from his own experience—he says,

> ". . . he that shall well consider the errors and obscurity, the mistakes and confusion, that are spread in the world by an ill use of words, will find some reason to doubt whether language, as it has been employed, has contributed more to the improvement or hindrance of knowledge amongst mankind. [15] . . . This, I think I may at least say, that we should have a great many fewer disputes in the world, if words were taken for what they are, the signs of our ideas only, and not for things themselves." [16]

Locke's remedies for the Abuse of Words are: No name without an idea for which it stands. The ideas themselves must be clear and distinct, if simple, like "yellow" or "white," and precisely determined if they are those collections of simple ideas, like "justice" or "law" which have "no settled object in nature." The words must be applied "as near as may be to such ideas as common use has annexed them to." But since common use has "not visibly annexed any signification to words," it is necessary to "declare their meaning." And, "if men will not be at pains to declare the meaning of their words," they "should at least use the same word constantly

---

[14] *The Works of John Locke*, Vol. II, Bk. III, Ch. 9, Sec. 4.
[15] *Ibid.*, Ch. 11, Sec. 4.
[16] *Ibid.*, Ch. 10, Sec. 15.

in the same sense." If this were done "many of the controversies in dispute would be at an end." [17]

Thus, Locke's *Essay* was not so much the philosophy of Skepticism, which it was supposed to be, as it was a handbook for consensus of opinion in practical affairs. It was a treatise on the meanings of words, to which we add the meanings of the ideas themselves, as tools of investigation, agreement, and action. His was a book on Method of Research.

If knowledge has to do only with ideas, and ideas are only copies of things and not the things themselves, so that even a "thing itself is only a collection of simple ideas," [18] then, can there be any certainty of knowledge? The only certain knowledge, according to Locke, is of that mathematical or logical and deductive character which perceives either immediately or by demonstration the connections, agreements, disagreements, and repugnancies between ideas. But if directly perceived—as that yellow is yellow, or that yellow is not white—this is "intuitive" knowledge, or as we should say, meanings. If indirectly perceived by demonstration—as that the three angles of a triangle are equal to two right angles—this is "rational" knowledge. The two together constitute the intellectual basis of Reason, and in so far they constitute that certain knowledge of which there can be no doubt. This holds true of our knowledge of an eternal, most powerful, and most knowing, wise and invisible being whose existence is deducible naturally from every part of our knowledge. The demonstration thus deducible, which makes us certain of this Being, arises from the idea of cause and effect, wherein the effect cannot be greater than the cause. The effect is the world, the cause is God.

This idea leads to two conclusions. Since one of these effects is man's intelligence, it follows that the original infinite cause must also have been an eternal mind. Second, the "order, harmony and beauty which are to be found in nature" could not have been produced had there not been a first eternal emotion, as well as intellect, which desired to see order, harmony, and beauty, and thus contained in itself "all the perfections that can ever after exist."

This idea of an eternal mind, which is simply the idea of perfection, makes us also certain that there is an eternal moral law, with its "measures of punishment," and this law is "as intelligible and plain to a rational creature, and a studier of that law, as the positive laws of commonwealths: nay, possibly plainer, as much as reason is easier to be understood, than the fancies and intricate contrivances

[17] *Ibid.*, Ch. 11, Sec. 26.
[18] *Ibid.*, Vol. III, Bk. IV, Ch. 11, Secs. 1, 2.

of men, following contrary and hidden interests put into words." [19]

Hence, Locke's notion of Reason was not merely that of an intellectual process. He injected into it an emotional meaning of ultimate purpose, which we name Happiness, and an instrumental meaning of natural laws contrived to reach that purpose, which we name Justification. He identified Reason with God and with Nature's Laws and Human Happiness, which, when it came to his *Treatise on Government*, became a beneficent providence, eternal, infinite, and unchangeable, which intended the welfare of mankind on principles of harmony, equality, peace, abundance, and the preservation of life, liberty, and property.

For this reason he has been characterized as utilitarian in philosophy. His utilitarianism was that of an infinite sovereign, not Bentham's earthly legislature. Of this infinite sovereign's intentions he had certain knowledge, deducible by demonstration, upon which he founded his law of nature, his theory of natural rights, his theory of value, and his justification of property and liberty. God, Nature, and Reason were identical, and they justified the Revolution of 1689.

We can thus see the basis of Locke's individualism. Human beings were not the product of habit and the customs of their time and place, but were rational units, like himself, who, by exercise of reason, could be certain of the infinite beneficent reason of the universe and the laws of nature designed to attain it. There is but one infinite reason, an infinite cause, which all individuals can know for certain because they themselves are the effects of that cause. This infinite reason is therefore Locke's own reason made eternal and unchangeable. He begins with his own individual mind as the center of the universe, and not with that repetition of events, practices, and transactions to which his mind had been so accustomed that they seemed natural, rational, and divine.

For this reason he was required to make the distinction between certainty and probability, a distinction which science since his time has made, for it deals only with probability. Yet he lacked the modern concepts of relativity, time, and motion, and sought for something fixed, like an individual soul, an infinite reason, a rational "frame" of the universe, to which all changes and probabilities might be referred.

Yet even Locke himself was a process of changing experience of the changing events about him. And so with every individual. Locke's certainty, after all, was only an idea in his mind, like the certainties of mathematics and logic which are not sciences but are mental tools of investigation. These tools, as he demonstrated, do

[19] *Ibid.*, Vol. V, *Two Treatises of Government*, Bk. II, Ch. 2, Sec. 12.

not exist in the universe without. Whatever comes from without and is therefore short of mathematical knowledge, "is but *faith or opinion,* but not knowledge, at least in all general truths" respecting the external world.[20]

If so, then that which passes for knowledge of the external world is only probability. Probability supplies the defect of knowledge "to guide us where that fails," and it "is always conversant about propositions, whereof we have no certainty, but only some inducements to receive them for true." The grounds of probability are "the conformity of anything with our own knowledge, observation and experience," and the "testimony of others, vouching their observation and experience."[21] Probability varies in degree, and the mind which

"would proceed rationally, ought to examine all the grounds of probability, and see how they make more or less for or against any proposition, before it assents to, or dissents from it; and upon a due balancing the whole, reject, or receive it, with a more or less firm assent, proportionably to the preponderancy of the greater grounds of probability on one side or the other."[22]

Thus, if probability, belief, opinion, experience, take the place of certain knowledge, the foundation is laid, not for skepticism, but for distinguishing reason from reasonableness. Reason may give us the immutable laws of God, Nature, Perfection, but Reasonableness gives us mutual assent to the preponderance of probability in the affairs of life. It is Locke's doctrine of Reasonableness, not his doctrine of Reason, that survives.

We need not here review the two centuries of philosophical discussion that followed Locke's physical method of treating ideas as atoms which could be observed by introspection and talked about like mechanisms. With Berkeley it meant that we could know nothing but ideas and that the world without was for us only the idea of God. With Hume it meant that even our own self was also only an idea. With Kant it meant that, of our own free will, we construct rational laws for the universe and for ourselves. These were doctrines of Reason, not of Reasonableness. They were ideas and not the meanings of ideas.

On the other hand, if we employ the word "meaning" as the emotional annex to Locke's word "idea," then the meanings are the changeable significance of events and practices in view of probabili-

[20] *Ibid.,* Vol. II, Bk. IV, Ch. 2, Sec. 14.
[21] *Ibid.,* Vol. III, Bk. IV, Ch. 15, Sec. 4.
[22] *Ibid.,* Ch. 15, Sec. 5.

ties and the changing meanings of reasonableness. The word is a substitute for what Santayana[23] intends perhaps by "essences"; not Plato's essences that preëxisted eternally and were pure ideas, but our own changeful meanings and values ascribed to things or events by that common sense which Santayana names "animal faith," equivalent to Locke's "faith or opinion." The word "meaning," as here used, carries Santayana's meaning of "essences," but without Plato's physical metaphor that implied the existence of essences outside the mind. If we interpret ideas, concepts, essences, and the like, to signify only the meanings and values which we assign, not only to words but also to objects and events, and even to Locke's ideas, we have terms suited not only to the changing interpretations of events and the changing interpretations of words, but also the changing ideas themselves, that have accompanied, not only the writings of economists, but, more important, the behavior of business men, laboring men, judges, legislators, whose meanings, valuings, and choices it is that economists write about. All of them act and induce others to act, not upon knowledge, but upon the meanings and valuings from which they construct their ideas.

Most important of all, the term "meaning" implies that a sensation, or feeling, or idea, does not exist abstractly as an isolated particle or atom bobbing against other ideas according to chemical "laws of association,"[24] but that it exists as a functioning part within the whole complex moving process of memory, expectation, and action. The meanings of ideas are much more than Locke's ideas—they are the repeating and variable guides to behavior, which are continually repeating but changing as the behavior itself repeats and changes from hour to hour, man to man, year to year, and century upon century. Locke's "ideas" are timeless, eternal, unchanging essences, but the *meanings* of ideas are a changeable function of events in the flow of time out of the remembered past, along the present action, into the expected future.[25]

Thus it is that meanings can be observed and are fitted for research and experiment. The important distinction can be made between the meanings assigned to words and the meanings assigned to ideas and events. Words, in economic behavior, as Locke commented generally, are used to conceal thought and to mislead, as well as to reveal thought and to lead aright. What business men, laboring men, courts, executives, politicians, and so on, really mean

[23] Santayana, George, *Skepticism and Animal Faith; Introduction to a System of Philosophy* (1923); *Realm of Essence* (1927).
[24] Literally so expounded by James Mill, the friend of Ricardo, in his *Analysis of the Phenomena of the Human Mind* (1828), which was avowedly a "chemical" theory of ideas.
[25] Below, p. 140, Hume and Peirce.

is not what they say, nor even what they think, but what they *do*. What they say and even think of God, Nature, property, liberty, etc., is their nominal meaning of words and of the ideas signified by the words; what they do is their real meaning, arising from their memory, activity, expectations, wishes, and alternatives. Thus meanings can be scientifically investigated in terms of activity. Such investigation is not the case with ideas and essences, for these are only mental formulae having no external reference except in the meanings, valuings, and choosings which they signify.

We may summarize and anticipate by saying that, while Locke's basic theory, like the theories of economists who followed him, was a theory of Individual Epistemology and Valuation, or how can an individual *know* and give *value* to anything; ours is a theory of the joint activity and valuations of individuals in all transactions through which the participants mutually induce each other to a consensus of opinion and action. It is not John Locke's theory of Reason, but is his theory of Reasonableness.[26]

2. *Value*

John Locke united Law, Economics, and Ethics in a single concept, Labor. The issue arose in his justification of the Revolution of 1689. Sir Thomas Filmer in 1680 had published his *Patriarcha,* though it had been written previously for private circulation during Cromwell's dictatorship. In this book he supported the "divine right of kings" as a natural right to dominion over the lives, liberty, and property of their subjects, answerable only to God from whom Kings derived the right.[27]

Locke replied with the divine right of Labor. This "glib nonsense" of Filmer, "an English courtier," said Locke, "had of late been publicly owned by the pulpit" [28] and made "the current divinity of the times." Against this doctrine of a divine right of political power Locke set up the "natural right of life, liberty, and property," derived from the right of labor to its own product. The difference between the two was the difference between Filmer's analogy of an organism, where the parts are subordinate to the whole, and Locke's analogy of a mechanism, where the whole is the sum of the parts.

These analogies applied both to individuals and to wealth. With Filmer, individuals were bound together by the original law of their heredity and social nature, like a family. With Locke, individuals

[26] Below, p. 140, Peirce.

[27] Figgis, J. N., *The Theory of the Divine Right of Kings* (1896, 1922), 149 ff. Citations are to the first edition.

[28] *The Works of John Locke*, Vol. V, *Two Treatises on Government*, Preface, 210.

came together for mutual convenience, like a convention. With Filmer, the wealth of the nation was the product of society, but with Locke, it was the sum of individual products. With Filmer, the individual's ownership of that wealth was derived from the Sovereign, but with Locke, private property preceded sovereignty. Hence, with Filmer, God and nature endowed the earthly monarch with rights by imposing duties on his subjects; but with Locke they endowed the individual with rights by imposing duties on the monarch. Each personified his own reasoning as the eternal reasoning of God and nature.

Locke founded his ideas upon a theory of Labor as the only source of value, and, on examination, it will be found that his idea of Labor-Value was a personification, in a "compound idea," of the private ownership of material things produced by labor. Out of this compound concept he resolved the good practices of manufacturers, farmers, merchants, and land-owners. Since Locke was the product of his time, we need to find the origins of this compound idea of labor, materials, and ownership.

Sir Thomas Smith, one hundred and twenty-five years before Locke's *Treatise,* had given a political meaning to the term "Common-wealth." [29] As ambassador from Elizabeth to the continent, he was struck by the difference between absolute monarchies, or dictatorships, and the Kingdom of England where the people participated in Parliament and had a hearing in the courts of the common law. The participating classes, in England, were the barons and the gentlemen, each of whom lived "without manual labor," and the yeomen, farmers, or freeholders, who were protected by the common-law courts and who "travailed to serve" the Commonwealth more than "all the rest." A fourth class, the "proletarii," were those who had "no free lande," such as the laborers, mechanics, copyholders, and even landless merchants and retailers. These had "no voice nor authoritie in our commonwealth, and no account is made of them but onlie to be ruled, not to rule others." [30]

This distinction made by Thomas Smith in 1565 between landed and landless classes remained the ruling distinction in the political meaning of *commonwealth* for more than three hundred years in England and more than two hundred and fifty years in colonial and agricultural America. The issue as to this meaning arose in the armies of the Commonwealth immediately after the final defeat of the King in 1647. There the Levellers demanded equal suffrage for all the soldiers regardless of ownership, but Cromwell and Ireton

[29] Smith, Sir Thomas, *De Republica Anglorum* (written about 1565, published 1583).
[30] See Commons, *Legal Foundations of Capitalism,* 222–224.

determined that only those who had a landed interest could be trusted to stand for the permanent interest of the Commonwealth. This was John Locke's political meaning of commonwealth. A political commonwealth was a participation in government by those who had a permanent interest in land.

The economic meaning of Commonwealth began with the political meaning. It arose from the confiscation of the monasteries, the conversion of arable land to pasture, and the enclosures of common lands. In 1540, those who had acquired these confiscated lands from Henry VIII and had raised the rents and evicted the tenants were denounced by Bishop Latimer as bringing "a common wealth into a common misery." They, in turn, denounced their attackers as "commonwealth men," equivalent to modern Communists, the leader and prophet of whom was the "Commonwealth called Latimer," who, from his office as bishop during the reign of Mary, denounced them in turn as "step-lords and rent raisers." A hundred years later, in the armies of the Commonwealth, the matter of suffrage in the new Commonwealth was debated at great length, wherein Cromwell and Ireton demanded that suffrage be restricted to property owners, while the Levellers demanded that suffrage be universal.[31] The Levellers, latterly known as Diggers, who were forerunners of American "squatters," homesteaders, and mining prospectors, extended the meaning of commonwealth to the common lands, which they began to prepare for crops and to clear for cottages, whereupon they were suppressed by the courts and Cromwell's army.[32]

Meanwhile, this economic meaning of commonwealth was extended by the common-law courts to the field of manufactures and merchandising. The distinction turned on the means by which a person becomes rich. If he gets riches by virtue of special or exclusive privileges of manufacture or merchandising granted by the sovereign, then his riches are a deduction from the commonwealth without a corresponding contribution on his part. But if he became rich by the activity of manufacturing, merchandising, retailing, importing commodities from abroad, or producing crops on his land, then his private wealth was equal to his contribution to the commonwealth. Commonwealth was the sum total of private wealth. This kind of private wealth could be acquired only by industry and frugality; the other kind by monopoly and oppression. This became Adam Smith's idea of the wealth of nations. It became the double mean-

[31] *The Clarke Papers*, I, 299–326, published by the Camden Society, Series 2, Vol. 49 (1891). These were shorthand reports of the debates in Cromwell's army after the capture of the King.

[32] *Ibid.*, 204–225. See also Gooch, G. P., *English Democratic Ideas in the Seventeenth Century* (1927), 214–219; Tawney, R. H., *Religion and the Rise of Capitalism* (1926), 255–261.

ing of wealth that has ruled orthodox economy from John Locke to the present time, namely, a material thing which is owned but is not monopolized.

Thus in 1599, a guild of tailors, though chartered by the king, was judged by the highest common-law court to be unlawful when it established a preference for its members in competition with non-members, because such a rule was "against the liberty of the subject and against the commonwealth." [33] In 1602, the same court declared that a monopoly granted by Elizabeth to a courtier was "against the commonwealth" in that the grantee had no mechanical skill and therefore no justification in his legal power to forbid others to compete who had the art and skill which are "profitable for the commonwealth." [34] Again in 1610, a merchant, Bates, was burdened by an extra import tax imposed by the king without consent of Parliament. On his refusal to pay, his attorneys unsuccessfully argued, before the Court of the Exchequer, that the wealth obtained by an importer of foreign goods was an equivalent addition to the Commonwealth. [35]

Lord Chief Justice Coke, who more than any other lawyer had developed this economic meaning that private wealth was equivalent to commonwealth, when not monopolized, was removed by King James in 1616, and his removal became the historic foundation for Locke's independence of the judiciary against arbitrary control by the king, accomplished by the Revolution of 1689 and written into law by the Act of Settlement, 1700.

The same equivalence of Private Wealth and Commonwealth was further developed by the Puritan divines, reaching its highest expression in Richard Baxter, contemporary of John Locke, who converted the village of Kidderminster from coarse living into a diligent and thrifty community.

"The public welfare," said Baxter, "or the good of many is to be valued above our own. Every man therefore is bound to do all the good he can to others, especially for the church and commonwealth. And this is not done by idleness, but by labour. As the bees labour to replenish their hive, so man, being a sociable creature, must labour for the good of the society which he belongs to, in which his own is contained as a part. . . . If God shew you a way in which you may lawfully get more than in another way (without wrong to your soul or any other) and if you refuse this and choose the less gainful way, you cross one of the ends of your calling, and you refuse to be God's steward, and to accept

---

[33] Davenant v. Hurdis, Moore K. B. 576 (1599), 72 Eng. Rep. 769 (Commons, op. cit., 47).
[34] Darcy v. Allein, Case of Monopolies, 6 Coke's Repts. 84 b., 77 Eng. Rep 1260-6 (1602).
[35] Bates Case, Lane 35 (1606), 145 Eng. Rep. 267, 2 Howell's State Trials 371.

his gifts, and use them for him when he requireth it; and you may labour to be rich for God, but not for flesh and sin. . . . That calling which conduceth most to the public good is to be preferred. . . . When two callings equally conduce to the public good, and one of them hath the advantage of riches, and the other is more advantageous to your souls, the latter must be preferred; and next to the public good the soul's advantage must guide your choice. . . . Prefer a durable good that will extend to posterity before a short and transitory good. . . . An oppressor is an Anti-Christ and an Anti-God . . . not only the agent of the Devil but his image." A selfish private spirit "careth not what the commonwealth suffereth, if he himself may be a gainer by it." [36]

Those whom Baxter could not win to his view of church and commonwealth were the wage-earners, journeymen, apprentices, and drunkards in the villages, who owned no property; and the landed gentry in the country who owned more property than they produced. These two classes were considered by him to be leagued together in opposition to church and commonwealth. As Tawney has pointed out, even Baxter and Bunyan, "who continued to insist on the wickedness of extortionate prices, rarely thought of applying their principles to the subject of wages." Baxter defended, not wage-earners, but tenants, as against landlords, who should not be "necessitated to such toil and care and pinching want as shall make them like slaves than free men." But, as wage-earners, he said, they need "a master who can establish a moral discipline among his employees which they would miss if they worked for themselves." [37]

Baxter's typical case of one who by becoming rich in material goods contributed yet more to the commonwealth was Thomas Foley, "who from almost nothing did get £5000 per annum or more by iron works, and with so just and blameless dealing that all men that ever he had to do with, that ever I heard of, magnified his great integrity and honesty, which was questioned by no one." Thus it was wealth acquired by industry, integrity, good management, and frugality, yet subordinate to church and commonwealth,

[36] Baxter, Richard, *Christian Directory* (reprinted 1838). It was Max Weber who first discovered the economic significance of Baxter. See Weber, Max, *Gesämmelte Aufsätze zur Religions-Soziologie*, I, 164 (1922, a part of which was translated as *The Protestant Ethic and the Spirit of Capitalism*, 1930); Commons, John R., Review of Tawney's *Religion and the Rise of Capitalism*, *Amer. Econ. Rev.*, XVII (1927), 63–68; Powicke, F. J., *A Life of the Reverend Richard Baxter, 1615–1691* (1925), 158–159; Tawney, Jeannette, *Chapters from Richard Baxter's Christian Directory* (1925); Tawney, R. H., *Religion and the Rise of Capitalism* (1926); *The Autobiography of Richard Baxter* (1696, ed. by Tawney, 1924); Commons and Perlman, Review of Sombart's *Der Moderne Kapitalismus*, *Amer. Econ. Rev.*, XIX (1929), 78–88.

[37] Tawney, R. H., *Religion and the Rise of Capitalism*, 268.

that marked the economic ideal of the Puritan spirit and the environment in which Locke got his ideas.

Tawney, in his *Religion and the Rise of Capitalism*, has well described the revolution that followed the year 1660 against both the
arbitrary rule of the Puritans and the arbitrary rule of the Stuart
kings; and we have seen how John Locke shared in this revolution.
The consequence was the demand that government should not inter-
pose to make private wealth subordinate to church and commonwealth. Locke was well prepared to support this demand both by
his skepticism of the human understanding and by his theory of
labor as the source of value. The kind of labor, however, which
he had in mind was that of Coke and Baxter: the busy and thrifty
tenant, freeholder, retailer, and proprietor of the common law and
of the Puritans, who worked and saved without compulsion, and
accumulated landed property, manufactures, and merchandise. It
was not the modern or Marxian labor of propertyless laborers, but
the labor of Foley and his iron works, Bates and his merchandise.

Neither Locke nor any of his Puritan contemporaries had made
the modern economic distinctions between rent, interest, profit, and
wages. Their attack was against persons, and not against the impersonal economic shares in distribution. All of these shares in distribution were combined in the single idea of personal compensation
for labor by a small farmer, a master workman, or merchant, who
was a proprietor, but not yet removed from manual work alongside
his journeymen and apprentices. Rent did not become an "unearned
income," like the income from monopolies and patents, until the
time of Ricardo, one hundred and twenty-five years after Locke.
It was only the excessive rent of rack-renting landlords and their
unjust enclosures that were classed by Baxter with the oppressors
and monopolists "against the commonwealth." Profit and interest
were not as yet theoretically distinguished, and indeed were not so
distinguished until Böhm-Bawerk, near two hundred years after
Locke.[38] Only usury, the excessive interest exacted by oppressive
money-lenders, was classed against the commonwealth, whereas
moderate interest charged for the use of one's property by others,
which one might have used himself, was a kind of profit. And
profit was hardly to be distinguished from wages where it was only

[38] Even Senior, in 1834, when he introduced the idea of "abstinence," did not distinguish interest as a payment for abstinence. Both profit and interest, for him, were
rewards of abstinence. He said (p. 89), "Abstinence expresses both the act of abstaining
from the unproductive use of capital [consumption], and also the similar conduct of the
man who devotes his labour to the production of remote rather than immediate results.
The person who so acts is a Capitalist, the reward of his conduct is Profit." Senior,
Nassau W., *Political Economy* (1834, 6th ed., 1872). Citation is to 6th edition.

the compensation for labor received by farmers, master workmen, and merchants who owned property yet worked harder for a profit than their employees for wages. Even in the time of Adam Smith, three-fourths of a century later, the employer was not distinguished from the laborer, nor profits distinguished from wages. If there were larger profits than ordinary compensation, the difference, as Tawney says, was only one of degree and not of kind.[39]

Locke's theory of value, thus derived from his Puritan contemporaries, was a theory based on a meaning of labor whose compensation was the ordinary compensation for the industry and thrift of a peasant farmer, a master workman, or a merchant, none of whom lived without work, and whose personal income, derived from the ownership of their output, partook of what afterwards became the impersonal incomes of rent, interest, profit, and wages. With him and others of his period, it was individuals, not functions, that were important.

Furthermore, with Locke and his Puritan contemporaries, all individuals were under a duty to work and accumulate—a duty imposed originally as punishment for the sin of Adam and Eve, and it was only those who actually worked and accumulated, and thus served the commonwealth, who fulfilled their duty to God. Labor was a punishment for sin, and consumption of wealth beyond one's personal needs was both a deduction from the commonwealth and a disobedience of God's commands. The Puritan worked and accumulated because it was his duty to God.

This was the kind of laborer who "produced value." Locke's meaning of value was that of productivity and accumulation which adds to the commonwealth, and not that of scarcity which deducts from the commonwealth. Consequently his idea of private property was the idea of production, usefulness, and happiness, each founded upon the idea of legal ownership for one's own use as a producer, or enjoyment as a consumer, of the products of his labor; not the transactional idea of reciprocally withholding from others what they need but do not own, nor the economic idea of scarcity as inducement to work, distinguished from the idea of labor as punishment for sin. Scarcity was personified as punishment for man's original sin at the Garden of Abundance. It is, however, this functional idea of scarcity that, after the time of Malthus, gave rise to the distinctions between rent, interest, profit, and wages.

With monopoly and oppression excluded as something derived from the arbitrary rule of monarchs, and with the scarcity idea of property and labor personified as Sin, it is evident that the produc-

[39] Tawney, R. H., *Religion and the Rise of Capitalism*, 207.

tivity idea of value is identical with both private wealth and commonwealth. Whatever augments private wealth, which can occur only in the sense of productivity, is an augmentation of commonwealth, and commonwealth is the sum of all private wealth.

Each of Locke's basic ideas, in his *Two Treatises on Government*, is founded upon this productivity idea of value, upon this proprietary meaning of ownership, and upon this moral idea of sin. He personified, in the single complex idea of labor, the constituent ideas of God, Nature, Reason, Perfection, Equality, Liberty, Happiness, Abundance, Usefulness, and Sin. God wills abundance but the sin of man compels him to work for it. Thus, he says:

> "Whether we consider natural reason, which tells us that men, being once born, have a right to their preservation, and consequently to meat and drink, and such other things as nature affords for their subsistence; or revelation, which gives us an account of those grants God made of the world to Adam, and to Noah, and his sons; it is very clear, that God, as King David says, Psal. cxv, 16, 'has given the earth to the children of men'; given it to mankind in common [and not, as Filmer says] to Adam, and his heirs in succession, exclusive of all the rest of his posterity." [40]

When Locke says that God's gifts were given in common, he, of course, does not mean common ownership in the historical sense of the primitive tribal communism, nor of the modern Marxian communism, nor of an organized group which rations to each individual his share. That meaning would not only have yielded to Filmer's contention of the natural authority of the head of the family to apportion shares to individuals as a dictator, but would also have contradicted his own idea of such original abundance that there was no injury to others by individual ownership and consequently no justification of any collective ownership that might obstruct free individual ownership. Locke's word "common" meant, not common ownership, by reason of scarcity, but equal opportunity universal in extent, by reason of abundance.

This idea of abundance is the presupposition of his idea of a natural right of property in "meat, drink and subsistence." His natural right of property does not arise from scarcity, but from abundance. Any individual can take what he needs from that abundance of God's gifts without taking it from anybody else, either by conquest or by unequal exchanges.

Upon whom, then, rests the correlative duty not to interfere with one's access to that which is so abundant that no conflict or compe-

[40] *The Works of John Locke*, V, *Two Treatises on Government*, Bk. II, Sec. 25.

tition can arise for exclusive possession of it? If it is as abundant as air or sunlight, then the idea of a right is meaningless, for there is no probability that any person will attempt to exclude any other from using as much of it as he needs. Yet, this is also Locke's idea of meat, drink, and subsistence. God in the original, and even present, state of nature, gives natural resources in such abundance that no person is compelled to ask consent of any other person to obtain access thereto. All that one needs to do is to take what he needs. But this "taking" is nothing but Labor in the form of meat, drink, and subsistence. This, however, is not merely manual labor, it is also intelligence. Rational labor, therefore, gives a title of ownership to whatever one takes from nature's abundance, which ownership, because the resources are abundant, does not deprive any other person of what he also may wish to take from that abundance.

"God, who hath given the world to man in common, hath also given them reason to make use of it to the best advantage of life, and convenience. The earth, and all that is therein, is given to men for the support and comfort of their being. And though all the fruits it naturally produces, and beasts it feeds, belong to mankind in common, as they are produced by the spontaneous hand of nature; and nobody has originally a private dominion, exclusive of the rest of mankind, in any of them, as they are thus in their natural state; yet being given for the use of men, there must of necessity be a means to appropriate them some way or other, before they can be of any use, or at all beneficial to any particular man. The fruit, or venison, which nourishes the wild Indian, who knows no inclosure, and is still a tenant in common, must be his, and so his, i.e. a part of him, that another can no longer have any right to it, before it can do him any good for the support of his life.

"Though the earth, and all inferior creatures, be common to all men, yet every man has a property in his own person: this nobody has any right to but himself. The labour of his body, and the work of his hands, we may say, are properly his. Whatsoever then he removes out of the state that nature hath provided, and left it in, he hath mixed his labour with, and joined to it something that is his own, and thereby makes it his property. It being by him removed from the common state nature hath placed it in, it hath by this labour something annexed to it, that excludes the common right of other men. For this labour being the unquestionable property of the labourer, no man but he can have a right to what that is once joined to, at least where there is enough, and as good, left in common for others." [41]

[41] *Ibid.*, Secs. 26, 27.

Thus Locke prepared the way for Adam Smith. Locke's idea of nature's abundance is also his presupposition of the natural right of liberty as well as property. "Every man has a property in his own person: this [property] nobody has any right to but himself." Thus his idea of labor is not merely manual labor and rational labor, and not merely the idea of productivity—it is also the idea of freedom and ownership. The laborer has a natural right to do as he pleases with his own body, and every other person is subject to the duty of letting him alone, while he takes his own property in meat, drink, and subsistence from nature's unlimited supplies. Locke's Labor is not slave labor—it is Free Labor, and this free labor is working on Free Land, which the laborer thereby reduces to his own private property.

At the time of Cromwell's victorious army, the Diggers, and other opponents of enclosures of the common lands by adjoining landlords, had based their claims to occupy the common lands upon the artificial scarcity of opportunities to labor. Locke based his advocacy of enclosures upon the natural abundance of land and the productivity of private property.

". . . he who appropriates land to himself by his labour, does not lessen, but increase the common stock of mankind: for the provisions serving to the support of human life, produced by one acre of enclosed and cultivated land, are (to speak much within compass) ten times more than those which are yielded by an acre of land of an equal richness lying waste in common. And therefore he that encloses land, and has a greater plenty of the conveniences of life from ten acres, than he could have from an hundred left to nature, may truly be said to give ninety acres to mankind: for his labour now supplies him with provisions out of ten acres, which were by the product of an hundred lying in common. I have here rated the improved land very low, in making its product but as ten to one, when it is much nearer an hundred to one." [42]

This was the argument of the American Homestead Law of 1862.[43] Hence, the productivity of the free laborer on free land is the same thing as the private property of the laborer, and this, according to Locke, is both a divine law and a natural law.

"God gave the world to man in common; . . . He gave it to the use of the industrious and rational. . . . He that had as good left for his improvement, as was already taken up, needed not complain, ought not to meddle with what was already im-

[42] *Ibid.*, Sec. 37.
[43] Commons, John R., and associates, *History of Labour in the United States* (1918), I, 562.

proved by another's labour. . . . God commanded, and his wants forced him to labour. That was his property which could not be taken from him wherever he had fixed it. And hence subduing or cultivating the earth, and having dominion, we see are joined together. The one gave title to the other. So that God, by commanding to subdue, gave authority so far to appropriate: And the condition of human life, which requires labour and materials to work on, necessarily introduces private possessions." [44]

The appropriation of any parcel of land, by improving it did not

"make prejudice to any other man, since there was still enough, and as good left; and more than the yet unprovided could use. So that, in effect, there was never the less left for others because of his enclosure for himself: for he that leaves as much as another can make use of, does as good as take nothing at all." [45]

Thus Locke united Law, Economics, and Ethics in the non-scarcity concept of land. It cannot be said that he was illogical, in view of the then sparse population of England and the world conquests that followed Elizabeth. The question arises, how much can such a laborer acquire as private property? Two answers are given by Locke, depending upon what goes before and what comes after the introduction of money. Before money was introduced the extent of property was

"set by the extent of men's labour, and the conveniences of life: No man's labour could subdue, or appropriate all; nor could his enjoyment consume more than a small part. . . . This measure did confine every man's possession to a very moderate proportion." [46] "The same law of nature, that does by this means give us property, does also bound that property too. 'God has given us all things richly,' I Tim. vi, 17. Is the voice of reason confirmed by inspiration. But how far has he given it us? To enjoy. As much as any one can make use of to any advantage of life before it spoils, so much he may by his labour fix a property in: Whatever is beyond this, is more than his share, and belongs to others. Nothing was made by God for man to spoil or destroy. And thus, considering the plenty of natural provisions there was a long time in the world, and the few spenders; and to how small a part of that provision the industry of one man could extend itself, and engross it to the prejudice of others; especially keeping within the bounds, set by reason, of what might serve for his use;

[44] *The Works of John Locke*, V, *Two Treatises on Government*, Bk. II, Secs. 34, 35.
[45] *Ibid.*, V, Sec. 33.
[46] *Ibid.*, V, Sec. 36.

there could be then little room for quarrels or contentions about property so established." [47]

This under-population argument was used against Filmer. If God made Kings the sole proprietors of the earth, a king

"may deny all the rest of mankind food, and so at his pleasure starve them, if they will not acknowledge his sovereignty, and obey his will." But it is "more reasonable to think, that God, who bid mankind increase and multiply, should rather himself give them all a right to make use of the food and raiment, and other conveniences of life, the materials whereof he had so plentifully provided for them, than to make them depend upon the will of a man for their subsistence." [48]

Thus the rule *before* the introduction of money was, "every man should have as much as he could make use of." But this "same rule of propriety" was not infringed when "larger possessions" were introduced by reason of the "invention of money." Here emerges Locke's mercantilism, which Quesnay and Adam Smith attacked, but which has not been overthrown, in fact, even to the present day. The acquisition of money, according to him, is both private wealth and an equivalent commonwealth.

For, with the "invention of money" it now became possible, without any encroachment on others, for an individual to own far more than he could subdue by his own individual labor. By "tacit agreement," a "little piece of yellow metal, which would keep without wasting or decay, should be worth a great piece of flesh, or a whole heap of corn." If he kept other commodities in large quantities he "wasted the common stock" because they "perished uselessly in his hands." But if he exchanged them for money or similar durable things, he gave away a part so that it perished not uselessly in his possession "and at the same time he might heap as much of these durable things as he pleased" and could not injure anybody, "the exceeding of the bounds of his just property not lying in the largeness of his possessions, but the perishing of anything uselessly in it."

The significance of money to the mercantilist Locke was its physical durability. For, he says, "thus came in the use of money, some lasting thing that men might keep without spoiling, and that by mutual consent men would take in exchange for the truly useful, but perishable, supports of life."

Then, by the use of money and commerce, large possessions be-

[47] *Ibid.*, V, Sec. 31.
[48] *Ibid.*, V, Bk. I, Sec. 41.

came profitable, "for I ask, what would a man value ten thousand, or an hundred thousand acres of excellent land, cultivated and well stocked too with cattle, in the middle of the inland parts of America, when he had no chance of commerce with other parts of the world, to draw money to him by the sale of the product? It would not be worth the enclosing." And this money thus "received in exchange for the overflow" may be "hoarded up without injury to any one; these metals not spoiling or decaying in the hands of the possessor." Thus private wealth, like the mercantilists' national wealth, is the accumulation of money acquired by exchange of commodities.

The introduction of money does not, in Locke's estimation, imply the disappearance of free land. Large possessions acquired by commerce and money were no more a reduction of the abundance of land than was the case before money was introduced.

Hence Locke's presupposition, by which labor, materials, and private property are made the center of his theory of value and government, is the presupposition of abundance of land granted to free men in common by a beneficent creator, with the duty to work and multiply. The economic term "abundance" is equivalent to Locke's theological term "beneficence."

With this presupposition of abundance there could be no contradiction between material things and ownership of the things. Not until property means scarcity and labor means abundance does the contradiction appear.

The introduction of gold and silver as money made it necessary for Locke to distinguish two kinds of value, each, however, founded on labor. "Value by tacit agreement or consent" is the value of gold and silver, but "the intrinsic value of things" depends only on "their usefulness to the life of man." This we shall later distinguish as scarcity-value and use-value, respectively. With Locke, however, each of these kinds of value was determined by the amount of labor, and it was this that led directly to Karl Marx's theory of value. The amount of intrinsic value—that is the quantity of use-value—is almost exactly identical with the amount of labor. Locke said, in repetition of his earlier statement:

". . . for it is labour indeed that put the difference of value on everything; and let anyone consider what the difference is between an acre of land planted with tobacco or sugar, sown with wheat or barley, and an acre of the same land lying in common, without any husbandry upon it, and he will find, that the improvement of labour makes the far greater part of the value. I think it will be but a very modest computation to say, that of the products of the earth useful to the life of man, nine-tenths are the effects of labour: nay, if we will rightly estimate things as they come to our use, and cast up the several expences about them, what in them is purely owing to nature, and what to labour, we shall find, that in most of them ninety-nine hundredths are wholly to be put on the account of labour." [49]

Quesnay and Smith did not go this far, but made nature *also* productive. McCulloch and Karl Marx adhered to Locke.

But gold and silver also have a value determined in amount mainly by the amount of labor. They are indeed "little useful to the life of man in proportion to food, raiment and carriage." They have but a "fantastical imaginary value: Nature has put no such upon them." [50] For this reason their value is not intrinsic but is "only for the consent of men." Yet labor makes "in great part, the measure of their value."

Thus Locke combined in a "complex idea" all that he had demonstrated elsewhere, both in his *Essay Concerning Human Understanding* and his treatises on Government and Toleration, respecting God, Nature, Reason, Property, Equality, Liberty, Happiness, Abundance, Usefulness, and Sin, and personified them in his meaning of Labor. God, Nature, and Reason are identical, for although the reasoning is Locke's own reason at work, yet he was given that power of reasoning out of God's own power, and he knows God's reason and can tell what God intended, not as a probability but as a certainty—a certainty derived not by intuition but by demonstration, like the eternal, timeless truths of mathematics. These intentions are: all men are treated alike by God who is identical with Nature and eternal Reason; all are to enjoy the happiness of having their wants satisfied from the useful qualities of nature's gifts; those useful qualities are given in abundance, such that no competition or dispute need arise respecting exclusive possession of them; this abundance is evidence that God's intentions are beneficent; with this abundance and this equality of treatment every person is equally at liberty to take all that he can use for himself, since enough will then be left for all others; under these conditions of abundance, therefore, life, liberty, and property may be designated as either natural rights, divine rights, or the rights which reason demonstrates, since reason is a logical justification from the universal benevolence of God.

The question arises, why should there be any need for Labor at all if God, nature, and eternal reason furnished everything in abun-

[49] *Ibid.*, V, Bk. II, Sec. 40.
[50] *Ibid.*, V, Bk. II, Sec. 50.

dance, like air, sunlight, meat, drink, and subsistence? Locke's answer was the Puritan's answer: Sin. It was Sin instead of Scarcity that forced man to work. Man's disobedience of God's commands was the occasion for condemning him both to the duty to work for a living and to the duty of subordination of the one whose sin was greater to the one whose sin was less. He used the same circumstance as Filmer, but interpreted it differently.

> "The words [at the expulsion from Eden] are the curse of God upon the woman, for having been the first and forwardest in the disobedience. . . . As helper in the temptation [as well as a partner in the transgression] Eve was laid below him, and so he had accidently a superiority over her, for her greater punishment . . . it would be hard to imagine, that God, in the same breath, should make him universal monarch over all mankind [as Filmer contended] and a day-labourer for his life; turn him out of 'paradise to till the ground,' v. 23, and at the same time advance him to a throne, and all the privileges and ease of absolute power. . . . God sets him to work for his living, and seems rather to give him a spade into his hand to subdue the earth, than a sceptre to rule over its inhabitants. 'In the sweat of thy face, thou shalt eat thy bread.' " [51]

Thus scarcity is personified as Sin, and poverty is justified as sinfulness. Sin is pictured as the judgment of an angry God, enforced by the penalty of expulsion from His Paradise of Abundance.[52] This became the theory of Adam Smith; and, a hundred and fifty years after Locke, slavery was justified in America as the penalty for sin, while all labor legislation, child-labor legislation, and trade unionism in America for a hundred years have been forced to distinguish punishment for sin from coercion by scarcity.[53]

Locke's meaning of Value is therefore a union of ethics, law, and economics in the personification of Labor, and contains, when reduced to physical measurements, three meanings, all of which exclude a functional concept of scarcity, and all of which, with

---

[51] *Ibid.*, V, Bk. I, Secs. 44, 45.

[52] Cf. Weber, *op. cit.*, on the duty to work contained in the doctrines of Aquinas, Luther, Calvin, and Baxter.

[53] Cf. Commons, John R., and Andrews, John B., *Principles of Labor Legislation* (1927); Commons, John R., and associates, *History of Labour in the United States*, especially on Imprisonment for Debt. Frank, T., *Economic History of Rome* (1920, 1927), 324, says, "The universal law of inertia that makes of every man a potential parasite has generally led naïve thought to the inference that labor must be the penalty of sin imposed at the exit gate of paradise. Ancient philosophers like Aristotle and Zeno while hardly satisfied with an explanation so simple arrived at an equally low estimate of a life spent in manual labor by dwelling upon the moral and intellectual futility to which years of constant drudgery led."

improvements, are found in Adam Smith. These may be summarized as:

(1) A physical, objective, embodiment of useful qualities—later to be distinguished as Use-Value—in that they are useful for production or for consumption, but their usefulness does not depend on scarcity and therefore does not diminish with an increase of supply nor increase with a reduction of supply. The sum total of these useful qualities is the economic meaning both of commonwealth and private wealth. Private use-value is identical with public use-value.

(2) The cause and measure of Value are the free will of the free laborer working on free land—condemned, however, to work and save for the future on account of his wilful disobedience of God's commands, and not on account of scarcity caused by ownership by others of his body, or of his opportunities to work, or of the products of his work.

(3) The fulfillment of this duty to work and save is, correspondingly, his right to private property in the product of his labor and frugality, and in the products of all other free laborers which he obtains from them by commerce and money. His rights are identical with his individual product on free land and with what he receives by free exchange.

3. *Custom*

At a luncheon of eight hundred business men in Philadelphia, in 1922, when the subject of discussion was the relations of employers to their employees, a statement of "Facts" was adopted and sent out as a leaflet, in part as follows: "We are all workers; the United States is our union; our allegiance is first to God and then to that union. Our nation is a living expression of belief in our Creator. Liberty is our human right by divine right."

This assertion of the divine right of liberty and property in 1922 goes back to John Locke in 1689.[54] We have noted above that Locke's idea of God, Nature, and Reason was his own idea made eternal, changeless, timeless, like mathematics. It existed, according to his *Essay Concerning Human Understanding*, only in his own mind, yet it was "certain." The question arises, How did it come to exist in his own mind? His philosophical answer was, divine beneficence equivalent to earthly abundance. For the finite in philosophy is scarcity in economics, and the infinite in philosophy is

[54] Cf. Hamilton, W. H., "Property According to Locke," *Yale Law Jour.*, XLI (April 1932), 864–880.

abundance in economics. But Locke had difficulty in working out his theory of abundance on the mercantilist assumption of a scarcity of money. Similar ideas of beneficence and abundance existed before, in the minds of Filmer and the popes and afterwards in the mind of Quesnay in France, Adam Smith in Scotland, Abraham Lincoln in America, and the employers of Philadelphia. Evidently, in the assumption of divine right of liberty and property, if the idea of God is deemed to be a God of scarcity (as afterwards it was with Malthus) instead of abundance, we must look elsewhere than to economics or philosophy to discover the origin of divine and natural rights. We find it in Custom.

The ideas of divine rights of property and liberty came from experience, as Locke contended, but the experience from which Locke's ideas obtained their meanings was his experience with what he deemed to be the good customs of those with whom he preferred to associate. So it was with Filmer and the Philadelphia employers. Locke was led to the publication of his special form of identification of God, Nature, and Reason by the popularity of Filmer's *Patriarcha* among the clergy and other adherents of King James, wherein God, Nature, and Reason had been identified with what Filmer deemed to be the good customs of those with whom he preferred to associate.

Filmer had written his book during the dictatorship of Cromwell, and he had two groups of opponents using similar arguments, against whom he must assert the divine right of King Charles. On the one side the Papacy, on the other side the Puritans, had identified God, Nature, and Reason with the right of the people to overthrow their kings and to assert, on the one side, the divine right of popes to govern the kings, and, on the other side, the divine right of small property-owners to choose the kings and regulate their behavior by law.

"Since the time that school divinity began to flourish," wrote Filmer, "there hath been a common opinion maintained, as well by divines as by divers other learned men, which affirms,—

" 'Mankind is naturally endowed and born with freedom from all subjection, and at liberty to choose what form of government it please, and that the power which any one man hath over others was at first bestowed according to the discretion of the multitude.'

"This tenet," says Filmer, "was first hatched in the schools, and hath been fostered by all succeeding Papists for good divinity. The divines, also, of the Reformed Churches have entertained it, and the common people everywhere tenderly embrace it as being most plausible to flesh and blood, for that it prodigally distributes a portion of liberty to the meanest of the multitude, who magnify liberty as if the height of human felicity were only to be found in it, never remembering that the desire of liberty was the first cause of the fall of Adam." [55]

Filmer then answers at length "the subtle schoolmen," especially Cardinal Bellarmine and the Jesuit, Suarez, "who to be sure to thrust down the king below the pope, thought it the safest course to advance the people above the king, that so the papal power might take the place of the regal." This doctrine of the "schoolmen," he goes on, "contradicts the doctrine and history of the Holy Scriptures, the constant practice of all ancient monarchies, and the very principles of the law of nature. It is hard to say whether it be more erroneous in divinity or dangerous in policy," for it is the doctrine of the "natural liberty and equality of mankind" on which is founded "the whole fabric of this vast engine of popular sedition." [56]

The doctrine of the divine right of Kings, which Filmer supported, was older, indeed, than the opposing doctrine, but, as Figgis points out, Filmer was the first to found it, not on the former notion of divine ordinance, nor on quotations from Scripture, but on human nature as formed by the Creator for existence in society.[57] Thus he identified divine law with the law both of nature and of human nature, and the divine right of kings became the natural right of Kings. Quesnay did the same for landlords and kings, and Locke, Smith, and the Philadelphia employers for manufacturers.

But Filmer gave a biological meaning to nature. The basic fact of human nature, he said, is not equality and liberty, but heredity and subjection. Babies are begotten by fathers, whereby, Filmer maintained, they fall immediately under the absolute paternal power of the father to do with them as he pleases in all matters of life, death, liberty, and property. Whatever they have of their own is obtained by grace and not by right. Their natural condition is slavery, and they may be exposed as in Rome, or sold, as in many historic cases of primitive society cited by Filmer, without any punishment imposed upon the father for so doing. But if the father did otherwise and preserved his children, it was not because nature imposed the duty but because he loved his children.

The same, argued Filmer, is true of a commonwealth as it is of a family. There is but one father of a commonwealth as there is

[55] Filmer, Sir Robert, *Patriarcha; or the Natural Power of Kings*, Ch. I, Sec. 1, p. 1, in Morley's edition of Locke's *Two Treatises on Civil Government* (2nd ed., 1887).

[56] *Ibid.*, 1–2.

[57] Figgis, J. N., *Theory of the Divine Right of Kings* (1st ed.), 149 ff.

but one father of a family. Filmer's "whole argument," says Figgis, "depends on the identification of the Kingdom with the family, and of royal power with paternal power." [58] He took this metaphor seriously. It was, as Figgis says, "far more substantial than the ordinary hotchpotch of quotations from Scripture" and "the popularity of the book is further evidence that the idea came to most men with the force of a discovery." [59]

The discovery was the identification of God with Biology, and the identification of Biology with the primitive customs of ancient families, tribes and nations, as well as the contemporary customs of the Kings of England and the adherents of the royal cause. Historically, Filmer was more nearly correct than Locke. The common law of England was, as he rightly says, not merely a "common custom," because

"for every custom there was a time when it was no custom, and the first precedent we now have had no precedent when it began; when every custom began, there was something else than custom that made it lawful, or else the beginning of all customs were unlawful. Customs at first became lawful only by some superior which did either command or consent unto their beginning. . . . The common law itself, or common customs of this land, were originally the laws and commands of kings at first unwritten." And the judges who built up the common law did "all receive authority from the king in his right and name to give sentence according to the rules and precedents of ancient times." [60] Filmer gives several citations.

So also with statute laws. The "king is the sole immediate author, corrector, and moderator of them also." Parliaments were called and dismissed by the king at his will. They were not founded on "the usage of any natural liberty of the people; for all those liberties that are claimed in parliament are the liberties of grace from the king, and not the liberties of nature to the people; for if the liberty were natural, it would give power to the multitude to assemble themselves when and where they please, to bestow sovereignty, and by pactions, to limit and direct the exercise of it. . . . The people cannot assemble themselves, but the king, by his writs, calls them to what place he pleases; and then again scatters them with his breath at an instant, without any other cause showed than his will." And the statute laws are not made by parliament but "by the King alone, at the rogation of the people." [61]

[58] *Ibid.*, 149.
[59] *Ibid.*, 151.
[60] Filmer, *op. cit.*, Ch. III, Sec. 9.
[61] *Ibid.*, Ch. III, Secs. 11–15.

All this, according to Filmer, is as reason says it should be, for otherwise the commonwealth is broken in pieces by sedition and civil war.

> ". . . although a king do frame all his actions to be according to the laws, yet he is not bound thereto but at his good will and for good example, or so far forth as the general law of the safety of the commonwealth doth naturally bind him; for in such sort only positive laws may be said to bind the king, not by being positive, but as they are naturally the best or only means for the preservation of the commonwealth. By this means are all kings, even tyrants and conquerors, bound to preserve the lands, goods, liberties, and lives of all their subjects, not by any municipal law of the land, so much as the natural law of a father, which binds them to ratify the acts of their forefathers and predecessors in things necessary for the public good of their subjects." [62]

Thus Filmer, equally with Locke, is the prophet of the manufacturers of Philadelphia. God, Nature, and Reason all agree and are identical in establishing a divine and natural right of kings according to what are deemed to be the practices, good or bad, of British kings and all kings from Adam to Charles, and afterwards of all employers toward their employees.

Filmer evidently exposed the divine right of kings naked and helpless before the nimble mind of Locke, who playfully tossed up and down Filmer's contradictory meanings of words and events. Filmer's importance for the theory, says Figgis, was "indeed great," for "he deserves to be remembered less as the most perfect exponent of the theory, than as the herald of its decadence." [63] His was exactly the kind of absurdity looked for by the clever author of the *Essay Concerning Human Understanding* in order to convert the divine right of kings into the divine right of property owners. But Locke's revision was the less absurd only because he spoke for the victorious party, Filmer for the defeated party.

Exactly like Filmer, Locke identified God, Nature, and Reason, but the meaning was different, for the customs out of which he constructed his meanings were the victorious customs of the farmers, manufacturers, merchants, and capitalists of 1689, whereas Filmer's were the decadent customs of primitive tribes, ancient civilizations, and papal adherents; the defeated customs of British kings, feudal lords, and royal adherents.

For custom is the mere repetition, duplication, and variability of

---

[62] *Ibid.*, Ch. III, Sec. 6.
[63] Figgis, *op. cit.*, 152.

practices and transactions. No repetition is exactly the same as its predecessor, and no duplication is exactly the same as its contemporary. Hence, there is always a variability of customs in successive times and at the same time. These variations in the course of history introduce new customs as variables, or as alternatives, of preceding or contemporary customs; there is always a decadence, or even a violent elimination, of old customs or competing customs, giving way to the new or different ones. Thus, there is a continual selection of customs going on, and consequently there is a survival of customs fitted to the changing economic conditions and the changing political and economic dominance. Since this occurs by operation of the human will, it is much like the artificial selection of Darwin's evolution, applicable, however, to practices and transactions suited to changing social conditions, instead of to Darwin's structures and functions of living organisms suited to changing geological conditions.

This analogy between the evolution of species and the evolution of customs, both by artificial selection, is close enough to warrant the assertion that there is a similar force at work which we name Willingness, both conscious and habitual. Customs cannot be changed radically or suddenly, since they arise from the most elementary fact of living creatures, Instinct and Habit, which are the mere repetition of acts found by experience to be preservative of life, of enjoyment, and of survival in the struggles of competition. This repetition goes from one generation to another in such a way that custom is analogous to heredity.

But custom is more than habit. It is the social habit which creates individual habit. We do not start as isolated individuals— we start in infancy with discipline and obedience, and we continue as members of concerns already going, so that conformity to repeated and duplicated practices—which is all that is meant by going concerns—is the only way to obtain life, liberty, and property with ease, safety, and consent. Neither do we start or continue as intelligent beings, presupposed by Locke's "original state of nature." We start and continue by repetition, routine, monotony— in short by custom. The intellect itself is both a repetition of action, memory, and expectation; and an imitation—or rather, duplication—of the acts, memories, and expectations of those upon whom we depend for life, liberty, and property.

If there is a feeling that keeps these repetitions and duplications agoing, it may be described as the feelings of Familiarity, Good Standing, and Social Compulsion. If these repetitions and expectations are found to be substantially invariable, and therefore highly familiar and quite compulsory if they are not adhered to, and if they are found to afford a good social standing that gives security of beneficial expectations, then they are likely to be personified as a kind of command issued before the event; whereas they are, as far as we know from the way in which they operate, only an expectation that similar beneficial behavior will be repeated. This personification of *good* customs was evidently the mental process of Filmer and Locke, who pictured the expected repetitions of physical nature and human nature, with which they were familiar and felt secure, as an eternal, timeless, presupposed, and unchangeable law of Nature, God, and Reason.

Yet, they are not unchangeable. They change with changes in economic and political conditions. The customs with which both Filmer and Locke were familiar were the repeated practices and transactions of landlords, tenants, kings, known as the feudal system; and the practices and transactions of merchants, master workmen, farmers, in the then period of capitalistic expansion through commerce and revolution.

The customs, however, which seemed divine and natural to Locke, were very recent in history, though they were older than Locke himself. Thus, the enforcement of voluntary contracts by the King's courts was hardly a hundred and fifty years old; yet Locke projected the practice back to the origin of society and founded upon it the obligation to obey the government which had been set up in the "original contract."

The judicial practice of reading into the behavior of parties an implied legal contract, arising out of what the court might assume by their acts to have been the intentions of the parties, was likewise of common-law origin, in the doctrine of *assumpsit* during the Sixteenth Century; but Locke, making, as he says, "the common distinction of an express and a tacit consent," founded upon it his doctrine that people in primitive times were supposed to make enforceable implied contracts similar to those in his own time. In general, Locke's doctrine of tacit consent, upon which much of his *Treatise* is founded, is nothing but custom. All customs, from the most primitive times, even slavery, may be interpreted as a practice of tacit consent; but Locke drew the line at those tacit consents which were to him familiar and deemed beneficial to those whose cause he espoused.

The inheritance of property by children, according to the custom of Englishmen, was a natural right of children, "and where the practice is universal, it is reasonable to think the cause is natural." [64]

[64] *The Works of John Locke*, V, *Two Treatises of Government*, Bk. II, Ch. 6, Sec. 88.

The subjection of women to their husbands, as then practiced in England, was founded on God's punishment of Eve, and on "the laws of mankind and customs of nations," so that there is a "foundation in nature for it." Her subjection was a divine and natural duty correlative to the husband's right, because familiar and beneficial in Locke's opinion. He objected only to the attempt of Filmer to apply the "sanctity of custom" to "a political power of life and death over her" which, Locke says, does not follow rationally from the sanctity of a "conjugal power" of property over her." [65]

Most important of all was the custom of private property, including in its meaning, "lives, liberties and estates," as practiced in the common law of 1689. Yet property, according to Locke, exists before the organization of society, and "the great and chief end, therefore, of men's uniting into commonwealths, and putting themselves under government, is the preservation of their property." [66]

If customs change, or conditions change, then a choice must be made between customs, and it is a conflict of reason and self-interest that determines the choice. Good customs should be selected and bad ones rejected. Speaking of the "rotten borroughs" represented in the British parliament, Locke says: "Things of this world are in so constant a flux, that nothing remains long the same. . . . But things not always changing equally, and private interest often keeping up customs and privileges, when reasons of them are ceased. . . . To what gross absurdities the following of custom, when reason has left it, may lead," may be seen, he said, in the unequal representation of these rotten boroughs in parliament. [67] This has happened, since Locke's time, to many of the customs he thought were divine, natural, and eternal. They have become more or less rotten.

On the other hand, the customs which were lacking in "a state of Nature" were those which the judiciary of England had developed into a common law in the time of Locke, after several centuries of slow selection of what were deemed, at the time, to be good practices. Locke's description of "a state of Nature" is exactly a state in which these customs had not yet been developed into a common law, but his participants were rational beings who knew about them anyhow, and who proceeded to organize a commonwealth to make them certain and enforceable.

[65] *Ibid.*, V, Bk. II, Sec. 83.
[66] *Ibid.*, V, Bk. II, Secs. 123, 124.
[67] *Ibid.*, V, Bk. II, Secs. 157, 158.

These new practices wanted but not yet found in the state of nature, were, according to Locke, first

"an established, settled, known law, received and allowed by common consent to be the standard of right and wrong; and the common measure to decide all controversies between them: For though the law of nature be plain and intelligible to all rational creatures; yet men being biased by their interest, as well as ignorant for want of studying it, are not apt to allow of it as a law binding to them in the application of it to their particular cases." [68]   Hence the need of independence of the judiciary.

"Secondly, in the state of nature there wants a known and indifferent judge, with authority to determine all differences according to the established law: For every one in that state being both judge and executioner of the law of nature, men being partial to themselves, passion and revenge is very apt to carry them too far, and with too much heat, in their own cases; as well as negligence, and unconcernedness, to make them too remiss in other men's." [69] Hence, again, independence of the judiciary.

"Thirdly, in the state of nature there often wants power to back and support the sentence when right, and to give it due execution. They who by any injustice offend, will seldom fail, where they are able, by force to make good their injustice; such resistance many times makes the punishment dangerous, and frequently destructive, to those who attempt it." [70]   Hence, the need of a constitutional monarch to enforce the decrees of the judiciary.

Thus the state of nature was that original state of isolated yet intellectual beings like Locke himself, who did not have the Common Law of England, an Independent Judiciary, a Constitutional Monarch, or a Sheriff subordinate to the judiciary.

The "state of war," on the contrary, is the state "not under the ties of the common law of reason" (where there is no common judge with authority), and where one may destroy a man "for the same reason that he may kill a wolf or a lion." In the state of nature, there is no appeal to an impartial earthly judge; this is true also of an unjust judge who refuses to obey the law. Princes owe subjection to the laws of God and Nature.[71]

So that there remains, in either case, only an "appeal to heaven," whereby the effort of all parties to enforce this divine and natural law is nothing else than the "state of war." The state of nature becomes the state of war, in the absence of an independent, impartial judiciary, or the absence of an executive obedient to the

[68] *Ibid.*, V, Bk. II, Sec. 124.
[69] *Ibid.*, V, Bk. II, Sec. 125.
[70] *Ibid.*, V, Bk. II, Sec. 126.
[71] *Ibid.*, V, Bk. II, Sec. 16.

law. What "puts men out of a state of nature into that of a commonwealth" is "the setting up a judge on earth." Thus Locke justified the Revolution of 1689, and put the burden of proof on the defeated king. The use of force by the king, without the authority of natural and divine law, "always puts him that uses it into a state of war, as the aggressor, and renders him liable to be treated accordingly." "The people have no other remedy in this, as in all other cases where they have no judge on earth, but to appeal to heaven." [72]

It is this "state of nature," not conquest by war, that is the origin of government. For the state of nature is a state of voluntary agreement without coercion. Herein Locke reversed English history but justified the revolution of 1689 and the American Civil War which abolished slavery.

> "Though governments can originally have no other rise than that before-mentioned, nor politics be founded on anything but the consent of the people; yet such have been the disorders ambition has filled the world with, that in the noise of war, which makes so great a part of the history of mankind, this consent is little taken notice of: and therefore many have mistaken the force of arms for the consent of the people, and reckoned conquest as one of the originals of government. But conquest is as far from setting up any government, as demolishing an house is from building a new one in the place. Indeed, it often makes way for a new frame of a commonwealth, by destroying the former; but, without the consent of the people, can never erect a new one." [73]

Locke searched for historical examples of his original state of nature, seeing that the objection was made that people are born under governments already existing, and could not have come together voluntarily out of a preceding state of separate individual existence. He mentioned the beginnings of Rome and Venice and the Indian tribes of America.

We may cite a later example. The nearest recorded approach to Locke's state of nature, which was also his state of abundance, was in the mining camps of California during the first year and a half of the gold discoveries, as described by Shinn.[74] During these eighteen months the miners had no government and no crimes; they had equality of claims staked off for diggings; they had individual liberty to acquire all the gold they could obtain by their own labor;

[72] *Ibid.*, V, Bk. II, Ch. 16.

[73] *Ibid.*, V, Bk. II, Sec. 175.

[74] Shinn, Charles Howard, *Land Laws of Mining Districts*, Johns Hopkins Univ. Studies in Historical and Political Science, II (1884), 12.

they had perfect private property in what they might obtain by labor, and common property in the sense of the public domain conquered from Spain and protected against the Indians. They were the Diggers of Cromwell's time, without the ejections by Cromwell's troops.

If we look for the explanation of their state of nature, we find that it was exactly John Locke's state of abundance. A gold digger could earn by his own labor as much as a thousand dollars a day in gold. Newcomers were, by the custom of the miners, permitted to take up claims, limited to the extent of their labor-power, alongside earlier claims. No one interfered with another's claim, since there was abundance for all. No one needed to work for wages, and thus each one was his own laborer, employer, landlord, and owner of his product, just as John Locke defined labor in 1689. No crimes, trespasses, or thefts occurred, because: what was the use when more money could be made by digging? This period passed with the inrush of gold seekers the second year, and abundance became scarcity. Then thefts, crimes, trespasses, courts, executives, and hangings emerged, and the State of Nature became the State of California.

Thus the fallacy of Locke's reasoning was the historic fallacy of Inverted Sequence. He reversed the time factor. He projected into primitive times intellectual beings like himself and the miners of California who came from a modern civilization. He projected backward the practices, to which he was accustomed and which he wished to see perpetuated, into an eternal reason binding upon men henceforth without change. What he figured to be a command issued in the past was an expectation of the future. Thus he transposed to an original state of nature the voluntary agreements which centuries of strong government and a king's judiciary had made the common law of England. He mentally constructed for a period of scarcity and violence the ideas belonging to a period of abundance and peace.

On the other hand, Locke appreciated the true historical process of custom when he rejected those customs that appeared to him to have outlived their rational basis and to be merely the perpetuation of unequal privileges. Reason had departed from such customs because they did not look good. Good customs are divine, natural, eternal; bad customs are human, unnatural, temporary.

Yet, what Locke had said of "rotten boroughs" is true of all customs. They begin as adaptations of human behavior to new conditions, and they survive after the "reason of them" has disappeared. And what Filmer said of the common law is also true.

Customs do not become law until the courts have decided disputes in conformity to them. They are "natural" in the human sense of security of expectations—not in the divine sense of unchangeable commands issued in the infinite past according to what the present individual thinks ought to have been issued.

The same is true of Locke's idea of the sanctity of property. By using the term Nature, he, like the manufacturers of Philadelphia, can picture liberty and property as a "fact," whereas they are only his justification of what he thinks they ought to be. Property is, in "real fact," only an expected repetition of managerial, bargaining, and rationing transactions, as variable as changing conditions and changing meanings; not a divine unchanging command issued in conformity to what present beneficiaries now think ought to be made unchangeable. The meaning of property has greatly changed from the time when Locke personified the customs of the frugal, laborious farmers, the master mechanics, and the merchants, as a divine command of unchanging nature and reason, to the time when property is absentee control over laborers and consumers throughout the world by a legalized credit and corporate system of management and a world-scarcity of opportunities. Locke's appeal to Heaven was his justification of the Revolution of 1689 against the divine right of Kings over their subjects. The Philadelphia manufacturers' appeal to Heaven in 1922 is their justification of a divine right of property owners over their employees.

This mental tool is not a good one for investigation of economic conditions, though it may be good for propaganda. It is a kind of oath, sworn even by those who are atheists, that, in the name of God, what they think is a fact *is* a fact and prevails over all research, investigation, and the opinions of others. We must therefore proceed to construct a new set of ideas that may, perhaps, be good tools for research.

John Locke was the spokesman of a Revolution that changed England from Feudalism to Capitalism. We find that other revolutions were presaged or followed by other revolutionary changes in economic and juristic theory. The French Revolution adopted the whole of Adam Smith's theory, and the classical political economy arose from the debate between Malthus and Ricardo during the world war and recovery that followed that Revolution. The Russian Communist Revolution adopted the theories of Marx, and we are now in the midst of a revolution in economic theory that grows out of another world war.

Locke set forth the labor theory of value, not mainly as a foundation for economics, but mainly as a justification of a revolution that supplanted rights of sovereigns by rights of property. He enlarged these rights of property by identifying money with both private wealth and common wealth. But this philosophy of Mercantilism served to split economic theory in two directions, the monetary and the non-monetary.

The monetary theories went off through Quesnay, Turgot, Malthus, until they reached the credit theories of MacLeod, Wicksell, Cassell, Knapp, Hawtrey, Keynes, and the other theories which presaged and followed a world war conducted on sheer credit.

The labor theories went off through Smith, Ricardo, Proudhon, and Marx, who sought to replace the nominal values of money by the real values of work and sacrifice, thereby presaging a hitherto unknown power of labor to dictate the terms on which war should be conducted. Thus the unfinished problems of the recent World War bring to the front the concerted action of labor, unknown to Locke, Smith, and Ricardo, in forcing its way into the possession of economic and political power; and economic theory changes from that of a physical equilibrium of competing individual property-owners to that of collective control of both economic transactions and government by both capitalistic and laboristic combinations. We shall proceed with some detail to follow these historical changes in economic theory in order to lay the foundations for the modern theories of transactions, working rules, and going concerns.

II. Transactions and Concerns [75]

1. *From Corporations to Going Concerns*

In the year 1893 the people of the State of Indiana made a demand upon the legislature for an equalization of taxes upon the property of the great public utility corporations—such as railways running across the state—with the property of farmers, manufacturers, and business men. Property at that time meant corporeal property and incorporeal property, the physical goods of lands, buildings, railway tracks, stocks of inventories on hand; and the debts and shares of stock owned by individuals or corporations. The incorporeal property escaped the assessors, partly because concealed, partly because the *situs* for taxation purposes followed the domicile of the owner, which, in the case of corporations, was deemed to be the state under whose laws the charter was granted

[75] This section is intended as an introduction or outline, to be developed in following chapters.

and in which the corporation was required to have its legal office. In response to the demand the legislature of Indiana changed the assessment of these corporations from the valuation of their physical property in Indiana to the total market value of their stocks and bonds, as bought and sold on the New York Stock Exchange, and then prorated that value to the State of Indiana in the proportion that the mileage in Indiana bore to the total mileage in all the states.

What happened was that a corporation which hitherto had only a legal existence in the state of its incorporation, because it was an invisible legal entity existing only in contemplation of law,[76] now became an economic going concern existing in its transactions wherever it carried on business and gained thereby the net income which gave value to its stocks and bonds on the stock exchange.

The State of Ohio copied this legislation and it went from Ohio to the United States Supreme Court where it was sustained in 1897. The Court found that the sum total of all the corporeal property of the Adams Express Company in Ohio was only $23,400; but Ohio's share, according to mileage, of the total market value of all the stocks and bonds was $450,000, an intangible property about twelve times as valuable as the corporeal property.[77] The Adams Express Company, instead of a corporation located in New York, becomes a going concern existing wherever it does business.

A similar transition from the legal to the economic meaning was made by the Supreme Court in the dissolution suit against the United States Steel Company in 1920. The company was incorporated as a holding company in the State of New Jersey. The Department of Justice brought suit to have the holding company dissolved, as a violation of the anti-trust laws, but the Court investigated the practices of its subsidiaries in different parts of the country and found them to be reasonable restraints of trade.[78] One of these practices, not brought before the Court in 1920, the so-called "Pittsburgh Plus" practice of discrimination, came before the Federal Trade Commission in 1923, on petition of a wide-spread Western Association of Rolled Steel Consumers. The practice consisted in quoting all prices of steel at Pittsburgh, plus the freight to the point of delivery, no matter where manufactured. The buyer, according to the contract, did not obtain title at Pittsburgh, but obtained title only at the point where he used the steel. This

---

[76] Dartmouth College v. Woodward, 4 Wheat 463 (1819).

[77] Adams Express Co. v. Ohio State Auditor, 165 U. S. 194; 166 U. S. 185 (1897). See Commons, *Legal Foundations of Capitalism*, 172.

[78] U. S. v. U. S. Steel Co., 251 U. S. 417 (1920).

practice, it was claimed by the lawyers in prosecution, created a monopoly located at the legal *situs* of the holding company in New Jersey. If this claim was correct, the remedy was dissolution of the holding company as a subterfuge to evade the anti-trust laws. Similar dissolutions, on that ground, had been ordered in the Standard Oil and Tobacco Company cases.

But the economists in the Pittsburgh Plus case, Fetter, Ripley, and Commons, argued that it was a discrimination rather than a monopoly, the discrimination existing wherever the corporation did business, and that the proper remedy was not dissolution, but the transfer of legal title to the product at any point where the steel was manufactured, whether Pittsburgh, Chicago, Duluth, or Birmingham. The company owned plants in all of these places, and the cost of production *plus freight* might be *less* when manufactured in Chicago and shipped to Iowa, *away* from Pittsburgh, than when manufactured in Pittsburgh and shipped to Iowa. But Iowa did not get the advantage of lower costs and shorter haul when the Chicago plant quoted its price on the Pittsburgh base plus freight from Pittsburgh. Furthermore the plant at Chicago selling *towards* Pittsburgh charged a *lower* delivered price to its customer than its delivered price to a customer who used the steel at a point nearer Chicago. This was the practice of "dumping," or selling in a distant market at lower prices than those charged in the home market. The issue was, whether there was a free competitive market when the thirty-year-old custom of the steel business designated as the *place of alienating legal control* the thousands of places of physical delivery to customers, or whether the ideal of equal opportunity and free competition required that *legal control* should pass at the point of manufacture.

The Federal Trade Commission, on this interpretation, ordered discontinuance of Pittsburgh as the basing point and the substitution of the places of actual manufacture as the basing points. The order did not fully carry out the interpretation of the economists that legal title should pass to the customer at the place of manufacture in order that all customers might have equal opportunity to *compete for legal control* at that place, but it substantially accomplished what the economists intended.[79]

The significant point, however, is that in the Adams Express and U. S. Steel cases mentioned, the Court or the Federal Trade Com-

[79] See Commons, John R., "The Delivered Price System in the Steel Market," *Amer. Econ. Rev.*, XIV (1924), 505. Fetter, Frank A., in his important book, *The Masquerade of Monopoly* (1931), investigates this picture and its economic effects in many American industries and court decisions. See below, p. 773, on Scarcity, Abundance, Stabilization.

mission [80] disregarded the domicile of the corporation in the state of its creation, and passed from a legal corporation existing only in law to an economic going concerning existing wherever it does business.

This transition in meaning, while it had been going on in many other cases, involved still another transition from the older economists' meaning of an "exchange," as a physical transfer of commodities, to the institutional meaning of a transaction as a legal transfer of ownership. It was ownership that fixed prices and permitted competition, and it was the transfer of ownership, instead of physical exchange, that determined whether competition was fair or discriminatory.

2. From Exchange to Transactions

John Locke's meaning of Labor was his personification of Law, Economics, and Ethics. Labor, with him, meant justification of ownership as well as the existence of material things that were owned. This double meaning of Ownership and Material Wealth continued to be the meaning of the orthodox economists for two hundred years, and they therefore concealed the field of institutional economics. It was this concealed ownership side of the double meaning of Wealth that angered the heterodox economists from Marx and Proudhon in the middle of the Nineteenth Century to Sorel at the opening of the Twentieth Century. We shall distinguish the two meanings and yet discover a correlation of materials and ownership, not in Locke's personification of Labor, but in a *unit of economic activity*, a Transaction, and in that expectation of beneficial transactions which is a larger unit of economic activity, a Going·Concern.

This falls in with an analogy to the recent correlation of the separate sciences of physics, chemistry, and astronomy, by the discovery of a unit of activity common to all of them.[81] Roughly speaking, the former units in physics had been molecules, the units in chemistry had been atoms, the units in astronomy had been planets and stars. And the "energies" which made these units go were heat, electricity, chemical affinity, gravity. But nowadays the unit common to all of them is a unit of activity, the interaction of corpuscular wave-lengths, and the concept of "energy" disappears. Four hundred million million vibrations per second are the

[80] The United States Steel Company did not appeal to the Supreme Court.

[81] A summary and elaboration of the following pages was made for the Jubilee Publication in honor of Dean François Gény, professor of Civil Law at the University of Nancy. I am permitted by the editor to make use of that article. See also title "Functionalism" and bibliography, *Encyclopaedia of the Social Sciences*.

color red in the human mind, but they are that many wave-lengths in physics, chemistry, and astronomy.

This analogy roughly describes the problem of correlating law, economics, and ethics. It is the problem of discovering a unit of activity common to them.

In the field of economics the units had been, first, Locke's and Ricardo's material *commodities owned* and the *individuals* who owned the commodities, while the "energy" was human *labor*. Next, the units continued to be the same or similar physical commodities and their ownership, but the individuals became those who *consumed* commodities and the "energy" became the stimuli of *wants*, depending upon the quantity and kind of commodity wanted. The first was the objective side, the other the subjective side of the same relation between the individual and the forces of nature, the latter, however, in the form of materials, owned by the individuals. An "exchange," so called, was a labor process of delivering and receiving commodities, or a "subjective exchange-value." In any case, by analogy to the older physical science, these opposing energies of labor and want, magnified into "elasticities" of supply and demand, could be physically correlated by the materialistic metaphor of an automatic tendency towards equilibrium of commodities in exchange against each other, analogous to the atoms of water in the ocean, but personified as "seeking their level" at Ricardo's "margin of cultivation" or Menger's "marginal utility." This equilibrium was accomplished by the "neo-classicists," led by Alfred Marshall (1890).

There was no need of a further correlation with law or ethics—in fact these latter were necessarily excluded, because the relations on which the economic units were constructed were relations between man and nature, not between man and man. One was Ricardo's relation between human labor and the resistance of nature's forces; the other was Menger's relation between the quantity wanted of nature's forces and the quantity available. Neither statute law, nor ethics, nor custom, nor judicial decision had anything to do with either of these relationships; or rather, all these might be eliminated by assuming that ownership was identical with the materials owned, in order to construct a theory of pure economics based solely on the physical exchange of materials and services.

The latter was done. This identity of ownership and materials was accepted as a matter of custom, without investigation. It was assumed that all commodities were owned, but the ownership was assumed to be identical with the physical thing owned, and therefore was overlooked as something to be taken for granted. The theories were worked out as physical materials, omitting anything of property rights, because they were "natural."

The historical and ethical schools of economists, led by Roscher, Schmoller, and others,[82] revolted against these eliminations of ownership. These schools, even in their culminating form of the "ideal typus" as proposed by Rickert and Max Weber,[83] never were able to incorporate into what remained merely descriptions or subjective ideals of historical process, the economic principles derived from Ricardo and Menger. This, however, can be done if we discover a unit of activity common to law, economics, and ethics.

If the subject-matter of political economy is not only individuals and nature's forces, but is human beings getting their living out of each other by mutual transfers of property rights, then it is to law and ethics that we look for the critical turning points of this human activity.

The courts of law deal with human activity in its relation, not of man to nature, but to the *ownership* of nature by man. But they deal with this activity only at a certain point, the point of *conflict of interests* between plaintiff and defendant. But classical economic theory, based on relations of man to nature, had no conflict of interests in its units of investigation, since its units were *commodities* and *individuals* with ownership omitted. These ultimate units produced, in fact, along with the analogy of equilibrium, a *harmony* of interests rather than a *conflict* of interests. Hence the ultimate unit to be sought in the problem of correlating law, economics, and ethics is a unit of conflicting interests of ownership.

But this is not enough. The ultimate unit of activity must also be a unit of *mutually dependent interests*. The relation of man to man is one of interdependence as well as conflict.

Still further, this ultimate unit must be one which not only is continually *repeating* itself, with variations, but also one whose repetitions are expected by the participants to continue, in the future, substantially similar to what they are in the present and have been in the past. The unit must contain security of expectations. This kind of expectation we name *Order*.

This meaning of Order is derived from the fact that the future is wholly uncertain except as based upon reliable inferences drawn

[82] Cf. Commons, John R., "Das Anglo-Amerikanische Recht und die Wirtschaftstheorie," in *Die Wirtschaftstheorie der Gegenwart*, III (1928), 293–317. I am permitted by the editors, H. Mayer, F. A. Fetter, and R. Reisch, and the publisher, J. Springer, Vienna, to make use of the last-named article.

[83] Rickert, H., *Die Grenzen der naturwissenschaftlichen Begriffsbildung; eine logische Einleitung in die historischen Wissenshaften* (1902); Weber, Max, "Die Objektivität sozialwissenschaftlicher und sozialpolitischer Erkenntnis," *Archiv f. Sozialwissenschaft und Sozialpolitik*, XIX (1904), 22–87. Below, p. 719, "Ideal Types."

from experiences of the past; and also from the fact that it may properly be said that man lives in the future but acts in the present. For these reasons the unit of activity contains a factor that indicates anticipation, or, literally, the act of seizing beforehand the limiting or strategic factors upon whose present control it is expected the outcome of the future may also be more or less controlled, provided there is security of expectations. This is indeed the dominant characteristic of human activity, distinguishing it from all the physical sciences. We shall later separate it out abstractedly and give it the general name of *Futurity*. But the orderly expectations, assumed by all economists under the name of "security," which is a special case of the general principle of Futurity, we name, for our present purposes, simply Order.

Thus, the ultimate unit of activity, which correlates law, economics, and ethics, must contain in itself the three principles of *conflict, dependence,* and *order.* This unit is a Transaction. A transaction, with its participants, is the smallest unit of institutional economics. Transactions intervene between the production of labor, of the classical economists, and the pleasures of consumption, of the hedonic economists, simply because it is society that, by its rules of order, controls ownership of and access to the forces of nature. Transactions, as thus defined, are not the "exchange of commodities," in the physical sense of "delivery," they are the alienation and acquisition, between individuals, of the *rights* of future ownership of physical things, as determined by the collective working rules of society. The *transfer of these rights* must therefore be negotiated between the parties concerned, according to the working rules of society, before labor can produce, or consumers can consume, or commodities be physically delivered to other persons.

When we analyze transactions, which are the transfers of ownership, we find that they resolve themselves into three types, which may be distinguished as Bargaining, Managerial, and Rationing transactions. These are functionally interdependent and together constitute the whole which we name a Going Concern. A going concern is a joint expectation of beneficial bargaining, managerial, and rationing transactions, kept together by "working rules" and by control of the changeable strategic or "limiting" factors which are expected to control the others. When the expectations cease then the concern quits going and production stops.

This going concern is itself a larger unit, and is analogous to that which in biology is Filmer's "organism," or in physics is

Locke's "mechanism." But its components are not living cells, nor electrons, nor atoms—they are Transactions.

We shall here anticipate our subsequent investigational trials and errors and shall set up the conclusions of our historical research by constructing a formula of a bargaining transaction, and then distinguish it from the formulae of managerial and rationing transactions.

(1) **Bargaining Transactions.**—By a study of the theories of economists, in the light of decisions of courts, the bargaining unit is found to consist of *four* parties, two buyers and two sellers, all of whom are treated legally as *equals* by the ruling authority that decides disputes. The resulting formula may be pictured in terms of the offers made by the participants, as follows, where the buyers offer to pay $100 and $90 respectively, for a commodity, and the sellers offer to accept $110 and $120 respectively.[84]

FORMULA OF BARGAINING TRANSACTION—LEGAL EQUALS

B $100	B^1 $ 90
S $110	S^1 $120

On the other hand, managerial and rationing transactions are, in law and economics, the relation of a superior to an inferior. In the managerial transaction the superior is an individual or a hierarchy of individuals, giving orders which the inferiors must obey, such as the relations of foreman to worker, or sheriff to citizen, or manager to managed. But in the rationing transaction the superior is a collective superior or its official spokesman. These are of various kinds, such as a board of directors of a corporation, or a legislature, or a court of law, or an arbitration tribunal, or a communist or fascist government, or a cartel, or a trade union, or a taxing authority, which prorates among inferiors the burdens and benefits of the concern. The formula of a managerial or rationing transaction is therefore the picture of a relation between *two* parties instead of four, as follows:

FORMULA OF MANAGERIAL AND RATIONING TRANSACTIONS
Legal Superior
Legal Inferior

It should be kept in mind that the formula of a transaction is not a copy of nature or reality—it is merely a mental configuration of the least unit of economic theory—a unit of investigation by means of which reality may be understood.

Here it is first necessary to distinguish the double and even

---

[84] Commons, John R., *Legal Foundations of Capitalism*, 66.

triple meaning of the word Exchange, already referred to as used by the early economists, which served to conceal the marketing process of bargaining from the labor process of managing, and from the authoritative process of rationing, as well as the legal from the economic process.

The concept of exchange had its historical origin in the pre-capitalistic period of markets and fairs. The merchant then was a peddler who carried his goods or coins to market and physically exchanged them with other merchants. Yet he really combined in himself two entirely different activities not made use of by the economists: the labor activity of physical delivery and physical acceptance of commodities, and the legal activity of alienation and acquisition of their ownership. The one was physical delivery of physical control over commodities or metallic money, the other was legal transfer of legal control. The one was an Exchange, the other a Transaction.

The difference is fundamental and was not incorporated in economic theory, because materials were not distinguished from their ownership. The *individual* does not transfer ownership. Only the state, or, in medieval times, the "market overt," by operation of law as interpreted by the courts, transfers ownership by reading intentions into the minds of participants in a transaction. The two kinds of transfer have been separated in capitalistic industry. Legal control is transferred at the centers of capitalism, like New York, London, or Paris, but physical control is transferred at the ends of the earth by laborers acting under the commands of those who have legal control. The transfer of legal control is the outcome of a Bargaining Transaction. The transportation of commodities and the delivery of physical control is a labor process of adding "place utility" to a material thing. This labor process, from the legal standpoint, we distinguish as Managerial Transactions.

The individualistic economists necessarily added to their meaning of Exchange the mutual grant of considerations. But this was treated, not objectively as alienation of ownership, but subjectively as a pleasure-pain choice between commodities; whereas, from the legal bargaining standpoint, it is the volitional negotiations of the persuasion or coercion between persons deemed to be legally equal and free, which terminate in reciprocal transfers of *legal control* of commodities and money by operation of existing law in view of the expectations of what the courts will do in case of dispute.

It was the latter meaning of an Exchange which the common-law judges of England, in the Sixteenth Century, recognized in their decisions of disputes between conflicting merchants, by taking over the bargaining customs of merchants on the markets and deciding disputes in conformity with those customs, in so far as they approved the custom. These customs, when taken over by the courts, became, in Anglo-American law, technically known as the doctrines of *assumpsit* and *quantum meruit*.[85]

Broadly interpreted these doctrines run as follows: Let it be inferred, in the ordinary course of trade according to the custom of merchants, that, when a person had acquired a commodity or money from another person, he did not intend robbery or theft or deceit, but intended to accept responsibility to pay for it or to deliver a commodity or service in exchange (*implied assumpsit*);[86] and further, he did not intend, by economic coercion or physical duress, to overcome the will of the other person as to the terms of the transfer of ownership, but intended to pay or perform what was fair or reasonable (*quantum meruit*).[87]

This inference of intention to accept responsibility and a moral duty to pay or perform was necessary because the courts were called upon, in case of a dispute, to create a legal duty by enforcing obedience of payment or performance implied in the negotiations. And this applied not only to deferred performance or payment, usually known as debt, but also to immediate performance or payment, usually known as a sale or cash transaction. It is these negotiations and intended alienation and acquisition of legal ownership, in consideration of payment or performance, that we name a Bargaining Transaction, leaving the physical "exchange" to the labor process, which we name physical delivery, enforced by the law of managerial transactions if necessary.

Parallel to these doctrines of *assumpsit* and *quantum meruit* the courts, in developing the law of freedom from duress, constructed an ethical standard of the "willing buyer and willing seller" by making inferences as to what was going on in the minds of participants. This willingness has been, since then, the standard set up for the decision of disputes arising from bargaining transactions, whether commodity bargains on the produce markets, wage bargains on the labor markets, stock and bond bargains on the stock exchange, interest bargains on the money markets, or rent and land

[85] *Assumpsit* and *quantum meruit* have a technical legal history growing out of many different kinds of cases—most of the early disputes being over rent and services or wages, but ending in the modern meaning of contract.

[86] Slade's case (1602, 2 Coke's Rep. 92b, 76 Eng. Rep. 1072, 1074), which epitomized a preceding century of decisions on particular aspects of *assumpsit*, and began to develop the law of contract which has superseded the older action of debt.

[87] The historical development of these principles may be found in the law books, especially Page, W. H., *The Law of Contracts* (3 vols., 1905), and their economic origins are being investigated for future publication by Mrs. Anna C. Davis.

bargains on the real estate markets. In all of these bargains the doctrines of *assumpsit, quantum meruit,* and *duress* have had an explicit or implied influence in questions of transfer of ownership.[88]

How, then, shall the economist construct a unit of activity, the bargaining transaction, which shall fit this evolution of the common law, derived, as it is, from thousands of decisions of courts? We have found that economists had already constructed the formula as above, applicable to markets. The bargaining consists of four parties, two buyers and two sellers, each, however, governed by the past and expected decisions of the courts in case of dispute, if a conflict of interests reaches that crisis.[89] Out of a universal formula which may thus be constructed so as to include these four participants offering to transfer ownership, and acting in line with customs approved in legal decisions, may be derived four economic and legal relations between man and man, so intimately bound together that a change in one of them will change the magnitudes of one or more of the other three. They are the issues derived from a fourfold conflict of interests latent in every bargaining transaction and the decisions of the American courts on economic disputes are readily classified in these four directions. Each decision has for its object the establishment of working rules as precedents which shall bring expectation of mutuality and order out of the conflict of interests. All of these relate to ownership of materials and not to the materials.

(1) The first issue is, Equal or Unequal Opportunity, which is the legal doctrine of Reasonable and Unreasonable Discrimination. Each buyer is choosing between the best two sellers, and each seller is choosing between the best two buyers. If a seller, for example a railroad company, or telegraph company, or steel corporation, charges a higher price to one buyer and therefore a lower price to that buyer's competitor, for exactly similar service, then the first buyer, under modern conditions of narrow margins of profit, is unreasonably discriminated against, and eventually may be bankrupted. But if there is good ground for the discrimination, such as a difference in quantity, cost, or quality, then the discrimination is reasonable and therefore lawful.[90] The same doctrine appears in many cases of labor arbitration and commercial arbitration.

[88] Cf. the historical development in Galusha *v.* Sherman, 105 Wis. 263 (1900); Commons, *Legal Foundations of Capitalism,* 57.

[89] Glaeser, M. G., *Outlines of Public Utility Economics* (1927), 105, 107, uses the terms "income bargain" and "cost bargain." His income bargain is equivalent to our seller's bargain, and his cost bargain to our buyer's bargain.

[90] Western Union Telegraph Co. *v.* Call Publishing Co., 181 U. S. 92 (1901). Below, p. 784.

(2) Another issue, inseparable from the first, is that of Fair or Unfair Competition. The two buyers are competitors and the two sellers are competitors, and may use unfair methods in their competition. The decisions on unfair competition have built up, during three hundred years, the modern asset of good-will, the biggest asset of modern business.[91]

(3) The third issue, inseparable from the other two, is that of Reasonable or Unreasonable Price or Value. One of the two buyers will buy from one of the two sellers. The price will depend on the three economic conditions, Opportunity for Choice, Competition of buyer with buyer and seller with seller, and Equality or Inequality of Bargaining Power between the actual buyer and the actual seller, who are nevertheless equals in law. This reasonable price is gradually constructed, in the minds of successive courts, on the three prerequisites of Equal Opportunity, Fair Competition, and Equality of Bargaining Power.[92]

(4) Finally, in the American decisions appears the dominant issue of Due Process of Law. It is this issue which we name a "working rule," which regulates individual transactions. The Supreme Court of the United States has acquired authority to overrule state legislatures, the Federal Congress, and all executives, in all cases where these are deemed by the Court to deprive individuals or corporations of property or liberty "without due process of law." Due process of law is the working rule of the Supreme Court for the time being. It changes with changes in custom and class dominance, or with changes in judges, or with changes in the opinions of judges, or with changes in the customary meanings of property and liberty. If a state legislature or the Federal Congress, or a lower court, or an executive, deprives any of the four participants in a transaction of his equal choice of opportunities, or his liberty of competition, or his bargaining power in fixing a price, that act of deprivation is a "taking" of both his property and his liberty. If the deprivation cannot be justified to the satisfaction of the Court, then it is a deprivation of property and liberty *without* due process of law, and is therefore unconstitutional and void, and will be enjoined.[93]

---

[91] Commons, *Legal Foundations of Capitalism*, 162; below, p. 773, Economic Stages.

[92] Cf. Commons' article on "Bargaining Power," *Encyclopaedia of the Social Sciences*, II; also *Legal Foundations of Capitalism*, 54.

[93] Cf. Commons, *Legal Foundations of Capitalism*. Summarized by Voegelin, Erich, *Über die Form des Amerikanischen Geistes* (1928), 172–238; Kröner, Hermann, *John R. Commons, seine wirtschaftstheoretische Grundfassung*, in Heft 6, Diehl, K., *Untersuchungen zur theoretischen Nationalökonomie* (1930); Llewellyn, K. N., "The Effect of Legal Institutions on Economics," *Amer. Econ. Rev.*, XV (1925), 665–683, "What Price Contract?—

Thus, if the formula of a bargaining transaction is properly constructed in the minds of both the economists and the lawyers, with its four participants ruled by the Supreme Court, with its essential attributes of conflict, dependence, and order (due process of law)— just as the formula of the atom or star is being reconstructed in physics, chemistry, and astronomy, with its constituents of protons, electrons, radio-activity, etc.—so also a unit of activity is constructed, common to law, economics, politics, and social ethics.

(2) **Managerial Transactions.**—But there are two other, yet inseparable, units of activity: the Managerial and Rationing Transactions, each exhibiting a legal, economic, and ethical correlation.

A managerial transaction grows out of a relation between two persons instead of four. While the habitual assumption back of the decisions in bargaining transactions is that of equality of willing buyers and willing sellers, the assumption back of managerial transactions is that of superior and inferior. One person is a legal superior who has legal right to issue commands. The other is a legal inferior who, while the relation lasts, is bound by the legal duty of obedience. It is the relation of foreman and worker, sheriff and citizen, manager and managed, master and servant, owner and slave. The superior gives orders, the inferior must obey.

From the economic standpoint the managerial transaction is the one whose purpose is the production of wealth, including what we have already named as the physical meaning of Exchange considered as the adding of "place utilities" by transportation and delivery of commodities; whereas the bargaining transaction has for its purpose the distribution of wealth and the inducements to produce and deliver wealth. The universal principle of bargaining transactions is scarcity, while that of managerial transactions is efficiency.[94]

Psychologically and ethically, also, the managerial transaction differs from the bargaining transaction. The ethical psychology, or what we name negotiational psychology of bargaining transactions is that of *persuasion or coercion,* depending on opportunity, competition, and bargaining power; because the parties, although deemed to be legally equal, may be economically unequal (coercion) or economically equal (persuasion). The negotiational psychology of managerial transactions is *command and obedience,* because one of the parties is both legally and economically inferior.

This managerial transaction, in the case of labor, is inseparable

An Essay in Perspective," *Yale Law Jour.,* XL (March 1931), 704–751; Grant, J. A. C., "The Natural Law Background of Due Process," *Columbia Law Rev.,* XXXI (1931), 56–81; Swisher, C. B., *Stephen J. Field, Craftsman of the Law* (1930), reviewed by Commons, John R., *Jour. of Pol. Econ.,* XXXIX (1931), 828–831.

[94] Below, p. 251, Efficiency and Scarcity.

from, but distinguishable from, the bargaining transaction. As a bargainer, the modern wage-earner is deemed to be the legal *equal* of his employer, induced to enter the transaction by persuasion or coercion; but once he is permitted to enter the *place of employment* he becomes legally *inferior*, induced by commands which he is required to obey. The distinction is clear if the two sets of terms are distinguished as the bargaining terms of employer and employee, or rather of owner and wage-earner, and the managerial terms of foreman or superintendent, and workman.

Here again is a double meaning of the historic word "exchange," based on failure to make use of the distinction between bargaining and managing. The proprietor, in modern industry, has two representatives, the agent and the foreman, often combined in one person. The agent is one whose acts are deemed legally to bind his principal, the employer, on the doctrine of Agency, which began long before the doctrines of *assumpsit* and *quantum meruit* but had the same underlying principle of implying an intention to transfer the ownership of property. The foreman is an agent for certain important purposes, such as liability of the employer for accidents or accepting an employee's output, where his behavior binds the employer to an assumed debt. He is, as such, an agent, but he is also only another employee placed in charge of the technological process. The distinction has been made clear by the modern differentiation of the "employment department" from the "production department." The employment department is governed by the law of principal and agent; the production department by the law of manager and managed.

Historically the failure of economists to distinguish, in their theories, between agent and employee traces back to the double meaning—legal and technological—of the terms employer and employee, master and servant, owner and slave. But this modern differentiation of two departments gives us the clue for going back and making the historical difference of meaning.

Apparently, therefore, no place was left, in the traditional economic meaning of the word "exchange," for this institutional distinction. Hence the word "exchange" is now found to have had a third meaning—the "exchange" of the laborer's product with a foreman, which is both a physical delivery under order and a transfer of ownership by the laborer of his product to the employer, acting through the employer's agent, in consideration of the transfer of ownership of money by the proprietor, or his agent, to the laborer. The latter transfer of ownership is a detail of the bargaining transaction, with its doctrine of persuasion or coercion, and the laborer is a wage-earner. The former is the managerial transaction of command and obedience, and the laborer is just a bundle of the mechanical labor-power of Ricardo and Marx.[95]

Recent economic theory, since the incoming of "scientific management," has furnished two pairs of terms and two units of measurement which permit the above-mentioned double meaning of "exchange" to be clearly distinguished. The units of measurement are the man-hour and the dollar. The pairs of terms are input-output and outgo-income. Scientific management has restored the labor-theory of Ricardo and Marx, but under the name of Efficiency. The ratio of output per hour (physical use-values) to input per hour (average labor) is the measure of efficiency. This is not an "exchange" at all—between the worker and the foreman— it is the physical process of overcoming the resistance of nature under the supervision of management. The unit of measurement of efficiency is the man-hour.

But the unit of measurement in the bargaining transaction is the dollar. It measures the ratio of outgo to income. The outgo is the alienation of ownership. The income is the acquisition of ownership. The dollar, then, is the measure of relative scarcities in bargaining transactions, while the man-hour is the measure of relative efficiencies in managerial transactions.[96]

There are many cases at common law setting down the rights and duties of these managerial transactions, distinguished from bargaining transactions.[97] They may be brought under the more general rule of the right of an owner to control the behavior of those who enter upon his premises, either as customers, visitors, trespassers, or employees. Hence, in the case of employees, the managerial transaction consists of the superior and the inferior, each governed by the law of command and obedience that has been created by the common-law method of making new law by deciding disputes which arise out of managerial transactions.

The managerial transaction has come to the front in recent years out of the investigations of scientific management. It involves, like the bargaining transaction, a certain amount of negotiation,

[95] Holden v. Hardy, 169 U. S. 366 (1898). See Commons, *Legal Foundations of Capitalism*, 63 passim. The foregoing analysis, we take it, underlies the rhetorical protest written into the Clayton Act, that "labor is not a commodity." As a *bargainer*, what the laborer sells is his labor-power, and the relation is persuasion, coercion, or duress. As a *laborer* he does not sell anything. He obeys orders by delivering his physical output of use-value.

[96] Below, p. 276, Input-Output, Outgo-Income.

[97] In my article, "Law and Economics," *Yale Law Jour.*, XXXIV (1925), 371–382, I treated efficiency as purely technological, because I had not then studied the law of managerial transactions.

even though, in law it is based solely upon the will of the superior. This inclusion of negotiation arises mainly from the modern freedom of labor, with its liberty of the laborer to quit without giving a reason. Under such an institutional set-up, it is inevitable that something that may look like bargaining comes to the front in managerial transactions. But it is not bargaining—it is managing, though it is an important phase in the negotiations of the bargaining transaction which accompany it.[98] As it is stated figuratively by an eminent manager of a great corporation, "We never give an order; we sell the idea to those who must carry it out." And Mr. Henry S. Dennison, from his own managing experience, has given the most careful analysis of the up-to-date managerial transaction, under the title, "job analysis of managing." His own summary gives an adequate idea of the most recent advance of scientific management in the meaning of managerial transactions.[99]

JOB ANALYSIS OF MANAGING

Understanding	*Observing* (Watching the operation, supervising, includes selecting what to observe and method of recording, mental or physical.) *Evaluating* (Interpreting the observed facts; relating them to other facts and to policies; determining relative significance.)
Devising	*Conceiving* (Imagining possibilities—goals.) *Analyzing* (Analyzing goal and possibilities and relating observed and evaluated facts thereto.) *Contriving* (Determining methods, means, incentives, operatives.)
Persuading	*Directing* (Giving orders—in absolute strictness not managing, but operating.) *Teaching* (Establishing the necessary understanding of goals, means, methods, and incentives.) *Inducing* (Inspiring—"instructing the desires"; the emotional partner to teaching.)

(3) **Rationing Transactions.**—Finally, Rationing Transactions differ from Bargaining and Managing Transactions in that they are the negotiations of reaching an agreement among several partici-

[98] Cf. Commons, *Legal Foundations of Capitalism*, 283–312, "The Wage Bargain."
[99] Dennison, Henry S., "Who Can Hire Management," *Bulletin of the Taylor Society* IX (1924), 101–110.

pants who have authority to apportion the benefits and burdens to members of a joint enterprise. A borderline case is a partnership transaction as to sharing the future burdens and benefits of a joint undertaking. A little more explicit is the activity of a board of directors of a corporation in making up its budget for the ensuing year. Quite similar, and more distinctive, is the activity of members of a legislative body in apportioning taxes or agreeing on a protective tariff—known as "log-rolling" in America. The so-called "collective bargaining," or "trade agreement," is a rationing transaction between an association of employers and an association of employees, or between any association of buyers and an association of sellers. Dictatorship and all associations for control of output, like cartels, are a series of rationing transactions. A judicial decision of an economic dispute is a rationing of a certain quantity of the national wealth, or equivalent purchasing power, to one person by taking it forcibly from another person. In these cases there is no bargaining, for that would be bribery,[100] and no managing which is left to subordinate executives. Here is simply that which is sometimes named "policy-shaping," sometimes named "justice," but which, when reduced to economic quantities, is the rationing of wealth or purchasing power, not by parties deemed equal, but by an authority superior to them in law.

We can distinguish two kinds of rationing, output-rationing and price-rationing. Fixing the quantities apportioned to participants without fixing the prices is output-rationing, but fixing the prices and leaving the quantities to the will of the buyer or seller is price-rationing. Soviet Russia and many cartels ration the output, but Soviet Russia also, in many of its "state trusts," like the post-office, fixes prices and leaves to individuals the decision as to quantities. The great field of taxation is a price-rationing, by charging to taxpayers the cost of public services, such as education or highways, without any bargaining by the taxpayer or any regard to the individual benefits he receives from the public services rendered.[101]

These three units of activity exhaust all the activities of the science of economics. Bargaining transactions *transfer ownership* of wealth by voluntary agreement between legal equals. Managerial transactions *create wealth* by commands of legal superiors. Rationing transactions apportion the burdens and benefits of wealth creation by the *dictation* of legal superiors. Since they are units

[100] Bribery of the courts was not illegal until after the sorry experience of Lord Bacon in 1621, and the substitution of salaries paid by the state for fees paid by the litigants.

[101] There may be arguments and pleadings, but these are not bargaining because there is no legal power of the taxpayer to withhold payment. Below, p. 805, The Police Power of Taxation.

of social activity among equals, or between superiors and inferiors, they are ethical in character as well as legal and economic.

(4) **Institutions.**—These three types of transactions are brought together in a larger unit of economic investigation, which, in British and American practice, is named a Going Concern.[102] It is these going concerns, with the working rules that keep them agoing, all the way from the family, the corporation, the trade union, the trade association, up to the state itself, that we name Institutions. The passive concept is a "group"; the active is a "going concern."

The difficulty in defining a field for the so-called Institutional Economics is the uncertainty of meaning of the word institution. Sometimes an institution seems to be analogous to a building, a sort of framework of laws and regulations, within which individuals act like inmates. Sometimes it seems to mean the "behavior" of the inmates themselves. Sometimes anything additional to or critical of the classical or hedonic economics is deemed to be institutional. Sometimes anything that is "dynamic" instead of "static," or a "process" instead of commodities, or activity instead of feelings, or management instead of equilibrium, or control instead of laissez-faire, seems to be institutional economics.[103]

All of these notions are doubtless involved in institutional economics, but they may be said to be metaphors or descriptions, whereas a *science* of economic behavior requires analysis into principles—which are similarities of cause, effect, or purpose—and a synthesis in a unified system of principles. And institutional economics, furthermore, cannot separate itself from the marvellous discoveries and insight of the pioneer classical and psychological economists. It should incorporate, however, in addition, the equally important discoveries of the communistic, anarchistic, syndicalistic, fascistic, coöperative, and unionistic economists. Doubtless it is the effort to cover by enumeration all of these uncoördinated activities that gives to the name institutional economics that reputation of a miscellaneous, nondescript, yet merely descriptive character, similar to that which has long since relegated from economics the early crude Historical School.

If we endeavor to find a universal principle, common to all behavior known as institutional, we may define an institution as Collective Action in Control of Individual Action.

[102] The German equivalent, *gutgehendes Geschäft.*

[103] Cf. *Proceedings* of the 43d meeting, Amer. Econ. Assn., December 1930, 134–141; also articles by Copeland, M. A., and Burns, E. M., *Amer. Econ. Rev.*, XXI (1931), 66–80; Atkins, W. E., and Others, *Economic Behavior, an Institutional Approach* (1931), 2 vols. This section is condensed in the article, "Institutional Economics," *Amer. Econ. Rev.*, XXI (1931), 648–657.

Collective action ranges all the way from unorganized Custom to the many organized Going Concerns, such as the family, the corporation, the holding company, the trade association, the trade union, the Federal Reserve System, the "group of affiliated interests," the State. The principle common to all of them is more or less control of individual action by collective action.

This control of the acts of one individual always results in, and is intended to result in, a benefit to other individuals. If it be the enforcement of a contract, then the debt is exactly equal to the credit created for the benefit of the other person. A debt is a duty capable of being enforced collectively, while a credit is an equivalent right created by creating the duty. The resulting social relation is an Economic Status, consisting of the expectations towards which each party is directing his economic behavior. On the debt and duty side it is the status of Conformity to collective action. On the credit and right side it is a status of Security created by the expectation of said Conformity. This is known as "incorporeal" property.[104]

Or, the collective control takes the form of a *tabu* or prohibition of certain acts, such as interference, infringement, trespass, and this prohibition creates an economic status of Liberty for the person thus made immune. But the liberty of one person may be accompanied by prospective benefit or damage to a correlative person, and the economic status thus created is Exposure to the Liberty of the other. An employer is exposed to the liberty of the employee to work or quit, and the employee is exposed to the liberty of the employer to hire or fire. This exposure-liberty relation is coming to be distinguished as "intangible" property, such as the good-will of a business, franchises to do business, patents, trademarks, and so on in great variety.[105]

The working rules which determine for individuals the limits of these correlative and reciprocal economic relationships may be laid down and enforced by a corporation, or a cartel, or a holding company, or a coöperative association, or a trade union, or an employers' association, or a trade association, or a joint trade agreement of two associations, or a stock exchange or board of trade, or a political party, or the state itself through the United States Supreme Court in the American system. Indeed, these economic collective acts of private concerns are at times more powerful than the collective action of the political concern, the State.

Stated in the language of ethics and law, to be developed below,

---

[104] Below, p. 78, Formula of Economic and Social Relations.
[105] Below, p. 402, MacLeod.

all collective acts establish social relations of right, duty, no right, and no duty. Stated in the language of individual behavior, what they require is performance, avoidance, forbearance by individuals. Stated in the language of the resulting economic status of individuals, what they provide is Security, Conformity, Liberty, and Exposure. Stated in language of cause, effect, or purpose, the common principles running through all economic behavior as a limiting and complementary interdependent relationship are Scarcity, Efficiency, Futurity, the Working Rules of collective action, and Sovereignty. Stated in language of the operation of working rules on individual action they are expressed by the auxiliary verbs of what the individual can, cannot, must, must not, may, or may not *do*. He "can" or "cannot," because collective action will or will not come to his aid. He "must" or "must not," because collective action will compel him. He "may," because collective action will permit him and protect him. He "may not," because collective action will prevent him.

It is because of these behavioristic auxiliary verbs that the familiar term "working rules" is appropriate to indicate the universal principle of cause, effect, or purpose, common to all collective action. Working rules are continually changing in the history of an institution, including the state and all private associations, and they differ for different institutions. They are sometimes known as *maxims* of conduct. Adam Smith names them *canons* of taxation, and the Supreme Court names them the *Rule of Reason,* or *Due Process of Law.* But, whatever their differences and different names, they have this similarity, that they indicate what individuals can, must, or may, do or not do, enforced by Collective Sanctions.

Analysis of these collective sanctions furnishes that correlation of economics, jurisprudence, and ethics, which is prerequisite to a theory of institutional economics. David Hume found the unity of these social sciences in the principle of scarcity and the resulting conflict of interests. Adam Smith isolated economics on the assumptions of divine providence, earthly abundance, and the resulting harmony of interests. Institutional economics goes back to Hume. Taking our cue from Hume and the modern rise of such a term as "business ethics," ethics deals with the rules of conduct arising from conflict of interests and enforced by the *moral* sanctions of collective opinion. Economics deals with the same rules of conduct enforced by the collective sanctions of economic *gain* or *loss.* Jurisprudence deals with the same rules enforced by the organized sanctions of *physical force.* Institutional economics is continually dealing with the relative merits of these three types of sanctions.

From this universal principle of collective action in control of individual action by different kinds of sanctions arise the ethical and legal relations of rights, duties, no-rights, no-duties, and the economic relations not only of Security, Conformity, Liberty, and Exposure, but also of Assets and Liabilities. In fact, it is from the field of corporation finance, with its changeable assets and liabilities, rather than from the field of individual wants and labor, or pains and pleasures, or wealth and happiness, or utility and disutility, that institutional economics derives a large part of its data and methodology. Institutional economics is concerned with the Assets and Liabilities of Concerns contrasted with Adam Smith's Wealth of Nations. Between nations it is the Credits and Debits in the balance of international payments.[106]

Collective action is even more universal in the unorganized form of Custom than it is in the organized form of Concerns. Yet even a going concern is also a Custom. Custom has not given way to free contract and competition, as was asserted by Sir Henry Maine.[107] Customs have merely changed with changes in economic conditions, and they may today be so mandatory that even a dictator cannot overrule them. The business man who refuses or is unable to make use of the modern customs of the credit system, by refusing to accept or issue checks on solvent banks, although the checks are merely private arrangements and not legal tender, simply cannot continue in business by carrying on transactions. These instruments are customary tender, instead of legal tender, backed by the powerful sanctions of profit, loss, and competition, which compel conformity. Other mandatory customs might be mentioned, such as coming to work at seven o'clock and quitting at six, or the customary standards of living.

But these customary standards are always changing; they lack precision, and therefore give rise to disputes over conflicts of interest. If such disputes arise, then the officers of an organized concern, such as a credit association, the manager of a corporation, a stock exchange, a board of trade, a commercial or labor arbitrator, or finally, the courts of law up to the Supreme Court of the United States, reduce the custom to precision and add an organized legal or economic sanction.

This is done through the Common-Law Method of Making Law by the Decision of Disputes. The decisions, by becoming prec-

---

[106] These balances, for a series of years, 1922 to 1930, are the basis of the enlightening book by Rogers, J. H., *America Weighs Her Gold* (1931).

[107] Maine, Sir Henry S., *Ancient Law: Its Connection with the Early History of Society, and Its Relation to Modern Ideas* (1861).

edents, become the working rules, for the time being, of the particular organized concern. The historic "common law" of Anglo-American jurisprudence is only a special case of the universal principle common to all concerns that survive, of making new law by deciding conflicts of interest, thus giving greater precision and organized compulsion to the unorganized working rules of custom or ethics. The common-law *method* is universal in all collective action, but the technical "common law" of the English and American lawyers is a body of decisions going back to feudal times. In short, the common-law *method,* or way of acting, is itself a custom, with variabilities, like other customs. It is the way in which collective action of all going concerns acts on individual action in time of conflict. It differs from statutory law in that it is judge-made law at the time of decision of disputes.

Collective Action is more than *control* of individual action—it is, by the very act of control, as indicated by the auxiliary verbs, a *liberation* of individual action from coercion, duress, discrimination, or unfair competition, by means of restraints placed on other individuals.

And Collective Action is more than restraint and liberation of individual action—it is *expansion* of the will of the individual far beyond what he can do by his own puny acts. The head of a great corporation gives orders which execute his will at the ends of the earth.

Since liberation and expansion for some persons consist in restraint, for their benefit, of other persons, and while the short definition of an institution is collective action in control of individual action, the derived definition is: collective action in restraint, liberation, and expansion of individual action.

These individual actions are really *trans*-actions—that is, actions between individuals—as well as individual behavior. It is this shift from commodities, individuals, and exchanges to transactions and working rules of collective action that marks the transition from the classical and hedonic schools to the institutional schools of economic thinking. The shift is a change in the ultimate unit of economic investigation, from commodities and individuals to transactions between individuals.

If it be considered that, after all, it is the individual who is important, then the individual with whom we are dealing is the Institutionalized Mind.[108] Individuals begin as babies. They learn the custom of language, of coöperation with other individuals, of

---

[108] Cf. Jordan, E., *Forms of Individuality; an Inquiry into the Grounds of Order in Human Relations* (1927).

working towards common ends, of negotiations to eliminate conflicts of interest, of subordination to the working rules of the many concerns of which they are members. They meet each other, not as physiological bodies moved by glands, nor as "globules of desire" [109] moved by pain and pleasure, similar to the forces of physical and animal nature, but as prepared more or less by habit, induced by the pressure of custom, to engage in those highly artificial transactions created by the collective human will. They are not found in physics, or biology, or subjective psychology, or in the German Gestalt psychology, but are found where conflict, interdependence, and order among human beings are preliminary to getting a living. Instead of individuals the participants are citizens of a going concern. Instead of forces of nature they are forces of human nature. Instead of the mechanical uniformities of desire of the hedonistic economists, they are highly variable personalities. Instead of isolated individuals in a state of nature they are always participants in transactions, members of a concern in which they come and go, citizens of an institution that lived before them and will live after them.

(5) **Assets** *versus* **Wealth.**—The three aspects, economic, legal, and ethical, which we shall endeavor to distinguish and then correlate in the concept of a going concern, turn on the meanings of Property and Liberty. We shall identify the economic meaning of Property as Assets, and the legal meaning of Assets as Property. The distinction between Wealth and Assets was concealed by the classical economists who defined wealth as materials and ownership. The ownership is not wealth—it is assets.

The term "property" cannot be defined except by defining all the activities which individuals and the community are at liberty or required to do or not to do, with reference to the object claimed as property. These activities are the three types of transactions. The only reason for making claims of ownership in the negotiations of all transactions is expected scarcity. David Hume first pointed out this identity of property and scarcity. Even radio wave-lengths, on account of their expected scarcity, are now reduced to property by rationing transactions prescribing who may make use of them, how much, and when. But scarcity is also a fundamental concept in economics. Both Ricardo's labor theory of value and Menger's diminishing utility theory of value were personifications of Scarcity in terms of the labor required and the satisfactions obtained in dealing with nature's limited physical resources.

---

[109] Below, p. 649, Veblen.

We use the term Scarcity instead of supply and demand. This latter term is used by business men as a name for thousands of different forces outside themselves which they cannot control and so they call them "supply and demand" and let it go at that. But we are compelled to analyze the forces and personifications hidden behind supply and demand, and so we give to them the broader name of scarcity, in its thousands of applications.

If the principle of Scarcity, then, is ultimate for law, economics, and ethical relations, it follows that the term Property has a double meaning, the economic meaning of scarcity known by economists as an "economic quantity" and by lawyers as the *"res"* or *"property-object"*; and the legal or ethical meaning of *property-rights,* which is the lawyer's meaning of "property." The latter meaning, however, we define as the *working rules* enforced by the community upon individuals in their transactions respecting that which is or is expected to be scarce.[110] This economic meaning of scarcity, when combined with forecasting, is expressed by the terms Assets and Liabilities; while the legal and ethical meaning of property is rights, duties, powers, liabilities, etc., as portrayed in the formula on page 78.[111]

The usefulness of this terminology, based on the economic, legal, and ethical aspects of scarcity, will be seen in the enlarged meanings which the Supreme Court of the United States has given to the terms Property and Liberty as used in the Federal Constitution, the supreme law of the land. This Constitution, including the Fifth Amendment (1791) and the Civil War Amendments (especially the Fourteenth, 1868), contains three provisions governing all legislative and executive authorities, whether state or Federal, in effect as follows:

(1) Private property shall not be taken for public use without just compensation.

(2) No state shall pass any law impairing the obligation of contracts.

(3) No person shall be deprived of life, liberty, or property without due process of law.

Arising out of the enlargements of meaning of the above several terms—such as property, liberty, person, and due process of law, as used in the Constitution—there are now to be distinguished three meanings of property in the sense of *rights*. Each of these

---

[110] These distinctions are derived from David Hume's unification of law, economics, and ethics on the common principle of scarcity. Below on Hume and Peirce, p. 140; on MacLeod, p. 397.

[111] Also Commons, *Legal Foundations of Capitalism*, 80 ff.

meanings is economic, legal, and ethical. The word "person" has come to mean a corporation owning assets, as well as a former slave who has become a citizen. Property (*res*), as decided in the Slaughter House Cases (1872),[112] meant "corporeal" property, namely, lands, machinery, slaves; "liberty" meant then the new "corporeal" liberty of the former slaves. Property also had the meaning of "incorporeal" property, the obligation and negotiability of debts. And the third meaning of property, not admitted by the majority in the Slaughter House Cases, but now known as "intangible" property, distinguished from "incorporeal," while it originally arose from the good-will cases three hundred years ago, arose also under the Fifth and Fourteenth Amendments to the Constitution from the later decisions of the Supreme Court enjoining legislatures against reducing the prices charged by business enterprises. To reduce prices by legislative enactment is now a "taking" of property, just as much as is the physical taking of corporeal property; although it takes only the *value* of the property. This, since 1890,[113] can be done only to the extent approved by the Supreme Court of the United States as consistent with the current but changeable meaning of "due process of law." [114]

Thus the three American meanings of property, as an economic asset, have arisen from the practice of the English and American courts in taking over the existing customs of private parties, in so far as deemed applicable and good, and giving to them the physical sanctions of sovereignty. In the feudal and agricultural period property was mainly corporeal. In the mercantile period (Seventeenth Century in England) property became the incorporeal property of negotiable debts.[115] In the stage of capitalism of the past forty years property becomes also the intangible property of liberty to settle upon whatever prices the seller or buyer can obtain. These meanings of both property and liberty, in construing the Constitution, were revolutionized by the Supreme Court in a line of decisions between the years 1872 and 1897; the revolution consisted in enlarging the meaning of property and liberty, from physical commodities and human bodies to bargaining transactions and the assets of individuals and corporations.

All of these meanings had, indeed, existed from the time of feudalism, but under different names and economic conditions.

---

[112] *Ibid.*, Chap. II.
[113] *Ibid.*, p. 15.
[114] On the changed meaning of "due process of law," see Commons, *Legal Foundations of Capitalism*, 333–342.
[115] *Ibid.*, 235–246.

"Incorporeal hereditaments," such as a franchise to collect tolls or services, were similar to intangible property. Sub-infeudation was the rights to the products of the land. Corporeal property was not absolute but was limited by these intangible properties, resting ultimately on rents derived from the products or services of tenants who actually cultivated the land. All were in the law from earliest times, but the American courts, in later days, chose to select and give different names, according to the new period of capitalism.

(6) **Liberty and Exposure.**—These changes in the meanings of the economic equivalent of property as assets and liabilities have made necessary a deeper analysis of the meanings of the term "rights" as used in jurisprudence. This analysis was materially advanced by Professor Hohfeld of the Yale Law School in 1913, and by the Yale Law faculty in the development of Hohfeld's analysis.[116] On the basis of their analysis the following formula is constructed showing a correlation of collective, economic and social relations, under the jurisdiction of the Supreme Court, and in so far as they apply to the three types of transactions concerned with economic quantities. The "social relations" are derived from Hohfeld's "legal relations," but are enlarged to include economic and moral concerns, as well as the State—his political or legal concern. The "economic status" is the correlated economic assets and liabilities; the "working rules" are individual action as controlled, liberated, and expanded by collective action.

In considering the formula a distinction is required, first, between Inducements and Sanctions. Inducements are individual inducements offered by individuals to each other—persuasion or coercion in the case of bargaining transactions, or command and obedience in the case of managerial transactions, or pleading and argument in the case of rationing transactions. Sanctions are collective inducements applied to individuals by the concern which controls, liberates, and expands their individual actions, by controlling, liberating, and enforcing their persuasions, coercions, commands, obedience, arguments, and pleadings.

These sanctions are distinguishable as' moral, economic, and legal sanctions, depending upon the kind of concern which exercises control. The legal sanction is violence, or threatened violence, and the concern is the State. The other sanctions are "extra-legal." The moral or ethical sanction is mere opinion, enforced by such concerns as churches, social clubs, and ethical associations like the many "trade associations" of business men who formulate a "code

[116] *Ibid.*, 91 ff.

FORMULA OF ECONOMIC AND SOCIAL RELATIONS
THE SUPREME COURT

SANCTIONS (MORAL, ECONOMIC, LEGAL)				INDUCEMENTS	SANCTIONS (MORAL, ECONOMIC, LEGAL)			
Collective Action	Working Rule	Economic Status	Social Relation	Transactions	Social Relation	Economic Status	Working Rule	Collective Action
Power	Can	Security	Right	Bargaining	Duty	Conformity	Must, Must not	Liability
Disability Immunity	Cannot May	Exposure Liberty	No Right No Duty^a	Managing	No Duty^a	Liberty	May	Immunity
				Rationing of economic quantities	No Right	Exposure	Cannot	Disability
Liability	Must, Must not	Conformity	Duty		Right	Security	Can	Power

^{a} Equivalent to Hohfeld's "privilege."

of ethics" whose enforcement rests only on the collective *opinion* of the members, if *not* supported by economic or legal penalties or rewards. The economic sanctions are enforced by such organizations as trade unions, business corporations, cartels, through the sanctions of profit or loss, employment or unemployment, or other economic gain or deprivation, but without violence.

These sanctions usually overlap, but, in following the usual methods of analysis, we here take extreme cases of the peculiar characteristic sanctions of each. We afterwards combine them in particular disputes as they arise, according to their relative "weights" employed in those disputes.

Often these moral and economic concerns also have their "courts" which decide particular disputes, under such names as "trials for heresy," "commercial arbitration," or "labor arbitration," performing functions similar to those in courts of law, but without the physical sanctions of the legal judiciary imposing the use of violence. In short, the formula applies to all collective action in control, liberation, or expansion of individual action, whether it take the form of moral, economic, or political concerns. It is, however, out of this universal formula of collective control, liberation, and expansion of individual action that the common-law courts derive their habitual assumptions whenever the physical violence of the state is called upon to decide disputes that cannot be decided by the use of moral or economic sanctions.

For these and other reasons, intimated above, the formula of correlation of law, morals, and economics does *not* mean that there is an *identity* between the legal relation and the moral or economic relations. It means only that the same legal relation holds for all economic practices, no matter how large or small the debt, the liberty, the exposure, etc., in particular disputes, or the relative *weights* of moral, economic, or legal sanctions. Hence it does not mean that the practices of individuals or of moral or economic concerns exactly conform to any rigid rule or "norm" that the legal judiciary lays down in its decisions. The formula represents a precise correlation only in a particular dispute where the judge or arbitrator actually decides what the particular disputants shall do or not do. Outside these disputes are billions of transactions that never get before the courts or arbitrators, and are highly variable. The formula is only a generalized formula, a creation of the mind in order to aid the mind in the process of analysis of moral, legal, and economic relations. Yet, if the parties do come before the court or arbitrator the formula contains all the possible legal, economic, or social relations that can be used in reaching a decision on the case, or that can be found in the billions of variable transactions or practices from which the judge or arbitrator derives his reasoning.

This is because there is also an *unorganized* and *inexact* collective action which we name Custom, to which the same formula applies and from which all courts derive their habitual assumptions in the common-law method of making more precise the relationships. Custom ranges in its degree of compulsion and lack of precision from mere variable *practices,* which have no binding effect, to *mandatory* customs. The use of bank checks is not mandatory in law but the business man who refuses to issue and accept negotiable bills on solvent banks cannot continue in business. The custom has become mandatory, though not precise, by the most powerful of sanctions, the economic sanction of profit and loss. But there may be no organized court to enforce it and give it precision. Mandatory custom, whether unorganized or organized as Going Concerns, tells individuals exactly or inexactly what they must and must not, can and cannot, may and may not, do.

The universal principle, or similarity of cause, effect, or purpose, which we can derive from all observations of collective control, liberation, and expansion of individual action, whether it be a going concern or a custom, we name a "working rule." It is these working rules which, in the decisions of American Courts, are summarized as "due process of law," or the "rule of reason." They are not something prefixed and eternal, or divine, as assumed by John Locke and the natural rights school of jurisprudence, but are simply the changeable rules, sometimes named "norms," which, for the time being, in view of changing economic and social conditions, the courts or arbitrators accept in issuing their commands to disputants in a litigation.

We can distinguish, as elaborated from the analysis and terminology of the Hohfeld school of law, four different volitional aspects of these commands, each of which gives rise to a collective capacity or incapacity of the opposite party to the dispute. If the court or arbiter orders the defendant to perform a service, to pay a debt, or to avoid interference with the plaintiff, then the auxiliary verbs "must" or "must not" are directed towards the defendant. Correlatively this means that the plaintiff has the "power" or "ability" to call upon collective action to aid him in enforcing his will upon the defendant who must or must not. This power is, volitionally, designated by the auxiliary "can."

On the other hand, if the court refuses to compel the defendant to act or not act, then the plaintiff "cannot" call upon collective action to enforce his will. Technically this is a "disability." And correlatively the defendant is in the position that he "may" do as he pleases in the matter at issue. This is an immunity.

Since, however, there is a reciprocal relation between the parties to the transaction, the plaintiff also "may" do as he pleases in other aspects of the matter at issue, and the defendant "cannot" have the aid of collective action in those respects in enforcing his will on the plaintiff. But if the plaintiff is commanded also to perform, or pay, or avoid interference on his side of the transaction, then, as before, the auxiliaries "must" or "must not" are correlative to the auxiliary "can."

In this way, it is the changeable working rules of a concern, expressed as the opinion of the court or arbitrator in using the sanctions of the concern, which determine, more precisely than is done by custom, what each party to a transaction can, cannot, may, must, or must not *do*.

Converting these volitional determinations into corresponding economic equivalents, there are four economic positions which the individual may occupy in his transactions, each of which places him in an Economic Status relative to other parties: The collective concern establishes for him (1) Security of expectations in so far as it requires (2) Conformity to those expectations on the part of others. If the court or arbiter withholds the aid of the collective sanction, then the one party is at (3) Liberty to do as he pleases and the other is (4) Exposed to gain or loss equivalent to the exercise of that liberty by the others. Thus, as illustrated above, an employer is exposed to the liberty of the employee to quit or not quit; and the worker is exposed to the liberty of the employer to "hire and fire."

When we turn further to the correlative social terminology, a "right" indicates that the individual "can," or has "power"—sometimes called "ability" or "capacity"—because he is a citizen, to call on the state or other collective concern for security of expectations, by imposing a duty of conformity by some kind of command; whereas, if no duty is imposed on either party, then the social relations are the reciprocal liberties and exposures of the parties to the exigencies of what, in economics, is "free competition."

This correlation enables us to distinguish the three meanings of property, which have evolved in the decisions of the United States Supreme Court during the past sixty years. The Constitution of the United States (Fifth and Fourteenth Amendments) prohibits the national and state legislatures from "taking" life, liberty, or property without due process of law. In a leading case in 1872 [117] the Court held that the meaning of property was corporeal property and the meaning of liberty was freedom from slavery. To "take" property or liberty, at that time, meant the working rule for the time being, that a state must not deprive a person of his security in doing as he pleases with corporeal goods or his own *corpus*—his "corporeal" body. This was a physical meaning of corporeal property, yet it had also an economic value.

To "take" property also meant, at that time, to deprive a person of his right to call upon the state to enforce a duty of performance or payment of an economic magnitude, the correlatives of which are a Credit or asset, and a Debt or liability. This "incorporeal property" or contract was also an "economic quantity." [118]

Quite different is intangible property, another "economic quantity" (such as the value of good-will, patents, franchises, etc.), whose meaning came into the American decisions after 1890. If it is decided that there is *no-duty* (Hohfeld's "privilege") in the case at issue, there is, of course, *no-right*. The economic correlative of *no-duty* is *liberty*, and the economic correlative of *no-right* is the equivalent *exposure* to the *liberty* of the other. The exposure of a merchant to an economic gain or loss is the "economic quantity" or commodity which the customer is at liberty to buy or refuse to buy; and the exposure of the customer to gain or loss is the liberty of the merchant to refuse to sell except at a price.

Then, if each party is treated equally, there is a reciprocity of liberty and exposure, as seen in the formula. This is the meaning of a bargaining transaction which fixes prices or wages, and of "intangible" property, distinguished from "incorporeal." The intangible property which the Court recognizes in these transactions is all those expectations of future beneficial transactions, known generally as the good-will of a business, or good credit, or good reputation, or that good-will of wage-earners known recently as "industrial good will," [119] all of which were formerly known as "liberty" but are now known also as property, because they are economic quantities having value. Following these decisions of 1890, [120] if a state or the Congress reduces the *prices* charged by a railroad corporation, or abolishes discrimination, or endeavors to equalize bargaining power between employers and employees, then this reduction of prices, or this interference with choice of opportunities,

[117] Slaughter House Cases, 16 Wallace 36 (1872).
[118] Below, p. 397, on MacLeod and the meaning of "economic quantity."
[119] Cf. Commons, John R., *Industrial Goodwill* (1919); also below, pp. 667–668, on Reasonable Value.
[120] Cf. Commons, *Legal Foundations of Capitalism*, 15, 36.

or this deprivation of bargaining power, is a "taking" of property, although what it takes or reduces is the *value* of the property, or the *behavior* of participants, and not the physical property.

Thus the meaning of "property," as used in the Constitution, was enlarged from corporeal goods to bargaining power, and the meaning of "liberty," from freedom of bodily movement to freedom of choice and freedom of bargaining power in all economic transactions.

(7) Time.—Finally, the question arises, What becomes of the traditional concept of commodities as employed since the time of Locke, Smith, and Ricardo? Their double meaning of commodities was materials and ownership. In 1856 MacLeod endeavored to build a system of political economy solely on ownership. But his theory was discarded by all economists because they thought he counted the same thing twice, once as a *material* thing, once as the *right* to the thing. But the economists themselves had already counted it twice in their double meaning of commodities as materials and corporeal property.

The difficulty of the classical economists was in the concept of Time. MacLeod was the first, though inconsistently, to point out that "the present" is a zero point of time between the incoming future and the outgoing past.[121] From this moving standpoint of "the present," ownership (as we reconstruct MacLeod) always looks to the future, but materials look to the labor of the past which produced them. But transactions occur at the present point of time at which rights of ownership are transferred. The concept of Time could not be important until economic theory changed from commodities to transactions. For Time is of the essence of a unit of activity.

Then, after the transaction, if a dispute arises, the court reads into the preceding transaction, as inferred from the then intentions of the parties, or from the intentions of the legislature, or from its own pragmatic philosophy of public policy, by means of various ethical doctrines, which together we name *habitual assumptions*,[122] certain expectations for the future, relative to commodities, prices, money, or other economic quantities. It is these future quantities, valued in the present, which are the Assets and Liabilities, the expected securities, conformities, liberties, and exposures of property, and the expected performance, forbearance, avoidance of individuals.

This mental process we have already mentioned in discussing the doctrines of *assumpsit* and *quantum meruit*, from which originated in part the modern doctrine of contracts. When once settled by a

[121] Below, p. 401, MacLeod on Time.
[122] Below, p. 697, Habitual Assumptions.

decision these habitual assumptions become, by the doctrine of precedent, the expectations of all parties concerning the future economic consequences of their present transactions. This is simply a special case of the principle of anticipation, or forecasting, which we name the principle of Futurity, a characteristic of all human behavior.[123]

The question has been raised and always will be raised, whether there can be a "science of Futurity." We answer, there *must* be such a science, if human activity is the subject-matter of the science. From the earliest times of soothsayers, magicians, and medicine men, through all the hypotheses formulated in all the sciences, down to the modern pessimism and optimism of business and the modern profession of the economic forecasters, it is always the principle of Futurity that dominates human activity. It may be that a science of Futurity is impossible; yet a science of the behavior of Transactions and Forecasting, tested by the observation of failures and successes, is a science of human activity. Indeed, it may be said that man lives in the future but acts in the present. Even the physical sciences have wide fringes of ignorance, prejudice, or overemphasis, which must be allowed for; [124] yet they are scientific, because it is their *method* of forecasting that is scientific.

This is even more true of a science of ownership and transactions —themselves forecasts of the future.

(8) **Transactional Meaning of Value.**—The concepts of Value and Capital have passed through three historic stages, which, in view of the present-day practical outcome of each, we may name the stage of Engineering Economics, the stage of Home Economics, and the stage of Institutional Economics.

The stage of Engineering Economics begins with Ricardo, is elaborated by Karl Marx, and culminates in the Scientific Management of Frederick Taylor. Here the working concept of Value and Capital is Use-Value, or the technological qualities of commodities and services, whose value per unit does not increase or diminish with demand or supply, but increases with the amount of labor and ingenuity which has been required to produce it, and diminishes with the amount of depreciation or wear and tear, or "using up." Use-value also changes with changes in civilization, as when bows and arrows give way to gunpowder or dynamite, or hoop skirts to bare legs. On account of these changes in invention or fashion, use-value may also be named Civilization Value, under

---

[123] Above, p. 83, and below, p. 714, on the Common-Law Method of Making New Law.
[124] Cf. Shapley, Harlow, *Flights from Chaos; a Survey of Material Systems from Atoms to Galaxies* (1930).

the two aspects of Obsolescence and Invention. If use-values were stored up to be used for further production in the future, that storage was Capital, in the classical meaning of the term. We name it Technological Capital; its attribute is use-value.

Use-value, or Technological Capital, is produced by labor—that is, the combination of Manual, Mental, and Managerial Labor as propounded by Karl Marx under the name "socially necessary labor-power." It becomes "scientific" when reduced to measurement. This measurement is the triumph of Frederick Taylor, the engineer, who, with his followers, systematized the three kinds of physical measurement required in the production of Use-Value: First is the physical quantity, such as *bushels* or *tons;* second is the physical quality such as *grade 1* or *grade 2;* third is the *man-hours per unit* required to produce it.

The outcome of engineering economics, when the time factor is introduced under the compound name of man-hour, is the concept of Efficiency, and the science of Efficiency is specialized in modern colleges of engineering and agriculture.

The stage of Home Economics begins with the hedonic, or pleasure-pain schools of Gossen, Jevons, Menger, Böhm-Bawerk; where, without the use of money, the individual proportions his varieties of food, clothing, shelter, land, equipment, and other production and consumption goods, so as to achieve the maximum total satisfaction out of the limited physical materials at his command. Here the concept of Value is that of a *diminishing* utility per unit of materials—diminishing with an increase in the quantity available; or an *increasing* utility per unit of materials—increasing with a *diminution* of the quantity available. Since this utility does not exist objectively, like use-value, but is subjective in the mind and feelings of the individual, it is generally included in the field of psychological economics. But its modern specialization is in the Science of Home Economics, or Consumption Economics, including the isolated farmer to the extent that he produces for his own use. In these cases the purpose is the maximum of human satisfaction to be derived from a variety of material goods, each of which, how-ever, in itself, yields a diminishing intensity of satisfaction per unit with an increase in quantity and an increasing intensity of satis-faction with a reduction in quantity.

Since, however, this psychological value is a special case of the universal principle of Scarcity we may name it simply Scarcity-Value, in contrast with Use-Value.

In this aspect scarcity-value may be converted from psychological economics to institutional economics, where *ownerships,* by means of transactions, are alienated and acquired. Here the unit of scarcity measurement is another institution, money, and the proprietary name is Price instead of the psychological name, "marginal utility."

Thus every unit of a commodity or service has two dimensions of measurable value, its use-value which does not diminish per unit with abundance nor increase per unit with scarcity, and its scarcity-value which diminishes per unit with abundance or increases per unit with scarcity.

Lastly, all commodities and services, when valued, are in the immediate or remote future, such that, on account of longer or shorter expected waiting, or greater or less expected risk, a future quantity is deemed to be less in value than a present quantity of like kind and amount. The psychological basis of this universal fact of human nature was elaborately expounded by Böhm-Bawerk,[125] who was seeking a psychological foundation for a universal fact of institutional economics. This universal fact appears on any market, where it is a factor in the negotiations that transfer ownership, and is the foundation of the credit and banking system. This present dimension of value compared with the expected dimension is a third dimension of the meaning of Value and Capital, usually named interest or agio, if added in the future, or discount, if deducted in the present.

Thus, the transactional or proprietary meaning of value has three dimensions, each highly variable on its own account: the Use-Value transferred from the engineering economics of Ricardo and Marx, the Scarcity-Value transferred from psychological economics, and the Transactional Value transferred also from psychological economics. All of these are combined in the proprietary expectations of a present transaction at a point of time, which we, following MacLeod, name an "economic quantity," instead of a physical quantity, because Futurity is one of its three dimensions, and all of them together constitute the modern meaning of capital.

The physical commodities of the classical and hedonistic schools do not disappear—they are merely transferred to the *future* through the institution of ownership. The future may be, indeed, so short that it is not worth measuring, but it is futurity nevertheless. Transactions are based on expectations of the immediate or remote future, secured by collective action consisting of the institutions of property, and available only after the closing of the negotiations which end in the transaction. Transactions are the means, under

[125] Böhm-Bawerk, E. von, *The Positive Theory of Capital* (tr. 1891).

operation of law and custom, of acquiring and alienating *legal* control of economic quantities, including legal control of the labor and management which will afterwards produce and deliver commodities towards the ultimate consumers.

Thus Institutional, or Proprietary, Economics is not divorced from the classical and psychological schools of economists—it transfers their theories to the *future* when physical goods will be produced, or physically delivered, or consumed, as an outcome of present transactions. It, however, separates *legal control* from the materials owned. The transfer of ownership is a present transaction, at an ever-present moving point of time. The future consequences may be the engineering economics of production of the classical and communistic economists, or the home economics of the hedonic economists, both of which depend on *physical* control. But institutional economics is *legal* control of commodities, of labor, or any other economic quantity, whereas the classical and hedonic theories dealt only with physical control. *Legal control is future physical control.* It may be modified as to the beneficiaries as in the laws of agency, receivership, trusteeship, etc., but these do not affect the transactions themselves, wherein it is legal control limited by the threefold dimension of use, scarcity, and futurity.[126]

It may seem quite the reverse of the assumptions of orthodox economists to say that it is legal control which has value, and not physical control. To them, physical control was necessary to create and consume wealth. In this they reached an evident conclusion, but they did not incorporate in their theories the idea that legal control is *future* physical control. They introduced futurity into economics by way of the psychology of Böhm-Bawerk. But futurity has always been there as property rights, which the psychological economists, however, rejected. Yet Böhm-Bawerk performed a distinguished service by running futurity back from the future psychology of consumption to the present labor of obtaining physical control for future uses. We run it back still further to the negotiational psychology which ends in the transactions that obtain the legal control which precedes physical control.[127]

(9) **Performance, Forbearance, Avoidance.**[128]—But legal control is not only an economic quantity, it is control of the future behavior of individuals upon which the dimensions of that economic quantity will depend.

The peculiar attribute of the human will in all its activities, dis-

---

[126] Below, p. 510, The Transactional Theory of Money and Value.
[127] Below, p. 438, From Psychological to Institutional Economics.
[128] Cf. Commons. *Legal Foundations of Capitalism*, 69 ff.

tinguishing economics from the physical sciences, is that of choosing between alternatives. The choice may be voluntary, or it may be an involuntary choice imposed by another individual or by collective action. In any case the choice is the whole mind and body in action —that is, the will—whether it be physical action and reaction with nature's forces in the production and consumption of wealth, or the negotiational activity of mutually inducing others engaged in the transactions.

Every choice, on analysis, turns out to be a three-dimensional act, which—as may be observed in the issues brought out in disputes— is at one and the same time, a performance, an avoidance, and a forbearance. Performance (including payment) is the exercise of power over nature or over others, in acquiring or delivering a physical or economic quantity. Avoidance is the exercise of power in one direction rather than in the next available direction; while forbearance is the exercise, *not of the total* power except at a crisis, or under compulsion, but the exercise of a limited degree of one's *possible* moral, physical, or economic power. Thus forbearance is the limit placed on performance; performance is the actual performance; and avoidance is the alternative performance rejected or avoided—all at one and the same point of time.

Forbearance and avoidance are usually combined in the legal word "omission," but as this word does not tell what is "omitted" we analyze it as either forbearance or avoidance.

It is from these three dimensions of choosing that the doctrine of reasonableness arises. Performance means either rendering a service, compelling a service, or paying a debt. Avoidance is non-interference with the performance, forbearance, or avoidance of others. Forbearance is the "reasonable" exercise of performance. Each may be a duty or a liberty, with a corresponding right or exposure of others; and each may be compelled, permitted, or limited by collective action according to the then working rules of the particular concern.

It is upon these three dimensions of the will in action—different altogether from Locke's concept of Power—that all collective compulsion, through legal or arbitrational procedure, operates. A command of performance has a similar implication to that of the legal doctrine of *quantum meruit,* that is, the economic quantity to which one is entitled. It is found in the American practice of regulating the amount of service to be rendered by, or of prices to be paid to, public service corporations. A command of avoidance is the most primitive and universal of all collective commands. It creates all rights of property and personal liberty, from the primitive *tabu* and the Ten Commandments, to all the varieties of modern corporeal, incorporeal, and intangible property. It creates the duty of non-interference, on the part of third parties, even of the first or second party, with the permitted expectations either of the use of land and materials (corporeal), or of the performance of services and pay-ment of debts (incorporeal), or of the expected beneficial transac-tions protected under the general name of good-will (intangible).

It is these duties of avoidance or forbearance which the United States Supreme Court commands upon legislatures and executives when they attempt to take property, or the value of property, or liberty, without due process of law. From the standpoint of eco-nomics, all of these collective commands, whether of performance, forbearance, or avoidance, are implied in the changing economic quantities known as assets and liabilities; from the standpoint of law they are property; from the standpoint of collective action they are working rules. From the standpoint of economic status they are security, conformity, liberty, and exposure. From the stand-point of the going concern itself, in its control of individuals, they are Power, Liability, Disability, Immunity.

(10) **Strategic and Routine Transactions.**—For more than a hundred years, economists have been developing a doctrine of com-plementary "goods," which in its more recent form becomes a doc-trine of limiting and complementary factors. However, looking at this doctrine from the standpoint of the human will in action amidst a conflict of interests, I name it a doctrine of Strategic and Routine Transactions.[129] Briefly I shall use the terms strategic or limiting, the word "strategic" referring to the volitional side, the word "limit-ing" referring to the objective side, of the same relationship of limiting and complementary factors.

The human will has the strange but familiar ability to act upon a single factor, out of hundreds and thousands of complex factors, in such a way that other factors shall, of their own inherent forces, bring about results intended. A very little potash, if that is the limiting factor, will multiply the yield of the land from 5 bushels to 30 bushels per acre. A very little control of an accelerator will set the automobile going 50 miles per hour. A very little exercise of control over a man who holds the strategic position among a mass of laborers will change a mob into a going concern. A very little security of legal control over the supply of a slowly increasing factor —such as a land site, needed by thousands of business men and laborers competing with each other for its use in centers of popula-

---

[129] Below, p. 867, Strategic and Routine Transactions.

tion—will compel the users of the land to deduct from their profits, interest, or wages enough to pay rent to the absentee owner.

Further, the limiting and complementary factors are continually changing places. What are contributory at one point of time may become strategic at the next point of time. At one time it may be potash, at a later time water; at one time it may be the accelerator, at another time the spark plug. At one time it may be the land site, when the rent bargain is made; at another time it may be a skilled mechanic or even laborers on strike, when the wage bargains are made; at another time it may be the banker when commercial credit is the limiting factor; at another time it may be a court of law or the Supreme Court, when everything else may stop until the lawyers obtain a decision. And so on in infinite variabilities of strategic and contributory factors. By operating upon, or furnishing a supply, or withholding supply, of what—at the particular time, place, or quantity—is the limiting factor in obtaining what one wants in the future, the whole complex of the universe may be brought under command of a physically puny human being.

Of course, if all the complementary factors become limiting factors at one point of time, then none of them is strategic, and the matter is hopeless. The concern dissolves in bankruptcy or revolution. For, generally, in a going concern, the limiting factors are *not cumulative* at a point of time—they are *successive* during a sequence of time. The most important of all investigations in the economic affairs of life, and the most difficult, as we shall find, is the investigation of strategic and contributory factors. It is none other than a universal principle of the human will in action—a principle that could not emerge with John Locke's concept of a passive mind analogous to physics, and emerges full-fledged only when economics becomes a science of the human will in all its activities.[130]

(11) **Negotiational Psychology.**—If institutional economics is therefore volitional economics, it requires a volitional psychology to accompany it. This is the psychology of transactions, which we may properly name transactional or negotiational psychology. Nearly all of the older schools of psychology are individualistic, since they are concerned with the relation of individuals to nature or to other "natural" individuals. Individuals are viewed, not as *citizens* with rights, but as physical or biological *objects* of nature. This naturalistic individualism is true of Locke's copy psychology, Berkeley's idealistic psychology, Hume's sensational psychology, Bentham's pleasure-pain psychology, the hedonistic marginal utility

---

[130] Below, p. 526, Margins for Profit; p. 867, Strategic and Routine Transactions.

psychology, James' pragmatism, Watson's behaviorism, and the recent Gestalt psychology. All are individualistic. Only Dewey's social psychology of custom may become negotiational.

The psychology of transactions is the social psychology of negotiations and the transfers of ownership. Each participant in the transaction is endeavoring to influence the other towards performance, forbearance, or avoidance. Each modifies the behavior of the other in greater or less degree. Thus each endeavors to change the dimensions of the economic values to be transferred. This is the psychology of business, of custom, of legislatures, of courts, of trade associations, of trade unions. In customary language it resolves into the persuasions or coercions, the advertising and propaganda, of bargaining transactions; the commands and obedience of managerial transactions; or the arguments and pleadings of rationing transactions. All of these are negotiational psychology. It may be observed that they are a special case of behavioristic psychology, directed towards the creation and transfer of ownership.

But these are only descriptions. A scientific understanding of negotiational psychology resolves it into the smallest number of general principles, or similarities of cause, effect, or purpose, to be found in all negotiations, but in varying degree.

First are the personalities of the participants in the transaction. Instead of enjoying the assumed equality of economic theory, the participants enjoy or suffer all the differences found among human beings, in their powers of inducing, and their responses to inducements and sanctions.

Then there are the similarities and differences of circumstance in which personalities are placed: First is scarcity or abundance of alternatives. This is inseparable from efficiency, or the capacity to bring events to happen. In all cases negotiations are directed towards future time—the universal principle of futurity. Working rules are always explicitly or tacitly taken into account, since they are the expectations of what the participants can, must, or may do, as controlled, liberated, or expanded by collective action. Next, in each transaction there is always a limiting factor whose control by the sagacious negotiator, salesman, manager, manual laborer, or politician, at the strategic moment, will determine the outcome of complementary factors in the immediate or remote future.

Thus, negotiational psychology is the transactional psychology which offers inducements and sanctions to transfers of ownership of economic quantities at variable valuations in terms of money, according to the variable personalities engaged in the negotiation, and to the present circumstances of scarcity, efficiency, futurity, working rules, and limiting factors.

Historically, this transactional psychology may be seen to have changed, and is changing continuously; so that the various philosophies of Capitalism, Fascism, Nazism, or Communism are variabilities of it. In the common-law decisions the change is evident in the changing distinctions between persuasion and coercion or duress; persuasion being considered the outcome of a reasonable status of either equality of opportunity, or fair competition, or equality of bargaining power, or due process of law. But economic coercion and physical duress are denials of these economic ideals, and nearly every case of economic conflict becomes an assumption or investigation, under the circumstances of the case, of the psychology of persuasion, coercion, or duress. Even the managerial and rationing negotiations come under this rule of institutional change, for the psychology of command and obedience is changed with changes in the status of conformity, security, liberty, or exposure. The modern "personnel management" is an illustration of this sort of change in negotiational psychology, as illustrated in the foregoing formula from Henry S. Dennison.[131]

All of this rests on what we have distinguished as three social relations implicit in every transaction: the relations of Conflict, Dependence, and Order. The parties are involved in a conflict of interests on account of the universal principle of scarcity. Yet they depend on each other for reciprocal alienation of ownership of what the other wants but does not own. The working rule is not a foreordained harmony of interests, as assumed in the hypotheses of divine or natural rights, or mechanical equilibrium of the classical and hedonic schools, but it actually creates, out of conflict of interests, a workable mutuality and orderly expectation of property and liberty. Thus conflict, dependence, and order become the field of institutional economics, builded upon the principles of scarcity, efficiency, futurity, working rules, and strategic factors; but correlated under the modern notions of collective action controlling, liberating, and expanding individual action.

Thus it may be seen how it was that the "natural rights" ideas of the economists and lawyers created the analogy of a framework, supposed to be created in the past, within which present individuals are supposed to act. It was because the economists and lawyers did not investigate collective action and negotiational psychology. They assumed the fixity of existing rights of property and liberty. But if

---

[131] Above, p. 67, Job Analysis of Managing.

securities, conformities, liberties, and exposures are simply the changeable working rules of all kinds of collective action, looking towards the future, then the framework analogy becomes no more than rhetoric, in the actual collective action of controlling, liberating, and expanding individual action in the immediate or remote future production, exchange, and consumption of wealth.[132]

Consequently, the final social philosophy—which we define as a belief regarding human nature and its goal—towards which institutional economics tends, is not something foreordained by divine or natural "right" or materialistic equilibrium, or "laws of nature." It may be Communism, Fascism, Nazism, Capitalism. If managerial and rationing transactions are the starting point of the philosophy, then the end is the command and obedience of Communism, Fascism, or Nazism. If bargaining transactions are the units of investigation, then the trend is towards the ideals of equality of opportunity, of fair competition, of equality of bargaining power, of due process of law, of the philosophy of Liberalism and regulated Capitalism. But there may be all degrees of combinations, for the three kinds of transactions are interdependent and variable in a world of collective action and perpetual change which is the uncertain future world of institutional economics.

III. IDEAS

John Locke's "ideas" began as simple copies of physical objects. These objects, in economics, were commodities and individuals. Then, by a passive association of ideas the more complex ideas of substance, relation, and mode became "collections" of ideas. These remained the concepts of economic theory for two hundred years.

But if the mind itself is a unit of activity, then it actually creates its own ideas. An idea is not a copy of reality—it is a useful imagination by which we get our living or get rich. And since getting a living is also resolved into units of activity, then a more complicated classification of ideas is required.

We shall endeavor to maintain the distinction above made, between Locke's "idea" and the "meaning," not only of words but also of ideas. Ideas are the intellectual tools with which we investigate. We shall reconstruct the familiar hierarchy of ideas in order to fit them to our subject-matter. This subject-matter is the transactions of human beings in producing and acquiring wealth by coöperation, conflict, and the working rules that control, liberate, and expand individual transactions. These outside activities come to us first as

---

[132] Below, p. 680, From Natural Rights to Reasonable Value.

mere sensations, and, as such, we cannot be sure whether they are caused by changes that happened outside our bodies or by changes that happened inside. As soon as the inside feeling is attributed to something that happened outside, we name it a Percept. A percept is the meaning we give to a sensation.

But, up to this point we get no further than animals or babies. The next step is the acquisition of language, by which we name our percepts as "Dick" or "Papa," and then classify them according to similarities, differences, and quantities.

There are, for our purposes, five kinds of similarities and differences, rising in a hierarchy from Locke's "simple ideas," which were percepts, to his most complex ideas. But instead of his complex ideas of "substance, relations, and modes," we construct five mental instruments of investigation, from simple ideas to ideas of high complexity.

The simplest idea (or instrument) is a *Concept*, derived from a supposed *similarity of attributes*, as Man, Horse, Use-Value, Scarcity-Value.

More complex is a *Principle*, by which we mean a supposed *similarity of actions*. While a concept involves no element of time, the flow of time is essential to the idea of a principle. From this idea of a principle is derived many special cases such as law, cause, effect, purpose. The so-called "law of supply and demand" is not a law; it is a special case of the principle of Scarcity, and, because a principle involves the sequence of time it is a *similarity of cause, effect, or purpose*. The principle of Scarcity, for example, may be either a cause of activity, an effect of activity, or a purpose intended by the actor. So with the other principles into which we can perhaps resolve the so-called "laws" of political economy as a cause, effect, or purpose of all economic activity, such as Efficiency, Futurity, the Working Rules of Collective Action, and the Limiting Factors whose control will control the complementary factors.[133]

Every science endeavors to reduce its complex activities to the simplest and most universal principles. If we do the same for political economy, distinguishing it from the physical and biological sciences as a branch of sociology, the simplest and therefore least specific similarity of cause, effect, or purpose is Willingness. Willingness is not the "will," nor is it Locke's "substance," or "existence," or "power"—it is only a supposed similarity of cause, effect, or purpose, derived from experience with human behavior.

Seeing, however, that the meaning of Willingness includes the

---

[133] See articles on "Law" and "Principle" in *Oxford Dictionary of the English Language*. The term "working rules" was first proposed to me by Professor R. T. Ely.

highly debatable and perhaps impassable gulf between psychology and economics, we shall take a hint from Ogden's "two-language hypothesis," wherein he makes the similar leap from physiology to psychology.[134] Ogden can use two languages for describing the same event. "Memory," for example, is the psychological language of which "retention" is the physiological language. This bi-lingual device does not solve the unsolvable problem of Locke and the modern "behaviorists," as to how unconscious physiology becomes conscious psychology, but it enables Ogden to shift from one to the other as needed, without binding himself irretrievably to either.

In the economics of Willingness, we need more than a two-language hypothesis; we need a three-language hypothesis of psychology, jurisprudence, and economics; indeed, a four-language hypothesis if we would accommodate, as Ogden does, the physiological behaviorists.[135] We need physiology when we study fatigue and salesmanship. Our four-language hypothesis of Willingness is psychology, jurisprudence, economics, and physiology. On the psychological side it is ideas, meanings, and valuings; on the economic side it is the valuing, choosing, acting, and forecasting which constitute the economic quantities of transactions and going concerns; on the juristic side it is the collective action of custom, politics, and the common and statutory law, which control, liberate, or expand the transactions or concerns; on the physiological side it is the glands, secretions, nerves, that set the body agoing or stopping.

This four-language hypothesis of the will recognizes the dualism and skepticism that Locke injected into all the sciences by his concept of ideas as a world within, copying a world without; but it transcends his dualism by the device of interpreting his term "ideas" as the fourfold activity of meaning, valuing, choosing, and conforming or not conforming, to the social rules of custom and law.

The unity of this four-language hypothesis of Willingness lies in the meaning of Future Time. Futurity has equally a psychological aspect of expectation, a measurable magnitude in modern economic theory, a juristic realization in the future, and a physiological response of the secretions which accompany inducements and sanctions.

Willingness thus becomes a general principle of cause, effect, or purpose, common to certain modes of motion, determined by the meanings given to words and events in view of the happenings expected; a mode of motion determined by the feelings of relative importance aroused in the minds of those who expect the happen-

[134] Ogden, C. K., *The Meaning of Psychology* (1926).
[135] Watson, J. B., *Behaviorism* (1925); *Behavior; an Introduction to Comparative Psychology* (1914). Also his article "Behaviorism," *Encyclopaedia Britannica*, 14th edition.

ings; a mode of motion restrained, liberated and expanded by the collective action which we name institutions. The motions themselves are a repetition of transactions in view of these meanings, valuings, and limitations. Thus the meaning of Willingness is the inseparable activity of meaning, valuing, transacting, and governing, wherein "meaning" is the semi-intellectual language; "valuing," the mainly emotional language; "transacting," the economic language; while ethics, law, and property are the working rules of collective, or institutional, language.

This four-language hypothesis enables us to avoid taking a position on the difficult problems of metaphysics, yet allows us to find a place for that which is non-physical, namely, the expectations that are inseparable from transactions and going concerns. For metaphysics, we substitute Futurity.

It also permits us to distinguish, as we shall do repeatedly, the two meanings of Analogy which necessarily run through all thinking, while at the same time making use of the rhetorical analogies which permeate all speech, instead of introducing unfamiliar words and signs, as the physical sciences are permitted to do. For analogy is simply the method of discovering similarities. Correct analogy is a true similarity. False analogies have arisen in the history of economic thought by transferring to economics the meanings derived from the physical sciences, as we have seen in Locke's derivations from the astronomy and optics of Sir Issac Newton, or from the more recent biological sciences of organisms, or even from the human will itself. These false analogies are often indicated by such terms as "hypostatizing," "reifying," "thingifying," "vivifying," "personifying," "eternalizing," "animism," "materialism." [136]

The false analogies may be condensed into the three analogies of mechanism, organism, and personification, since they consist in transferring to economics the ideas properly employed in physics, physiology, or individual psychology. These, we conceive, may be avoided by substituting the two ideas of transactions and going concerns, and recognizing that, in speaking of them, we are using the four languages of psychology, jurisprudence, economics, and physiology to indicate four aspects of the same behavior. These going concerns and transactions are to economics what Whitehead's "organic mechanism" and "event" are to physics,[137] or the physiologists' "organism" and "metabolism" are to biology, or the total

[136] Cf. Frank, L. K., "The Principle of Disorder and Incongruity in Economic Affairs," *Pol. Sci. Quar.*, XLVII (1932), 515–525.
[137] Whitehead, A. N., *Science and the Modern World* (1925).

personality of the Gestalt psychology to the particular acts of will.[138]
Wherever one or another of these migratory meanings from mechanism, organism, or individual psychology have crept in, we consider
the resulting intellectual tools unfitted for economic research, although, on account of the paucity of language we are often compelled
to use them by way of allowable dramatic analogy.

Still more complex than a principle is a Formula, constructed by
the mind to investigate a relation between the parts and the whole.
It reaches its amazing triumph in the pure mathematics of imaginary
lines and numbers. Other mental formulae which we construct are:
the relations of buyers and sellers to a transaction in which they
participate; the relations of transactions themselves to the going
concern of which they are parts; the relation of the individual to
society, of the citizen to the Commonwealth; and so on in endless
variety. However simple or complex the formula, it is always a
mental picture of a relation between the parts and the whole.

Max Weber, followed by Sombart and preceded by Rickert, constructed something similar to a formula, which he named the "ideal
typus." It was intended to eliminate subjective factors and to furnish a strictly objective formula of what are the essentials for
investigation and understanding of all social facts in their relations.
Hence their ideal type held no implication of right or wrong. But,
even so, as has been pointed out by Kröner and Schelting, different
investigators differ as to what is essential, or they differ in the
weights given to different essentials. Thus Weber created the ideal
type of the "capitalistic spirit," or the "handicraft spirit." This
ideal type remains fixed for the investigator, and, if the facts do not
correspond, then the ideal type is not changed and brought into
conformity with the facts, but the facts are introduced later as
"frictions," although frictions are just as important as the type.
But the formulae of transactions and concerns avoids these difficulties because it starts with actual behavior instead of with the several
feelings or "spirits." There is no need to find an inward principle,
like the capitalistic spirit, for an explanation of similarity of behavior. This principle is itself objective when derived from the
working rules of a concern.[139]

The most complex idea is a Social Philosophy, usually described

---

[138] Köhler, W., *The Mentality of Apes* (1917, tr. from 2d ed., 1925); *Gestalt Psychology*
(1929); Koffka, K., *Growth of the Mind; an Introduction to Child-Psychology* (tr. 1924);
Petermann, Bruno, *The Gestalt Theory and the Problem of Configuration* (tr. 1932).

[139] See Kröner, *op. cit.;* Schelting, Alexander von, "Die logische Theorie der historischen
Kultur-Wissenschaft von Max Weber und im besonderen sein Begriff des Idealtypus,"
Archiv f. Sozialwissenschaft und Sozialpolitik, LXIX (1922), 623–752. Below, p. 719,
Ideal Types.

with the suffix *ism,* such as the philosophies of individualism, socialism, communism, anarchism, fascism, capitalism, agrarianism, trade unionism. European economists use the term "ideology," where we use "social philosophy." "Ideology," we take it, is purely intellectual. It has no feelings, activity, or punch. But a social philosophy has two main poles of relationship—it is based on an ethical emotion regarding human nature and it sets up a wished-for goal in the future. Here it is a similarity of *purpose* that stands out predominant, subordinating to itself the meanings of all concepts, principles, and formulae. The philosophy is not always a clear idea. It is usually half-conscious. If a man starts out to prove a thing, it is wonderful how he can select the facts that prove it. It is our social philosophies that unconsciously select for us our facts and definitions. Yet a social philosophy, for purposes of investigation, is only a compound idea, having, as Locke said of justice, law, or of God, "no settled object in Nature," but deducible from all other ideas.

Our meaning of "ideas" bears a resemblance to E. W. Hobson's definition of science as a "conceptual scheme fitted to percepts." [140] It is different, however, in that, with us, the subject-matter of our science is human beings, who themselves have their own "conceptual schemes." The economic scientist, therefore, has two "conceptual schemes," his own by which he constructs his science, and those of human beings, his subject-matter, who construct theirs for their own purposes.

Thus we construct and reconstruct in our minds, by a process which we call Theorizing, five mental tools for investigation and understanding, which, taken together, we name Ideas and their Meanings. Ideas, interpreted as meanings, are Percepts, Concepts, Principles, Formulae, and Social Philosophies. They are inseparable, and it is on account of their interdependence that we construct a sixth idea which we name Theory.

More properly, theory is the active process of theorizing, and theorizing is a method of thinking. Various methods of theorizing have had an important influence on economic theory. Hegel, the philosopher, described it as thesis, antithesis, and synthesis. Thesis is a first assertion, antithesis is its opposite, and synthesis is the reconciliation of the two on a larger scale. This formula was applied by Hegel to the evolution of the "world spirit" embodied in the

---

[140] Hobson, E. W., *The Domain of Natural Science* (1923). An apparently contrary view of science is that of Cohen, Morris R., *Reason and Nature, an Essay on the Meaning of Scientific Method* (1931), and *Law and the Social Order; Essays in Legal Philosophy* (1933).

political evolution of the German race; then by Marx to the materialistic evolution of society, and by Proudhon to the economic contradiction of efficiency and scarcity. A mental formula was given an objective existence.[141]

Then, since *evolution* of the external world was evidently a part of the formula, the process of thinking came to be described as analysis, genesis, and synthesis. Analysis is the process of classification, by which we compare similarities and distinguish differences, and are able to break up the subject-matter into concepts, principles, formulae and philosophies. Genesis is analysis of the changes that are continually going on in all of the factors, named by Darwin Natural Selection. Synthesis is the union of analysis and genesis into a formula of the changing relations of the parts to the whole. Thus by analysis we classify, subdivide, and give meaning to the various concepts of value, or to the principles of efficiency and scarcity. By genesis we show changes in prices, or the unfolding of early customs into multitudes of modern customs, or the evolution of inventions from the stone age to wireless. By synthesis we unite the changing parts into a changing whole.

The incoming of this formula of thinking about the economic facts of the world led, in the latter part of the Nineteenth Century, to the distinction of statics and dynamics, which were taken over from the earlier physical sciences. If we examine what was done by economists whose method of thinking was described as "statical," we find that it consisted in assuming that all other factors were constant, except the one factor the changes of which were being investigated. This method was practicable in the laboratory sciences and has resulted in the great discoveries of those sciences, because—by ingenious devices—all of the factors except the one investigated, can actually be kept constant, and the subject-matter investigated utters no protest and puts up no individual or collective resistance. But in economic science the subject-matter is *living human beings,* who act individually and collectively, and who will not permit the laboratory experiments to be carried out. Hence, the static analysis must be only a mental hypothesis based on mere assumption that other factors remain constant; there can be no possibility of testing the theory by keeping any of them actually constant.

At the time when the earlier economists were writing, there was not available either the statistics or the mathematical theories necessary to investigate a problem of multiple change. In fact, these

---

[141] Below, p. 366, on Marx and Proudhon.

statistics and theories did not become fairly well available until the post-war investigations, especially in America. All the factors are changing at the same time and are breaking up into subfactors also changing relatively to all the others. The problem of multiple change is world-wide; mathematical economists in many countries are at work endeavoring to bring the problem to a synthesis of the measurable relations of the changing parts to the changing whole.

But here arises a distinction in the meaning of the word "dynamics." We distinguish it as "multiple change" and "multiple causation." In the physical sciences, causation is entirely eliminated, because the subject-matter has no will of its own. The mathematical economists necessarily endeavor to treat economic science in a similar way and to rule out causation. The ideas of cause, effect, and purpose are strictly of human invention; they come about by the endeavor of the human will, in its individual and mass action, to control and subordinate all the other human and non-human factors to itself, or to resist such control and subordination. By assuming harmony of interests, the older economists thought to eliminate all of these human factors as "frictions"—as the mathematical economists do in their theories of multiple change. But not until a theory of the human will in action is developed so as to fit these arbitrary, unaccountable, passionate, and war-like activities of human beings, can it be said that the whole of political economy is reduced to a workable economic science.

This we endeavor to do by the formula of strategic and routine transactions. The human being, in constructing its formula of part-whole relations, is seeking to discover what is the limiting factor, the strategic control of which will produce changes in other factors, each of them acting through their own forces. Here the idea of cause, effect, and purpose originates; a theory of multiple change in physics becomes a theory of multiple causation in economics.

While the term "synthesis" might be applied to this process, yet a more precise term is needed. Max Weber gave to it the name "understanding." Dean Akeley gives to it the name "insight." We follow Akeley's terminology, and reduce the method of thinking to analysis, genesis, and insight.

The meaning of Insight will appear if we examine the economists' controversy of fifty years ago over the "deductive" and "inductive" methods of investigation. The deductive method seems to be the method of the syllogism, with its major and minor premises from which flow an inevitable conclusion. Thus, man is mortal—the major premise; Socrates is a man—the minor premise; therefore Socrates is mortal—the inevitable conclusion.

What we want to know, however, as Akeley has said,[142] is whether this particular Socrates now on the operating table will die and how soon, at the hands of the surgeon. Here we have a hundred major premises, some of which give us hope that he will live, others, fear that he will die. What we need here is insight.

So it is in economics. We are investigating the major premises themselves, and trying to discover whether, here and now, they can be controlled. The "law of supply and demand," or, as we should say, the Principle of Scarcity, is inevitable, true enough, and, like death or the law of gravitation, cannot be avoided. But what we want is to control, if we can, or to find out who it was that controlled, death, gravitation, and supply or demand. If I throw a man out of a ten-story window, was he killed by me or by the law of gravitation? If a great corporation charges some of its customers a high price and their competitors a low price for the same commodity or service, were the high-price customers bankrupted by the "law of supply and demand" or by an unfair use of the principle of Scarcity by the corporation? It is *insight* that we need.

Hence there are two meanings of the word "induction," or inductive method of investigation, involving also deduction. Induction may be a collection of illustrations as minor premises, which, when assembled, merely restate the major premises. In which case we are reasoning in a circle. Or induction may be, as Akeley has said, a new Insight into the complexity of major and minor premises, all of which must be weighed and balanced for the particular situation and the consequences that have followed or may follow.

This kind of induction is what Akeley substitutes for synthesis. Synthesis is not merely deduction or induction—it is insight into the relationship between the limiting and complementary parts of the whole situation in a world of change and perpetual discovery. It is Illumination, Understanding, and an Emotional Sense of the fitness of things. When it comes to action, it is strategy. Great and new insights have marked the progress of economic thinking. Every one of the economists, from whom we proceed to derive our present theories, has contributed a new insight, not seen before or not clearly seen. The older controversies about deduction and induction dis-

[142] See articles by Akeley, Lewis E., Dean of the College of Engineering, University of South Dakota, in *Journal of Philosophy*, XXII (Oct. 1925), 561; XXIV (Oct. 1927), 589; XXVII (Feb. 1930), 85; *Journal of Engineering Education*, XVIII (Apr. 1928), 807–822. Below also, p. 719, on Rickert and Max Weber. Similar articles on methodology in jurisprudence by Cook, W. W., "Scientific Method and the Law," *Johns Hopkins Alumni Magazine*, XV (1927), 3. See articles in *Encyclopaedia Britannica*, 14th ed., on "Analogy," "Causality," "Logic," "Scientific Method"; Wolf, A., *Essentials of Scientific Method* (1930) Cf. Commons, "Das Anglo-Amerikansche Recht und die Wirtschaftstheorie," in *Die Wirtschaftstheorie der Gegenwart*, III, 313 ff., on the methods of Menger and Schmoller.

appear in the great movement to obtain Insight and Understanding. The process is never finished. There is plenty of room for more insight. The older insights have been wonderful and important for their time and place—never to be forgotten or set aside. The new insights are needed, and in turn they need the aid of the old, because "the world's economic dilemma" [143] is more puzzling than ever before, and yet similar dilemmas have occurred in the past.

Thus a theory, as we make use of the term, is a complex activity of Analysis, Genesis, and Insight, actively constructed by the mind in order to understand, predict, and control the future. Often the word theory, or theoretical, is a name of reproach uttered by the practical man who claims to be dealing only with Facts. He does not usually have a similar objection to the word "philosophy." The investigator should not ask him what is his "theory," but what is his "philosophy." By this term he undoubtedly means insight and understanding. But the practical man is a theorist when he predicts that the prices of stocks will rise and therefore buys as much as he can. If, instead, the prices fall and he is bankrupt, it is not because he is practical but because his theory was wrong. He did not analyze all the facts; did not take into account all the changes that were going on; did not combine analysis and genesis into a correct insight of the changing multiple relationships. In other words he did not guide his practice by a correct theory. He was a poor theorizer. Hence the word theory means a correct or incorrect insight among the limiting and complementary factors. It is not a fact, but a prediction of facts. If correct, then it is an insight that will fit all the future facts needed. If not correct, then it is simply a blunder and needs correction.

Yet, there is another meaning of the word Theory, which is Pure Theory, whereas the meaning just now given is Pragmatic Theory, and is Peirce's meaning of *Science*.[144] Economists may be distinguished as Pure Theorists, in so far as their reasoning is carried on and enjoyed on any presupposition which they may happen to accept, without regard to whether their deductions will work or not when tested by experiment; or they may be distinguished as Pragmatic or Scientific Theorists, in so far as they have an eye on the worthfulness of their reasoning for understanding, experimentation, taking chances, and guiding themselves and other participants in the future. Pure theory must always start with assumptions, that is, a general principle taken for granted. Given these assumptions the theory works itself out logically.

[143] See the important book under this title by E. M. Patterson (1930).
[144] Below, p. 140, Hume and Peirce.

All sciences make this distinction. Mathematics will illustrate it. Pure mathematics is not a science, it is a Formula. It is constructed in the mind by means of the language of number. Any consistent way in which numbers can be combined in the mind on the basis of any presupposition is a correct formula which may possibly be useful sometime. Euclid thought his assumptions or axioms were self-evident and therefore led to a certain deduction that no two lines could be drawn parallel through a given point. He confused an assumption with external reality. But Lobachevski (1829), by a new insight, worked out an equally consistent formula which showed that through a given point can be drawn two parallels to a given straight line. Each was pure theory, but they started with different assumptions; Euclid with flat space and stationary points, and Lobachevski, or his successors, with moving space and relative time. Each theory was consistent because it came out correctly upon the assumptions with which each started. Seventy-five years after Lobachevski, using modifications by intervening mathematicians, Einstein applied the hitherto useless formulae to rapidly moving points of light across the universe, instead of to supposed stationary points on the earth; he is reported as saying that he made his discoveries by questioning every assumption. Then experiments verified the usefulness of the formulae for a new order of facts. This was an instance of pragmatic theory which we name science.[145]

It is the same in economics. Every school of economic thought has contributed something of pure theory, derived from its own assumptions of a limited number of facts or axioms, from which the concepts, principles, formulae, and social philosophies may ultimately be derived as mental tools for theorizing, research, invention, experiment, planning, and acting.

Yet the pure theory in economics cannot be identified with that in physical science, because physical materials have no purposes, wills, rights, or interests. The economist is himself a part of the purposeful subject-matter of his science. This may not appear until he is forced by a crisis to choose between conflicting interests; then his pure theory is perhaps found to contain the assumptions which directed his choice.

The foregoing is a classification of pure Ideas according to their *subjective* meanings as percepts, concepts, principles, formulae, philosophies, and theories. Ideas may also be classified according to similarity of *objective attributes,* such as use-values, scarcity-values, and human, or ethical, values. Or, again, they may be

---

[145] Below, p. 140, Hume and Peirce; p. 649, Veblen; p. 386, Absolutism and Relativity.

classified according to similarity of *social relations*. The principal ones which we shall use are bargaining, managerial, and rationing transactions, custom, and sovereignty.

These three principles of classification we may name classifications of *concepts*, sometimes known as "statics," wherein questions of time and causation do not arise. But when we look upon them as units of activity, sometimes known by analogy to the older physics as "dynamics," then a causal or purposeful classification of ideas according to time sequence is required. This is the classification according to similarity of cause, effect, purpose, or so-called "laws" which, however, we name *Principles*. These principles may be reduced to the five similarities of scarcity, efficiency, futurity, working rules, and strategic factors. For the sake of convenience of reference we tabulate this classification of ideas as follows. It must be noted that these ideas are not really separable in fact. They are simply mental tools which must be combined somehow for purposes of investigation:

CLASSIFICATION OF IDEAS

1. According to Similarity of *Mental Instruments*
   a. Percepts (meaning of sensations)
   b. Concepts (similarity of ideas, attributes, relations)
   c. Principles (similarity of cause, effect, purpose)
   d. Formulae (part-whole relations)
   e. Social philosophies (human nature and ultimate goal)
   f. Theory (insight, experimentation).
2. According to Similarity of *Objective Attributes* (concepts)
   a. Use-values (civilization values)
   b. Scarcity-values (demand and supply)
   c. Future values (present discount values)
   d. Human values (virtues and vices).
3. According to Similarity of *Social Relations* (concepts)
   a. Bargaining transactions
   b. Managerial transactions
   c. Rationing transactions
   d. Custom (extra-legal control)
   e. Sovereignty (legal control).
4. According to Similarity of *Cause, Effect, or Purpose* (principles)
   a. Scarcity (bargaining)
   b. Efficiency (managing)
   c. Futurity (forecasting, waiting, risking, planning)
   d. Working rules (rationing, going concerns, custom, sovereignty)
   e. Strategic and routine transactions (volitional control).

Finally, the Big Idea is Ceaseless Change, the ultimate difference which two centuries have brought about from the ideas of Locke to the ideas of the Twentieth Century. It is the transition from *objects* to *activities* as the subject-matter. Objects have attributes and relations, but human activities have cause, effect, purpose, strategic and supplementary factors. Instead of dealing merely with attributes and relations we deal also with activities. Instead of dealing with individuals and physical things we deal with transactions and going concerns. Instead of Locke's concepts, substances, relations, and modes, we construct principles, formulae, and philosophies of desired and undesired expectations.

The foregoing classification of ideas which we find useful in subsequent pages may be summarized by comparison with other systems:

First, the idea of a passive mind reflecting the external universe descended from John Locke through the Eighteenth and Nineteenth Centuries of economic thought. This did not begin to give way to the idea of an active mind formulating its own ideas for purposes of investigation and insight until long after Darwin had formulated his theory of the struggle for survival. Ideas are the greatest of human inventions for overcoming nature and other people in the struggle for supremacy. It is the terms "meaning" and "valuing," introduced in recent psychology, that connect the former purely intellectual ideas of philosophy and logic with the emotions and activities that maintain existence and supremacy in the conflict of interests.

But survival is not merely individual survival—it is collective survival. This fact, though of course well known, did not begin to find its place in economic theory until after the rise of sociology beginning with Auguste Comte and more recently revised and summarized by E. A. Ross.[146] But this social psychology extends to the total population, whereas our "social philosophy" extends only to the 48,000,000 people engaged in "gainful occupations" by means of their participation in the rights of citizenship. What is meant by social psychology is what we mean by collective action in control of individual action by way of the variety of working rules needed in all collective action.

The individualistic psychology, so far as our discussion is concerned, takes three forms: the economic individualism of two centuries, the recent "behavioristic" psychology, and "Gestalt" psychology.

Economic individualism may always be identified as "net income" economics. The individual is pictured as receiving a net income determined by the difference between his outgo of work or money

[146] Ross, E. A., *Social Psychology, an Outline and Source Book* (1931).

and his income of pleasure or money. It is this that makes the individual isolated and conceals the conflict of interests. But our transactional economics is always a transfer of titles of ownership. This transfer always creates two debts, a debt of performance and a debt of payment. It is gross income and gross outgo, instead of individual net income. The gross outgo of one person is the identical gross income of the opposite person or persons in the transaction, and it is the *size* of this outgo-income that occasions conflict of interests. In every transaction there are two transfers of ownership, the ownership of a material object or service, and the ownership of another "object," which is a promise to pay. The transaction creates two debts. It might be named a debt economy enforced by collective action, were it not that we begin with the activity that creates the debts. This makes it possible to introduce a transactional or negotiational psychology which is itself a social psychology, leading up to the double transfers of ownership and the double creation of debts.

This negotiational psychology takes three forms according to the three kinds of transactions: the psychology of persuasion, coercion, or duress in bargaining transactions; the psychology of command and obedience in managerial transactions; and the psychology of pleading and argument in rationing transactions.

The fact that this is a behavioristic social psychology requires distinction to be made from the individualistic behavior psychology of those who reject ideas altogether as merely subjective and unmeasurable, basing their psychology on the glands, muscles, nerves, and blood currents, etc. Negotiational psychology is strictly a psychology of ideas, meanings, and customary units of measurement.

Negotiational psychology approaches more nearly to the "Gestalt" psychology, which, however, is distinctly an individualistic psychology, concerned with the mental growth of the individual from infancy. The resemblance consists in the fact that the Gestalt psychology is a part-whole psychology, wherein each particular act is connected with the whole configuration of all acts of the individual. But the mental concept which we use as a tool for investigating this part-whole relationship in its social implications is a "formula." It is by the construction of a formula that the economic or social investigator learns the prime method of investigation which resolves itself mainly into a constructive method of interviewing.[147]

---

[147] For example, see Bingham, W. V. D., and Moore, B. V., *How to Interview* (1931); *Interviews, Interviewers, and Interviewing in Social Case Work*, Family Welfare Association of America, 130 E. 22d St., N. Y. (1931); Lindeman, E. C., *Social Discovery; an Approach to the Study of Functional Groups* (1924).

Auguste Comte, the founder of sociology, classified the methods of theorizing in three stages of historical evolution, which he named the Theological, Metaphysical, and Positive stages.[148]   Our study of economists, from Locke to the present day, leads us to a similar three stages, which we name the stages of Personification, Materialism, and Pragmatism.

In the stage of personification, two stages of personification are really called for, in order to fit Comte's classification.   The first is the stage of Superstition, or the presupposition of arbitrary wills, comparable to the human will, governing human events.   This was Comte's "theological" stage, named by anthropologists "animism."   The second is the stage of Rationalism, or Comte's "metaphysical" stage, wherein the presupposition is that of a non-arbitrary but benevolent, rational will, governing human events; this stage is illustrated by Locke, Quesnay, Smith, and the bulk of economic and legal reasoning of the Eighteenth and Nineteenth Centuries.

In the subsequent stage of materialism—a non-benevolent kind of metaphysics, illustrated by Ricardo, Karl Marx, and the supply and demand theorists—the causes were found, again by analogy, in certain foreordained "forces" or "laws," or in an automatic "equilibrium" of physical nature, which operated independently of the human will in a world of supposed certainty.   It is, however, often difficult to determine whether the metaphysical economist is a benevolent rationalist or a non-benevolent materialist.

Comte's "positive" stage retained something of personification, metaphysics, and fore-ordination.   We have not space to develop this allegation, but by observation of the conflicting way in which economists and people of affairs are thinking and acting, especially since the World War, our third stage is that of perpetual investigation and experiment which, following Peirce, we name Pragmatism. In the stage of Pragmatism, a return is made to a world of uncertain change, without fore-ordination or metaphysics, whether benevolent or non-benevolent, where we ourselves and the world about us are continually in a changing conflict of interests.   And, like Locke, we investigate how our own minds and the world about us actually behave in a society of human beings whose future is frankly recognized as unpredictable but which can be controlled somewhat by insight and collective action.

This we conceive to be the problem of Institutional Economics. Institutional economics is not something new—it always has been the obvious accompaniment of all economic theories.   For this reason

[148] Comte, Auguste, *Cours de philosophie positive* (1830–42, 5th ed., 1892).

it may often seem to be superficial, since it is so commonplace and familiar. But this may be the very reason why it needs investigating and why it is most difficult to investigate. The whole progress of all the sciences has been from the most remote objects—even thousands of light-years away—to the most intimate, which are our own wills in action. It has been the progress of science not only from the simple to the complex but also from the remote to the commonplace.[149]

IV. CONFLICT OF INTERESTS

The Science of Political Economy has fluctuated between extreme individualism and extreme collectivism. While each school of economists has arisen out of conflict of interests, each has rejected the conflict from which it sprang as something unnatural, artificial, and temporary. Even the collectivist dictatorship is designed to wipe out conflicts of interest. The individualist schools looked forward to a future harmony of interests based on private property; the collectivists to a future harmony based on collective property. We may therefore look upon all economic theories as idealisations of future harmony, not as scientific investigations of existing conflicts and the ways in which order arises from conflict.

There were several reasons for the individualistic idealism of the Eighteenth and Nineteenth Centuries. First was the assumption of divine beneficence and earthly abundance—there would be no conflict of interests if divine law were not thwarted by earthly sin.

Another was the concept of net income instead of gross income. Net income is an individual's difference between gross income and gross outgo. But gross income of one individual is gross outgo for another, and gross outgo of one is gross income for another. There is no conflict of interests in the concept of net income; the conflict arises out of gross income for one and the identical gross outgo for another.

This harmony and conflict of interests is traceable to the ultimate units of investigation. The commodity was identified with corporeal property—the ownership of materials—and therefore ownership, from which conflicts of interest arise, was omitted. And when incorporeal property or debts had to be accounted for, they also were treated in the same way as commodities, the buying and selling of which were simply a means of obtaining a net income. Not until the concept of a transaction was introduced, which meant the transfer of two ownerships and the consequent creation of two debts,

[149] Below, p. 386, From Absolutism to Relativity.

could gross income be distinguished clearly from net income. But we resolve a transaction not only into conflict of interests, but also into mutual dependence and collective efforts to bring order out of conflict.

The Science of Political Economy has therefore arisen out of conflicts of interest, and out of efforts to convert conflict of interests into an idealistic harmony of interests. Economic conflicts become political conflicts and wars, and these arise from scarcity; while economic classes arise from the similarities of interest in obtaining and retaining ownership of shares of the world's limited supply of wealth. There are not merely two classes, as Marx maintained, but there are as many economic classes as there are differences among the similarities of interest. The widest classification has usually been based on the difference between producers and consumers of wealth, but these, as proprietors, are broken up into many classes of buyers, sellers, borrowers, lenders, farmers, laborers, capitalists, landowners; these again into wheat farmers, cotton farmers, bankers, manufacturers, merchants, skilled and unskilled laborers, mine owners, railway owners, and so on indefinitely in classes, subclasses, and subdivisions of subclasses.

The importance of investigating instead of idealizing these economic classes and their conflicts lies in the fact that the classes have been organizing and consolidating for concerted action, according to similarities in their economic interests. Thousands of these organizations appear and disappear, some on a national or even international scale, with headquarters at great centers of economic or political strategy, such as New York, Washington, London, Paris; some on a local or district scale according to the areas within which their interests are similar.[150] Everywhere has occurred the rise and fall of collective action along a wide or narrow similarity of interests; out of these conflicts arise either a workable harmony of interests, or a standstill, or a crash which requires the strong arm of still another collective action—practical politics and war—to bring, not Harmony, but Order out of Conflict.

Since the time when the study of economics began to be distinguished from philosophy, or theology, or physical science, the point of view which investigators took was determined by the nature of the conflict deemed uppermost at the time, and by the attitude of the investigators towards the conflicting interests. It is these differences among economists that are known as "schools" of economic

[150] The Federal Trade Commission has issued a directory of several thousand of these associations.

thought. We may summarize them here but develop them more fully in later chapters.

The first school was that of the Scholastic economists of the Thirteenth Century and after, whose leaders were the Church Fathers, especially St. Thomas Aquinas (1225–1274). They lived in an age of Feudalism and sheer violence of the powerful; where, however, the merchant class had begun its efforts to obtain liberty from the dominance of nobility and church. The new economic problems became the conflicts between buyers and sellers and between borrowers and lenders. St. Thomas attacked both the civil law inherited from Roman jurisprudence, and the Hebrew law of lending money to gentiles. According to the Roman law, it was lawful to sell a thing for more than its worth and to buy it for less than its worth; and it was lawful, according to both Roman and Hebrew laws (the latter only in lending to gentiles), to take usury for money lent. St. Thomas set up the Divine law of the Church Fathers, to the effect that, since all men were brethren, to sell something for more than its "worth" or to buy for less than its "worth" would be the sin of cheating; and to charge a price for the use of money would be the sin of selling what did not exist, therefore tending to inequality which is contrary to justice. He set up Brotherhood in place of Conflict as the ideal of economic theory.

This solution of conflict of interests recurs even today in considering the problem of what would be fair and reasonable if coercion, secrecy, and inequality were eliminated from economic life. In solution of the problem there have been created railroad commissions, market commissions, commercial arbitration, labor arbitration, courts of justice, in endless number and variety. Since St. Thomas based his idea of reasonable value on labor cost, his was the first of the labor theories of value.

Next came the school of Mercantilists, with the decline of Feudalism and the rise of the formerly despised merchant class into political power. The purpose of the Mercantilists was to show how the monarch or legislature might best promote the national interest by promoting the interests of merchants through protective tariffs, or bounties on exports, or monopolistic charters for joint stock companies, or navigation laws, or the exploitation both of colonies and their own agriculturists; thus creating such a favorable balance of exports over imports as would bring gold and silver into the country at the expense of other nations. The Mercantilists flourished in the Seventeenth Century, culminating with John Locke and the British Revolution of 1689. Indeed, they continue to flourish today;

but the modern names of the school are Nationalism, Protectionism, Fascism. Nazism, or the Republican Party.

The first protest against Mercantilism was made by the French Physiocrats, known in their day as "the economists." Their leader, François Quesnay, beginning in 1753, contended that the mercantilist policy was ruinous to an agricultural country like France, in that it favored manufacturers, merchants, bankers, and their corporations, whereas these classes were unproductive and only the forces of nature were productive. Gold and silver, moreover, were not wealth—they were only a circulating medium for the exchange of wealth. This wealth, if not interfered with by government, would flow naturally, like the blood, wherever it was needed for the exchange of commodities.

From this physiological analogy of the blood Quesnay and his followers derived the doctrine of free trade—let Nature take its course without putting government in business. For Nature was deemed beneficent and productive of wealth, and needed not the artificial scarcities created in the interest of merchants and manufacturers. Mercantilism discriminated against agriculture—the only occupation where Nature produced more than the producers consumed, the surplus going to the non-productive classes. The Physiocratic doctrine is repeated today when American farmers claim that they feed and clothe the world, but cannot make a living or maintain the fertility of the soil, because the business classes, whom they call the "Capitalists," control the government and discriminate against agriculture. The Physiocrats flourished in France for thirty years, but the School also flourishes today under the names of Agrarianism, Agricultural Economics, Single Tax, Progressivism, or, until recently, the Democratic Party.

Next came the Classical School of economists, whose leaders, for seventy years from 1776, were the quite divergent Adam Smith, Thomas Malthus, David Ricardo, and John Stuart Mill.

Smith took over the Physiocrats' doctrine of free trade and their opposition to Mercantilism, but he belonged to a nation that was leading the world in manufactures. Hence, for him and his followers, free trade would keep the leadership for England's manufacturing and shipping interests, leaving the production of raw materials and food to other nations. He represented the conflict between Mercantilism and Industrialism, just as the Physiocrats represented the conflict between Mercantilism and Agrarianism. Hence he rejected that part of the Physiocratic doctrine which held that Nature alone was productive of wealth, and went back to Aquinas and John Locke. It was now labor that was productive.

The labor in manufactures, commerce, and shipping also produced wealth, although he conceded to the Physiocrats that in agriculture the beneficence of nature augmented the work of labor.

Meanwhile Malthus in his famous *Essay on the Principles of Population* (1798), showed that population increased faster than the productivity of nature and labor, and he introduced scarcity, passion, stupidity, misery, as fundamentals in economic science. These were later taken over by Darwin and extended to all living creatures, in his *Origin of Species* (1859).

In 1817, Ricardo, a shrewd capitalist, took over the scarcity theory of Malthus and substituted the niggardliness of nature for the Eighteenth Century beneficence of God and nature. It was a change from theology to materialism: Nature does not aid man—she resists him, even in agriculture. From this changed point of view regarding nature, Ricardo developed the conflicting interests of landlords against the interests of capitalists and laborers. The pressure of population forced labor and capital outward to lower extensive margins of cultivation, or downward to lower intensive margins of production, so that there was always a tendency to reduce wages and profits to a minimum, which was equivalent to the amount that could be obtained on these lowest margins. Then competition equalized profits and wages throughout the nation so that on the better land, where nature's resistance was less, capital and labor obtained no greater income than on the least productive land in actual use. This left a surplus which Ricardo called rent (named by J. S. Mill the unearned increment), belonging solely to landowners without the expenditure of any labor or business enterprise on their part. This rent was further augmented in England by the protective tariff on food. Consequently, Ricardo furnished the grounds upon which manufacturers were able, thirty years afterwards (1846), to overcome the resistance of landlords in Parliament against repeal of the protective tariffs which had been enacted by landlords to keep up the prices of food.

The pessimistic theory of Ricardo and Malthus, of diminishing wages and profits caused by overpopulation, provoked into existence the schools of Socialists, Communists, Anarchists, Land Nationalizationists, Single Taxers, and Syndicalists.

The Communist school—as developed by Karl Marx in his debate with the anarchist, Proudhon, in 1846—retained Ricardo's conflict of interests but refused to make his distinction between Land and Capital. Ricardo's analysis had united capitalists and laborers against landlords on the tariff. But Marx made landlords and capitalists identical in their interests by defining each as mere property-owners whose joint control of government was used to exploit the laborers, a proletariat of non-property-owners. The remedy was a future harmony of interests, beginning, however, with confiscation of all private ownership in order to reduce all capitalists to a proletariat. This, as reaffirmed and led by Lenin and Stalin, reached unexpected success in the Russian Revolution of October 1917. The reaction against Communism developed as Nazism in Germany.

While Marx and the communists spoke for the interests of wage-earners, Proudhon and the anarchists spoke for the interests of the small peasant farmer against the great land-owner; for the small business man, the shop manufacturer or contractor and the retailer, against the big wholesaler, the jobber, and their alliance with the bankers who controlled money and credit. Proudhon's exploiter was a Merchant Capitalist, while Marx's was an Employer Capitalist. From Proudhon's mutualism of small proprietors, and his paper money representing labor-power, have arisen coöperative production, coöperative marketing, credit unions, greenbackism, populism, all endeavoring to displace the middleman and banker by coöperative or political action of farmers, laborers, or small business men.

Ultimately a combination of Marx's communism and Proudhon's anarchism was effected by Sorel, at the opening of the Twentieth Century, under the name Syndicalism. The reaction against this developed into the Fascism of Italy.

Another outcome of Ricardo's pessimism was the Land Nationalization School of which John Stuart Mill and Henry George, in the latter half of the Nineteenth Century, were the leaders. Mill, though included in the list of classical economists, differed from them in the important particular that he dropped Ricardo's labor theory of value and substituted money as the measure of value. He accepted Ricardo's theory of rent, and, in order to avoid confiscation, proposed the national ownership of all *future* unearned increments of rent. Henry George followed Ricardo more exactly, proposing a Single Tax on Rents and the abolition of all taxes on capital and labor. The American people, without the aid of economic theory, have made a special use of this principle of unearned increment, in the law of special assessments on the owners of land in payment for the construction of highways, streets, and irrigation ditches, in so far as the improvement increases the value of the land and the assessment does not exceed the cost of the improvement.

Meanwhile the pessimistic conclusion of Ricardo, which had led to communism and anarchism, and would later lead to Syndicalism, Fascism, and Nazism, had been flatly contradicted, during the long period of unemployment that culminated in the European revolutions of 1848, by the school of harmony of interests, known as Optimists. The leaders of this school, in the middle of the century, were the American, Henry C. Carey and the Frenchman, Frederic Bastiat. Carey favored protective tariffs in the interest of American manufacturers, but Bastiat favored free competition in the interest of French property-owners. The latter formulated his theories in a long debate with Proudhon, the anarchist.

According to Carey and Bastiat, and contrary to Ricardo and the communists and anarchists, the landlord or capitalist rendered a service to the community as much as did the laborer. The value of this service was the alternative price which the employer or laborer would be compelled to pay if he did not pay rent to the landlord, or profit and interest to the capitalist. He was better off by paying rent for superior land than he would be by going to the margin of cultivation where no rent was paid, and better off by paying profits and interest to capitalists than by working for marginal capitalists who made no profits. The optimists' theories survive in the justifications of private property, in the value theories of American courts, and in the theories of choice of opportunities. They are modified, however, by more modern doctrines of equal opportunity and equality of bargaining power.

The optimists were deemed superficial by the classical economists, although, as we shall see, their theories are the theories of the American courts. The economists, however, took property rights as self-evident and not needing justification or investigation; and founded their theories therefore on a contradictory definition of wealth as materials and the ownership of the materials. Carey and Bastiat were indeed originators of the modern ideas of *intangible* property. But the economists had only the doctrine of *corporeal* property. Hence they took the proprietary side as equivalent to the material side, therefore not needing investigation, and based their theories on cost of production of the material things, by devoting themselves to an analysis of the physical conditions of production, consumption, risk, and exchange of wealth.

MacLeod, shortly afterwards, went to the opposite extreme of this double meaning of the word "commodity" as wealth and its ownership. He attempted to eliminate physical things altogether and to construct political economy solely on the concept of the negotiability of debts and other property rights. But property rights, the economists objected, were superficial and involved double counting of the same thing, as when MacLeod, adopting a fallacy of Anglo-American law, argued that if a farm is valued at $10,000, then a debt of $5,000 secured by a mortgage on the farm is an additional "property," making the total value $15,000, whereas it is only $10,000. It was deemed necessary by the orthodox economists to disregard property rights and to analyze only production, exchange, and consumption of the physical things and services rendered by labor.

This explicit elimination of property rights was the method of the new school, the Psychological economists, which followed the European revolutions of 1848, and whose originators during a period of thirty years were the unknown Gossen (1854) and the well-known Jevons (1871), Menger (1871), and Walras (1874). Böhm-Bawerk (1884), and J. B. Clark and Fetter afterwards carried the Psychological School of economics down to more recent times. Upon an analysis of this Psychological School we find it to be the immediate precursor of the school of institutional economics.

During the Nineteenth Century the so-called Historical school arose in Germany (Roscher, Hildebrand, Knies), which rejected the entire method of reasoning of the other schools, and introduced into economics the method of historical research, which at the present time has become an important method. They explained the existing system of production and bargaining as an evolution imposed upon the present by the changing conditions of the past. This school brought into the science the concepts of Custom, Property, and conflicts of interest, which had been avowedly excluded by the classical and psychological schools. The Historical school led to the Ethical and Institutional schools (Schmoller, Veblen) which emphasized custom, legislation, property rights, justice and injustice, as the important factors in economic science.

In an entirely opposite direction the school of mathematical economists arose also from the psychological school. But mathematics and statistics have become, not a solution of problems, but tools of research which any school can use according to the assumptions which it takes as presuppositions for mathematical calculations.

The Twentieth Century blossoms with a third stage of capitalism which we name Banker Capitalism. We have noted above the clash between Proudhon and Marx—Proudhon speaking for the small proprietor, the master workman and the peasant farmer, against the great merchant capitalists and bankers who controlled access to credit and markets; Marx speaking for the wage-earners in the factories of the employer-capitalists. Marx dealt with the technological stage of capitalism, where the employer becomes the capitalist, with mass production suited to the enlarged markets previously developed by transportation and controlled by the merchant.

We can even set an approximate date, by consulting the records of patents granted, for the shift in the United States from merchant capitalism to employer capitalism. It is the two decades from 1850 to 1870. During these twenty years the number of patents leaped from less than 1,000 per year to more than 12,000 per year. This is the period when the railways created a national market and the patent office a factory system.

The third stage, Banker Capitalism, had its forerunner in the commercial banking of the decades of merchant capitalism with their short-time credits needed for the marketing of commodities. But the banking syndicates, or the investment bankers, of the Twentieth Century, affiliated with commercial banks, rise to a dominant position in the consolidation of industries, the sale of securities, and control of boards of directors whose corporate securities they have sold and for which they have become supposedly responsible. They saved defaulting establishments in times of depressions, by taking them over and then financing them on the upturn of prosperity. Millions of scattered investors now automatically enroll themselves under the lead of trusted bankers to whom they have transferred the management of their savings. One company has nearly 600,000 stockholders. Industry is largely owned by an invisible army of investors who are controlled by an invisible syndicate of bankers. Through international affiliations the syndicates are world bankers. Each nation erects a Central bank, the latest American approach to which is the Federal Reserve System. Nations, localities, industries, laborers, become subject to this official and semi-official control; the Twentieth Century economics becomes the Institutional Economics of collective action by bankers in a world-wide control over merchants, employers, employees, and even nations.

Thus the post-war science of Political Economy is an inheritance from seven centuries of economic conflict and a dozen resulting schools of economic thought. It returns somewhat to the Reasonable Value of Thomas Aquinas, yet it is a subject as complicated as all the conflicting interests throughout the world that have come to the front out of the World War and the history that preceded the war. A former world war, the twenty-five years which followed the French Revolution of 1789, started the Nineteenth Century schools of economic thinking. Then, the long depression preceding the Revolutions of 1848 brought in the heterodox economists of anarchism, communism, socialism, and optimism. Now the new World War with its Russian Revolution, Italian Fascism, German Nazism, and Banker Capitalism, has started thousands of economists, the world over, on another revision of the foundations of economic science.

We may, therefore, re-classify the foregoing schools of economists with reference to the way in which they fit a classification of present-day opinions of the millions of people who are in the midst of the fluctuations of prosperity and depression and the inequalities of wealth and poverty. There are the Let-Alone opinions: We can do nothing about it; it is inevitable. There are next the Exploitation opinions: Everything goes by sharp practice and taking it out of others without giving much in return. There are, finally the Pragmatic opinions: Let us investigate and come to an understanding as to what should and can be done, and then act together, if possible, to establish a régime of reasonable practices and reasonable values.

Or, again, these schools of economists may be classified from the standpoint of the ultimate unit of investigation from which they start their theories—as, the Commodity theorists, the Psychological theorists, the Transactional theorists. But the psychological theorists were also commodity theorists, and we name them also the orthodox economists, because their idea of a commodity was the idea of material things equivalent to the contradictory idea of the ownership of the things. Neglecting the ownership side, a commodity (such as a loaf of bread) may be looked upon from two standpoints, the objective and the subjective. *Objectively* it is the product of *labor* which has added useful qualities to the otherwise uncontrolled forces of nature. To these qualities we give the name employed by Ricardo and Karl Marx, Use-Value, the proper meaning of *Wealth*. But, *subjectively,* the same commodity is the means of satisfying the *wants* of a particular individual at a particular time and place. This individual wants not too much nor too little, but just enough. To this individualistic relation between supply and demand we give the name Scarcity-Value, or *Assets,* because it turns on the scarcity or abundance of the commodity and is equivalent to property rights.

But, for the transactional theorists, the ultimate unit is an economic activity, in the disposition of ownership of future material things and the creation of debt. This we name a transaction, and we distinguish transactions as managerial, bargaining, and rationing transactions. These three types of transactions are our ultimate units of activity into which all economic relations can be resolved.

Our classification thus differentiates two types of economists, according to the ultimate unit of investigation which they employ:

The *commodity* economists, of the objective and subjective schools, the former making the usefulness of the commodity (use-value, objective), the latter making the feelings dependent upon the commodity (diminishing-utility, subjective) their ultimate unit of investigation; and the *transactional* economists who make the various kinds of transactions their units of investigation.

But the transaction is a proprietary relation—a relation between Man and Man—whereas the commodity, where ownership is omitted from its definition, is a relation between Man and Nature—either the physical relation of production of wealth, or the psychological relation of satisfaction of wants. Hence the transaction, as a proprietary or institutional unit of investigation, contains within itself all of the issues on which economists have divided. These issues we have named Conflict, Dependence, and Order.

In every economic transaction there is a Conflict of Interests because each participant is trying to get as much and give as little as possible. Yet nobody can live or prosper except by Dependence on what others do in managerial, bargaining, and rationing transactions. Hence, they must come to a working agreement, and, since such agreements are not always possible voluntarily, there always has been some form of collective compulsion to decide disputes. If these decisions are accepted as precedents and are conformed to as a matter of course in succeeding transactions, then the deciding authority need not intervene and does not usually intervene unless the conflict again reaches the crisis of a dispute between plaintiff and defendant. This process we name the Common-Law Method of Making Law by Deciding Disputes. To the entire process we give the name, Working Rules of Going Concerns, the purpose of which is to bring Order out of Conflict.

Still a third cross-classification of the Schools may be made according to the kind of transaction which they make the ultimate unit on which the social philosophy of each is builded. This classification differentiates the Bargaining school, the Managerial school, and the Collective school of economists. The first makes the bargaining transaction its unit; the extreme of the school being Anarchism, which totally rejects managing and rationing. The second makes the managerial and rationing transactions its ultimate units; the extreme case being the philosophy of Communism. The third school combines rationing, managing, and bargaining in a hierarchy of collective action; the modern outcomes of which are the various kinds of socialisms (distinguished from communism) such as guild socialism, state socialism, Fascism, Nazism (National Socialism), as well as syndicalism, pluralism, trade unionism, banker capitalism.

This leads to another cross-classification of economists according to the way in which they look upon society and upon collective action within society, whether as Mechanism, Machinism, Organism, or Going Concern.

If it be a theory of Mechanism, or, using the term of Pareto,[151] a "molecular theory of society," then the theorists follow the analogy of the physical and chemical sciences, wherein society is only a population, rather than a society, and the blind forces of nature act without cause, effect, or purpose, like the waves of the ocean or the stars or planets. These schools tend towards the Let-Alone opinions.

Quite different from the analogy of a Mechanism is the analogy of a Machine. A machine is an *artificial* mechanism devised by man, but a Mechanism is a "natural" movement of atoms, waves, vortexes, or whatever they turn out to be. But the machine is "artificial," and, as an analogy to society, worked out as a philosophy of Machinism, it has come to the front on account of the dominance of the Engineer in the business and politics of a Machine Age. The machine becomes what we name a Going Plant of an entire nation, or even the world, if we take into account the steamship, the wire, and the wireless. It has its power generating prime movers, its batteries of power transmission, its organization of materials, of labor, and of output to fit the "social machine" as a whole. All are governed by the technological ability of the modern scientist and the scientific engineer. This analogy becomes the Managerial School of economists, tending towards different forms of dictatorship, whether communistic, fascistic, or capitalistic; or towards a National Economic Planning Council, or the more recent Technocracy, or, in general, towards what we name Engineering Economics. The analogy tends, by no means, towards let-alone opinions. It tends towards the opposite: Let's do everything by science and scientific management.

Next, somewhat similar, but derived from biology rather than physics, is the analogy of an Organism. Here society is governed by a central power, such as the "social will," or "social value," operating through "social labor power," all of it analogous to the human will. Its valuations and activities, as well as all individuals, disappear into specialized hands, ears, eyes, stomach, obeying the commands of a single will. These schools tend towards the older theories of Thomas Filmer, or the various kinds of dictatorial socialism (such as Fascism or Nazism), or even towards the supremacy of banker capitalism.

[151] Below, p. 677, From Individuals to Institutions.

But these are analogies drawn from other sciences. We name them Dramatic or Poetic Analogies, contrasted with the Scientific Analogies which every investigator constructs within the confines of his own particular science. That which appears in "society" as similar to Mechanism or Machinism in physical science, or Organism in biological science, becomes that which, taken over directly from the language and customs of business and the decisions of courts, is known in England and America as a Going Concern. It is these going concerns of collective action with their working rules, in unlimited variety, each looking towards the future, and controlling individual action, which we make, not an analogy derived from other sciences, but the real thing which we are investigating. They were talking poetry, we are talking prose.

Growing out of these notions of mechanism, organism, machine, and going concern, the schools of economic opinion may again be classified according to the ideas of cause, effect, or purpose towards which they look for explanation of what happens, such as the theories of equilibrium, of process, and of institutions. These terms are not to be considered exclusive, for all of them appear in different degrees in all theories.

The "equilibrium" theories, or rather automatic equilibrium or molecular theories of a natural mechanism, by personification, inject a *purpose*, like the waves of the ocean "seeking their level," or the "harmony of the universe" with its "music of the spheres." Their model is Sir Isaac Newton's "laws of motion," in his *Principia* (1687). They tend towards theories of harmony of interests and they look upon law and its conflict of interests as "pathological," not belonging to economics.

The "process" theories direct their attention to the *changes* and the evolution that results from infinitesimal but *unintended or accidental* changes. Their model is the "natural selection" of Charles Darwin, in his *Origin of Species* (1859), where he developed the fivefold process of heredity, over-population, variability, struggle for existence, and survival of the fit, the whole process derived from the Malthusian principle of Scarcity.

The institutional theories, or, as we term them, the going concern theories, are built upon both the equilibrium and the process theories. Their attention, however, is directed towards *intended* or *purposeful* changes, and to a *managed* equilibrium instead of an *automatic* equilibrium. This purposeful control was named by Darwin "artificial selection," by which was meant that the minds of men, by individual or collective action, control evolution itself according to their own ideas of fitness. These theories have arisen out of the new science of sociology, whose American pioneer in stating them is E. A. Ross in his book *Social Control* (1901).

Thus, we have several cross-classifications of the schools of economic thought: first, as to their historical origin out of class conflicts; second, as to their social philosophy of laissez-faire, exploitation or workability; third, as to their ultimate units of investigation, whether commodities, feelings, or transactions; fourth, as to the kind of transactions on which their philosophy is based, as bargaining, managerial, or rationing; fifth, as to their methods and analogies, whether mechanism, machinism, organism, or going concerns, or whether equilibrium, process, or collective action.

In this maze of conflicting schools and opinions which reach different conclusions in the study of economics, we cannot start with assumptions universally accepted and then reason down deductively to their practical application to the problems before us. Rather should we start at the beginning, as did John Locke in the midst of a similar maze of theological and political dogmatisms of the Seventeenth Century which led to confusion, intolerance, and civil war. We should examine our own minds in order to discover how much we can really know and what are the mental tools with which we may investigate and understand. Our subject-matter is the transactions of human beings in producing, acquiring, and rationing wealth by coöperation, conflict, and the rules of the game. These activities come to us first as mere sensations, and, as such, we cannot be sure whether they are caused only by predispositions and social philosophies inside ourselves, or by activities outside ourselves. It is only by carefully examining these predispositions, which we name Habitual Assumptions,[152] that we can prepare ourselves for investigation and understanding. And the way in which we can best do this is to continue, as we began with John Locke, to examine the way in which the various schools of economic thought have or have not injected into their theories their own peculiar social philosophies. We shall continue, not with all economists and philosophers, but with those whom we name Pioneers of New Insight. Each of them has contributed something which, in the wind-up, must be given due weight along with the conflicting or contradictory opinions of all the others. It is this due weight that we name Reasonable Value.

V. Economic Backbone of History

The Collective Action of modern history runs from Feudalism to the Merchant Capitalism of England at the Revolution of 1689,

---

[152] Below, p. 697, Habitual Assumptions.

then towards Employer Capitalism at the middle of the Nineteenth Century, then towards Banker Capitalism of the Twentieth Century. But this institutional development was accompanied by a monetary development, from metallic money to paper money and then to credit money, in terms of which debts, taxes, and prices of anything salable were stated, and, if need be, enforced by law.

Although wholesale price changes are but one of many factors yet they stand out in such a way historically that, by a biological analogy, they may be named the economic backbone of history (Chart I). It matters not whether the theories of price changes

CHART 1
WHOLESALE PRICES IN THE UNITED STATES AND ENGLAND
1790 — 1932

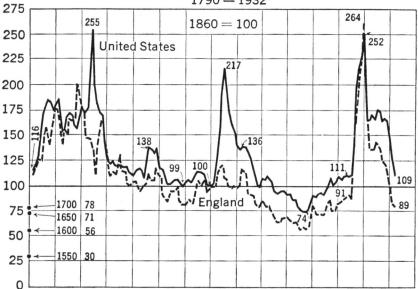

The computations of relative changes from 1500 to 1790 in wholesale prices are indicated by the vertical line of dates at intervals of 50 years. These estimates for preceding centuries are reduced to the base 100 for the year 1860, by checking with the data collected by Abbott Payson Usher, "Prices of Wheat and Commodity Price Indexes for England, 1259–1930" in *Review of Economic Statistics*, XIII (Aug. 1931), 103. The computations for 1792 to 1933 were made, for England, by S. Jevons (1791 to 1860), A. Sauerbeck (1860 to 1920), Board of Trade (1920–1933). The computations for the United States were made by H. V. Roelse (1791 to 1801), *Jour. Amer. Stat. Assn.*, XV (Dec. 1917), 840–846, Alvin H. Hansen (1801 to 1840), *Jour. Amer. Stat. Assn.*, XIV (Dec. 1915), 804–812, R. P. Falkner (1840 to 1891), in Aldrich Report, Vol. 3 of Senate Reports for 52nd Congress, second session and special session, Appendix A; and for the period from 1891 to date by the United States Bureau of Labor Statistics in Bulletin 284 and subsequent bulletins.

are "monetary" or "non-monetary,"[153] nevertheless it is by means of prices that all individuals and classes measure their success or failure in a world of money and credit. Moreover, wholesale prices hold the control position, since they are the prices received by producers, out of which the bulk of wages, interest, profits, and rents are paid. "Society" is bound together or torn apart by this "cash nexus" or cash disruption.

The theories of economists and the conflicts of interest cannot easily be understood without reference to the history of changing price levels. The threefold rise of prices, after the discovery of America and the clipping of currency by monarchs, to the middle of Elizabeth's reign had much to do with the rise of the capitalist farmers, the mercantile and manufacturing classes, by reducing greatly the burden of their rents, debts and taxes. Yet, at the same time the condition of the laboring classes was greatly depressed by the institutional change from serfdom to cash wages.[154]

By the time of John Locke at the end of the Seventeenth Century, with a continuing rise of prices, the capitalistic classes had become wealthy enough to stage a revolution against the decadent feudal classes, though in France this did not occur until one hundred years later. Not until 1732 did David Hume introduce into economics the important distinction between a stationary price level and a rising or falling price level, as an interpretation of the changes that had been going on under Merchant Capitalism. So disturbing was this newly recognized factor of world-wide price changes that the classical and hedonistic economists, beginning with Adam Smith, relegated it from their theories as merely "nominal values," and substituted what seemed to them the more realistic labor-pain, pleasure, and labor-power, as the measure of "real value."

While Locke's theories came towards the end of the Seventeenth Century, when the index of prices had risen over threefold in 200 years, Hume's came in 1732, Quesnay's in 1758, Smith's and Bentham's in 1776. But Malthus' and Ricardo's labor theories came in the decade after 1815, when prices were falling precipitately, and the heterodox theories of Marx, Proudhon, Bastiat, and the American Carey came after the long-continued fall of prices in the 1840's. They also sought something more fundamental than the superficial price changes. The psychological economists, Jevons, Menger, and Walras, also seeking something more fundamental

[153] Below, p. 590, World Pay Community.
[154] Jacob, William, *An Historical Inquiry into the Production and Consumption of the Precious Metals* (1832), 261 ff. The institutional historians, as far as I can find, did not give much weight to Jacob's monetary reasons for the rise of the capitalist class.

than prices, came in the decade of the 1870's, when falling prices were again a disturbing factor. But the statistical and institutional economists, concerned with the price changes themselves, did not begin to have influence until the Twentieth Century, especially after the fall of prices following 1920.

Thus throughout the Eighteenth and Nineteenth Centuries the various schools of economists were unable to incorporate in their more fundamental theories of nature and man these superficial and nominal changes in the general movement of prices. The theories of money, credit, and general price changes came in from a different direction, namely, statistics and mathematics, which have nothing to do with labor, pain, or pleasure. And not until the Twentieth Century, especially after the World War, did statistics acquire a theoretical foundation and terminology of its own which, if the science is perfected, may make it possible to measure, correlate, and forecast the process of such vital social changes as prices, prosperity and depression, employment and unemployment, going concerns and bankruptcy, optimism and pessimism, changes in the distribution of wealth, and even the great institutional changes from Feudalism to the successive stages of Capitalism. Instead of mere "nominal" values these wide-spread general price changes, whether of wholesale or other prices, become the very real values of Institutional Economics.

CHAPTER III

QUESNAY

I. THE NATURAL ORDER

François Quesnay, founder of the Physiocratic school known to France and to Adam Smith as "The Oeconomists," was—even more than John Locke—an originator of physical analogies guided by reason. Locke had based his economics on Labor, the bounty of Nature, and the Accumulation of Metallic Money. Quesnay omitted Labor and based his economics on the bounty of Nature and the Flow of Money. Smith afterwards based his economics on the Division of Labor. Modern Economics comes back to money, not as a physical commodity, nor as a flow, but as a repetition of transactions.[1] A favorable balance of trade obtained by depressing the prices of one class of people in order to enable another class to get rich and to undersell foreigners abroad, thus bringing a continually accumulating fund of metallic money into the country, was the monetary fallacy of Mercantilism. David Hume had exposed it in 1752 and Quesnay followed in 1758 by reducing money to a circulation instead of an accumulation.

While Locke, in 1692, started with the Individual, Quesnay, in 1758, started with the Commodity. The individual now became a kind of steering wheel for the Commodity, guiding it along the same beneficent highway of God, Nature, Reason, and Abundance. But Quesnay found something different from Locke's findings of what interfered with this preordained Happiness. He condemned, not Locke's absolute monarch, but Locke's Mercantilism. Sovereigns should be absolute—that was as natural and divine for Quesnay as for Filmer. But they should guide themselves by the natural order implanted by God in Man's Reason; not by tariffs, bounties, corporations, and other privileges for the gain of merchants and manufacturers at the expense of agriculture.

The astonishing effect which Quesnay's *Tableau économique* had upon the intellectual life of France for twenty years after 1758 can be likened only to the effect of Darwin's *Origin of Species* on the

[1] Below, p. 510, Transactional Theory of Money and Value.

scientific world after 1859. The elder Mirabeau exalted Quesnay's discovery to the level of the other two greatest discoveries of civilization, Writing and Money.[2] Its originality was its introduction of mechanics into economics. Where Darwin afterwards substituted for the will of God a blind mechanism of heredity, variation, struggle, natural selection, and survival, Quesnay subordinated an absolute monarch to a bountiful mechanism of Nature, Reason, and God. Where Mercantilism sought to control prices arbitrarily in order to accumulate metallic money, Quesnay substituted a natural flow of money in one direction and a flow of commodities in the opposite direction, leaving prices to be adjusted by "nature."

Quesnay was a landlord and a physician at the court of Louis XV. He believed in absolute monarchy and his theories were lessons on management addressed to an incompetent dictatorship which was failing to observe the "laws of nature."[3]   The only science which Quesnay had to work with was a physiological science which Harvey had created in 1628 when he demonstrated the circulation of the blood. It was this circulation of the blood which would now explain, as a branch of physics, the production and circulation of wealth. For wealth is to the social organism what blood is to the animal organism. The social organism—that is, an agricultural kingdom— like the animal organism, takes up food, textiles, timber, minerals from the soil, from the air, from the sunshine and rain; manipulates and digests them, then circulates them to all parts of the social body. Each part of the body takes out what it needs for sustenance, and the whole is continually renewed from the earth. Quesnay's theory is aptly named by Böhm-Bawerk a Fructification theory.[4] It was a theory of the Life Forces in which production of wealth is the augmentation of the *volume* of vital force, and in which "circulation" is not productive, since it merely carries that volume of energy to different members of the system, consuming much of

[2] Smith, Adam, *Wealth of Nations*, Cannan ed. (1904), II, 177.

[3] Quesnay, François, *Tableau économique* (1758), *Maximes générales du government économiques d'un royaume agricole* (1763). References are to edition of Quesnay's writings by August Oncken, *Oeuvres économiques et philosophiques de F. Quesnay* (1888), hereafter cited as "Quesnay." See also Daire, E., *Physiocrates* (1846). N. J. Ware's important article on the Physiocrats, *Amer. Econ. Rev.*, XXI (1931), 607–619, applies mainly to the followers of Quesnay and not to Quesnay himself, the originator. Economists generally take Turgot as representative of the Physiocrats, but his theories were decidedly different at important points. See below, p. 487, Turgot.

[4] Böhm-Bawerk, E., *Capital and Interest* (tr. 1891), 63 (discussion of Turgot's use of Quesnay's theory). Turgot accounted for the productivity of mines by a geological process. "The land produces fruit annually but a mine produces no fruit. The mine itself is a garnered fruit." Cited by Gide and Rist, *History of Economic Doctrines* (tr. of 2d, 1913), 14. Quesnay held that, not the agriculturists, but the *subsistence* of the agriculturists, looked upon as circulating capital, was productive.

it on the way. Neither are merchants and manufacturers productive since they either consume the commodities outright and send none of them back into circulation, or they send back only the equivalent, in the form of manufactures, of what they consume. They cannot send more and hence cannot produce a surplus.

Quesnay argues that it is only Life Force that is productive, since by its energy not only is something *reproduced* in the same volume as the original but the volume is *augmented*. This augmentation is a surplus, *un produit net;* and it is this augmentation that is productive, while the *reproduction* of the same volume is unproductive. Other forces, including the labor of man, only reproduce, in a different form, the equivalent of what they consume. Vital force does that, but it also produces a surplus of its own kind of energy. Other forces are reproductive. Vital force is productive. Thus reproduction is sterility, production is vitality. Hence only the cultivators of the soil are productive; all merchants, artisans, manufacturers, and intellectuals are sterile; not because the cultivators alone produce *use-values*—Quesnay conceded that others did that—but these use-values were only changes in the *form* of things, not enlargement of their bulk. And the enlargement of bulk was the enlargement of exchange-values.

But it turns out that the cultivators of the soil themselves are productive only by courtesy. They only assist the really productive vital forces of nature which alone have power to enlarge the volume of things. Cultivators, in reality, are sterile, because they do not add to the volume of things. They simply put the seed in the ground and breed the animals, and carry the feed to the livestock. Nature does the rest. Their own food and sustenance is productive, but their *labor* is not productive. Only that force which we call Life, whether in man or nature, is productive, because it alone can enlarge a seed of wheat to 50 seeds, a calf into a cow, a baby into a farm hand. It is this enlargement of bulk that constitutes Quesnay's famous "net product" of agriculture.

But this net product of Quesnay's, strangely enough, is not a product of use-value; it is a product of exchange-value.

Here occurs the confusion of Wealth with Assets, of materials with their ownership, which runs through much of economic theory for two centuries. It might almost be said that, had Quesnay and the early economists known the institutional science of corporation finance—with its equivalence of assets and liabilities, its net worth of assets over liabilities—much of the confusion and conflicts of opinion would have been avoided. To us wealth is use-values which *increase* with abundance. Assets are the ownership of scarcity-values which *decrease* with abundance. We shall find this confusion through a hundred and fifty years of theorizing; Quesnay affords us the first opportunity to discover how it came about, and to observe some of the devices by which the two diametrically opposite concepts of wealth and ownership of wealth have been fused into one.

It must be noted, in extenuation, that, not only at the time of Quesnay, but even from primitive times to the present, the prevailing concept of Value has been that of Power, Strength, Valor, Vigor, Weight, Influence, Force, Validity. The term, Exchange-Value, is therefore the extension of this meaning to commerce. Exchange-Value is Power-in-Exchange, Purchasing Power, Power to Command the commodities and services of others. When the business man or common man says, "What is my automobile worth? What is its real value?" he thinks of its power to command, especially money, in exchange. All men in commercialized nations are intuitive mercantilists. It was, indeed, a great service of Quesnay and his followers, the Physiocratic Economists—indeed, the most difficult and never-ending service of economic theory—to get behind this common sense, empirical, intuitive thinking, and to show that the substance of Real Value in Exchange is not Power to Command Money, but Power to Command Commodities and Services in Exchange for one's own commodities and services. Prior to Quesnay, nobody had ever been able to offer a *physical* explanation of exchange-value. The church and moralists declaimed against Money; there was a prejudice against money-dealers and money-makers; and the concepts of usefulness, use-value, welfare, or service were set up as ethical contrasts to money. But nobody had been able to show, in physical quantitative terms, the mechanism needed for reasoning out the hidden nature of exchange-value. Hence the enthusiasm over Quesnay's *Tableau économique*.

Quesnay eliminated use-values, as being merely the personal uses which individuals might make of the physical things which they took out of circulation. He focussed attention on exchange-value as power to command, not money, but commodities, in exchange: A nation's "wealth" is augmented by increasing the quantity of physical things having this power-in-exchange.

Whence comes this augmentation of Power? It comes, says Quesnay, from a bountiful force of nature which augments the quantities of materials out of which food, clothing, shelter are afterwards manufactured. It is this augmentation of materials by the forces of nature that augments the volume of exchange-values, thus augmenting the power of the nation. Value is identical with exchange-value, which is power-in-exchange, as the common sense of everybody agreed. But the source of this power was agriculture, not manufactures or merchandising.

Why was it, then, that the agriculture of France was so depressed when it was only through agriculture that this bountiful energy could produce abundance of material, food, clothing, and shelter for mankind? Quesnay's answer was: the artificial scarcities imposed by the policy of Mercantilism which did not permit exchange-value to conform to the benevolent enlargement of value. Agriculture was being depressed by the mercantilist policy of France. Special privileges of marketing were being given by the government to the monopolies and guilds of merchants and manufacturers, under the mistaken notion that agricultural products should be furnished cheaply to them in order that they might sell manufactured products abroad and bring home silver in exchange. Nature is the beneficent force which enlarges the life of the Nation. She multiplies her products, and what the cultivator does is only to unite his life with hers and restore what he has taken from her. Therefore, everything taken from the cultivators and consumed by merchants and manufacturers who merely transport and manipulate the material but do not enlarge its bulk, is so much sheer loss; even though, in doing so, they add to the uses of the material by changing its kind, form, and place. The merchants and manufacturers, indeed, are also productive in so far as they send back implements, fertilizers, and food to help out the cultivators; but they are "sterile" to the extent of what they consume or what they send on to others, equally sterile, to consume.

Cultivators, merchants, and manufacturers must all have a minimum of subsistence. This was, indeed, all that the cultivators (peasants) were getting in Quesnay's time; but, while the subsistence of the sterile classes contributes nothing to restore the soil, the subsistence of the cultivators does contribute, and is therefore productive. Thus, that which is productive is that which goes back to agriculture in the form of circulating wealth and fixed wealth. Circulating wealth (*avances annuelles*) was seed, manure, the restoration of wear and tear of machinery, and the subsistence of the peasants. Fixed wealth were of two kinds, *avances primitives* of the peasant cultivators, such as machinery and improvements, and *avances foncières*, or fixed improvements of the landlord, such as fences, drains, buildings, and improved fertility.

The owners of these fixed products were, indeed, entitled to interest, but not because their fixed improvements, as a whole, were productive. The only part of fixed improvements which created a net product was that part distinguished as wear and tear, depreciation or depletion, and which, therefore by definition, was to be classed along with seeds, fertilizers, and sustenance of cultivators, as circulating wealth. These circulating objects alone produced a net product over and above their own quantity, by virtue of going in to the cultivation of the soil, and it was out of this net product that the proprietors and the monarch obtained their revenues. An increase in the number of the sterile classes reduces by just that much the net product for the succeeding years, because it takes out of the circulation that which might have gone back to the soil as circulating products.[5] In short, Quesnay's *Tableau économique* is the point of view of American farmers who complain that the middlemen, manufacturers, and urban residents take so much from their product that they cannot keep up the improvements and fertility of the soil and must eventually abandon their farms and move to the cities. Quesnay was the original agricultural economist.

Quesnay's difficulty was in his use of these physical concepts, pertaining to conservation of natural resources, as identical with scarcity concepts pertaining to the exchange-value of commodities. He made "wealth" the exchange-value of wealth, or power to command commodities in exchange, that is, assets instead of wealth. He thereby excluded the idea of relative scarcities, and thus confirmed economic theory in the idea of eliminating money, the instrument for measuring scarcity. He got back to a physical barter economy where, according to him, the wealth of nations is abundance of goods with high exchange-values in terms of other goods, rather than a mercantilists' high scarcity-value of money and low scarcity-value of commodities. The Physiocrats wanted commodities, and these commodities are to be obtained in large quantities only when one's own commodities are both abundant and have high exchange-value. Money is merely nominal value—it is an instrument of exchange and measurement by which we can tell whether our own commodities have high exchange-values or not. It must be noted that when Quesnay speaks of "prices" he means exchange-values in terms, not of money, but of other commodities.

Money, then, is a measure of the exchange-values of commodities. But for Quesnay measurement and circulation do not produce wealth—they merely accommodate the back flow of commodities at their previously determined exchange-values, in terms of commodities. Thus wealth (*richesses*) he contended, was not abundance of goods, but abundance of goods at good prices (*bon prix*)— that is, not abundance of use-values, but abundance of exchange-

[5] Haney, L. H., *History of Economic Thought* (1911), 175, 176.

values. The savages of Louisiana had abundance of goods (*biens*) such as water, wood, game, fruits of the earth, etc., but these did not become wealth (*richesses*) until they acquired exchange-value with France, England, Spain, etc., that is, not until they circulated and brought back other commodities.[6]

What the state needs is large quantities of commodities at high exchange-values per unit in command of other commodities from other nations. The nation's net product is not the use-values of commodities—it is the abundance of exchange-values of commodities. The mercantilists believed the power of the state to reside in large quantities of ready money, which required low exchange-values of raw material, in order to encourage exports of manufactures and bring in the money through foreign trade. That meant high exchange-value of money and low exchange-values for agriculture. But Quesnay saw the power of the state residing in large quantities of raw material at high exchange-values in domestic and foreign trade, whereby the net product would be increased, for it was out of this that taxes could be paid.

The more these exchange-values follow the "natural order" (which is the bountiful order) while in the process of circulation, that is, without interference by arbitrary restraints and privileges granted by government which depress farm prices for the sake of manufacturers and merchants; then the more profitable are the nation's agricultural products in both foreign and domestic trade, and the more do they enable the farmer to restore the fertility of the soil and make successful the agriculture on which population, as well as wages, of all classes depend.

But the policy of France was the reverse. The merchants and manufacturers increased their power by purchasing farm products at low prices, in order, by the resulting low prices of exports, to bring in gold and silver. Quesnay would increase the state's power by selling farm products at high prices. The commercial classes buy of the farmers at low prices and sell at high prices—their interests are opposed to those of an agricultural nation whose proprietors should sell at high prices in order to enlarge agriculture and thereby enlarge the very flow of products on which the permanent gains of commerce itself depend.[7] One should not depress the exchange-value of provisions within the kingdom, in order to furnish cheap raw materials for export, for that is ultimately disadvantageous in trading with foreigners. If exchange-values are high, so is revenue. And this leads to Quesnay's paradox: "Abun-

---

[6] Quesnay, 353.
[7] *Ibid.*, 322–324, 344.

dance without exchange-value is not wealth. Scarcity with high prices is poverty. Abundance with high prices is opulence." [8] This is not a paradox if nature is bountiful and if scarcity is the artificial scarcity imposed by government.

Nature, or rather "the natural order," which is the bountiful order of benevolence, if left to itself will produce high exchange-values (*bon prix*) since the "natural order" implies the self-interest of each person guided by the same benevolent order that guides agriculture, and this means that each person chooses those lines of action wherein Nature has previously provided high exchange-values and abundance.

Eventually Quesnay saw the predicament. He had eliminated the mercantilist fallacy of a foreign balance of trade designed to increase the nation's import of precious metals, but had fallen into the fallacy of increasing the supply of agricultural commodities without reducing their exchange-value. This predicament led him, in 1765, seven years after his *Tableau économique,* to a practical abandonment of his earlier distinction between productive and sterile classes. [9]

For, evidently, from the standpoint of conservation of resources, the greater the *absolute* abundance of agricultural products the greater is the wealth of the nation; but, from the standpoint of business and marketing, the greater the *relative* abundance of agricultural products the less is their exchange-value, and therefore the less is the wealth of the nation. So when, in 1765, Quesnay faced this predicament, he modified his distinction between the sterile and productive classes. The "sterile" classes, he now said, are not sterile unless they produce *more* products than the agriculturists will take at a favorable price (*bon prix*). But they are sterile in so far as they produce *more* than the farmers will take in exchange. In that case the excess product is "illusory wealth" (*une augmentation illusoire des richesses*). In other words, defining wealth, not as use-value of commodities, but as their exchange-value, it follows that the sterile classes do produce wealth if they do not produce too much of it. His *"illusory wealth"* was assets, not wealth.

The same is true of the farmers, Quesnay continued in his new analysis. If they produce too much raw materials for the rest of the nation to buy at favorable exchange-values to themselves, they too, are producing, not wealth, but "illusory wealth." Hence, as Quesnay now said, in 1765, the sterile classes are only *relatively* sterile and not absolutely so, and the productive classes are only

---

[8] *Ibid.,* 335; Gide and Rist, *op. cit.,* 14 ff.
[9] In his *Le droit naturel,* Quesnay, *op. cit.,* 359 ff.

relatively productive, depending upon the relative quantities which each produces for exchange with others. Each class is productive if it does not produce more than its proper proportion of the total. He emphasizes this: *"Je dis à proportion des richesses du pays."* [10]

Hence, having at first defined productive classes as those who, through the bounty of nature, add a net surplus of physical quantities to the total circulation of commodities, and sterile classes as those who do not add materials; Quesnay finds, when he squarely faces the difference between material things, which we name "use-values" or wealth, and the "scarcity-values" of private ownership, which we name assets, that what he really meant was that all classes are productive to the extent that the quantities of their use-values are proportioned properly to each other, according to their relative scarcities. If properly proportioned then their products of use-value are real wealth, because they have favorable exchange-values; but if one commodity is over-supplied it becomes "illusory wealth" because it has little or no exchange-value. He shifts from the physical concept of augmenting the flow of physical goods or wealth, by augmenting their use-values, to the scarcity concept of the best proportioning of the various quantities of use-values in order, by preventing the abundance of some products from reducing their prices and the scarcity of others from raising their prices, to stabilize the scarcity-values. His "illusory wealth" is assets.

Quesnay, however, insisted on his original definition of sterile classes, and his followers adhered to it, so that his modification in 1765 has escaped, apparently, the notice of his later critics. His attempted reconciliation of the physical concept of agricultural abundance with that of high exchange-values of agricultural products was made by asserting that the "natural" part played by the sterile classes was so small anyhow, that, in a natural, bountiful order of the universe, where government did not favor the sterile classes, the latter classes would have but little effect on exchange-value and might be disregarded. As though a vice is not a vice if it is a little one!

The natural scarcity of nature's fertility, according to Quesnay, may be taken for granted and disregarded as not having any functional importance in determining other values, provided the artificial or collective scarcity of Mercantilism is eliminated. And this follows from the fact that, according to the "natural order," people who have liberty in the acquisition of property prefer to go into manufactures rather than agriculture anyhow, since its hardships are

---

[10] *Ibid.*, 391.

less and life in towns is preferable to life in the country. Consequently individuals would distribute themselves "naturally" in such proper proportions that exchange-values of agricultural products would be high, notwithstanding their abundance, were it not for governmental obstructions and privileges at the expense of agriculture.[11] Also, his reconciliation was effected by saying, in 1765, that what he meant by sterile classes was only that part of such classes as was occupied with luxuries.

Yet, the physical and scarcity concepts are contradictory. One is wealth, the other is assets. The physical concept of use-value implies that the quantity of valuable energy embodied in each unit of a commodity does not diminish with an increase in supply. Water quenches thirst, and a thousand gallons of water will quench a thousand times as much thirst as one gallon. This is use-value which does not diminish per unit, with an increase in quantity. Likewise with Quesnay's exchange-value. Exchange-value, with him, unless interfered with by artificial or governmental scarcity, was a physical circulation of a predetermined physical force of nature embodied in commodities, but having power to command other commodities; it would follow that a million bushels of wheat should have a million times as much exchange-value as one bushel. This extreme case makes the argument absurd, but Quesnay's "natural order" did not permit absurdities.

Quesnay's philosophy was discredited by his term "sterile classes," which was corrected somewhat by Adam Smith, who partly substituted Labor for Nature. Yet his physical concepts of "circulation" and exchange-value were afterwards taken over by Karl Marx, instead of Smith's division of labor. There were two systems of circulation, the circulation of money and the circulation of commodities. The latter takes commodities, which come from nature, to all parts of the body. The former takes back to each person the exchange-value of what he has passed on to others. Circulation does not add anything, it merely transfers to others what has previously been created by nature. That previous creation was value in the sense of power, the bountiful but hidden force of nature. Circulation, if left to its natural course, merely revealed as exchange-value that which had previously been embodied as the bounty of Nature.

Turgot, Adam Smith, Ricardo, and Marx gave to Quesnay's *avances annuelles* and *avances foncières* the name of "capital": Capital was *saving* in the form of both circulating and fixed goods, that is, salable commodities; while the circulation and vendibility

[11] *Ibid.*, 391, 392.

of those commodities yielded again, in the theory of Ricardo and Marx, a physical concept, exchange-value, but equal to a different embodied energy, the power of labor, instead of Quesnay's power of nature.

II. THE MORAL ORDER

Quesnay, having acknowledged the discrepancy between physical concepts and scarcity concepts, bridged it, as we have seen, by means of his notion of the "natural order" which would not permit the discrepancy to happen. It was another branch of this Natural Order that justified, for Quesnay, the income of the landlords and the monarch. Adam Smith took over bodily this branch of Quesnay's Natural Order, but used it to justify the capitalists instead of the landlords or monarch. For, argued Quesnay, how were the landlords and monarch to be justified in taking interest on their fixed capital (*avances foncières*) and, indeed, in taking the whole of the net product, when it was not their fixed capital, as a whole, that produced a surplus, but only that part of it which "circulated," namely, the equivalent of the wear and tear, or depreciation, or depletion, of fixed capital,[12] including the subsistence of cultivators? They were entitled to take out exactly what they put in, namely, the equivalent of their circulating commodities as above defined, just as the present cultivators and the sterile classes did. But why should they take interest and the net product also, on account of that part of fixed capital which still remained in their hands unused and not passed on either to nature for augmentation, nor into circulation for reproduction? Why should not the cultivators take the whole of the net product and eliminate the landlords—as they actually did in the French Revolution when the peasants took over the estates—since it was their subsistence and not the landlord's ownership that produced it?

Quesnay justified the cultivators and sterile classes by "the natural order" and the "natural right." The cultivators and the sterile classes got the subsistence necessary for their existence from the landlords and monarch. They got the equivalent of what they put in—that was as natural as any law of physics.[13]

But there was another branch of the natural order, the "moral order," which was just as binding on mankind by nature as the physical order. It was this that justified the landlords and monarch in taking the net product of rents, interest, and taxes.

[12] Below, p. 267, Averages.
[13] See his justification of the income of the sterile classes as distinguished from the luxurious classes. Quesnay, *op. cit.*, 390–391.

Yet this moral order was nothing else than the prevailing custom of the landlords and monarchs of France in 1758. The Physiocratic view of a nation was that of great landed proprietors enjoying their privileges from a monarch, who, like their monarch, had their manor courts which made them sovereigns over their subjects. Quesnay did not distinguish sovereignty from private property. He had in mind the France and Germany of 1758, with their feudal estates which were also sovereignties, with their manorial courts and armed officials. The proprietor was sovereign, acting through officials who executed his power.[14] Nine-tenths of his subjects were agricultural laborers and peasants; others were hand-workers in their little shops, manipulating the wool, leather, pork, which the agricultural laborers turned over to them; or they were domestic servants and literally *manu*-facturers, manipulating the products furnished them by the landlords. They were not citizens of a commonwealth. The sovereign proprietors did not get a share because they produced it, but because of their position in the moral order with which Quesnay was familiar. They were the nobility, who, simply because they were noble, were supreme by moral right. Without them nothing could be done, for their ancestors had provided the soil originally, and they themselves furnished security and subsistence to the cultivators as well as to the sterile classes.

What Quesnay wished was, not that the landlords and monarch should be ousted or restrained by constitutional or proprietary limitations. He wished only that the landlords and monarch, in the disposition of their sovereignty, should follow the "natural order" rather than try to impose their ignorant commands upon the production and circulation of wealth. They held their positions by the moral order but were not obeying the natural order.

For nature was intelligent, benevolent, and bountiful, like John Locke's Nature. Therefore physical law, according to Quesnay, was "the regulated course of all physical events, in the natural order evidently the *most advantageous for the human race.*" And moral law, having the same benevolent origin, was "the rule of all human actions in the moral order conforming to the physical order evidently the *most advantageous for the human race.*" Out of these natural laws proceed natural rights. Natural right, said Quesnay, is "the right which a man has to things fit for his happiness"; and justice—the rule of natural law which determines natural rights—was "a natural and sovereign rule, recognized by the light of reason, which determines *obviously* what belongs to self or to another." [15]

[14] Gide and Rist, *op. cit.*, 19.
[15] In *Le droit naturel*, Quesnay, 359, 365. Italics mine.

These definitions of the Natural Order, including the Moral Order, enabled Quesnay to reconcile all the contradictory notions of philosophers regarding natural law, natural rights, and natural justice; for his was a flexible notion of natural rights such as would fit the circumstances of any time and place, but which thereby reduced "natural rights" to their natural absurdity. Thus the apparently contradictory natural rights of all philosophers were all true, *relative* to the time and circumstances in which they were *obviously* true. Justinian was correct in holding that natural right is that which nature reveals to animals, *provided* they are animals. So, in a state of isolation, the individual's natural right is whatever he obtains by his own force and intelligence, *provided* he is isolated. Even Hobbes' unlimited right of "all against all" is right, *provided* it is a state of anarchy. Likewise those are correct who say that natural right is that which is general and sovereign, *provided* we are talking about a nation which has a sovereign authority in control of all persons. Likewise those are also correct who hold that natural right is not absolute but is limited by tacit and explicit agreements, *provided* such agreements are customary. Even those were correct who denied natural rights *in toto*, *provided* they were talking about persons who had no knowledge of natural right. Knowledge is the "light" without which reason cannot see, and the natural order exists, in a state like France, only for those who have both reason and knowledge.

Hence, to Quesnay and the Physiocrats, the fundamental positive law to be enacted by a monarch was that of public and private instruction in the laws of that natural order which is the "light to reason." The greatest crime is that of keeping people in ignorance, for it is knowledge of natural law that guides reason to the maintenance of authority, property, abundance, and the security of landlords and the Bourbon dynasty.

In short, Quesnay's idea of natural law, natural right, and natural order was merely the Custom of the time and place, distinguished from the edicts of sovereignty. Custom was nature; sovereignty was mercantilism. But custom, for Quesnay, became an enlightened sense of fitness, an educated common sense, an obvious intuition, which makes things look natural if they are customary, and unnatural if the state intervenes. Custom is harmony of interests and harmonious proportioning of labor and resources. This harmonious proportioning would follow from the fact of nature's bounty, which, if not interfered with by sovereignty, would cause individuals to flow into the channels where nature was most bountiful, and not to flow into other channels where they extracted from circulation more than nature's own proportioning of her bounty. If they followed this natural order, then not too much of any product would be encouraged by government where nature was niggardly, at the expense of too little of other products where nature was bountiful. In short, the natural order was a good economy, as seen by Quesnay, and the artificial order was the bad economy supported by the Mercantilists and Louis XV.

These natural laws, thus perceived by the light of Reason, had, according to Quesnay, the two qualities of intelligence and benevolence needed to create abundance, since they were laid down by an Intelligent Being for the happiness of man. Hence, they were "immutable, unbreakable, and the best laws possible." [16] Quesnay had in mind, by way of contrast, the positive and therefore artificial laws of the then arbitrary rulers of Europe. These positive laws differed from the natural laws in that they created scarcity whereas nature produced abundance. This difference arose from the circumstance that the positive laws might be mistaken, corrupt, coercive, capricious, and therefore violations of natural law, which, on the other hand, was immutable, intelligent, benevolent, and bountiful. Consequently these natural laws of the natural and moral order, as understood by an intelligent and benevolent landlord like Quesnay at the Court of Louis in the year of 1758, should be made the magic formula for positive laws.

Thus where Locke had looked on natural law as justifying manufacturers and merchants against kings and landlords, Quesnay saw it justifying kings and landlords against merchants and manufacturers. Each identified God, Nature, Reason, and Abundance. They differed respecting the beneficiaries.

It seems almost a paradox that Quesnay, while justifying the rent of landlords by the natural order and moral order, should have reached the practical conclusion that all taxes should be levied on the landlords' rents, and all other taxes eliminated. The explanation is twofold:

His taxable "net product" did not include the landlord's *maintenance* of the fertility, nor the *improvement* of the fertility. These were the landlord's "advances" which must not be taxed if the landlord is expected to restore original fertility. It was only the net product from *original* fertility that should be taxed.[17]

The other explanation is that he had in mind only agricultural rents and mainly such taxes as sales taxes, import taxes, and highway taxes. The taxes of France, at the time, were not only taxes

[16] *Ibid.*, 375.
[17] Below, p. 348, Ricardo; p. 805, The Police Power of Taxation.

on foreign imports but taxes on domestic imports from the farms to the towns (*octrois*), and the compulsory labor on the highways (*corvées*). These taxes interfered with the circulation of goods, and oppressed the peasants. They increased the costs of agricultural production and reduced the net revenues derived from the sale of agricultural products. By eliminating these taxes, agricultural rents would be greatly increased, and these increased rents would be available for increased taxation. Quesnay was proposing, what often happens in fact, that a dominant class, the landlords and guilds of monopolistic manufacturers and merchants, should voluntarily forego their privileges in the expectation that the increased productivity of the nation as a whole would benefit them also. When Turgot afterwards, in one of the provinces, had removed these obstructions to commerce, he demonstrated the validity of Quesnay's theory and brought increased prosperity to the province. But when, on a national scale, Turgot attempted similar reforms, the nobility were able to have him removed from office (1776), because they had their own ideas of the natural order.[18] It has often been said that Turgot's physiocratic reforms might have prevented the French Revolution, but the beneficiaries of things as they are did not see that far. The revolution divided up their estates among the peasants and abolished the guilds of merchants and manufacturers.

Forty years after Quesnay, Malthus substituted nature's scarcity for nature's abundance. Sixty years after Quesnay, Ricardo founded the idea of value on labor's power in overcoming the natural scarcity of nature's resources. Ninety years after Quesnay, Karl Marx took over Quesnay's circulation, Ricardo's labor, nature's scarcity, and eliminated landlords, monarchs, and capitalists. A hundred and twenty years after Quesnay, Henry George took over Quesnay's natural rights, nature's bounty, and Ricardo's rent, to develop his single tax proposal. Meanwhile, eighteen years after Quesnay, Adam Smith rejected, in part, his productivity of nature, and went back to John Locke's theory of labor. But prior to Smith and even to Quesnay, David Hume had, unnoticed by either, substituted scarcity for abundance, as not only the foundation of economics but also as the origin of the rights of property.

[18] Below, p. 487, Turgot.

CHAPTER IV

HUME AND PEIRCE

I. Scarcity

While Locke and Quesnay correlated Law, Economics, and Ethics on the principle of abundance, David Hume correlated them on the principle of Scarcity. Adam Smith speaks of him as "by far the most illustrious philosopher and historian of the present age," yet Smith rejected his foundations and returned to Locke whom Hume had rejected. Said Hume in 1739,

> "Reverse, in any considerable circumstance, the condition of men: Produce extreme abundance or extreme necessity: Implant in the human breast perfect . . . humanity or perfect rapaciousness and malice: By rendering justice totally *useless,* you thereby totally destroy its essence, and suspend its obligation upon mankind. . . . Few enjoyments are given us from the open and liberal hand of nature; but by art, labour, and industry, we can extract them in great abundance. Hence the ideas of property become necessary in all civil society: Hence justice derives its usefulness to the public: And hence alone arises its merit and moral obligation." [1]

By "utility" Hume meant public utility—equivalent to the modern "social utility"—or public welfare, or the good of society. Bentham afterwards meant private utility, or the pleasure and pain of the individual. Hume's public utility influenced individuals by subordinating to it the motive of self-interest. Bentham's private utility was self-interest, made by him identical with public utility. [2]

If public or social utility is, for Hume, the sole origin of justice and the sole foundation of its merit, in what way does it operate on individuals, for whom, according afterwards to Bentham, only their own pleasure and pain are operative? Hume's answer is, the degree of Scarcity and the Character of the People.

---

[1] *The Philosophical Works of David Hume,* 4 vols., ed. by T. H. Green and T. H. Grose (1875, reprint 1898), IV, 183. Citations are to reprint of 1898.
[2] Below, p. 218, Bentham *versus* Blackstone.

"Let us suppose," he said, "that nature has bestowed on the human race such profuse *abundance* of all *external* conveniences, that, without any uncertainty in the event, without any care or industry on our part, every individual finds himself fully provided with whatever his most voracious appetites can want, or luxurious imagination wish or desire. . . . It seems evident, that, in such a happy state, every other social virtue would flourish, and receive tenfold encrease; but the cautious, jealous virtue of justice would never once have been dreamed of. For what purpose make a partition of goods, where everyone has already more than enough? Why give rise to property, where there cannot possibly be any injury? Why call this object *mine*, when, upon the seizing of it by another, I need but stretch out my hand to possess myself of what is equally valuable? Justice, in that case, being totally USELESS, would be an idle ceremonial, and could never possibly have place in the catalogue of virtues." This state of abundance was "the *poetical* fiction of a *golden age*" and "the *philosophical* fiction of a *state of nature.*"[3]

Thus Justice and Private Property arise from *relative scarcity*. But communism, he goes on, arises from *total scarcity*.

"Suppose a society to fall into such want of all common necessaries, that the utmost frugality and industry cannot preserve the greater number from perishing, and the whole from extreme misery: It will readily, I believe, be admitted, that the strict laws of justice are suspended, in such a pressing emergence, and give place to the stronger motives of necessity and self-preservation. Is it any crime, after a shipwreck, to seize whatever means or instrument of safety one can lay hold of, without regard to former limitations of property? . . . The Use and Tendency of that virtue [justice] is to procure happiness and security, by preserving order in society: but where the society is ready to perish from extreme necessity, no greater evil can be dreaded from violence and injustice. . . . The public, even in less urgent necessities, opens granaries, without the consent of proprietors. . . . Would an equal partition of bread in a famine, though effected by power and even violence, be regarded as criminal or injurious?"[4]

Hume then gives historical examples from Sparta and the Agrarian laws of Rome, but concludes that the customs of property of Englishmen in his day, such as ownership of one's own product, alienation by consent, enforcement of contracts, inheritance, were generally more useful to the public, and therefore more just, than common or equal ownership.

[3] Hume, *op. cit.*, IV, 179, 180, 184.
[4] *Ibid.*, IV, 182.

However, the argument is changed from Locke's laws of Nature and Divine Reason in a state of Abundance to Hume's necessity and convenience in a state of Scarcity.

"Examine the writers on the laws of nature," says Hume, "and you will always find, that, whatever principles they set out with, they are sure to terminate here at last, and to assign, as the ultimate reason for every rule which they establish, the convenience and necessities of mankind. A concession thus extorted, in opposition to systems, has more authority, than if it had been made in prosecution of them." [5]

Extremes of human character likewise make public utility and justice a matter of change and relativity.

". . . suppose, that, though the necessities of human race continue the same as at present, yet the mind is so enlarged, and so replete with friendship and generosity, that every man has the utmost tenderness for every man, and feels no more concern for his own interest than for that of his fellows: It seems evident, that the *Use* of justice would, in this case, be suspended by such an extensive benevolence, nor would the divisions and barriers of property and obligation have ever been thought of. . . . Why raise landmarks between my neighbor's field and mine, when my heart has made no division between our interests? . . . the whole human race would form only one family; where all would lie in common, and be used freely, without regard to property." [6]

Hume mentions the various virtues of honor, generosity, bravery, conscientiousness, good faith, and all that Adam Smith afterwards included under the name of Sympathy, and based his ethics and economics on the two principles of personality and scarcity. On these principles he attempted to refute the ethical theories of both Locke and Hobbes, "who maintained the selfish system of morals," [7] as well as the economic and ethical theories taken over from them by Adam Smith, Bentham, and the economists for a hundred years, who based their economics on self-interest.

"We have found instances," he says, "in which private interest was separate from public; in which it was even contrary: And yet we observed the moral sentiment to continue, notwithstanding this disjunction of interests. And wherever these distinct interests sensibly concurred, we always found a sensible increase of the

[5] *Ibid.*, IV, 189.
[6] *Ibid.*, IV, 180, 181.
[7] *Ibid.*, IV, 267.

sentiment, and a more warm affection to virtue, and detestation of vice . . . Compelled by these instances, we must renounce the theory, which accounts for every moral sentiment by the principle of self-love. We must adopt a more public affection, and allow that the interests of society are not, even on their own account, entirely indifferent to us. Usefulness is only a tendency to a certain end; and it is a contradiction in terms, that any thing pleases as means to an end, where the end itself no wise affects us. If usefulness [public or social utility], therefore, be a source of moral sentiment, and if this usefulness be not always considered with a reference to self; it follows, that every thing, which contributes to the happiness of society, recommends itself directly to our approbation and good-will." [8]

This Adam Smith afterwards denied. Yet if we are familiar with modern trade union "ethics" and the business "ethics" of industry, commerce, and banking, we shall find that it is exactly Hume's Scarcity of opportunities with their resulting conflict of interests that gives rise, out of the conflict, to all the economic virtues of honesty, fair dealing, fair competition, reasonable exercise of economic power, equal opportunity, live-and-let-live, good-will, and reasonable value, which subordinate the immediate interests of self to that sharing with others of limited opportunities which makes possible the peaceful conduct of transactions and going concerns. Scarcity operates, as Hume says, both as self-interest and as self-sacrifice, and an economics based on Hume's scarcity permits a union of economics, ethics, and jurisprudence; whereas the economics of self-interest, following Adam Smith or John Locke on the assumptions of abundance and divine beneficence, divorced economics from ethics and law. For this reason we make Scarcity, and not the "law" of supply and demand or self-interest, for both economics and jurisprudence, a universal principle.

Hume again reverses his extreme supposition.

"Suppose likewise, that it should be a virtuous man's fate to fall into the society of ruffians. . . . He . . . can have no other expedient than to arm himself, to whomever the sword he seizes, or the buckler, may belong: To make provision of all means of defence and security: And his particular regard to justice being no longer of Use to his own safety or that of others, he must consult the dictates of self-preservation alone, without concern for those who no longer merit his care and attention." [9]

Hume then abandons these extreme cases and proceeds to the

[8] *Ibid.*, IV, 207.
[9] *Ibid.*, IV, 182–183.

actual complexity of historical society. "The common situation of society," he says, "is a medium amidst all these extremes." [10] They do not operate as extreme cases. They operate with extreme complexity and extreme variability, according to character and circumstance. In order to discover the historical differences in public utility and justice, we must, he says, have recourse to "statutes, customs, precedents, analogies and a hundred other circumstances; some of which are constant and inflexible, some variable and arbitrary." [11]

All of these may be reduced, from another point of view, to Hume's three ideas of repetition, variability, and futurity, which he recites under the name of Custom.

II. FROM HABIT TO CUSTOM

Hume differed from Locke in that he reduced all ideas to mere subjective feelings, instead of allowing them to exist as intellectual copies and rational reflections. Bishop Berkeley had prepared the way, and to him Hume ascribed "one of the greatest and most valuable discoveries," which Hume then adopted.[12]

Berkeley had pointed out the double meaning of "idea" in Locke's theory—a *feeling* and a *felt body*, and had showed that, as mere sensation, a feeling does not yield the relations of order, coherence, and unity in the universe. Locke's "idea of a thing" was nothing more than an "idea," and an idea was nothing but a feeling, but, for Berkeley, it must be a feeling of the orderly, coherent relations between feelings. Hence, for Berkeley, the reality of a felt body disappears altogether and only the reality of God remains, whom we directly feel as an orderly, coherent, beneficent will guiding us and the world.

But Hume went further and held that the mind itself was neither Locke's nor Berkeley's "soul" which knows its own feelings, but only the succession of feelings themselves which cannot know themselves.[13] "The mind is not a substance," a continuing organ that has ideas; the mind is only an abstract name for the series of ideas; "the perceptions, memories and feelings *are* the mind; there is no observable 'soul' behind the processes of thought." [14] Thus Hume reached his ultimate skepticism that the world is only a succession

---

[10] *Ibid.*, IV, 183.

[11] *Ibid.*, IV, 191. Hume's "public utility" should not be confused with the modern more restricted use of the term, such as "public utility corporations."

[12] *Ibid.*, I, 325.

[13] *Ibid.*, I, 326; also Green's summary of Berkeley and Hume, I, 149 ff.

[14] Durant, W., *The Story of Philosophy* (1926), 281.

of feelings, and that the mind as intellect, never perceives any real connection between these feelings.

Hume continues, indeed, to speak of ideas as "copies," but they are not Locke's dry pictures of external objects—they are faint feelings which repeat more vivid feelings. "Two ideas of the same object can only be different by the different feelings." [15] "Our ideas are copied from our impressions" and "they differ from each other only in the different degrees of force or vivacity." [16]

Thus, according to Hume, every impression or perception, whether external or internal, whether of the bulk, motion, and solidity of bodies or of their colors, tastes, smells, sounds, heat or cold, or of pains and pleasures arising from them, are originally on the same footing—they are impressions. Those impressions are internal and perishing existences; hence we do not know them as related either to any external substance that continues to exist or any internal soul that retains its identity. The soul does not observe itself feeling these impressions—the soul is merely the succession of the perishing feelings themselves.

Thus, philosophically, Hume reaches utter skepticism. But practically it is not so. Hume's explanation is Activity and Custom.[17] Activity gives us experiences, and experiences are conjunctions of ideas having resemblance, contiguity, and causation. Causation is the most extensive and appears in the two relations of motion and power. Motion is produced by one object in another object, but power is the capacity to produce such motion. Motion is actual, power is potential. Therefore cause and effect, actual or potential, are

"the source of all the relations of interest and duty, by which men influence each other in society, and are placed in the ties of government and subordination. A master is such-a-one as by his situation, arising either from force or agreement, has a power of directing in certain particulars the actions of another, whom we call servant. A judge is one, who in all disputed cases can fix by his opinion the possessions or property of any thing betwixt any members of the society. When a person is possessed of any power, there is no more required to convert it into action, but the exertion of the will." [18]

Thus the will is activity. Power is the capacity to move by act

[15] Hume, *op. cit.*, I, 560 (Appendix).

[16] *Ibid.*, I, 396. In the Appendix, p. 560, he corrected this statement by omitting the word "only," but nevertheless retained differences of feeling as the only differences of ideas.

[17] Hume identified habit with custom, which we distinguish.

[18] Hume, *op. cit.*, I, 320–321.

of will. But Hume repeats the physical analogy of Locke in failing to analyze Choice.[19]

As ideas these same experiences are the familiar but less vivid feelings which remain or are repeated after the original experience, and thus these are the "reflections" of impressions which we understand by memory and imagination. Ideas are internal repetitions of impressions from without and these are capable of producing a new kind of impression—the impressions of Reflection, which are also feelings, but looking mainly to the future, such as desire, aversion, hope, fear.

It is these feelings of reflection that constitute Hume's notion of Opinion and Belief which we choose to designate, Meanings. A belief cannot arise from a present sensation, yet neither can it arise without a present sensation. It is inseparable from the repetitions, which Hume names Habit or Custom.[20]

". . . the present impression has not this effect by its own proper power and efficacy, and when considered alone, as a single perception, limited to the present moment. I find, that an impression, from which, on its first appearance, I can draw no conclusion, may afterwards become the foundation of belief, when I have had experience of its usual consequences. We must in every case have observed the same impression in past instances, and have found it to be constantly conjoined with some other impression . . . the belief, which attends the present impression, and is produced by a number of past impressions and conjunctions . . . arises immediately, without any new operation of the reason or imagination. Of this I can be certain, because I never am conscious of any such operation, and find nothing in the subject, on which it can be founded. Now as we call every thing CUSTOM,[21] which proceeds from a past repetition, without any new reasoning or conclusion, we may establish it as a certain truth, that all the belief, which follows upon any present impression, is derived solely from that origin. When we are accustomed to see two impressions conjoined together, the appearance or idea of the one immediately carries us to the idea of the other." [22]

He then reverses his experiment and finds, if the idea exists without the present impression,

"that tho' the customary transition to the correlative idea still remains, yet there is in reality no belief nor persuasion. A present

[19] Below, p. 301, Choices and Opportunity.
[20] Cf. Boucke, O. F., A Critique of Economics (1922), 151–152.
[21] Or Habit.
[22] Hume, op. cit., I, 402–403.

impression, then, is absolutely requisite to this whole operation; and when after this I compare an impression with an idea, and find that their only difference consists in their different degrees of force and vivacity, I conclude upon the whole, that belief is a more vivid and intense conception of an idea, proceeding from its relation to a present impression." [23]

Thus an opinion or belief is "a lively idea related to or associated with a present impression." [24] It is, as we would say, the meaning of the impression.

Thus Hume converts the idea of a "law of nature" not only from that of Locke's and Quesnay's divine command issued in the past and from their idea of a harmonious law of nature, but also from the idea of a necessary connection between cause and effect as well as from "arguments" of any kind. He makes the laws of nature mere expectations "derived entirely from habit, by which we are determined to expect from the future the same train of objects, to which we have been accustomed. This habit or determination to transfer the past to the future is full and perfect; and consequently the first impulse of the imagination in this species of reasoning is endowed with the same qualities" of expectation. If there is a contrariety of past experiments then this "first impulse is . . . here broken into pieces" and we judge that "when they do happen, they will be mixed in the same proportion as in the past." The result here is a less degree of probability, but in any case, "the supposition, *that the future resembles the past* . . . is derived entirely from habit." [25]

"Thus all probable reasoning is nothing but a species of sensations. 'Tis not solely in poetry and music, we must follow our taste and sentiment, but likewise in philosophy. When I am convinced of any principle, 'tis only an idea, which strikes more strongly upon me. When I give the preference to one set of arguments above another, I do nothing but decide from my feeling concerning the superiority of their influence. Objects have no discoverable connexion together; nor is it from any other principle but custom operating upon the imagination, that we can draw any inference from the appearance of one to the existence of another." This bias is unconscious. "The past experience, on which all our judgments concerning cause and effect depend, may operate on our mind in such an insensible manner as never to be

[23] *Ibid.*, I, 403.
[24] *Ibid.*, I, 396.
[25] *Ibid.*, I, 431, 432.

taken notice of, and may even in some measure be unknown to us." [26]

Sometimes, he admits, the reflection seems to produce the belief without the custom. We can even "attain the knowledge of a particular cause merely by one experiment." The mind then "draws an inference" concerning either the cause or the effect. But this seeming difficulty will vanish if we notice that we have many millions of experiments to convince us of the principle *"that like objects, placed in like circumstances, will always produce like effects."* Thus our experience is transferred to instances of which we have no experience, either expressly, directly, tacitly, or indirectly.[27]

Thus it is, as we interpret Hume, that in all our affairs, whether of common life, or science, or philosophy, it is not our intellect, as Locke maintained, but is our past feelings repeated, which determine "that lively idea related to or associated with a present impression" which is, therefore, not intellectual knowledge, but that individual bias, which is the individual's meanings attributed to the impressions from without.

The same applies to Hume's idea of morals. Where Malebranche, Cudworth, and Clarke set out with moral relations as purely intellectual constructions, Hume asserted that such intellectual relations are mere tautological assertions like those of mathematics, which cannot be felt; then he rested his ethics, as we have already observed, on the feelings of social utility and scarcity.[28]

Hume's Hegelian editor, T. H. Green, writing in 1875, revolts against this reversal of the laws of nature and morals from their old foundation on universal intellect to Hume's foundation on individual feelings and expectations:

"That a doctrine which reduces the order of nature to strength of expectation, and exactly reverses the positions severally given to belief and reality in the actual procedure of science, should have been ostensibly adopted by scientific men as their own . . . would have been unaccountable if the doctrine had been thus nakedly put or consistently maintained. . . . Expectation is an 'impression of reflection,' and if the relation of cause and effect is no more than expectation, that which seemed most strongly to resist reduction to feeling has yet been so reduced. . . . In an expectation made up of such expectations, there would be nothing to serve the purpose which the conception of uniformity of nature actually serves in inductive science . . . Upon that 'interrogation of nature' by which, on the faith that there is a uniformity

---

[26] *Ibid.,* I, 403–404.
[27] *Ibid.,* I, 405.
[28] *Ibid.,* IV, 190.

if only we could find it out, we wrest from her that confession of a law which she does not spontaneously offer . . . uniform relation between phenomena is neither impression nor idea and can exist only for thought." [29]

From this citation Green concludes, "if the relation of cause and effect is merely custom, the extension of knowledge by means of it remains to be accounted for; the breach between the expectation of the recurrences of familiar feelings and inductive science remains unfilled; Locke's 'suspicions' that 'a science of nature is impossible,' instead of being overcome is elaborated into a system." [30]

Durant likewise expresses Green's revolt.

". . . Hume was not content to destroy orthodox religion by dissipating the concept of soul; he proposed also to destroy science by dissolving the concept of law. Science and philosophy alike, since Bruno and Galileo, had been making much of natural law, of 'necessity' in the sequence of effect upon cause; Spinoza had reared his majestic metaphysics upon this proud conception. But observe, said Hume, that we never perceive causes, or laws; we perceive events and sequences, and *infer* causation and necessity; a law is not an eternal and necessary decree to which events are subjected, but merely a mental summary and shorthand of our kaleidoscopic experience; we have no guarantee that the sequences hitherto observed will re-appear unaltered in future experience. 'Law' is an observed *custom* in the sequence of events; but there is no 'necessity' in custom.

"Only mathematical formulas have necessity—they alone are inherently and unchangeably true; and this merely because such formulas are tautological—the predicate is already contained in the subject; '3 × 3 = 9' is an eternal and necessary truth only because '3 × 3 and 9' are one and the same thing differently expressed." [31]

Yet modern science does exactly what Hume expounded under the name of habit and custom. Hume was distinguishing two concepts of the mind, the passive concept accepted by Locke and Green and the active concept of the mind constructing its own tools for investigation and action, including the mental tools of law, cause, effect, necessity, and so on. If the mind is passive then it perceives no relations between its "perishing sensations." But if the mind is active, then it actually creates, feels, and acts upon a supposed relationship between the parts and the whole of the perishing sensations. What Hume's skepticism destroyed was the idea of a passive mind. What he foretold was the idea of an active mind.

[29] *Ibid.*, I, 275, 276–277, 286.
[30] *Ibid.*, I, 285.
[31] Durant, *op. cit.*, 281.

III. PRAGMATISM

It was the founder of American Pragmatism, C. S. Peirce, in 1878, who dissolved Hume's skepticism by creating the concept of an active mind. A physical scientist associated with the Geodetic Survey of the Federal Government, he profoundly investigated the Habit and Custom to which Hume had taken refuge in considering practical affairs. Peirce actually made Habit and Custom, instead of intellect and sensations, the foundation of all science. He gave to his system the name Pragmatism, but by this he meant merely the *method* of scientific investigation. In this way he avoided both the radical skepticism of the passive mind of Hume's psychology, and the pre-determined "order of nature" of Hume's critics. It is just because Peirce, the physical scientist, expounded the psychology of all scientific investigation that we endeavor to follow him and to accept the term Pragmatism as the name of the method of investigation which we attempt to apply to economics in this book.

We do not forget the hundred and forty years from Hume to Peirce,[32] with its philosophical forerunners of pragmatism, such as Dugald Stewart and William Hodgson. We simply find Peirce's method more useful for our purposes. Nor do we forget the fifty years since Peirce, with such successors as William James, John Dewey, and Schiller, nor the Gestalt psychology of Köhler and Koffka.[33] Peirce afterwards protested against the use made of his term "pragmatism" by James and Schiller, saying that his was a theory of knowledge and a test of truth, while theirs was a philosophy of life, value, or desire. James, he said, construed the test of truth of an idea not merely as to whether it leads to expected consequences, but also whether it leads to *desirable* consequences, such as individual happiness, or Dewey's *desirable social* consequences.[34]

We are compelled, therefore, to distinguish and use two meanings of pragmatism: Peirce's meaning of purely a method of scientific investigation, derived by him from the physical sciences but applicable also to our economic transactions and concerns; and the meaning of the various social-philosophies assumed by the parties themselves who participate in these transactions. We therefore, under the latter meaning, follow most closely the social pragmatism of Dewey; while in our method of investigation we follow the pragmatism of

[32] See especially Voegelin, Erich, *Über die Form des amerikanischen Geistes* (1928), 19 ff.

[33] James, William, *Pragmatism* (1906), *Essays in Radical Empiricism* (1912); Dewey, John, especially *The Quest for Certainty: a Study of the Relation of Knowledge and Action* (1929); Schiller, F. C. S., *Humanism* (1903); on Köhler and Koffka, see above, p. 97.

[34] See Peirce's articles in *The Monist*, XV (1905), 161–181, 481–499; XVI (1906), 147–151, 492–546.

Peirce. One is scientific pragmatism—a method of investigation—the other is the pragmatism of human beings—the subject-matter of the science of economics.

Peirce, in his scientific pragmatism, began by clearly distinguishing and incorporating into the feelings themselves the *relationship* between sensations which Hume rejected because he could not explain them as feelings.[35] Peirce illustrated the method by noticing two sorts of elements of conscious feeling. "In a piece of music there are the separate notes, and there is the air." Hume's impressions and ideas were the "notes," which are isolated feelings at separate points of time. But not the "air," for this is a continuity of feeling through a flow of time.

"A single tone," says Peirce, "may be prolonged for an hour or a day, and it exists as perfectly in each second of that time as in the whole taken together; so that, as long as it is sounding, it might be present to a sense from which everything in the past was as completely absent as the future itself. But it is different with the air, the performance of which occupies a certain time, during the portions of which only portions of it are played. It consists in an orderliness in the succession of sounds which strike the ear at different times; and to perceive it there must be some continuity of consciousness which makes the events of a lapse of time present to us. We certainly only perceive the air by hearing the separate notes; yet we cannot be said to directly hear it, for we hear only what is present at the instant, and an orderliness of succession cannot exist in an instant. These two sorts of objects, what we are *immediately* conscious of and what we are *mediately* conscious of, are found in all consciousness. Some elements (the sensations) are completely present at every instant so long as they last, while others (like thought) are actions having beginning, middle, and end, and consist in a congruence in the succession of sensations which flow through the mind. They cannot be immediately present to us, but must cover some portion of the past or future. Thought is a thread of melody running through the succession of our sensations."[36]

Thus thought itself, for Peirce, was not a pure intellectual abstraction, nor was it, as for Berkeley and Hume, a series of sensations; it was what we name a "meaning." It was the overtone of feeling through memory and expectation that runs through the

[35] Peirce, Charles S., "How to Make Our Ideas Clear," one of a series of six articles he published in *Popular Science Monthly* (1877–1878), XII, 1–15, 286–302, 604–615, 705–718; XIII, 203–217, 470–482. Reprinted in *Chance, Love, and Logic* (1923). Citations are to the reprint.

[36] *Ibid.*, 39, 40.

repetition of sensations. Thought, says Peirce, differs from other systems of relations, such as music, in that "its sole motive, idea, and function is to produce," not intellectual knowledge, but the feeling of "Belief." Belief has four properties:

> ". . . it is something that we are aware of; . . . it appeases the irritation of doubt; . . . it involves the establishment in our nature of a rule of action, or, say for short, a *habit*. . . .   The *final* upshot of thinking is the exercise of volition. . . .   The essence of belief is the establishment of a habit . . . the whole function of thought is to produce habits of action; and . . . whatever there is connected with a thought, but irrelevant to its purpose, is an accretion to it, but no part of it. . . . To develop its meaning, we have, therefore, simply to determine what habits it produces, for what a thing means is simply what habits it involves. . . . What the habit is depends on *when* and *how* it causes us to act. As for the *when*, every stimulus to action is derived from perception; as for the *how*, every purpose of action is to produce some sensible result. Thus, we come down to what is tangible and practical," for which reason Peirce gave it the name Pragmatism, "as the root of every real distinction of thought, no matter how subtle it may be. . . .   Our idea of anything *is* our idea of its sensible effects." [37]

And he concludes with a rule for obtaining scientific clearness in our ideas. "Consider what effects, which might conceivably have practical bearings, we conceive the object of our conception to have. Then our conception of these effects is the whole of our conception of the object." In other words, Pragmatism is Futurity.

Here, however, the provisional ending is only Hume's individual bias, which differs according to the different feelings of different persons. Peirce proceeds further in order to get that scientific belief which is not biased. This is the problem of reality and is what we distinguish as the difference between Habit and Custom.

For, Peirce's solution of the metaphysical problem of the ultimate and fundamental reality becomes, not an individual bias, but a social consensus of opinion. The real is that whose characters are independent of what anybody may think them to be. "The opinion which is fated to be ultimately agreed to by all who investigate, is what we mean by truth,[38] and the object represented in this opinion is the real. That is the way I would explain reality." [39]

[37] *Ibid.*, 41, 43, 44, 45.
[38] Peirce, as a scientist, did not mean ultimate truth. He meant the existing state of knowledge which changes with further truth.
[39] Peirce, *op. cit.*, 57.

Thus the meaning of metaphysics is changed. It is no longer a problem of an individual's intellectual knowledge of ultimate reality, as it was with Locke, Berkeley, and Hume. It is a problem of the expectations which those who are competent to investigate agree upon in predicting as to the world's events, such that they feel confidence in acting alike for the future, in so far as they continue to agree. This is not merely Hume's biased belief—it is scientific belief, and is the unbiased meaning of meaning. Where Hume had to go back to his individual experience which he could see or remember,[40] in order to get something "beyond which there is not room for doubt or enquiry," Peirce requires only social confirmation by all who see, remember, and confirm by experiment, in order that there may be no room for doubt and inquiry. This is the difference which we shall make between bias and science, and between Habit and Custom. Bias is individual opinion. Science is consensus of opinion. Habit is individual repetition. Custom is a kind of social compulsion imposed on individuals by the collective opinion of those who feel and act alike.

Thus Peirce reveals Hume's shortcomings. They are first, Hume's idea of the mind, like that of Locke, as a mere passive receptacle of impressions from without, existing only for a point of time; [41] whereas Peirce's idea is that of an active, continuing organizer and reorganizer of impressions. Second, the impressions exist longer than Hume's mathematical point of time, for they retain the past impression which is memory, they repeat and change in the moving present, and they expect a feeling in the immediate future which is always becoming the present. Time, with Hume, is successive mathematical *points* of time, each without duration. Time with Peirce is an *instant* of time containing in itself past, present, and future. Thus Hume was a sensationalist, but Peirce was—a pragmatist.

Since Peirce's concept of the mind was that of an active organizer of impressions, Hume's "impressions" themselves are now seized upon in their external relations of parts related to the whole activity, past and future, instead of coming in to the mind as separate impressions associated only by resemblance, contiguity, and succession. The mind does not wait for impressions, it is continually looking for them, breaking them up into parts, and reconstructing them into new feelings. Those new feelings are not Hume's passive impressions, but are Peirce's active beliefs reaching forward for future action. It is this relation of the part to the whole and of the past

---

[40] Hume, *op. cit.*, I, 384.
[41] Durant, W., *op. cit.*, 295.

experience to future expectations that becomes the psychology of our transactions and going concerns.

Peirce also enables us to see that Hume's skepticism was derived from his individualism and the isolated speculations of great philosophers of his age unaided by the coöperation and criticism of scientific investigators. Hume's skepticism was his distrust of the mere individual intellect as an instrument for discovering the metaphysical ultimate reality of things, as it had been relied upon by Locke and most philosophers who preceded himself. Hence he rejected the intellect as something abstracted from both feelings and society. His meaning of intellect was an empty interval between feelings, and therefore nothing. Hume was frank enough about this skepticism.

> "I am first affrighted and confounded with that forlorn solitude, in which I am placed in my philosophy. . . . Every step I take is with hesitation, and every new reflection makes me dread an error and absurdity in my reasoning. . . . Can I be sure, that in leaving all established opinions I am following truth? . . . There are two principles, which I cannot render consistent; nor is it in my power to renounce either of them, viz., that all our distinct *perceptions are distinct existences, and that the mind never perceives any real connexion among distinct existences.* . . . Most fortunately it happens, that since reason is incapable of dispelling these clouds, nature herself suffices to that purpose . . . I dine, I play a game of backgammon, I converse, and am merry with my friends. . . ." [42]

Thus Hume forgets his skepticism when he becomes the pragmatist.

Green's criticism of Hume is sound in one respect and unsound in another. It is sound in the conclusion that Hume's idea of an individual's experiences can never be a foundation for science, since it is only the unconcerted experiences of an individual, which is bias, not science. But Green is wrong in insisting that science requires a predetermined uniformity in order to have a "law" of nature. All that science requires is Peirce's uniformity of expectations on the part of those competent to investigate, which uniformity therefore has the binding effect of custom upon the individual investigator.

Hume's manly skepticism was the individualism of his century and the isolation of a pioneer. Peirce's reality is the consensus of· a world of scientific investigators. This is borne out by Hume's idea of education. He attributes to custom all belief and reasoning,

[42] Hume, *op. cit.*, I, 544, 545, 548, 559.

but he does not distinguish Custom from Habit. Hence when he comes to education, he looks upon it as "an artificial and not a natural cause" though it "operate upon the mind in the same manner [as] the senses, memory, or reason." [43]

Yet if we distinguish custom from habit, then custom is none other than education, for it is the repeated impressions of fellow beings from childhood, which impose conformity of habitual assumptions upon individuals, whereas Hume's Custom was identified with individual habit, which he might obtain from the repetitions of physical nature or of other human beings, not influenced by the moral compulsion of collective opinion. Habit is indeed an individualistic term in that it is limited to the experience, feelings, and expectations of an individual; but custom is that portion of experience, feelings, and expectations derived from other persons who act collectively alike, which is education in its broadest meaning. Habit is repetition by one person. Custom is repetition by the continuing group of changing persons. It has a coercive effect on individuals, and, instead of education accounting for "more than one-half of those opinions that prevail upon mankind," as Hume contended, it accounts for practically all of them. Hence education is not artificial—it is the usual social process of acquiring habits through life-long repetition of dealings with others and the necessity of conformity enforced by collective action. Education is the acquiring of habit by conformity to custom. And so it is with Peirce's consensus of opinion. It is the consensus of belief by scientists which has the force of custom in creating new habits for the individual.

Thus we approach, through Hume in 1739 and Peirce in 1878, the meaning of meaning. This meaning, however, is not yet complete for our economic purposes, because Hume was an individualist and sensationalist, while Peirce's field of research was the physical sciences. Not until we reach John Dewey do we find Peirce expanded to ethics, and not until we reach institutional economics do we find it expanded to transactions, going concerns, and Reasonable Value. Yet Hume's "belief," as interpreted by Peirce, is what we mean by meaning.

Belief, or Meaning, is first of all bias. Says Hume, "After the most accurate and exact of my reasonings, I can give no reason why I should assent to it, and feeling nothing but a *strong* propensity to consider objects *strongly* in that view under which they appear to me." "My feelings," he says, "are always biased, and therefore

[43] *Ibid.*, I, 416.

I am skeptical intellectually, but still my biased feelings are the meanings I give to appearances."

These meanings arise from experience. "Experience is a principle which instructs me in the several conjunctions of objects from the past." These, he says, are resemblance, contiguity and causation.

Experience repeated becomes habit. "Habit is another principle, which determines me to expect the same for the future."

Experience and habit become imagination. "Both of them conspiring to operate upon the imagination, make me form certain ideas in a more certain and lively manner than others, which are not attended with the same advantage. . . . The memory, senses and understanding are, therefore, all of them founded on the imagination or the vivacity of our ideas."

But all of these feelings are called into existence only when an impression from without excites them, and their inference from that impression is belief. "An opinion, therefore, or belief, may be most accurately defined, a lively idea related to or associated with a present impression." These beliefs we shall name habitual assumptions.[44]

This belief "is a more vivid and intense conception of an idea," and, according to its relative intensity compared with accompanying passions, pains, and pleasures, it "actuates the will."

Thus according to Hume, beliefs are the individual's biased meanings of events. It requires still further Peirce's consensus of belief of all who competently investigate, in order to eliminate bias and to attain scientific confidence of expectations.

Thus Peirce's Pragmatism is none other than the scientific method of investigation. The charge is often brought against the so-called "philosophy" of Pragmatism that it is based on the fallacy that "whatever works" is true and right. If a business man is successful, he is right. If a bank-robber gets away with the goods, he is justified. But Peirce's meaning was not so. He meant, if a *theory* "works" when tested by experiments and verified by others, then the *theory* is true and right, so far as present knowledge is concerned and all the known facts are included.[45]

IV. From Nature to Going Concerns

Something similar is the test in economic science, as Peirce found in physical science. But the essential difference is that physical science deals with knowledge of the activities within the body of

---

[44] Below, p. 697, Habitual Assumptions.

[45] On the further development of pragmatism see Geyer, D. L., *The Pragmatic Theory of Truth as Developed by Peirce, James and Dewey* (1914). See below, p. 649, on Veblen.

the cosmos, including human beings as nature's objects; while economics deals with the individual as a citizen endowed with rights, duties, liberties, and exposures, in varying degrees imposed by various concerns. It is this distinction that requires a negotiational psychology, different from the historic psychologies and different even from what is currently known as social psychology. Its field is bargaining, managing, and rationing, within the working rules of collective action. The historic psychologies are individualistic, as indeed they must be, since their subject-matter is human beings as natural objects and not human beings as citizens or members of going concerns. Peirce's pragmatism, applied to institutional economics, is the scientific investigation of these economic relations of citizens to citizens. Its subject-matter is the whole concern of which the individuals are members, and the activities investigated are their transactions governed by an entirely different law, not a law of nature but a working rule, for the time being, of collective action.

CHAPTER V

ADAM SMITH

I. SELF-INTEREST AND MUTUALITY

David Hume had substituted Scarcity and Public Utility for
Locke's Abundance and Commonwealth, and it was in this sense
of public good or social utility that Adam Smith understood
Hume's meaning of Utility. But, while consenting, as a philosopher, to Hume's idea of public utility, Smith, in his *Theory of
Moral Sentiments*, 1759, denied that, as a "sentiment" common to
mankind, it could be effective on individuals. The idea, he said,
was derived from a "philosopher's reflections," and was not a direct
motive of the individual to support justice. The usefulness "of any
disposition of mind is seldom the first ground of our approbation"
either to ourselves or the community, but rather do we intuitively
appreciate, without reflection, both in ourselves and others, the
virtuous human qualities such as reason, good understanding, self-
control, humanity, justice, generosity, public spirit, "without
thought of their utility to the community"; and we directly disap-
prove and hate the opposite qualities of greed, selfishness, and vice
without reference to their effect on the community as a whole.
The idea of the usefulness to the public of all qualities of this kind
is "plainly an afterthought and not what first recommends them
to our approbation." [1]

Thus Smith substituted innate emotions for Locke's innate ideas.
He converted Locke's "compound ideas," derived from reflection,
into a compound feeling of sympathy and antipathy not derived
from reflection. These compound feelings he named "sentiments,"
not "reflections." The reflections were the "philosopher's afterthought."

The highest compound of all the emotions was the "sense of
propriety," equivalent perhaps to our idea of the "sense of fitness," or "insight." This sense of propriety was innate in our very
being and was the summation of all the sentiments, whose special
cases were the feelings of sympathy, antipathy, conscience, and its

[1] Smith, Adam, *The Theory of Moral Sentiments* (1759, citation to 1822 ed.), 205, 216,
217, passim.

sense of duty. Taking his cue from Hume's "vivid ideas," Smith substituted a "lively imagination" for Locke's cold ratiocination. We do not, of course, he said, actually feel the identical emotions of others, rather do we proceed through a "lively imagination" to place ourselves in the position of another, and, in doing this, we exercise judgment as to the propriety or impropriety of their conduct and our own. This sense of propriety can then be personified as an "impartial spectator," "a man within the breast," "the great judge and arbiter of our conduct," a "vice-gerent" of "divine providence," who subordinates our conduct to the virtues with which we sympathize and sets us against the vices which we antipathize.

Thus, in 1759, having safeguarded the Virtue of Nations, Smith proceeded, in 1776, to safeguard the Wealth of Nations. Here also was a vice-gerent of divine providence that needed not the help of Church, or State, or any Collective Action. It was "a certain propensity in human nature to truck, barter and exchange one thing for another." This innate propensity was planted there to become a *cause;* it was not an *effect* of the division of labor, as has been supposed.

"The greatest improvement in the productive powers of labour," he said, "and the greater part of the skill, dexterity, and judgment with which it is anywhere directed, or applied, as well as a great number of machines, seem to have been the effects of the division of labour. . . . It is the great multiplication of the productions of all the different arts, in consequence of the division of labour, which occasions, in a well governed society, that universal opulence which extends itself to the lowest ranks of the people. . . . This division of labour, from which so many advantages are derived, is not originally the effect of any human wisdom, which foresees and intends that general opulence to which it gives occasion . . . [but is the] consequence of a certain propensity to truck, barter, and exchange one thing for another, . . . a consequence of the faculties of reason and speech."[2]

While Smith has sometimes been charged with exalting self-interest regardless of consequences, yet his idea of self-interest was, like that of Locke and Quesnay, subordinate to his idea of divine beneficence. It was this, that had planted in the human breast an instinct of mutuality of interests, which he named the "sense of propriety," and which, in turn, led to division of labor, exchange, and earthly abundance. Self-interest was subordinate to self-sacrifice, in the unseen intentions of Providence. While consciously

[2] Smith, Adam, *An Inquiry into the Nature and Causes of the Wealth of Nations* (1776, ed. by Cannan, 1904), I, 5, 12, 15. Citations from Cannan's edition.

seeking to promote only his self-interest the individual unconsciously, guided by this divine instinct, like the bees in a hive, promotes the general welfare. If he thinks of it afterwards, it is—like a philosopher's afterthought—only a pretense and a hypocritical justification of what his conscious selfishness had led him to do.

> "As every individual," says Smith, "necessarily endeavors as much as he can both to employ his capital in the support of domestic industry, and so to direct that industry that its produce may be of the greatest value; every individual necessarily labours to render the annual revenue of the society as great as he can. He generally, indeed, neither intends to promote the public interest, nor knows how much he is promoting it. By preferring the support of domestic to that of foreign industry, he intends only his own security; and by directing that industry in such a manner as its produce may be of the greatest value, he intends only his own gain, and he is in this, as in many other cases, led by an invisible hand to promote an end which was no part of his intention. Nor is it always the worse for the society that it was no part of it. By pursuing his own interest he frequently promotes that of the society more effectually than when he really intends to promote it. I have never known much good done by those who affected to trade for the public good. It is an affectation, indeed, not very common among merchants, and very few words need be employed in dissuading them from it." [3]

This conscious intention of self-seeking is unknown to animals, which act only by unconscious instinct. But in human beings, "the faculties of reason and speech" create both the instinct of private property and the propensity to truck, barter, and exchange. These are

> "common to all men, and to be found in no other race of animals, which seem to know neither this nor any other species of contracts. . . . Nobody ever saw one animal by its gestures and natural cries signify to another, this is mine, that yours; I am willing to give this for that. . . . But man has almost constant occasion for the help of his brethren, and it is vain for him to expect it from their benevolence only. He will be more likely to prevail if he can interest their self love in his favor, and shew them that it is for their own advantage to do for him what he requires of them. Whoever offers to another a bargain of any kind, proposes to do this: Give me that which I want, and you shall have this which you want, is the meaning of every such offer;

[3] *Ibid.*, I, 421.

and it is in this manner that we obtain from one another the far greater part of those good offices which we stand in need of. It is not from the benevolence of the butcher, the brewer, or the baker, that we expect our dinner, but from their regard to their own interest. . . . Nobody but a beggar chuses to depend chiefly upon the benevolence of his fellow citizens." [4]

Thus whether it were sympathy or self-interest, it was mutuality in either case, arising from the sense of propriety planted there by divine Providence. Those who contend that Smith in his *Wealth of Nations* contradicted his *Theory of Moral Sentiments* overlook his theology of divine beneficence which, as in the theories of Locke and Quesnay, was equivalent to earthly abundance. Hume derived both self-interest and justice from Scarcity, but Smith, Locke, and Quesnay derived them from Abundance. If there is abundance of nature's resources, no person can injure any other person by taking from him all he can get, if he does this by exchanging his own labor for that of the other. The other has abundance of alternatives to which he can resort if he is not satisfied with the terms of exchange offered. And the one who makes the offer does not suffer if it is not accepted, because he also has abundance of alternatives. Enough will be left for others to take all they can get by a similar method. Self-interest cannot injure anybody in a world of abundance, as Locke had shown, though self-interest does injure others in a world of scarcity, as Hume had shown. But Smith's was not a world of Scarcity.

Modern economic society has given us a means of testing both Hume and Smith. A cycle of prosperity is Smith's Abundance; a cycle of depression is Hume's Scarcity.

Hence Smith was consistent in his *Moral Sentiments* and his *Wealth of Nations*. In the former book he was dealing with the sacrifice of self to the wants of others *on account of* their virtues, in a world of abundance. In the latter he was dealing with the sacrifice of self to the wants of others *regardless* of their virtues or vices, also in a world of abundance. For, the two sentiments of sympathy and of propensity to bargain were each subordinate to a higher vice-gerent, the "sense of propriety," which is a divine sense of fitness, conscience, and harmony in a world of abundance. Sympathy promotes by self-sacrifice the welfare of those whose virtues are approved. But the propensity to exchange benefits even those whose vices the sentiment of antipathy disapproves. The one supplements and does not contradict the other. Each requires self-

---

[4] *Ibid.*, I, 15, 16.

sacrifice, but the sacrifice in either case is unimportant in a world of pre-ordained abundance.[5]

But this pre-ordained abundance does not fit the facts of history. Had Smith investigated the growth of the common law in England as expounded by Coke and Blackstone, and had he accepted Hume's principle of Scarcity as the explanation, in place of the current deism of beneficence and abundance, he might have discovered a different consequence of his "faculties of reason and speech." Instead of a divine instinct of mutuality of interests, planted in the breasts of individuals, he would have found that this very mutuality itself was an historic product of collective action in actually creating mutuality of interests out of conflict of interests. Instead of an unseen hand guiding the self-interest of individuals towards general welfare he would have seen the visible hand of the common-law courts, taking over the customs of the time and place, in so far as deemed good, and enforcing these good customs on refractory individuals, in conformity to Hume's "public utility." Within this institutional history of collective action controlling and at the same time liberating and expanding individual action, he would have found the reasons why, in his England of the Eighteenth Century, the human animal had reached the stage where he could say, "This is mine, that is yours; I am willing to give this for that."

But Smith did not take recourse to the common law. He unconsciously personified and eternalized the common law of his time as a sense of propriety and fitness to an existence in social life. His conscious attention was directed to statutory law. He was substituting the statutory law of Divine Providence for the statutory laws of Mercantilism. As in the case of John Locke his familiarity with the current customs of the common law made them equivalent to divine law.

---

[5] James Bonar traces Smith's idea to Mandeville's *Private Vices, Public Virtues*. See Bonar, J., *Philosophy and Political Economy in Some of Their Historical Relations* (1893), 154 ff. This alleged origin is plausible, but it is because Smith's propensity to exchange overcomes antipathy to the vices of others just as it disregards sympathy with the virtues of others, in a world of abundance. Jacob Viner holds that Smith, in his *Theory of Moral Sentiments*, gave to "benevolence" but a "minor rôle" in economic matters. See Viner, J., "Adam Smith and Laissez Faire," *Jour. of Pol. Econ.*, XXXV (1927), 198, 206. But, as we have stated above, Smith in his theory of value actually ridiculed benevolence and gave it even a hypocritical rôle in economic matters. He could do this consistently because in neither case was it individual benevolence nor individual self-interest that promoted the "public utility." It was divine benevolence and the equivalent earthly abundance which, as with Quesnay, identified the moral order with exactly the opposite economic order in promoting public welfare. Having rejected, as we shall see, all collective action, he resorted to theology to provide the earthly abundance needed for the common welfare.

II. LIBERTY, SECURITY, EQUALITY, PROPERTY

The Mercantilist policy, as understood by Smith, operated directly by what it did and indirectly by what it permitted. Directly it was a policy of government in aid of private business by protective tariffs, bounties, colonial and navigation laws, charters of incorporation; indirectly it was permission allowed for private collective arrangements by which individuals adopted rules or followed customs restraining the perfect liberty of individuals from engaging in unlimited competition. And, according to him, the only duties of a government in sustaining a system of natural liberty were "protecting the society from the violence and invasion of other independent societies"; protecting "every member of the society from the injustice or oppression of every other member of it, or the duty of establishing an exact administration of justice," including the enforcement of individual but not collective contracts; "the duty of erecting and maintaining certain public works and certain public institutions . . . because the profit could never repay the expense to any individual or small number of individuals." [6] This excluded all bounties, protective tariffs, corporate franchises, regulations of trade, labor legislation, child labor laws, and so on.

Yet his idea of government is not completely laissez-faire, as was that afterwards set up by the anarchists. It is a government which actively holds every individual away from every other individual. Each individual, in the language of anthropology, is *tabu*, but each may voluntarily raise the tabu [7] for a short period of time and may voluntarily authorize the government to enforce his promises upon himself for the benefit of others. If this is done, then every individual has "perfect liberty." This perfect liberty means that he is free to seek his self-interest in any way he pleases. He is free to choose what he will do with his own body, or with the objects of nature which he owns, or with the output of his labor; or with the output of other people's labor which he has received in exchange; and the state will lend its physical power to enforce his individual will. The innate "sense of propriety" was enough to prevent abuse of liberty, although that liberty had the aid of the state to enforce it.

This concept of free self-interest, backed by law, is inseparable from that of Security, for if there is no firm expectation that other people will be held off in the future as well as in the immediate present, or that they will do what they have promised to do, then

[6] Smith, Adam, *An Inquiry into the Nature and Causes of the Wealth of Nations*, II, 185.
[7] Cf. Frank, Lawrence K., "The Emancipation of Economics," *Amer. Econ. Rev.*, XIV (1924), 17–38.

such a creature as man, who lives by expectation, can have little inducement to produce, save, or exchange.

It also means Equality of opportunity, for if some individuals are held off from others, but the latter are not held off from the former, then the former are not free but the latter are free. If this is the logical consequence, then we have the very outcome of the mercantilism or landlordism which he condemned because it authorized or permitted privileged classes to infringe upon the freedom of the industrious and thrifty merchants, manufacturers, and farmers upon whom he relied for productivity, thrift, and exchange.

In short, the self-interest of the individual is attained both by holding other people off and by binding them together by contracts, so that each may operate in any direction deemed most advantageous to himself. Smith's meaning of self-interest was not completely that of a laissez-faire government; it was a common-law meaning of liberty, security, equality, and property, enforced by the independent judiciary of John Locke. It meant, in fact, judicial, not legislative, sovereignty.

But legislatures are not the only collective action that interferes with liberty and equality. Equally to be prohibited, according to Smith, were all customs and all private associations that made arrangements, rules, or gentlemen's understandings, which limited individual competition. "People of the same trade," he said, "seldom meet together, even for merriment and diversion, but the conversation ends in a conspiracy against the public, or in some contrivance to raise prices." Thus he condemned trade associations and the live-and-let-live understandings of modern business ethics. These contradict a state of "perfect liberty." Though these meetings cannot be prevented consistently with "liberty and justice," yet the law should "do nothing to facilitate such assemblies; much less to render them necessary." He would have ruled out, in modern life, all city directories and telephone directories, for there should be even no "public register" of their names which "connects individuals who might never otherwise be known to one another." With the aid of directories and telephones, they might agree to give up their perfect liberty and be bound by rules. Likewise, regulations which enable "those of the same trade to tax themselves in order to provide for their poor, their sick, their widows and orphans, by giving them a common interest to manage, renders such assemblies necessary." [8] So even charity organizations and mutual insurance violate liberty.

[8] Smith, Adam, *An Inquiry into the Nature and Causes of the Wealth of Nations*, I, 130.

Likewise with masters and their workmen. "The masters, being fewer in number, can combine much more easily; . . . we seldom, indeed, hear of this combination because it is the usual, and one may say, the natural state of things which nobody ever hears of." These combinations "sink the wages of labour even below this [natural] rate," [9] which would not occur if masters did not give up their perfect liberty by submitting to rules of their own making.

But most obnoxious of all the restraints on the perfect liberty of self-interest is the provision that "makes the act of the majority binding upon the whole." In a free trade an effectual combination cannot be established except by the unanimous consent of every single trader, and it cannot last longer than every single trader continues of the same mind. But the majority of a corporation can enact a by-law with proper penalties which will limit the competition more effectively and durably than any voluntary combination whatever. "The pretense that corporations are necessary for the better government of the trade, is without any foundation. The real and effectual discipline which is exercised over a workman, is not that of his corporation, but that of his customers." [10]

Thus Smith, in restoring the natural and divine right of perfect liberty and equality of all individuals, had no misunderstanding as to the nature of custom, or the by-laws of corporations, or the working rules of going concerns, or the compulsion of what we know in recent times as "business ethics," or the stabilizing practices of business, the live-and-let-live policies of fair competition, the "follow-the-leader" practices of modern price-making, or the shop rules of unions. All of these impose restrictions upon the output of the individual through collective control of his liberty to do as he pleases. Smith's meaning of liberty was therefore not merely an absence of statutory compulsion imposed by legislation, but an absence of every moral or economic compulsion imposed by custom, or trade practice, or business ethics, or collective pressure, or collective bargaining, such as nowadays condemn the price-cutter, the scab, or blackleg, who takes more than his share of limited resources or of the limited purchasing power of the consumers. Smith's labor was free labor beyond anything known on earth.

The explanation is that his was the idealism of Divine Beneficence, Universal Abundance, the Age of Reason, and the Sense of Propriety. There would therefore be no disproportionate overproduction, no artificial scarcity caused by corporations or other collective

[9] *Ibid.*, I, 68, 69.
[10] *Ibid.*, I, 130, 131. By corporations he included guilds and similar trade associations, as well as joint stock companies.

activity. With this theory of abundance, beneficence, and propriety, he, like Quesnay, condemns all statutory regulations by governments, all tariffs, all restraints of custom, and even calls in question the support by taxes of free education and its consequent subjection to politics.[11]   He sets up a divine law of purely individualistic self-interest and perfect liberty through abolition of customs and working rules which restrain individuals; he substitutes the guiding hand of a bountiful Providence, and its vice-gerent the sense of propriety, for the entire regulative policy of Europe, even declaring against the common sentiments of sympathy which unite people in associations to care for their poor, sick, widows, and orphans.   In this he expressed the sentiments of the age, and the French Revolution carried out his ideas by abolishing church, landlords, associations, and unions.[12]   Smith came as near to creating the Age of Anarchy as Napoleon's dictatorship would permit.

Smith's idealism could not be otherwise if he abolished all collective action in economic affairs.   If collective action is abolished, then the theorist must find in the individual breast a set of instincts that keep society agoing.   These instincts must be placed there by some external power that intended the welfare of mankind.   This external power was God.   Only three instincts were necessary for his purposes—sympathy, truck and barter, and the sense of propriety.   These take the place of all collective action in economic affairs.

Property, with Smith, as with Locke, was the protection by law of the laborer in holding for his own exclusive use, against all of the world, the physical products of his labor.   This was the physical, colonial, or agricultural concept of *corporeal* property, found also in Locke and Quesnay and not based on any concept of scarcity but on the physical holding of objects having use-value.   Smith could not base Property on the principle of scarcity, as Hume proposed, because that would lead to repudiation of God and to justification of the monopolistic or preferential practices of mercantilism, with its pretense of benefiting the public by restricting supply. But his definition of liberty had included all that is contained in the meaning of individual property.   Liberty included exclusive holding, for one's own use, of the physical objects which he could use or abuse as he pleased.   It included liberty to sell or not sell that property, liberty to charge such prices as he could, security for the future, and equality with all other individuals before the law.

But this private property is strictly individual property, and his

---

[11] *Ibid.*, I, 131–136; 437–462; II, 249–299.
[12] *Le lois chapelier*, 1791, and other legislative acts.

meaning is carefully distinguished from all notions of corporate property, or associated property, or any subordination of the will of the proprietor to any custom, trade practice, or by-law. Hence if we use the term "individual property," we have the essential idea of what Smith meant by terms as seemingly divergent as "labor," "individual," "self-interest," "exchange," "productivity," "frugality," "commodity," and even "wealth of nations." His laborer is always an individual owner of corporeal property. His commodities are always individually owned. His Wealth of Nations is the sum of individual wealth. He thus had the double meaning of wealth as materials and their ownership. His self-interest is the free will of an unregulated individual owner. In short, the term "individual corporeal property," and not merely private property which may be corporate property, is Smith's idea of willingness of the individual to produce wealth and exchange it with others.

This meaning of property was taken over by the United States Supreme Court in interpreting the Fourteenth Amendment, but without Smith's limitation to individual property, or his exclusion of corporate property.[13] Later the Supreme Court went further, owing to its desire to bring modern business practices within the meaning of property and liberty protected against legislatures, and gave to freedom of transactions and price fixing themselves, the meaning of property. The court followed John Locke and Adam Smith in their ideas of God, Nature, and Reason; but it enlarged the meaning of property to include corporations, transactions, and even unincorporated associations, as well as the right to buy and sell at prices fixed in transactions. This extension in meaning is the basis of intangible property which is the basis of the idea of a going concern, whose life and death is the expectation of beneficial transactions. Such may be said to be the present constitutional meaning of property in the United States, not attained until after 1890. It includes not only Smith's individual self-interest, but, by including the right of association, which Smith excluded, the meaning of property becomes the corporate self-interest of a personified association of both stock holders and bond holders in the exclusive use of all objects that are scarce. Thus the meaning of property includes corporate liberty to withhold from others, corporate liberty to alienate to others, corporate liberty to acquire from others, and corporate liberty to combine with others. Each of these rights and liberties applies, not to physical things, but to their ownership, and the meaning of property becomes the expectation of transactions between individuals and concerns.

[13] Commons, John R., *Legal Foundations of Capitalism* (1924), 11 ff.

Hence the meaning of property enlarges from physical things to transactions and the expected repetition of transactions, and from use-values to scarcity values, expressed as prices. Smith did not include in his meaning of property and liberty either its transactions or its scarcity values. The latter were the evils of mercantilism. The former were already included in liberty. The theories and practices of mercantilism confronted him, based entirely on the fact of scarcity and the pretense of public utility. This pretense, employed as the justification of associated control of individual transactions, was hypocritical, he said, whereas perfect individual liberty to labor and to accumulate in one's own self-interest is the honest method of taking care of the public welfare. The principle of scarcity, for him, left economic theory to the arbitrariness of physical nature, or the political control of governments, or the monopolistic practices of guilds and corporations—all comprehended in his meaning of "mercantilism."

Against this false doctrine of what we may name Collective Scarcity, or Concerted Scarcity, he set up a doctrine of individual productivity, operating through, not the institution but the natural law, of individual property, uncontrolled by governments, corporations, customs, or any other associated action. So that his three main topics, productivity, thrift, and effective demand, turned on his idea of an individual will induced by perfect liberty to produce, to accumulate, and to exchange in a world of abundance. This became individual corporeal property, in opposition to any form of corporate, collective, or governmental property or control imposed by the policies of mercantilism or corporationism in a world of artificial scarcity.

Thus, in making his substitution of individual property for corporate property or collective control, Smith rejected Hume's realistic foundation of property on scarcity, but founded it, like Locke, on natural order, divine beneficence, and abundance. What he actually did, therefore, was to substitute Individual Scarcity arising out of the common law of property, for a collective scarcity arising out of the regulations and restrictions of sovereignty, or associations, or corporations, authorized and permitted by statutory law. He conceived property to be based, not on the *fact* of scarcity, nor on the *fact* of custom, but on his *justification* of ownership of the products of one's own labor. Like Locke he merged a fact with its justification.

But we draw the distinction between the object of property, the rights of property, and the justification of property, a distinction which Smith did not draw, as was inevitable, since his social philosophy was that of a moral order of the universe wherein a custom and its justification are inseparable. In short, his idea of Reason was, like that of John Locke, a union of Happiness and Justification.

If we make these distinctions, then Property as a corporeal fact is the exclusive holding of physical things because they are scarce; rights of property are the collective securities, compulsions, liberties, and exposures that go with this exclusive holding. These rights of property were justified by Smith on the foundation of labor. But property, itself—or rather assets, including corporeal, intangible, and incorporeal property, and distinguished from both rights and reasons—is simply the scarcity circumstances of individuals, determining, according to prevailing rules, their transactions with other individuals. Smith could not contemplate the later developments of collective property in any of its forms of corporations or concerted movements where individual liberty and individual property are subordinated to collective rules of concerns. While scarcity is ultimately, as Hume understood, a scarcity of food, clothing, shelter, and land, yet for the business man, working man, creditor, debtor, landlord, tenant, scarcity is a scarcity of proprietors. These proprietors are buyers, sellers, lenders, borrowers, landlords, tenants, who own, or have the prospect of owning, the food, clothing, shelter, and land. It is this proprietary scarcity for which prices are paid, and the price is not the price of the food, clothing, shelter, or land —it is the price paid for the right, as MacLeod afterwards asserted (1856),[14] to have the government exclude everybody else from the said food, clothing, shelter, or land. Scarcity, as an immediate fact of business and the subject-matter of economics, is scarcity of those who have legal control, not scarcity of goods. It is only for the wants of wild animals that scarcity is scarcity of food. For the wants of mankind scarcity is scarcity of actual and potential owners of food, willing to give orders to agents for the transfer of ownership and to laborers for the production of use-values.

This distinction runs counter to what was common sense in the time of Adam Smith. But modern absentee ownership, corporations, syndicates, unions, high financing, and wholesale marketing have changed what to Smith was common sense. Goods have physical dimensions, handled by laborers, but ownership has scarcity dimensions negotiated by business men. Business men are specialists in scarcity. The distinction was not apparent nor of great importance in a period of small manufacturers, merchants, and farmers, who did their own working, accumulating, and exchanging.

[14] Below, p. 397, MacLeod.

III. Labor-Pain, Labor-Power, Labor Saved

Smith went further than John Locke in the significance which he attributed to Labor. He not only derived property rights from the right of the free laborer to his own product, as did Locke, but he gave three meanings to Labor which he considered as equivalent, but which served afterwards to split economists into three schools, the Ricardo-Marxian School of Labor-Power, the Carey-Bastiat School of Labor Saved, and the neo-classical school of Labor-Pain.

These three meanings are found in his famous chapter on the real and nominal price of commodities:

"The real price of every thing, what every thing really costs to the man who wants to acquire it, is the toil and trouble of acquiring it. What every thing is really worth to the man who has acquired it, and who wants to dispose of it or exchange it for something else, is the toil and trouble which it can save to himself, and which it can impose upon other people. What is bought with money or with goods is purchased by labour, as much as what we acquire by the toil of our own body. That money or those goods indeed save us this toil. They contain the value of a certain quantity of labour which we exchange for what is supposed at the time to contain the value of an equal quantity. Labour was the first price, the original purchase-money that was paid for all things. It was not by gold or by silver, but by labour, that all the wealth of the world was originally purchased; and its value, to those who possess it, and who want to exchange it for some new productions, is precisely equal to the quantity of labour which it can enable them to purchase or command." [15]

Since these three meanings of Labor-Pain (toil and trouble), Labor-Power, and Labor Saved were deemed, by Smith, equivalent in magnitude, any one of them could be used as his measure of value. If Smith did not accept Hume's explanation of property on the ground of scarcity, and since he rejected all forms of collective control of supply as the artificial values of mercantilism, he found an automatic principle of restriction of output in Labor-Pain. Pain was his personification of scarcity.

Elie Halévy has suggested an ethical reason why Smith defined value as a function of labor instead of a function of scarcity.[16] Puffendorf, he says, had made the value of a thing a function of its fitness to satisfy wants, and its price a function of its scarcity.

---

[15] Smith, *An Inquiry into the Nature and Causes of the Wealth of Nations*, I, 32–33. It is significant that Georg Simmel (*Philosophie des Geldes*, 1900) builds upon the similar idea of "exchange" with Nature. The idea goes back to Sir William Petty in the Seventeenth Century; see *Palgrave's Dictionary of Political Economy*.

[16] Halévy, Elie, *La formation du radicalisme philosophique*, 3 vols. (1901), I, 172 ff.

Hutcheson, Smith's teacher, had made value a function of fitness to produce pleasure and of difficulty of acquisition, the latter looked upon by him as identical with scarcity. We note that, in the concise terminology of later economists who followed Bentham, these meanings would have been expressed as utility and scarcity. But we note also that it was John Locke whom Smith followed. Locke had in mind a juridical theory of the rights and liberties of property as against the arbitrary claims of British monarchs before the Revolution of 1689. He justified that right by a labor-power theory of productivity and a labor-pain theory of punishment for sin.

Smith agreed with this "natural and inviolable" right of property, but it should be noted that when he defined value as a function of labor-pain instead of a function of scarcity, he had already personified scarcity as this labor-pain, the equivalent of Hutcheson's "difficulty of attainment." Labor-pain is something that immediately recommends itself to the laborer who feels it—he does not feel scarcity and he does not feel his labor-power—he feels the labor-pain that increases with scarcity of natural resources and decreases with their abundance. If scarcity is the philosopher's after-thought, pain is Smith's human feeling.

Smith's two meanings of Labor [17] as Pain and Power became afterwards the ground of division between Malthus and Ricardo, Malthus using Smith's Labor-Pain and Ricardo using Smith's Labor-Power.[18] They are the subjective and materialistic meanings of the same personification of Scarcity. But the differences went much further in the course of a hundred years following Malthus and Ricardo. The materialistic meaning of Power became Power over Nature, which, when taken over by Karl Marx, led to the Russian Revolution; whereas we shall find that it leads merely to the unpersonified principle of Efficiency. The subjective meaning of Pain, at the hands of both Smith and Malthus, was a personification of Price; and when Money, Smith's "nominal" value, was substituted for Labor by later economists, money became, not a price paid to Nature, but a de-personified purchasing power which commands the services of other people and terminates in the institutional principle of a measure of Scarcity.

Since Smith included, in his personification of labor, nearly all of the concepts and principles on which succeeding schools divided, we necessarily anticipate their theories when we analyse Smith's meaning of Labor. Whitaker has pointed out that the early labor

---

[17] Smith's third meaning, "labor saved," became Carey's personification of scarcity in 1837. Below, p. 310, Value of Service.
[18] Below, p. 348, Ricardo and Malthus.

economists confused the three ideas of Cause of value, Regulator of value, and Measure of value, basing his distinction in part on Wieser's suggestion that Adam Smith put together two theories, a philosophical and an empirical theory, which contradict each other.[19] Smith's "philosophical" view, however, was not philosophy but personification. It consisted in personifying labor and nature; it was this personification that controlled his empirical view, leading him to the paradox that the actual historical development of European economic policy was exactly the opposite of the "natural order." The personified natural order was one which would have worked out in history along the principles of a divine reason which intended abundance of goods and happiness of man, and his so-called empirical and historical chapters were intended to show how man, by collective action, had inverted the natural order. His so-called "inductive" method was not inductive. It was a collection of illustrations designed to show that mankind had reversed the natural sequence of events. "Nature" began with liberty, security, equality, property. But man had begun with slavery, insecurity, inequality, and subordination of individuals to collective action.

So with Smith's personification of labor. Labor was conceived as carrying on an exchange with beneficent nature that works along with man; then the laborers exchange their products with each other, not according to the natural order, but under regulations of collective action in violation of the natural order. For these reasons his personification of labor and nature was a personification of all the bargaining, managerial, and rationing transactions which we have noted, but without any collective action whatever, which he considered artificial and contrary to nature. It was these personifications that made his theories an economics of man's relation to nature, instead of man's relation to his fellow-men.

In this way Smith's Cause of Value was the individual human will dealing with materials furnished by a divine will that was generous; his regulator of value was an idea of divine government laying down laws for dealings with nature and mankind, which would have been attained if collective action had not substituted its working rules for the divine order; and his labor, used as a measure of value, was a personification of what would have been a stable measure if money and collective action had not interfered.

It is impossible to separate the three ideas of cause, regulator, and measure, since, if a cause or regulator is to be described quan-

[19] Whitaker, A. C., "History and Criticism of the Labor Theory of Value in English Political Economy," *Columbia University Studies in History, Economics, and Public Law*, XIX, No. 2 (1904); Wieser, Friedrich von, *Natural Value* (tr. 1893), xxvii.

titatively, the description can be made only in terms of measurement. Modern physical science has abandoned the ideas both of cause and regulator and contents itself with repetition and measurement. Under the influence of mathematics, this also is becoming the attitude in economics, mistakenly we think.

For it is evident that cause and regulation cannot be eliminated from economics if it is to be considered a science of human volitions. Cause, regulation, and even measurement, are ideas derived from human purpose, which physical sciences rightly attempt to eliminate. But if economics deals with the transactions of human beings, then these purposes directed to the future are the subject-matter of investigation. Locke, Quesnay, and Smith were not mistaken in the search for causes—their mistake was in their personification of nature and labor as the cause, regulator, and measurer, where they should have sought it in transactions, customs, and working rules of collective action. They placed *causation* in the intentions of divine Providence, whereas it should have been placed, as by Hume and Peirce, in the intentions of human beings. They sought for their *regulator* an ultimate or fundamental cause, which with Locke, Quesnay, and Smith was the natural law of a benevolent universe. And they sought for a *measure* in terms of this ultimate, natural cause, namely labor and nature, guided by divine beneficence; whereas measurement is a purely artificial and collective device of custom and law constructing arbitrary units by which the universe and human activity can be reduced to the language of number.

1. *Cause of Value*

"The word Value, it is to be observed," said Smith, "has two different meanings, and sometimes expresses the utility of some particular object, and sometimes the power of purchasing other goods which the possession of that object conveys. The one may be called 'value in use'; the other, 'value in exchange.' The things which have the greatest value in use have frequently little or no value in exchange; and on the contrary, those which have the greatest value in exchange have frequently little or no value in use. Nothing is more useful than water: but it will purchase scarce anything; scarce anything can be had in exchange for it. A diamond, on the contrary, has scarce any value in use; but a very great quantity of other goods may frequently be had in exchange for it." [20]

For these reasons Smith rejected use-value from economic theory, as did his successors, and considered that economic science had to

[20] Smith. *An Inquiry into the Nature and Causes of the Wealth of Nations*, I, 30.

do only with exchange-value. But modern scientific management has brought back use-value into economics, and Smith must have had a different meaning of use-value which led him to reject it. We find, indeed, that Smith actually employed the idea of use-value in all his reasonings. In fact, his whole philosophy was based on a theory of use-value, which we proceed to analyze by the various ways in which he formulated it.

This requires, as we have already intimated, an analysis of his term Value into its two components, use-value and scarcity-value.[21] For value, as we know from modern statistical requirements, is a quantity of use-value, measured by its own physical units, *times* its scarcity-value per unit measured by money. For example, the *value* of a quantity of that *use-value* named wheat is the number of bushels *times* the price, or scarcity-value per bushel.[22] Since Smith approached his analysis with the presuppositions of divine abundance and human sinfulness, we shall find in these presuppositions his meanings of use-value and scarcity-value.

(1) **Cause of Use-Value.**—We have used the term labor-pain as equivalent to Smith's "toil and trouble," and distinguished it from labor-power. Smith did not develop separately a theory either of labor-power or use-value, because his theory of abundance flowing from the beneficence of nature and his theory of labor-pain as the equivalent of Locke's penalty for sin, did not call for a theory of power to overcome nature's resistance, as was required by Ricardo when he afterwards contemplated the niggardliness of nature. Yet, by examining Smith's theories of production and exchange we may infer what he means by labor-power as the cause of use-value. Thus inferred, his idea of use-value was John Locke's dualistic idea of the mind within copying the world without. The physical world without was use-value. The psychological world within was happiness.

But Smith's quantity of labor-pain was, for him, equivalent to a quantity of labor-power. Consequently the quantity of product created by labor-power was accompanied by an equivalent quantity of pain within. We may name this equivalence, which is the copy theory of Locke, Psychological Parallelism, to be distinguished alike from what we shall name Functional Psychology and Transactional Psychology. Psychological Parallelism follows Locke's idea of the mind within copying the world without.

We have drawn four diagrams (Charts 2, 3, 4, 5) to illustrate what we conceive to be Adam Smith's original value formula and the formulae of succeeding schools of economists. Each of them

---

[21] See below, p. 390, for third component, Futurity.
[22] Cf. Fisher, Irving, *Nature of Capital and Income* (1906), 13 ff.

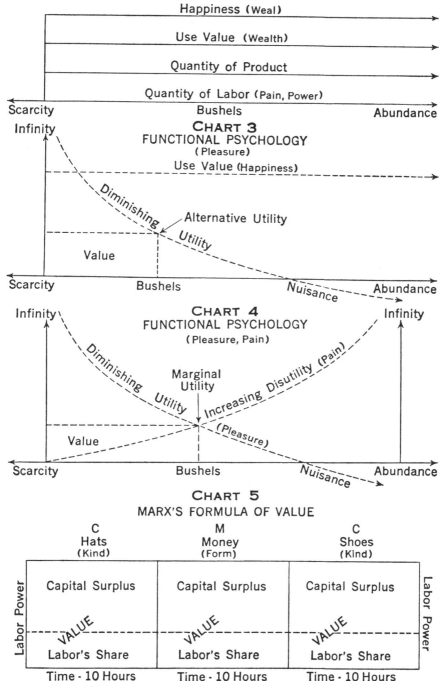

CHART 2
PSYCHOLOGICAL PARALLELISM
(Smith, Ricardo)

Happiness (Weal)

Use Value (Wealth)

Quantity of Product

Quantity of Labor (Pain, Power)

Scarcity   Bushels   Abundance

CHART 3
FUNCTIONAL PSYCHOLOGY
(Pleasure)

Infinity

Use Value (Happiness)

Diminishing Utility

Alternative Utility

Value

Scarcity   Bushels   Nuisance   Abundance

CHART 4
FUNCTIONAL PSYCHOLOGY
(Pleasure, Pain)

Infinity   Infinity

Diminishing Utility

Marginal Utility

Increasing Disutility (Pain)

(Pleasure)

Value

Scarcity   Bushels   Nuisance   Abundance

CHART 5
MARX'S FORMULA OF VALUE

C Hats (Kind)	M Money (Form)	C Shoes (Kind)
Capital Surplus	Capital Surplus	Capital Surplus
VALUE	VALUE	VALUE
Labor's Share	Labor's Share	Labor's Share
Time - 10 Hours	Time - 10 Hours	Time - 10 Hours

Labor Power   Labor Power

will be described more fully in its proper place, but all of them rest upon the same economic concept of scarcity-abundance. This base-line, for purpose of illustration, may be said to be a scarcity or abundance of the commodity wheat, measured by bushels. As a point on the base-line moves to the right, indicated by the arrow, the quantity of wheat increases towards abundance. As the point moves towards the left the quantity of wheat moves towards scarcity. Towards the right abundance increases; towards the left scarcity "increases"; so that abundance is diminishing scarcity, and scarcity is diminishing abundance.

An increase in the quantity of product, according to Smith and Ricardo (Chart 2), is an increase in the quantity of use-value and this is paralleled by an increase in the happiness of mankind. The assumption back of it is that human wants in general are unlimited, and Smith rejected use-value because, for him, it meant the un-limited *subjective* Happiness and not its parallel *objective* use-value.

But this *objective* use-value is identical with the quantity of product, for product is none other than a quantity of use-value. Hence an increase in quantity of product, which, for him, was an equal increase in the quantity of labor-pain or labor-power, was also an equal increase in the quantity of use-value in its *subjective* meaning of Happiness. This psychological parallelism was not in-deed exactly parallel, for happiness was also increased gratuitously by divine beneficence.

Chart 2 is intended to show how simple it was for Ricardo, forty years after Smith, to reject Smith's labor-pain and use only Smith's labor-power. The change involved, indeed, a profound change in the ultimate philosophy of Nature, from nature's divine abundance to nature's overpopulation and niggardliness, introduced by Malthus in 1798. But the change did not involve any change in the parallelism of use-value and happiness. An increase in abundance is an increase in the quantity of labor-power required to produce it; this is the same as an increase in the quantity of physical products whose attribute, the use-value of the wheat, increases at the same rate, which is also the rate at which happiness of mankind is augmented.

The reason for this parallelism is evident, as may be illustrated by comparison with Chart 3. Neither Smith nor Ricardo had the concept of diminishing utility *per unit*, which we name functional psychology, since it depends on scarcity and abundance. This aspect of psychology was discovered independently after the middle of the century by Gossen, Jevons, Walras, and Menger. Now it turns out that subjective happiness (pleasure) is not unlimited (for a given product) but it diminishes *per unit* with an increase in abundance and increases *per unit* with an "increase" of scarcity. In the direction of abundance it may become a "nuisance," like a flood of water that drowns the recipient. In the direction of scarcity water may become the "infinite" utility of life or death on a waterless desert.

This functional psychology was not known to Smith or Ricardo, and therefore no meaning of use-value could be given except the meaning of happiness in general. But nevertheless Smith had a meaning for use-value and its parallel happiness, none other than his "wealth of nations." In confirmation of this meaning of use-value we cite Edwin Cannan.

Cannan has pointed out that the term wealth is etymologically but a longer form of the word "weal," [23] and that wealth in the older sense signified the kind of welfare that is "so dependent on the possession or periodical receipt of certain external objects, such as bread, meat, clothes, or money, that the word came to be applied to those objects themselves as well as the state of body and mind produced by access to them." When Adam Smith adopted the word wealth, its meaning had come to be this external object instead of the subjective weal, and "had become so common that lexicographers forgot to mention the older sense." [24]

This agrees with what we find in the Sixteenth and Seventeenth Centuries, culminating in John Locke. Common weal and Common wealth were then used interchangeably as economic quantities, and each had also the political meaning of a government.[25] When it came to Adam Smith, his rejected term "value-in-use" had the similar meaning, weal and wealth—weal, the subjective use-value of happiness or welfare, paralleling the objective use-value or wealth, as indicated in our Chart 2.

But Cannan also points out that when it came to Adam Smith, Ricardo, and all the physical economists, except Lauderdale, wealth had come also to mean exchange-value [26]—a fatal extension of meaning, for it was this threefold meaning of value, as weal, wealth, and exchange, that became the paradoxical meaning as understood by Proudhon, Marx, the American Greenbackers, and in fact by all

---

[23] Chart 2.

[24] Cannan, Edwin, *A History of the Theories of Production and Distribution in English Political Economy from 1776 to 1848* (1894), 1, 2.

[25] The interchangeability of these meanings is evident in *A Discourse of the Common Weal of This Realm of England* (probably written in 1549—first published in 1581. Reprinted and edited from the MSS. by Elizabeth Lamond, 1893). Commonly attributed to W. S., unknown.

[26] Cannan, *op. cit.*, 5 ff. Lauderdale, Earl of, *An Inquiry into the Nature and Origin of Public Wealth* (1804).

paper money theorists who demanded a supply of money equal to the abundance of values (use-values) produced or owned.[27]

From the foregoing we conclude that, parallel to the psychological use-value of Smith and Ricardo, was a physical use-value, measured by physical units of bushels, gallons, etc., equivalent to his meaning of Social Wealth, or Wealth of Nations Its peculiarity is that it does not diminish *per unit* with abundance, nor increase *per unit* with scarcity, contrasted with the later meaning of diminishing utility which diminishes *per unit* with abundance and increases *per unit* with scarcity.   Use-value is abundance-value, but functional value is scarcity-value.   In short, use-value was Smith's subjective meaning of what he meant objectively by goods and wealth, which increased with abundance.

If so, then use-value, or goods, may be described as a kind of value which changes with physical and cultural differences, but not with supply or demand.   The physical differences are differences in kind, as shoes or wheat; differences in quality, as spring wheat or winter wheat, grade 1, grade 2; differences in deterioration, depletion, or exhaustion, or wear and tear.   The cultural variables we distinguish as Civilization Values, since they are changes, not in supply or demand, but in style or fashion, religion or morals, and in the inventions or discoveries of civilization which change the objects of desire from arrows to dynamite, from horses to autos, from paintings to movies.   The diminishing use-value of these civilization values is to be distinguished as Obsolescence, and its increasing use-value as Invention.

In other words, use-value is a physical and civilization attribute, not a scarcity attribute of things or persons; but, like scarcity, it also has a psychological language.[28]   Its psychological value depends upon its physical qualities but not upon their quantity; upon happiness and not scarcity; upon the existing civilization and not on supply and demand.   Hence use-value should be defined in the same way as the color, or shape, or weight, or bulk, or volume, of objects. Use-value has indeed quantitative dimensions, but these are physical quantities, with their own units of physical measurement, such as yards of cloth, cords of wood, kilowatt-hours of electricity.[29]

[27] Below, p. 591, A World Pay Community, on Kellogg.

[28] Modern economists, influenced by the hedonic economists, usually read back into the early meanings of use-value their meaning of diminishing utility.   By so doing they give a double meaning to utility, the early meaning which does *not* diminish, *per unit* with increasing abundance, and the later meaning which *does* diminish, *per unit*, with increasing abundance.   The later meaning, we hold, was not known to the classical economists nor to their follower, Karl Marx.

[29] Böhm-Bawerk, E. von, in *The Positive Theory of Capital* (tr. 1891), eliminates these "technical" relations from political economy, whereas in them we find the concepts of efficiency and managerial transactions.

It will be seen that in this meaning of physical use-value, while it has both objective and psychological language and is therefore the idea of a relation between things that satisfy human wants and the wants themselves, yet there is no idea of the actual dependence of the individual here and now upon having a greater or less quantity of a particular use-value. It is John Locke's dualistic idea, which we name Psychological Parallelism, but it also is the similar two-language hypothesis of weal and wealth—weal, the psychological language of happiness of which abundance of wealth is the economic language.

Smith was concerned with the differences in the exchange-values of *different* commodities, and not with the increase of pain required to produce the *same* commodity under different conditions or in different quantities. The amount of pain (or its equivalent power) required to produce a bushel of wheat is greater than the amount required to produce a bushel of potatoes. Hence two or three bushels of potatoes exchange for one bushel of wheat. Ricardo had the same exchange-value in mind when he changed from labor-pain to Smith's equivalent labor-power. Wheat contained two or three times as much labor-power as potatoes and this accounted for the exchange-ratio of wheat and potatoes.

A different problem came up after the hedonic economists had noticed the diminishing utility *per unit* of an increasing quantity of the *same* commodity (Chart 3). If the utility *per unit* diminishes as supply increases, does not also the dis-utility, or pain *per unit*, increase with the increase in fatigue required to produce an increase in supply? This oversight had been a defect of the Austro-hedonic school. They asserted that, with the substitution of machinery for labor, we had passed out of the "pain economy" of primitive times which Smith wrote about, into a "pleasure economy." But pain still remains and increases with an increase in the effort required to produce an increasing output of the same commodity. So the classical economics came back as neo-classicism, whose schematic formula may be shown as in Chart 4. If there is no supply at all, then utility (not use-value) may rise, in some cases like water, to infinity, and there is obviously no labor-pain in producing it. But if labor increases, then the intensity of the pain of labor *per unit* increases as the pleasure *per unit* decreases.

But trees do not grow into the sky. At some point, say the point of marginal utility, the supply stops increasing because the diminishing pleasure equals the increasing pain.

Hence there are two versions of marginal utility—the Austro-hedonic and the neo-classical. In the painless economy of the former the diminishing pleasure of the one commodity reaches a descending point where the pleasure of an alternative commodity exceeds it; consequently an equilibrium is reached by choosing among all diminishing utilities of all commodities (Chart 3). The point of choosing between alternatives sets the margins equally for all and becomes the point of equilibrium. This version appears, at the hands of Böhm-Bawerk in 1890, as the doctrine of "utility cost," or the marginal gain obtained by choosing the better of the optional alternatives.[30]

But the marginal utility in the neo-classical version is the point of balance where the pain of continuing production balances the pleasure of continuing consumption of the same commodity (Chart 4).

Thus at the end of the Nineteenth Century Smith's parallelism had become functional psychology by changing the meaning of use-value to diminishing utility and the meaning of pain to increasing dis-utility. The concept of Value remains, as it had been, a two-dimensional concept, this time the marginal-utility, or scarcity-value, *times* the quantity of product, or use-value, where it had previously been labor-pain *times* the quantity of use-value.

There was another reason why Smith could find no place for value-in-use in his economic theorizing, namely, personal services. These are apparently intangible and disappear as soon as performed. But they certainly are useful, and their usefulness continues after the service is performed. Smith and his followers contented themselves by distinguishing "productive" from "unproductive" labor. The physician or surgeon, the lawyer, statesman or politician, the minister or priest, the teacher, the musician or actor, the scientist, the domestic servant, the housewife, were "unproductive" because the usefulness of their labor did not appear in a commodity which could be saved and sold on the markets, or exchanged directly for other commodities or for the labor of others. The only way in which the *value* of such services could be measured was in terms of money, as wages and salaries, or in terms of the commodities directly exchanged for them. For this reason labor itself could be treated only as a commodity, whose value was its exchange-value. Personal services had exchange-value, but their use-value appeared only in the happiness of other people and there were no units of measurement, like tons and yards, which could measure happiness.

It was different with labor "embodied" in a commodity. Labor gave to that commodity an added value, but since even its "use-

---

[30] Below, p. 307, Cost of Service and Cost of Product.

value" was looked upon as psychological, the added value could be measured only as an added exchange-value.

A hundred and fifty years of economic theorizing has puzzled over the problem of giving a decent status to these personal services. If they are use-values how can we measure them except by the dollar? But the dollar measures their scarcity-value and not their use-value. It measures their supply and demand, or their bargaining power, or the power of custom, but not their usefulness. This century and a half of theorizing has introduced various concepts and devices by which the usefulness of personal services may be assimilated to the usefulness of "productive" labor in a general concept of use-value. One of the concepts is the "average-man-hours" introduced by Karl Marx and given precision in the theories of scientific management. Another is the concept of "overhead" labor, measured by man-hours, which does not add use-value to any particular commodity but adds it to all commodities produced by a going concern. This concept of overhead is a special case of the modern formula of the part-whole relationship. Another is the concept of the mental labor of scientists, inventors, and engineers, which, looked upon as "overhead" labor for a particular establishment, turns out to be the most productive of all kinds of labor, since it enlarges the capacity to create an output of use-values more than all other human abilities combined. Along with this is what may be distinguished as the national overhead labor of teachers, ministers, priests, statesmen, politicians, policemen, et al., whose work as a whole enlarges the capacity of the nation as a whole to increase the output of use-value, regardless of the compensations they receive, whether from taxes or any other source.

Another concept is the analysis of the meanings of the term use-value itself as the fourfold meaning of elementary, form, time, and place "utilities." [31] The elementary utilities are the forces of nature which must be utilized, and their utilization is the changes in form, time, or place—how, when, and where needed—regardless of their exchange-values or prices or wages paid. The so-called personal services of physicians, surgeons, domestic servants, housewives, even musicians and actors, are the addition of form, time, and place uses to the otherwise useless elements of nature. They increase directly the physical use-values of things, but the compensations received for these services are in the entirely different fields of bargaining power, custom, scarcity, opportunity, alternatives, and all the circumstances of economic dependence or independence at the time and place when and where the services are rendered.

[31] *I.e.*, use-values.

It was exactly this discrepancy between service to others and power over others, between production and acquisition, between use-value and scarcity-value, which split the various schools of economists, but which Smith left open on account of his preoccupation with the one issue of Individualism versus Mercantilism.

Lacking these refinements introduced during the succeeding century, what was Adam Smith's concept of the cause of use-value? It was anything which increases abundance. There were, with Smith, five factors which increased this abundance, distinguished from labor-pain which restricts abundance; namely, Labor-Power, Division of Labor, Exchange, Saving, and the Beneficence of Nature in agriculture.

Karl Marx afterwards elaborated the kind of labor-power implied by Locke and Smith, as manual, mental, and managerial power. If we attempt to give them further precision, we should reduce them to terms of motion, in which case manual power means the power to move one's body or other physical bodies by the use of nerves, muscles, and bones. It is properly physical power, rather than "manual" power. It is the physical power to move things, or self, or other persons by direct impact. It is physical force, and may be violence.

But mental power is power to move things indirectly at a distance in space or future time, by means of moving other bodies directly, such that the latter set in motion physical forces of their own. Tools, machines, prime movers, airplanes, are caused by mental power.

Managerial power, likewise in terms of motion, is power to move other people to move things and persons by their physical, mental, and personality power.

Taken together, these three aspects of power are more properly to be named man-power, and such was indeed the meaning of Labor as employed by Locke, Smith, and Marx, for their laborers were evidently physical, mental, and managerial laborers. It is man-power that increases the abundance of use-values and the wealth of nations.

But the greatest productivity of this man-power arises from Division of Labor, which permits specialization and requires exchange. Smith's entire work is a commentary on the increased productivity through the many varieties of division of labor, beginning with shop division, then proceeding to industrial, territorial, and international division of labor, all of which require the exchange of products.

Consequently Exchange-Value is looked upon by Smith as the "form" that labor-power must take if it produces, by specialization, the largest amount of use-value. If labor-power is a cause of use-value, it can operate only within an environment of civilization that determines the kind and form which its product of use-value will take.

It was Karl Marx who afterwards formulated these implications of cause, kind, and form contained in Smith's idea of use-value. (See Chart 5, p. 175.) The *cause* or "substance," in the terminology of Locke and Marx, is Labor-Power. The *kinds* of use-value are determined by the physical and civilization conditions, such as hats and shoes. The *form* of value, with Smith, took the two forms, productive and unproductive labor, the former being the cause of products destined for exchange, the latter of products for immediate consumption. Both were useful, but productive labor created use-value in the form of exchange-value, while unproductive labor created it in the form for immediate consumption.

Hence the form in which labor was productive, reading back from Marx, was the form of exchange-value imposed by division of labor, and the form in which it was unproductive was the form of consumption goods which had no exchange-value. The former is what is meant by a "commodity." A commodity is a use-value in the form of exchange-value.[32] Whatever facilitates exchange-value, without cost, augments production, and, for this reason, the banking system and paper money, which substitute a costless medium for costly gold, thereby augment production.[33]

Herein Smith differed from Quesnay. Quesnay belonged to an agricultural community whose prosperity, for him, turned on abundance of agricultural products at high exchange-values. But Smith, like Locke, belonged to a country both agricultural and manufacturing whose prosperity turned on the exchange of agricultural for manufactured products. Quesnay pictured the situation as a flow of commodities; Smith pictured it as a territorial and occupational division of labor.

Admitting, said Smith, that the revenue of every country consists in "the quantity of subsistence which their industry could procure to them," yet by "means of trade and manufactures, a greater quantity of subsistence can be annually imported into a particular country than what its own lands, in the actual state of their cultivation, could afford. The inhabitants of a town, though they frequently possess no lands of their own, yet draw to themselves by their industry such a quantity of the rude produce of the lands of other people as supplies them, not only with

[32] Cf. Marx, Karl, *Capital* (tr. Kerr edition, 3 vols. 1909, original 1867), I, Chap. 1. Below, p. 251, Efficiency and Scarcity.
[33] Smith, Adam, *An Inquiry into the Nature and Causes of the Wealth of Nations*, I, 279–283.

the materials of their work, but with the fund of their subsistence. What a town always is with regard to the country in its neighborhood, one independent state or country may frequently be with regard to other independent states or countries. . . . A small quantity of manufactured produce purchases a great quantity of rude produce. . . . While, on the contrary, a country without trade and manufactures is generally obliged to purchase, at the expense of a great part of its rude produce, a very small part of the manufactured produce of other countries." [34]

Yet these low exchange-values of agricultural products and high exchange-values of manufactures were not oppressive to the farmers, as Quesnay had contended, provided there were no artificial scarcities intervening. They were the automatic and therefore natural exchange-values that followed the division of labor and the enlarged productivity of labor through specialization and exchange. If the farmers had to do their own manufacturing, then their crops would be reduced in volume. It was their increased productivity, through territorial division of labor, that made the low exchange-values of their products beneficial to the farmers themselves. They made up by enlarged productivity more than they lost by low prices. Smith's excellent historical research respecting trade between town and country, between nations, and between nations and their colonies, was designed to demonstrate the reciprocal benefits obtained when exchange-values were permitted to conform to the differences in productivity of labor.

But this was a change in the meaning of productivity. Quesnay had made productivity turn on the *bulk* of commodities having exchange-value—and only the vital forces of nature can increase the bulk. But Smith made the meaning of productivity turn on the *use-value* of commodities having exchange-value—and labor-power adds use-values to the raw material produced by nature, without enlarging the bulk. Hence it was their differences as to whether wealth consisted in the bulk of commodities having exchange-value, or in the accrual of use-values upon the bulk, that actually caused Smith and Quesnay to agree in part but to differ considerably in their meanings of productive and unproductive labor. Productive laborers, for Smith, were those who produced for exchange with others; Quesnay's productivity of Nature was also production for exchange. Unproductive laborers were those who produced for *consumption* by self or others, and this, for Quesnay, made nature also unproductive. To be productive for Quesnay, Nature must increase the bulk of things having *exchange-value;* but, for Smith, Labor-

[34] *Ibid.*, II, 175.

Power must increase the *usefulness* of things having exchange-value.[35]

Thus, productive labor for Smith was that which produced use-value in the form of exchange-value. For him, only exchange-values constituted the wealth of nations, because these values existed only where division of labor was enlarging the abundance of use-values having exchange-value.

But the *form* of exchange-value has no significance except as it is a form that increases the abundance of use-values. Smith's idea of exchange-value furnished him with his most important discovery in combating mercantilism: the distinction between effective demand and money demand. Effective demand consists in the production of goods for exchange, not in the possession of money, and this production is not effective as demand except in the form of exchange-value. The Mercantilists had argued that an increase of demand could be secured by increasing the supply of money. But Smith showed that money distributed itself to nations and sections only in proportion to the production of goods (use-values) for exchange. It is not money that creates effective demand for labor and commodities—it is commodities. And commodities are created, not by money, but by labor. It is productive labor, then, producing use-value in the form of exchange-value, that is the effectual demand for other productive labor; hence exchange-value is more than mere form of physical things—it is the inducement that all classes of productive laborers offer to each other to increase their productivity. But when we come to this meaning of inducement, we have shifted the meaning to money prices, which Smith excluded.[36]

Smith's idea of effective demand turned on his Division of Labor, which eliminated both money and diminishing utility. It was division of labor that converted Quesnay's idea of circulation into a relation of "effectual demand." Quesnay could not construct such an idea in terms of nature. He had two circulations—money in one direction, goods in the opposite direction. But Smith eliminated money in his meaning of exchange-value. According to Quesnay the merchants and manufacturers merely extracted quantities arbitrarily, through the privileges of mercantilism, from the circulation of goods as they went along. But, according to Smith, the manufacturers, who accumulated use-values of commodities instead of consuming them, created thereby an effective demand, that is, power to command in exchange not only other commodities but also labor. The augmentation by labor of use-value having the form of ex-

---

[35] *Ibid.*, I, 30 ff.; II, 161 ff.
[36] Below, p. 555, The Business Law of Supply and Demand.

change-value becomes a demand for labor itself and for other use-values produced by labor. And, since it is use-values instead of masses of materials that consumers want, it follows that the total demand for labor is the total augmentation of use-values accumulated by capitalists and offered to laborers as subsistence and maintenance in exchange for the further use-values produced by them. Both the effective demand for labor and the effective demand for other products, including of course foreign imports, are limited by the quantity of use-values accumulated by capitalists and available for exchange. The use-value that is consumed in the instant of its production leaves behind no such power of command, or effective demand, as Smith also named it. This use-value has passed out of existence, and of course its exchange-value, or power to induce commodities to be produced by others, has disappeared with it. But that which is created in a transportable and cumulative form of use-value becomes an effective demand for labor and other commodities. It actually comes out upon the markets and can be seen performing a demand; whereas that which is consumed, but leaves no equivalent reproduction appearing upon a market, is unproductive.

Thus the term "productive," as used by Smith, is equivalent to effective demand, and the term "unproductive" means failure to create effective demand. Hence it is not money but commodities, not scarcity but abundance, not distribution but production, that creates effectual demand for commodities and for labor; and it does so only in the form of exchange-value.[37]

From Smith's idea of effective demand was derived the conclusion, later perfected by James Mill, that there could be no such thing as "overproduction."[38] It was a logical conclusion from the concept of use-value which does not diminish per unit with increasing abundance. For Smith it would also have been an invidious reflection on divine beneficence if there could be overproduction in a predetermined world of harmony and abundance. Not until diminishing utility was discovered and money restored to economic theory; indeed, not until Malthus had previously created a new idea of God, did it become possible to offer a rational explanation of starvation by unemployment in the midst of abundance.

It was this idea of effective demand, through exchange-value, division of labor, and productive labor, that furnished to Smith his other great cause of abundance of use-values—Thrift, Parsimony, Saving. Here Smith followed Turgot,[39] and established for a hun-

[37] Smith, Adam, *An Inquiry into the Nature and Causes of the Wealth of Nations*, I, 313 ff.
[38] Below, p. 348, Ricardo and Malthus.
[39] Below, p. 487, Capital and Capitals.

dred and fifty years of economic science the physical and legal equivalents of the process of saving.[40]

The legal equivalent of saving is private property. The physical equivalent, according to Smith, consists in preserving, even for a few days, the output of labor and agriculture. The saving is not saving money, it is saving use-values. The merchant saves in the form of commodities. The farmer saves in the form of vegetables, grain, and livestock. The manufacturer saves in the form of machinery and commodities. While the legal equivalent is ownership, the physical equivalents are, not money, but commodities, improvements, machinery. And these are saved because they or their expected products have exchange-value and therefore effectual demand for other use-values in the form of goods and services.

After Ricardo, economists looked upon production as the effort to overcome the resistance of nature and yield any service that satisfies wants. But Smith had covered that idea in his concept of willingness induced by property. His "productive" labor, therefore, was that labor which created a vendible commodity which could be saved and could thereafter constitute an effective demand to the extent of its use-value. The other kind of labor-power was "unproductive," in that it created only a service that perished at once; or, if it were a physical product, it perished at home without coming out where it could be effective upon the markets. His use-values were inventories for future exchange without the intervention of money. Production, for him, was not therefore the production of mere use-value. A use-value for him was an attribute that existed physically and could be accumulated and passed on in exchange. Production was the production of exchange-value—a paradox it may seem, but not a paradox when we consider that it was not scarcity nor money that concerned Smith most. What concerned him was willingness to create an abundance of use-values for the sake of their effective demand for the commodities and services of other nations.[41] This was to be accomplished by means of productivity, thrift, and exchange, instead of by either the ineffectual demand of mere wishes or the mere purchasing power of money. Commodities, for Smith, are purchased by commodities, not by money.

Productive labor was thus the production of effective demand, but unproductive labor perished without leaving anything that the

---

[40] This reasoning was based on the elimination of money. It was a concept of physical saving, not pecuniary investment or debt. Assumptions later made of the identity of physical saving and pecuniary investment were called in question by the followers of Wicksell. Below, p. 598, From Marginal Productivity to Capital Yield.

[41] It was this paradox which occasioned the controversy between Proudhon and Marx. Below, p. 366.

capitalist could save for the sake of its effective demand. Hence it is that the technological problems of production, efficiency, labor-power, in the several later meanings of diminishing and increasing returns, balancing the factors, labor management, and the credit and money problems of inflation and deflation, did not emerge for Smith. Both production and accumulation, for him, were simply the outcome of willingness to work, save, exchange, and thus increase the abundance of use-values—with money as a colorless medium.

It was this doctrine of Thrift that marked a leading distinction between Quesnay and Smith. Accumulation with Quesnay was accumulation of physical quantities produced by nature, but accumulation for Smith was accumulation of use-values added to these physical quantities by labor. One was conservation of natural resources, the other was thrift. Hence, while Smith agreed with Quesnay respecting the unproductiveness of all domestic servants, all officers of government, all sovereigns, professional classes, musicians, armies, navies, etc., whose work was admittedly useful and had exchange-value, yet Smith's reason for considering them unproductive was different from Quesnay's. The work of these classes, for Smith, "perished in the very instant of performance" and "therefore could not be saved." For Quesnay, their work did not add to the bulk of physical things, but actually deducted the amount of their exchange-value from that bulk. Quesnay applied the same reasoning to "artificers, manufacturers, and merchants." They were unproductive because they did not add to physical bulk, but deducted from it. But for Smith their work was productive because it did not perish in the instant of performance, and because it produced an additional use-value having an additional exchange-value equal to the use-values which they consumed. Accumulation consists in saving this additional use-value in the form of commodities which can be exchanged, to bring back equivalent use-values.[42]

Nature, for example, produces fifty bushels of wheat from one bushel of seed, but when that wheat comes back from the miller in the shape of flour, the farmer finds that he gives up several bushels of wheat in exchange for the flour made from one bushel. Quesnay stigmatized this deduction from the farmer's wheat as the exchange-value of the unproductive labor of the miller. Smith dignified it as the exchange-value of an additional use-value contributed by the productive labor of the miller. With Quesnay the miller was unproductive because his consumption of wheat reduced the bulk of

---

[42] Smith, Adam, *An Inquiry into the Nature and Causes of the Wealth of Nations*, I, 314; II, 173-175. As previously stated we use the term use-value as the equivalent of Smith's "wealth."

wheat on the markets. With Smith the miller was productive because the augmented use-value of flour given to the farmer in exchange for his wheat was equal to the lesser use-value of the wheat given by the farmer to the miller. The miller saved the additional use-value of flour above the use-value of wheat, to the extent that he sold it to the farmer, instead of consuming it himself. Thus his labor is productive if it produces use-value to be exchanged with the farmer.

Thus, Smith's doctrine of saving is inseparable from his doctrines of labor-power, division of labor, exchange-value, and use-value. Quesnay's process of circulation was itself, for Smith, a process of saving instead of a process of deduction from the bulk of goods, since it was a process of augmenting use-value in the form of augmented exchange-value, which, when thus augmented, was "stocked up and stored to be employed if necessary upon some other occasion." It is not bulk of things that is saved—it is accruals of use-values having exchange-values.

It is thus the saving of use-values having exchange-values that distinguishes not only productive labor from unproductive labor, but also productive consumption from unproductive consumption, accumulation from consumption, wealth from poverty, and effective demand from wishes or money. Productive labor is that which, through saving, accumulates use-values having exchange-value. Productive consumption of use-values is that which is replaced by at least an equivalent accumulation of use-values from productive labor. This accumulation is merely saving, while wealth is abundance, not merely of use-values, but of use-values having exchange-values in the form of abundance of commodities, improvements, and machinery that are saved. Effective demand arises only when wishes are backed by commodities which have an exchange-value, and this is the meaning of Smith's "productive labor."

It is to be taken for granted that ultimately these accumulations of commodities will themselves produce consumable use-values, and that these improvements and machinery will enlarge the volume of use-values and therefore of exchange-values. But these final use-values, whose abundance brings happiness, will be psychological when they arrive and as divergent as the tastes of consumers. Hence Smith's exclusion of use-value from economics. Meanwhile, the important value is their stored up use-values having the form of exchange-value, that is, their enduring power of effective demand. Augment the quantities of use-values in the form of exchange-values, and the ultimate consumers' use-values may be left to individual psychology.

This concept is quite the same as the common-sense ideas still prevailing. The "productive" labor of a nation is, even to this day, considered to be that which produces commodities having exchange-value on the markets, while that which produces for the home or farm is unproductive.

But there is a difference from Smith's notion of exchange. Smith, like Quesnay, excluded money from his meaning of exchange-value. Money was merely an unstable measure of value. But modern life and debts turn on sales for money. It is inflation and deflation of assets and liabilities. Its vagaries pay no attention to use-values, labor-pain, or labor-power. The elimination of money as something superficial left orthodox economics unable to deal with modern economy.

Yet Smith retained a curious remnant from Quesnay, a remnant retained also by modern common sense and "agricultural economists," a relapse from the deeper insight of John Locke. Locke had figured that Labor, in agriculture, produced as much as 99 per cent of the total value, and Nature only one per cent. Quesnay had figured that Nature, in agriculture, produced 100 per cent of the total value produced by the nation, and Labor produced nothing. Smith, just because he excluded use-value from his theory of economics, as afterwards included by Ricardo,[43] failed to see that it is Labor, or rather man-power, that alone produces use-value. Likewise, because he carried the assumption of Nature's beneficence and abundance, contrary to Malthus and Ricardo, he did not fully distinguish between the use-value produced by man-power and the physical bulk produced by Nature

"In agriculture," he said, "nature labours along with man; and though her labour costs no expense, its produce has its value, as well as that of the most expensive workmen. . . . Rent . . . may be considered as the produce of those powers of nature, the use of which the landlord lends to the farmer. . . . No equal quantity of productive labour employed in manufactures can ever occasion so great a reproduction. In them nature does nothing; man does all. . . . The capital employed in agriculture, therefore, not only puts into motion a greater quantity of productive labour than any equal capital employed in manufactures, but in proportion too to the quantity of productive labour which it employs, it adds a much greater value to the annual produce of the land and labour of the country, to the real wealth and revenue of its inhabitants." [44]

[43] McCulloch, *The Works of Ricardo* (1888), 169. See also below, p. 257, Efficiency and Scarcity.
[44] Smith, *An Inquiry into the Nature and Causes of the Wealth of Nations*, I. 343, 344.

Thus Smith's concession to Quesnay respecting the greater productivity of agriculture was an abandonment of John Locke. Locke had made labor the producer of 99 per cent of all value. Smith conceded that agricultural labor was more productive than manufacturing labor, but refused to say, as Quesnay had said, that the former was wholly "productive" and the latter wholly "unproductive." "As a marriage," he said, "which affords three children is certainly more productive than one which affords only two; so the labour of farmers and country labourers is certainly more productive than that of merchants, artificers and manufacturers. The superior produce of the one class, however, does not render the other barren or unproductive." [45]

Yet, contrary to both Quesnay and Smith, we conclude that it is not bulk that labor produces—it is usefulness of the bulk. Nature multiplies the bulk, but she may prefer to multiply weeds instead of food. Does nature raise a crop of wheat, or does man, by using some of nature's forces and weeding out the others, raise the crop of wheat? Are nature's forces in raising wheat more productive than nature's forces in moving an ocean liner 30 miles an hour or an airplane 200 miles an hour? Or is production Man's ingenuity in doing something with nature that nature never thought about? It required Ricardo's change from nature's abundance to nature's resistance, even in agriculture, in order to confute Smith's fallacy that nature is more productive in agriculture than in manufactures, and thus to get back to John Locke. The fallacy lay in the confusion between nature increasing the bulk and man directing natural resources towards the increase of use-value.

Three-quarters of a century after Smith Karl Marx, following Ricardo, made his materialistic analysis of both labor-power and use-value. But even now the confusion of bulk and use-value is only in process of being cleared up, as the social meaning of Efficiency takes the place of the concept of productivity of nature's forces.[46]

Through his division of labor and consequent exchange of products, Smith obtained a further ethical justification of property. Locke's justification went only so far as to justify ownership by the laborer of what he individually has produced, and Locke had difficulty in justifying the ownership of *other* people's product, obtained in exchange by the intervention of money. Smith supplied the justification by his division of labor, without the intervention of money: If there is perfect liberty in the exchange of products, then

[45] *Ibid.*, II, 173.
[46] Below, p 251, Efficiency and Scarcity.

the laborers would see to it that the quantity of labor which they gave up would be quite equal, or "supposed to be equal," to that which they received in exchange. No person could therefore become wealthy without making other people equally wealthy, for the accumulation of one's labor, put into exchange, would be equal to the accumulation of other people's labor received in exchange. Herein Smith's theory again is false, because he omitted money, credit, and bargaining power, whereby some are made wealthy by extracting wealth from others. But by eliminating money, his division of labor and perfect liberty, along with Locke's abundance and divine beneficence, justified not only private property in one's own product, but also private property in other people's products acquired by means of exchange.

Likewise with Hume's concepts of scarcity and public utility. With abundance substituted for scarcity, Hume's "public utility," or public welfare, as a motive of individual action totally disappeared. And with collective action eliminated, so that perfect liberty of individuals resulted in getting wealthy only by making others equally wealthy, then the interference of the state should be permitted only in the most exceptional and urgent cases.[47] If left to this natural state of perfect liberty and nature's abundance then each individual would have only his own toil and trouble as his measure of both his own product and the equivalent product of others. These needed no concept of public utility or public welfare, since the invisible hand of Providence, which operated through abundance and the instinct of truck and barter, were adequate for the public interest. Smith's was a philosophy of Abundance, not Hume's philosophy of Scarcity.

(2) Cause of Scarcity-Value. *a. Psychological and Proprietary Scarcity.*—We have elaborated the double meaning of Labor as Pain and Power, which afterwards divided Ricardo and Ricardo's successor, Marx, from Smith and Malthus. The Ricardian group is usually known as the materialistic economists, while Smith and Malthus belong to the general group of psychological economists. But we make the more fitting distinction between the two groups by naming them psychological and proprietary economists. Considered as labor-pain the "real price" is the amount of toil and trouble sacrificed. Considered as labor-power the "real price" is the quantity of that power *owned* by the laborer and *sold* to an employer. The former is psychological, the latter is proprietary.

Smith's laborer is pictured as having on hand a limited stock of

---

[47] Smith, *An Inquiry into the Nature and Causes of the Wealth of Nations*, II, 32, 43, 83, 184–185. War, highways, etc.

"ease, liberty, happiness," a part of which he "lays down" in a personified exchange with Nature. This was the "real price," the "original price," the "real cost" which must be paid to nature, and gave to everything its value. To Smith this was not personification —it was "real."

But Ricardo and Marx afterwards looked upon the laborer as the common law had come to look upon him—as the free laborer who owns his body, or rather owns his physical, mental, and managerial abilities, the use of which he can sell on the open market. This labor-power is also a limited stock, not of happiness, the sacrifice of which is pain, but of power to produce goods and services, the sacrifice of which is alienation of ownership. This was also the idea of John Locke, who took it from the common law. His laborer was a free laborer owning his labor-power, and when the laborer "mixed" that power with nature's resources, the resulting output was his private property which he could sell to others if he wished.

The shift in meaning from Smith to Ricardo and Marx came about by a different philosophy of Nature from that of Smith and Locke. It was the shift from Nature as beneficent to Nature as niggardly, brought about by the overpopulation theory of Malthus.[48] In the hands of Ricardo and Marx this was a shift from theology to materialism, a shift which Auguste Comte would have described as a shift from theology to metaphysics.[49] It involved a change in meaning of the natural cause of scarcity-value. Ricardo found this natural cause objectively in the resistance of nature to labor-power; but Smith, for whom nature meant abundance, found his cause of scarcity-value subjectively in the resistance of human nature to toil and trouble.

When it came to Karl Marx, that which was implied by Ricardo became explicit: The laborer is free, and therefore owns his labor-power. But he sells it, not to nature, as Smith had personified, but to an employer, as Ricardo had understood.

This turns out to have been the common-law concept of property. The common law, in its treatment of transfers of ownership, paid no attention to pain or happiness. It paid attention only to the will. Did the laborer *intend* to sell his labor-power to the employer, and how much did he expect to receive in exchange? The logic of intentions was derived, not from pain or happiness, but from the customs and current usages of the time and place, according to the early doctrines of *assumpsit* and *quantum meruit*.

---

[48] Below, p. 244, Malthus.
[49] Above, p. 107, Comte.

It is this scarcity-value which we name proprietary scarcity,[50] and we have three historical stages in the meaning of scarcity: Smith's psychological stage of resistance of the laborer to labor-pain; Ricardo's materialistic resistance of nature to Smith's labor-power; Marx's proprietary resistance of the free laborer against selling his own labor-power for low wages.

Back of each, actually the source from which each was derived, was the Eighteenth Century common-law concept of a free wage-worker, not wholly propertyless, but owning and selling his man-power at whatever price he could get on the markets of the time and place. Still further back is Auguste Comte's picture of the historical stages through which ideas themselves evolve, which we have revised to mean the personification stage of Smith, the materialistic stage of Ricardo and Marx, and the transactional stage of the way in which institutions actually work.

Adam Smith took the common-sense view, without investigation, that human wants are unlimited and therefore human happiness is limited only by the total quantity of all use-values produced for the satisfaction of those wants. But while Smith made use-value equivalent to the "utility of a particular object," he did not distinguish between the abundance of *all* useful objects and the abundance of a *single* useful object, nor between the subjective and objective meanings of use-value.

Smith's view, however, is another common-sense view, known, of course, to all the physical economists but not incorporated in their analysis simply because they did not distinguish the whole from the parts which compose it. It was not until nearly a hundred years after Smith that this distinction was made by the later school of psychological economists. Everyone knows that the want for a particular object is not unlimited, but the want diminishes with an increase of quantity available at the time and place, going often as far as to become a nuisance instead of a utility, a pain instead of happiness. Everyone knows also that this subjective intensity of a want for a particular object increases with a *decrease* in the quantity available when and where wanted, going as far as a matter of life and death. This dependence of the individual upon a particular object, which we name Scarcity-Value, is properly distinguished as a functional psychology not taken care of in Locke's prevailing dualism of mind within and world without. Hence the physical econ-

---

[50] Cf. Llewellyn, K. N., "The Effect of Legal Institutions upon Economics," *Amer. Econ. Rev.*, XV (1925), 665–683. Llewellyn, like Hume, makes proprietary scarcity the basis of his correlation of law and economics. Knies and Ely had previously set forth a similar idea.

omists either disregarded this functional fact, or minimized it—as did Quesnay with his "illusory wealth"—or substituted personification or materialism.

Yet Smith's view also appeals to common sense. While labor-power was the cause of use-values and tended towards abundance and lower prices, labor-pain caused a restriction of the supply of use-values and tended towards scarcity and higher prices. The difference between labor-power and labor-pain is the difference between the cause of a kind of value that increases with abundance and the cause of a kind of value that increases with scarcity; labor-power causes use-value, labor-pain causes scarcity-value. If anything that increases abundance is a cause of use-value, then anything that restricts abundance is a cause of scarcity-value.

Smith's scarcity-value was therefore partly avowed and partly implied. His *avowed* scarcity-values were the artificial monopolies that restricted output, and their cause was collective action which prevented individuals from entering privileged occupations. His *implied* scarcity-value was the restriction of output by individuals in a state of nature where there was no collective action, and the cause of this natural scarcity-value was labor-pain.

He identified his avowed scarcity-value with monopoly and identified monopoly with collective action, whether it be the state or private associations. This was his meaning of mercantilism. 'Monopoly of one kind or another, indeed, seems to be the sole engine of the mercantile system." [51] Smith could not, therefore, like Hume, attribute private property to scarcity, since he had identified scarcity with the collective action of mercantilism. Collective action was an artificial cause of scarcity because it restricted the output of individuals. Since scarcity, however, is an evident fact, he must find its cause planted divinely in the breast of each individual.

In this respect Smith only followed common sense. Scarcity, in popular and empirical contemplation, is equivalent to difficulty of attainment from whatever cause; therefore the greater the degree of scarcity the greater is the pain of labor, in terms either of greater intensity of effort or longer duration of work. This is true, also of exchange-value. The pain of producing something abundant in order to obtain in exchange something that is scarce, requires an amount of pain equivalent to that of the scarce object to be acquired. Hence labor—interpreted as pain, effort, toil, trouble, difficulty of attainment—increases with nature's scarcity and diminishes with nature's abundance. If the product is abundant, like air or water, there is little or no pain connected with its acquisition, and its value

[51] Smith, *An Inquiry into the Nature and Causes of the Wealth of Nations*, II, 129.

therefore is small. If it is scarce, like shoes or hats, then a corresponding amount of pain, either in intensity or duration, is required, and its value is great. Consequently, if we can eliminate all artificial scarcities, as is done when we eliminate collective action, whether private or governmental, then the degree of natural scarcity of objects desired is identical with the quantity of labor-pain required to get the objects, directly, or indirectly by exchange. The greater the scarcity, the greater the labor-pain; the greater the abundance, the less the labor-pain. Labor-pain is the common-sense personification of scarcity and the cause of scarcity-value. It is this which immediately "recommends itself" to each individual; and thus Smith substitutes a personification of scarcity for Hume's "philosophical afterthought" of scarcity.

But Hume's "afterthought" was not psychological scarcity—it was proprietary scarcity. Evidently a similar scarcity ratio of income to outgo may be derived from the proprietary standpoint and from the psychological standpoint. If the laborer is looked upon as a free laborer who owns his body, including its physical, mental, and managerial abilities, then what he owns is a very finite, limited, and scarce fund of labor-power. His outgo now, not of labor-pain which he suffers, but of labor-power which he alienates, is a deduction from his limited supply of man-power, which, because it is scarce, is entitled to the name given to all scarce objects held to the exclusion of others—property. This was the idea of John Locke. Locke's laborer was a free laborer owning his labor-power, and when he mixed it with nature's abundant resources the resulting income of use-value became an augmentation of his property in recompense for the equivalent outgo of his property. Locke, however, did not inject the scarcity idea into his meaning of property, as did the more realistic Hume, because he was bent on divine abundance and the original sin of man. But neither did he go back to the psychological roots, as Smith did.

Hume's is the more correct interpretation. He brought together, under the simple idea of Scarcity, all that may be distinguished as property, law, and ethics. Smith separated them into his three ideas of (1) a physical object having use-value, (2) a personification of nature as benevolence and abundance, like Locke, and also (3) Locke's ethical justification.

If, however, we look upon Property, either private property or associated property, as an expected repetition of transactions, then property is, as Hume maintained, a function solely of scarcity. Rights of property do not exist except as to what is scarce or expected to be scarce.[52]   The value of property is always a scarcity-value.   Man's efforts to acquire ownership, individually or collectively, pushed on by scarcity, is as instinctive as life itself, and its threefold meaning might be distinguished as the Object of property, the Instinct of property, and the Common Law of property.   The instinct may be as destructive of others as it is preservative of self, and the word "instinct" is proper enough, since it may be interpreted to mean the behavior of all living creatures, whether animal or human, in so far as moved by scarcity of resources.   The instinct of property is the instinct of scarcity, while the object of property is the things that are scarce.

Every enduring community of mankind, therefore, sets up rules governing individuals in this pursuit of exclusive possession of what is scarce; and these rules, arising directly out of repeated practices and decisions of disputes, become, when thus authoritatively decided, a common law of property.   Smith, like Locke and Quesnay, saw no distinction between a benevolent providence that subjectively intended to give to labor a sacred right of property and an historical fact of custom or law that gave it.   Hume did distinguish facts from their justification: The facts were the effects of scarcity, the justification was man's own ideas of public utility, public welfare, or public necessity.   Yet, the distinction between fact and its justification could not be made until science was distinguished from theology.   The distinction is as far from being made today as it was in the time of Locke, Quesnay, and Smith.   Justifications are asserted as facts, and Adam Smith shows us how it was done.

A fact is, after all, as Locke contended, only a mental construction expressed in words and intended to convey to other people information regarding what happened.   As such, however, the element of persuasion is a constituent part of a fact.   Its persuasiveness consists in its capacity to elicit acceptance by others.   Since, therefore, a fact is a mental construction arrived at by selecting certain qualities from the great complex of experiences, this persuasiveness of the fact is accomplished by selecting the qualities that will persuade.   Smith selected labor-pain as his own persuasive meaning of acquisition and accumulation.   Labor-pain is sufficiently ambiguous to include all of the economic, legal, and ethical meanings, and sufficiently appealing to carry consent.   It can be recognized by every one as a fundamental fact of human nature, underlying all activity.   It has an ethical appeal inseparable from the many physical, scarcity, and proprietary meanings.   Labor-pain

---

[52] This distinction was not brought out until MacLeod, eighty years after Smith. Below, p. 397, MacLeod.

is, in short, a fact, a personification of scarcity and a justification of Smith's substitution of individual labor for the concerted acts of Mercantilism.

It is the foregoing Proprietary Scarcity of the common law which we name Bargaining Power. Smith himself took note of it:

> "Wealth, as Mr. Hobbes says, is power. But the person who either acquires, or succeeds to a great fortune, does not necessarily acquire or succeed to any political power, either civil or military. His fortune may, perhaps, afford him the means of acquiring both, but the mere possession of that fortune does not necessarily convey to him either. The power which that possession immediately and directly conveys to him, is the power of purchasing; a certain command over all the labour, or over all the produce of labour which is then in the market." [53]

This proprietary scarcity, thus commented on by Smith, has always been the live problem. The question naturally arises, why, for more than a hundred years from Smith and the original "classic" economists to the present day neo-classicists, did his personification of scarcity as pain remain the basis of economic theory? The reply must be found in the issue of mercantilism and in all issues of individualism *versus* collectivism. Collective transactions caused artificial scarcity. Labor-pain caused natural scarcity. Smith's labor-pain, operating through division of labor and perfect individual liberty, was his substitute for the theories and practices of Mercantilism and all collective action. Mercantilism, whether political or through private associations, restricted supply artificially; labor-pain restricts it naturally.

What has happened, however, is that Smith's Mercantilism, in all the forms of collective control through political parties, tariffs, private corporations, syndicates, or unions, has become more dominant than Smith could imagine. Scarcity is caused by the same political and proprietary collective action as that which he denounced as the artificial monopolies of mercantilism, not by personification of labor-pain which he announced as the divine rule of justice. The economics of today is the revised Mercantilism of proprietary scarcity in a world of relative scarcities, not the feeble personification of scarcity as Labor-Pain in a world of abundance.

b. Liberty and Abundance.—Smith's defect resided in his double meaning of words—an ethical and an economic meaning. His ethical meaning was the *justice* that would obtain if there were no collective action, and the *injustice* that actually obtained on account of col-

[53] Smith, *op. cit.*, I, 33.

lective action. His economic meaning was the *natural abundance* that would obtain without collective action and the *artificial scarcity* that is actually imposed by collective action.

Thus his term "liberty" had both an economic and an ethical meaning. Economic liberty was abundance, ethical liberty was freedom from collective compulsion. The state of nature was a state of liberty because it was a state of abundance but not collective action. So with his meaning of scarcity. His ethical meaning of scarcity was labor-pain as a regulator of reasonable value. His economic meaning was the artificial scarcities of collective action.

Hence the opposite of pain, for Smith, is not pleasure but liberty. Liberty *increases* as pain diminishes, for liberty means abundance of alternatives. Liberty *decreases* as pain increases, for pain means scarcity of alternatives. This is, truly enough, the economic meaning of liberty. But for Smith the same liberty was the opposite of collective action: Liberty diminishes as collective action increases, or increases as collective action diminishes, for liberty is freedom from collective compulsion. This is his ethical meaning of liberty.

Smith's ultimate defect lies in his personification of proprietary scarcity as psychological scarcity. Proprietary scarcity is the common and statutory law that regulates the security and liberty of property-owners, including the enfranchised owners of merely their own labor-power. Individuals do not choose between the alternatives offered by nature—they choose between the alternatives offered by owners. You cannot walk down the street and appropriate anything you want in proportion to its marginal utility. A proprietor and the police stand on guard. Laborers cannot choose to work according to the amount of pain. They work or do not work according to the alternatives that custom and law permit proprietors to offer and withhold. The value of property consists in its scarcity value. Therefore the proprietor under conditions of free competition (which means liberty from collective action) is free to refuse to produce a commodity, or free to withhold its use from others when it is produced. This is the only way in which he can maintain the scarcity-value of the commodity in the process of exchange.

Thus, even when all collective compulsions are eliminated and therefore the proprietary liberty of the common law is perfect, the situation is yet proprietary scarcity, consisting both in liberty to offer and accept inducements to create abundance through productivity, and inducements to restrain too much abundance. But it is the abundance of alternative *sellers* that constitutes proprietary liberty for the buyers, and abundance of alternative *buyers* that constitutes proprietary liberty for the sellers. The workingman and the job-giver have equal *proprietary* liberty in that each has equal liberty to work or not work, to hire or not hire—the officials of government are required both to keep their hands off and keep other people off. But each may not have equal *economic* liberty, because the alternative for the workingman may be the onerous alternative of enlarging his total labor-pain as the price he must pay, while the alternative for the job-giver may be only the inconsequential alternative of foregoing one out of hundreds or even thousands of laborers in filling the jobs in his concern.[54]

Other similar illustrations might be given in all of the transactions of buyers and sellers, landlords and tenants, financiers and business men. In order that there may be "perfect liberty" there must be, not only absence of legal duties, there must also be abundance of economic opportunity.

These many instances of proprietary scarcity which vary somewhat inversely to proprietary liberty, were eliminated from Adam Smith's concept of private property because he assumed that— when all scarcity depending on the legislative compulsion of mercantilism had been eliminated, and all associated property with its economic compulsion had been eliminated, as well as all inequalities —then the division of labor among equal individuals would create such abundance through productivity, thrift, and exchange, that there would remain no onerous alternatives for anybody. This idea was taken over by the Optimists, Carey and Bastiat, seventy-five years after Smith.[55]

Thus Smith, like Quesnay, had in mind the Mercantilist legislative policy of scarcity by collective action, and in this respect Smith's contrasted notion of automatic scarcity was his failure to distinguish the legislative meaning of deprivation of liberty from the common-law meaning. This liberty of choice of would-be competitors, in the case of scarcity by legislation, is limited by the legal duty to refrain from competition, and the liberty of choice of would-be consumers or producers is limited by the resulting scarcity of goods or of raw materials furnished by preceding producers. Smith assumed that, when this legislative scarcity should be eliminated then all scarcity would be eliminated by becoming identical with quantity of labor-pain, and it would follow that economic liberty would be attained when legislative liberty was attained.

Yet the common law of private property itself is based upon

---

[54] Commons, John R., *Legal Foundations of Capitalism*, 58 n.; Coppage v. Kansas, 236 U. S. 1 (1915). Below, p. 331, Limits of Coercion.

[55] Below, p. 310, Value of Service and Value of Product.

scarcity of resources, whereas Smith conceived it to be based on a natural right to the products of one's own labor. And the scarcity meaning of property still remains, as the withholding of that which is scarce relative to the wants of others. Liberty and scarcity vary inversely, if to liberty is given the economic meaning of choosing between abundant accessible alternatives, whether the abundance arises from absence of compulsion imposed by superior authority or from the automatic division of labor. If there is perfect liberty of choice there is no scarcity, for the objects desired are so abundant, like air, that all consciousness of choosing disappears in the abundance of supply. If there is perfect scarcity, which signifies no supply at all, then there is no liberty. This was Hume's "afterthought."

Yet Smith's is the common-sense, empirical view of the matter. The workingman who discovers that no jobs are offered to him except on onerous terms makes no distinction between scarcity of jobs and loss of liberty. He has, indeed, the proprietary liberty of refusing to work, for he owns his labor-power. And the owners of the opportunities have the equal proprietary liberty of refusing to hire him. Each has the ethical meaning of liberty. Conversely, it was upon this distinction that the socialists and communists invented the term "wage-slavery."

But, back of proprietary liberty is the economic meaning of liberty. The workingman's liberty of choice increases with abundance of jobs and diminishes with scarcity of jobs; inversely, his resulting labor-pain diminishes with abundance and increases with scarcity of jobs. But it is the common law of property, not the abundance of nature's benevolence, that regulates. The regulation may be good or bad, wise or ignorant, just or unjust. It may expand liberty even more than it restrains liberty. But it is not pain, it is collective action of going concerns.

2. *Regulator of Value*

The various empirical policies known as Mercantilism were developed along with the rise of monarchies and markets against the opposition of Feudalism, and along with the accompanying experience that exchange-value as a means of livelihood for manufacturers and merchants depended upon control of supply or demand. A centralized government in England furnished this control both for foreign and colonial markets and for the local guilds of manufacturers and merchants in the domestic markets. This regulation was always justified on the basis of public welfare—a hypocritical justification according to Smith, because it always favored a privileged few whose private welfare was represented by them to be identical with the public welfare. John Locke substituted parliament for the monarch in the exercise of this collective control, but Adam Smith substituted, in fact though not in philosophy, the judiciary for both monarch and parliament.

Each based his argument on a return to the natural law of divine benevolence instead of the arbitrary regulation of supply and demand by the king, for Locke, but by parliament and guilds for Smith. Smith therefore required a natural regulator of supply and demand in place of collective regulation, and he found it, not in the common-law courts, but in the breast of every industrious and thrifty manufacturer and merchant.

> ". . . the private interests and passions of individuals naturally dispose them to turn their stock towards the employments which in ordinary cases are most advantageous to the society. But if from this natural preference they should turn too much of it towards those employments, the fall of profit in them and the rise of it in all others immediately dispose them to alter this faulty distribution. Without any intervention of law, therefore, the private interests and passions of men naturally lead them to divide and distribute the stock of every society, among all the different employments carried on in it, as nearly as possible in the propo·tion which is most agreeable to the interest of the wh· le society." [56]

Thus Smith agreed with Quesnay regarding the problem of illusory wealth. Illusory Wealth would correct itself because individuals would be compelled, against their natural preferences if necessary, to change their labor from products whose prices were falling to products whose prices were rising. But while Quesnay dismissed the problem as inconsequential because Nature produced wealth, Smith showed how it would be done where labor produced the wealth.

In the first place, says Smith, this state of nature is a state of perfect liberty, security, equality, property, and mobility, without any interference by money and debts. Each individual can shift himself promptly from one occupation to another; he is not tied down by custom, habit, fear, or any collective restraint. It was, as Pareto afterwards said, a "molecular" concept of Society.

In the second place the wants of society as a whole are unlimited This assumption can be utilized in two ways, either from the side of demand or from the side of supply Smith employed both. The

---

[56] Smith, Adam, *An Inquiry into the Nature and Causes of the Wealth of Nations*, II, 129.

demand side is founded on his idea of effectual demand, the supply side on the idea of labor-pain. The two together result in a tending towards equilibrium, without the need of collective action.

The equivalence of demand and supply was later formulated by James Mill,[57] followed by Ricardo, although Mill added nothing but lucidity to Smith. Restated in our own meanings of words, if man's wants are unlimited, his happiness can be carried to unimagined extent by creating greater abundance of use-values. There would therefore be no decline in exchange-values if the different kinds of use-value were augmented proportionate to the new wants as they unfolded. Each augmented the demand for all other kinds of output, and there could be no overproduction if production were permitted to expand to its greatest limit. If by division of labor, for example (assuming perfect mobility and eliminating time), every physical product could be doubled by doubling the productivity of labor, then everything doubled in quantity would double the effectual demand for every other thing also doubled in quantity, and there would be no alteration in their exchange-values per unit.

But even this theory of unlimited demand required a factor that would be effective in restricting supply of particular products if they became too abundant, and in augmenting the supplies that were deficient, so that all prices would be regulated proportionate to the amount of this regulating factor contained in each. Ricardo afterwards found this factor in the marginal laborer. Smith found it in the toil and trouble of all laborers. His labor-pain as a *cause* of scarcity-value operates by restriction of output; his labor-pain as a *regulator* of scarcity-value operates by proportioning output among the different occupations so as to equalize the labor-pain in all. As a *cause* of scarcity-value, output is restricted when the income is believed to be too low relative to the amount of pain. As a *regulator* of scarcity-value, output is enlarged in some employments where the income is large relative to pain, and restricted in other employments where the income is low relative to pain, so that the pain per unit of income is equalized. Thus, while pain as a *cause* of scarcity operates on particular employments, pain as a *regulator* operates on all employments.

Ricardo's marginal laborer, who, according to him, regulated value, was the least productive laborer, and this fitted his theory

[57] Mill, James, *Commerce Defended* (1807); restated in *Elements of Political Economy* (1821), 186–195. Previously stated by Jean Baptiste Say, *Traité d'économie politique* (1803), English translation, 4th ed., 76 ff.

of the niggardliness of nature. The marginal laborer was the one who worked against the greatest resistance of nature. This laborer, in a free market and with mobile labor, regulates, by competition, the exchange-value of the product of other laborers where nature is more prolific, and also regulates the exchange-values of all products, since all laborers shift from low paid to high paid employment. The productivity of the least efficient laborer regulates the exchange-value of the output of all laborers.

But Smith's regulation of value was not the least efficient labor—it was the most painful labor. Man was condemned to labor—that was true on account of the original sin. He was compelled to lay down a portion of his ease, liberty, and happiness, in order that goods might be produced. But this should be done fairly. No individual should be compelled to suffer more than any other individual in his activity of producing, accumulating, and exchanging use-values for the good of his fellow men. The existing state of mercantilism was not only inefficient, but also unjust, in that it regulated individuals arbitrarily by collective action instead of leaving them to be regulated automatically by the invisible hand that had placed in the breast of each a principle of just distribution proportionate to pain.

This principle was the ratio between income of use-value and outgo of labor-pain, that is, the "real price" paid for the use-value. The private interests and possessions of men lead them to distribute their labor among different employments, without the aid of collective action, in such proportions that this ratio of income to pain would always be substantially equal for all.

To accomplish this purpose of regulation, however, Smith had to eliminate the isolated individual, with whom he started, and substitute the *average* labor-pain of all individuals at all times and places. In doing this his average labor-pain became both a regulator of value and a measure of value, as follows:

"Equal quantities of labour, at all times and places, may [58] be said to be of equal value to the labourer. In his ordinary state of health, strength and spirits; in the ordinary degree of his skill and dexterity, he must always lay down the same portion of his ease, his liberty, and his happiness. The price which he pays must always be the same, whatever may be the quantity of goods which he receives in return for it. Of these, indeed, it may sometimes purchase a greater and sometimes a smaller quantity; but it is their value which varies, not that of the labour

[58] Cannan notes that in Smith's first edition this read, "Equal quantities of labor *must* at all times and places be. . . ."

which purchases them. At all times and places that is dear [scarce] which it is difficult to come at, or which it costs much labour to acquire; and that cheap [abundant] which is to be had easily, or with very little labour. Labour alone, therefore, never varying in its own value, is alone the ultimate and real standard by which the value of all commodities can at all times and places be estimated and compared. It is their real price; money is their nominal price only."[59]

Herein both the regulator of value and the measure of value, in a state of nature where collective action has been eliminated, becomes average labor-pain. Smith eliminates the personal differentials arising from differences in character, and the repetition differentials arising from differences in fatigue. Neither did the historical passage of time disturb his average pain. It is the same in the Middle Ages as in the Eighteenth Century. In all periods and places the average laborer lays down the same portion of his ease, liberty, and happiness during the similar unit of time. It is the average pain regardless of individuals, hours of labor, fatigue, time, place, or race. Hence it is both a regulator of value in a state of nature and a stable unit for measuring value in any state of society. Labor-pain was no particular pain of any particular person—it was a mathematical formula endowed with toil and trouble.

It must be noted that Smith did not have Ricardo's idea of differentials but contented himself with these averages. Yet had he possessed Ricardo's differentials, he might have come out at a similar result. Ricardo's labor-power, which caused, regulated, and measured value, was the least efficient labor-power—the marginal laborer. This would have been equal, perhaps, to the most painful labor-pain. But Smith did not operate with differentials—he operated with averages, and these averages applied both to labor-pain and labor-power. If so, then each unit of labor-pain might be considered to be, on the average, equal to each unit of labor-power, on the average. And this seems to have been his view—each average unit of labor-power is accompanied by an equal average unit of labor-pain. In other words, each unit of power which increases the quantity of use-value is accompanied by an equal unit of pain which resists the exercise of that power. It was both personification and materialism.

Of course, if the matter were left at that point, things would come to a standstill, and nothing could be produced. But they are not left there, except in the case of indolent laborers, the aged,

[59] Smith, Adams, *An Inquiry into the Nature and Causes of the Wealth of Nations*, I, 35.

and the young. Smith's typical laborer had the ambition to work, to accumulate, and exchange, induced by security of private property, and this overbalanced the pain-resistance. Hence Smith could pass from labor-power to labor-pain without catastrophe to his system, because private property created a willingness to work that subdued the pain of work. Yet this willingness was not without limit. Pain finally asserts itself and resists further outgo of ease, liberty, and happiness.

Smith takes great pains with his process of averaging labor-pain, and this indeed is necessary because it is intended to serve both as a regulator of reasonable value and as a stable measure of real value. It is this average labor-pain that shifts the average laborer quickly from one employment to another "in his ordinary state of health, strength and spirits," and thus tends to reduce the differences in pain imposed by these differences in employments. This tends to equalize the inequalities in different occupations, so as to "make up for a small pecuniary gain in some employments and counterbalance a great one in others." The differences in occupations, which he mentions, are hardship, cleanliness or dirtiness, honorableness or dishonorableness, ease or difficulty of learning the business, regularity or irregularity of employment, small or great trust reposed in the workmen, and probability or improbability of success.[60] All of these are accompanied by pecuniary differences of income, either as wages or as profits, but these pecuniary differences were eliminated by Smith, because he eliminated money and substituted the exchange-values directly between commodities. These exchange-values, however, are justifiable if they coincide with differences in average labor-pain. And it is this average labor-pain, which, by restricting the supply of labor in the more painful occupations and enlarging the supply in the less painful occupations, regulates the exchange differences so that they coincide with the pain differences.

So, his regulation of value is a regulator of "real value" provided collective action and money are not allowed to intervene. If this collective action is eliminated, then there will emerge divine benevolence, abundance, perfect liberty, perfect equality, and security, such that exchange-values will be regulated according to their real value.

This "real value" of Smith's is "reasonable value," but without the leading constituents of reasonable value, namely, collective action, scarcity, money, custom, and collective opinion. Reasonable

60 *Ibid.*, I, 102 ff.

value, as formed in the practices of courts, juries, commissions, arbitration arrangements, and so on, is a concept of collective action in terms of money, arrived at by consensus of opinion of reasonable men—"reasonable" in that they are men who conform to the dominant practices of the time. Reasonable value changes with new combinations of circumstances and collective control, and is in process of evolution through changes in efficiency, scarcity, custom, politics, and dominant interests. But Smith's real value in terms of labor-pain is an automatic principle for all time, that regulates behavior for the good of man, but without collective action. It is his personified equivalent of the "just price" of Thomas Aquinas and the collective action of courts and arbitration.

The distinction between the two meanings of reasonable value turns on two concepts of willingness, the collective wills of going concerns and the individual wills of private property. Smith conceived correctly that, in a world of abundance where individual property was perfectly protected against violence, no conflicts over scarcity could occur. In such a world therefore it required only willingness of individuals and benevolence of the deity to work out reasonable prices in the distribution of that abundance.

Having identified his automatic regulator of scarcity-value with the quantity of labor-pain, Smith proceeds to inquire why it is that, upon the labor market, the price (exchange-value) of labor does not, under existing conditions, coincide with the quantity of labor-pain delivered in exchange for the produce. All of these discrepancies we shall find to be various aspects of artificial scarcity controlled by custom, sovereignty, or other collective action, instead of regulated automatically by quantity of labor-pain. They were, as already mentioned, the artificial or collective scarcities imposed by sovereignty which grew out of the principles of collectivism and conflicted with the principle of perfect liberty. Among these restrictions were exclusive privileges of corporations (guilds), long apprenticeship, understandings between competitors, free education at public expense, state regulation of wages, price fixing, tariffs, bounties levied in order to maintain a favorable balance of trade, and obstructing the free circulation of labor and stock [capital] by poor laws.[61]

But even if these mercantilist interferences with liberty were eliminated, there were still two other proprietary claimants, the landlords and the capitalist employers, who, even under conditions of perfect liberty, prevented the accurate proportionment between

---

[61] *Ibid.*, I, 120 ff.; 437 ff.; II, 141 ff.

labor-pain and wages. These other claimants, who introduced the factor of proprietary scarcity, were examples of the Common Law of Private Property. "As soon as the land of any country has all become private property, the landlords, like all other men, love to reap where they never sowed, and demand a rent even for its natural produce." "The rent of land, considered as the price paid for the use of the land, is naturally a monopoly price." [62] And wherever, therefore, rent was paid, it was evidence of prices regulated by proprietary scarcity in disregard of labor-pain.

The same was true of Smith's concept of profits. They were determined solely by supply and demand for capital amongst the owners. There was no question here of labor-pain or labor-power, and not even of any so-called labor of "inspection and direction." Profits "bear no proportion to the quantity, the hardship, or the ingenuity of this supposed labor of inspection and direction." [63] They are regulated in two ways, which turn out to be special cases of proprietary scarcity. First, by the value of the stock employed; second, by the combination of masters to keep down wages.[64]

The value of stock was the quantity of raw material and subsistence for laborers, that is, "circulating commodities," required relative to the number of employees, ranging in the illustrations given by Smith from £35 to £360 per employee.[65] Evidently the profits *per employee*, in the latter case mentioned by Smith, would be over ten times as great as in the former case, provided the *rates* of profit were the same.

The second factor of scarcity in determining profits is collective scarcity. The rate of profits varies also with the ability and willingness of masters to combine in the joint control of their property —a willingness and ability usually greater than that of the laborers.[66]

With reference to wages, however, there is a third principle which may keep wages continually above the natural price. This is an increasing demand for labor owing to the increasing growth of wealth under abundant natural resources compared with population, as in North America where there was a great "scarcity of hands" compared with a more nearly stationary country, like China.[67]

Hence, even in a state of perfect liberty, exchange-values would not be proportionate to labor-pain, owing to the fact that rent and

[62] *Ibid.*, I, 51, 146.
[63] *Ibid.*, I, 50.
[64] *Ibid.*, I, 68, 69.

[65] *Ibid.*, I, 50 ff.
[66] *Ibid.*, I, 68, 69.
[67] *Ibid.*, I, 73.

profits, arising from private property without labor, were able to claim a share out of their exchange-values; while wages themselves differed owing to differences in the pressure of population and not to differences in labor-pain.

But even these were not all of the circumstances under which, even in a state of perfect liberty, exchange-values were determined by proprietary scarcity rather than by the amount of labor-pain. In order that prices of commodities might be equal to the quantity of labor-pain of each employment, three more general circumstances were necessary. "First, the employments must be well known and long established in the neighborhood; secondly, they must be in their ordinary, or what may be called their natural state; and, thirdly, they must be the sole or principle employments of those who occupy them."[68] That is, in order that wages may be equal to the toil and trouble, even after proprietary rents and profits, as well as pressure of population are eliminated, there must be publicity, normality, and independence, each of which introduces the factor of collective regulation of scarcity in the guise of custom or trade practices.

Lack of publicity, says Smith, that is, Secrecy, prevents competitors from moving into the field where wages or profits are high, even though they have perfect liberty to move. Normality, or the "natural state," is an elimination of changes in biological scarcity arising from the forces of nature, since, according to Smith, "normality" is the absence of seasonal fluctuations of demand as well as the variations of good and bad seasons in agriculture.

The requirement of "independence" eliminates all complementary products or integrated industries by which the laborer supports himself without charging his labor up to his main product, such as products of home workers, cottagers, the house rents charged by families who take in lodgers, and the labor of out-servants to landlords. In other words, even though there is perfect liberty of the individual, vouchsafed by the common law, yet wages are determined by scarcity regardless of pain, in all cases of secrecy, fluctuations of seasons, and the complementary goods of integrated industries.[69]

If, then, all of this array of exceptions is conceded by Smith, the question remains, Is it not collective action, including custom,

[68] *Ibid.*, I, 116–118.

[69] *Ibid.*, I, 116–120. Viner, in the article referred to above (p. 162), interprets Smith as including within the "natural order" many of these exceptions which I interpret him as *excluding* from the "natural order." I hold that Smith excluded custom, all collective action, and all exceptions not accounted for by labor-pain. These were "artificial" and not "natural."

after all, that determines the value of labor itself as well as commodities? Smith excludes collective action only by "supposition." His condition of perfect liberty "supposes" that there are no interferences, no exceptions, no duties, no trade practices, no customs, no habits, no secrecy, no seasons, no complementary goods or integrated industries, no money or collective enforcement of contracts, such that each laborer is a physical unit guided by increments of pain. Such a set of labor atoms will promptly transfer their labor-power as accurately as a flow of water from products whose prices are low relative to pain, to products whose prices are higher, thus tending to raise the prices of the former and reduce the prices of the latter, and bringing about an equilibrium such that the quantity supplied of each will be so regulated that a unit of average labor-pain devoted to one product will receive the same compensation as a unit of labor-pain devoted to any other.

This personification resolved human nature into physical molecules, and prepared the way for the anarchists and for Bentham, Ricardo, and the hedonic economists of the Nineteenth Century.

3. *Measure of Value*

But Smith had something very real in view—it was a stabilized measure of value when collective action should be eliminated. "The price which he pays [in toil and trouble] must always be the same, whatever may be the quantity of goods which he receives in return for it. Of these, indeed, it may sometimes purchase a greater and sometimes a smaller quantity; but it is their value which varies, not that of the labor which purchases them." [70]

Thus, while labor-pain was Smith's *regulator* of value applied to a state of nature, now, as a *measure* of value, he applies it to the actual state of manifold collective action and existing money prices. He will measure, by this stabilized average labor-pain, not only the inequalities, injustices, and accidents of the actual society, but also, the rents, profits, and wages concealed behind money prices.

"The real value of all the different component parts of price, it must be observed, is measured by the quantity of labor which they can, each of them, *purchase or command*. Labor measures the value not only of that part of price which resolves itself into labor, but of that which resolves itself into rent, and of that which resolves itself into profit." [71]

---

[70] Smith, *An Inquiry into the Nature and Causes of the Wealth of Nations*, I, 35.
[71] *Ibid.*, I, 52 and footnote. Italics mine.

All money prices may fall continuously if all labor becomes more efficient or money becomes scarce. All money prices may rise if labor becomes less efficient, or money more abundant, or if paper money is substituted. Some prices may rise and others fall. High prices may be reached owing to monopoly, or low prices through competition. Prices may be extortionate or reasonable. Labor-pain will measure their departure from or coincidence with reasonable value. It is *their* values which diverge, not the value of the labor-pain, and the divergence is measured by larger or smaller quantities of pain required to purchase them.

Thus it is that Smith's measure of value turns on his distinction of real and nominal price. The real price is the expenditure of pain, the nominal price is the expenditure of money. The distinction is between the feelings of individuals and the artificial units of measurement collectively agreed upon by man.

If we examine these artificial units we find that they have been standardized by custom or law for the purpose of reducing to numbers various dimensions employed in the science of economics, such as quantities of use-values, degrees of scarcity, rates of output, lapse of time, etc. All of these, indeed, have behind them intense human feelings of happiness, misery, pleasure, pain, hope, fear, justice, injustice, and these are real values for human beings. But we have for these feelings no units of measurement standardized by custom or law.

All measurements, therefore, are as nominal as money, just as all units of measurement are artificial. They are a form of language—the language of number. They may be signs, indeed, that intense feelings are happening, but they do not measure the feelings —they measure the superficial behavior. Adam Smith wished to create a unit of emotion that would measure the justice and injustice of economic life. When he came to the actual affairs of life, he found himself measuring transactions by units of length, area, weight, scarcity, productivity, and time. All of these were nominal —none were real.

But this is true only if the economic behavior of conflict and coöperation is nominal and individual feelings alone are real. Units of measurment in economics are collective devices used to measure transactions for the three great social reasons of accuracy, security, and justice. These are real if society and transactions are real.

Every transaction employs three kinds of measurement, a physical measurement, a scarcity measurement, and a time measurement. The physical measurements are of two kinds, quantities of goods and rates of output or of income. The scarcity measurements are of two dimensions of time, the present moment and the future lapse of time. It was not until the coming of Karl Marx and scientific management that the rates of output were reduced to measurable dimensions, and not until Böhm-Bawerk that the future lapse of time was separated out as a measurable dimension.

Every unit of measurement must be of the same character as the dimension to be measured. Use-values are the expected uses of "goods" and these are measured by physical units of tons, yards, bushels. Scarcity values are the prices of goods, and these are measured by the scarcity unit, the dollar. The two are always found together in all transactions. Wheat is $2.00 *per* bushel. Cotton is ten cents *per* yard. Pig iron is $30.00 *per* ton. The bushel, yard, ton, measures the quantity of use-value. The dollar and cent measure their scarcity-value. We do not measure the scarcity of wheat by units of physical dimension. The price of wheat is simply the scarcity dimension of wheat in terms of a scarcity standard of value, the dollar; whereas the useful attribute of wheat is measured in terms of standards of bulk—the bushel—and of quality—a certain quality of wheat.

Each unit is standardized by custom or law as the first requisite of accuracy, security, and justice in transactions. If a dispute arises and a court decides, then the court decides upon the basis of the physical unit deemed lawful and the scarcity unit, also created by law. It is these legal units that measure legal tender and legal performance. A legal performance of delivery of wheat is so many lawful bushels. A legal tender of payment is so many lawful dollars, or what the court deems to be an equivalent. Adam Smith's state of nature had no legal tender and no legal units of measurement, because these are artificial units.

A certain commodity, gold, has been standardized by custom and law in its physical dimensions but not in its scarcity dimensions. Its physical dimensions were 23.22 grains of pure gold, for the American dollar. Its scarcity dimensions were its general purchasing power upon the markets. The two dimensions are separable, and have often been separated by the law which declares legal tender. Legal tender paper money has been substituted for physical quantities of gold as the measure of relative scarcities. But neither denominations of paper nor grains of gold are measures either of real value or nominal value, in Smith's sense of the feelings of individuals—they are legal measures of economic transactions, where accuracy, security, and justice are wanted. They do not measure real value in the sense of an isolated individual dealing with the forces of nature. They are artificial units of physical and scarcity dimensions imposed by the collective action of custom, law, and courts. When Smith measured reasonable value by labor-pain he was measuring psychological scarcity; but money measures proprietary scarcity. Units of pain may, perhaps, measure subjective feelings in a state of nature; but money measures economic power, equality of opportunity, fair and unfair competition, reasonable and unreasonable values, in a state of politics, law, or other forms of collective action. Reasonable value is reasonable scarcity-value measured in terms of money.

The error of Smith is that of starting at the beginning of things, either of time or fundamentals, instead of starting with a cross-section of going concerns in all their complexities at a point of time, already built up, no matter how, by accruals from the past, and moving on to a future not yet finished but changeable.

Smith's effort, like that of Locke and Quesnay, was an effort to find something ultimate, in the nature of things and divine reason, that already had a fixity and stability for all time. But as far as we know, for human purposes, there is no such stability. Everything is flying around wildly, regardless of man's security and expectations. The only stability that we know is that which man himself creates by collective action. Units of measurement are one of the instruments of stability, but these do not exist in nature. They are artificial structures devised by man for accuracy and security. Smith could not find his unit of pain because man had not artificially constructed such a unit. Man had, however, in course of time, constructed a unit of scarcity by collective action —legal tender money or what the courts deemed to be its equivalent. It required more than a hundred years following Smith for economists to see the importance, and then to devise methods of stabilizing, that purely artificial, collective and "nominal" unit of measurement—the scarcity-value of money. And the reasons for this stabilization are the social reasons of making more accurate, secure, and just the present and expected transactions. While the physical dimensions of gold had been reduced to a stable unit of measurement in terms of weight by John Locke and Isaac Newton, nearly two hundred years elapsed before attempts were made to stabilize the scarcity dimensions of gold in terms of purchasing power. What actually has been happening is the discovery that Smith's very superficial measure of nominal value is the very vital measure of changing scarcities in a world, not of individuals, but of collective action regulating individual action.

It has thereby been learned that these scarcity-values employed in transactions must be taken as constructed for an already going concern, existing through centuries of custom, property, and sovereignty; experimented upon happily or disastrously, but capable of being artificially measured and then perhaps stabilized by collective regulation.

Hence it cannot be said that Smith's *average* of labor-pain was fallacious. It was a personification of average purchasing power. As such it is exactly the process of averaging which is followed with fair success, in modern times, in constructing "index numbers" of the average movement of prices, whether of commodities, wages, stocks, bonds, etc. In these index numbers the unit is the unpersonified purchasing power of the dollar instead of the pain of labor. Compiled in averages, the average for index numbers, in the modern case, is the scarcity of money relative to the average of the various scarcities of commodities, of wages, or of securities. In Smith's usage it is the average scarcity of commodities in terms of the average pain of production. The principle of averages itself is sound enough as a mere working rule. His error was his personification of money as average labor-pain.

This error proceeded from his effort to obtain a stable measure of real value, in terms of human toil and trouble, instead of a stable measure of scarcity, in terms of money. He wished to avoid a "pecuniary" economy by substituting a "natural" or "welfare" economy. The intention was good enough but too fundamental. A more superficial but pragmatic process is that of continuing the historical experimenting on methods of obtaining reasonable values by means of stabilizing the measure of scarcity in a pecuniary economy. For, after all, it is reasonable value that is "welfare economy."

If we now compare Wieser's and Whitaker's analyses (above, p. 171) of cause, regulator, and measure of value, we can see how inseparable they are. Measurement is inseparable from regulation because it is by means of measurement that regulation is accomplished. And cause is not predetermined; it is the human purpose to be effected by measurement and regulation. While Smith pictured the causes of value to be derived from a benevolent and just purpose ruling the movements of man and nature, his causes were really his own purposes transferred to nature. His regulator was his ideal of a just regulation of value without collective action, but with liberty, security, equality, and property. His measure of value was his measure of reasonable value applied in criticism of the existing artificial and arbitrary values of mercantilism and the vagaries of gold, silver, and paper money.

IV. Social Utility

Smith contended that Hume's idea of public utility was a philosopher's afterthought and not a direct motive of the individual to support justice. He must therefore find in the breast of each individual something that would automatically promote the public welfare, and besides, something that could not be placed there by any form of collective action, since practically all kinds of collective action must be eliminated from his scheme of morals and economics.

This something must therefore have been placed in the breast by an external divine Providence which intended the harmony and happiness of mankind. But it must be placed unconsciously in such a way that the individual himself did not know it was there for that purpose, so that consciously he could go ahead just as he felt inclined to love or to hate, or to seek his own self-interest by persuading others that the bargains he offered them would promote their self-interest more than they would promote his own self-interest.

When it comes to looking for these motives divinely planted by Adam Smith in the human breast, we find that they cannot be reduced by him to less than six; namely: sympathy, self-interest, the sense of propriety, the propensity to truck and barter, labor-pain placed there to regulate output by preventing over-production, and a divine or natural right to be free from almost every kind of collective action except punishment for fraud and violence or for national self-defense.

Each of these implanted instincts or motives took the form of a more or less clear opinion or supposition in the breast of each individual at the time when he was engaged with other individuals having similar suppositions. Take Smith's supposition regarding labor-pain:

> Money and goods, he said, "contain the value of a certain quantity of labour which we exchange for what is supposed at the time to contain the value of an equal quantity. . . . But though labour be the real measure of the exchangeable value of all commodities, it is not that by which their value is commonly estimated. It is often difficult to ascertain the proportion between two different quantities of labour. The time spent in two different sorts of work will not always alone determine this proportion. The different degrees of hardship endured, and of ingenuity exercised, must likewise be taken into account. There may be more labour in an hour's hard work than in two hours' easy business; or in an hour's application to a trade which it cost ten years' labour to learn, than in a month's industry at an

ordinary and obvious employment. But it is not easy to find an accurate measure either of hardship or ingenuity. In exchanging indeed the different productions of different sorts of labour for one another, some allowance is commonly made for both. It is adjusted, however, not by any accurate measure, but by the higgling and bargaining of the market, according to that sort of rough equality which, though not exact, is sufficient for carrying on the business of common life." [72]

It appears then, after all, that it is not labor-pain that determines value in exchange—it is transactions, which may be persuasive or coercive, depending also on opinion as to whether one party is more necessitous or less intelligent than the other, more efficient or less efficient, or does not have a better alternative than the one offered, or is exposed to competition more seriously than the other party. These inequalities, however, were ruled out of a state of nature where each party is perfectly free and perfectly equal to the other. Smith abandoned his labor-pain standard in the statement of it. Labor-pain was only an individual opinion. The only place where either Hume's subjective public utility or Smith's sympathy, self-interest, sense of propriety, propensity to truck and bargain, or natural rights, can be investigated is in the transactions, whether bargaining, managerial, or rationing, and in the collective action of statute or common law, or customs, or political parties, business concerns, labor unions, farmers' coöperatives, banks, and indeed all associations that furnish the social conditions within which individuals act in the production, pricing, and consumption of commodities.

We may give to the theories of Smith and his imitators for a hundred and fifty years the name "fundamentalism." They rested their case on the feelings of Man and God. Transactions and customs were too superficial, too behavioristic, too familiar, too commonplace. Economics, for them, must get back somehow to something more fundamental—an ultimate essence of God, Nature, Reason, Instinct, Physics, Biology. The most familiar things are the last to be investigated.

Yet it is these familiar transactions controlled by collective action that are the wages, profits, interest, rents, employment, unemployment, welfare, misery, of nations and individuals.

It is only in so far as these kinds of collective action control individual action that either Hume's public utility emerges in behavioristic form that can be observed and measured, or that Smith's

---

[72] *Ibid.*, I, 32, 33. Continuation of preceding quotation, p. 210 above.

several substitutes for public utility can emerge from fundamentalism to transactionalism.

Meanwhile, in the same year of Smith's *Wealth of Nations,* Bentham established, for the next hundred years or more, the methodology by which economists could eliminate law and custom and could consolidate Smith's substitutes into a single substitute for collective action—pleasure.

CHAPTER VI

BENTHAM VERSUS BLACKSTONE

It was Bentham who separated Economics from Law and Custom. The "wonderful year" 1776 produced Bentham's *Fragment on Government*, Smith's *Wealth of Nations*, Watt's steam engine, and Jefferson's Declaration of Independence. The first was the philosophy of happiness, the second the philosophy of abundance, the third the technology of abundance, the fourth the revolutionary application of happiness to government. Eleven years before, Sir William Blackstone had published his *Commentaries on the Laws of England*, agreeing with Smith's Divine Origins but finding their earthly perfection in the Common Law of England. Jeremy Bentham's *Fragment* was his critique of Blackstone, substituting Greatest Happiness and Legislative Codes for Divine Origins and Common Law.[1] This was followed, in 1780, by his *Morals and Legislation*, revised in 1789, wherein he eliminated *duty* and derived ethics from happiness. Henceforth, for more than a hundred years, political economy separated itself from law, and law separated itself from happiness.[2] The law rested on past custom and divine justice; economics on present happiness and individual wishes. Bentham taught James Mill and James Mill taught Ricardo, so that Bentham said that Ricardo was his spiritual grandson.[3] His great-grandsons were the hedonistic economists of a hundred years later. Bentham was really the founder of Nineteenth Century economics, divorced from law, custom, and ethics.

Blackstone had shown, and even avowed, himself, according to Bentham, to be a "determined and persevering" enemy to reform of the laws of England as called for by the axiom of the "greatest happiness." Instead of expounding the laws, he "justified" them

---

[1] Bentham did not originate the greatest happiness principle—he got it first from Priestley. See Bowring's "History of the Greatest Happiness Principle," in Bentham's *Deontology, or The Science of Morality*, ed. by Bowring (1834), I, 298.

[2] Cf. Bonar, James, *Philosophy and Political Economy in Some of Their Historical Relations* (1893), 218; Carter, John C., *Law, Its Origin, Growth and Function* (1907), 233-240, showing the grounds on which the leading American lawyer of his time rejected Bentham's principles of happiness. Carter was arguing for the new custom of mergers of great corporations contrary to the older anti-trust laws.

[3] *The Works of Jeremy Bentham* (ed. by Bowring, 1843), I, 498. Hereafter cited as Bentham, *Works*.

as derived from "authority" that supported custom, or from an "original contract" on the part of the people to obey the sovereign. His justifications were his "reasons." Blackstone, says Bentham, "takes upon him to give reasons in behalf of it . . . the very idea of a *reason* betokens approbation." Even when he officially adopts the reasons of others, "he makes them his own." If Blackstone had tested the laws of England by their tendency to promote or obstruct the happiness of the people, then his "reasons" would not have led to a "kind of *personification*, . . . as if the Law were a living creature," or to a "mechanical veneration of antiquity," by which "the merit of justifying a law when right, should have been thought greater than that of censuring it when wrong." [4]

Thus Bentham identified custom with tradition supported by authority, and rejected it on this account: Judge every act, not by conformity to ancient custom but by its effect on the general happiness. Bentham claimed that his *Fragment on Government* was the "very first publication by which men at large were invited to break loose from the trammels of authority and ancestor-wisdom on the field of law." [5]

If custom is rejected, where, then, shall Bentham find his justification of the law? He will find it in his *wishes*. This was, he says, where Blackstone also found his justification. Blackstone simply *wished* the laws to remain as they were.

Blackstone's definition of municipal law, said Bentham, was not a description of rights and duties, but was an opinion of right and wrong. "Municipal law," according to Blackstone, is " 'a rule of civil conduct prescribed by the supreme power in a state, commanding what is right and prohibiting what is wrong.' " [6] Blackstone founded this opinion, according to Bentham, on the law of nature, commanded by a Being of infinite power, wisdom, and goodness. But it was, in fact, Blackstone's wish. "A great number of people," said Bentham, "are continually talking of the law of nature; and then go on giving you their sentiments of what is right and wrong; and these sentiments, you are to understand, are so many chapters and sections of the law of nature." [7]

If Blackstone, therefore, wishes to follow ancestor-wisdom, Bentham wishes to promote the general happiness.

[4] *Ibid.*, I, 229, 230 (Preface to first ed. of *Fragment*).

[5] *Ibid.*, I, 260 n. (Introduction to *Fragment*).

[6] Blackstone, Sir William, *Commentaries on the Laws of England*, Introduction, Sec. II, p. 44 (ed. by Cooley, 1884; original edition 1765). Blackstone's common-law theories were treated in my *Legal Foundations of Capitalism*, and this chapter is devoted mainly to Bentham, the founder of Nineteenth Century economics.

[7] Above, p. 125, Quesnay.

"When I say the greatest happiness of the whole community [8] ought to be the end or object of pursuit, in every branch of the law, . . . what is it that I express?—this and no more, namely that it is my wish, my desire, to see it taken for such, by those who, in the community in question, are actually in possession of the powers of government. . . . In making this assertion, I make a statement relative to a matter of fact, namely that which, at the time in question, is passing in the interior of my own mind; —how far this statement is correct, is a matter on which it belongs to the reader, if it be worth his while, to form his judgment." [9]

Blackstone's wish, said Bentham, was concealed in his double meaning of the word "wrong," an ethical wrong, *opposed* to ethical right, and a legal duty *correlative* to an equivalent legal right. Yet, as Bentham maintained, a legal right may be ethically wrong and a legal wrong may be ethically right. *Right* is a compunction of conscience. *Rights* are compulsions of law. The history of slavery shows this contradiction. Blackstone, in fact, had no working concept of change, or process, or novelty, or history, as an essential feature of the Common Law. The law had always existed in the divine reason, which was his meaning of natural law, and the function of the judge was to find that reason and apply it to the particular case in hand. The judge does not create new law when he decides a dispute, which thereupon changes the law itself; he merely finds the natural justice which was always there but which the disputants and judge had not known about. Blackstone's concept was Locke's copy concept of a passive mind.

But Bentham, also, knew nothing of historic process or of change as an essential feature of the common law. He was forever building up *codes* of law on his principle of universal happiness. Hence, neglecting history, he was logical in his ultimate analysis both of Blackstone and himself. Codes and the common law were each founded on wish. Blackstone wished the law to be as he conceived it to be, which to him seemed divine and natural. Bentham wished it to be different and said so. And this is the only alternative to a theory of change and experiment. For, in lieu of historic research founded on a theory of the novelty of changes in customs and of experimental adaptation to other changes, wherein the change itself is the subject-matter of investigation and experiment, the only basis left for law and economics is Wish. Blackstone and Bentham were wishers, not scientists.

[8] Bentham saw that the greatest happiness of the "greatest number" might lead to despotism of majorities, hence he substituted greatest happiness of all.

[9] Bentham, *Works*, IX, 4 (Intro. to *Constitutional Code*).

The distinction between codes and the common law goes back to the distinction between the deductive method and the experimental method of thinking in both law and economics. The code method is similar to the deductive method in that each starts with a fixed scheme of social organization from which all individual cases are variations; but the experimental method is that which starts with changes and novelties within a general rule of stability. In the code method each particular case is its own independent variable; its decision makes no change whatever in the code. Having disposed of a particular case in its peculiarity, that case has no lasting effect as a precedent. The judicial mind, in the next case, comes back to the code in its clear-cut pristine vigor.

But the experimental method is the common-law method of judge-made law wherein each particular case, when decided, becomes itself a change in the code, constitution, or statute, because it has a lasting effect as a precedent. And then when a new case arises it is not merely a matter of going back to a fixed code or primordial principle that had always existed in law or economics, or even of discovering a previously unknown divine intent applied to that case. It is a matter of reasoning from many conflicting precedents or experiences, some of which would lead to a decision towards one side of the case, and others to a decision on the opposite side of the case. Thus in a common-law country the code, or statute, or constitution, itself changes experimentally with changes in the practices of the people and the decisions of disputes.[10]

Bentham makes plain that his method of thinking is the code method of statutory law imposed from above on the people, and not the experimental method of the common law derived from the people themselves. This follows from his fundamental "principle of utility" and rejection of custom. The common law arises from changing customs of the people, but his concept of utility is a sentiment of approval or disapproval by the sovereign. Utility is an "act of the mind," a "mental operation" which, "when applied to an action, approves of its utility, as that quality of it by which the measure of approbation or disapprobation bestowed upon it ought to be governed." And that quality of action in question is its "tendency . . . to augment or diminish the happiness of the party whose interest is in question . . . not only of every action of a private individual, but of every measure of government."[11] Thus Bentham's "principle of utility" is not merely his statement of pleasure and pain as the sovereign master of man, it is his asser-

[10] Below, p. 692, Analytic and Functional Law and Economics.
[11] Bentham, *Works* (Intro. to *Morals and Legislation*), I, p. A1, and footnote.

tion that sovereigns should bind their subjects to the sovereign's ideas of what is happiness for them. Custom and the precedents of the Common Law have nothing to do in restraining the sovereign.

Bentham meets this inference of the arbitrariness of his code by the *ad hominem* argument of charging the same arbitrariness to the common-law courts. It was "wishes" also, which animated them when they changed the laws by resorting to fictions. In the eyes of the lawyer a "fiction" is evidence of "progress" in the common law. In the eyes of Bentham it was a willful "usurpation" by the courts of the legislative power which had created the code. As stated by the common-law lawyer, a fiction is resorted to for the furtherance of justice. The courts are confined to the administration of existing statutes, codes, or rules. They lack, in the English system, the legislative power to change these rules. Thus they have frequently

> "avoided the injustice that their application to the actual facts might cause, by assuming, in behalf of justice, that the actual facts are different from what they really are. . . . The employment of fictions is a singular illustration of the justice of the common law, which did not hesitate to conceal or affect to conceal the fact, that a rule of law has undergone alteration, its letter remaining unchanged." [12]

But Bentham claimed,

> "a fiction of law may be defined—a wilful falsehood, having for its object the stealing of legislative power, by and for hands which could not, or durst not, openly claim it,—and but for the delusion thus produced, could not exercise it. . . . Thus it was that, by means of mendacity, usurpation was, on each occasion, set up, exercised and established." [13]

Thus Bentham consciously rejected the common-law method of making law by experiments, which Smith had merely overlooked, and placed his faith in legislative sovereignty.

One of the fictions on which Blackstone depended was the fiction of an original contract. "The people on their part," said Bentham, "promised to the King a general obedience; the King, on his part, promised to govern the people in such a particular manner always as should be subservient to their happiness." But why the need of such a fiction, when the real test consists in determining at what point the people are justified in resisting obedience?

[12] Bouvier's *Law Dictionary*, title "Fiction." The simpler and more general method in the United States is the common-sense method of changing the meanings of words used in the statute or constitution.

[13] Bentham, *op. cit.*, I, 243 (Preface to 2d ed. *Fragment*).

". . . They should obey, in short, *so long as the probable mischiefs of obedience are less than the probable mischiefs of resistance:* . . . taking the whole body together, it is their *duty* to obey just so long as it is their *interest,* and no longer . . . Suppose the constant and universal effect of an observation of promises were to produce *mischief.* Would it *then* be men's *duty* to observe them? would it *then* be *right* to make Laws, and apply punishment to *oblige* men to observe them? . . . Now this other principle that still recurs upon us, what *other* can it be than the *principle* of Utility? The principle which furnishes us with that *reason* which alone depends not upon any higher reason, but which is itself the sole and all-sufficient reason for every point of practice whatsoever." [14]

Thus Bentham's reliance on codes ends in *revolutions,* whereas the common-law method *gradually* eliminates the enforcement of contracts when found, in particular cases, to work injustice.

What, then, is the meaning of that Utility which sets up codes instead of experiments? Bentham revised Hume's idea of public or social utility. Hume, according to Bentham, had employed the term with several meanings. Sometimes the meaning was "usefulness considered as an end, no matter what"; sometimes the meaning was "a quality inhering in a physical instrument, a machine, a house, or piece of furniture, where utility is conduciveness to the end that is sought"; sometimes it meant "pleasure as an end," but never indicating that avoidance of pain is also pleasure, and never intimating that the "idea of happiness is to be inseparably connected with the idea of utility." Neither did Hume derive from "utility" a criterion of "right or wrong," nor an "answer to the question 'What ought to be done, and what left undone?'" Thus Hume did not distinguish the utility that *is* from that which *ought to be.* Hume's enumeration of the virtues was a mere classification without showing the "proportion in which they are conducive to happiness. . . He introduces, without any attempt to show their relationship or dependence, pleasures, pains, desires, emotions, affections, passions, interests, virtues, vices and other entities, in the direst confusion." [15]

But Bentham simplified this confusion by converting all of these meanings of utility into a single Force, or Energy, that compels man to act.

"Nature has placed mankind under the governance of two sovereign masters, *pain and pleasure.* It is for them alone to

[14] *Ibid.,* I, 271–272.
[15] Bowring's "History of the Greatest Happiness Principle," in Bentham's *Deontology,* I, 291–294.

point out what we ought to do, as well as to determine wha we shall do. On the one hand the standard of right and wrong, on the other the chain of causes and effects, are fastened to their throne. They govern us in all we do, in all we say, in all we think: every effort we can make to throw off our subjection, will serve but to demonstrate and confirm it. In words a man may pretend to abjure their empire; but in reality he will remain subject to it all the while. The *principle of utility* recognizes this subjection, and assumes it for the foundation of that system, the object of which is to rear the fabric of felicity by the hands of reason and of law. Systems which attempt to question it, deal in sounds instead of sense, in caprice instead of reason, in darkness instead of light." [16]

Bentham further simplified the matter by making private utility identical with public utility, whereas Hume set them in opposition. Where Hume had derived from scarcity both self-interest, or private utility, and self-sacrifice, which was his public utility, Bentham now derived public utility from Smith's self-interest and abundance. The "greatest happiness" was the sum total of the greatest self-interest of all. Instead of Hume's scarcity which requires subordination of self to the good of others, Bentham's abundance permits the aggrandizement of self without injuring others. This abundance is a reason, often cited, for American indifference to political and financial corruption. Smith's theories were correct, according to Bentham, except in the one particular where Smith had agreed with Blackstone, namely, the justification of an original state of nature, for which Bentham substituted utility. But Bentham's utility was not Hume's utility. It was the utility of abundance, not the utility of scarcity.

In the first place, the "community" is not an organized association which restrains individuals for the common good—this is again a fiction. "The community," says Bentham, "is a fictitious *body*, composed of the individual persons who are considered as constituting, as it were, its *members*. The interest of the community then is, what?—the sum of the interests of the several members who compose it." [17] And he substituted Parliament for the community.

In the second place, the wealth of the community consists in the "sum of the particular masses of the matter of wealth belonging respectively to the several individuals of whom the political community—the nation—is composed. Every atom of that matter, added by any one such individual to his own stock, without being

[16] Bentham, *Works*, I, 1 (Intro. to *Morals and Legislation*).
[17] *Ibid.*, I, 2.

taken from that of any other individual, is so much added to the stock of national wealth." [18]   Thus Bentham's concept of property was corporeal property; his concept of national wealth excluded scarcity and bargaining, and included only the sum of all private production of use-values.

It follows that the interest of the community is only an arithmetic sum of individual interests—not an expectation of transactions between individuals as members of a going concern.   And public utility is the *sum* of private utilities.   Hence, Bentham's utility is Smith's subjective side of use-value, equivalent to Bentham's "enjoyment of wealth" and parallel to the objective use-values, equivalent to Bentham's "matter of wealth." [19]   Greatest happiness is greatest enjoyment, greatest enjoyment is greatest abundance, greatest abundance is greatest volume of use-values (wealth).   Public and private utility are identical on account of abundance, whereas, with Hume, they were opposed on account of scarcity.

This concept of society was, for more than a hundred years, *not a society but a population* of molecules [20] of the classical and hedonic economists, revolted against by the Marxian and Christian socialists and by modern social philosophy.   Starting with individual pleasures and pains, society is but a *sum* of individuals, and wealth is a *sum* of physical goods.   Economics was thus divorced from ethics, as it had not been by Hume, for, with Bentham, there was no scarcity relation between individuals in the acquisition of wealth. In order to bring in the ethical considerations, economists had to make a new start which they called ethics.   The omission of Hume's principle of Scarcity became the dualism of individual and society, of economics and ethics.

But this dualism rested on two theories of the origin of ethics. One was the individualistic theory of the maximum of pleasure in a world of abundance, where the individual could not injure others by taking all he wanted.   The other was the social theory of conflict of interests in a world of scarcity, where the individual *may* injure others if he takes all he wants.   On the foundation of the latter theory ethics is a historical process developing out of the decisions of economic disputes, and there is no dualism of ethics and economics.   On the foundation of the former theory, ethics becomes Bentham's individual wishes, and the dualism of individual and society is inevitable.

The difference is plain if we start with transactions instead of

[18] *Ibid.*, III, 40 (*Manual of Pol. Econ.*).
[19] Above, p. 175, Chart 2.
[20] Below, p. 678, Pareto.

individuals, and with scarcity instead of self-interest. Here we start with the social relation itself which is not a harmony of many self-interests, but is an inseparable relation of *self* interest to the *collective* interests that require the rules and regulations of concerted action respecting the shares which each disputant shall obtain from the limited opportunities available for self and others. The individuals now become, if their interests are respected as property or liberty, not *atoms* of a *population*, but *citizens* of a *commonwealth*, kept together by the inducements and sanctions of scarcity; and their membership consists in their expected orderly repetition of transactions with others which determine daily, hourly, and for the indefinite future, both the quantities to be produced and the shares to be obtained out of the total but limited quantity available.

Bentham formulated the calculus of wishes by which his *sum* of individual interests, constituting the aggregate *population* interest, could be ascertained. Herein he constructed a common denominator, a unit of pleasure, which is also a unit of avoidance of pain, which should be thereby a unit of wish to serve as a measure not only for Smith's subjective use-values but even also for Blackstone's customs and laws, and Bentham's own codes. The value of everything, from food to religion, from rights to wrongs, is reduced to the following computation of the variable number of units of satisfaction of wish which go to make up a given quantity of that utility which is the arithmetic sum of pleasure. This calculus a century afterwards became almost bodily the calculus of the hedonic economists. We condense his enumerations.[21]

(1) The intensity of the sensation of pleasure or pain caused by the custom or the commodity.

(2) The length of time during which the sensation is felt.

(3) The degree of risk, or certainty and uncertainty of that sensation.

(4) The futurity, or degree of propinquity or remoteness expected to intervene before the actual sensation occurs.

(5) The fecundity, or chance that the sensation will be followed by sensations of the same kind.

(6) The purity, or chance of not being followed by sensations of a different kind.

(7) The extent, or number of persons enumerated in the population census, who get the total quantity of pleasure and suffer the total quantity of pain to be derived from the commodity or custom.

If, then, a legislator, or magistrate, or private citizen, wishes to

[21] Bentham, *Works*, I, 1–16 (*Morals and Legislation*).

consider the general tendency of his proposed act either in law, ethics, or economics, he begins with any one person most immediately affected by it, and considers the "value" ("quantity") of those produced after the first, that is, the fecundity and purity of the first pain or pleasure; then he "sums up" the values ("quantities") of all the pleasures and all the pains, takes account of the number of persons concerned and arrives at the general good tendency of the act, if on the side of pleasure; or at the general evil tendency, if on the side of pain.[22]

Truly Bentham was the high peak of the Eighteenth Century Age of Reason and the Nineteenth Century classical and hedonic schools of economics.

The foregoing, continues Bentham, has to do with pleasure as the *end* which individuals and governments should wish to obtain. But the same pleasures and pains are *instruments* which have the Force or Energy needed to obtain these ends. As instruments this energy is Motives and Sanctions.

Motives precede the act, in that the individual looks beyond the act to the expected consequences of it. The order of sequence, we figure out, seems to be as follows: (1) expected event that will probably cause pain or pleasure; (2) present belief that it will cause pain or pleasure; (3) present pain or pleasure occasioned by present belief; (4) present motive to avoid or obtain expected pain or pleasure; (5) resulting act of will to avoid or obtain expected pain or pleasure.

Bentham did not connect this sequence with a *structural* concept of the mind, and this was accomplished by James Mill, the pupil of Bentham and tutor of Ricardo. Mill explained Bentham's sequence of pain, pleasure, belief, motive, and will by the "association of ideas," and constructed what his son, John Stuart Mill, making use of Lavoisier's then recent "affinities" of chemistry, unknown to Bentham's Newtonian physics, described as an "intellectual physics or spontaneous chemistry of the mind." [23] Pain and pleasure are sensations that may originate from the same external sources, but association of ideas may pull one person in one direction, another person in another direction, according to the "disposition" of each. Bentham had explained the functioning of the mind; [24] James Mill's association of ideas explained its structure. Its structure and function proceeded from sensations to ideas; then to associations of

[22] *Ibid.*, I, 16.

[23] Mill, James, *Analysis of the Phenomena of the Human Mind* (1828); citation to 1869 ed., Preface by J. S. Mill, I, ix.

[24] Mitchell, W. C., "Bentham's Felicific Calculus," *Pol. Sci. Quar.*, XXXIII (1918), 161.

ideas accompanied by feelings of pain, pleasure, desire, or aversion; then to muscular action. It was this association of ideas that connected an expected pleasure with the economic instruments by which it can be obtained. It was John Locke's corpuscular ideas converted into a chemical analogy.

"The sound of a violin is the immediate cause of the pleasure of my ear; the performance of the musician the cause of that sound; the money with which I have hired the musician the cause of that performance. The money is, in this case, the cause of the cause of the cause of the sensation, or the cause, at two removes. . . . The mind . . . is deeply interested in attending to the cause; that we may prevent, or remove it, if the sensation is painful, provide, or detain it, if the sensation is pleasurable. This creates a habit of passing rapidly from the sensation, to fix our attention upon its cause." [25]

It will be seen that, by reason of the fact that Bentham and James Mill explained the functions and structure of the mind by *physical* and *chemical* analogies, they could not introduce the scarcity concept of "diminishing utility," which does not occur in physics or chemistry. Bentham noted it but left it unsettled.[26] The result was that, although Bentham *seemed* to introduce a psychological factor by means of his emphasis on pains and pleasures, it was merely an intellectual succession of ideas correlated with external physical forces, causing, not pain and pleasure, but *ideas* of pain and pleasure. Hence, when he speaks of pain and pleasure he is really speaking of the physical objects that cause ideas. In other words, Bentham's concept of utility is essentially Locke's and Smith's parallelism of the world without and the copies within. It is this passive and intellectual concept of the human will that justifies Veblen's gay comment that the hedonic man, who is Bentham's man and the "economic man" of the Nineteenth Century, is

"a lightning calculator of pleasures and pains, who oscillates like a homogeneous globule of desire of happiness under the impulse of stimuli that shift him about the area, but leave him intact. He has neither antecedent nor consequent. He is an isolated, definitive human datum, in stable equilibrium except for the buffets of the impinging forces that displace him in one direction or another. Self-imposed in elemental space, he spins symmetrically about his own spiritual axis until the parallelogram of forces bears down upon him, whereupon he follows the line of the resultant. When the force of the impact is spent, he comes

[25] Mill, James, *op. cit.*, II, 187–188.
[26] Mitchell, *op. cit.*, 170, 171.

to rest, a self-contained globule of desire, as before. Spiritually, the hedonistic man is not a prime mover. He is not the seat of a process of living, except in the sense that he is subject to a series of permutations enforced upon him by circumstances external and alien to him." [27]

With this physico-chemical analogy of the will, moved by the force of pain and pleasure, it follows that the force itself. which moves him to action, acquires the name of Sanctions. A sanction, says Bentham, "is a source of obligatory powers or *motives:* that is, of *pains* and *pleasures;* which, according as they are connected with such or such modes of conduct, operate, and are indeed the only things which can operate, as *motives.*" [28]

"There are four distinguishable sources," continues Bentham, "from which pleasure and pain are in use to flow: considered separately, they may be termed the *physical*, the *political*, the *moral*, and the *religious:* and inasmuch as the pleasures and pains belonging to each of them are capable of giving a binding force to any law or rule of conduct, they may all of them be termed *sanctions.*" [29]

The "physical sanctions" are the powers of physical nature operating on the individual, "not purposely modified by the interposition of the will of any human being." But it is these sanctions that are made use of wherever there is an interposition of other wills, and even of religion, "insofar as the latter bears relation to the present life." In other words, the physical sanctions are land and commodities; the physical sanction is equivalent to the physical term, use-value, which now becomes utility, or the sanctions of expected pleasure or avoidance of expected pain, operating through physical goods.

If these physical sanctions operate *without* the interposition of any other will, they are wealth, or rather, the "matter of wealth" in its two forms of subsistence and enjoyment.[30] If they operate through the will of a judge or other person "according to the will of the sovereign or supreme ruling power in the state," then they are, not "matter of wealth," but "matter of security." Bentham presumably has in mind prisons, munitions, guns, and policemen's clubs. These are the political sanctions operating through their peculiar "form" of physical use-value. But if the sanctions operate

"at the hands of such *chance* persons in the community, as the

[27] Veblen, Thorstein, "Why Is Economics Not an Evolutionary Science," reprinted in *The Place of Science in Modern Civilization and Other Essays* (1919), 73, 74.

[28] Bentham, *Works*, I, 14 n. (*Morals and Legislation*).

[29] *Ibid.*, I, 14.

[30] *Ibid.*, II, 194; III, 41, 42.

party in question may happen in the course of his life to have concerns with, according to each man's spontaneous disposition, and not according to any settled or concerted rule . . . then the binding force may be said to 'issue from the moral or popular sanction.' "

Thus Bentham's moral sanction is not that of custom, nor any of the rules of concerted action, but is the "chance" meeting of individuals in a population of molecules, with whom bargains or conversations may occur.

Likewise, the religious sanction issues from a "superior invisible being," employing the motives of expected pleasures and pain, "either in the present life, or in a future." If in the present life, then the religious sanction operates through physical instruments which embody "the powers of nature," presumably church buildings, Bibles, and paraphernalia—another peculiar "form" of use-value. Here also the concerted beliefs and movements cf fellow-believers, the trials for heresy, and so on, which we associate under the names of custom and common law, do not appear in Bentham's classification. These fellow-believers are "chance" persons.[31]

It is with the political sanctions operating through the physical use-values of guns and prisons, that the bulk of Bentham's writings have to do. His "moral sanctions" occur as accidents—the "chance" hitting upon other persons who are animated by the chance wishes that happen to be moving them around like his own.

These moral sanctions are partly allowed for by Bentham under the name, "sanction of sympathy," which is "the pleasure or pain . . . in the breast of some other person in whose well being the person in question experiences an interest, produced by the force of the sympathetic affection." But he treated this sympathy as something like Smith's instinct of truck, barter, and exchange.

". . . how can a man be happy, but by obtaining the friendly affections of those on whom his happiness depends? And how can he obtain their friendly affections, but by convincing them that he gives them his own in exchange? And how can he best convince them, but by giving them these friendly affections in reality; and if he give them in reality, the evidence will be found in his words and deeds. . . . The first law of nature is to wish our own happiness; and the united voices of prudence and efficient benevolence, add . . . seek your own happiness in the happiness of others. . . . He who secures for himself a pleasure, or avoids for himself a pain, influences his own happiness *directly;*—he who

[31] Cf. *ibid.*, I, 14 (*Morals and Legislation*); II, 192 ff. (*The Rationale of Reward*); III, 33 ff. (*Manual of Political Economy*).

provides a pleasure, or prevents a pain to another, indirectly advances his own happiness." [32]

Thus sympathy is a profitable exchange of happiness.

While sympathy could thus be explained in terms of self-interest, it was not so with duty. Here it is a one-sided transfer, with no pleasure to be obtained in exchange, and only pain suffered for the sake of others.

"It is, in fact, very idle to talk about duties; the word itself has in it something disagreeable and repulsive; and talk about it as we may, the word will not become a rule of conduct. A man, a moralist, gets into an elbow chair, and pours forth pompous dogmatisms about *duty*—and *duties*. Why is he not listened to? Because every man is thinking about *interests* . . . in the moral field it cannot be a man's duty to do that which it is his interest not to do." When "interest and duty are considered in their broadest sense, it will be seen that in the general tenor of life the sacrifice of interest to duty is neither practicable, nor so much as desirable; . . . and that if it could the happiness of mankind would not be promoted by it. . . . It may be safely pronounced, unless it can be shown that a particular action or course of conduct is for a man's interests, the attempt to prove to him that it is his duty, will be but a waste of words." It is just because duty is not an effective motive that legislation, with its physical sanctions of reward and punishment is required. "All laws which have for their end the happiness of those concerned, endeavor to make that for a man's interest which they proclaim to be his duty." [33]

Thus Hume was right. The sense of duty proceeds from Scarcity and not from Bentham's Abundance.

"Pleasures then, and the avoidance of pains," said Bentham, "are the *ends* which the legislator has in view; it behoves him therefore to understand their *value*. Pleasures and pains are the *instruments* he has to work with; it behoves him therefore to understand their force, which is again, in another point of view, their value." [34]

Thus the term "value" is shifted from Smith's pain to Bentham's pleasure, or rather to the arithmetic net income of pleasure after pain is deducted. It is this net income of pleasure that is the Force which moves mankind. Its sovereignty is exercised by the two sanctions, Want and Enjoyment.

[32] Bentham, *Deontology*, I, 17, 19.
[33] *Ibid.*, I, 9–12.
[34] Bentham, *Works*, I, 15 (*Morals and Legislation*).

"Want, armed with every pain, and even death itself, had commanded labor, had sharpened courage, had inspired foresight, had developed all the faculties of man. Enjoyment, the companion of every satisfied want, had formed an inexhaustible fund of rewards for those who had overcome the obstacles and accomplished the designs of nature. . . . Before the idea of law was formed, *want* and *enjoyment* had done, in this respect, everything which should have been done by the best concerted laws." [35]

Thus we see that Bentham eliminated Custom in three ways. He substituted the sovereignty of wants and enjoyment for habits and customs. He substituted "chance" individuals for the collective action of custom and going concerns. He substituted the legislature for the common law.

These substitutions carry with them the elimination of his "moral sanctions" and his "religious sanctions"; since it leaves these in the shape of a mere accidental concourse of individuals impinging on one another according to physical laws, and without any hopes or expectations of repeated transactions that hold together those of similar beliefs and interests, either in a going business, a family, a fraternity, or a church.

The result is that there remain just two sources of sanctions, Wealth and Parliament—the physical use-values of wealth, and the physical powers of sovereignty. Wealth provides physical sanctions that control human behavior in the production, exchange, and consumption of commodities. Parliament provides physical sanctions that create and protect private property. It was Adam Smith simplified for oncoming economists. There is no intervening collective action, no rule of custom, no common law, between the individual and the legislature or magistrate. Just as Bentham merged all economics, ethics, and law into the pleasures and pains of individuals, so he merged all kinds of inducements under the general name of Sanctions. Sanctions are any kind of pleasure and pain, whether physical, moral, legal, or economic, when looked upon as proceeding from external inducement to act.

Admitting the all-prevalence of pleasure and pain, yet we infer that, for the practical purpose of dealing with situations as they arise, the generalization is too sweeping. Pleasures differ in kind as well as quantity. This Bentham allows, but, for him, these differences in kind are not important. The two most important differences met with in economics, are those founded on inducements offered by individuals to each other and the inducements offered by the various kinds of collective action. Pain and pleasure are

[35] *Ibid.*, I, 303 (*Civil Code*).

found in each, and they are important motives appealed to. The distinction may be preserved by naming the one Inducements and the other Sanctions.[36] Inducements pertain to transactions between individuals; sanctions to the customs and rules of *collective induce-ments*. Bentham, like Smith, had no place for collective action, and, indeed, no place for the persuasions, coercions, and commands of bargaining, managerial, and rationing transactions. He was dealing only with individuals, sovereigns, and commodities; he made no distinctions between the different kinds of pleasures and pains that distinguish individual action from collective action. His sovereign masters were pleasure and pain, not habit and custom.

What Bentham did by his chemical analogy was to give to pains and pleasures a physical existence. This physical existence was—money. Wesley C. Mitchell has shown how this was done. He quotes from Bentham's unpublished manuscript, unearthed in 1901 by Halévy:

"If then between two pleasures the one produced by the pos-session of money, the other not, a man had as lief enjoy the one as the other, such pleasures are to be reputed equal. But the pleasure produced by the possession of money, is as the quantity of money that produces it: money is therefore the measure of this pleasure. But the other pleasure is equal to this; the other pleasure therefore is as the money that produces this; therefore money is also the measure of that other pleasure. It is the same between pain and pain; as also between pain and pleasure . . . if we would understand one another, we must make use of some common measure. The only common measure the nature of things affords is money. . . . Those who are not satisfied with the accuracy of this instrument must find out some other that shall be more accurate, or bid adieu to Politics and Morals."[37]

Thus Bentham abandoned his unit of wish in his unpublished manuscript, and it was unfortunate for all hedonists in ethics and economics that he neglected to publish. For, as Mitchell proceeds,

"This formulation of the mental operation of an ideally perfect money-maker can be converted into a passable formulation of Bentham's hedonism by merely turning pecuniary into psycho-logical terms. Substitute pleasure for profit and pain for loss, let the unit of sensation stand for the dollar, replace accounting by the hedonic calculus, interpret self-interest as the maximizing

---

[36] Above, p. 78, Formula of Economic and Social Relations.
[37] Cited by Mitchell, *op. cit.*, 169–170.

of net pleasures instead of net profits, and the transformation is complete." [38]

Thus Bentham's "greatest happiness of all" terminates in the greatest pecuniary profit of the business man. Yet it is not pleasure or pain that is measured by money—it is scarcity. When pleasure and pain become dollars and cents, they shift from happiness to relative scarcities, and these then become the force, cause, and regulator of human actions. Pleasure and pain are too fundamental. Our problem is the more superficial but behavioristic problem of what is actually done in a money and credit economy, influenced by scarcity, futurity, custom, and sovereignty. Bentham's pleasure and pain blur the distinctions. Pleasure, for him, is both positive income of pleasure and negative avoidance of pain. But the latter is choice of alternatives, the former is acquisition of income. Avoidance is choice of a greater instead of a lesser income, or of a lesser instead of a greater outgo.[39] Acquisition and avoidance cannot be added together, they are two dimensions of the same act—which is a performance in one direction by avoidance in another direction.

Bentham's pleasure and pain blur the distinctions between individual transactions and collective control, between inducements and sanctions, between self-interest and ethics, between happiness and scarcity, feelings and money. The problems of economics are more superficial—they lie on the surface. But they are more specific— they are the problems of buying and selling, borrowing and lending, hiring and firing, managing and managed, plaintiff and defendant. They may all be resolved, indeed, into pleasure and pain—but that is too fundamental and elusive, for then they dissolve into wishes. But practices and prices of collective and individual action turn on dollars and quantities.

Bentham's "sovereign," also, was not an outcome of the customs or other collective action of the mass of individuals who constituted his "community." His individuals were a population, not a society; they were "chance" individuals, not a going concern; and his sovereign was an outsider, not a part of the society. His sovereign was apparently quite absolute, in that he was free to choose the laws which he would enact, unrestrained by the habits, customs, corporations, unions, political parties, that put him there on the expectation that he would do their bidding. Bentham "wished" that this sovereign should adopt the general happiness principle. But sovereigns have acted differently. The British Constitution

---

[38] Mitchell, W. C., "The Rationality of Economic Activity," *Jour. of Pol. Econ.*, XVIII (1910), 213; cf. Bonar, *op. cit.*, 218.

[39] Below, p. 304, Choices and Opportunities.

arose from conquest and the common law. The common law arose from the customs of the people in so far as approved by the judges appointed by the crown. Political parties now displace the crown and select the judiciary. Collective business organizations control political parties, and custom and organization, more than pain and pleasure, regulate politicians and people.

Bentham reduced sovereignty to security, as he had reduced pleasure to money. Political Economy, according to Bentham, is both a science and an art. It is the science of pleasure and pain. It is the art of legislation employing the instrument of pleasure and pain for the sake of "the maximum of wealth and the maximum of population."[40] This end is a "final cause"; the several sanctions of pain and pleasure are the "efficient causes or means."[41] The legislator, when inquiring more particularly in what the happiness of the body politic consists, finds that it is fourfold—subsistence, abundance, equality, and security.[42] Subsistence and abundance are the province of political economy. Security is the province of the law; equality is secondary, because there is a continual progress towards equality in a nation which prospers by agriculture, manufactures, and commerce under the care of security. "Legislators have often shown a disposition to follow the counsels of equality under the name of *equity*, to which greater latitude has been conceded than to *justice:* but this idea of equity, vague and ill-developed, has rather seemed a matter of instinct than of calculation."[43]

Security, then, is all that political economy demands of the law, and even "liberty" is but a branch of security. "Personal liberty is security against a certain species of injury which affects the person. Political liberty is . . . security against the injustice of the members of government." Liberty, with Bentham, is a breaking away from custom and resting one's behavior on utility. In his *Defense of Usury* it is "blind custom" that is the sole basis, which either the moralist In his rules and precepts, or the legislator in his injunctions, can have to build on, when they prevent people from paying and receiving such rates of interest as they might freely wish. But "custom" is an arbitrary guide. It varies from age to age and country to country. "Mutual convenience of the parties, as manifested by their consent," and not the custom of my neighbors, nor the fiat of legislators, is the only standard that tells whether

[40] Bentham, *Works*, III, 33 (*Manual of Political Economy*).
[41] *Ibid.*, I, 14 (*Morals and Legislation*).
[42] *Ibid.*, I, 302 ff. (*Civil Code*).
[43] *Ibid.*, I, 307; also see Williams, A. T., *The Concept of Equality in the Writings of Rousseau, Bentham, and Kant*, Columbia Univ. Teachers College Series, No. 13 (1907).

borrower and lender are each obtaining the maximum of happiness under the circumstances.[44]

What, then, are the attributes of subsistence and abundance, with which political economy is concerned, and how do they come into existence under the care of security and liberty? Bentham says that they consist in physical objects rather than in the services obtained from other people. These physical objects are created under the pressure of the physical sanction, namely, want and enjoyment. Nothing "can be added, by direct legislation, to the constant and irresistible power of these natural motives? But the law may indirectly provide for subsistence, by protecting individuals whilst they labour, and by securing to them the fruits of their industry when they have laboured." [45]

But these wants and enjoyments go further than subsistence. ". . . after having raised the first ears of corn [they] . . . erect the granaries of abundance, always increasing, and always full. . . . Opulence . . . does not arrest this movement when once it is begun."

And in what does this opulence consist? It consists of abundance created through one's own labor, not through the prices paid to others for their labor. For "in what does the wealth of society consist if not in the total of the wealth of the individuals composing it?" [46]

True enough, we may say—but just as Bentham conceives society to be made up of self-contained human units, so he conceives the wealth of society to be the sum total of physical units owned by these individuals. This sum total is equivalent to "a lot of happiness." Just as money has disappeared in pleasure and pain, and scarcity and "assets" have disappeared in the concept of "wealth" there results a physical concept of both wealth and happiness, suited, perhaps to a colonial or primitive period of isolated farmers, to abundance of natural resources and corporeal property, but not to a society where one's wealth ("assets") comes through marketing, buying and selling, and a price system dominated by the concerted movements of capitalists, farmers, laborers, merchants, bankers, and governments. What, then, does security, the principal object of the laws provide?

"Law alone, has been able to create a fixed and durable possession which deserves the name of Property. The law alone could accustom men to submit to the yoke of foresight, at first

[44] Bentham, *Works*, III, 4 (*Defense of Usury*).
[45] *Ibid.*, I, 304.
[46] *Ibid.*, I, 304.

painful to be borne, but afterwards agreeable and mild: It alone could encourage them in labour—superfluous at present, and which they are not to enjoy till the future. . . . The law does not say to a man, '*Work and I will reward you*'; but it says to him '*Work, and by stopping the hand that would take them from you, I will ensure to you the fruits of your labour*, its natural *and sufficient reward, which, without me, you could not preserve.*' . . . The idea of property consists in an established expectation—in the persuasion of power to derive certain advantages from the object, according to the nature of the case. . . . The legislator owes the greatest respect to these expectations . . . when he does not interfere with them, he does all that is essential to the happiness of society." [47]

Security, therefore, is the security that the laborer shall have in the ownership of what his labor has produced. But, it is objected, says Bentham, that the laborers have no property, and Baccaria had said, "The right of property is a terrible right, and may not perhaps be necessary." This is surprising, says Bentham, from so judicious a philosopher. The poor, who have no property are far better off than they would be "in a state of nature." It follows that the legislator

"ought to maintain the distribution which is actually established. . . . When security and equality are in opposition, there should be no hesitation: equality should give way. . . . The establishment of equality is a chimera . . . the cry for equality is only a pretext to cover the robbery which idleness perpetrates upon industry." [48]

From these remarks it will be seen that Bentham's concept of property was the corporeal property of lands, buildings, tools, held for one's own exclusive use, not in anywise the intangible property of modern society that consists in access to markets and obtains wealth (assets) by controlling the scarcities of services and enforcing the contracts to pay those scarcity-values. His arguments have no application whatever to a modern society where a person's property ("assets") is taken from him by prices, not by legislation. And the objectionable doctrine of equality is interpreted to mean, not the equalizing of bargaining power, nor equal opportunity, nor fair competition, but the dividing up equally of the physical possessions of proprietors. It was primitive agrarianism that he had in mind.[49] Such a "levelling" system, according to Bentham, is not

[47] *Ibid.*, I, 307 ff.
[48] *Ibid.*, I, 311, 312.
[49] Cf. Commons and associates, *History of Labour in the United States*, I, 522, on the Agrarianism of the first American Labor Party, 1829.

only impossible in practice but the desire to establish it has its roots, "not in virtue, but in vice; not in benevolence, but in malevolence." [50]

We may conclude then that when Smith's abundance was accepted but Blackstone's custom and Hume's public utility were rejected in Bentham's concept of utility, the economists were furnished with the following molecular method of reasoning: Man is a *passive* but selfish being, moved by self-interest under the name of utility. Society is a *sum* of individuals whose pleasures and pains can be added, subtracted, and balanced by the quantity of commodities. Money is the *measure* of pleasure and pain employed in this accounting system. Self-interest cannot harm anybody, because there is *abundance*. This pleasure-pain is imputed, by the *association of ideas*, to physical commodities. Since money is an artificial creation by the collective action of institutions and therefore is *nominal*, we get closer to the thing measured when we state our theories either in units of the physical labor and physical commodities that create and constitute wealth, or in units of pleasure and pain that constitute utility and disutility; in either case we state our theory, not in the collective units of a nominal measure of happiness, money, but in dimensions of pleasure-pain that operate as uniformly as the laws of physics and chemistry. Political economy derives, from the common law and from custom, only useless *traditions* and *ancestor-wisdom*. It requires from statute laws and codes, only *security* of possessions and contracts. This security must maintain things as they are, for any effort to introduce *equality* is both impossible and vicious. The laws of political economy, provided security be cared for, are nearly as accurate as the laws of gravitation. They can be reasoned out mechanically, like the equilibrium of physics or the affinities of chemistry, from sensations, ideas, pleasures, pains—which are subjective *copies* of the existing production and consumption of commodities.

In this calculation of Bentham's there were two omissions— scarcity and custom. They were omitted because misapprehended and not fitted to the models of the only sciences then known— physics and chemistry. Scarcity was familiar enough, but it was associated with the concerted action of the governments, monopolies, and corporations of mercantilism; whereas scarcity is none other than private property itself. With mercantilism thus rejected, scarcity took on, not the institutional form of property, but the physical form of a preordained law of equilibrium of supply and demand operating on fluid individual atoms like the waves of the ocean.

[50] Bentham, *op. cit.*, I, 358–361 (On the Levelling System).

And custom was looked upon as the ancient tradition of the common law—as Blackstone portrayed the common law and lawyers even yet portray it, when they consider that we have passed from the period of custom to the period of liberty and contract. When it comes to such customs as good-will, trade practices, going concerns, standard forms of contracts, the use of bank credit, the modern practices of stabilization, and so on—these are given the name "practices," as though there were a difference between custom and practice. But there is no difference except in the degree to which they compel uniformity and permit variability. The practice of using bank checks in America and England is as compulsory as was the custom of working on the estate of a feudal landlord. A business man has no more liberty to use gold or silver instead of checks than the medieval tenant had to become an outlaw with Robin Hood. He has much the same empty liberty of contract. He simply cannot continue in business if he refuses to receive or to pay bank checks. The case is similar with many other trade practices. A workingman cannot hold a job, if he comes at eight o'clock when the others come at seven. This is either a "practice" or a "custom." But, like the use of bank checks, the "practice" is as compulsory as custom. For custom is not merely something that happened when man was stupid; it is that expected repetition of transactions that must be observed by individuals if they expect, by dealings with others, to make a living or get rich. And private property, which Hume reduced to the principle of Scarcity, is itself only an evolving custom; for private property is all the changing repetitions of transactions that acquire, alienate, and permit the use of things that are scarce or expected to be scarce, under existing rules.

Bentham and Blackstone looked for custom in the past. That is true, but effete. Customs originated in the past. But they also changed in the past, and they are changing in the present. But this is not their sole distinction. Custom is also the *expectation*, based on experience, that practices will be repeated in the future, and it is this that gives to them that power of concerted action to compel uniformity of individual action, to which the name custom applies now, as always, rather than the individualistic and non-compulsory terms "practice" and "habit."

There are variabilities, of course, as conditions change. It is these variabilities that make possible the evolutionary changes of custom. The common law itself is only the decisions of disputes according to prevailing customs, each decision operating as a precedent. Between the multitude of conflicting precedents there is opportunity for the judges to select, so that the common law changes and "grows" by "artificial selection" looking towards future consequences, instead of being Blackstone's voice of God, characterized by Bentham as ancestor-wisdom.

Bentham and the molecular economists did not even look upon the standard of living as a custom, as was done first by John Stuart Mill and as it has obviously been looked upon in modern wage arbitrations which set wage and salary differentials according to differences in standards of living. For the early economists, the standard of living was a physical minimum of existence, like the physical minimum of coal needed to keep a steam engine going. It was not a custom, it was physiology.

Had the two items, scarcity and custom, been included in Bentham's calculus, then his concepts of the individual, of society, of commodities, of wealth, and of sovereignty would have broken down. Each individual's activities would then have become a function of the activities of all other individuals, instead of a mere addition of production, and a deduction by consumption, of physical goods. The total wealth of a nation would not have stopped as a mere sum of physical goods at a point of time. It would have become also the "assets" of individuals and concerns, obtained by a process of proportioning the ownership of the different kinds of goods and the different activities of producers in their transactions of holding, withholding, bargaining, and choice of alternatives, individually and collectively.

The customs, which Bentham had eliminated as mere ancestor-wisdom, would necessarily have come back in the practices of extortion, discrimination, and economic coercion; in the inequalities of opportunity and bargaining power; in the corporations, holding companies, unions—in fact, in all of the good and bad practices of a national economy which determine prices and quantities. And the function of sovereignty would have become not merely that of protecting the producers and owners of materials, but would have come back to something like the mercantilist policies of proportioning the activities of individuals, associations, and even of nations with regard to what was deemed by the political parties and dominant economic interests to be the best for classes and nations.

It was not until the time of the psychological economists that the principle of scarcity attained its first functional significance in the economic psychology of pleasure and pain. Bentham mentioned the principle of diminishing utility with increasing abundance, but his application of it had nothing to do with prices, nor with the bargains of individuals, nor with trade practices and customs. His application of diminishing utility pertained only to his discussion of security and the inequalities in the quantities of physical goods possessed by individuals. A larger quantity of commodities possessed by a rich person than by a poor person does not increase his happiness proportionately, and the total happiness is greater where there is equality of possession than where there is inequality.[51] This principle might lead to a system of progressive taxes or inheritance taxes, the latter of which Bentham advocated;[52] but the principle was not applied by him or the other physical economists to psychology or to prices and markets. For this reason we class Bentham as a physical economist, rather than as a psychological economist. His pleasures and pains were only copies of commodities and metallic money.

Bentham's elimination of custom and scarcity, by substituting money in the guise of pleasure, and sovereignty in the guise of wishes, prepared the way not only for the classical economist Ricardo and the hedonic business economists who substitute pleasure for money, but also for both the utopian socialists and the Marxian communists. The utopians took over Bentham's "equality," which he had subordinated to "security." The Marxians took over his sovereign, and made it the dictatorship of the Proletariate. Neither custom nor scarcity functioned in their theories.

By eliminating custom and scarcity, Bentham resolved economics and ethics into the wishes of independent individuals. Like Locke and Smith, as well as the entire school of individualistic moralists and economists who followed their lead through the Nineteenth Century, he was concerned with the individual process of arriving at moral and economic judgments and individual conduct. But if we consider the historical process by which custom becomes common law and even statute law and constitutional law, we find that it has been a collective process arising from the conflicts of interests, which he refused to concede. Instead, therefore, of starting with an individual, we start with the transactions between individuals and the expected repetition of those transactions—which, from the organized point of view is going concerns, and from the unorganized point of view is custom. Each bargaining transaction is in itself

---

[51] " . . . throughout the whole population of a state, the less the inequality is between individual and individual, in respect of the share possessed by them in the aggregate mass or stock, of the instruments of felicity—the greater is the aggregate mass of felicity itself: provided always, that by nothing that is done towards the removing of the inequality, any shock be given to security." Bentham, *Works*, II, 272 (*Constitutional Code*).

[52] "When property is vacated by the death of the proprietors, the law may intervene . . . with the design of preventing too great an accumulation of property in the hands of a single person." *Ibid.*, I, 312 (*Civil Code*).

a collective process. In its most extreme simplicity the transaction cannot be resolved into individual units, but requires the actual or potential presence of at least five individuals who bear to each other the several relations of equal or unequal opportunity, fair or unfair competition, moral, economic, or physical power, and the joint expectation of a decision of possible disputes by a fifth party representing the collectivity of which the five individuals are members.

This is the concerted process of arriving at both economic and ethical judgments and conduct, by the several participants concerned. The "conduct" of individuals, which formed the problem of ethics and economics, becomes the repeated, duplicated, and expected transactions of many individuals, which is but another name for custom evolving into the working rules of organized concerns. Lacking this historical and collective process of arriving at both economic and ethical judgments, the individualistic economists and moralists had to inject either a principle of divine benevolence, as did Locke and Smith, to take the place of custom and the common law, or, like Bentham, had to leave the matter in the realm of individual wishes.

But, beginning with the transactional point of view, we have for investigation the actual process, freed of the personifications of Locke or Smith, the skepticism of Hume, the physical analogies of Bentham, the divinity and ancestor-wisdom of Blackstone. Each transaction is in itself a possible harmony of interests out of a conflict of interests and a collective regulation of the conflict. It is a harmony of interests, as contemplated by Smith and Bentham, because it is the reciprocal relation of rendering a service to each other It is a conflict of interests, owing both to the competition for access to limited opportunities and the inequalities of individuals in their exercise of bargaining power. It is an ethical regulation of the conflict through the concerted operation of rules and decisions of disputes. Out of this regulation arise the current but changing ideals of equal opportunity, fair competition, equality of bargaining, and due process of law, which constitute the combined ethical, economic, and juristic problem of reasonable practices and reasonable prices.

Thus arises the volitional (distinguished from Bentham's hedonic) concept of value—not the traditional volitionism of individualistic ethics, but collective volitionism. This is a concept of choosing between opportunities that are scarce; it is therefore an economic concept of the will, as against the introspective concept of pleasure and pain. These opportunities are the property of self and other people; and this property depends on the concerted action, not only of the state, but also of corporations, syndicates, and unions, which determine by moral, economic, and physical sanctions what shall be the securities, conformities, liberties, and exposures of the individual in his choice of opportunities, exercise of power and competition. It is a concept of membership, citizenship, or participation, within a great variety of collective compulsions, differing in degrees of compulsion—as against Bentham's mass of individua atoms added together to constitute his fiction, the "community.

It is a concept of both individual and concerted action, governing and being governed—as against Bentham's passive individual, moved to act by accidental sanctions and an external sovereign. It is a concept of Blackstone's custom, common law, routine, ancestor-wisdom, even stupidity, operating in the field of money, credit, debts, taxes, practices, and prices—as against Bentham's lot of intelligent "lightning calculators" measuring off a "lot of happiness."

CHAPTER VII

MALTHUS

The Age of Reason ended in the French Revolution. The Age of Stupidity began with Malthus. Godwin, the anarchist, had proposed, in 1793,[1] that the principles of the French Revolution should be imported into England. Malthus, the theologian, replied, in 1798, with the principle of Overpopulation and a new idea of God.

It was Benjamin Franklin who, in 1751, first suggested overpopulation as the cause of the wage system.[2] He had a practical purpose. It was an argument against the Mercantilism of England's colonial policy which prohibited manufactures in America. England need have no fear of competition from American manufactures, because a wage system could not arise in this land of abundant natural resources. Franklin went back to biological scarcity and ended with proprietary scarcity.

"There is, in short, no bound to the prolific nature of plants or animals but what is made by their crowding and interfering with each other's means of subsistence. Was the face of the earth vacant of other plants, it might be gradually sowed and overspread with one kind only, as, for instance, with fennel; and were it empty of other inhabitants, it might in a few ages be replenished from one nation only, as, for instance, Englishmen. . . . In countries full settled . . . all lands being occupied and improved to the height, those who cannot get land must labor for others that have it; when laborers are plenty their wages will be low; by low wages a family is supported with difficulty; this difficulty deters many from marriage, who therefore long continue servants and single. . . . Land being thus plenty in America, and so cheap as that a laboring man, that understands husbandry, can in a short time save money enough to purchase a piece of new land sufficient for a plantation, whereon he may subsist a family, such are not afraid to marry. . . . There are supposed to be now upwards of one million English souls in North America (though it is thought scarce eighty thousand has been brought over by sea) and yet perhaps there is not one the fewer in Britain, but rather many more, on account of the em-

[1] Godwin, William, *An Enquiry Concerning Political Justice and Its Influence on Virtue and Happiness*, 2 vols. (1793).

[2] Franklin, Benjamin, "Observations Concerning the Increase of Mankind and the Peopling of Countries" (1751) in *The Works of Benjamin Franklin* (ed. by Jared Sparks, 1882), II, 311. Citations are to the Sparks edition.

ployment the colonies afford to manufactures at home. . . . But notwithstanding this increase, so vast is the territory of North America, that it will require many ages to settle it fully; and, till it is fully settled, labor never will be cheap here, where no man continues long . . . a journeyman to a trade, but goes among those new settlers, and sets up for himself . . . in proportion to the increase of the colonies, a vast demand is growing for British manufactures, a glorious market wholly in the power of Britain, in which foreigners cannot interfere. . . . Therefore Britain should not too much restrain manufactures in her colonies. . . . The labor of slaves can never be so cheap here as the labor of workingmen is in Britain. . . . [Americans purchase slaves] because slaves may be kept as long as a man pleases, or has occasion for their labor; while hired men are continually leaving their masters (often in the midst of his business) and setting up for themselves. . . . The danger therefore of these colonies interfering with their mother country in trades that depend on labor, manufactures, etc., is too remote to require the attention of Great Britain." [3]

Franklin's appeal in 1751 to the British Mercantilists fell unnoticed. Malthus did not discover it until he revised his *Essay on Population* for the second edition in 1803. The Malthusian argument, in 1798, was not, like Franklin's, a futile petition to the self-interest of England; but like Franklin's, it had a practical purpose. Its purpose was the disillusionment of the Age of Reason and a justification of existing institutions.[4]

The French had logically combined Adam Smith's sympathy, self-interest, sense of propriety, and rejection of concerted action, and, under the name of liberty, equality, fraternity, had abolished landlords, church, and all collective action of guilds, corporations, and any other association. Godwin, the father of all the anarchists, had carried Smith's rejection of collective action into a rejection of the State itself, and had carried Smith's natural liberty, equality, and sympathy into the equal perfectibility of all men if only the organized coercion of government, which afforded Smith's security of property, were eliminated.

Five years later, Thomas Malthus, the theologian, brought against Godwin's natural equality of man the natural sinfulness of man, which should be expected to nullify all schemes based on the supposed liberty, equality, and sympathy. He converted Smith's divine abundance for the purpose of human happiness into divine scarcity

[3] *Ibid.*, II, 312–319.
[4] Malthus, T. R., *An Essay on the Principle of Population as It Affects the Future Improvement of Society* (first edition, 1798), 173 ff.

for the purpose of evolving the human mind and moral character out of the "clay of the earth." Not only the wage system, but also vice, misery, poverty, and war were incidental to the divine principle that population should increase faster than the means of subsistence. This Malthus named the "principle of population," which is none other than the biological foundation of the principle of Scarcity. It is this principle that is the basis of what he called the "mighty process of God . . . for the creation and formation of mind; a process necessary, to awaken inert, chaotic matter, into spirit; to sublimate the dust of the earth into soul; to elicit an aethereal spark from the clod of clay." [5]

The economists of the Nineteenth Century took from Malthus only the materialistic basis of overpopulation developed in the first half of his book, whereas Malthus himself considered that his great contribution was his theory of Moral Evolution in the latter half of his book. From the overpopulation argument the economists preached race suicide to the wage-earners. From the spiritual conclusion, Malthus preached the moral evolution of human character out of what afterwards was called "the struggle for existence." He was the first scientific evolutionist, indeed the first scientific economist, in that he derived his theory, not from assumptions, like Smith's reversal of the historic process, but from investigation of the process itself. From these investigations he developed the economic principle of scarcity, and this is the reason why both Darwin and Wallace got their idea of evolution immediately after reading Malthus. But his was the Origin of Morals. Theirs was the Origin of Species. Both proceeded from Overpopulation.[6]

Wallace has stated his process of reasoning immediately after he had read Malthus.[7] He proceeded from the *positive* checks of war, poverty, vice, misery, not from the preventive, *volitional* checks, which Malthus named *moral* checks. These non-volitional, or positive checks, yielded only the Biological Evolution of Darwin and Wallace, not the Moral Evolution of human character, which was the aim of Malthus.

This was the Malthusian break from the older ideas of divine

---

[5] *Ibid.*, 353.

[6] We quote from the first edition of Malthus (1798). In his second edition (1803) he emphasized the preventive restraints which afterwards the classical economists adopted as preachments to wage-earners in their efforts to raise wages. Articles on Darwin and Wallace in *Encyclopaedia Britannica* bring out the way in which they obtained their insight from Malthus.

[7] Wallace, Alfred Russel, *My Life, A Record of Events and Opinions* (1905, 2 vols.), I, 232, 240, 361.

beneficence and earthly abundance which descended from Locke to Quesnay and Smith. We should not, said Malthus, "presume to reason from God to nature," but "should reason from nature up to nature's God," whose thoughts are above our thoughts "as the heavens are high above the earth." That which first awakens the mind in this divine process of Moral Evolution is the stimulus of wants of the body, for the mind is created only by activity.

> "It can scarcely be doubted, that these stimulants could not be withdrawn from the mass of mankind, without producing a general and fatal torpor, destructive of all the germs of future improvement. . . . To urge man to further the gracious designs of Providence, by the full cultivation of the earth, it has been ordained, that population should increase much faster than food." [8]

Thus the divine abundance of Locke, Quesnay, and Smith becomes the divine scarcity of Malthus. The one would leave man a lazy, stupid animal; the other makes him work, think, and plan for future progress.

But it is not only Smith's abundance and Smith's self-interest, it is also Smith's sympathy that springs from overpopulation.

> "The sorrows and distresses of life form another class of excitements, which seem to be necessary, by a peculiar train of impressions, to soften and humanize the heart, to awaken social sympathy, to generate all the Christian virtues, and to afford scope for the ample exertion of benevolence. . . . It seems highly probable, that moral evil is absolutely necessary to the production of moral excellence." The principle of population "undoubtedly produces much partial evil; but a little reflection may, perhaps, satisfy us, that it produces a great overbalance of good." [9]

But it follows that all men cannot be equally free and perfectible. It is the "middle regions of society" that are best suited to this intellectual and moral improvement. Both luxury and poverty produce evil rather than good; yet we cannot have middle classes without having upper classes and lower classes. "If no man could hope to rise, or fear to fall, in society; if industry did not bring with it its reward, and idleness its punishment, the middle parts would not certainly be what they now are." [10]

"Godwin," said Malthus, "considers man too much in the light of a being merely intellectual"—as indeed also did Locke, Quesnay, Smith, Bentham, and the other philosophers of the Age of Reason.

[8] Malthus, *op. cit.*, 350, 359, 361.
[9] *Ibid.*, 372, 375, 361–362.
[10] *Ibid.*, 369.

To consider man a "rational being" is like "calculating the velocity of a falling body in vacuum." He is a "compound being" whose "corporeal propensities act very powerfully as disturbing forces." Indeed they usually predominate over his reason.[11]

Thus Malthus introduced the passions into economics, whereas, for the philosophers of the Eighteenth Century, culminating in Smith, Bentham, and Godwin, what they called "feelings" were only intellectual counters which rational beings used to calculate forces, probabilities, supply and demand, greatest happiness, and greatest profits. But, for Malthus,

"the question . . . does not merely depend, upon whether a man may be made to understand a distinct proposition, or be convinced by an unanswerable argument. A truth may be brought home to his conviction as a rational being, though he may determine to act contrary to it, as a compound being . . . hunger . . . liquor . . . woman, will urge men to actions, of the fatal consequences of which, to the general interests of society, they are perfectly well convinced, even at the very time they commit them."[12]

If this is true, then not only coercion and punishment by the state are necessary[13] but also private property. Godwin's error consisted in attributing vice and misery to human institutions instead of human nature.

"Political regulations, and the established administration of property, are with him the fruitful sources of all evil. . . . Yet, in reality, they are light and superficial, they are mere feathers that float on the surface, in comparison with those deeper seated causes of impurity that corrupt the springs, and render turbid the whole stream of human life. . . . Man cannot live in the midst of plenty. All cannot share alike the bounties of nature. . . . Suppose all the causes of misery and vice . . . removed. War and contention cease and universal benevolence take the place of selfishness." If so, condensing his argument, then marriages will be contracted without the duty of providing for the children, since, on the principle of equality, the community will provide for them if the parents do not. Population would therefore increase geometrically but subsistence only arithmetically. He goes on: "What becomes of the picture? . . . The hateful passions that had vanished reappear . . . in so short a period as within fifty years. . . . Violence, oppression, falsehood, misery, every hateful vice, and every form of distress, which degrade and sadden the present

[11] *Ibid.*, 252 ff.
[12] *Ibid.*, 254, 255.
[13] *Ibid.*, 259.

state of society, seem to have been generated by the most imperious circumstances, by laws inherent in the nature of man, and absolutely independent of all human regulations." [14]

Godwin's community "would call a convention."

"The question was no longer, whether one man should give to another, that which he did not use himself; but whether he should give to his neighbor the food which was absolutely necessary to his own existence. . . . Imperious necessity seemed to dictate that a yearly increase of produce should, if possible, be obtained at all events; that in order to effect this first, great, and indispensable, purpose, it would be advisable to make a more complete division of land, and to secure every man's stock against violation by the most powerful sanctions. . . . It seems highly probable, therefore, that an administration of property, not very different from that which prevails in civilized states at present, would be established, as the best, though inadequate, remedy, for the evils which were pressing on the society. . . ." [15]

"It is, undoubtedly," concludes Malthus, "a most disheartening reflection, that the great obstacle in the way to any extraordinary improvement in society, is of a nature that we can never hope to overcome. . . . Yet . . . no possible good can arise from any endeavors to slur it over. . . . Sufficient yet remains to be done for mankind, to animate us to the most unremitted exertion." [16]

His later book, in 1821, *Principles of Political Economy*, was his puzzled but humanitarian reply to Ricardo's materialism. [17]

Thus Malthus restates in the language of piety, the conclusions of the skeptical Hume, that not only self-interest and private property, but also self-sacrifice, sympathy, and justice, proceed from the principle of scarcity which is none other than his principle of population. Henceforth the passions of man claim a place along with Smith's natural liberty and Bentham's intellectual calculus of pleasure and pain. Darwin and Wallace each acknowledge their debt to Malthus. The struggles of politics and war for life and property take the place of Smith's divine abundance, while ignorance, passion, envy, habit, custom, scarcity, take their place above reason, liberty, equality, and fraternity. [18] Smith's optimism disappears in what

[14] *Ibid.*, 176–191.

[15] *Ibid.*, 195–198. The refusal of Russian peasants, after the triumph of Communism, to raise grain when it was commandeered for the urban communities is one of many instances of the validity of this argument.

[16] *Ibid.*, 346, 347.

[17] Below, p. 348, Ricardo and Malthus.

[18] The elaborate emotional philosophy of the Nazi government of Germany, as portrayed in detail by Calvin B. Hoover, is a special case of this Malthusian principle. See Hoover, Calvin B., *Germany Enters the Third Reich* (1933).

Malthus admits is a "melancholy hue of human life," but which he finds, nevertheless, really "in the picture," because he starts with human nature in its hard reality and does not confuse facts with justification, nor what *is* with what he *wishes*, nor nature with what nature ought to be. His justification of the ways of God to man, with which we began this chapter, was not the beginning of his book. It was the social philosopher's conclusion of his *Essay on Population*.

Thus Malthus, at the collapse of the Age of Reason, proclaimed the Age of Stupidity. It stretched from the anarchistic philosophy of the French Revolution to the communistic philosophy of Russia, to the fascistic and nazistic philosophies of Italy and Germany, and to the individualistic philosophy of American capitalism. The concept of Nature changes from Locke's abundance at the Garden of Eden to Darwin's scarcity and survival of those who survive—not because they are morally fit, as Malthus hoped, but just because they fitted the moral and economic environment, as Hume had philosophized. Malthus began the disillusionment of an Age of business cycles, overproduction, underproduction, unemployment, mass migrations, tariffs, monopolies, political and economic struggles of landlords, peasants, farmers, capitalists, and laborers; an age that split economists into capitalistic, anarchistic, communistic, syndicalistic theorists; an age that brought another world war with its revolutions, dictatorships, tariffs, imperialism, futile American efficiency and drastic American exclusion of the overpopulation of Europe—the "melancholy hue" of Malthus vindicated and even frightfully overdone.

CHAPTER VIII

EFFICIENCY AND SCARCITY

I. Materials and Ownership

Throughout the Nineteenth Century, and even back to John Locke, the double meaning of the word Wealth lay at the root of the conflicting schools of economic thought. It was the meaning of Wealth as materials and as their ownership. This we name the orthodox meaning of wealth. Those who first clearly made the distinction between materials and ownership were the heterodox communists and anarchists. But the orthodox schools always assumed that wealth meant the same thing as ownership of the wealth. The standard instance was the meaning of a commodity: A commodity was physical material which was owned.

The double meaning arose from the fact that the customary meaning of property was corporeal property Corporeal property evidently expands and contracts with the corporeal thing which is the object of ownership. If my colt grows to a horse, then my corporeal property grows from ownership of a colt to ownership of a horse. The earlier economists had no place in their meanings of wealth for incorporeal or intangible property. They treated them as commodities, though they were debts and opportunities for profit. And, even operating with the idea of corporeal property, they made no distinction between materials and the ownership of the materials.

The contradictory mèanings of materials and ownership were exposed by the Communists and Anarchists in the middle of the Nineteenth Century, but the orthodox economists, including the later psychological economists, continue the orthodox double meaning to the present day.

This double meaning appears plainly as late as 1906 when Irving Fisher published his notable book on *The Nature of Capital and Income*. Fisher, at that time, as, however, only a part of his total system of economic science, followed the prevailing usage of the commodity economists by defining wealth as *"material objects owned by human beings."* [1] His analysis did not stop with the former mere assumptions of ownership involved in the term corporeal prop-

---

[1] Fisher, Irving, *The Nature of Capital and Income* (1906), 3.

erty; he carried the double meaning forward to its contradictory conclusions. "According to this definition," he says, "an object, to be wealth, must conform to only two conditions: it must be material and it must be *owned*."

". . . some writers," adds Fisher, "add a third condition, namely that it must be *useful*. But while utility is undoubtedly an essential attribute of wealth, it is not a distinctive one, being implied in the attribute of appropriation; hence it is redundant in a definition. Other writers, like Cannan, while specifying that an object, to be wealth, must be useful, do not specify that it must be owned. They therefore define wealth as 'useful material objects.' This definition, however, includes too much. Rain, wind, clouds, the Gulf Stream, the heavenly bodies—especially the sun, from which we derive most of our light, heat, and energy —are all useful, but are not appropriated, and so are not wealth as commonly understood."

Here are the two meanings of utility, the use-value and scarcity-value. It is the latter meaning which Fisher excludes as "not a distinctive" meaning of wealth, because it is "implied in the attribute of appropriation." This is certainly accurate, but leads to contradiction. The basis of ownership is scarcity, as Hume pointed out. If a thing is expected to be so abundant that everybody can get it without asking consent of anybody or of government, it becomes the property of nobody. If limited in supply it becomes private or public property. The sun is not appropriated, but limited supplies of sunlight are appropriated by owning favorably located land sites, factories, and homes. The Gulf Stream, though limited, is made free for all, outside a three-mile limit, by international agreement. One nation might own it if its navy drove all other navies from the oceans. Hence proprietary economics is the world-wide economics of scarcity. Of course, objects must have use-value, in what we have defined as the technological economics of engineering and the physical sciences. But if useful things are not scarce or expected to be scarce they will not be produced and there will be no struggle for ownership—they will not be owned, privately or publicly. Hence we identify property-value with scarcity-value, which we name assets, not wealth; but wealth we identify with use-value which has no scarcity dimensions of supply and demand. This, we concede, contradicts the current orthodoxy of "diminishing utility." But the latter concept lies at the foundation of the confusion of wealth with assets.

Fisher rightly criticises other writers who insist that an article, to be wealth, must be "exchangeable," since this would exclude parks, Houses of Parliament, and much other trusted wealth. "Although it is essential that wealth should be owned, it is not essential that it should continually change owners." Of course, the reason why wealth is owned is because it is scarce. The first essential of ownership is scarcity; the collective action of society constructs the rules of exchange of ownership.

"Again," says Fisher, "many writers, like MacLeod, omit the qualifier 'material' altogether, in order to make room for the inclusion of such 'immaterial wealth' as stocks, bonds, and other property rights, and for human and other services. Property and services are, it is true, inseparable from wealth, and wealth from them, but they are not wealth. To embrace all these under one term involves a species of triple counting. A railway, a railway share, and a railway trip are not three separate items of wealth; they are respectively wealth, a title to that wealth, and a service of that wealth." [2]

Here, of course, Fisher recognizes the distinction which we point out. But he had previously defined wealth as a material thing, the railway, which must be owned. The ownership is the title.

We may even carry the analysis further and have quadruple counting. We have the railway as a technological going plant turning out a "service" of wealth as an output of use-values, the trips. This is "wealth." We have also the ownership of the railway, a business organization charging a price for the trip and thereby bringing in an income for the owners. This is assets and income. But we have the word "service" with the double meaning of an *output* of .managerial transactions turning out use-values regardless of prices, and as an *income* of money values for the owners, derived by bargaining transactions with those who can pay for the services.

The significance of these meanings will appear in Fisher's criticism of those economists who, like Tuttle,

"have endeavored to break away from concrete objects entirely. The term 'wealth,' they maintain, applies, not to concrete objects, but to the *value* of these objects. Much may be said in support of this contention. But as the question is chiefly verbal, that is, not a question of finding a suitable concept, but of finding a suitable word for a concept, it does not seem advisable to depart from the prevailing usage among economists." [3]

The question would, indeed, be only verbal were it not for the

[2] *Ibid.*, 4.
[3] *Ibid.*, 4.

two kinds of value, use-value and scarcity-value, and the resulting difference between *output* and *income* which rests on the difference between materials and ownership, between wealth and assets. The technology of production of materials simply yields output regardless of who owns or enjoys it. Rights of property convert it into income. This is not a verbal difference. It is the difference between output and income, between technological capital which enlarges output, and proprietary capital which obtains ownership of it and limits its demand or supply. If the output of wealth (use-value) is already defined to include income from that wealth, then, of course it is double counting to count also the property rights by which that output becomes income. But it becomes double counting only because it had previously been a double meaning of wealth—wealth and assets.

The working out of engineering or technological economics is illustrated by Fisher, but under the concepts of *income* and *ownership* rather than *output* and *input*. He says,

"Various classes of wealth may be distinguished. Wealth which consists of the earth's surface is called *land;* any fixed structures upon it, *land improvements;* and the two together, constituting immovable wealth, *real estate.* All wealth which is movable (except man himself) we shall call *commodities.* A third group includes human beings—not only slaves who are owned by other human beings, but also freemen who are their own masters." [4]

This classification of human beings as wealth to the extent of their labor-power, had matters of ownership, liberty, and income been excluded, would have been quite accurately the engineer's concept of wealth as the output of use-value derived from the input of nature's forces, including human nature. When engineers write or philosophize on economics, this is the way they do it.[5] Fisher cites also a large number of economists who have "included man in the category of wealth", namely, Davenant, Petty, Cunard, Say, McCulloch, Roscher, Willstern, Walras, Engel, Weiss, Dargun, Ofner, Nicholson, and Pareto. Others might have been added, such as Ricardo and Karl Marx. Indeed, it was Marx who gave to this engineering economics its classic conclusion. It is a quite legitimate and necessary part of the whole of political economy, for it is the concept of productivity and efficiency, regardless of property rights or feelings. These several economists had not clearly recognized

[4] *Ibid*, 5.
[5] Ingails, W. R., *Current Economic Affairs* (1924); Taylor, F. W., *The Principles of Scientific Management* (1911); Dahlberg, Arthur, *Jobs, Machines and Capitalism* (1932).

the need of distinguishing the opposing fields of political economy—efficiency and scarcity—and had not the advantage of the engineering terms input and output, contrasted with the business terms outgo and income, which would have made the distinction clear. Taking society as a whole, but omitting property and the proprietary outgo or income, this is the social organization of production, whose behavioristic language is the managerial transactions of command and obedience; whose measurement is man-hours input and use-value output; whose economics is efficiency and whose human beings are power machines.

Fisher recognizes this paradox of including human beings as wealth, but his apology would not have been needed had he perceived that he was talking two languages at once, engineering and business. The field of engineering needs no apology except when it is set up by engineers for business economy or political economy. The difficulty arises when slaves are emancipated. Fisher says,

> "It is true that freemen are not ordinarily counted as wealth; and, indeed, they are a very peculiar form of wealth, for various reasons: first, because they are not, like ordinary wealth, bought and sold; secondly, because the owner usually estimates his own importance so much more highly than any one else; and finally, because the owner and the thing owned in this case coincide." [6]

This apology to human beings is unnecessary if engineering economy is intended. The engineer, as such, treats human energies the same as the other forces of nature. They are man-power. They are not owned, as far as the engineer, *per se,* is concerned. Yet Fisher goes on: Human beings, like other wealth, are "material" and "owned."

> "These attributes, and others which depend upon them, justify the inclusion of man as wealth. But in order to concede as much as possible to popular usage, the following supplementary definition is framed: By wealth (in its more *restricted* sense) we mean *material objects owned by man and external to the owner.* This definition obviously includes slaves, but not freemen. But it is more difficult of application than the wider definition first given, as it requires us to separate into arbitrary classes those persons who are intermediate between freemen and slaves, such as vassals, indentured servants, long-time apprentices, and negroes held in peonage. . . . most workers in modern society are 'hired,' *i.e.* bound by contract to some extent and for some period of time, even though it be for no more than an hour, and to that extent

[6] Fisher, Irving, *op. cit.,* 5.

are not free. In short, there are many degrees of freedom and many degrees of slavery, with no fixed line of demarcation." [7]

These puzzles are unnecessary if institutional economics is distinguished from engineering economics. Institutional economics is the relation of man to man, but engineering economics is the relation of man to nature. The engineers' concept of wealth excludes all reference to the proprietary economy, which is the historical and institutional economy of the evolution of rights, duties, liberties, and exposures. The engineers' concept of wealth, if it excludes ownership, is quite the correct concept of wealth. Wealth is merely the physical attribute of use-values, no matter who owns the materials, or labor, or output, and no matter if the *use-values* are oversupplied and their *scarcity-value* is thus so diminished that nobody cares to own them. So far as the engineer is merely an engineer, not under the business man's orders, he goes on producing indefinitely. Today, he has become surprised that the world's business organization will not permit him to use his abilities for the good of mankind. But the business man sees that, although the greater the efficiency of the producing organization, which the engineer brings about, the *greater* is the production of wealth. Yet he also sees, from the private standpoint of ownership, of income, of demand and supply, or ability to pay, that the *less* is their proprietary value, or assets.

From the standpoint of engineering, as such, all human relations take on the single aspect of managerial transactions where there is no freedom for the worker, and the relation, for the time being, is only command and obedience. The total man-power of the nation is the total input, and the total physical control over nature's forces is the total output. But the institutional aspect is the *sharing* of that output and the *inducements* that keep the concern agoing. Two systems of measurement are used, the engineer's man-hour and the business man's dollar.

With this double meaning of wealth—the engineering meaning of output of materials (use-value) and the business meaning of income from ownership (scarcity-value), we are confronted by the very situation that reveals the conflict between business economy and engineering economy. It is the double meaning of the word "service," referred to above. Fisher describes service as the "income" derived from capital or wealth. "An instrument renders a service when, by its means, a desirable event is promoted or an undesirable event prevented." [8]

[7] *Ibid.*, 5–6.
[8] *Ibid.*, 336.

Thus, "A paper manufacturer . . .," he says, "was offered a round sum" by his competitor "if he would close his mills. This he did," and "the contract which he made with his rivals constituted a kind of property for them; the wealth by *means* of which his promise was made good was evidently his own person, together with his plant; and the service performed was the inactivity of both." [9]

According to this double meaning, a paper mill yields the "services of wealth" when it is making paper and when it is not making paper. By the same reasoning a bricklayer performs a service when he lays brick and when he is out on a strike. Running a loom is a service and shutting it down is a service. Restricting output is a service and increasing output is a service. Increasing the scarcity of goods is a service, and increasing the abundance of goods is a service.

These contradictions are plainly a confusion of output with income, of materials with ownership of materials, of efficiency with scarcity, of wealth with an owner's assets. Output is a service rendered to other people regardless of the price; income is the price received by the owner, based on his right to withhold service from others in the proprietary process of bargaining or waiting until the others will pay a satisfactory price. *Income* is the proprietary acquisition of assets; *output* is the engineering augmentations of wealth, or Cromwell's commonwealth. Restricting output is not a service—it is bargaining power. The resulting scarcity is not a service. It is a means of acquisition. Efficiency is a service, even though nothing is paid for it.

When wealth, capital, income, service, are defined with these contradictory meanings, only doubtful social programs can be built upon the definitions. They are a confusion of efficiency with scarcity, of production with ownership, of output with restriction of output, of engineering economy with business economy, of private income with social output, of assets with wealth.[10]

Yet there is a different sense in which private ownership renders a service to society. It is not by *production*, but by the *regulation* of production. The regulation must be made by somebody, either by the rationing of Communism or the self-interest of Capitalism. This double meaning runs back to Quesnay and all the orthodox

[9] *Ibid.*, 28.

[10] Cf. Commons, John R., "Political Economy and Business Economy: Comments on Fisher's Capital and Income," *Quar. Jour. of Econ.*, XXII (1907), 120 ff. Fisher, in a later article (*Quar. Jour. of Econ.*, XXIII, 536), stated that he was considering only the causes of market valuation, "which seldom, if ever, exactly registers utility to society." The discrepancy, he said, belongs to "social pathology and therapeutics." But we are considering the need of therapeutics.

economists, and serves to confuse the meanings of efficiency and scarcity. If the engineer, as such, goes on producing independently without regard to falling prices, the business man, who is always in control of the engineer, gives orders to restrict the output of that commodity, and turns, if he can, to the production of other commodities whose prices are not falling. If the farmer finds that the price of wheat is falling, but the price of hogs is rising, he turns his labor-power from wheat to hogs. He supplies a more intense demand by producing hogs, and a lesser demand by producing wheat.

This is indeed a service to society, *if it is well done*. The Eighteenth Century economists believed the *regulation of production* would be well done by relying only on private property and self-interest. But they had to bring in Divine Beneficence to guide self-interest, and earthly abundance to render it harmless. The Nineteenth Century *materialistic* economists believed regulation would be well done by private property and self-interest, but they had to bring in a kind of beneficent "natural" law, an overruling natural right, or an analogy to Newton's laws of equilibrium. If these were not enough, they had to go back to the Eighteenth Century and appeal to God and Patriotism.[11]

But the Nineteenth and Twentieth Centuries contradicted them at every point. Depressions, scarcity, and misery became as natural and divine as Prosperity, Abundance, and Happiness. Hence they and all others turn to many kinds of collective action in lieu of God or Nature, in order to regulate private property and self-interest. They realize that the scientist or engineer has done only too well in his work of controlling physical nature. By collective action they must find a way to control human nature.

Yet, by means of an idealized society and an idealized human nature, guided divinely or naturally towards an assumption of *continuous prosperity*,[12] they read into certain evident facts a principle of *ideal regulation* of production by private property and self-interest. The proprietor renders a service to society, without intending to do so, by apportioning and economizing the productive forces of society so that *not more* is produced of one thing than is wanted, at the expense of producing *less* than is wanted of other things.

Hence the confusion of the double meaning of production, as producing and regulating production, which is the confusion of efficiency and scarcity, as a social service. The sagacious business man, or proprietor, is "productive" in the sense of regulating pro-

---

[11] Above, p. 13, John Locke.
[12] Below, p. 719, Ideal Types; above, p. 158, Adam Smith.

duction proportionate to supply and demand, as evidenced mainly by *changes in prices*. But the scientist, or engineer, is productive in the sense of enlarging man's control of the forces of nature, *regardless of prices*.

It is on account of this double meaning of productivity as enlarging supply and proportioning supply, that we substitute the more modern terms of activity in the various kinds of transactions. Activity requires the introduction of time, velocity, rate, turnover, repetition, etc. At this point we analyze them as the principle of Efficiency and the principle of Scarcity. By efficiency is meant, in terms of managerial transactions, the *rate of output per unit of input, the man-hour*, thus increasing the power over nature but regardless of the total quantity produced. By scarcity is meant, in terms of bargaining transactions, the *rate of proprietary income* from other persons relative to the *rate of proprietary outgo*, measured by the dollar. Inefficiency means a *slower rate* of output per unit of input, but weak bargaining power means a *lesser rate* of income per unit of outgo.

It is the changes in terminology from production to efficiency, from supply and demand to scarcity, that have been brought about by introducing the *time* concepts of velocity, rate of turnover, visible and invisible supply, etc. The introduction of this time factor makes more clear the difference between the two kinds of service rendered to society. Efficiency tends to increase the abundance of goods, or to reduce the man-hour costs, or to reduce the hours of labor. Scarcity distributes the output to those who can pay and withholds it from those who cannot pay, or increases the hours of labor, or reduces the pay to laborers who do not have equal bargaining power.[13]

Efficiency and Scarcity are here treated each abstractly in order to distinguish them. In fact, they set limits to each other, according to the principle of limiting and complementary factors.[14]

II. REAL AND NOMINAL VALUE

The preceding discussion was intended to show that the institution of property was tacitly accepted by all schools of commodity economists, whether the classical objective school or the hedonic subjective school, as the starting point in their definitions of wealth, resulting in the revolutionary schools of Marx and Proudhon and the confusion of scarcity with efficiency. When converted into

[13] Below, p. 276, Input-Output, Outgo-Income; p. 294, From Circulation to Repetition.
[14] Below, p. 627, Strategic and Routine Transactions.

terms of activity, then the concept of property, with its rights, duties, liberties, and exposures of bargaining transactions, is the volitional equivalent of scarcity; while materials, with their managerial transactions, are the volitional equivalent of efficiency. A similar volitional and materialistic confusion runs through meanings of real and nominal value. The distinction turns on what is deemed important or unimportant and what seems to be actual, when everything is changing. As we have noted in Chapter II, each of the schools of economic thought has its following at the present day, for each selected a part of the whole, and built its system on that part by taking the others as self-evident or unimportant. Indeed every student of political economy repeats in his own mind the historical evolution of the schools, and a study of the history of economic theory is not an academic curiosity—it is a recapitulation of the evolution of our own thinking.

Practically everybody, in our civilization, begins his working life as a Mercantilist, because money is the familiar and all-important instrument by which he gains a living. The more money he can acquire, the richer and more successful he is, and the more money a nation can acquire from other nations and the less it must pay to them, the more prosperous does the nation seem to be. He remains a Mercantilist if he is successful and the nation is prosperous. Everything of value is measured by money.

But if he is thoughtful or unsuccessful, or the nation is depressed, or debtor nations cannot pay, he begins to ask, What are the Real Values back of money or more important than money? Then he begins to distinguish money as nominal value or institutional value, and something else as real value. Here his puzzles begin, and practically all the schools of economic thought which accompanied or followed Mercantilism have been involved in the puzzles which every individual meets in distinguishing real value from nominal or institutional value.

Do we mean by real value that which is fair and reasonable as between all parties because there is no coercion or misrepresentation? If so, then nominal value is the actual price but real value is what ought to have been the price. This was the answer of the theological school whose leader was Thomas Aquinas, and it is the answer of modern institutionalists.

Or do we mean by real value a "natural" value which would ensue if there were no monopolies or interferences by government, such that all values were fixed by perfectly free competition of labor and capital? If so, then nominal value is scarcity-value but real value is what would have been the price if labor alone were the measure of value. This was the answer of Smith, Ricardo and Marx, as well as Aquinas.

Do we mean by real value the happiness which we enjoy from consumption, or the pain which we suffer in production? If so, then nominal value is again the actual money price but real value is our satisfactions or our sacrifices. This was the answer of the psychological school and Adam Smith.

Do we mean by real value the quantities of commodities which we can purchase with our money? If so, then nominal value is money-value but real value is the quantity of commodities and services acquired by paying out money. This is the meaning of modern economists.

Finally, nominal value is itself a very real value for the person who is called upon to pay his debts or buy his food immediately, and cannot sell his products or labor for enough money to pay his debts or buy his food. This is the meaning in all business economy, and the reason why people are mercantilists.

When confronted with these various meanings of real value contrasted always with the institutionalist or monetary meaning of nominal value, and when we find that the various schools of commodity economists agree on these meanings of nominal value but differ on the meanings of real value, we infer that we must go deeper into these meanings of nominal value and real value. We find, on examination, that by nominal value what they really meant was scarcity-value, depending on the institution of property whose measure is a unit of another institution of scarcity-value, money; and that by real value was meant whatever was deemed important, including money itself. Having taken scarcity for granted as a constant factor, when they came to any variability from that constancy they named it nominal value.

The difficulty resides in the instability of the conventional measure of scarcity. It may be gold, or paper, or credit. The gold dollar was stabilized in its physical dimensions of use-value as 25.8 grains nine-tenths fine, but its scarcity-value was its average purchasing power. Only when modern index numbers were invented did it become possible to measure the changes in the scarcity-value of money. Each commodity, including money, has its own changing scarcity-value. Scarcity itself is a changing social relation between the total quantity wanted and the total quantity available in any or all bargaining transactions. The total quantities wanted and available are vaguely known as demand and supply. But we have no means of measuring directly demand and supply. We can only measure their effects on transactions. It is similar to the measurement of heat or weight.

We measure a change in heat indirectly by measuring its effects on a column of mercury marked off arbitrarily in fixed units of length. So we measure changes in scarcity by their effects on the price paid for a unit of scarce commodity marked off arbitrarily in units of dollars and cents.

But these units themselves are not fixed, like units of length. They are more nearly like units of weight, which weigh less at high elevations than they do at the sea-level, and must be corrected mathematically to their sea-level equivalents. So with the unit of money. Its variability must be corrected to an assumed level of its average purchasing power at a point of time, say the year 1913, or 1926, and then the changes in its scarcity-value are the inverse of the changes in its average purchasing power above or below that level. From this base level the changes in relative scarcities of individual commodities become the "dispersion" of their prices from the average.

Hence average purchasing power is a statistical substitute for the effort to distinguish nominal value from real value. It is merely a unit of measurement of the scarcity-value of money, which varies inversely to its average purchasing power. As prices rise the value of the money unit falls, or as prices fall the value of the money unit rises. It is this average that is used as a base-line, and not any notion of real value, from which to measure the dispersion of individual prices. It is a theory of measurement and not a theory of real or nominal value.

Thus the statistician, taking the average purchasing power of money for the year 1913 as 100, measures the subsequent changes in relative scarcities of individual commodities, no matter what may have been the *causes* of the change, by their dispersion from the average. During a succeeding period the average, perhaps, of the prices of the same commodities rose 10 per cent, showing that the scarcity of money, relative to the average of all other scarcities, had declined 9 per cent.

Lacking this mathematical device of index numbers of averages and dispersions the early economists searched for something which should be not only more stable than money, which measured only nominal values anyhow, but should be more substantial in measuring real value. At first, consistent with their theories of nature's abundance and beneficence, they looked upon scarcity, not as natural, but as the artificial scarcities imposed by the policy of Mercantilism. The Physiocrats substituted the different producing powers of nature as determining the real exchange-values of commodities. Adam Smith substituted the quantity of average common labor which the owner of wealth could purchase with his money or with his wealth converted into money. Average common labor was not only a stable measure of value for him, but it also measured the real value of the commodities and services which the labor of others could procure for self from nature's resources.

Smith's idea appeals to us at first sight. The extent of our real enjoyment of necessaries, conveniences, and luxuries depends evidently upon the amount of labor which we can command from others in rendering services to us. But the idea was evidently inadequate to mark off the artificial scarcities which Smith had mainly in mind. The owner of a monopoly can command more labor, just as much as he can command more money, than he could if his business were competitive.

Ricardo corrected this. Real value was not the quantity of labor which we can *command* from others, nor even the quantity of commodities, but was the quantity of labor which it had cost to produce the commodities and services, while his nominal value was the quantity of commodities produced or purchased at the fluctuating prices in money or the artificial scarcities created by monopolies and restraints of trade.

This again appeals to us as something real. Everything of value is produced by labor. Indeed, Ricardo gave to this labor-cost of production the name Value. He assumed apparently that it was the only Real Value. It applies to gold and silver as well as all commodities and services, and served to distinguish paper money from real money as well as artificial scarcity from real value. If there were no paper money created by government and no artificial restraints or privileges, then everything, including metallic money, would exchange with each other in proportion to the amount of labor which it cost to produce them. This was, indeed, with modification, the theory of the scholastic economists, five hundred years before Ricardo. Commodities and services, if there were no artificial restraints, nor coercion, nor misrepresentation, would exchange in proportion to their real value, measured by labor-cost. That commodity which cost more labor (not wages) had more value than that which cost less labor to produce it, and therefore equal labor exchanged for equal labor.

Herein Ricardo, by changing the meaning of real value from *command* over labor to *labor-cost* of production, confuted the fallacy of the Physiocrats and Adam Smith and the fallacy that remains to this day, that *nature* in agriculture is productive. He exposed also the related fallacy that nature is productive in manufactures and transportation. Indeed, the proposition that all use-values are the product of labor runs counter to the usual assumption that nature aids man in the production of wealth and that nature therefore is also productive. We see the forces of nature at work everywhere. A steam engine, a waterfall, the fertility of the soil, the improvement of wine that grows more valuable with age, and so on, are the forces of nature at work. It seems mere common sense to say that nature, as well as man, is productive, and, in confuting this idea, Ricardo is the greatest of economists, not even yet understood.

He merely reversed the interpretation of the ratio between output and input. Where those whom we may call the theological economists held that the output was increased by the aid of nature, those whom we may now call the efficiency economists, led by Ricardo, held that the rate of output was increased because, with the aid of man's inventions, the resistance of nature was overcome. The older view went back to the theological assumptions of John Locke, Quesnay, Adam Smith, and Malthus, contrasted with Ricardo's materialistic assumptions, regarding man's relation to nature. Is nature beneficial to man, therefore aiding him in the production of wealth, or is nature inimical to man, therefore resisting him in the production of wealth? In either case her benefits or resistances are differential. She benefits him more, or resists him less, in some directions than she does in others. If an acre of fertile land yields 20 bushels, and an acre of marginal land yields only 10 bushels, for the same amount of labor, the theological economists would say that on the first acre nature produced twice as much as on the poorest acre, but the efficiency economists, led by Ricardo, would say that on the first acre nature's resistance was half as much as on the marginal acre. Or when electricity carries a message 3,000 miles in less than a second and a steam engine requires four days, the theological economists would logically be led to say that nature aids man more by electricity than she does by the expansion of vapor. But the efficiency economists would say that man's power over nature is greater when he invents and uses electricity than when he invents a steam engine. It is the same comparison of two mathematical ratios of output to input, but in one case it is interpreted as nature's differential benefit to man, in the other case as man's power over nature's differential resistance to man.

Ricardo made the distinction clear when he classified both machinery and fertility, not as capital or land, but as increased productivity of the labor of man.[15] When we say a piece of desert land is not productive, what we mean is that man cannot produce a crop by cultivating it. The land is not productive. Only the mental,

[15] See below, p. 348, on Ricardo.

manual, and managerial labor of man is productive, and he searches for ownership of the places and materials of nature where his labor is more productive. If the Physiocrats and Adam Smith were right in identifying nature with a beneficent God, then the deity furnishes wealth gratuitously to some but compels others to work for it. If Ricardo was right, then nature is the physical forces which man strives to own and control for his own purposes, and the differentials are due, not to God, but to the institution of property which gives to some owners protection against taking from them the differential advantages over marginal land to whose ownership others are relegated. What man seeks to own is not the productivity of nature but the differential resistances of nature. This was understood by Karl Marx who made rent a matter of private property and not a result of the productivity of nature.

But Ricardo's concept of real value was not worked out by him in all its details. This was done by Karl Marx, who substituted the man-hour for Ricardo's man-month or man-year, and this made more clear the change from productivity to efficiency. Henceforth we are able to see that the ultimate difference between Communism and Capitalism is in the choice of the unit of measurement of Value. Communism measures value by the man-hour, and is therefore a theory of Differential Efficiency.[16] Capitalism measures value by the dollar, and is therefore a theory of Differential Scarcity.

The distinction may be found in the difference already mentioned between wealth and assets. A great manufacturer of leather, in 1921, found that the value of his hides and leather had suddenly fallen 50 per cent by a fall in the average of prices. He had to borrow $5,000,000 in order to make good his loss in assets. But the paradox remained that his Wealth, in the form of machinery, buildings, hides, leather, and the efficiency of his plant was not diminished at all in quantity or quality. For Ricardo and Marx the real value of the wealth was the quantity of labor required to produce it. This had not diminished. But the value of the Assets was a nominal value because it was merely the institution of property valued at the prices at which he could sell his hides and leather.

Here, of course, the distinction between nominal and real breaks down. Assets are as real in one sense as is wealth in another sense. We abandon the terms nominal and real except as used by modern statistical economists, and substitute the institutional terms scarcity-value and use-value in order to fit the facts. Use-value is wealth produced by labor (manual, mental, and managerial), which, as such, does *not diminish* with a fall in prices, nor increase with a

---

[16] On the distinction between Communism and Socialism, see below, p. 531.

rise in prices. Its variability is its wear and tear, depletion, depreciation, obsolescence, and invention. But Scarcity-value is prices paid for legal control measured in terms of money. Value itself is Assets, or the value of ownership; a dollar multiple of the quantity of use-value *times* the dollar price.[17]

This compound meaning of Value is neither nominal nor real. It is statistics and accountancy. It does not answer the question, What is really or truly valuable according to our notions of ultimate reality. It is only a customary formula of two highly variable magnitudes, use-value and scarcity-value, combined in another highly variable magnitude, Value. This meaning of Value therefore turns only on the practice of measurement, and measurement is not ultimate—it does not tell what is really true—it is only the language of number in terms of artificial units not found in nature but put there by collective action to facilitate transactions.

Thus we separate the theory of measurement from the theory of reality. Afterwards we can read into the measurements any conclusions which we think important according to our ethical assumptions, whether of communism, socialism, capitalism, anarchism, fascism, nazism, unionism, or what-not. It was Ricardo and Marx who constructed what they thought was real value, but what was merely the man-hour unit for measuring changes in the efficiency of human ability in creating use-values out of nature's resources.

Ricardo had not analyzed in detail his meaning of labor. Labor seemed to be a commodity, like a horse or engine, bought, sold, stoked, or fed by capitalists. But Marx corrected him not only by defining labor as social labor-power but also as mental and managerial as well as manual labor. Yet Marx and his followers, like Ricardo, continued to emphasize manual labor. Not until the revolutionary inventions of the Nineteenth and Twentieth Centuries and the more recent rise of scientific management have mental and managerial labor acquired even a more important position in the theory of production than manual labor. For, what is an automatic machine, or an automatic plant like a flour mill, or the modern machinery of agriculture, or even the sustained fertility of the soil, except the mental labor of past generations repeating itself in the minds of present-day scientists and engineers? They are the result of centuries of mental labor. There are said to be 200,000 chemical compounds unknown to nature. These are the output of mental labor, more than manual labor, which overcomes the resistance of nature, and manual laborers must themselves be mental, else monkeys could do their work. Managerial labor, too, is mental labor coupled

---

[17] Including discount; see below, p. 390, on MacLeod and Futurity.

with the institution which determines the extent of command and obedience.

It is this evolving repetition and coördination of manual, mental, and managerial labor, which may be named Social Man-Power or the Marxian Social Labor-Power. The term is intended to give to mental and managerial ability its due weight along with manual labor. It is intended to distinguish engineering economy from proprietary economy, which Marx was the first clearly to distinguish. It does not determine the exchange-values of products, as Marx contended, since these are determined by scarcity and bargaining power. But the term signifies the associated human energy at work in overcoming the resistance of nature by creating social use-values.

We thus have two meanings of Human Ability—producing power and bargaining power. Producing power is the mental, managerial, and manual ability which is power to create *wealth,* but bargaining power is the proprietary ability to withhold products or production pending the negotiations for transfer of *ownership* of wealth. The one creates use-value, the other determines scarcity-values. Each is human ability in action, and, though inseparable socially, they can be distinguished by analysis or division of labor, and measured separably.

III. Averages

First, how shall we construct a unit for measuring the total quantity of all use-values? There are hundreds of units of such measurement, such as the bushel of wheat, the size of a building, the number of suits of clothing, the ton of iron, the acre of land, the kilowatt-hour, and so on in unknown variety. But there is one unit common to all of them, just as money is common to all of them, and that unit, as contended by Ricardo and Marx, is the unit of labor-power required to produce them.

This unit is a time-unit as well as a quantity unit. It measures a process. It changes economics from "statics" to "dynamics." Ricardo had not fixed upon a particular unit of time. He used the man-year, the man-month, or the man-day. Marx made it the man-hour, and thereby formulated, for the first time, what has now become the unit of scientific management for measuring the efficiency of the individual laborer, or of all labor organized in a plant or nation.

But Marx's man-hour was an *average* man-hour. There are two opposing fallacies regarding the use of averages, which may be named the individualistic and the communistic fallacy. These should be examined, for, in economics, we use many averages. The value of the dollar is the inverse of its average purchasing power. The efficiency of labor is its average producing power. Averages are needed in economics because we deal with mass movements, and they are the common everyday usage of conversation. Yet the average is only a formula existing in the mind. There is no such thing as an average man or an average purchasing power. There are only individual producers and individual prices. Hence the individualistic fallacy rejects totally the use of averages because only individual men or individual prices have real existence, and science cannot deal with fictions—it must deal with concrete reality.

But in using the average we do not assert its real existence. We use it only as a mental formula for investigation and action. Its validity as a formula depends upon its fitness to the particular problem in hand. An average of cows and men may not be a useful average for some purposes. But the average life of mankind is the basis of life insurance.

The communist fallacy of averages is just the opposite. It wipes out individuals altogether by reducing each individual to a number of aliquot parts of the whole. On this fallacy Karl Marx constructed his concept of Social Labor-Power. Individuals disappeared as such, and reappeared as multiples or fractions of aliquot parts of a total social labor-power. The common laborer working one hour was his aliquot part of the total. The skilled workman was two or three aliquot parts, the child one-half, the woman two-thirds of a man, and so on. While the individualistic fallacy rejected the average because only individuals really existed, the communistic fallacy rejected individuals because only social labor-power was the real existence.

But individuals do exist, and they exist as social man-power. This is what we mean by a going concern. They exist as participants in transactions. Their participation in managerial transactions is the "going plant," turning out use-values by their social labor-power. Their participation in bargaining transactions is their "going business," acquiring each a share in the use-values produced by the social man-power of the world. The results of their participation in managerial transactions are their joint efficiency. The sharing of their product by bargaining transactions is determined by control of relative scarcities.

Evidently, then, if we are to compare the efficiency of one plant with that of another, or the changes in efficiency of the same plant at different times, or the efficiency of one nation with another nation, we must construct a mental unit, the average man-hour. And if we are to compare the shares obtained by participants we must construct another mental unit, the average purchasing power of money.

On examination of Marx's communist fallacy which caused the individual to disappear and made only social labor-power the real existence, we find that he was unknowingly constructing a *weighted average*. The skilled mechanic counted as 3, the common laborer counted as 1, the woman as 0.66, the child as 0.5. Individuals do not really disappear, but in a weighted average we give to them different numerical values. The communist fallacy gave real existence to a weighted average. To this kind of fallacy is sometimes given the name Metaphysics, or "reifying" a mental formula. It is a common error of the credulous and Pythagoreans, who thought that numbers were real existences and settled disputes.

But in the construction of a weighted average there may be a more important fallacy. It is the confusion of efficiency with scarcity. Should the general manager at $20,000 per year be given 20 times the weight of his stenographer at $1,000 per year? If we were constructing the formula of an average income this would be a proper weighting. But if we are constructing the formula of average efficiency, we cannot tell whether the manager is more efficient than the stenographer. They do different kinds of work which are incomparable, yet each is an essential part of the whole. We know that the manager gets more wages, but that may be only because managers are scarcer. If managers were as abundant as stenographers, their wages would probably be no higher. This has become distressingly evident to "white collar" workers. And the scientist or inventor, whose mental work contrived the machinery or layout which perhaps increased the efficiency of the plant more than all others combined, probably gets less wages than the manager, because scientists and inventors are more abundant or have less bargaining power than managers. All that we know of their comparative efficiency is that each is necessary to the efficient working of the particular concern, or of the social man-power of the nation as a whole. Hence no error is made, which is worth while correcting, when we construct a simple average, counting each individual as one. Individuals can, indeed, be compared with other individuals when doing the same kind of work. But when doing different kinds of work the only measurable difference is their wages, and wages measure relative scarcities, not relative efficiencies. Hence the average man-hour unit is a simple average, where each individual counts as one.

Nor can we compare the efficiency of different concerns producing different kinds or qualities of use-value. We cannot compare the efficiency of an automobile factory with the efficiency of a clothing factory. We can compare them by dollars, but this changes the comparison to earning power or bargaining power, away from efficiency. We can only compare the efficiency of different establishments producing the same kind and quality of product, and we can compare the efficiency of the same establishment in 1920 with its efficiency in 1929.

The usefulness of this kind of comparison by averages depends ultimately on our concept of Political Economy itself. Is economics a *process*, or is it an *equilibrium* of forces seeking their level? Is it static, or is it dynamic? If it is a process, then *Change* is what we measure. This is the problem of index numbers, of averages and dispersions. In measuring changes in efficiency the *man-hour* is the proper unit. In measuring changes in relative scarcities the *dollar* is the unit. The one gives the changes in the average producing power of mental, managerial, and manual labor; the other the changes in the average purchasing power of money.

Having constructed the average man-hour as a unit of measurement, how shall the formula be applied to the process of production? Karl Marx was the first to analyze this technological social process which we now call *efficiency* but which he called the "creation of *surplus value*." [18] Marx constructed two concepts, "constant capital" and "variable capital," in order to develop his idea of surplus value, but which, taken together, turn out to be merely the concept of efficiency. He said:

"... The means of production on the one hand, labor-power on the other, are merely the different modes of existence which the value of the original capital assumed when from being money it was transformed into the various factors of the labor-process. That part of capital then, which is represented by the means of production, by the raw material, auxiliary material and the instruments of labor, does not, in the process of production, undergo any quantitative alteration of value. I therefore call it the constant part of capital, or, more shortly, *constant capital*.

"On the other hand, that part of capital, represented by labor-power, does, in the process of production, undergo an alteration in value. It both reproduces the equivalent of its own value, and also produces an excess, a surplus-value, which may itself vary, may be more or less according to circumstances. This part of capital is continually being transformed from a constant to a variable magnitude. I therefore call it the variable part of capital, or, shortly, *variable capital*. The same elements of capital which, from the point of view of the labor-process, present them-

[18] This is not represented in our Chart 5, p. 175. That chart represents the process of *exchange* on the markets, not the process of *production* in the shop.

selves respectively as the objective and subjective factors, as means of production and labor-power, present themselves, from the point of view of the process of creating surplus-value, as constant and variable capital." [19]

It should not be inferred that, by his terms constant and variable, Marx intended anything like the "fixed" and circulating capital of the classical economists. By "constant" capital he meant the *depreciation* and *obsolescence* of fixed capital combined with the transformation of "circulating" capital into the output of a shop, factory, or farm. Thus, to use his illustration, the total value of a fixed capital in the form of machinery may be $1,054, but the wear and tear of the machinery in the production of a certain amount of output is only $54. It is the value of this wear and tear that is his "constant" capital which the capitalist advances in producing that output. In this way a capitalist advances say $500 in a process of production. This is "split" up as follows. "Constant" capital $410, "variable" capital $90, and, at the end of the process, the original capital has enlarged from $500 (C) to $590 ($C^1$). The enlargement, $90, is "surplus value."

But the constant capital ($410) is itself composed of three constituents, $312, the value of raw material; $44, the value of auxiliary material; and $54, as above, the value of the wear and tear of the machinery. We name these, materials and depreciation. The total value ($410) is his "constant capital advanced for the production of value."

Since the total value of the machinery employed is supposed to be $1,054 but only $54 is used up in the process, there remains a value of $1,000 "which still continues in the machinery." The value of the wear and tear is "constant" just because it is not "fixed." It "circulates," just as the value of the materials circulates. By "circulation" he means, as did Quesnay, the *transfer* of "value" without increase or decrease. For the same reason the value of the materials (raw and auxiliary) is "constant" capital. It is the sum of these values ($410) that is "transferred" without change to the value of the product while it is passing through the shop in the process of production.

But the $90 paid for labor-power is "variable" capital. It is variable in that it is the active force that is continually transforming constant capital into a "variable magnitude." He names this active process the "subjective factor," while the "means of production" (materials and depreciation) are the "objective" factors in

[19] Marx, Karl, *Capital; a Critique of Political Economy* (tr. 1909, Kerr ed.), I, 232–233; same citations for what here follows.

the process. From the "point of view" of "the elements of capital" purchased by the capitalist, they are means of production and labor-power; from the point of view of the "process of creating surplus value" the same "elements" are "constant and variable capital."

Extended to the whole social process over a period of time, that part of Marx's "constant" capital, which he identifies with materials and depreciation, uses up the whole of the "remaining machinery" ($1,000 in his illustration) and transfers its value to the whole of the social product. Thus the so-called "fixed" capital is reduced by Marx, through the concept of "wear and tear," or depreciation, to the same concept of "constant" capital as the "materials," in that the *value* of each, without augmentation or deduction, is transferred to the social product.

It is this social process that, following recent economists, we shall name the Social Technological Turnover. Marx's theory was evidently based on a return to Quesnay's concept of "circulation" which had been tacitly abandoned by Smith when he substituted division of labor.[20] And his term "value" which, like Ricardo, he identified with the amount of labor-power embodied in the product throughout the entire social process of "transferring" the "constant" value of materials and depreciation into the "value" of the product, we convert into the *output* of his social use-value relative to the *input* of man-hours of his social labor-power. This, again, is the modern meaning of efficiency.

Evidently here, in the concept of efficiency, is the origin of his concept "surplus value." If "output" of use-value is given the name "value" because it is created by labor and measured by man-hours, while "input" is given the name "value of variable capital" because it is the man-hour cost of furnishing subsistence to laborers during the productive process, then the spread between output and input might be named "surplus value," because it belongs to the employer and not to the laborer.

One problem for Marx is, how to take care of changes going on *outside* the shop. His process of creating surplus value occurs only inside the shops, factories, or farms where production takes place. He takes care of these outside forces by means of two considerations: the *socially necessary* labor-time, and the *constant proportion* between constant and variable capital.

He gives and explicitly justifies a double meaning of "necessary labor-time."[21] One is the labor-time necessary to produce the value of the total social product, including "surplus value." This would

---

[20] Below, p. 294, From Circulation to Repetition.
[21] Marx, Karl, *op. cit.*, 240 n.

include the time necessary, by depreciation, to use up the "fixed" capital.[22] The other is the labor-time necessary to produce "only the value of his labor-power, that is, the value of his means of subsistence." In either case the "socially necessary labor-time" is "limited by social conditions."

These social conditions, outside the individual shop, we may distinguish, following his usage, as threefold: changes in natural conditions, changes in inventions and obsolescence, and changes in the general level of prices.

Changes in natural conditions are typified by him in the case of changes in agricultural production.

"If the time socially necessary for the production of any commodity alters—and a given weight of cotton represents, after a bad harvest, more labor than after a good one—all previously existing commodities of the same class are affected, because they are, as it were, only individuals of the species, and their value at any given time is measured by the labor socially necessary, *i.e.*, by the labor necessary for their production under the then existing social conditions." [23]

This means a change in value of his *constant* capital. It is "constant," not that it does not change in value, but that it does not transfer to the product more or less than its then value.

"Suppose," he says, "the price of cotton to be one day sixpence a pound, and the next day, in consequence of a failure of the cotton crop, a shilling a pound. Each pound of the cotton bought at sixpence, and worked up after the rise in value, transfers to the product a value of one shilling; and the cotton already spun before the rise, and perhaps circulating in the markets as yarn, likewise transfers to the product twice its original value." [24]

The same is true if the value of the cotton is measured by man-hours instead of money. The function of constant capital is to transfer to the product, through the value of the raw material and the value used up in depreciation, the number of man-hours of value necessary to produce the output under the changeable conditions of physical nature. And the "socially necessary" labor is merely Ricardo's *highest* labor-cost (man-hours) necessary to produce the most expensive part of the product on the margin of cultivation. This highest labor-cost, by the process of free competition, gives the similar exchange-value to all competing units on the same market at

[22] Below, p. 598, on Böhm-Bawerk's "period of production."
[23] Marx, Karl, *op. cit.*, 233–234.
[24] *Ibid.*, 233.

the same time, regardless of the man-hour cost of each. Hence the *differential* efficiencies, or differential efficiency profits, of individual establishments are not considered when attention is directed to the whole social process of production and to the measurement of changes in social efficiency. This is one reason why Marx eliminates Ricardo's theory of Rent. His "socially necessary" labor is Ricardo's marginal laborer, whose labor-cost determines the exchange-value of all supermarginal products.[25]

Invention and obsolescence of machinery is another "social condition" arising outside the individual shop.

"If in consequence of a new invention, machinery of a particular kind can be produced by a diminished expenditure of labor, the old machinery becomes depreciated more or less [becomes obsolescent] and consequently transfers so much less value to the product. But here again, the change in value originates outside the process in which the machine is acting as a means of production. Once engaged in this process, the machine cannot transfer more value than it possesses apart from the process." [26]

Here it may be said that the term "outside the process," refers to the "mental labor" of scientists and inventors, and is included in Marx's meaning of "social" labor-power. It is not, for him, a part of the shop process, but is a part of the entire social process of invention and obsolescence, operating on the individual shop through the agency of free competition.

Finally, "outside the process" of production in the shop is a general rise or fall of prices. This is a "social condition" that affects more or less alike all market values of materials, of capital equipment and of the means of subsistence of labor-power. And here it becomes clear, as Marx maintained in regard to the other "social conditions," that it was not any *absolute* difference between constant and variable capital that he made the foundation of his system. It was a "proportion" or *relative* difference between the two. If all money prices and wages rise or fall equally, then it is evident that the *proportion* between the amount of social labor-power necessary to produce the total output and the amount needed to produce the means of subsistence of the laborers does not change.

Thus, rightly enough, any change in particular prices or in all prices generally, must be eliminated if it is desired to ascertain just how much is the change in social efficiency, which is his change in "surplus value." What he says of external changes in technical

[25] See also below, p. 348, on Ricardo and Malthus.
[26] Marx, Karl, *op. cit.*, 234.

conditions coming from inventions and obsolescence is true of all changes in prices including changes in agricultural conditions of good crops and bad crops. The *proportions* do not change.

"The technical condition," he says, "of the labor process may be revolutionized to such an extent, that where formerly ten men using ten implements of small value worked up a relatively small quantity of raw material, one man may now, with the aid of one expensive machine, work up one hundred times as much raw material. In the latter case we have an enormous increase in the constant capital [depreciation and materials] that is represented by the total value of the means of production used, and at the same time a great reduction in the variable capital [means of subsistence], invested in labor-power. Such a revolution, however, alters only the quantitative relation between the constant and the variable capital, or the proportions in which the total capital is split up into its constant and variable constituents; it has not in the least degree affected the essential difference between the two." [27]

Thus Marx was the first economist to formulate all of the factors necessary, and exclude the factors not necessary, to the modern concept of efficiency. His reasoning was rejected, not on account of its inaccuracy, but on account of his social philosophy and the odd meanings of words which he introduced to support that philosophy. It is not surprising that the communist followers of Marx, in Russia, should have staked their whole fortune on a revolution in technology, regardless of the many "social conditions" which Marx had rightly eliminated if only a theory of efficiency was being formulated, instead of an all-round theory that should include such "external" factors as habits and customs of the people, international complications, money and credit, the rise and fall of prices, etc. Confined to the more modest dimensions of a mere formula of efficiency as one of several factors in the social process, he formulated a principle which has only begun to come into economics from the "outside" profession of engineering. But these engineers also, when they proceed to add a social philosophy to their efficiency concepts, come out, as we shall see, at practically the same conclusion as did Marx, namely, Communism, or the inverted communism known as Fascism.

We proceed to reconstruct Marx's theory into a theory merely of efficiency, as we can observe it coming in as a part of a whole theory of political economy.

[27] *Ibid.*, 234.

IV. Input-Output, Outgo-Income

In the year 1920 a certain clothing factory required 10 man-hours of *operating* labor to produce a standard suit of clothes, but in 1929 it required only 5 hours per suit. The efficiency was increased 100 per cent. During the same period the average wage was increased from 80 cents per hour to 90 cents per hour, and the wholesale price of the suit was reduced from $33.00 to $24.00 per suit. The efficiency is measured by man-hours, the scarcity of labor or scarcity of suits is measured by dollars.

Evidently confusion of efficiency and scarcity would arise if we should use the terms input and output in the sense of input of dollars and output of dollars' worth of product. The input would be 80 cents or 90 cents per hour of labor, and the output would be $33.00 or $24.00 per suit. Hence we substitute the terms outgo and income to indicate the scarcity ratio measured by dollars, while output and input indicate the efficiency ratio measured by man-hours. The *input* per unit of *output* fell from 10 man-hours to 5 man-hours, indicating an increase of 100 per cent in efficiency. The *outgo* to labor from the employer's assets increased from 80 cents to 90 cents per hour, indicating an increase of 12½ per cent in the scarcity of labor; and the *income* from the sale of suits decreased from $33.00 to $24.00, indicating a decrease of 24 per cent in the scarcity of suits.

Yet a confusion of this efficiency with this scarcity arises wherever common sense uses the dollar instead of the man-hour to measure efficiency, and wherever economists indiscriminately use "input" of money instead of "outgo" of money. The reason why economists use "money input" as the measure of efficiency is set forth recently by J. D. Black in his *Production Economics*,[28] and it goes back to Ricardo's similar use of the pound sterling when he meant labor-hours. They did not use *actual* money input but only a figurative stable purchasing power of money, in order to eliminate money from the calculation. This is proper enough for purposes of analysis and separation of the factors, but leads to social fallacies.

Black distinguishes "physical" input from "price" input, and holds that "when physical inputs are all converted to a price basis, they can be combined into one input figure." He illustrates,

"If the price of 32 minutes' use of a machine is $0.64; of 32 minutes of labor, $0.56; of 640 horsepower-minutes, $1.20; and of 115 bushels of wheat, $140.00; and the output is 25

[28] Black, John D., *Introduction to Production Economics* (1926), 314 ff.

barrels of flour; then the input per barrel of flour is $142.40 divided by 25, or $5.65. Thus the one operation of converting input data to a price basis overcomes the two shortcomings of the physical input data." [29]

These shortcomings, according to Black, are as follows:

First, the impossibility of "adding the use of a machine for 32 minutes, the 32 minutes of man-labor, the 640 horsepower-minutes, and the 115 bushels of wheat used in producing 25 barrels of flour." Second, "the . . . defect of physical input data is that in themselves they include none of the effects of fluctuating prices. . . . In a period when wages are high and machinery cheap, manufacturers use less labor if possible and substitute machinery for it at every turn; but if the reverse is true, labor would tend to take the place of machinery on many operations." [30]

Based on these price measurements Black constructs a formula of the "least-cost combination per unit of output," which is the point of greatest efficiency. These least costs are determined at the point where the sum of all fixed and variable "inputs per unit of output in cents" is the lowest. Thus the "least-cost combination of machine inputs" in producing flour, in an illustrative mill, is at the point where the input of wheat, at a constant price per bushel, is 6,750 bushels. That is the point where, at the constant prices paid for factors of production, the sum of all the money inputs per bushel is lowest, including the money input for interest, depreciation, taxes, repairs, and maintenance. If other factors of input are taken into account, at supposed constant prices, such as buildings, labor-power, supervision, fixed machines, and variable machines, then the least-cost combination per bushel of wheat occurs at an input of something less than the money cost of 9,000 bushels. [31]

These computations by Black are highly important and useful in the private management of agricultural concerns, and indeed of any concern. We use them as a starting point to show the changes to be introduced in order to move from the private to the collective or social point of view.

First is the distinction between materials and ownership, previously considered. But the term "materials" is not adequate. We substitute the term "use-values," to include, under one name, all useful services of a technological sort to whomsoever rendered. In this way the "personal services" rendered by labor are use-values as much as the "material services" rendered by commodities. Both

[29] *Ibid.*, 315.
[30] *Ibid.*, 314.
[31] *Ibid.*, 391, 392.

are rendered by labor, the one directly, the other through the intervention of materials.

The term "ownership" also, in collective action, includes all transfers of ownership. This means transfers of ownership, not of materials, but of the use-values directly or indirectly augmented by labor.

These meanings are altogether separated from any subjective or psychological valuations. Subjective values are individualistic. Objective "values" are values only by analogy. They are only relations or processes subject to change from any cause whatever. By "objectivity" is meant anything which changes independently of the individual will. Hence there are two kinds of objective values, physical use-values and proprietary scarcity-values, the one proceeding from collective labor-power, the other from that collective power over individuals which we name institutions. One of these institutions is money, in the sense of a collective instrument for the creation, negotiability, and release of debt by individuals.

Property, therefore, or ownership is as objective as materials, or labor, or use-values. In other words, all emotion, feelings, or volitions are eliminated and we take, for the time being, the position that pure science is supposed to take, the position of pure intellect, analyzing without emotion or purpose the collective action of labor-power in controlling nature's activities, and the collective action of institutions in controlling individuals' activities.

Hence the distinction between labor-cost and proprietary cost. The latter might be named institutional cost. The two are the double meaning of the familiar "cost of production." In order to keep the distinction clear, by converting it into terms of activity, we use the term "input" for labor-cost and the term "outgo" for proprietary cost. Labor-cost is of three kinds, manual, mental, and managerial input. Proprietary cost is of two kinds, the alienation of ownership of use-values and the alienation of ownership of the negotiable instrument, money.[32]

This analysis results in a threefold relation of use-value. It may mean output and it may mean outgo or income. As *output* it is the technological qualities of usefulness related to the input of labor. Here it means creation of *Wealth* for "society." As *outgo* it is the *alienation* of legal control, either by a laborer who produced it or by one who has acquired its ownership from the laborer. Here it means decrease of *Assets* for the individual by alienation. As *income* it is *acquisition* of ownership either *from* the laborer or from any other preceding owner who alienates it; or *by* the laborer

[32] See next chapter, Futurity.

from an employer or merchant. Here it means increase of Assets for the individual by acquisition.

Since Money, an institution, is not productive in the technological sense, its relations between individuals are only twofold, *outgo,* or alienation, and *income,* or acquisition. And, since modern society is mainly a money-credit economy we are accustomed to identify proprietary cost with money-cost, and this elision may be practiced if it is borne in mind that money-cost is always an alienation-cost, not different in kind from alienation of ownership of any use-value.

The distinction may be made in our foregoing example of a clothing factory. The *labor-cost* of making a suit of clothes had been reduced from 10 man-hours to 5 man-hours, a reduction of 50 per cent. We name it a reduction of labor-input per unit of labor-output (use-value). But the *money-cost* to the employer in payment for the average man-hour of labor had been increased from 80 cents to 90 cents, an increase of $12\frac{1}{2}$ per cent. This we name money-outgo in exchange for ownership of the labor output. It is the difference between producing power and bargaining power. The increased producing power had doubled the *output* of *wealth* (use-value) per man-hour, but the increased bargaining power of the laborers had increased the labor *income* 10 cents per hour and reduced the employer's *assets* the same 10 cents per hour. If efficiency is measured by dollars, then the employer who beats down wages is more efficient than the one who raises wages, just as he is more efficient when he introduces machinery and better organization by which he reduces the amount of labor input per unit of output.

Thus efficiency, when measured by dollars, has the double meaning of reducing wages and reducing the amount of labor required to produce the commodity. The first is bargaining power which takes advantage of relative scarcities. The other is producing power which takes advantage of relative efficiencies. Both are "costs" of production, but they are two different kinds of cost. We distinguish the one as proprietary cost, or outgo, determined by bargaining transactions and measured by money, the other, not as cost, but as input, determined by managerial transactions and measured by man-hours.

The similar contradiction exists at the selling end of his business. If efficiency is measured by dollars, then the employer who can sell at higher prices is more efficient than the one who sells at lower prices, just as he is more efficient when he increases the output per unit of labor. Raising prices may be monopolistic or artificial scarcity, which Ricardo named "nominal" value, but increasing the output per unit of labor is reducing Ricardo's "real" value. We should now say: increasing the business man's selling prices increases his assets, but increasing the output of his going plant increases the rate of production of wealth. And the distinction now can be made, which Foreman makes in his notable analysis of the confusions in court decisions,[33] between efficiency profits and scarcity profits. Efficiency profits are obtained by increasing the rate of output *per unit of labor,* which is the same as reducing the rate of input of labor *per unit of output.*[34] But scarcity profits are made by raising prices received or reducing prices and wages paid.

Thus there is no similarity between producing power and bargaining or purchasing power, a similarity implied when both are measured by the same unit, the dollar. They are as different as man's relation to nature and man's relation to his fellow-men. The difference is to be tested by the unit of measurement. If the quantity can be measured by man-hours, it is power over nature; if by dollars it is power over fellow-men. The terminology must be constructed to fit the difference. Input-output signifies man's power over nature. Outgo-income signifies power over other persons. It is this that makes the distinction between engineering economy and proprietary economy. Input-output are terms derived from physics and engineering. Outgo-income are terms fitted to the diminution or augmentation of that ownership which is assets. All of the terms are confused in the usual terms cost and value.

The contrasted terms, input and output, are appropriate in that they are derived from physics and engineering. They indicate the quantity of "energy" of one kind as input, converted into a quantity of energy of another kind, the output. But here must be distinguished three meanings of the terms input and output as used respectively by the scientist, the engineer, and the political economist.

The physical scientist is interested in the conservation of energy throughout the universe. One form of energy is converted into other but equivalent forms. It appears now as electricity, now as gravitation, now as chemical action, now as food or clothing, now as the living human body, now as the dead human body passing off into other forms of energy. Nothing is lost or wasted. Indeed in many cases, the scientist can actually account for the equivalent energy in different forms of repeated input and output of energy. Thus an input of one horse-power of steam pressure per second equals an output of 550 pounds weight raised one foot per second,

---

[33] Foreman, C. J., *Efficiency and Scarcity Profits; an Economic and Legal Analysis of the Residual Surplus* (1930).

[34] This must be distinguished from increasing the rate of output by increasing the *quantity* of labor-input. See below, p. 284, on Production, Productivity, and Efficiency.

and this, as input, equals an output of 746 watts of electricity per second, which, again as input, equals an output of 178 calories of heat per second, and so on even to the equivalent chemical input and output of the human body. These equivalents we may name the ideal efficiency of science, because, if the theory of conservation of energy is correct, then nothing is lost and all energies are accounted for in changing from one form to another form.

But, for the engineer, distinguished from the scientist, most of these energies are lost and wasted. He is interested in useful energy (use-value), not useless. He is content with practical efficiency, for he introduces human control into the operations of the universe. The best efficiency of a steam engine is said to be about 10 per cent of the potential calories embodied in the coal; of a compound condensing steam engine about 25 per cent of the calories; of a gasoline or oil engine as high as 40 per cent of the heat energy released inside the cylinders; of dynamos 90 per cent of the input of mechanical energy delivered as output of electric energy. The sun is said to deliver a quantity of energy somewhat equivalent to lifting 15,000 tons one foot upon an acre during a crop season, but man-power gets out of it only one-tenth of a foot-ton in the stored-up energy of 50 bushels of wheat. Man-power is only $\frac{1}{75,000}$ efficient. The scientist attempts to account for the 15,000 foot-tons of energy in the heat, electricity, vibration, weeds, straw, wheat and so on, but the agricultural engineer is content if he can increase the crop from 30 bushels to 40 bushels per acre. He is interested in useful work, not useless work.

It depends on what the engineer wants. If he wants noise, then he constructs his motor and equipment to produce as much noise as possible, and every other output is wasted. If he wants to move a sewing machine, then the energy that goes off in noise and friction is wasted. This is what we mean by engineering economy and use-value. Use-value is not something passive—it is a consequence of the activity of nature's energies directed by human intelligence for human purposes with as little waste as possible.

But the political economist narrows still further the meanings of input and output, because he is interested in human energy. The physical inputs of the engineer become outputs of human energy for the economist. They are the forces of nature which human energy converts into buildings, soil fertility, chemical compounds. The engineer does not care what kind of energy he uses as input. He uses whatever kind which, compared with other energies, is the more efficient in creating use-values. Neither is he interested, as such, in the prices paid for labor, materials, or energies. That is the business man's puzzle. If, in the existing state of the arts, steam-power is more efficient than labor-power, he uses steam-power. Each is a machine, and thus we have what may be named the engineer's machine-theory of labor, distinguished from the merchant's commodity-theory. The commodity-theory of labor turns on the prices that must be paid on account of the scarcity or abundance of labor. This was the classical theory of economics. The machine-theory of labor turns on the greater or less efficiency of labor compared with other machines. This is the theory of Frederick Taylor, the engineer. But the political economist's theory of labor turns on the participation of individuals as citizens in the managerial, bargaining, and rationing transactions of a going concern. Human labor appears as a person, that is, a citizen, who alone has rights, duties, liberties, and exposures, and not as a commodity or machine.[35]

Hence it is that the economist, distinguished from the engineer, picks out only one kind of energy, human energy measured by the input of man-hours, and converts the input of all other kinds of energies into the output of human energy. This distinction between man and nature is disregarded by the physical economists who combine into one homogeneous input the money prices of Capital Goods, Land, and the Human Agent, though he may find it useful for his purposes.[36] Thereby the input of capital goods is the prices paid for the use of tools, machines, buildings, roads, goods in process, fuel, feed, horses, cows, crops, organization, and money. The input of land is the rent paid for uses of artificial and natural crops, forests, pasture, building sites, railroad rights of way, mines, quarries, water, oil, gas. The input of the human agent is the wages and salaries paid for physical, mental, and managerial effort. These are, indeed, the historical distinctions and groupings made possible when all are reduced to money-cost of production, or so-called money "input," contrary to the engineer who, as such, makes the classification in terms other than money. No distinction is made by the engineer nor by the business man between human power and mechanical power. The output of each is the output of a machine.

Ricardo and Karl Marx first made the distinction, not because they looked upon laborers as citizens with property rights, but

---

[35] A labor leader whose union had concluded arbitration and unemployment insurance agreements with his employers stated that his fellow members now felt themselves to be "citizens" of the whole industry, even more interested in the efficiency and continuous prosperous existence of the industry than the employers themselves. See also article by Commons, John R., "Constitutional Government in Industry," *Review of Reviews* (1903).

[36] Cf. Black, *op. cit.*, 383–467.

because they sought to distinguish real value from nominal value. Hence they have not been followed, except by the communists. If, however, we look upon their theories merely as theories of measurement, instead of theories of real value, then they formulated the measurement of efficiency. The economist's principle of efficiency is the ratio of labor-output to labor-input. The activity to which this principle applies is the thousands and millions of managerial transactions which, through organization and concerted action, make up the rate per man-hour at which wealth (use-values) is produced. To this total of all relations between all managerial transactions and all production of wealth Marx gave the names Social Labor-Power and Social Use-Value. Social Use-Value is the total output, but Social Labor-Power, or rather Social Man-Power, including mental, managerial, and manual labor, is the total input. It is the measure of national efficiency. Thus, for example, we roughly guess that during the past hundred and twenty years, while the total population of the United States has increased seventeen-fold, and the average hours of labor have been reduced from twelve to nine, making the increase in man-hours ten-fold, yet the total production of wealth (use-values) has increased fifty-fold. If so, then national efficiency, measured by man-hours, has increased approximately five-fold. Probably five times as much use-value (wealth) per man-hour was produced in 1930 as the rate of production in 1810. The estimate is the ratio of output of use-values to input of social man-power.

This is certainly a moderate estimate, but is only a guess. First had come the physical inventions, like the cotton gin, which increased the laborers' output 1,500 times. Then the energy inventions such as the use of water power, steam power, electricity, and gasoline; finally the personnel and psychological inventions of scientific management. During the hundred and twenty years they have certainly increased the man-hour efficiency of labor more than five-fold. Even during the past thirty years, with the use of mechanical power and personnel management the average man-hour efficiency must have doubled, perhaps trebled.

Now we make a further discovery—the difference between the social and the individual point of view. Use-value is the social concept of *wealth*. Scarcity-value is the individual concept of *assets*. Our leather manufacturing firm had as much social use-value, in the form of hides and leather, after the 50 per cent fall in prices as before the fall. But it would bring to the firm only half as much money if sold at prevailing prices. Thus, again, use-value is social wealth, scarcity-value is prices, and the economist's Value is the business man's Assets, a multiple of use-value and scarcity-value. When we speak of a "wealthy man" we instinctively feel that there is this distinction, but we also instinctively confuse the distinction. Is he wealthy because he owns large quantities of physical things useful for society, or because he can acquire from society large quantities of other things? We speak of him as wealthy if he can acquire other things but poor if what is really his great share of the nation's wealth will not buy much of anything. This double meaning of wealth is distinguished when we measure wealth by the social man-power required to produce it, and measure assets by money. Assets are scarcity, wealth is abundance.

This is what we mean by Capitalism, the double process of creating use-value for others and restricting its supply so as to create scarcity-value. Hence capitalism, unlike the Marxian Communism,[37] requires two units of measurement, the man-hour and the dollar. The one measures the quantity of use-value created, the other measures its scarcity-value. The one measures wealth, the other measures assets. Capitalism is both a producing society and an acquisitive society. It is not merely acquisitive as it seems to be when dollars are used as the unit of measurement.[38] It is productive when man-hours are used, and acquisitive when dollars are used.

This requires us to recur to the distinctions in the meaning of production, productivity, and efficiency. Production, as used by the classical economists and their followers, relates to the quantity produced relative to demand, as seen in their terms "productive" and "unproductive." But productivity and efficiency relate to the *rate* of production, regardless of the total amount produced or the amount demanded. More accurately, efficiency is the velocity of production. Its measurement is the rate of output per man-hour, that is, "man-hour costs"; while productivity is this rate multiplied by the number of man-hours. Of two plants with equal efficiency, the "productivity" of the one with a thousand employees is ten times the productivity of the other with a hundred employees.[39]

A problem which arises is that of converting dollar measurements into man-hour measurements. We are dealing again with averages. The average hourly wage of all manual, mental, and managerial

[37] The Lenin and Stalin Communism employs money, not as a bargaining instrument but as a rationing instrument. In so far as they have permitted free buying and selling, money becomes a bargaining instrument.

[38] Cf. Tawney, R. H., *The Acquisitive Society* (1920).

[39] This conforms to the distinctions of "capacity, efficiency, and productivity" made by W. T. Spillman, *Farm Science* (1918), and by H. C. Taylor, *Outlines of Agricultural Economics* (1925), 133 ff., but with "input" limited to input of human energy and converting their inputs of other energies into the net output of human energy.

labor engaged in production, transportation, and delivery, but not in selling, buying, or financing, is the man-hour unit at that date. By eliminating the changes in average wages at other dates, the average man-hour becomes a constant unit of measurement. Thus if the average wages are 90 cents per hour and are afterwards changed to $1.00 per hour, the number of man-hours is ascertained by eliminating the change in wages. This is a simple average, because we cannot distinguish the efficiency of the machine operator from that of the superintendent. All workers are necessary. Each is a part of the whole concern.

The meaning of "production" formerly pertained to the proprietary economy of supply and demand and this was its meaning when the early economists distinguished productive from unproductive labor. Productive labor, for them, was producing for sale or exchange—a confusion of efficiency and scarcity. But the meaning of efficiency pertains to engineering economy. The engineer, as such, is not interested in the quantity produced. He is interested in the *rate* of production. But the business man is interested in the *quantity* produced. He restricts production when his prices are expected to fall, or increases production when his prices are expected to rise, while endeavoring always to have his engineer increase the velocity of production. The latter is, indeed, the engineer's problem. He is not concerned with prices. He is interested in the ratio of output to input, but the business man is interested in the ratio of income to outgo—the velocity of acquisition. The ratio of output to input is efficiency or productivity. The ratio of income to outgo is price, determined by the rate at which output is offered on the market relative to the rate at which there are offers to take it off the market. The more the engineer can increase the rate of output relative to the rate of input of man-power, the greater is his command over nature. The more the business man can increase his rate of income relative to his rate of outgo, the less is his production relative to demand, and the greater is his command over other people. Man's power over nature is productivity, measured by man-hours. His output is augmentation of wealth (use-value). Man's power over others is measured by dollars (scarcity-value). It is the quantity of production relative to the quantity wanted, and restriction of output is augmentation of prices, values, and assets.

It was this confusion of production with productivity that permitted the economists to abandon Ricardo's man-power and substitute the dollar as the measure of efficiency. This confused producing-power with bargaining power. To buy at low prices and sell at high prices became a definition of efficiency, whereas it is a definition of bargaining power. The latter consists in taking advantage of the relative scarcities or abundance of labor and commodities on the markets. The former consists in taking advantage of the relative powers of man over nature's forces on the farm and in the factory. If it is wished to apply the term "efficiency" to both, then it should always be asked, which kind of efficiency is meant? Is it power over nature measured by man-hours, or power over others measured by dollars? Is it the engineering economy of input and output or the proprietary economy of outgo and income? Is it efficiency in production, or effectiveness in bargaining?

The classical economists took scarcity and property for granted. Nobody would be foolish enough to produce anything in excess of what was wanted at profitable prices. Consequently the term "production" had the antithetic meaning of production and withholding production. This confused the two ways of making a profit —the efficiency profits, obtained by reducing the man-hour input relative to output, and the scarcity profits, obtained by increasing income relative to outgo. And the further confusion resulted of production of *goods,* or wealth, with "production" of *value,* or assets. It is on account of this double meaning of production that we distinguish the terms "engineering economics" and "business economics." Engineering economy increases output regardless of its money value on the markets. Business economy restricts and regulates the quantity produced in order to maintain or augment its money value. The confusion of the two started from the double meaning of wealth as materials and ownership.

Thus the classical economists did not distinguish output from income, or outgo from input. The distinction was concealed in the double meanings of cost and value. They assumed that, of course, a man's output was his income. Or, if they saw the difference, they did not make use of it. Back of the confusion of income with output were the ethical assumptions of personal freedom and rights of ownership. "In the ordinary sense of the term," says Black, *"human effort cannot be owned by somebody else."* [40] This assumption is true enough for modern society, but the point is that, even here, the *output* of human effort, under the wage system, is owned by somebody else. The output of labor is the use-value added to the employer's property. It belongs to the employer on the doctrine of *assumpsit* which reads into its acquisition by the employer a debt owed by the employer to the

[40] Black, J. D., *op. cit.,* 447.

employee. What happens is twofold—a physical process and a proprietary process. The physical process is the input and output of labor-power, regardless of ownership and assets. The proprietary process is the outgo of money from the employer's assets which is the income of money for the laborer, augmenting his assets; and the outgo of money-value from the laborer's assets when the ownership of the output is transferred to the employer, for whom it becomes an income in augmentation of his assets.

The reason why the physical economists did not make use of the distinction between engineering and proprietary economics, and therefore took it for granted that output was income, is found, as said above, in their proper enough assumption that nobody would willingly work unless he expected his output of use-value to become his income of use-value. This could be taken as self-evident when they started with an isolated Robinson Crusoe. His output is, of course, his income, because there is no intervening transaction. But when there are Robinson and Friday at work, or when there are millions at work, output is not income. It depends on who owns the output. The output of the slave is the income of the owner. The output of the laborer is the income of the employer. The input of the laborer is man-power. His output is use-value. The money outgo of the employer and equivalent income of the laborer is the money wage. There is no necessary or natural connection between the use-value and money. They are measured by two different systems of measurement, which are inconvertible. The output varies inversely to the input, and the ratio of use-value as output to man-hours as input is the measure of efficiency. But the money income of the one is the same as the money outgo of the other. One is the changeable rate at which use-value (wealth) is augmented; the other is the changeable price paid for the unit of use-value.

The appropriateness of the terms "outgo" and "income" arises from their fitness to describe the process by which scarcity is increased by outgo but diminished by income. It involves the distinction between commodities and money. If an owner has a stock of goods on hand and delivers a part of it to his customer, then the money-value of the part delivered is his commodity-outgo. It reduces the quantity of stock on hand—his inventory—and thus increases its scarcity for him. But if he buys from the wholesaler or manufacturer a consignment of goods, then the quantity received is his commodity-income which augments his stock on hand and increases its abundance for him.

So also with money outgo and income. He has an available

quantity of money in the form of cash or a deposit account at the bank. If he pays to the wholesaler a part of this money, it is money-outgo, decreasing for him the amount of available money. But when he receives from his customer a money-payment and then deposits it at his bank, he receives a money-income which augments his quantity of money available at the bank.

Thus the terms outgo and income pertain to the changing scarcities of goods or money for the individual. Their meaning is proprietary. Income augments the quantity owned, and outgo diminishes it. Hence the ambiguous word "cost" is to be distinguished as proprietary outgo of money or of commodities at their money value, thereby reducing the value of assets owned. And income obtains its proper double meaning of money, or money-value of commodities acquired, thereby increasing the value of assets owned. The ratio of income to outgo is the velocity of acquisition of assets.

Consequently when economists reduce all inputs to money inputs they reach the confused conclusion that the least cost, or greatest efficiency, is the least money cost of the several factors of interest, labor, depreciation, taxes, repairs, materials, etc.[41] This confusion is the everyday confusion of common sense which measures everything by money, and is excusable on the plea that economic science has not yet taken over into its theories the man-hour measurements used by Karl Marx and scientific management, and has not had time enough to grasp the engineer's concept of input and output in contrast to the proprietary and business concepts of outgo and income, and therefore has not fully distinguished wealth from assets. The distinction was clearly pointed out by Ricardo more than a hundred years ago, but when economists, following John Stuart Mill after 1845, quietly dropped Ricardo's labor-power measure of value and substituted the monetary measure of value, the orthodox economists, distinguished from the communist economists, have accepted the popular delusion of defining the greatest efficiency as the least money-cost of production, whereas the greatest efficiency is the least man-hour cost. The least money cost is the least outgo per unit of income; the least man-hour cost is the least input of labor per unit of output.

This may be illustrated further by returning to our clothing factory which reduced the average number of hours of operating labor, required to make the standard suit, from about ten hours per suit to about five hours per suit. We can here say that the *labor-cost*, in the sense of man-hour cost, was reduced 50 per cent.

[41] Cf. Black, *op. cit.*, 391, 392.

This is the same as saying, inversely, that the shop efficiency was increased 100 per cent.

There are other ways of stating the same thing. Formerly one hour of average labor produced one-tenth of a suit—now it produces one-fifth of a suit. The increase is 100 per cent. Or, where formerly five hours of labor produced 50 per cent of a suit, five hours now produce 100 per cent of a suit. This is an increase of 100 per cent of a suit in five hours, which is the same as an increase of 100 per cent in efficiency. One way of stating it is the inverse of the other, which is possible because efficiency is a ratio. If the labor-hours per suit are reduced 50 per cent, then the suits per hour of labor are increased 100 per cent. Either way of putting it is the same as saying that efficiency has increased 100 per cent.

Nothing is here said about money, or wages, profits, prices, money cost, or money income. These latter are business problems of the relative scarcities of things. But we are now considering only the producer's technological problem of relative efficiencies of different methods of production and differing willingness of labor to work. The dollar is the business man's unit of scarcity-measurement— the man-hour is the producer's unit of efficiency-measurement. We measure efficiency by the output of product *per* input of man-hours; we measure scarcity by the prices or wages paid in dollars. We cannot measure efficiency by prices or wages, nor scarcity by man-hours.

This is the evident distinction between producer and seller, and between manufacturer and merchant. The producer, or "manufacturer," as such, is a technologist, an engineer, a manager, a laborer. His problem is, how to increase the output per man-hour of input— that is, how to increase the efficiency (*ratio* of output to input) of industry and agriculture. But when he becomes a seller he becomes a merchant, that is, a business man. Now his problem is prices and wages—how to increase the prices received for what he sells, or to reduce the prices and wages which he must pay for what he buys. Business can make profits in both ways—by efficiency and scarcity. If, solely as producer, the manager and his laborers are able to increase the hourly output of goods per hourly input of labor, then they are the successful producers—the specialists in efficiency. But if, solely as seller and buyer, the employer increases his dollar net income by higher prices received or by lower prices and wages paid, he is the successful business man—the specialist in scarcity.

The two, however, are under the same business control. In

which function shall this business control be induced to make the larger profit? Shall it be as producer or as buyer and seller?

But we must first go further in distinguishing producer and efficiency from business and scarcity. It is often said that the great increase in modern efficiency has come from the substitution of machinery for labor, and that machinery displaces labor. But machinery has not been substituted for labor, nor has machinery displaced labor, except temporarily or when falling prices reduce profits. What has happened is that direct labor has been transferred to indirect labor. A hundred years ago it required nine farmers' families to support ten families, including themselves. Now three farmers' families support ten families, including themselves. Agricultural efficiency has been increased perhaps threefold in a hundred years. What happened was that six farmers' families were transferred from the *direct* production of agricultural products to the *indirect* production of agricultural products. They now produce coal, iron, lumber, fertilizers, railways, highways, steamships, agricultural machinery, delivery of goods to warehouses, and so on, all of which indirectly produce agricultural products. What happened was that nine families were formerly employed in the *direct* production of agricultural products and one family in the *indirect* production, whereas now only three families are engaged in the direct production, and seven families are engaged in indirect production of agricultural products. The efficiency of agriculture is not to be measured by the output of direct labor but by the output of both direct and indirect labor. The whole nation has contributed to the increased efficiency of agriculture, just as the increased efficiency of agriculture has released labor for the increased output of the whole nation.

But this applies to the nation as a whole and not to any particular agricultural establishment. The particular establishment buys its agricultural machinery from an implement factory which had bought its materials from other owners, and had employed labor to manufacture and transport the implements. What the particular farmer bought was a particular quantity of indirect labor, "stored-up" and furnished to him from preceding industries. And this stored-up labor is employed by him as *his share* of the nation's indirect labor, along with his own direct labor, to produce his crop of wheat.[42]

This indirect labor, stored up in farm implements, fertilizers, and other improvements, depreciates by use or obsolescence and must be replaced by new and more efficient implements, fertilizers, and

[42] Below, p. 560, Margin for Profit, on "materials."

improvements. If it wears out or becomes obsolete in five years, on the average, then he must calculate that he is employing each year one-fifth, or 20 per cent, of the total amount of stored-up labor which he obtained from other industries. In order, then, to find how much labor he has actually employed he must add to the number of man-hours of direct labor per year one-fifth of the number of man-hours of labor stored up in his farm implements, fertilizers, and improvements.

A set of terms that fits this distinction is "operating labor" and Karl Marx's "embodied labor." The farmer's use of embodied labor is equivalent to the depreciation and obsolescence of his farm implements, fertilizers, and improvements. If they depreciated 20 per cent a year, on the average, then he employed each year 20 per cent of the total embodied labor which he has on hand. This is the number of hours of indirect or embodied labor which he must add to the number of hours of direct or operating labor, in order to find how much labor he has actually employed in producing his crop of wheat. It is his *share of the total indirect labor* of the nation devoted each year to his crop of wheat, and added to his own direct labor.

Evidently, then, the calculation of increasing efficiency of an agricultural establishment or of a clothing factory is exaggerated if we measure it only by the operating labor. This is a mistake usually made. Our divisor—the input of labor—must be increased so as to include, as input, not only the direct, or operating labor, but also the indirect, or embodied labor.

This calculation reduces the apparent increase in efficiency, when the increased use of machinery is taken into account. The above calculation of 100 per cent increase in efficiency of a certain clothing factory was made on the basis of only direct or *operating* labor. The increase of efficiency was really less than that because the depreciation and obsolescence of the newly added *embodied* labor in the form of added machinery was not included in the calculation. Had it been included then the increased efficiency of *both* direct and indirect labor would have been less than 100 per cent. If the output of *direct operating* labor per man-hour is increased 100 per cent because the indirect labor embodied in machinery has been introduced, that does not mean that the efficiency of *operating labor* has been increased that much, because we have not counted the additional amount of labor required to make the machinery. We must allow that some of the labor formerly devoted to the operating production is diverted to its indirect production by constructing, in the case of our increased efficiency of agriculture, the steel-producing machinery and the agricultural equipment used in the direct operating production of wheat.

This indirect production by embodied labor may be named the process of Technological Capital. The quantity of such capital should be measured by man-hours, and then distributed as depreciation and obsolescence *overhead* by adding it to the operating man-hours.

We name this kind of capital, thus calculated in man-hours, Technological Capital in order to distinguish it from Business Capital, measured in dollars. It approaches the capital concept of the classical economists, though it is more properly named "capital instruments," and "inventory."

Business capital is sometimes considered to be the market-value of plant or farm and equipment, but this changes with the changes in prices, profits, and wages. Or business capital is sometimes the amount of investment, but this changes with the market values of stocks, bonds, and land values, depending on expected profits and rents. Business capital earns interest and profits which we shall name the financial margin.[43] But technological capital does not earn anything—it is *output, not income.* The value of business capital depends upon *future* prices and quantities of output and this means the expected scarcities of different outputs, measured in dollars. But the amount of technological capital depends upon the past and present quantity and efficiency of all labor, embodied and operating, measured in man-hours.

Hence we have two different kinds of "overhead," the business overhead of interest and taxes, known as "fixed charges"; and the technological overhead of embodied man-hours, known as depreciation and obsolescence. Each kind of overhead is becoming enormously important, in proportion as the labor-power of the nation is transferred in all industries from direct labor to indirect labor, that is, from operating labor to embodied labor.

The two, again, are under the same business control. In which direction does public policy suggest that business men should be induced, in self-interest, to guide their establishments? Is it towards enlarging business capital, or towards enlarging technological capital? This means, Is it towards enlarging fixed charges of interest and customary profit or towards enlarging fixed charges of depreciation and obsolescence?

There is still another kind of overhead labor that is increasing in importance. It is the "white collar" overhead. This may be

---

[43] Below, p. 574, Financial Margin. On the reasons for excluding rents see below, p. 348, on Ricardo and Malthus.

named Operating Overhead, instead of Embodied Overhead. All scientists, engineers, managers, clerks, accountants, designers, superintendents, foremen, required to carry on and enlarge the efficiency of industry, are a part of the man-power which, taken together, is named simply Management. The increasing importance of management means an increasing transfer of labor from manual to clerical and managerial labor.

These undoubtedly increase the efficiency of labor, but if they are left out of calculation, as is usually done when speaking of the increasing efficiency of labor, two mistakes are made. It is not mere manual labor that increases its own efficiency. It is mental, managerial, and manual labor together that increase efficiency. And they must be counted together, otherwise the calculation of increased efficiency is exaggerated when labor is shifted from manual to managerial and mental. The "average" man-hour which measures the increase of efficiency is an average of all the manual, mental, and managerial labor whether it be operating labor, operating overhead labor, or embodied overhead labor.

And, in computing the average, every individual counts as one, whether it be the general manager or the errand-boy, whether it be man, woman, or child. The fact is, as already said, we cannot tell whether the manager is more efficient than the errand-boy. We know that he gets more wages, but that is because managers are scarcer, not because they are more efficient. If they were as abundant as errand-boys, their wages would probably be no higher. This increased abundance is today the situation of "intellectuals," and perhaps the largest factor in the rise of Fascism and Nazism. If the intellectual and white collar employees get less wages than manual laborers, it is not because they have become less efficient—they have become more abundant. All that we know respecting their comparative efficiency is that each is necessary to the efficient working of the concern as a whole.[44]

With these explanations we return to our clothing factory which increased its efficiency 100 per cent when calculated only in direct operating manual labor. But calculated in both operating labor and management and in the embodied labor of depreciation and obsolescence, I have estimated the increase in efficiency in that establishment at 75 per cent instead of 100 per cent. In other words, the number of man-hours required to make a suit of clothes was reduced in the proportion 10 to $7\frac{1}{2}$ instead of 10 to 5. Thus an increase of 75 per cent in the output per man-hour of average labor of all kinds was a decrease of $33\frac{1}{3}$ per cent instead of 50

[44] On this subject cf. Clark, J. M., *Overhead Costs: Social Control of Business* (1923).

per cent in the number of hours per suit of clothes. By either calculation the efficiency increased 75 per cent instead of 100 per cent.

In these calculations an improvement in *quality* of output is considered equivalent to an enlargement of *quantity* of output. For the quality also can often be calculated in man-hours. If the quality improves *without* an increase in man-hours, then the efficiency is increased that much. If it required a corresponding increase in man-hours to improve the quality, then efficiency was not increased. A "standard" suit is one in which quality is not changed, and all other garments and all improvements in quality have been reduced by the accountant of that establishment to an equivalent in man-hours with the standard suit. Thus, by reducing quality to quantity, it is calculated that the efficiency of the establishment as a whole increased 75 per cent; or, inversely, the man-hours per standard unit of output were reduced 33⅓ per cent.

Two things happened in the establishment when efficiency was increased 75 per cent. The price of the suit was reduced, but not enough to deprive the producers of their gain in efficiency. The physical speed of the workers was not increased, because they had already been speeded up by piecework, and therefore the increased efficiency came solely from more and better machinery and more and better management. But the second thing that happened was that the hours of labor were considerably reduced, the wages and salaries per hour were greatly increased, and the profits of the establishment were decidedly increased. Had the prices of clothing been reduced 33 per cent, when the efficiency increased 75 per cent, then the *buyers* of clothing would have obtained all of the gain from increased efficiency, and the producers would not have gained the shorter hours, higher wages, higher profits, and increased amount of interest on increased investment, which came from their higher efficiency.[45]

V. FROM CIRCULATION TO REPETITION

From Quesnay to the Twentieth Century economic theory was dominated, in large part, by his analogy of Circulation of commodities and money. In the latter part of the Nineteenth Century it began to take over the analogy of Turnover. The one is the analogy of a "flow," the other of a "wheel." The wheel analogy retains one of the dimensions of the circulation analogy—a relatively constant total quantity represented by the size of the wheel, but

[45] Below, p. 789, Prices.

adds another kind of quantity, a dynamic energy which drives or slows down or stops the wheel, that is, changes the velocity of circulation. Eliminating the physical analogies, what is meant by turnover is the *rate of repetition* of transactions.

In order to construct this formula there is needed the artificial concept of the beginning and ending of a process which however has no beginning and no ending; a total but changing quantity, the size of the wheel, that persists during that period of time; and the repetition of enough parts whose sum, during the period of time, will be equal to the total quantity. By a useful physical analogy it is "velocity" or rate of "turnover," but, without analogy, it is rate of repetition, or rate of recurrence.

The above formula is not a "copy" of nature. It is only an artificial construction created by statistical imagination in order to be useful for control of nature or business. In this respect, the rate of turnover, or more properly, the rate of repetition, has undermined practically all of the older physical analogies of an economic mechanism, such as equilibrium, flow, tendencies, circulation, whose time factor could not be measured. It has prepared the way for mathematical theories of process, trends, cycles, rates of change, velocities, lags, forecasts, upon which individual or concerted action may somewhat control the process. In fact, this concept of rate of repetition has almost obliterated the older meanings of all the terms employed by the commodity and hedonic economists. The concept originated in the practical conduct of business, followed by the theoretical analysis of economists.

The term turnover seems first to have been used in retail trade, where the rate of turnover is figured as the average period of time required for the value of the sales to equal the average total value of the stock of goods on hand. The value of the stock on hand is a part of business "capital," the value of sales is gross income during the period of time. If the rate of turnover of the total capital-value, including both materials and capital instruments, is five times per year, then the capital can earn five times as much as the capital of a competitor whose turnover is only once per year, and consequently he can sell at lower prices or higher profits. The idea has been applied to labor-turnover during recent years, but our main concern now is its application to proprietary and industrial turnover. The rate of turnover is the velocity of repetition.

The proprietary turnover is the rate at which titles of ownership are transferred. A relatively constant volume of bank deposits, say 30 billion dollars, accomplishes during a year, say, 750 billion dollars worth of transfers of ownership, a turnover of the whole amount once in 25 days. It indicates that on the average, the total volume of bank money has been debited to depositors in payment for transfers of ownership of commodities and securities about 12 times per year, although without this formula the quantity of money would seem to persist constantly the same, like a circulation. This rate of proprietary turnover, or repetition of transactions, may be distinguished as the turnover of assets. It is measured by dollars, and is the turnover of scarcity-values.

But the technological or industrial turnover is measured in man-hours. The national increase in efficiency which we have previously estimated at fivefold in 120 years, was brought about by inventions and management. Most of these inventions required a large equipment of capital instruments involving much labor for their construction as intermediate products before the ultimate consumer could get the increased quantity of consumption goods. Hence older phenomena appear with new importance—depreciation and obsolescence. The total amount of wealth appears to increase at a possible rate of 4 per cent per year, but it is composed of new instruments to take the place of the depreciated and obsolete. The rate at which the old disappears and the new is substituted is the industrial turnover, equivalent to Böhm-Bawerk's "average period of production." Mitchell has estimated that "the man-made equipment with which the American population works represents a value equivalent to between three and four years' effort of its money-earners." [46] Since for other countries the estimate runs as high as six or seven years, and since we include not only equipment but also materials up to the point of delivery to ultimate consumers, we may, without waiting for further investigation, estimate the rate of material turnover at once in five years.

In other words, if the physical turnover of output measured by man-hours is once in five years, then the proprietary turnover of ownership measured by dollars is about 70 times in five years. The proprietary velocity of bargaining transactions is 70 times the technological velocity. Legal control is transferred 70 times as rapidly as goods are produced.

It is this double formula of industrial and proprietary turnover that makes feasible the concept of a going concern with its two aspects, the going plant and the going business. The going plant is the whole of the fixed capital and inventory, measurable by the man-hours required for its production, which continues relatively constant although the parts are changing at different rates

[46] Mitchell, W. C., *Business Cycles; the Problem and Its Setting* (1928), 98.

of turnover. The going business is the whole of the capital assets, measurable by money, which remains relatively constant although the parts are continually changing by buying and selling. The correlation of proprietary and industrial turnover, of going plant and going business, by the principle of limiting and complementary factors,[47] is the going concern.

The terms "internal economy" and "external economy" are sometimes used to distinguish these two aspects of a going concern.[48] But the "internal" economy turns out to be the engineering economy of managerial transactions producing use-values; the external economy becomes the proprietary economy of bargaining transactions which maintain or enlarge, if possible, the total value of assets. The two are interdependent, but they differ as does efficiency from scarcity.

Other applications of the turnover analogy may be found in the genesis of the meanings of use-value. It formerly meant happiness derived from the use of physical goods and was therefore immeasurable and rejected by economists. But happiness had the double meaning of enjoyment of the whole of one's possessions, and the enjoyment of its parts, such as sugar or bread. The whole of one's happiness might be increased with abundance of possessions while the part-happiness derived from sugar or bread was actually diminishing with its own abundance. Hence the term use-value, which had meant the whole, came to have the latter meaning of part-happiness under the name, diminishing utility, and the whole is kept relatively constant, if possible, by changing and replacing the diminishing parts.

Failure to understand this relation of the whole to its parts led critics of the psychological school at first to deny the principle of diminishing utility with increasing abundance, for happiness evidently increases with abundance. The analogy of turnover reconciles the contradiction. Happiness as a whole increases with abundance, while various kinds of happiness are diminishing with their own abundance, and are therefore repeating themselves at different rates of recurrence.[49] It was not until the middle of the Nineteenth Century that this part-whole relation was discovered by the hedonic economists. It is a special case of the analogy of turnover.[50]

But the discovery of diminishing utility led to another double meaning, the meaning of use-value. Every commodity, whether

[47] Below, p. 627, Strategic and Routine Transactions.

[48] Foreman, C. J., *Efficiency and Scarcity Profits: an Economic and Legal Analysis of the Residual Surplus* (1931), 100 ff.

[49] Plehn, Carl C., speaks of the "law of recurrence," applicable to "the concept of income as recurrent consumable receipts," *Amer. Econ. Rev.*, XIV (1924), 1-2.

[50] Above, p. 201, Adam Smith.

land, machinery, labor, or food, was subject to the principle of diminishing utility with increasing abundance. It was also subject to diminishing use-value by wear and tear, depreciation, obsolescence, and consumption. The difference between the two should be evident, but it is obscured when each is measured by money. Therefore the term use-value or wealth is given the double meaning of a physical process of production and a bargaining process of acquisition. The one is physical turnover measured by man-hours, the other is proprietary turnover measured by dollars.

The confusion of meaning is further concealed in the evident fact that both use-value and scarcity-value depend upon the wants of buyers. A use-value that does not satisfy wants is useless; it is also useless if produced in greater abundance than is wanted. But this is a double meaning of uselessness. Hence the word "wants" itself has a double meaning which we distinguish as Civilization-values and Scarcity-values. Bows and arrows are no longer use-values except for amusement. Explosives and guns take their place. Hoopskirts are no longer use-values. Close-fitting skirts take their place. We may distinguish these changes in civilization-values as obsolescence, under the two meanings of invention and style. They operate by the forces of competition. Invention creates new use-values which, by greater efficiency or changes, render the old obsolete. These are changes in civilization, which is merely a name for all customs considered as a whole. We name them civilization-values, since they have a psychological base, and a change in civilization is obsolescence of old and invention of new use-values.

These changes in customs which make up the total changes in civilization are not like ancient customs which endured for centuries. They may be sudden and sweeping. Andrew Carnegie is said to have scrapped a million-dollar blast furnace within six months after its construction in order to substitute the new invention of the continuous process of changing iron ore into finished steel before it could cool down as pig iron. The former custom was obsolete within six months, and all of his competitors were compelled to adopt the new custom, or be driven from that field of industry.

Besides obsolescence, use-value diminishes also by depreciation, but scarcity-value diminishes by abundance. Depreciation takes various names, according to the nature of the use-value. It is wear and tear of machinery, exhaustion or depletion of soil fertility and other natural resources. This is the "using-up" of use-values, which must be replaced by man-power. And it is this depreciation, obsolescence, and re-creation that is the meaning of technological turnover.

We are, as usual, dealing with averages. The rate, or velocity, of turnover is an average rate for the whole concern or the nation. It may therefore be broken up into the many separate rates of turnover of the various parts which constitute the average rate of the whole. The classical and popular terms used to make this distinction are circulating capital and fixed capital. Circulating capital is raw material, partly finished goods and finished goods when they cease circulating, because they reach the hands of the ultimate consumer. Fixed capital is soil fertility, buildings, machinery, highways, bridges, etc.

But this distinction does not accurately fit the process. There is no fixed capital whatever. All is circulating, but at different rates of turnover. A pile of coal in the bins is "fixed," for the time being. Its rate of turnover, according to its size and use in the concern, depleted by output and augmented by input, may be, say, twelve times a year, or once per month. So with all other inventories of circulating capital. But the building, or machinery, by depreciation and obsolescence, may need to be replaced in one, ten, twenty, or thirty years. Its rate of turnover may be once in thirty years, or say, 3 per cent per year. So with other fixed capital. The average rate of turnover for the fixed capital of the plant, through obsolescence and depreciation, may turn out to be once in 12 years, or 8 per cent per year.

It is this important fact of depreciation and obsolescence that is concealed in the popular distinction—and in the distinction made by older economists—between fixed capital and circulating capital. Many a prosperous coöperative telephone company, run by farmers and charging low rates to its members, has suddenly found itself bankrupt when its illusory "fixed" capital must be replaced on account of depreciation or obsolescence. Often thirty-year bonds are issued by counties to build cement roads which must be replaced in ten years, and then another thirty-year bond must be issued for another turnover of ten years. Eventually the road is burdened by a debt three times as great as the cost of the road. Often corporations have paid high dividends while their property was depreciating or obsolescent, and then have issued bonds or new stock under the misleading allurement of new capital to enlarge their alleged prosperous business.

What they have been doing, in all such cases, is commonly known as "paying dividends out of capital." It is more accurately described as paying dividends instead of maintaining or enlarging efficiency with the incoming of new inventions. If the average rate of turnover of the plant is found, by the engineers, to be 10 years, then there must be withheld from dividends, in one way or another, 10 per cent annually of the total value of the plant. Otherwise dividends are "paid out of capital" instead of paid out of income from gross sales. An important result of the public regulation of railroads and public utilities was the prohibition against this practice of "paying dividends out of capital." This was one of the deceptions known as "high finance," but it is only an advantage taken by financiers of the popular illusion of "fixed capital" in place of the rapid turnover of capital equipment.

On the other hand, a marked advantage of the modern big corporation is its provision for "depreciation reserves," along with the refusal by boards of directors to declare excessive dividends when earnings are excessive, but to build up a "corporate surplus," additional to depreciation reserves, and then declare "stock dividends" of ownership instead of annual dividends of income. We shall consider this recent phenomenon under the name of Profit Cushion.[15]

Thus the turnover of "fixed capital" is equal to the rate of depreciation and obsolescence. With the great speed of modern machinery and especially the obsolescence on account of new inventions, the man-hours of labor embodied in the machinery may be used up at a rapid rate. Hence the increase in efficiency is exaggerated when measured only by the man-hours of operating labor. In the foregoing illustration of a clothing factory the efficiency of *operating* labor increased 100 per cent in ten years, or, inversely, the labor input was reduced 50 per cent. Either statement is exaggerated. New and improved machinery had been introduced. The extent of the exaggeration depends on the man-hour magnitude of the fixed capital and its rate of depreciation and obsolescence. We have named this magnitude and its rate of depreciation, following Karl Marx, the "embodied overhead," measured by man-hours.

Thus, on the analogy of turnover, we convert Marx's "constant and variable" capital, measured as he did by man-hours, into a going plant, whose magnitude is the recurrent but variable input of labor and output of wealth. His "variable capital" becomes merely the variable ratio of labor-input to labor-output, which is the varying efficiency of the plant. "Fixed" capital and circulating capital (materials) are merged into a single concept of an average rate of turnover in the activity of converting the physical energies of the universe into a useful output. The varying efficiency of the plant is the total output relative to the total input of both operat-

---

[51] Below, p. 582, the Profit Cushion.

ing labor and embodied labor, over the average period of time during which both the fixed capital and the materials are used up.

Thus we are able to distinguish and measure the process by which wealth is augmented from the process by which assets are augmented. Wealth is increased by increasing the ratio of output to input, assets by increasing the ratio of income to outgo. If the number of suits of clothing, which are the output of wealth, is increased 75 per cent per man-hour, then this increase is the *rate* at which that form of wealth is increased.

A farmer's combined reaper, thresher, and sacker costs less, measured by man-hours, than his former separated horses, reaper, and thresher; but two men can turn out more wheat per hour than twenty did before. Efficiency reduces present man-power by the accumulated mental and manual power of the past. But there are no heirs who inherit property-rights in mental-power after the patents have expired. Consequently the man-hours required to measure the magnitude of technological capital are only the man-hours actually employed in its creation.

It is the deceptions and illusions that accompany these transactions that make important the distinction between the turnover of wealth and the turnover of assets. It involves a double meaning of the word capital, its technological meaning and its proprietary meaning. The one was formerly named capital, the other is capitalization. But capitalization is named capital by business men. This is capital in the sense of assets; the other is capital in the sense of wealth. One is scarcity-value, or expected *income;* the other is use-value, or expected *output.* The confusion arises from employing one unit of measurement, the dollar, which measures the magnitude of business men's capital, which is assets (scarcity-value), for measuring also the magnitude of the social meaning of capital, which is wealth (use-values). Both fixed capital and circulating capital are wealth when measured by man-hours, and an increased velocity of output relative to input is increased efficiency. Both are assets and liabilities when measured by dollars, and an increased velocity of income relative to outgo is an increased rate of accrual of a business firm's assets.

VI. Ability and Opportunity

1. *Physical and Legal Possession*

Hence we arrive at the distinction between ability and opportunity. Ability is capacity to act. Opportunity is the limited alternatives between which choices are made in acting. But abilities are operated in the two directions of power over nature and power over others, distinguishable as producing power and bargaining power. And the limited alternatives, therefore, between which choices are made are natural opportunities and proprietary opportunities.

This distinction, though obvious, is concealed in economic theory by the double meaning of wealth, which we have noted means material things and their ownership. But the term ownership is thereby given a double meaning of physical possession and legal possession. This double meaning is used by J. D. Black as follows:

"Many of our wants are definitely associated with *ownership* of things rather than some property of the things themselves. In many cases, ownership is necessary before the good can satisfy our wants properly. No one will dispute this in the case of clothes or toothbrushes or lap dogs. It is true to a large extent for land, houses, automobiles, books, pictures, musical instruments. Hence possession must really be looked upon as a fourth [52] circumstance determining power to satisfy wants. This same grouping can be applied to services as well as to material goods." [53]

Here the words ownership and possession are used in what may be distinguished as the physical meaning of holding the materials of nature for one's own use in production or consumption, and the proprietary meaning, which economically is exactly the opposite, namely the right to exclude others and to withhold from them what they want but do not own.[54] We cannot quietly walk down the street or into our neighbor's field and pick up whatever we need for production or consumption. We must come to terms with the owner. Hence the double meaning of possession, as used in economics, is physical control and legal control. Before physical possession can be obtained, legal possession must be negotiated.

This seems to have been the oversight of the physical and hedonic economists. They always meant physical possession and not legal possession. This was involved in their double meaning of wealth as materials and ownership. But if the economist

[52] His other three are form (including substance), place, and time.

[53] Black, J. D., *Production Economics*, 29. See below, p. 378, on Menger, for the similar double meaning.

[54] The technical *legal* distinction between *ownership* and *possession* is not material to the economic meaning here considered. Each means the right to exclude others from entering upon (that is, using) the property without the consent of the owner or possessor. On account of this legal distinction we use the more inclusive term, "legal control," as meaning either legal ownership or legal possession.

should attempt to produce or consume without previously obtaining legal possession he would go to jail. By physical possession we have opportunity to increase the production or consumption of wealth, if we have previously obtained legal possession. By legal possession we have power to exclude others and to bargain for a transfer of ownership. Physical possession is holding, legal possession gives the right of holding or withholding. One is opportunity to choose among nature's forces; the other is opportunity to choose between buyers or between sellers.

It is, in fact, upon this distinction that we distinguish not only between Materials and Ownership, but also between Wealth and Assets, between Property and Property Rights. Wealth is the use-values added by mental, managerial, and manual ability to the otherwise useless raw materials of nature. But if the materials of nature are so abundant, like air, that they can be had without asking, then they have, of course, no scarcity-value, and no one would be foolish enough to claim exclusive possession of them as his own property. Air, although it is the most useful of all the materials of nature, has no value on account of abundance, and therefore nobody claims an exclusive possession of it. But if air becomes scarce, like air artificially warmed in the North or air artificially cooled in the South, or wave-lengths for wireless communication, then conflicting claims of ownership arise. Even a Radio Commission is created to apportion to individuals exclusive use for limited periods of the limited wave-lengths. Wavelengths are wealth, but their legal possession is assets.

Thus we distinguish between property and property rights. Property is the claim to exclusive control for one's own use, or for the use of others if a price is paid, of the materials of nature which are scarce or expected to be scarce. But property rights are the collective activities of government or other concerns apportioning to individuals an exclusive claim against others in the use of anything that is expected to be scarce enough to create conflicts over exclusive use. Thus property is not only a claim but is also a conflict of claims to whatever is scarce, but rights of property are the concerted action which regulates the conflict.

Of course, we distinguish here between analysis and justification. The analysis is the relation between scarcity, property, and property rights. The justification of property rights is the reasons advanced for maintaining or changing them. With these justifications we are not now concerned. The analysis is intended to show the double meaning of "possession." In its physical meaning it is power over nature's forces. In its proprietary meaning it is collective power granted to individuals to withhold from others what one claims for his own use. In the one meaning it is the prerequisite of efficiency; in the other it is the prerequisite of bargaining power.[55]

2. *Choices*

But in either case ability resolves itself into choices, and choices are choices between scarce opportunities. In the physical meaning choice is choice between natural, that is, material or physical, opportunities. In the proprietary meaning it is choices between buyers, or sellers, or borrowers, or lenders, or laborers, or employers, or lessors, or lessees, etc. It is choices between the alienations and the acquisitions of ownership. In the physical meaning the choices pertain to an increase of power over nature's forces. In the proprietary meaning they pertain to an increase of power over other persons. The one is relative efficiency, the other is relative scarcity.

In the physical meaning of possession it is by choosing among nature's opportunities that wealth is produced or consumed. "Choosing," says Black, is a "form of production." Black's terminology rightly includes consumption in his meaning of production, if by choosing we mean the *act* of choosing and not merely the subjective valuing of alternatives which results in the act.

> "Before eating can begin," he says, "a *decision* or *choice* has to be made as to what will be eaten. . . . The choice may be between goods or services to use in commodity production, or to use in service production. . . . There can be no question about these being production. But choosing food, clothing or recreation for oneself are as surely production." [56]

If we inquire how it is that the act of choosing is productive of wealth we must examine more closely the meaning of a choice between alternatives. It is a choice of the direction and force with which we use our man-power of mental, managerial and manual abilities. In this sense every choice is threefold in its dimensions of acting upon the materials of nature. It is a performance, an avoidance and a forbearance at one and the same instant of choosing, as may be seen from the formula on the following page.[57]

[55] The distinction between property and property rights is deduced from MacLeod, below, p. 397.
[56] Black, J. D., *op. cit.*, 41.
[57] Cf. Commons, John R., *Legal Foundations of Capitalism*, 69.

In one direction, AC, the man-power, or ability to control the forces of nature, may be deemed to be greater than in the alternative direction, AB. But, in that direction, it is not deemed useful

FORMULA OF CHOICE

Man-Power

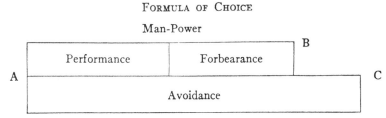

to exert one's ability. Hence a choice is made between the two alternatives. The rejection of the one we name Avoidance; the choice of the other we name Performance.

But only in periods of crisis, or intense speeding up, is Performance equal to the total man-power in that direction. The difference between actual performance and possible performance we name Forbearance. Hence each choice is a double choice of alternatives, a choice of Performance limited both by Forbearance and by the next best alternative avoided. Performance is the actual effort of moving one of the alternative factors available at the moment. Avoidance is the rejection of alternative factors not deemed effective for the purposes intended. Forbearance is the degree to which performance is exerted, not to its full possible ability, but restrained by the will because too much energy exerted is deemed to defeat its purpose.

Thus every choice has a threefold limit. First, the capacity, that is, *possible* ability, whether managerial or manual, guided by mental foresight. Second, the choice between a greater or lesser degree of force, in which case performance is less than possible ability in that direction. Third, the choice between performing in one direction by avoidance of other directions.

Thus reduced to the mere physical dimensions of human ability we have, nevertheless, a volitional guidance by the will, and it is in this way that choosing is productive. We name it the Will-in-action. It is control over the direction in which nature's energies shall work by choosing the degree of human force employed in actual performance, by forbearing to use more force than is necessary, and by avoiding its use in alternative directions. Hence, choosing is productive because it is performance, forbearance, and avoidance.

It is this analysis of the act of choosing that gives significance to the principle of limiting and complementary factors as a guide to managerial transactions in the production of wealth. If sagacious, we choose a performance limited by forbearance, upon that factor which, at the time and place of decision, is deemed to be the limiting factor, and avoid, for the time being, the complementary factors,[58] though afterwards they may be chosen successively as the then limiting factors. It is this process of choosing between limiting and complementary factors of nature's forces which we distinguish as choice of natural opportunities, or production of wealth.

The distinction, however, must be made between rational, habitual, and accidental choices, as Black has done.[59] The choice actually made may not be the actually limiting factor, in which case the effort is wasted. The degree to which rational or scientific choices are made, as opposed to habitual and accidental, we designate as Timeliness. Its field is mental and managerial ability. It differs widely among persons, reaching its lowest degree in merely manual labor. For Timeliness is the degree to which choices of exerting human abilities are effective in so far as the changeable limiting factors are selected at the right time, right place, right form, and right quantity.

Thus the three limiting factors in man's choosing among nature's material forces are man-power, opportunity, and timeliness. Man-power is mental, managerial, and manual ability. Opportunities are the limiting and complementary factors among the forces of nature. Timeliness is performance, forbearance, avoidance, at the right time, place, form, amount, and degree of human energy. This engineering process of choosing is specialized in managerial transactions, but its prototype is Robinson Crusoe for whom only physical possession was taken into account. Measured in terms of the highest obtainable efficiency it is the least input of man-hours or largest output of use-values within the existing limits of ability, natural opportunities available, and best judgment of timeliness. The outcome of these dimensions of choice in control of nature's forces we name efficiency.

But curiously enough, the same dimensions of choice are to be found in the field of economic power, or relative scarcities, which is the proprietary meaning of possession. Here the dimensions of Bargaining Power are also performance, avoidance, forbearance. We name these Economic or Proprietary Opportunities since they are the relative scarcities which afford the opportunities, whereas the others were Physical Opportunities, where relative efficiencies afforded the opportunities. Opportunity is the objective side of

[58] Below, p. 627, Strategic and Routine Transactions.
[59] Black, J. D., *op. cit.*, 41.

which ability and choice are the volitional side. The analysis of choice of opportunities has only gradually worked itself into economic theory, although always assumed as obvious and therefore not needing investigation, and we shall here endeavor to mark the stages of its development. For it is choices of opportunities that are the legal meaning of value, as against the physical concepts of cost of production and the hedonic concepts of pleasure and pain.

3. *Opportunity*

(1) **Cost of Service and Cost of Product.**—In Böhm-Bawerk's criticism of Senior's abstinence theory[60] is the beginning of recent doctrines of "utility cost" and "opportunity cost," the latter of which we find is the equivalent of the judicial doctrine of reasonable cost of service. Böhm-Bawerk uses the hedonistic language of pleasure derived from material services, namely, "utility-cost"— which we can readily convert into the proprietary language of money, or "opportunity-cost."

He distinguishes two kinds of loss of well-being, the "positive" kind, where "we inflict on ourselves positive injury, pain, or trouble"; and the "negative" kind, where "we do without a happiness or satisfaction which we otherwise might have had." This alternative avoidance is his utility-cost.

These two methods of measuring cost are not cumulative. The one cannot be added upon the other. They are alternative. "Since in the economic life of today," says Böhm-Bawerk, "we have an infinite number of possibilities of turning our work to fruitful account," the measurement of sacrifice in terms of labor-pain "almost never occurs." At the present time "we estimate by far the greater number of cases not by the pain of work, but by the profit or advantage we have renounced."[61]

Thus he changes his economic philosophy from Senior's pain economy of abstinence and scarcity to a pleasure and abundance economy of choosing between a greater and lesser pleasure. The generality of this principle is undoubted. We choose (with modifications hereafter to be considered) the larger pleasure and reject the smaller pleasure. We gain a surplus of pleasure.

To this renounced advantage Böhm-Bawerk gives the paradoxical name, "negative cost," or "utility-cost," whereas to the sacrifice, pain, or trouble of Adam Smith and Senior he gives the name

[60] Böhm-Bawerk, E. von, *Capital and Interest: a Critical History of Economical Theory*, 275 (1884, tr. by W. H. Smart, 1890), 275 ff.
[61] *Ibid.*, 284.

"positive cost." Since, however, the terms "positive" and "negative" are here given a meaning different from the mathematical meaning of positive and negative, because the meaning here intended is evidently the volitional meaning of choosing between alternative pleasures, we use his term "utility-cost" of alternative pleasure avoided, contrasted with the mathematical "positive cost" or positive pain of the classical school. The positive cost or pain leads to the idea of *net income* when the positive "income" of pleasure is set against the positive "outgo" of pain. But the concept of utility-cost leads to the idea of a *surplus* when a lesser pleasure avoided is compared with a larger pleasure acquired.

This will appear more familiar when we turn from Böhm-Bawerk's natural economy of materials and pleasures to the proprietary economy of a monetary community. Here everything is owned by somebody, and before the individual can have access to nature he must bargain with owners. Hence we convert the psychological term "utility-cost" into the pecuniary term "opportunity-cost." Here the activity is not physical, yet it is behavioristic. It is the act of closing the negotiations by agreeing on the transfer of legal control.[62] Opportunity-cost arises from choice of abundant opportunities for selling. Thus, in our formula of a bargaining transaction,[63] the seller S has before him two opportunities to sell to two competing buyers. He cannot sell to both in one transaction because in each transaction he is offering to sell one commodity, however large or small, and therefore he must choose between the two buyers. Buyer B offers $100 but buyer B^1 offers only $90. If seller S cannot induce buyer B to pay more than $100, then S, in accepting $100 for his commodity, thereby rejects the $90 offered by B^1. This $90 is to S his opportunity-cost—and the meaning is "negative," even paradoxical, because it is not a cost in the positive sense of outgo, but in the alternative sense of a lesser share, which he avoids, of an abundant existing supply of goods purchasable by money.

But the positive cost for S is, say $80, which, as a buyer, he pays to a seller in a *preceding* transaction. Thus "opportunity-cost" and "positive cost" are not cumulative. They are, in fact, the difference between *positive outgo* and *alternative income*. The buyer B^1 stands for the *next best* of all proprietary opportunities open to S to sell his commodity, while Buyer B stands for the *best* of all proprietary opportunities available at the time. For this reason we name it opportunity-cost.

[62] Above, p. 90, Negotiational Psychology.
[63] Above, p. 59.

Hence we arrive at a distinction to be made, but not usually made, between "surplus" and "net income." *Net income* is the difference between the gross income of S ($100 received from B), and his gross outgo ($80 paid to a preceding seller) in *two* transactions—in this case $20. But surplus, in this case, is a difference between two *gross incomes* in *one* transaction, the income $100 for S offered by B, and the alternative lesser income $90 offered by B^1. In this case the *surplus* is $10. The surplus and net income are not cumulative, which would be $30. They are the two ways of measuring value, by cost and by choice of opportunities.

In the case of "surplus" the surplus income is an "unearned" income, or "quasi-rent," of $10, arising from mere freedom to choose, without cost, between two proprietary opportunities represented in the persons of two proprietors, B and B^1, on the *same market at the same time*. But net income is the $20 difference between a positive outgo, $80, and a positive income, $100, on *two markets at different times*. In other words, surplus is the difference between two opportunities to sell in *one* transaction, but net income is the difference between positive outgo and positive income in *two* transactions.

It is upon this magnitude of surplus rather than net income, and of its measurement as opportunity-cost rather than positive cost, that the courts, as we shall see, construct their concept of reasonable cost of service. It is also a distinction which mathematical economists are only beginning to grasp in their theoretical use of statistics.[64]

In order to preserve this distinction, however, it will be necessary to have a term that will signify positive cost and distinguish it from the opportunistic cost of service. We shall distinguish it as "cost of product," whereas the opportunistic concept is "cost of service." Cost of product is the classical or pain idea of cost as positive *outgo* of money or pain in exchange for positive *income* of goods or pleasure. But cost of service is the volitional *alternative income* avoided because the individual is finite and cannot have both incomes at once and therefore chooses the larger. Thus cost of product is *outgo*, but cost of service is *alternative income*. All business is actually conducted on the alternative income, or cost of service principle, and the cost of product is merely a factor in the "mark-up" which the seller intends to get if he can.

It is to D. I. Green and H. J. Davenport that we owe the first

---

[64] See Morton, W. A., in an appendix to Ellis, L. S., *The Tariff on Sugar*, publication of The Rawleigh Foundation, Dec. 1932.

formulation of this idea of opportunity-cost.[65] While Green, says Davenport, was "the first to formulate the doctrine in entire definiteness," he was not "the first to give it systematic application." This Davenport did by means of a detailed examination of the leading theorists of the classical and hedonic schools, to which the reader is referred in his book, *Value and Distribution*. He found that Böhm-Bawerk and the Austrian school had recognized this principle, yet they did not adhere to it "without vacillation," and the doctrine had also been stated or implied by several later economists under such names as "displacement-cost," "quasi-rent," and especially the "substitution" cost of Alfred Marshall.

We have followed Davenport's exhaustive analysis and his contrast with the older theories, by reducing it to the foregoing formula of a transaction, and giving to it his name of "opportunity-cost," "distributive cost," or "distributive share." These terms describe quite accurately the active process of choosing which occurs in every bargaining transaction. What each seller chooses is that one which is largest of all the alternative shares of the total social output offered to him by buyers in the form of money. This may be named his "distributive share," the share which he accepts. In making the choice, however, he foregoes or rejects the next smaller share of the total social output offered to him by the next best buyer in the form of money. This is the "distributive cost," and it is nearly identical with the concepts of substitution cost, displacement cost, or Green's and Davenport's opportunity-cost. The "distributive share" is the claim to that share of the social output which he actually receives as the purchasing power of "money income." The opportunity-cost is the claim to a smaller share which he rejects and which therefore becomes a "cost," in the volitional sense of a lesser share not accepted in order to obtain the larger share accepted. The difference between the two is a quasi-rent, a surplus, an unearned income, obtained without cost by merely choosing, but serving as one of the constituents that go to augment his net income.

(2) **Value of Service and Value of Product.**—But if the individual can gain a surplus, which augments his net income, by having the opportunity to choose the *larger* of two gross incomes, cannot he also augment his net income by having the opportunity to choose the *lesser* of two gross outgoes? We look for the beginnings of this analysis in the writings of Henry C. Carey from 1837

[65] Green, ·D. I., "Pain Cost and Opportunity Cost," *Quarterly Journal of Economics*, VIII (1894), 218; Davenport, H. J., *Value and Distribution, a Critical and Constructive Study* (1908); *The Economics of Enterprise* (1913).

to 1847. His analysis was taken over and popularized without acknowledgment, even to the words and illustrations, by Bastiat in 1850.[66] What each of them really did was to go back to Adam Smith's concept of "labor saved," which Smith had made equivalent to "labor-cost" and "labor-commanded."[67] Each of them used Smith's concept of "labor saved" to overthrow Ricardo's doctrine of cost and rent, but Carey used it to support a protective tariff while Bastiat used it to refute the anarchist Proudhon, and to support free trade.

Carey and Bastiat employed the term "value of service" to distinguish their meaning of "labor saved." On examination of the value theories of the American courts and of business men from whose habits the courts derive their theories, we find that this is exactly their meaning of "value." The legal and capitalistic theory of value is a *labor-saved theory*, and therefore is not found in the "positive" cost or value theories of the classical or orthodox economists, nor in the theories of their communistic, anarchistic, hedonistic, or heterodox followers and dissenters.

"Labor-saved," however, is a personification of money or money-value, and the legal-capitalistic theory is a money-value theory. While Carey and Bastiat eliminated money in order to get at their concept of labor-saved, yet they also converted labor-saved into money-saved. Hence, in expounding the origins of their theory we are expounding the legal and capitalistic theory of value. We find, however, their theory embedded in our formula of a transaction, where it evidently is a volitional theory of choice of opportunities.

Bastiat, like Carey, begins with a social philosophy the opposite of Böhm-Bawerk's. Instead of an *abundance* of opportunities, between which we choose the *most remunerative* and therefore disregard the pain of sacrifice, Bastiat starts with a *scarcity* of opportunities and therefore with the pains of sacrifice, between which we choose the *least onerous*, and disregard the positive income of either money or pleasure. This, he rightly says, proceeds from the universal law of scarcity, namely, that wants exceed the supply and therefore require labor to produce a supply. But since labor is disagreeable the value of products to the buyer, who acquires

---

[66] Carey, H. C., *Principles of Political Economy* (1837); *The Past, the Present and the Future* (1847); Bastiat, Frederic, *Harmonies économiques* (1850), citations are to *Harmonies of Political Economy* (tr. by P. J. Stirling, 1860). See Carey's claim to priority in his *Principles of Social Science* (1858), I, iii. Citations are made to the edition of 1868. Carey's claim is verified by Gide, Charles, and Rist, Charles, *History of Economic Doctrines* (1913 tr.), 327, and Haney, L. H., *History of Economic Thought* (1911, 1930), 304.

[67] Above, p. 170, on Smith.

them in exchange, is not proportioned to his *own labor-cost* in producing them but to the labor which it *would have cost* him if he had produced them himself instead of acquiring them from another. Their value is thus measured by Adam Smith's labor *saved,* not by Ricardo's labor-*cost.* He states it in the form of labor, but it may be stated in the form of money.

"... the value," says Bastiat, "far from bearing a necessary proportion to the labour *performed* by the person who renders the service," as had been the labor-cost doctrine of Ricardo and afterwards of Marx and Proudhon, "may be said rather to bear proportion to the labour *saved* to the person who receives it. This general law of value, which has not, so far as I know, been observed by theoretical writers, nevertheless prevails universally in practice. ... it has its principle and foundation less in the effort of the person who *serves* than in the effort saved to him who *is served.*" [68]

Thus we may name Bastiat's "subjective value" a "negative" value, or, paradoxically, a dis-utility-value, the *value* to self of *avoiding* a more onerous alternative pain, just as Böhm-Bawerk's negative cost, or "utility-cost" was the *cost* to self of *foregoing* a lesser alternative pleasure. Converted into monetary terms this is technically a *dis-opportunity-value,* equivalent to the legal concept (which was also Carey's and Bastiat's concept), the value of service.

This is the same as the popular meaning of "nuisance value," which is the price a person would pay to get another person to remove a nuisance which was reducing the value of the property which he owned. The term has obtained legal recognition as a refutation against a claim for good-will value.[69]

This technical dis-opportunity-value, or the familiar nuisance value, we have seen is the "distributive," rather than the negative, meaning of value. It is the value to self of avoiding a greater outgo to others by having the opportunity to choose a lesser outgo. If a payment has to be made for this opportunity, it is a nuisance value. The situation may be seen in the formula of a bargaining transaction (above, p. 59).

In our formula the buyer B or B¹ has two alternatives. He can buy his commodity from S at $110 or from S¹ at $120. As a buyer, seeking his own advantage by choosing between the disagreeable alternatives imposed upon him, he selects the less disagreeable and pays $110 to S. The difference measures a nuisance value. This seller at $110 has therefore performed a service for him—a service

[68] Bastiat, F., *Harmonies of Political Economy* (tr. 1860), 114.
[69] See Commons, John R., *Legal Foundations of Capitalism*, 202; Consolidated Gas Co. *v.* N. Y., 157 Fed. (1907), 849.

which has *saved* him from the next worst alternative, or nuisance, of paying $120. The magnitude of the service is the *surplus* thus "saved," namely $10, towards augmenting his net income. This $10 is the nuisance value which he would pay to S^1, if he did not have access to S. In the latter case it is, not an "unearned income," but an unearned "saving," a "quasi-rent," arising from costless freedom to choose the lesser of two alternative positive costs (outgo) imposed upon him by the legal institutions that compel him to pay for the commodities which are needed by him but are limited in supply and owned by others.

It is upon this concept of choosing the lesser of two evils that the courts build their concepts "value of service" and "nuisance value." But since, as in the other case, there are two meanings of value, the *positive* value of expected money income and the distributive or *negative* value of avoiding an alternative higher money outgo, we shall need again a pair of terms to preserve the distinction. They are "value of product" and "value of service." Value of product is the classical and hedonistic idea of value as expected positive income of money or pleasure received in exchange for positive outgo of goods or pain. But value of service is the volitional alternative higher outgo *avoided,* or nuisance value if it cannot be avoided, because the individual is finite and cannot endure both outgoes at once, and therefore chooses the lesser or pays the nuisance value if he has no alternative. Thus value of product pertains to income, but value of service to alternative higher outgo. Value of product is one factor of *net income,* the other being the cost of the product. But value of service is another volitional *surplus,* the other being cost of service, both of which augment net income.

This concept of value of service was not something new in economic theory—it was a new name and a new application of Ricardo's doctrine of "comparative cost" in international trade. Ricardo had said, "The same rule which regulates the relative value of commodities in one country, does not regulate the relative value of the commodities exchanged between two or more countries." [70] Carey builded upon these "two rules" of Ricardo, and constructed out of them his theory of a protective tariff, contrary to Ricardo's and Bastiat's free trade. In one country, like America, he says, the positive quantity of labor may be a measure of relative values, as Ricardo held, because all labor has "an equal power to command the services of nature. The product of two carpenters in New York or Philadelphia can generally be exchanged for that of two masons." So also the product of different laborers in different parts of France,

[70] *The Works of David Ricardo* (ed. by McCulloch, J. R., 1888), 75.

or England, or India, are about equal and will exchange at rates proportionate to labor-time within the country.

But this is not true in foreign trade. "The time of a laborer in Boston is nearly equal in value to that of another in Pittsburgh, Cincinnati, or St. Louis; but it will not be given for that of a laborer in Paris or Havre. . . . The people of Italy give a year's exertions for less than those of England obtain in half a year." [71] This statement of Carey's was Ricardo's doctrine of comparative cost.

Yet, as Ricardo held, in supporting free trade, foreign trade is advantageous because each country exports that on which its own labor is more efficient, and imports that on which its own labor is less efficient. Thereby it *saves* the higher amount of its own labor required for its own high-cost products, and can devote that labor to its low-cost products for export. It is but a step from this doctrine to say, as did Carey, that the measure of the value of the service rendered by the foreigner is the alternative amount of home labor "saved," in the sense that it would otherwise be required to produce the goods imported.[72] It was this idea of choosing the lesser of two labor-costs that Carey and Bastiat expanded into a universal law of value, applicable in both domestic and foreign trade, and thus changed Ricardo's and Marx's doctrine of positive labor costs as the measure of value, to Ricardo's comparative labor costs as the measure of value, and to Smith's "labor saved" as the measure of value. By giving to it the name "value of service," measured by alternative *higher* labor cost avoided, instead of "value of product," measured by its own labor-cost, they placed it on the map as something universal, where Ricardo had seen it only in foreign trade. But it changed the whole concept of value from the positive classical and communistic labor-cost to a competitive choice of the lesser of alternative costs.

It is rather strange that Davenport, who developed so brilliantly the companion doctrine of opportunity-cost, did not develop also this doctrine of dis-opportunity-value. It is possibly because, like most economists, he had dismissed Carey and Bastiat as irrelevant freaks, and therefore devoted his attention to the classical and hedonic economists. He dismissed the concept of dis-opportunity-values as "competition." But the other also arises from competition. Davenport does make use of the one contribution made by Carey which had been immediately accepted by all economists,

[71] Carey, H. C., *Principles of Social Science* (1868), I, 155.

[72] Carey, in his earliest theorizing, was a free trader, but afterwards he saw that this doctrine of value would support a protective tariff against cheap foreign labor.

namely his substitution of "cost of reproduction" for the "cost of production" of the older economists,[73] but he gives to this no particular attention. As a matter of fact, Carey's "labor-cost of reproduction" was an entirely new concept, not merely equivalent to, but contradictory of, Ricardo's and Marx's "labor-cost of production." It was not a theory of labor-cost at all but a universal theory of opportunity to choose the lesser of two alternative labor-costs. But it has been accepted generally by economists and courts without noticing the discrepancy, just as Adam Smith did not notice the discrepancy between labor-cost and labor-saved. Yet it becomes, as generally used, an idealistic volitional concept of alternatives, constructed in imagination as an "ideal type"[74] of what the price *would* be if there were free competition, regardless of what had been the preceding positive labor-costs of production, as apparently maintained by Ricardo. Its universality, however, is unquestionable, and readily appears when reduced to the formula of that ultimate unit of economic theory, the bargaining transaction, wherein four competing participants are endeavoring to choose, not only as sellers the larger of two gross incomes, but also as buyers the lesser of two gross outgoes.

This suggests another reason for Davenport's oversight of disopportunity-value. It was his failure continuously to make use of the distinction between *gross income* and *net income*. Had the two constituents of net income, namely gross income and gross outgo, been always carried in mind, then the concept would have been called for of choosing the lesser of two gross outgoes as much as the concept of choosing the larger of two gross incomes. He does, indeed, parenthetically by way of caution, make it clear that opportunity-cost, the choice between gross incomes, should not be confused with what we might name *occupation-cost,* the choice between *two net incomes,* representing two different occupations. ". . . the doctrine of opportunity-cost," he says, "rightly understood, does not point fundamentally to the question of how much could be realized of gain in some alternative occupation or activity, but only to how much must be realized in the occupation or activity . . . in order to insure its continuance."[75] In other words, the choice is not that of changing occupations, but is that of choosing between buyers who patronize the same concern. The buyer who pays the higher price is chosen by the seller, and the buyer rejected measures opportunity-cost, or cost of service to the seller. But

[73] Davenport, H. J., *Value and Distribution: a Critical and Constructive Study,* 322.

[74] Below, p. 719, on Ideal Types.

[75] Davenport, H. J., *op. cit.,* 92–93.

somehow there was overlooked the companion series of choices by the same person, now as a buyer, wherein his choice lies between two sellers. These are such as the sellers of raw material or sellers of labor, wherein the seller who sells to the buyer at the *lower* price is chosen and where the seller *avoided* by the buyer measures the dis-opportunity-value, or value of service.

Davenport seems to pass this off as the self-evident fact of competition. The buyer *does* choose the lesser price asked by competing sellers which he calls "competition," but so does the seller choose the higher price offered by competing buyers, which also is competition. According to Davenport, choice of opportunity should not be confused with competition, because he looks on sellers as competitors, but his opportunity-cost is a choice by a seller between two buyers. Yet these buyers are also competitors as may be seen from the formula. Competition is a rivalry between buyers as much as it is a rivalry between sellers, and the buyer is choosing between two sellers just as the seller is choosing between two buyers. Competition and opportunity occur on both sides of the transaction.

A further explanation may be offered from a study of court decisions on reasonable cost of service and reasonable value of service. Both of these concepts appear in court decisions and a study of these decisions reveals, as above stated, that they reject the Ricardian and classical economists' notions of positive cost of production and positive value of the product, since these are believed to be private matters, unless a public concern is introduced when there is alleged to be unfair competition or discrimination. In order to discover the magnitude of the latter public welfare issues the courts resort to the comparative method of measuring alternative prices received, or prices paid, by others in a similar market, which might be shown to be the reasonable alternatives open to buyers or sellers if they were free to choose similar alternatives, under the existing conditions of supply, demand, custom, and the usual practices of persons in similar circumstances. When resolved into economic terminology this is Ricardo's comparative costs, Carey's cost of reproduction and value of service, or the more technical dis-opportunity-value, as well as Davenport's opportunity-cost, or cost of service. Here, in the legal forum, the comparative and distributive concept, value of service, is as often at issue as the similar comparative and distributive concept, cost of service.[76]

A still more likely explanation of the omission of the value-of-

[76] For historical development of this legal doctrine see below, p. 773, Scarcity, Abundance, Stabilization.

service concept is the absurd meanings given to it by Carey and Bastiat. The term was to them an old acquaintance from Ricardo, quite inconsistent with his usual doctrine, but suddenly discovered as throwing a new halo around the abused head of Capitalism in Bastiat's case and Protectionism in Carey's case. To discover the source of these absurdities we are required to examine what is reasonably and properly meant by the volitional concept of choice of alternatives.

(3) **Inaccessible Alternatives—Free Will and Free Choice.** —When Bastiat illustrated his concept of value of service he took Proudhon, who had been declaiming against rent, interest, and private property, back to "a primitive forest and in sight of a pestilential morass." [77] "Here," he said to Proudhon, "is land exactly like what the first clearers had to encounter. Take as much of it as you please. . . . Cultivate it yourself. All that you can make it produce is yours. I make but one condition, that you will not have recourse to that society of which you represent yourself as the victim. . . . A labourer," he continues, now obtains with 15 days' work a quantity of goods which he "would formerly have had difficulty in procuring with 600 days' work." [78] Hence six hundred days' work is the "value of the service" which landlords and capitalists render to the laborer in the form of food. The positive labor-cost, or cost of *production,* is fifteen days' labor. That was Ricardo's and Proudhon's idea of value. But the labor *saved,* by virtue of the lower cost of *reproduction* brought about by "society," from its original condition as a morass was the surplus of 585 days' labor. The laborer pays the cost of *reproduction,* not the cost of *production.* The difference—585 days' labor—is the value to the laborer of the services rendered by landlords and capitalists, as representatives of "society," in return for which, of course, rent, interest, or profit, is an insignificant payment.

Similarly when the regulation of railway rates was in its infancy, the legal representatives of the railways took the farmers back seventy-five years and argued that the value of the service rendered by the railways was what it would cost the farmers, *if there were no railroads,* for the transportation of wheat over dirt roads by horse carriage. This was estimated at least as 50 cents per ton-mile whereas the railway charge was only some 3 cents per ton-mile. The value of the service rendered by railways to farmers was therefore 50 cents, for which the railways charged an insignifi-

[77] Bastiat, *op. cit.,* I, 201. Similar illustrations had been used by Carey to disprove Ricardo's theory of rent.
[78] *Ibid.,* 201–202.

cant 3 cents, and the farmers got a surplus of 47 cents. Hence it
would be unjust if their railway rates were reduced.

This, too, is the instinctive argument of business men when they
expound the value of their service to labor by furnishing employment, or advertise the value of their service to consumers by emphasizing "service" instead of price-reduction.

The argument is good but is liable to fallacy which may be named
the *fallacy of non-concomitant alternatives,* or *inaccessible options.*
It is in fact a fallacy respecting the human will. The will is
limited to here and now. Bastiat's laborer does not choose between
the cost of food *now* and the cost a thousand years ago. The railroad's farmer does not choose between shipping by rail *now* and
shipping by dirt road fifty years ago. This would be a choice
between the railway and the inaccessible option of hauling his wheat
to market by horses and trucks. This is "no choice." He does
not choose between an accessible and an inaccessible alternative in
space, nor between an alternative that has disappeared in time past
and one that is here in time present. He chooses between the two
least onerous alternatives accessible at the same time and same
place. It is his misfortune if the next alternative is unreasonably
onerous, but if it is so, then it nevertheless is the actual value of
service under the circumstances, even though it is shocking to common sense.

In such case it remains only to construct in imagination an
"ethical typus" [79] that shall be a "reasonable" value of service, and
this is the imaginary "cost of reproduction" under existing conditions by an alternative but imaginary railway. It soon was
discovered that the railway contention, like Bastiat's contention, was
absurd. Its absurdity rested on the common-sense observation that
we do not choose inaccessible alternatives. It is the absurdity of
a free will instead of a free choice. The reasonableness may be
imaginary, but that is the way it always starts. Extensive investigation may be necessary to carry it through.[80]

It was these fallacies of inaccessible and non-concomitant alternatives that gave to Carey and Bastiat the name of the "optimist"
school. They were optimist because they did not deal with a finite
human will. More valid than Bastiat's inaccessible alternatives was
his other illustration of accessible alternatives, which is the theory

[79] Below, p. 719.

[80] On the contest of the past forty years over these doctrines of cost of service and
value of service, see especially Ripley, W. Z., *Railroads: Rates and Regulation* (1905), 167;
Sharfman, I. L., *Railway Regulation* (1915), *The American Railway Problem* (1921), *The
Interstate Commerce Commission* (2 vols., 1931); Glaeser, M. G., *Outlines of Public Utility
Economics* (1927). Consult indexes of these books.

of value from which the courts derive their theory of reasonable value. He says:

"I take a walk along the sea-beach, and I find by chance a magnificent diamond. I am thus put in possession of a great *value*. Why? Am I about to confer a great benefit on the human race? Have I devoted myself to a long and laborious work? Neither the one nor the other. Why, then, does this diamond possess so much value? Undoubtedly because the person to whom I transfer it considers that I have rendered him a great *service*,—all the greater that many rich people desire it, and that I alone can render it. The grounds of his judgment may be controverted—be it so. It may be founded on pride, or vanity— granted again. But this judgment has, nevertheless, been formed by a man who is disposed to act upon it, and that is sufficient for my argument." [81]

Here our terminology is applicable. There are three methods of determining value.

(1) The value of the diamond is "value of the product" to the seller, and this is the price, under all the circumstances of demand and supply, which he can actually sell it for to a buyer. And the "cost of the product" to the seller was the insignificant labor of finding it. The difference is net income for the seller. This was the classical and orthodox way of stating it, in terms of "positive" value, diminished by "positive" cost. It is a *net income* concept.

(2) But the "cost of service," or "opportunity-cost," to the *seller* was the *lower* price which the next rich man offered to pay but which the seller rejected, because he had the better alternative. The difference is *surplus* for the seller. This was the Böhm-Bawerk, Green, and Davenport way of stating it.

(3) On the other hand, the "value of the service," or "dis-opportunity-value" to the *buyer* was the *higher* price he would have been compelled to pay had not the finder of the diamond "saved" him from that expense by selling at a lower price. The difference between the two is *surplus*, this time for the buyer. This was Carey's and Bastiat's way of stating it.

Carrying Bastiat's analysis to his next step, while the "positive" cost to the finder of the diamond was the insignificant labor of finding it, there was a "dis-utility-value" measured by the greater labor-cost of digging for the diamond. This was, as Bastiat meta-phorically but solemnly said, the "value of the service" rendered by the *sea-beach*—one of nature's many "gratuitous services"—to the finder by *saving* him from the greater labor-cost of digging.

[81] Bastiat, *op. cit.*, I, 113–114.

Or, applicable to Böhm-Bawerk, the buyer of the diamond doubtless obtained greater satisfaction (income) from the diamond than from an equal consumption of food. The "utility" of the rejected food was the "utility-cost" to him of choosing to enjoy the diamond instead of the alternative food.

The fallacy of inaccessible options, or non-concomitant alternatives, suggests a related fallacy regarding the value of service. It is said that in choosing the least onerous alternative the individual rejects, not only the "next worse" alternative but *all alternatives* inclusive, from the next worse to the "most worse" of all. Therefore the value of the service to him is the *sum* of all the avoided alternatives, which, of course, might conceivably rise to infinity.

This fallacy may be named the *fallacy of infinite alternatives.* Only an infinite being can enjoy all possible alternatives at the same time and place: but then he would not choose—he would take them all at once, regardless of space or time. The economist's well-known analysis of a free market will correct this fallacy.

It was these fallacies of inaccessible, non-concomitant and infinite alternatives that rendered the "optimist" school of Carey and Bastiat absurd. Yet, applied to the economist's finite beings on a market, their discovery, like that of Davenport, becomes a notable contribution to economic theory. A finite being, who is the economist's being, is limited to but one of the infinite possibilities of the world at the moment of choosing. He may be in error as to which is best and next best, or worse and "worser." That was his mistake. But anyhow he can only take one at a time, though the magnitude of that one may be big if he is rich, or small if he is poor. He cannot take both alternatives at the same time and place.

Hence he is forced into the predicament of choosing. In the mental process that precedes the act of choice, which we name negotiational psychology, and more so if the process is instinctive, he has already rejected all of the remote alternatives, and has narrowed his choice down to the two that are deemed to be the "two best" or the two "least worse," only one of which he can get with his limited resources. Here the final predicament is resolved, and the negotiations are closed, not by thinking but by acting. This acting is the act of choosing. It must be distinguished from the preceding "mental acts," or psychology of "choosing." It is the actual behavior of choosing, which, from the behavioristic standpoint we have resolved into performance, avoidance, forbearance.

The measure of this active advantage in choosing is either the next best *income* which he foregoes, which therefore is the "cost" to him of being compelled to choose, or the next worse *outgo* which he avoids, which is the "value" to him of the opportunity to avoid that next worse alternative outgo. The finite choice of economics is the behavioristic choice of the better of two accessible alternatives. By avoiding or foregoing one of the two he has left all of the others to the world at large.

An opposite fallacy occurs in Böhm-Bawerk's criticism of Senior's abstinence theory, above noticed. Böhm-Bawerk was led to eliminate pain and sacrifice from economic consideration on account of his theory of abundance of opportunities under modern conditions, so that we do not choose between pains, we choose between pleasures. Hence, for him, all costs were utility-costs—the next best alternative *income* avoided. But what he did was, not *actually* to eliminate positive pain and positive cost, but, by the usual device, *virtually* to eliminate them by supposing them to be constant, just as Bastiat virtually, but not actually, eliminated positive pleasure and positive income by supposing them to be constant. This oversight, we see, arose from failure to perceive that net income is the outcome of *two* variables, gross income and gross outgo. By assuming *outgo* as constant, then the variable, with Böhm-Bawerk, was the pleasures of utility or gross income. But by assuming *income* as constant, the variable with Bastiat was dis-utility or gross outgo.

The same is apparently true of Davenport's opportunity-cost. He virtually eliminated outgo or pain as constant, so that his choice was a choice between alternative incomes.

But this process of virtual elimination is only a mental device as a substitute for the laboratory methods of actual elimination. There is really, in every transfer, a variable gross income for one which is the identical gross outgo for the other, because its ownership is merely transferred. But a transaction is two transfers. If one of these is virtually eliminated by keeping it constant, then the others are the variables. In the repetition of *selling*, it is the gross money *incomes* that are considered to be variable. In the repetitions of *buying* it is the gross money *outgoes* that are considered to be variable. But it is the conjunction of the two variables in two transactions that yields the actual dimensions of net income.

Here we recur again to the third concept of choice of alternatives, previously noted, namely, the choice between two net incomes. This net income concept of opportunity is quite different from the gross income concept. Opportunity-cost refers to the single choice of a seller between two *gross* incomes offered by two buyers, but choice between *net* incomes is the *two* choices of a person, who is both buyer and seller, between two gross outgoes as buyer and two gross incomes as seller. For this reason we have assigned to this choice of net incomes the name of *occupation-cost* instead of "opportunity-cost." For, consider what is the situation of a person who both obtains gross income by selling and suffers gross outgo by buying. He is evidently a person who occupies a position such as a job, or even an entire going concern in all its relations of buying materials and labor and selling the finished product. This position in the social mechanism is his occupation, and "occupation-cost" must therefore be a *choice between two occupations,* wherein the chooser abandons the occupation having the lesser *net* income and chooses the occupation having the larger net income. He chooses between occupations, not between buyers of his product and not between sellers of labor and raw material. He changes his occupation—not his customers or laborers or materials.

While this concept is proper enough for an economic situation where a person leaves one job and takes another job, or where a whole establishment abandons one occupation, say the manufacturing of bicycles, and transfers to another, say the manufacturing of automobiles, yet it conceals what happens when he remains in the same occupation. What happens there is the social phenomena of bargaining and the social relation of sellers and buyers, upon which are founded most of the issues that come up for decision. Thus, "occupation-cost" conceals the gross income that is paid as social cost for services rendered, as well as the gross outgo of service rendered to others. It makes impossible, therefore, the analysis of utility-cost, opportunity-cost, or the legal concept of cost of service, as well as the analysis of dis-utility-value, dis-opportunity-value, or the value of service of Bastiat and the courts. Only in case gross income and net income happen to be identical, because positive costs have been eliminated by contract, as is done in the case of contract-interest or contract-rent, does gross income happen to coincide with net income. Therefore, in that case, occupation-cost happens to coincide with what we define as opportunity-cost. But in all such cases as jobs and going concerns, where the two variables of gross income and gross outgo determine net income, the separation of buying from selling must be made in theory, for it is actually made in practice.[82]

We are now in position to summarize why it was that Böhm-Bawerk and Davenport have left their theory of opportunity unfinished. Having eliminated positive cost (pain or money outgo) by resorting to *distributive cost* (utility-cost or opportunity-cost), they have failed to eliminate positive value (pleasure or money income) and thus have not resorted to *distributive value* (dis-utility-

[82] Below, p. 526, Margin for Profit.

value or dis-opportunity-value). The reason is the failure to distinguish value as net income and value as gross income.

Back of this oversight are the two reasons, already suggested, why the concept of dis-opportunity-value has not been unearthed, as it had been by Carey and Bastiat. One is the optimistic assumption that we live in a pleasure economy of abundance and hence do not choose between pains. The other is the individualistic assumption of classical theory that we seek the largest possible *net* income regardless of the effect on other people. The first eliminates positive costs by assuming that they are equal and therefore negligible. The second conceals positive costs in the individualistic notion of net income. But they are not concealed, and the social relations of persuasion, coercion, bargaining power, etc., are brought into the open, if we start with the social concept of transactions instead of individuals.

This is the significance of the distinction between opportunity and occupation. The notion of opportunity instead of occupation, as here defined, brings to the front the concealed notions of gross income and gross outgo. This reveals the concealed issue of opposition of interests and the resulting need of courts or similar tribunals to bring about a reasonable harmony of interests. The concept of an individual is a concept of *net income* for one person from his private occupation. It is an individual matter and involves no conflict with other individuals, no tribunals to decide between them, and no issue of public interest.

But the concept of a transaction is a gross income equal to a gross outgo for two persons, and here are the conflicts of interest. Gross income for the seller is gross outgo for the buyer in *one transaction*, whereas net income or loss is merely the excess of one over the other for *one individual* in two transactions. The same is true when the equivalent terms are expressed as value and cost. Positive value, that is, gross income, for the seller is the price which he receives when he sells; positive cost, that is, gross outgo, for the buyer in that transaction is the same magnitude of price which he pays. Hence an increase in gross income is a gain for the seller and an equal loss for the buyer. The conflict of interest is irrepressible in every price. It is the reason for bargaining, compromising, and the intervention of the state, in reconciling the conflict of interests.

But an increase in *net income* conceals this conflict of interests in buying and selling. The latter are the legal facts of transferring legal control over a share of the social output of commodities and services. As such, they involve negotiation, choices between offers and bids made by others, partial or complete control of supply and demand, inducements, persuasion, coercion, duress—in short, bargaining. The familiar terms employed in economic theory, from the time of Quesnay, of "circulation" of goods, "flow" of income, "exchange," and so on, derived, as they are, from analogy to physics and engineering, conceal this economic act of bargaining and this conflict of interests. This concealment is not noticed, partly because the transfer of ownership is not distinguished from the delivery of things; partly because, by starting with the individualistic notion of net income, the bargains by which net income is determined are not brought into the problem.

But, by starting with the notion of gross income and gross outgo, repeated continuously, which means starting with a repetition of transactions instead of self-centered individuals, the bargaining as well as managing and rationing transactions, and therefore the inherent opposition of interests, are brought to the front and can be measured somewhat. While the notion of choice between net incomes, which means the individualistic notion of *both* buyer and seller, conceals the bargaining activities that may or may not harmonize the opposing interests, the notions of choice between *either* gross incomes or gross outgoes, measured by "opportunity-cost," or "cost of service," and "dis-opportunity-value," or "value of service," are the measure of the gains and losses derived by one person from another person in the bargaining transactions themselves. The conflict of interests also exists in managerial and rationing transactions, because in these transactions the principle of scarcity also plays a part.

The foregoing analysis of bargaining activities enables us to distinguish more fully the meanings of good-will and competition. If bargaining transactions are stripped of all misleading advertising, deception, nepotism, monopoly, and coercion—in order to arrive at the price concept of a willing buyer and willing seller, each of whom has thereby freedom of choice—then we arrive at the concepts both of good-will and fair competition. Customers' good-will is willingness of the free buyer to pay to a concern the *same or higher* price for the similar service than the buyer would pay elsewhere, that is, a "fair price." But free competition is willingness of the buyer to pay only the *same or lower* price for the similar service than he would pay elsewhere, that is, a "cut price," even a destructive price at bankrupt sales. Here the magnitude and social consequences of the gains and losses of individuals in their dealings with each other becomes increasingly a matter of public importance.

We therefore ask, What were the historical circumstances which led to the incoming of these notions of choice of opportunities as a substitute for the classical notions of cost of production? This leads us to the notable but then heterodox transition made in the first half of the Nineteenth Century from individuals to society.

(4) From Division of Labor to Association of Labor and Public Purpose.—In the decade of the 1840's the "association of labor" was "in the air." We have said elsewhere that this decade and the preceding one were "the hot air period of American history." All economists, reformers, and practical men began to take account of "association." [83] The formulation took different names and shapes according to the different inclinations of the progenitors. For most of them it was named coöperation; for the anarchists it was "mutualism"; for Robert Owen or Karl Marx it was Socialism or Communism; for Auguste Comte it was "sociology"; for practical business men it was freedom of incorporation; for labor it was trade-unionism; for Carey and Bastiat it was "association of labor." For all of them it was "society" distinguished from government. Society, and not an aggregate of individuals, produced wealth.

In this respect the period was not only a reaction against Adam Smith's Division of Labor substituted by him for the Mercantilism of governments; it was also a reaction against Smith's antagonism to all forms of incorporation and association which controlled individuals. Smith's division of labor made each individual independent and the sole producer of wealth, while his concept of association, like that of Bentham's, was merely that of *adding* one's product to the product of others, and then exchanging it with others. But the new associationism of a coöperative society now produced the wealth and then individuals owned and transferred it to each other.

There were naïve ideas and magic fallacies springing from these newly formulated concepts of society. Carey and Bastiat looked upon theirs as an unlimited historical accrual of social services from the stone age to the present age, equivalent to an accrual of value in the form of land, fixed improvements, and machinery. But, strangely enough, society, for them, was the capitalists and landlords, who owned all of this historic accrual of wealth. Yet, as they argued, all of this social accrual of value was freely available to present laborers who did not own it, and thereby "saved" them from the labor they would otherwise be compelled to perform, as individuals repeating the past history of society, in order to obtain the present necessaries and luxuries. Whether they called it social wealth, or social value, or value of service, was indifferent because

---

[83] Cf. Commons and associates, *History of Labour in the United States*, I, 493 ff.; Commons, John R., "Horace Greeley and the Working Class Origins of the Republican Party," *Pol. Sci. Quar.*, XXIV (1909), 225.

its value, like that of Ricardo and Marx, was the amount of labor-power historically embodied in it.[84]   This saving of present labor by the accrual of social value was almost infinite, as when Bastiat, in the fore-mentioned case of a morass, estimated its accrued value at 60 times the amount of present operating labor required to produce the crop.   It was indeed infinite, from the standpoint of what was possible for any finite being in the present generation.   We name it a fallacy of infinite accrual of social value, as well as what we have previously named, from the individual standpoint, the fallacy of inaccessible or non-concomitant options.

By means of this fallacy Carey worked out his rebuttal of the Ricardian unearned rent and the Malthusian pessimistic law of population.   Population does not expand from higher to lower margins of productivity in agriculture, but expands from lower to higher margins.   Settlement begins on the less fertile but easily cultivated hill tops with primitive tools, and expands towards the more fertile lands requiring huge capital equipment, created by the social labor-power of the past, for drainage, highways, forest removal, deep plowing, etc.   This is the accrual of socially created physical capital with its augmented power over nature.   None of this fertile land could possibly be *reproduced* by the individual settler in its present cultivated condition, because, in order to do so, he would individually have to go through the historic stages of his ancestors up to the present.   Not even the Ricardian unearned increment of rent, no matter how great it might be, is equivalent to the value of what, in the history of the race, has been expended by society to bring the owner's land up to its present yield.   Hence the Carey-Bastiat reasoning, like that of Marx, eliminated the distinctions between rent, interest, and profit.   Each of these functional divisions of the social product, and all of them together, are evidently less than a fair return on what society has historically invested in the present value of land and capital.[85]

But this physical concept of social accrual of wealth involved Carey and Bastiat in a contradiction of their new meaning of private property, from which John Locke and Adam Smith had escaped by their concept of the individual as the owner of what he had individually produced, and Marx escaped by his idea of common property. According to Carey and Bastiat the individual proprietor owns, not

---

[84] Cf. the more recent similar formulation of the social concept by Anderson, B. M., *Social Value, a Study in Economic Theory, Critical and Constructive* (1911); *The Value of Money* (1917).

[85] It must be noted that neither Carey, Bastiat, nor preceding economists had a theory of urban rents. This came later in an application of the theory of opportunity-cost. Below, p. 805, Police Power of Taxation.

what he produced, but what society has produced. This was not the case with Locke and Smith, whose individuals exchanged with other individuals what each had previously produced, and the total social product was merely the sum of all individual products.

Evidently Carey and Bastiat were involved in a naïve use of the newly discovered principle of association of labor. Rightly regarded, they fell into the hands of Karl Marx. Their argument was a fallacious special pleading in order to more than justify whatever is actually taken by present proprietors as rent, interest, and profits against the current attacks of the newly emerging socialists, anarchists, and communists, who based their arguments on the same social production instead of individual production.[86]

Modern economics, from the time of Ricardo, provoked more intensely by the social theories of the 1840's, is increasingly busied with the problem of measuring the limited services rendered to the social output by finite individuals and concerns, and comparing their value with the present and deferred compensations received from society by individuals for the services. The mental tools for exposing the associational fallacies of the 1840's are found in several new concepts and practices, such as the accrual of ideas instead of accrual of wealth;[87] the use of accounting records which show a *net* accrual of uncompensated services for a single concern[88] in place of the infinite gross accruals from all the services of the past; and the *turnover* of wealth, on account of depreciation, in place of the accumulation of wealth.[89]

Carey and Bastiat saved themselves by substituting *cost of reproduction* for Ricardo's *cost of production* as the price which present generations pay for the services of the past. They could not, except for purposes of fallacious justification of private property, hold that an infinite accrual of past social services is embodied in all present values of land and capital equipment. The services of the past have disappeared by depreciation, wear, tear, obsolescence. In their place have reappeared new services and improvements on old services, based, not on the accrual of wealth, but on the repetition and accrual of ideas, along with an enormously increased efficiency in the production of wealth. Consequently, referring to our formula of a bargaining transaction, the present value of any accumulated wealth cannot exceed the present cost ($110) of reproducing that wealth.

---

[86] See other comments on Carey and Bastiat by Böhm-Bawerk, E. von, *Capital and Interest;* Gide and Rist, *History of Economic Doctrines;* Haney, L. H., *History of Economic Thought* (revised ed. 1933); Scott, W. A., *The Development of Economics* (1933).

[87] Below, p. 649, Veblen.

[88] Commons, John R., *Legal Foundations of Capitalism*, 203.

[89] Above, p. 294, From Circulation to Repetition.

This is obviously because the buyer of any accumulated wealth from the past, no matter how great or small its specific labor cost at the time of production, has *now* the alternative of purchasing its equivalent from a competing seller ($110) at the present cost of reproduction. This is the base-line of Carey's and Bastiat's value of service (or dis-opportunity-value), and measures the *saving* of labor by having access to an alternative producer who sells at the present lower costs of production because he makes use of the historic increase, not in social wealth, but in social efficiency.

Hence Carey's cost of *reproduction* rescues him and Bastiat from the fallacy of his preceding ethical justification of private property in the ownership of what, not the owner, but society had produced. It was his answer to the advocates of common ownership, and a needed correction of their use of Ricardo's *cost of production*, since they had used the latter concept to condemn private ownership of what society had produced. But, for Carey, private owners do not get more or pay less of the social wealth than the present cost of reproduction. This applied equally to rent, interest, and profit, as well as wages.

For it is evident that, upon their assumptions of free, equal, and prompt competition, the equilibrium point between the price charged by the seller and the same price paid by the buyer is at the cost of reproduction. Hence, on these assumptions of equilibrium, the later doctrines of opportunity-cost of Böhm-Bawerk, Green, and Davenport are identical, from the seller's standpoint, with the doctrines of dis-opportunity-value of Carey and Bastiat, from the buyer's standpoint. While apparently, in our formula of a bargaining transaction, the opportunity-cost is measured by the difference between buyer 100 and buyer 90, and the dis-opportunity-value is measured by the difference between seller 110 and seller 120, yet if 110 is the cost of reproduction, and if free, equal, and prompt competition bring down the price to that cost of reproduction, then the opportunity-cost for the seller is measured by the difference between 90 and 110, and the dis-opportunity-value for the buyer by the difference between 120 and the same 110. Each gains by the transaction at 110, but the gain is not the unmeasurable psychological gain of the pain and pleasure economists—it is the measurable economic gain of choosing the cost of reproduction instead of alternative prices demanded by the next best seller (120) or offered by the next best buyer (90).

Yet, if the three assumptions that underlie the doctrine of equilibrium, namely freedom, equality, and promptness, are rejected, then we shall find that our formula does apply to the legal doctrines of the limits of coercion.[90] We can see how this happens by contrasting, with Carey and Davenport, the theory of Alfred Marshall, the culminating exponent of the "neo-classical," or equilibrium economists.

(5) **The Law of Substitution.**—That the two concepts, opportunity-cost, or cost of service, and dis-opportunity-value, or value of service, may be used interchangeably without noticing their difference, when free competition is assumed, may be seen in what Marshall calls "the great Law of Substitution," often, he says, "referred to the action of competition." [91] He states the two sides of his principle of substitution, namely, "to obtain *greater results* with a *given expenditure,* or *equal results* with a *less expenditure.*" The first, we see, takes the standpoint of the seller, and is Davenport's opportunity-cost. The second takes the standpoint of the buyer, and is Carey's and Bastiat's dis-opportunity-value.

Marshall then uses one or the other as equivalent. The business man, he says, "is continually comparing the efficiency and the supply prices of different factors of production which may be used in obtaining the *same result,* so as to hit upon that combination which will give the largest incomings in proportion to any *given outlay;* or, in other words, he is ceaselessly occupied with the Law of Substitution." [92]

This is Davenport's opportunity-cost, where the *outlay is constant* and the income is variable.

But Marshall goes on: "The sum of the supply prices of those factors which are used is, as a rule, less than the sum of the supply prices of any other set of factors which could be substituted for them. Whenever it appears to the producers that this is not the case, they will, as a rule, set to work to substitute the *less expensive method.*" [93]

This is Carey's and Bastiat's dis-opportunity-value, or "cost of reproduction" where the *income is constant* and the outlay is variable.

It turns out, therefore, that Marshall's "law of substitution" is none other than Carey's "cost of *reproduction*" contrasted with Ricardo's "cost of *production.*" H. G. Brown [94] makes a similar identification of the opportunity-cost of Davenport and the dis-opportunity-value of Carey, both being equivalent to "cost of repro-

[90] Below, p. 331, Limits of Coercion.
[91] Marshall, A. C., *Principles of Economics* (2d ed., 1891, cited; not materially changed in 8th ed., 1930), 401–402, 414–415, 554–559.
[92] *Ibid.*, 414.
[93] *Ibid.*, 554. Italics mine.
[94] Below, p. 805, The Police Power of Taxation.

duction," although the latter concept comes from Carey and not Davenport.

It may seem over-captious to insist on these double meanings of Marshall's law of substitution, but it is not so when we are making the shift from the individualistic to the social point of view and to the value theories of the courts which perforce must take the social point of view. Marshall is considering the individual entrepreneur and his *net income,* where there is no conflict of interests, but the courts are comparing one individual, as plaintiff or defendant, with what is customary among all individuals similarly situated. The judge, or arbitrator, is asking what are the *reasonable* alternatives which *would* be available to either party if all were treated equally before the law.[95] This requires an investigation into what is customary at the time and place. Reasonable value of service is what other *buyers,* similarly situated, would pay for the service rendered; reasonable cost of service is what other *sellers,* similarly situated, would receive in compensation for the service rendered. Marshall's problem of *free* competition and his equilibrium margin of utility or profitableness, which, however, may be destructive, extortionate, or discriminatory in actual practice, give way to the problem of *fair* competition, *equal* opportunity, and *reasonable* value. In this respect all of the customs and opportunities of the time and place are compared with those of the individual plaintiff or defendant who asks society, in the person of a judge or arbitrator, to bring collective force to aid the execution of his will against the will of the other party or all parties.

It may seem also that we have entered upon a too meticulous insistence on the obvious relations already attributed by economists, as Marshall said, to competition, but it is not so if we observe the very fundamental changes which this choice of alternatives makes in all cases where, contrary to equilibrium theories, competition is not wholly free, equal, and prompt; and further, if we observe that these concepts of opportunity mark a transition from the classical idea of positive cost of production and the hedonic ideas of positive pain and pleasure to the volitional ideas of choice of alternatives. The lawyer, who epitomizes the institutional point of view in most cases of conflict of interest, asks neither about feelings nor "fundamentals." He gets everything down to dollars and cents. He asks, What is the next best alternative which my client is up against on account of the action of the opposite party? And the damages must not be estimated in feelings (except in the domestic law of "heart balm"), but in the alternative dollars and cents which it will cost

[95] Below, p. 719, Ideal Types.

to bring his client out financially equal with his opponent in enjoying the opportunities which society is supposed to be rendering equally to all its members. If competition were always ideally free, as assumed in the working hypotheses of non-institutionalists, then there would be no measurable difference between competition and choice of opportunities. But the lawyer, though more "opportunistic" and less "fundamental" than the economists, is, for that reason, closer to the everyday experiences of inequalities of all classes of people. He is dealing directly with individual experience in its relation to the social opportunities owned, controlled, or withheld by other individuals, in a world where there is no equilibrium at the cost of reproduction simply because there is not perfect freedom, perfect equality, or perfect promptitude of competition. We must therefore turn to the more realistic alternatives that people are up against. These we name the limits of coercion.

(6) **Limits of Coercion.**—Here we approach a third dimension of the bargaining transaction, which we name bargaining power, instead of cost of reproduction. In our formula it is evident that seller S cannot force buyer B to pay more than $120, since above that margin his competitor S^1 would take his place as the seller. Neither can buyer B force seller S to accept less than $90, since below that margin his competitor B^1 would purchase from S. These limits, $120 and $90, may be named, for this assumed transaction, the Limits of Coercion. They are the limits, under the circumstances, where S and B have *free* but *unequal* opportunity.

We have placed these limits far apart, which may seem absurd to those accustomed to think in terms of free, equal, and prompt competition which brings both cost and value to an equilibrium at the cost of *reproduction*. But these extreme limits were exactly the situation of scarcity faced in the Middle Ages when the *markets overt*, the guilds and the sovereigns adopted their rules regulating trade, and they continue to be typical of many situations of less capable bargainers with which modern rule-making attempts to deal. For, within these limits of coercion, determined by accessible alternatives, where shall the price be determined? If S is the stronger bargainer, having control of a commodity limited in supply, but having, however, such abundance of resources that he can afford to hold out longer than the buyer B, then he can force the price up to the limit of free opportunity offered to B by the next strongest competitor, S^1. If, inversely, the buyer B is the stronger bargainer, having less need of buying than S has of selling, then he can force the price down to the margin where S has the free alternative of selling to B^1 at $90. Somewhere between these limits of coercion,

$120 and $90, will be found the actual price agreed upon between seller S and buyer B. It is the difference between free competition and equal opportunity.

Here arise the two problems which have come to the front on account of the two characteristics of modern economics, the rise of concerted action and the narrowing of margins for profit. These have begun to reach the courts in endless variety during the past three or four decades and have required the creation of commissions with powers of investigation not available to the courts. They are the problems of reasonable or unreasonable discrimination, free or fair competition, and reasonable price. The problem may be illustrated from our formula of the bargaining transaction.

Each of these problems has to do with the negotiational psychology of persuasion and coercion, and is an investigation of the point where coercion begins and persuasion ends. In our formula, if a corporation S sells to B at $100 and to B^1 at $90, then the question arises whether the lower price $90 was a reasonable cost of service, and therefore the surplus $10 obtained from B was an unreasonable discrimination against B and in favor of B^1. In neither case does either the classical economic problem of cost of production, or the Carey-Bastiat cost of reproduction, arise. Or if the buyer B pays to S $110 and to his competitor S^1 $120, the issue is whether the $120 was the reasonable value of service and the $110 a discrimination therefore of $10 in favor of S against his competitor S^1. We shall see that this economic and ethical issue of discrimination and reasonable value or cost of service did not reach a solution by the Supreme Court of the United States until the year 1901.[96] It is, economically, the issue of ascertaining the reasonable limits of coercion. Similar issues arise in abundance in all labor transactions, in the rates of interest charged to borrowers and so on. Its investigation may take the form of positive costs of production as one of the factors to be considered but the social problem is reasonable and unreasonable discrimination.

Or, take the other issue of free and fair competition, which, from our formula, will be seen to be inseparable from the issue of reasonable and unreasonable discrimination. A change in either one causes a change in the other. The two issues go back hundreds of years in the *law merchant* and the common law, but they reach their extreme social importance in the modern age of great corporations and narrow margins for profit. If, in our formula, the seller S^1 wants $120 for his product, but claims that his competitor S is cutting prices unfairly to $110; or, if the buyer B^1, who can afford

[96] Below, p. 773, on Scarcity, Abundance, Stabilization.

to pay only $90, complains that his competitor B is pulling away his laborers or material men by offering them $100, then, in either case the issue is raised as to whether the free competition was fair competition. In the seller competition the issue is whether $110 or $120 was the reasonable cost of service to the seller, and in the buyer competition the issue is whether the $100 or the $90 was the reasonable value of the service to the buyer. Neither the costs of production nor the resale prices enter into the problem, except as matters of evidence, for the social issue at stake is whether, in this transaction, the competitors are acting fairly towards each other.

In either case, as we have said, the third problem of reasonable price exists, and here, therefore, arises the negotiational psychology of persuasion and coercion, which may possibly be reconciled by the hedonic economists as a special case of their doctrine of pain and pleasure. Yet it is so highly different that the hedonic concepts are meaningless. But it is a kind of psychology which must be measured in dollars. The line must be drawn between persuasion and coercion, and the effort of the courts to draw that line in dollars and cents is again the problem of Reasonable Value. Starting with the criterion of reasonableness as a value agreed upon between a willing buyer and a willing seller, the point must be ascertained where each may be said to persuade the other, since, of course, at that point neither coerces the other. What is really being decided, in such case, by the court which takes the social point of view, is whether one individual is obtaining a larger share, and the other is obtaining a smaller share, of the whole social product than is justified by the reasonable cost of service and the reasonable value of service of each. If one is obtaining a larger share than thus justified, then he is coercing the other and the other is coerced. The *outgo* of one is of course equal to the *income* of the other. That is a commonplace of classical economics. But the social problem is whether one is giving up a larger share, and the other is therefore receiving a larger share of the social output than is "reasonable." If each is obtaining a share justified by his reasonable cost of service and the reasonable value of his service, no matter how much his positive cost or positive income to himself, then the price is persuasive and the value is reasonable.

It must be conceded that the ascertainment and measurement of this point between persuasion and coercion is difficult and complicated, and is partly subject to feelings and emotions, but mainly to the historical development of bargaining power. On this account it is important, because, by deciding one way or another, billions of dollars' worth of the social output are transferred by judicial opinion from one individual or class of individuals to another individual or class. Indeed, upon a single decision on this problem of Reasonable Value has been decided whether ten billion dollars shall go to railway companies in high freight and passenger rates, or to millions of people in lower freight and passenger rates.

We have used the terms opportunity-cost and dis-opportunity-value in order to distinguish the various meanings of cost and value, but they are merely technical terms for what is familiar in the negotiations that accompany bargaining transactions. A university professor receiving $5,000 salary is offered $9,000 by another institution and begins to negotiate with the university which employs him for an increase of his $5,000 salary. He decides to stay at $5,000. What does it cost him to stay? It costs him $4,000, not because his *outgo* costs are increased $4,000, but because he loses an *alternative* $4,000 income by merely choosing to stay.

But what is the value of his service to the university? What are his services worth? Nobody can tell except by comparison with what he can get elsewhere. The university gets for $5,000 a service which the next alternative buyer deems to be worth $9,000. These may be said to be only "talking points" in the negotiations because there are considerations other than money which also are talking points. But "talking points" are of the essence of negotiational psychology. If there are no talking points except money, as is the case in ordinary bargaining transactions, then we have simply the money considerations by which to measure cost of service and value of service. The professor is "worth" $9,000, since he renders a service to the university worth $9,000 elsewhere. And the university gains a surplus because it pays him $4,000 less than the value of the service. The $9,000 is, *to the university*, a dis-opportunity-value, or value of his service. Whether the professor is worth that much to the community, or society, is another question—the question of *reasonable* value of service.

On the other hand, the professor is donating $4,000 to the university because, by choosing to stay, he sacrifices that amount of alternative income. The $9,000 is, to him, his opportunity-cost, or cost to him of the service he renders.

Other illustrations may be given. A wage-earner is in urgent need of immediate cash but has only his expected wages of $20.00 to be paid at the end of two weeks. He makes an assignment of his wage to a salary-purchasing agency which pays him $18.00. What he is really paying to the lender is $2.00 for the use of $18.00 two weeks in advance of the wage-payment, equivalent to eleven per cent for two weeks or about 40 per cent per month. Calculated on a yearly rate, he is paying interest at the rate of 240 to 280 per cent per year.

On the strength of this and similar experiences of small borrowers, the question of *reasonable* value of service arose. There was devised the so-called uniform "small loan law" which created licensed companies authorized to charge, on sums of $300 or less, a rate of 3½ per cent per month, or 42 per cent per year, on unpaid balances, and making illegal any rates on small loans in excess of that rate. This law was adopted by a number of states. It was their standard of the *reasonable* value of the service rendered by loan companies to necessitous small borrowers. Here it is that organized society attempts to offer to the necessitous borrower an alternative, which its spokesmen, the legislature, deem reasonable.

Yet, on first impression the states were legalizing an usurious rate of interest. But, considering the only alternatives previously available to this class of borrowers who were unable to borrow at commercial banks at the usual legal rates of interest, a rate of 3½ per cent per month was materially less than the previous alternatives. In the instance above cited, instead of $2.00 for the use of $18.00 for two weeks the interest payment at 3½ per cent per month would have been approximately 32 cents.

This, again, is a special case of dis-opportunity-value, or the value to a person of having the opportunity to avoid an alternative higher outgo. Although the rate of 3½ per cent is high and usurious compared with what would be paid to commercial banks by persons with good credit acceptable to the banks, yet for the person without credit and in necessitous circumstances, the rate is decidedly less than his next worse alternative rate. He is better off than he would be under his actual economic circumstances, and, although his positive sacrifice is very great indeed at 3½ per cent per month, it is less than it would be at 10 or 20 or 40 per cent per month.[97]

We need not here give further illustrations of these interdependent relations of opportunity, competition, and price. The formula is universal and applies to all cases. They recur with great variety and complexity, since every one of the three factors is highly variable in the billions of transactions to which, however, the formula affords the clue. We proceed to lead up to the formula by way of the hypothetical history of the classical and hedonic economists.

[97] On the Small Loan Laws see Ryan, F. W., *Usury and Usury Laws* (1924); King, W. I., *The Small Loan Situation in New Jersey in 1929*, published by New Jersey Industrial Lenders Association, Trenton, N. J. (1929); Fisher, C. O., "Small Loans Problem: Connecticut Experience," *Amer. Econ. Rev.*, XIX (1929), 181; *Personal Finance News*, published by the Amer. Assn. of Personal Finance Companies, Washington, D. C.; Townsend, Genevieve, *Consumer Loans in Wisconsin* (1932).

(7) **From Crusoe to Going Concerns.**—To begin with Böhm-Bawerk's hypothetical history, suppose Robinson Crusoe is on an island by himself. This is the proper enough method of virtual elimination of society. Crusoe has to work in order to eat. Eating is utility, and the choice of rabbits instead of fish is the choice of a higher utility, rabbits, at the expense of foregoing the lesser utility, fish.[98] The avoidance of the fish is the utility-cost of choosing the rabbits, and the difference is surplus utility.

Convert this to Carey and Bastiat. Crusoe must have the rabbits because there are no fish. He can get the rabbits by trapping them or chasing them. He chooses trapping as the easier way. He "saves" the labor of chasing. The magnitude of this avoided labor is the disutility-value to him of the easier labor of trapping them, and the difference between trapping and chasing is pure surplus labor "saved."

But suppose there are two persons on the island—Crusoe and Friday. Neither has any alternative opportunity but must deal with the other or else get along with his own isolated labor. There is no government to enforce rights or protect liberties. Each relies on his own power, and the things which each holds as his own product are anything needed by the other.

Two kinds of coercion are conceivable, which we distinguish as Duress and Coercion. Both parties resort to violence. The stronger robs the weaker. Duress. Afterwards, without violence, the stronger continues to rob the weaker by threats of violence. Duress is not only violence—it is also the threat of violence. Violence is the alternative, the inducement. The duressed individual is offered two alternatives and chooses the less onerous. We may say that he has "no choice." But he has. He chooses the lesser pain of work. The greater pain of violence avoided is the value to him of the service which Crusoe renders by offering to him the lesser pain of slavery. Friday gains a surplus and is better off.

But suppose each of the parties is physically the equal of the other. Two Crusoes. Violence and threats of violence are nullified by equalization. Each wants or needs what the other produces and holds. Each has the equal degree of physical power to withhold from the other. Each now submits to the other a different set of alternatives. The alternatives now are not the duress of violence but are the scarcity of going without what he needs but which the other withholds.

But the power of scarcity, like the power of duress, may be un-

---

[98] Böhm-Bawerk, E. von, *Capital and Interest, A Critical History of Economical Theory* (1922), 278 ff.; *The Positive Theory of Capital* (tr. by Smart, 1891), Book III, on Value.

equal. This is what we name Coercion. It depends on the relative wants and resources of the opposite parties. But, since resources are but the means of satisfying the corresponding wants, and since the satisfying of wants exhausts resources in course of time, the power of each to determine the ratios of exchange depends upon their relative power to wait for the other to give in. The one with larger resources or less wants can wait longer than the other. He has the larger power of abundance which gives him larger power of waiting and can eventually impose a higher value on his own product in terms of exchange for a larger quantity of the services of the other. Thus, if the physical power of withholding is equal and if there are no alternative opportunities, then value in exchange is determined by the relative scarcity of possessions and its inverse economic power of waiting. But in either case the value of the service which each renders to the other, when the exchange is finally made, is the greater pain he would suffer than the pain he actually suffers by giving up to the other what he does give up. This greater pain which he avoids is the value of the service which one renders to the other. It is Ricardo's comparative cost and Carey's and Bastiat's value of service.

But suppose, finally, that resources relative to wants are equal; that each has equal waiting power; that thus the economic power of scarcity has been nullified by equalization just as the physical power of duress has been nullified by equalization. Each then must resort to that moral power which we name "persuasion." Each must offer to the other a service which the other is free to reject, and so each must win over the other by appealing to his freedom of choice; must depend on "good-will"; must depend on persuasion; and they have attained the "ideal type" of jurisprudence, the "meeting of minds" of "a willing buyer and willing seller."

But suppose the powers of persuasion of Crusoe and Friday are unequal. One is a better salesman than the other. There still remain the further inequalities of fraud, misrepresentation, ignorance, stupidity. These also can conceivably be eliminated by equalization, as is supposed to occur when Greek meets Greek, or Jew meets Scotch.

We have thus analyzed, by elimination, four stages of psychology. First is the stage of man's relation to the forces of nature where the terms utility-cost and dis-utility-value seem technically appropriate. Second, the stage of man's relation to man where the terms opportunity and dis-opportunity seem appropriate. But this takes on three different stages of human ability: physical force, economic power, and moral power. The first we name duress, the second coercion, the third persuasion. Duress is the direct or threatened compulsion of physical force. Coercion is the indirect coercion of economic power to withhold. Persuasion is the moral power of inducement.

Each of these is supposed successively to be eliminated by supposed equalizations, for they do not reveal themselves as force, power, or coercion when they are supposed to reach equilibrium by the supposition of equalization.

But in order to get this ideal equalization we must leave our island and begin again. Suppose population surrounds Crusoe and Friday and that a government rules them. Physical duress now is equalized, not by supposition but by government. Friday may be the slave of Crusoe, not because Crusoe is physically, economically, or morally superior, but because the state compels Friday to obey and it both relieves Crusoe of dependence on his own doubtful superior power and excludes third parties from offering to Friday alternative opportunities. Whether Crusoe persuades, coerces, or whips Friday is a matter of indifference, for Friday is a thing, not a citizen, and the only relation between them is the managerial transaction of command and obedience, not the bargaining transactions of buying and selling.

But suppose the state grants to Friday personal and property rights—passes the Thirteenth and Fourteenth Amendments; converts him into a citizen. What it grants, from the economic standpoint, is equal physical power to withhold services and products. Physical force is presumably eliminated by equality of citizenship and a judiciary. Private violence and the private threats of violence are prohibited, and only sovereignty threatens and exercises physical duress. Each must now resort to the economic coercion of waiting until the other gives in.

But the state cannot enforce equality of economic coercion. The best it can do is to set upper and lower limits. In order to enforce economic equality, it would be necessary to enforce equality of wants, equality of pains, and even equality of opinions regarding the value of things. Conceivably the state might grant equal division of resources through a communistic rationing instead of private bargaining, as the soviets are doing. But though resources might be made mathematically equal, measured by a supposed money of account, yet they would not be psychologically equal, for the differences in wants and aversions of individuals would immediately ascribe differences in the values of things, although they were supposed to be equal in quantity and quality.

Neither can the state, if it authorizes private bargaining, equalize persuasion. Persuasion is that psychological power, without duress or coercion, of one over another by which each induces the other to render a service at a favorable ratio of exchange. Just as wants and aversions are different in their degree of power to induce action, so also is persuasiveness different in its degree of power to induce action. Indeed, it is these differences in desires, aversions, and salesmanship that constitute personality. In lieu of equalizing them, and indeed in the interest of avoiding their equalization in order to enlarge the scope of personality, the state may set upper and lower limits of coercion or fraud, beyond which economic power is not permitted to be substituted for personality. If a state does not set these limits between the persuasions of personality and the coercion of economic power, then private associations attempt to do so under such names as business ethics, trade union ethics, professional ethics, commercial or labor arbitration, and so on.[99] If the courts adopt and enforce these rules, then custom becomes common law.

We therefore now pass to the psychology of judges and arbitrators relative to bargaining transactions. This necessarily takes a historical character, instead of the preceding supposititious character. Decisions of disputes arising from opposition of interests must promptly be made in order not so much to obtain justice as to avoid anarchy and violence and thus to keep transactions agoing. Justice is an afterthought, historically and logically. Hence the psychology of judges follows dominant custom and current practicality, as Bentham protested against Blackstone, rather than happiness and justice.

Historically the Seventeenth Century was a struggle in England, victorious in 1689, to separate judges from the dominance of the king in order that they might be free to base their opinions on the public standpoint, known then as commonwealth, against what was then deemed to be the private standpoint of king and courtiers. Since that time, in England and America, the courts represent the same social standpoint as the economists' theories which we have examined. It is the standpoint which, since Ricardo, raises the economic question whether the shares of the social output going to individuals or classes, as the social cost of inducing individuals to contribute, are proportionate to the contributions which those individuals or classes make towards the total output; in other words, whether private wealth is proportionate to private contributions to the commonwealth.

This distribution of social wealth, however, comes up for judicial decision mainly out of the conflicts of interest inherent in the trans-

[99] Below, p. 874, Personality and Collective Action.

actions of individuals. It is founded on the presuppositions of individual property, freedom, and personality. The courts and arbitrators therefore necessarily disregard the *net* incomes obtained by individuals. Hence they necessarily adopt, when this issue of coercion arises, the comparative method of ascertaining whether the *gross* income obtained or *gross* outgo imposed, in the disputed transaction bears a similarity to what is customary in analogous transactions. Thus arises the principle of comparative costs and comparative values, which we have distinguished as dis-opportunity-values and opportunity-costs. These lose their paradoxical aspect when once the social, distinguished from the private, method of measurement is comprehended. This also is the method of reasoning, not by way of the psychological economists' ideas of happiness and pain of individuals, nor by way of the anarchists' ideas of ethics and justice, nor by the business man's net income, but by the social method of ascertaining objectively what is customary, dominant,. and therefore reasonable.

If the courts feel called upon to give reasons for their opinions, as is their situation more or less in England and America, then their psychology mounts to the intellectual level of rationalizing, of justifying, and of socializing what they instinctively and intuitively feel to be the principles of public welfare applicable to the case in hand. The lower courts are thus relieved of the necessity of thinking upon the social problems involved, for they are merely called upon to follow precedent and authority where clearly expressed, or to make suggestions to the highest court when doubts arise. In America this has gone further; all acts of legislatures and the Congress are tentative suggestions to the Supreme Courts as to what acts the latter might perhaps be led to believe are in the public interest. This is so because, even if the court is called upon to decide only whether the legislative act conflicts with the superior constitution, the written constitution is highly elastic and may readily, and often has been, changed by changing the meanings of words.

Out of this genetic and institutional psychology of the courts have arisen, finally formulated by superior legal minds after many trials and errors, certain generalizations, principles, or maxims, believed to reconcile and harmonize the centuries of preceding intuitive decisions rendered to settle disputes promptly as they arose. Among these the most general of all, believed to reconcile public and private interests in the largest variety of disputes arising under the system of buying and selling, is that principle which describes a free bargain as the meeting of the minds of a willing buyer and a willing seller. These terms of willingness are again defined by comparisons with what is customary and dominant; but in general they mean the reasonable elimination of what are currently believed to be duress, coercion, and unethical persuasion.[100]

Applying this mode of reasoning to our formula of a transaction, if the seller S sells to buyer B at $100 and the similar commodity to B^1 at $90, we reach the inference of unequal opportunity, unequal freedom, or discrimination. This may or may not have social significance, depending on whether it is customary or not. If deemed to be customary, then to it is given the meaning of equal opportunity.

Likewise, if S sells at $100 while his competitor S^1 is selling at $120, we may reach the inference of unfair competition, whose social significance again depends on what is deemed to be customary. If deemed to be customary, it acquires the economic name of fair competition.

In these two illustrations we reach the two terms, equal and unequal opportunity—equal opportunity being reasonable value of service or reasonable cost of service, while unequal opportunity is unreasonable cost or value of service.

Or finally, if S takes advantage of B by forcing him to pay $120 because that is his best alternative opportunity, or if B takes advantage of S by forcing him to accept $90 because that is his best alternative, we may infer that there is evidence here of coercion, depending again, however, for its social significance on comparison with what are deemed to be the dominant and customary transactions.

It will again be seen that, in our formula of a bargaining transaction, there are three variable dimensions. We have to observe that these include all of the economic issues that come before the courts for decision on the question of reasonableness. These are the issues of discrimination, or equal and unequal opportunity; of free competition and fair competition; of equality or inequality of bargaining power.

It will also again be seen that in any transaction it is possible for any one of the four participants to bring forward one or all of the three issues. Our seller S may bring suit against B on the ground of discrimination or of extortion, and against S^1 on the ground of unfair competition, depending upon the point at which any one of the three variable dimensions of the transaction seems most patently to impinge. The same is true of the other participants.

It will also be seen that if a decision is rendered on any one of

100 Cf. Galusha v. Sherman, 105 Wis. 263 (1900); Commons, J. R., *Legal Foundations of Capitalism*, 57.

the three issues, it will change the economic magnitudes of the other two. A decision on fair competition will modify both discrimination and price, and so on with decisions on the other issues. This functional relation between the four parties to a typical transaction as well as between the three dimensions of value will appear when we pass at a later point, from hypothetical to real history.[101]

(8) **Bargaining Power.**[102]—Bargaining power does not emerge as a distinct subject for economic theory until legal support is furnished for concerted economic action. The two principal methods of concerted action are the corporate and the regulative. In the corporate form the individuals authorize a board of directors and a manager to make the bargains which legally bind the share-holders. Individual bargaining is eliminated. But in the regulative method the participants, whether individuals or corporations, yield to the rules, laws, or regulations which determine limits upon their individual or corporate bargaining power. Individual bargaining continues, but is limited.

The presuppositions of the individualistic, communistic, and anarchistic economists did not include these presuppositions of bargaining power. Adam Smith, in basing his economic theory on the legal rights of the individual to liberty, equality, and property, strongly opposed both forms of concerted action. He set up, as against concerted action, a deistic, quasi-mechanical competition which controlled individuals in their bargaining.[103] The "corporations" which he so vigorously criticized, were of the regulative kind [104]—guilds which imposed limits upon the individual bargains of its members. So also were the tariffs, bounties, and trade privileges of mercantilism granted by governments to individuals or classes. They increased the individual or concerted domestic bargaining power of citizens by lifting favored individuals above the menace of foreign competition. This individualistic and mechanistic presupposition of Smith dominated the classical and psychological economists. They were carried to the extreme by the anarchists. They were abolished entirely by the communistic economists whose presupposition eliminated both individual and concerted bargaining by substituting rationing by the state, the exact opposite of bargaining.

As long as these individualist, anarchist, and communist doctrines prevailed, there could be no scientific theory of that intermediate

---

[101] Below, p. 773, Scarcity, Abundance, Stabilization.

[102] Reprinted in part by permission from *Encyclopedia of the Social Sciences.*

[103] Cf. Knight, F. H., "Historical and Theoretical Issues in the Problem of Modern Capitalism," *Journal of Economic and Business History* (Nov. 1928), 121.

[104] Named below Syndicate Capitalism, p. 883.

process between the individual and society which is the concerted bargaining power of individuals. All such action was denounced as monopolistic by the individualists and anarchists, or as mere palliatives by the communists.

But meanwhile, in the decade of the 1850's, both in England and America—unforeseen by Smith, Marx, or Proudhon, and unseen by later economists and courts—a new legal right was recognized by the legislatures: the universal right of association, additional to the rights of liberty, equality, and property. Corporations were not prohibited, as Adam Smith and the anti-monopolists demanded. They were universalized by general corporation laws, instead of being created by special acts of legislatures. At the same period, in England and America, labor organizations abandoned their ideas of coöperative production or socialism, and adopted the ideas of collective bargaining.

The foregoing right to incorporate was made the equal right of all who chose to incorporate—not because this device would increase their bargaining power, but because it would increase their productive power by attracting capital with the promise of limited liability. And unions were suffered to exist, until, twenty or thirty years later, it was found that they had thereby acquired new bargaining power. About the same time it was discovered that the corporations also, by concerted action, had acquired similar bargaining power. Thus we reach, at the end of the Nineteenth Century in America, the period of anti-trust laws applied to both corporations and unions.

After a period of vigorous prosecutions under these laws, the courts finally discovered that, in the effort to abolish drastically these schemes of concerted action, they were striking at the very base of property and liberty—the right to withhold from others what they need but do not own. Hence, in 1911,[105] the words "reasonable restraint of trade" were introduced into the decisions, repeating a similar change during the Seventeenth Century in the common law. Then when, in 1920, following this rebirth, in 1911, of the idea of reasonableness, it was found, in the dissolution suit against the United States Steel Corporation,[106] that that corporation had practiced only reasonable restraint of trade, the recognition of bargaining power was attained in law.

This recognition came to a more specific determination in the price maintenance cases, where it was found that, if the prohibition of price maintenance were carried to its effective limit, the corpora-

---

[105] Standard Oil Co. of New Jersey *et al. v.* the United States, 221 U. S. 1 (1911); United States *v.* American Tobacco Co., 221 U. S. 106 (1911).

[106] United States *v.* United States Steel Corp. *et al.*, 251 U. S. 417 (1920).

tion must be compelled to deliver its commodities to any buyer who might come along, and that this would both deprive it of liberty and lead to price-fixing by government.[107] This has been done in the case of public utilities. When rates were fixed by law, compulsory service was also ordered. But in the price maintenance cases, the right to withhold was limited by restricting it to reasonable restraint of trade. Similar discovery had previously been made in the case of laborers. It had been found that to prohibit laborers, by a decree of specific performance, from withholding their services even though they had contracted to work, was a denial of the personal liberty guaranteed under the Thirteenth Amendment to the Constitution of the United States.[108] Business enterprises might, without such violation of the Constitution, be compelled to specific performance if they had made contracts to deliver commodities. But they could not lawfully, except as public utilities, be compelled to make such contracts. Thus, with the legal power to withhold commodities and services finally recognized in law, reasonable restraint of trade, according to the court's ideas of reasonableness but contrary to the anti-trust laws, comes to have a standing in law; and its equivalent bargaining power, or intangible property, comes to have a standing in economics. For restraint of trade *is* bargaining power, and reasonable restraint of trade is reasonable bargaining power.

During this transition period of the past thirty years, distinguished as the period of admitting the process of reasonable bargaining power into the domain of law and economics, the process itself has obtained popular appeal under such names as stabilization of industry, stabilization of prices, orderly marketing, stabilization of employment, or production. Such schemes of stabilization appeal to the wish for restraint against unlimited individual bargaining. The connotations of the terms "stabilization" and "orderly marketing" are similar to the connotations which, in labor economics, were formerly known as "equalization of bargaining power over the competitive area." The purpose, in this instance, was to prevent the individual bargaining of competing employers and workers from reducing wages and increasing hours of labor to the disadvantage of their competitors who paid higher wages or worked less hours per day. Indeed, in this instance, it is the bargaining transactions, individual or collective, which set the rules and regulations for those

[107] Great Atlantic and Pacific Tea Co. *v.* Cream of Wheat Co., 224 Federal Reports 566 (1915); United States *v.* Colgate and Co., 250 U. S. 300 (1919); Federal Trade Commission *v.* Beech Nut Packing Co., 257 U. S. 441 (1922).

[108] These cases are exhaustively covered by Witte, E. E., *The Government in Labor Disputes* (1932).

managerial transactions which have become the special subject-matter of the new discipline, "scientific management."

Extended to the business community, under such names as business ethics, it is the purpose, by means of this newly permitted bargaining power, to prevent that individual bargaining of competitors which steals customers by cutting prices, or steals labor by raising wages. It is now coming to be believed—a belief not contemplated by the early economists—that both the purchasing power of the public and the supply of labor-power are limited. Therefore, the new ethical doctrine of "live-and-let-live" indicates that the proper procedure—instead of the practice of competing by individual bargainers in order to pull customers or laborers away from competitors by lower prices or higher wages—is to get only a reasonable share of that limited purchasing power or limited labor-power. This cannot be done without stabilization and its reasonable restraint of trade. The clear road for this theory of reasonable bargaining power was prepared by the above cited decisions in the steel dissolution and the price maintenance cases.

Hence the practical theories of today, in the United States, are not the older theories of individual competition, individual property, the liberty of individual bargaining, the mechanism of free competition, nor even the communist theories of prohibition of bargaining. They are the theories of reasonable bargaining power. These come before economists and courts under the four groupings of discrimination, or unequal opportunity for individual bargaining; fair competition instead of free competition; reasonable price instead of normal or natural competitive price; and equal or unequal treatment of the different kinds of bargaining power, such as that of laborers and employers, farmers and capitalists, etc.

A sketch of the historical expansion of this doctrine of reasonable bargaining power would involve analogies and citations of cases on each of these economic aspects of reasonableness. It is enough to notice its historical development by classification of the various kinds of bargaining power. Labor organizations were the first to move towards this later doctrine of reasonable bargaining power by collective action, because they were the first to feel the pinch of the limited number of jobs and of the resulting discriminations and destructive competition. Railways and other public utilities next were forced by law to come under the doctrine, because the supply of their services was evidently limited, and their huge corporate form enabled them to set their own rules for the individual bargains of shippers and passengers. Manufacturing industries next came within the theory, the issue, in their case, culminating in the cases cited above. Then the most comprehensive of all industries, the banking industry, was admitted to the process, under the Federal Reserve Act which authorized concerted action of eight thousand banks, guided by twelve Reserve banks, in regulating the prices to be charged for, and the volume to be issued of, bank credit. Then the farmers, by enlarging the meaning of coöperation from coöperative production to coöperative marketing, are in the struggling process of obtaining a larger share of the world's purchasing power by their own collective bargaining power. Last of all, the Federal government, through its National Industrial Recovery Act, and its Agricultural acts, with their codes and regulations under the direction of the President, extends wholesale the doctrine of reasonableness by collective action to practically all manufacturers and agriculturists.

In all of these cases may be seen, in varying degree, an historical shift from concerted action in order to increase the production of wealth, highly favored in the past by the economists and courts, to concerted action in order to restrict the production of wealth, highly disfavored by them in the past. For, it is the shift from producing power to bargaining power, which, when authorized by law, becomes reasonable restraint of trade. We have noted this shift in the case of corporations and labor unions. The similar process was also noted in the change of meaning, above referred to, of farmers' coöperation from improvement of scientific agriculture to improvement of bargaining power. The Federal Reserve System was created in 1913 for the "accommodation of business and commerce," but, in 1922, it shifted to restrictions upon the free granting of credit in the private transactions of member banks, which freedom had proven disastrous in 1919–1921.[109]

We also have noted that the historical shift to bargaining power has occurred, not only towards the corporate form of consolidations, mergers, and holding companies, but even more towards the regulative form of fixing maximum or minimum standards for the individual and corporate bargains of buying, selling, lending, hiring, and excluding competition. Looked at in this way, the first break from the classical economic doctrine of free trade in the United States was in the protective tariff of 1842 which increased the domestic bargaining power of manufacturers. Consistently with this, but eighty years afterwards, was the restriction of immigration which markedly increased the bargaining power of both organized and unorganized labor.

In these cases it was positive governmental action. In other cases it was negative governmental action—as in the Federal Reserve

[109] Below, p. 590, A World Pay Community.

System, or the stabilization policies of competitive industries, or the collective bargaining of farmers' coöperatives and trade unions—the negative action of permitting that to be done, by means of bargaining power, which was deemed to be reasonable or indifferent, while positively restraining that which was deemed to be unreasonable or injurious to the public. In the negative case of governmental permission, there remained for the effectiveness of private concerted action only such economic sanctions as loss of profit, exclusion from markets, loss of employment, etc., which might be brought to bear upon those recalcitrants who attempted to break away and act independently.

Permission to impose these economic sanctions was granted in the Federal Trade Commission Act of 1914, by the proviso that it should not be deemed unlawful to "meet competition." Acting under this permission to meet competition, or even to threaten to meet it, the independent action of a competitor was likely to become even more destructive to himself, economically, than was conformity to the practices and prices observed by the others. According to this proviso it is not unreasonable restraint of trade for all the smaller competitors to "follow the leader"—a leader who obtains leadership through prestige or through economic power to cut prices below the level at which the small competitor can live. Thus the economic coercive sanctions of collective bargaining power become increasingly effective, even without resorting to the corporate form, but merely by resorting to the stabilization form.

Other practices, incidental to the strengthening of their bargaining power, are the new and more exact methods of statistical forecasting, by means of which individuals may more promptly withhold or expand production in concert with their competitors. The wide general acceptance of the principle of bargaining power is seen in the disappearance of nearly all resistance to high protective tariffs, and in the substitution of universal log-rolling whereby farmers concede high protection to the bargaining power of manufacturers in exchange for high protection of the farmers' bargaining power. Likewise, the conservation of natural resources takes on new and interested recruits when it is seen that the opening up of new lands for cultivation or new mines and oil wells for exploitation, reduces the bargaining power of owners of natural resources.

Other cases might be mentioned. Concerted bargaining power, with its sanctions of economic coercion, rises to a preëminence even more comprehensive and world-wide than the formerly dreaded political power with its physical duress, because it actually controls the state. The state, indeed, becomes one of the instruments of bargaining power, either by its own direct act or by its permission of concerted action. Through the use of this political instrument the struggle for bargaining power reaches its preëminence. The economic theories of free competition and laissez-faire, deductively worked out from the presuppositions of liberty, equality, self-interest, individual property, and the mechanism of competition, give way to pragmatic theories of the reasonable use, under all the circumstances, of that bargaining power which may be equally or unequally shared by individuals, by classes, or by nations.

These theories of concerted bargaining power are directed towards the economic, legal, and ethical problems of unfair discrimination, unfair competition, unreasonable price, and unequal treatment of the bargaining power of associations of manufacturers, farmers, laborers, merchants, bankers, or others. It is the emergence of these issues out of the new predominance of bargaining power that has recently occupied the attention of higher courts, as never before, upon economic, legal, and ethical theories of prices, values, practices, and transactions.[110]

VII. RICARDO AND MALTHUS

With the coming of Malthus and Ricardo, after Smith, economic science began its Nineteenth Century conflicts of opinion which terminate in the present-day distinctions of scarcity and efficiency. Malthus and Ricardo were intimate friends, but they differed on every point. Nineteenth Century political economy developed from their conversations and publications during the period of depression and unemployment that followed the battle of Waterloo.

Malthus has been called muddle-headed; Ricardo has been called the greatest logician of economics. But Malthus was muddled because he found political economy a highly complex and contradictory subject. Ricardo was logical because he avoided the complexities and assumed a single principle of great simplicity, from which everything could be derived. Yet his principle was not simple. It contained the contradiction of materials and ownership. Classical economics, communistic economics, syndicalistic economics, single tax economics, all flowed logically from this contradiction. The puzzle is one of method—how to combine in a simplified way the complexity of Malthus and the logic of Ricardo. Each was a genius of new insight; but the insight of each was predisposed by

---

[110] The first notable effort to construct a theory of bargaining power was John Davidson's *Bargain Theory of Wages* (1898). Further development is found in the theories of the historical and institutional economists. See Commons, John R., *Legal Foundations of Capitalism*.

the divergent social philosophies which they habitually assumed. Malthus was a minister of the gospel, a humanitarian, pained by the poverty and unemployment of his period. Ricardo became a millionaire capitalist through his cleverness on the Stock Exchange. Malthus was a theist, Ricardo a materialist, and they saw the same things from opposite angles.

Their differences originated in their theories of rent, and extended to their theories of labor, of demand and supply, and of unemployment. Each discovered his theory of rent at about the same time, but Malthus published his in 1815 and Ricardo published his contrary version in 1817. To this Malthus replied in his *Principles of Political Economy* in 1821. The evidence that each contemporaneously discussed the matter appears in the letters of Ricardo to Malthus, 1816 to 1823.[111]

Their theories of rent may be distinguished as the Differential Abundance theory of Malthus and the Differential Scarcity theory of Ricardo. They turn out to be quite the same. But they take opposite views of supply and demand—views which persist to the present day. Ricardo's theory, after passing through the hands of Karl Marx and the engineer Frederick Taylor, came out as the efficiency theories of scientific management, and through the hands of Henry George came out as the Single Tax. The Malthusian theory of rent, after passing through the psychological economists, came out as the specific productivity theory of J. B. Clark.

The Malthusian theory of rent was provoked by the theories of Smith and Quesnay, who had given to rent, as said by Malthus, the characteristics of a monopoly.[112] But Malthus was interested in maintaining a protective tariff on wheat to the advantage of agriculture and the landed interest, whereas Ricardo was interested in the free importation of wheat in order to reduce the manufacturers' wage-cost of production.

Malthus therefore distinguished three kinds of monopoly: an artificial monopoly like a patent; a natural "total" monopoly, like certain vineyards of France; and a partial monopoly "fairly applicable" to rent.[113]

The scarcity of land, Malthus said, is not enough to account for the high price of raw produce. This high price is to be explained

---

[111] Malthus, T., *An Inquiry into the Nature and Progress of Rent and the Principles by Which It Is Regulated* (1815); *Principles of Political Economy Considered with a View to Their Practical Application* (1821); *Letters of David Ricardo to Thomas Robert Malthus* (1810–23; ed. by Bonar, J., 1887); *The Works of David Ricardo* (ed. by McCulloch, J. R.).

[112] Malthus, T., *An Inquiry into the Nature and Progress of Rent and the Principles by Which It Is Regulated*, 3–7, 15–16, 20.

[113] *Ibid.*, 8. Repeated in his *Principles of Political Economy*, 110 ff.

on the principle of population. The fertility of the soil yields more necessaries of life than is required for the maintenance of the persons employed on the land; and these necessaries have the peculiar quality, derived from his theory of population, of "raising up a number of demanders in proportion to the quantity of necessaries produced."

These qualities of fertility therefore are different from those of all artificial or total natural monopolies, in that the latter do not create their own demand, but soil fertility does. Hence, the prices received by monopolists diminish with abundance and increase with scarcity, since "the demand is exterior to, and independent of, the production itself." But, "in the case of strict necessaries, the existence and increase of the demand, or the number of demanders, must depend upon the existence and increase of the necessaries themselves." Thus the cause of high prices of food and other necessaries above cost of production, "is to be found in their abundance, rather than their scarcity," and is therefore "essentially different from the high prices occasioned by artificial . . . and natural . . . monopolies," which is to be found in their scarcity rather than their abundance.

With this immense distinction, Malthus asks, Is not rent, instead of being a monopoly, or a nominal value, or a mere transfer, "on the contrary a clear indication of a most inestimable quality of the soil, which God has bestowed on man—the quality of being able to maintain more persons than are necessary to work it"? [114]

Malthus conceded a third peculiar quality, also derived from his theory of population—the "comparative scarcity" or "partial monopoly" of more fertile land. This arises from the expansion of population which drives cultivation down to less fertile land.

"While fertile land is in abundance . . ." he said, "nobody of course will pay a rent to a landlord. But . . . Diversities of soil and situation must necessarily exist in all countries. . . . the accumulation of capital beyond the means of employing it on land of the greatest natural fertility, and the greatest advantage of situation, must necessarily lower profits; while the tendency of population to increase beyond the means of subsistence must, after a certain time, lower the wages of labor." Consequently, "The expense of production will thus be diminished, but the value of the produce, that is, the quantity of labor, and of the other products of labor besides corn, which it can command, instead of diminishing, will be increased." [115]

[114] Malthus, Thomas, *An Inquiry into the Nature and Progress of Rent*, 12–16.
[115] *Ibid.*, 17–18.

Thus no rent would be paid on the last portion of land brought into cultivation, even though profits and wages are low on that land. But since the price of food, in terms of power to "command" labor in exchange, has increased, and this price will be received by the cultivators of richer land, the latter would either pay rent to a landlord, or cease to be "mere farmers," and become landlords as well as farmers, "a union by no means uncommon."

Yet even these "partial monopolies" received by landlords under the name of rent "are neither a mere nominal [scarcity] value, nor a value unnecessarily and injuriously transferred from one set of people to another," as is the case with total monopolies. They are "a most real and essential part of the whole value of the national property, and placed by the laws of nature where they are, on the land, by whomsoever possessed, whether the landlord, the crown, or the cultivator." [116]

Thus Malthus, while he explained artificial monopolies and natural total monopolies on a principle of scarcity, explained the partial monopolies of rent upon a principle of differential abundance. Differential abundance applied only to soil fertility. Fertility of the soil creates population but monopoly does not. His principle of population comes in to explain the high price of food by pressure towards lower margins of cultivation; but it was the beneficence of God that explained rents on lands superior to marginal land.

As soon as Ricardo had read the Malthusian theory of rent he wrote to Malthus:

"I think . . . that rents are in no case a creation of wealth; they are always a part of wealth already created, and are enjoyed necessarily, but not on that account less beneficially to the public interest, at the expense of the profits of stock. . . . The arguments . . . of those who contend for a free trade in corn remain in their original full force, as rents are always withdrawn from the profits of stock." [117] And again he wrote, "rent being always a transfer, and never a creation of wealth—for before it is paid to the landlords as rent it must have constituted the profits of stock, and a portion is made over to the landlord only because lands of a poorer quality are taken into cultivation." [118]

Where Malthus, therefore, by using the fact of diminishing returns in agriculture, had identified the interest of the landlord with the interest of the public in maintaining a larger population, Ricardo, as he wrote later (1817), made

[116] *Ibid.*, 18–20.
[117] Bonar, J., *op. cit.*, 59; McCulloch, J. R., *op. cit.*, 243.
[118] Bonar, J., *op. cit.*, 155.

"the interest of the landlord . . . always opposed to that of the consumer and manufacturer. . . . All classes . . . except the landlords, will be injured by the increase in the price of corn. The dealings between the landlord and the public are not like dealings in trade, whereby both the seller and the buyer may equally be said to gain, but the loss is wholly on one side, and the gain wholly on the other." [119]

Meanwhile Ricardo proceeded to construct his theory of value and rent which should fit this difference between himself and Malthus. He had to invent a new definition of "rent." He distinguished between the exhaustible and the "original and indestructible" qualities of the soil. The *exhaustible* qualities were *not* the divine free gifts to man which Malthus supposed—they had to be restored by the same kind of labor that constructed improvements on the land. The inexhaustible qualities seem to have been such as those vineyards of France whose fertility had to be restored but whose sunlight, topography, and situation were inexhaustible. It was only to these inexhaustible qualities that the theory of rent should apply; it was they that should be considered the "partial monopolies" of Malthus. The difference between the two was that Malthus considered rent a payment for divine-made fertility; but Ricardo considered fertility man-made, the return of which was profit and interest. But Ricardo's rent was not man-made.

Therefore Malthus was mistaken, according to Ricardo, in his theory of value. His was indeed the "prevailing" idea which placed the origin of value in the wants of consumers. But Ricardo now placed its origin in the efforts of labor. This was the reason why Malthus measured value by its power to *command* labor or money in exchange; but Ricardo considered value to be the amount of labor-cost *embodied* in producing the product. The Malthusian rent was measured by the quantity of money or labor it would *command;* the Ricardian rent by the amount of labor it would *cost* to produce it. The prevailing idea, said Ricardo, confounded value with wealth or riches, and

led to the contradiction "that by diminishing the quantity of commodities, that is to say, of the necessaries, conveniences and enjoyments of human life, riches may be increased." But, if you "double the quantity of utility . . . the quantity of what Adam Smith calls value in use," you do "not double the quantity of value" if the quantity of labor required to produce it is no greater. Then he went on to say, "the wealth of a country may be increased in two ways: . . . by employing a greater portion

[119] McCulloch, J. R., *op. cit.*, 202–3.

of revenue in the maintenance of productive labour, which will not only add to the quantity, but to the value of the mass of commodities; or it may be increased, without employing any additional quantity of labour, by making the same quantity more productive, which will add to the abundance, but not to the value of commodities." [120]

The distinction here made by Ricardo between "value" on the one hand, and "utility," "value in use," "wealth," or "riches" on the other hand, has bothered some economists, so that his chapter on "Value and Riches" has seemed to be a confusion. But the distinction was considered by McCulloch as the one great service of Ricardo to economic science, and, we think, has been so recognized generally. It was really the distinction between wealth or riches as private assets versus commonwealth, and value as the labor-cost of production, instead of the power to command labor in exchange.

"Its discovery," said McCulloch, "has shed a flood of light on what was previously shrouded in all but impenetrable mystery. . . . What the researches of Locke and Smith did for the production of wealth, those of Ricardo have done for its value and distribution." [121]

What Ricardo was trying to get at, in this analysis, was the meaning of value as a multiple of use-value and scarcity-value. But his scarcity-value was the resistance of nature to labor's power of production, whereas value had previously meant the wants of consumers. "Value in use," as he considered to be the meaning of Adam Smith, meant utility; its meaning was abundance of wealth or riches for the nation, since if you double the quantity of use-value you double the quantity of necessaries and conveniences. Use-value therefore varies directly with physical quantity, as two million bushels of wheat have double the quantity of use-value of one million bushels. Use-value means necessaries and conveniences, which constitute the wealth or riches of nations.

But Ricardo's "value" of the two million bushels remains the same if the same quantity of labor produced it. If so, then the *value* of one bushel has fallen one-half, since it requires only half as much labor to produce it; therefore it will exchange for only one-half as much of other things which have not changed in value. Its exchange-value had fallen one-half though its use-value remains the same, or, inversely, its use-value has doubled though its exchange-

[120] *Ibid.*, 166–169, chapter on "Value and Riches, Their Distinctive Properties."
[121] McCulloch, J. R., Introduction to his edition of *The Works of David Ricardo*, xxiv–xxv.

value remains the same. Hence Ricardo's "value" was neither use-value alone, nor exchange-value alone. It was a multiple of the quantity of use-value, measured by bushels, *times* the exchange-value per unit, measured by labor-power.

Ricardo's concept of exchange-value, contrary to that of Malthus, grew out of his concept of resistance of nature to the labor of man. He got this idea from Malthus himself, but he carried out logically the Malthusian theory of overpopulation and changed the philosophy of nature from Abundance to Niggardliness. Here evidently Malthus was muddle-headed, because he tried to reconcile divine beneficence with rent. But Ricardo was logical, because he was a materialist and identified scarcity with the resistance of nature to man's efforts.

We can say, as Ricardo did, that there is a larger quantity of labor-power required, or "embodied," as Marx would say, where nature's resistance is greater than where nature's resistance is weak Or, we can say that the productivity of labor varies inversely to the resistance of nature. If productivity doubles, it means that nature's resistance is diminished one-half. It would be equally true, then, to say, as Ricardo did, that exchange-value varies *inversely* to labor's productivity, or that it varies *directly* with nature's resistance.

Consequently, Ricardo paralleled his concept of value as a multiple of a quantity of use-value *times* its exchange-value with his concept of labor as a quantity of labor-power *times* the resistance of nature—or, as he actually put it, a quantity of labor-power *times* the *inverse* of the productivity of labor. Hence the "value" of a total product—say a million or two million bushels of wheat—can be stated either as a multiple of its use-value *times* its exchange-value (omitting the wants of consumers and all questions of supply and demand), or as a multiple of the number of laborers *times* the resistance of nature to their labor-power. The measure of this resistance becomes the *labor-time* required to overcome it, for a given labor-power varies inversely to the time required to produce a given output.

The concept of value thus devised by Ricardo, which sets aside the wants of consumers and their supply and demand of commodities is evidently not a concept of value—it is a concept of efficiency, for efficiency is the ratio of output of use-value to man-hour input of labor-power.[122] Efficiency, therefore, for Ricardo, was a personification of scarcity. Where Smith and Malthus had personified scarcity as labor-pain imposed as punishment for sin in a world

[122] Above, p. 276, Input-Output, Outgo-Income.

of abundance, Ricardo personified scarcity as nature's resistance to labor-power in a world of scarcity. The two personifications are exactly the opposite. Pain diminishes as power increases. If nature's resources are scarce owing to pressure of population towards lower margins, then it was labor-power, not labor-pain, that overcame the resistance of nature. This was not a price paid to God on account of sin, it was a price paid to nature on account of scarcity. Hence the quantity of labor-power needed to overcome the resistance of nature was the "natural" price of commodities. Nature offers very little or no resistance in the case of water or air, but greater resistance in the case of wheat or gold. These relative resistances to labor-power were Ricardo's "natural" exchange-values.

Ricardo, like Smith, and unlike Malthus, must get away from Mercantilism—a policy based on money and the artificial scarcities of monopoly and restraints of trade. Hence, instead of this artificial scarcity, he, like Smith, substituted natural scarcity, but, unlike Smith, he substituted the resistance of nature for Smith's sinfulness of man. He passed, according to Comte's geneology of the sciences, from the theological to the metaphysical stage of the science, or, as we should say, from personification to materialism.

These were two kinds of personification of scarcity. Smith, whom Malthus followed, considered the quantity of labor-pain that could be *purchased*, but Ricardo considered the quantity of labor-power required to *produce* the product, each, however, as a "natural" instead of an "artificial" price. But since price is the price *per unit*, and *value* is the sum of the prices of all the units of a product, it followed, for Ricardo, that the "quantity of value" was compounded by the two dimensions—the quantity of use-value and the labor-power per unit. The latter was his labor-price. The multiple of the two was Value.

Consequently, when "productivity doubles," the meaning is that the quantity of use-value (happiness, riches) doubles—but the labor-power remains the same. Stating it in terms of money: if the quantity of wheat rises from one billion to two billion bushels, the wealth, riches, or happiness of the world is doubled as to that commodity; but if the price falls consequently from one dollar to 50 cents per bushel because the productivity of labor is doubled, then the "quantity of value" remains where it was. This is an increase of riches, or wealth for consumers, but not an increase of value for producers.

But Ricardo, by eliminating money which measures relative scarcities, and by substituting labor-power which measures relative

resistances, confused scarcity with efficiency and, in effect, personified price as an exchange with nature, whereas price is an exchange
with man.

Yet it is no wonder that Ricardo's discovery excited the enthusiasm
of McCulloch. It was, indeed, revolutionary at the then theological
and metaphysical stage of economics. His personification of scarcity
as the equivalent of labor-power in production served to confute
Malthus and the fallacies that came down from Mercantilism, which
personified value as inverse to labor-pain that could be commanded
in exchange.

This idea of scarcity had been associated with the monopolies
of Mercantilism. Ricardo saw the same idea in the writings of men
like Lauderdale and Malthus. Lauderdale had said, according to
Ricardo, that if water becomes scarce and exclusively possessed
by an individual, you will increase his riches because water will then
have value: and if wealth be the aggregate of individual riches, you
will by the same means also increase wealth.[123] This was exactly
the fallacy of Mercantilism, and Ricardo replied, as we have indicated, by distinguishing monopoly scarcity from natural scarcity.
A monopoly was artificial scarcity, but the scarcity of nature's resources was natural. In the case of monopoly the individual
monopolist would charge higher prices for the same supply, and
would thereby be richer, but others would be poorer, because "all
men 'must' give up a portion of their possessions for the sole purpose of supplying themselves with water, which they before had
for nothing."[124] Likewise in the case of a general scarcity of
water not monopolized, all individuals would be worse off, and in
this case also they would have to devote a part of their labor to
procuring water and they could therefore produce only less of other
commodities. "Not only would there be a different distribution of
riches, but an actual loss of wealth."[125] That is to say, the *value*
of water would be *greater* in case of general scarcity because more
labor is required to procure it, but the *wealth* of the community
would be *less* because a smaller quantity of use-values is produced
by a larger quantity of labor. This was the "flood of light" that
enthused McCulloch.

Thus we can see that the alleged confusion of Ricardo in his
chapter on "Value and Riches" arises from two sources. The first
is Ricardo's personification of money and scarcity as labor-power

[123] Ricardo had misapprehended Lauderdale who made public wealth equivalent to
abundance and private wealth equivalent to scarcity. Cf. Lauderdale, J. M., *Inquiry
into the Nature and Origin of Public Wealth* (1804; citation to 1819 ed.), 7 n., 14.

[124] McCulloch, *op. cit.*, 167.

[125] *Ibid.*, 167.

instead of its real meaning of efficiency. The second is that of reading back into Ricardo's meaning of utility the later meanings of diminishing utility, whereas what he and Smith meant by utility was the physical, or technological qualities of objects, measured by physical units such as tons or bushels, which therefore do not diminish per unit with a decrease of demand or an increase of supply.[126] This meaning of utility, as use-value, to which Böhm-Bawerk gives the name "material services" (*Nutzleistungen*),[127] is Riches or Wealth. It indeed also diminishes in value but the diminution is physical deterioration, wear and tear, to be distinguished as physical "depreciation," and not subjective "diminishing utility."

There is, however, also the subjective meaning, previously mentioned, of even this physical "use-value," namely, the "necessaries, conveniences, and enjoyments of human life." But this kind of meaning, as used by Ricardo and Smith, we have named Civilization Value, or Cultural Value, since it changes, not with supply or demand, but with changes in civilization—as the change from arrows to dynamite, from horses to automobiles.

This meaning of utility as use-value was also identified by Bentham with Happiness, since happiness had not yet attained, even with Bentham, the meaning of diminishing utility which diminishes with an increase of supply or decrease of demand. An increase in the quantity of utility was an increase in the quantity of Happiness. Hence the meaning of utility, with Smith, Bentham, and Ricardo, was a kind of civilization value which increases with invention and decreases with obsolescence. Its increase, therefore, is identical with an increase in riches, wealth, and happiness. This is Ricardo's meaning when he said: if you double the quantity of utility, you therefore double the quantity of riches or wealth. This was identical with Bentham's doubling the quantity of happiness. This meaning of utility we have distinguished as use-value; it may also be distinguished as abundance-value, since it does not diminish per unit with increase of quantity.

Ricardo evidently looked upon this civilization concept of utility (Smith's "value-in-use," or "abundance-value") as a subjective valuation. He held with Adam Smith that the riches which "consisted in necessaries, conveniences, and enjoyments of life," were subjective, and therefore could not be measured. Ricardo says, "one set of necessaries and conveniences admits of no comparison

---

[126] Above, p. 175, Psychological Parallelism.
[127] Böhm-Bawerk, E. von, *Capital and Interest, a Critical History of Economical Theory*, 223.

with another set; value-in-use cannot be measured by any known standard; it is differently measured by different persons." [128]

But there was a way for Ricardo by which all use-values could be reduced to a common measure. It was not by money which measured artificial scarcity. It was by labor-power which measures natural scarcity. But when this metaphorical unit of measurement is introduced, it is not riches or wealth that is measured—it is Value. And exchange-value becomes an exchange with nature, which varies inversely to the labor-power required to produce the quantities exchanged.

The much simpler way, and the one actually used in commerce, free from personification and metaphor, is the measurement of use-values by physical units and technological qualities—as a bushel of wheat grade 1 or grade 2. It seems strange that Ricardo and all the physical economists who were men of common sense, did not use this common-sense method of measuring use-value objectively, instead of resorting to labor-power or labor-pain, or even money.[129] The physical units of measurement were at hand and visible everywhere. But they tried to be too profound. They must have been afflicted by the metaphysics of the age of reason, which did not distinguish between cause and measurement. Labor-power is, indeed, a cause; use-value is its effect. But each has its own system of measurement, and the ratio between the measure of the effect (use-value, output) and the measure of the cause (labor-power, input) is the measure, not of value, but of efficiency. It required nearly a century, until the arrival of scientific management, to get rid of Ricardo's metaphysics.

But, for his time and age, Ricardo's was a new insight. He saw the difference between Nature's abundance-value of preceding economists and the scarcity-value of the Malthusian nature's resistance to labor. His change in the meaning of value was indeed revolutionary. It changed not only the meanings of labor and productivity, it also changed all the terms used in political economy; or rather it perpetrated a double meaning of all the terms, which persists to the present day.

It changed primarily the meaning of nature. Malthus initiated this change by his doctrine of overpopulation. But he did not carry the doctrine out consistently, because he retained vestiges, in his theory of rent, of the theological doctrine of beneficence and abundance. But Ricardo was a materialist, a pessimist, and a deductive economist. He carried out logically the niggardliness of

---

[128] McCulloch, J. R., *op. cit.*, 260.
[129] Below, p. 510, Transactional Theory of Money and Value.

nature. Hence the double meaning of rent which persists to the present day. Ricardo eliminated soil fertility, which was the essential part of the Malthusian theory. Malthus saw the more productive fertility yielding a larger output per man-hour of labor than the marginal fertility; but Ricardo saw the more productive non-fertility requiring a lesser input of labor than the marginal land.

The second main difference followed upon this difference in the theory of rent. It is the difference in meanings of supply, demand, and markets. Ricardo wrote to Malthus in 1814, "I sometimes suspect that we do not attach the same meaning to the word 'demand.' If corn rises in price, [you] perhaps attribute it to a greater demand." This Malthus did, for he attributed it to an increase of population. "I should [attribute it to] a greater competition," said Ricardo, meaning by "greater competition" a greater productivity of labor.

"The demand cannot, I think, be said to increase if the quantity consumed be diminished, although much more money may be required to purchase the smaller than the larger quantity. If it were to be asked what the demand was for port-wine in England in the years 1813 and 1814, and it were to be answered that in the first year she had imported 5,000 pipes and in the next 4,500, should we not all agree that the demand was greater in 1813. Yet it might be true that double the quantity of money was paid for the 4,500 pipes." [130]

This was, indeed, the difference between Malthus and Ricardo. It was the difference between production and bargaining. Value, for Malthus, was scarcity-value determined by bargaining, whose ultimate inducement was the demand of consumers and whose measure was price. But for Ricardo scarcity-value, determined by bargaining and measured by money, was only a "nominal value." The "real value" was the quantity of use-value measured by the labor cost of "pipes" of wine produced and marketed. For Ricardo, a higher price paid for wine was a nominal price, wherein scarcity-value was equivalent to "nominal" value. Malthus was interested in the prices themselves determined by demand and supply, and believed that quantities would follow prices. But Ricardo was interested in quantities and the labor cost of the quantities, and did not care what became of the prices. For Ricardo an increase from 4,500 to 5,000 pipes of wine (use-value) was an increase in wealth and riches, although the price might fall from $2.00 to $1.00. But for Malthus a fall in price was a *decrease* of wealth because the *inducement* to produce wealth was thereby reduced.

[130] Bonar, J., *op. cit.*, 42.

The difference resolves itself into the difference between power to *produce* wealth and power to *induce* its production.

"We agree," said Ricardo, "that effectual demand consists of two elements, the *power* and the *will* to purchase; but I think the will is very seldom wanting where the power exists, for the desire of accumulation will occasion demand just as effectually as a desire to consume; it will only change the objects on which the demand will exercise itself. If you think that with an increase of capital, men will become indifferent both to consumption and accumulation, then you are correct in opposing Mr. Mill's idea, that in reference to a nation supply can never exceed demand." [131]

James Mill, referred to by Ricardo, had developed Smith's idea, derived from non-diminishing use-value, that it is production, not consumption nor money, that creates effectual demand.[132]

"I go much further than you," said Ricardo, "in ascribing effects to the wants and tastes of mankind; I believe them to be unlimited. Give men but the means of purchasing, and their wants are insatiable. Mr. Mill's theory is built on this assumption." [133]

But, for Malthus, wants were limited. "It is unquestionably true," he said, "that wealth produces wants; but it is a still more important truth that wants produce wealth." [134]

Thus the difference between Malthus and Ricardo was the difference between the increasing wants of an increasing population thereby maintaining scarcity-values, and the increasing productivity of all producers, thereby increasing the quantity of all use-values.

The issue between these two concepts of demand and supply arose with the widespread depression, unemployment, and falling prices that followed the Napoleonic wars and aroused this discussion between Malthus and Ricardo. Malthus needed actual demand in order to increase a nation's wealth, whether this demand arose from the possession of money, or the possession of labor-power, or the increase of population, or the possession of rents, or even the protective tariffs on grain that increased the purchasing power and therefore increased the demand by landlords for labor. Without this demand there would be nothing produced, and it was the falling off of demand, or the purchasing power of consumers, to which he attributed the existing depression and unemployment.

[131] *Ibid.*, 43–44.
[132] Mill, James, *Commerce Defended* (1807); above, p. 158, Adam Smith.
[133] Bonar, J., *op. cit.*, 49.
[134] Malthus, T., *Principles of Political Economy Considered with a View to Their Practical Application* (1821), 363.

Hence Malthus was not disturbed by the fall of *profits*. He was disturbed by the fall of prices. If profits were too high, then too much would be produced relative to existing demand. There must be an increase of consumption which keeps up prices, not an increase of production which increases competition and reduces prices. Therefore Malthus proposed an increase of consumption by an increase of taxation and public works as a remedy for unemployment. But Ricardo wrote, "It is against this . . . doctrine that I protest, and give my decided opposition." [135]

What Malthus proposed in order to increase consumption was an increase of taxation, an increase in tariffs on wheat, an expansion of public works, and an increased expenditure by the wealthy on their estates, all of which was "unproductive consumption," since it did not produce commodities that came upon the markets and reduced prices.

A hundred years later, following another world war, this was almost exactly the remedy proposed by a National Unemployment Conference called by President Harding, and held under the direction of Secretary Hoover. The conference recommended an increase in public works during periods of unemployment, to take up the slack in private employment.[136] The Harding Conference was Malthusian economics, opposed to Ricardian economics. Malthus would have called their proposal "unproductive consumption," but he meant the same thing that the Conference meant by public works, which produce a product that is not sold. It would be "unproductive" because it would not create a product that comes upon the market and would therefore not add to the existing unemployment by reducing the prices received by private employers.

Ricardo, too, needed actual demand in order to increase a nation's wealth, but his demand, contrary to Malthus, must come from an increase in production by capitalists at the lower levels of prices, and this increase was prevented when the capitalists could not make a profit at those lower levels. The reason, therefore, for the then existing unemployment, was not the falling prices caused by a falling demand—it was the high rents, high taxes, and high wages, the latter caused by the obstinacy of labor. "The labourers are immoderately paid for their labour, and they necessarily become the unproductive consumers of the country." If wages should be reduced "there would be little diminution in the quantity of com-

---

[135] Bonar, J., *op. cit.*, 186.

[136] *United States Monthly Labor Review*, Nov. 1921, 129–132; *Report of the President's Conference on Unemployment*, 89–107, Superintendent of Documents, Government Printing Office (1921).

modities produced; the distribution only would be different; more would go to the capitalists and less to the labourers." [137]

Thus Malthus and Ricardo stated the two arguments usually advanced by capitalists as a remedy for unemployment. Raising the tariff and increasing public employment come from Malthus; reducing taxes and wages comes from Ricardo.

Starting with the opposite terms of the same efficiency ratio they converted them into opposite concepts of supply and demand, and, therefore, into opposite concepts both of national wealth and the remedy for unemployment and overproduction. For Malthus it was abundance of purchasing power that would increase the demand for production and therefore increase the national wealth. But this purchasing power was withheld by landlords and wealthy tax-payers. They should improve their estates and build public works which would create a demand for labor without reducing prices.

But, for Ricardo, it was producing power that created the demand for labor, and the inducement to produce was withheld from capitalists by high rents, high taxes, and high wages.

For Malthus there were general overproduction, low prices, and unemployment because demand was limited. For Ricardo there was no limit to demand, but the semblance of overproduction was the inability of capitalists to earn a profit at low prices, high wages, high taxes, and high rents.

Thus where Malthus and others found their meaning of wealth and riches in the scarcity-values that depended upon the wants and demand of consumers, Ricardo found his meaning of wealth and riches in the total quantity of use-values supplied by producers. But the contradiction turned on two meanings of demand and supply, which persist to the present day. The Malthusian meaning of increased demand was *higher prices,* higher taxes, higher tariffs, higher wages, higher rents, all of which meant larger consumption of wealth by larger purchasing power. The Ricardian meaning of increased demand was *larger quantity* of production at lower prices, lower taxes, lower tariffs, lower wages, and lower rents, but higher profits, in order to induce capitalists to employ laborers. The two had reached an impasse which has been repeated for more than a hundred years. It is the contradiction between a greater *share* of the national wealth going to consumers and a greater margin for profit going to capitalists, as the remedy for unemployment.[138]

This double meaning of demand and supply turned finally on a double meaning of markets and exchange. Ricardo held that

[137] Bonar, J., *op. cit.,* 189.
[138] Below, p. 526, The Margin for Profit.

marketing and exchange were a process of production. Malthus held that they were a process of bargaining. If marketing and exchanging is a process of production, then it is a labor process clear through to the ultimate consumers. If it is a process of bargaining, then it is a proprietary process of buying at a lower price and selling at a higher price. But both Malthus and Ricardo eliminated money as the measure of value and substituted labor as the measure of value. Hence they must have two meanings of "labour" which Hollander has rightly distinguished as "commanded labour" and "embodied labour." [139]

But back of Hollander's distinction is the difference in the meaning of markets as the productive process of physical delivery and the scarcity process of bargaining. Hollander seems to hold that Ricardo included scarcity in his meaning of value-in-use,[140] but this interpretation reads back into Ricardo the later ideas of diminishing utility which were not there prior to the Austro-hedonic economists. Neither Smith, Malthus, Bentham, nor Ricardo associated use-value with diminishing utility or scarcity. Use-value, with them, meant abundance of riches and its psychological parallel, happiness, measured physically by tons and bushels. If so, then the "commanded labour" of Smith and Malthus was their personified measure of scarcity in the process of bargaining, using commanded labor as the measure; but the "embodied labour" of Ricardo and Marx was their personified measure of scarcity in the productive powers of labor overcoming the resistance of nature.

The fact that Malthus followed Smith in the concept of "commanded labour," although Smith based his meaning on the quantity of labor-pain and Malthus on the demand of consumers, is explained by the two sides of the scarcity ratio between quantity wanted and quantity available. If value means scarcity-value, then it is a social relation between a quantity wanted (demand) and a quantity available (supply),[141] which can be expressed as a *ratio* between two quantities. This scarcity-ratio can be changed by changing either the demand side or the supply side. Smith, like Ricardo, assumed demand to be unlimited, and therefore his cause, regulator, and measure of scarcity was labor-pain which limited the *supply* side of scarcity. But Malthus asserted that demand was limited by the number of demanders who could be sustained by the existing food supply or by the possession of land or money.

[139] Hollander, J. H., "The Development of Ricardo's Theory of Value," *Quar. Jour. Econ.*, XVIII (1904), 455 ff.

[140] *Ibid.*, 458–459.

[141] Below, p. 378, Menger.

Hence he directed his attention to the *demand* side of scarcity; his cause, regulator, and measure were the consumer's "will and power" which augmented or reduced the demand. Thus, while Smith's regulator of scarcity-value worked out by changing the supply side, Malthus' regulator worked by changing the demand side, of the same scarcity ratio between demand and supply.

Each paid attention to what, for him, was the limiting factor in the same scarcity relation. For Malthus the cause of scarcity-value was the demand of consumers for an increase of supply; for Smith it was labor-pain which limited the supply. For Malthus the regulator of value was the proper proportioning of demand for labor among the different occupations by the will of man collectively; for Smith the regulation of value was the automatic proportioning of labor-pain among occupations by individuals separately. For both Malthus and Smith the personified measure of scarcity-value was the amount of labor that could be *purchased* by commodities or money. Thus "commanded labour," a special case of bargaining power, became, for Smith and Malthus, the measure of scarcity-value, whether that scarcity was caused by Smith's labor-pain of producers or by Malthus' limited demand of consumers.

But Ricardo's cause of scarcity-value was not the demand of consumers, which, for him, was unlimited. His cause was the resistance of nature, and this resistance was identical with the quantity of labor required to overcome it. Hence "embodied labour" became his measure of "natural" scarcity-value. But the quantity of embodied labor varies inversely to the productivity of labor. Therefore the quantity of use-value for Ricardo is regulated by the productivity of labor, and the degree of scarcity-value varies inversely to the productivity of labor. Labor produces use-value, but the unwillingness of labor causes scarcity-value. It is the double meaning of markets with the double personification of scarcity. If marketing is bargaining, then commanded labor is the measure of scarcity. If marketing is production, then embodied labor is the measure of efficiency.

With Ricardo, as afterwards with Marx, a market was a part of the whole process of production, and not a process of bargaining. The market consisted in a labor process, all the way from extraction of raw material, manufacturing it in new forms, transporting it, delivering it physically to the wholesaler in exchange for another physical delivery, until finally the finished goods are delivered physically by the grocery boy to the ultimate consumer who himself is another laborer, physically producing or delivering in return his own commodities or services. Money was also one of these physical commodities that could be physically delivered, not different from the others.

In more modern terminology, this meaning of marketing, as transportation, is the creation of "place utility" by labor not different from labor's creation of "form utility." But utility, in this meaning, is physical use-value. Labor is not really "creating" anything. It is only changing the form and place into use-values of the elementary materials furnished by nature. Thus marketing and exchanging were a labor process of augmenting the use-value of materials up to the point of ultimate delivery to ultimate consumers. This technological process of a marketing mechanism, considered as a part of the process of producing use-values, we distinguish as the technology of marketing. The other meaning is the institution of bargaining. These meanings are the difference between managerial transactions and bargaining transactions.

For bargaining is not a physical process of delivery and exchange. It is a business process of negotiation as to the prices and quantities which shall afterwards be physically delivered by the labor process. The things delivered in this business process of bargaining are not physical commodities, they are legal claims of ownership. Hence we have distinguished physical delivery by labor from legal delivery by bargaining; and the double meaning of markets and exchange are the labor process of delivering and exchanging use-values, and as the bargaining process of agreeing upon scarcity-values and delivery of ownership at these values.

This double meaning of marketing and exchanging was the root of the difference between Malthus and Ricardo. It persists, with practical consequences, in modern economics. One is the technology of markets, the other is the pricing and valuing upon the markets. It turns on the difference between use-value and scarcity-value. The double meaning runs through the debate between Marx and Proudhon and gives a double meaning in the discussions of the past hundred years on coöperative marketing. In the technological meaning of coöperative marketing the purpose is the *displacement* of the middleman by a coöperatively owned machinery of marketing. In the bargaining meaning, coöperation does not displace the middlemen but enters upon *collective bargaining* with them. Farmers' "coöperatives" are going through the process of distinguishing between coöperative marketing and collective bargaining, just as labor coöperatives, eighty years ago, suddenly changed from the socialistic coöperative production and marketing intended to displace capitalists, to the less revolutionary collective bargaining with capitalists on wages, hours, and conditions. The farmers are in a different position because they need warehouses for storage and therefore they actually displace the middleman. But the two processes are distinguishable. In the first meaning of marketing and exchanging, as used by Ricardo and Marx, the terms indicated the last step in the production of wealth by physical delivery and physical exchange, which increased the *quantity* of wealth by increasing the quantity of use-value. In the second meaning, as used by Smith, Malthus, and Proudhon, marketing was the first step of bargaining by agreeing upon the prices, which thereby changed the ownership of wealth.

VIII. MARX AND PROUDHON

It will have been seen that all of Ricardo's double meanings of words turned on his assumption of the stability of the purchasing power of money. All of his illustrations were stated in terms of money, and this was possible because he had virtually eliminated money by assuming its purchasing power to be stable for each particular commodity. In this way what he really did was to work out; not a theory of value, but a theory of efficiency. His unit of measurement was a unit of man-power, figuratively stated as the pound sterling. It was Karl Marx who substituted the man-hour for Ricardo's man-day, man-month, and man-year, and then worked out what he also thought was a theory of value, but which was a theory of efficiency.

Meanwhile, Ricardo's labor theory of value gradually disappeared from the classical political economy, except for McCulloch's post-mortem gasp in 1886.[142] The labor theory was really buried when John Stuart Mill, in 1848, quietly substituted money-cost for labor-cost, scarcely realizing what he had done.[143] But meanwhile the theory was executing a marvellous resurrection at the hands of Karl Marx, who rightly proclaimed himself the true Ricardian. It is from Marx, the inverted Hegelian philosopher,[144] that we derive our best understanding of the confused language of the plain business man, Ricardo.

Marx arrived at his analysis, in the course of his debate with

[142] McCulloch, J. R., began his exposition of Ricardo in 1818, and the last edition of his *Principles* was published in 1886.

[143] Mill, J. S., *Principles of Political Economy with Some of Their Applications to Social Philosophy* (1848, 1897).

[144] Hook, Sidney, in his recent *Towards the Understanding of Karl Marx, a Revolutionary Interpretation* (1933), reads back into Marx the modern doctrine of Pragmatism. He makes a good case. But if Marx was "pragmatic" in action, he was Hegelian in theory.

another Hegelian, Proudhon. It was this discussion which, for the first time, split the Ricardian labor theory into anarchism and communism. Prior to and even after this discussion, in the decade of the 1850's, both anarchism and communism were looked upon as the same thing, Socialism. The discussion ended with Marx's "utopian socialism" applied to Proudhon, and with Marx's "scientific socialism" applied to himself. But both were utopian and neither was scientific.[145] Each was Hegelian metaphysics.

The Hegelian methodology was not the scientific method of hypothesis, investigation, experiment, verification, to fit the changing facts of observation; it was the philosophical method of beginning with a big idea foreordained to be realized in the future and then analyzing it into little ideas that inevitably lead forward to the big idea. This dialectic took on two aspects: the analytic, espoused by Proudhon, and the genetic, espoused by Marx. These were two versions of the same idea of the universe. The analytic was the mental process of thesis, antithesis, and synthesis. The genetic was the historical swing of civilization from the thesis of primitive communism to the antithesis of Eighteenth Century individualism, and back to the inevitable synthesis of future communism. This was indeed an inversion of Hegel's idea of the world-spirit. Whereas Hegel's "spirit" would culminate in a future German world-empire, Marx's materialism would culminate in a future world-communism.[146]

But Proudhon, like Smith and Ricardo, started with the idea of an individual who produces use-values for himself; who then turns to other individuals, and proposes an exchange of the *surplus* not needed by himself. Thus Proudhon separated production for self from marketing with others, and made use-value the opposite and contradictory of scarcity-value. Hence, his term *contradictions l'économiques* was the basis of his philosophy. Proudhon's "utility-value" was Smith's and Ricardo's physical use-value, which *increases* with abundance and is produced by labor—described by Proudhon as "the capacity possessed by all products, natural or industrial, to serve the subsistence of man." It is therefore the equivalent of Bentham's Happiness. Proudhon's exchange-value was scarcity-value which *decreases* with abundance, described as "the capacity" which the same products "have of being given in exchange for each other." This capacity depends therefore on the relative scarcities of two use-values in the process of bargaining. So his use-value was

---

[145] Cf. Marx, K., and Engels, F., *The Communist Manifesto* (1848).

[146] On the Hegelian metaphysics see article "Hegelian Philosophy," *Encyclopaedia Britannica*, 14th ed. On the "left wing" Hegelianism, see article on Feuerbach, L. A., in the *Encyclopaedia of the Social Sciences*, Vol. VI, 21-22.

thesis; his scarcity-value was antithesis; his "synthetical value," which brought the two together in a unity, was what he called "constituted value," determined by what he called "opinion." But by "opinion" he really meant what we call the negotiational psychology of agreeing on price, quantity, and time of delivery, in a *free* bargaining transaction.

This bargaining transaction was to be freed from all physical coercion by government and from all economic coercion by "property." And, since property itself was created by government, he would destroy government in order to destroy property. "Property is Robbery," according to Proudhon, because it is the power of physical duress brought to the support of economic coercion. This coercion of property must be eliminated, in order that bargaining agreements as to prices and quantities may be made solely by the free and equal "opinion" of the bargainers.

Consequently, the difference between Proudhon and Marx was the difference between bargaining and rationing. Proudhon would have free and equal bargaining by eliminating government; Marx would have perfect rationing by eliminating bargaining.

It is Proudhon's free and equal bargaining that is merely the similar concept of "reasonable value" intended in Anglo-American common law. His "constituted value" is the reasonable value of the courts, since it is a valuation agreed upon by "a willing buyer and a willing seller." But Proudhon—not being familiar with the historic ideals of the common law—had to Hegelianize it as the "synthetic value," or "constituted value," which reconciled the antithesis of use-value and scarcity-value, if the parties were perfectly free.[147]

But in order to reconcile the two on the basis of a willing buyer and a willing seller, Proudhon must destroy the power of the state enforcing the rights of property to rob both the buyer and the seller. This robbery appeared as all forms of money income derived otherwise than from the *labor* of the participants, in the bargaining transactions, such as interest, profits, rents, high prices charged by capitalists and excessive salaries. These were property, and these were robbery.

It must be seen, therefore, that by his meaning of property as "robbery," Proudhon did not mean the individual property that a person owns resulting from his own labor or from free negotiations with others whose property also resulted from their own labor. He would not abolish this kind of property, but he thought it would

[147] Cf. Proudhon, P. J., *Système des contradictions économiques; ou Philosophie de la misère* (2 vols., 1846, 2d ed., 1850), Book I, Chap. 2.

survive if government were abolished. Indeed, Anarchism means the most extreme inalienable, exchangeable, and *individual* property, provided it be based on labor and the freedom and equality of bargaining. The eminent Russian anarchist, Kropotkin, found an ideal of anarchism in the farms and county fairs of Iowa.[148]   So it is with Proudhon. The division which economists had made between rent, profit (including interest), and wages had no meaning for him, just as it has no meaning for the Iowa farmer in so far as he supports his family on the use-values of their joint labor, and then sells his *surplus* on the markets by free and equal bargaining at the county fairs. The economists' impossible separation of that farmer's income of use-value into rent, profit (interest), and wages was for Proudhon, as for the farmer, merely the joint compensation which the farmer received for his combined ownership, management, and labor. If he could agree with other farmers, at the county fairs, on the exchange values of their surplus, without compulsion on either of them, then that exchange value, thus "constituted," was what he called "synthetic value." But it was that which, in the language of the common law, would be called the "reasonable value" of a willing buyer and a willing seller.

The explanation is that Proudhon based his theory on Merchant Capitalism and Landlordism, while Marx based his theory on Employer Capitalism. It was Merchant Capitalism and its commercial banking that dominated France; it was Landlordism and tenant farming that dominated the rest of Europe. This latter is the distinction which, in America, is coming to be known as the difference between the "dirt farmer" and the "landlord" farmer and between "little business" and "big business." Proudhon stood for the dirt farmer and for little business. His stand was against the merchant capitalist and banker who controlled the access to markets, and thereby reduced little business to a condition of sweatshop competition; and against the landlord who rack-rented his tenants. Against these Proudhon hurled his definition of property as robbery—not against the small property of the sweated working farmers, master workmen, and retailers. In his newspaper, *Le Peuple,* he said, in 1849, "We desire that every one should have property. We wish for property without usury, because usury is the stumbling block to the growth and universalization of property." By usury he meant not only excessive interest but all excessive prices, profits, rents, and salaries. When it came to preparing his remedy and setting up his Bank of the People during the Revolution of 1848,

---

[148] Kropotkin, P., *Fields, Farms, Factories, Workshops, or Industry Combined with Agriculture and Brain Work with Manual Work* (2d ed., 1901), 75 ff.

it turns out that all he proposed was voluntary coöperative marketing and coöperative credit (the more recent "credit unions"), but not even coöperative production, for that would subordinate the individual producer to the coöperative producers.[149] Proudhon's anarchism was his world-wide synthesis of individual property and voluntary coöperation in marketing and borrowing. Hence his thesis was the use-value that increases with *abundance;* his antithesis was exchange-value which increases with *scarcity;* his synthetic value was the *reasonable value* of equality and liberty in bargaining transactions. After three years in jail for these revolutionary proposals, it was no contradiction in Proudhon that he accepted the politician, Napoleon III, who released him from jail and made Proudhon's liberty and equality the catchwords of his own dictatorship.

But Marx looked upon Employers as Capitalists, while Proudhon looked upon Merchants and Bankers as Capitalists. Marx had his eye on the factory system of England, Proudhon upon the handicraft system of France. Marx expected landlordism to become a factory system. Proudhon expected to split up landlordism (in other countries than France) into small-farm ownership. In the factory system, which Marx saw in England, the employer had transformed Proudhon's master workman into a foreman, and the wage-earners into a mass of homogeneous labor.[150] Hence, while Proudhon would oust the wholesale merchants and their bankers by means of voluntary coöperation and individual bargaining, Marx would oust the employers from the factories by common ownership and governmental administration, and would abolish bargaining by the communist system of rationing. Proudhon did not distinguish rent, interest, profit, and wages when paid to small producers. They were merged into one compensation for labor. The same was true of Marx for socialized producers. Not only Ricardo's rent, but also his profits of employer-capitalists and his interest paid to bankers and investors, were merged into one common fund of exploitation by property owners whereby the social use-value produced by labor-power was extracted from laborers, not in the process of bargaining as held by Proudhon, but in the very ownership of the materials in the process of production. Proudhon was Ricardo anarchized; Marx was Ricardo communized. Where Marx likened his social labor-power to a hive of bees and the associated employer-

---

[149] See "Proudhon" in Palgrave's *Dictionary of Political Economy* (1923 ed.); Dana, Charles A., "Proudhon and his Bank of the People" (1850), in Henry Cohen's *Proudhon's Solution of the Social Problem* (1927).

[150] Below, p. 763, Merchant, Employer, and Banker Capitalism.

capitalists to the owners of the hive extracting the honey by means of their control of government, Proudhon pictured his millions of individual laborers as property-owners themselves, while the merchant capitalists, bankers, and landlords were their robbers by aid of government in the process of bargaining.

Hence, when it came to Proudhon's antithesis of production and exchange and his corresponding antithesis of use-value and scarcity-value, Marx denied both the antithesis and the need of the synthesis. Where Proudhon proposed a system of free and equal bargaining, Marx proposed compulsory rationing. The first was anarchism; the second, communism.

Their difference was partly in the double meaning of marketing. With Marx, marketing itself was a process of production whereby social labor-power adds the more recent "place-utility" (use-value) until the commodity is delivered to the ultimate consumer. With Proudhon, marketing meant bargaining power, whereby the relative scarcity-values of money and commodities were agreed upon, through economic coercion, between strong and weak bargainers. For Marx, commodities were produced for exchange—just as Smith, Malthus and Ricardo intended when they distinguished "productive" labor as labor whose product is destined for exchange, from "unproductive" labor whose product is destined for home consumption by the one who produced it. Marx seized upon this meaning of "productive labor," and made it universal under the modern factory and transportation system where nobody consumes what he produces, but always consumes what others produce, and where the output, therefore, is not owned by its producers.

Consequently, Marx claimed that there are no such surplus products, above family consumption, as Proudhon had assumed when he carried overproduction for self into a surplus sold to others. The product now is "social" use-value, not individual use-value, and social use-value includes transportation, wholesaling, retailing, and physical delivery to the consumer by all the social labor-power which binds the world together by production, transportation, and physical delivery.[151] Production and exchange, the latter in the meaning of physical delivery, are one and the same labor process of production. Production does not end before exchange is thought of, but exchange is itself the labor process of two physical deliveries of two physical commodities, including those "services" which merely add use-values to commodities.

This is on account of the division of labor. But Marx got com-

[151] Marx had some trouble as to whether transportation was always "productive." But this was because he did not have the more recent idea of adding place-utility (use-value).

munism out of the division of labor, where Smith got individualism. In either case it meant the same thing as exchange. "From the moment," says Marx, "that you suppose more than one hand assisting in production you have already supposed a whole system of production based on the subdivision of labor," [152] and therefore on the exchange of physical delivery. Other individuals are indeed "collaborators," as Proudhon proposed, following Smith. But they were not Proudhon's or Smith's *voluntary* collaborators, whose collaboration consisted in their bargaining transactions. The collaboration was the *compulsory* fitting of laborers into the technological system, so that the labor of each becomes merely an aliquot part of a world-wide machine-process of delivering to each other the accrual of use-values under the name of "exchange." [153] Thus, says Marx, "the collaborators, and the diverse functions, the division of labor and the exchange which it indicates are all existing already. . . . It would have been just as well to have supposed exchange-value in the first place." [154]

The way in which Marx constructed this social division of labor and thereby eliminated Proudhon's bargaining may be seen by a diagram of his famous formula, C-M-C.[155] Here he distinguished, in Hegelian fashion, the Substance of Value, the Form of Value, and the Kind of Value. The "substance" was simply labor-power *times* labor-time. The "form" of value was its exchange-value embodied in money which had no use-value. The "kind" of value was the kinds of commodities exchanged through the medium of money.

Measuring horizontally, in Chart 5, the Labor Time in each kind of production is 10 hours. Measuring vertically, the labor-power is the efficiency of labor which varies inversely to nature's resistance. The multiple of time and efficiency is the "substance" of value.

This substance takes "form" in the process of exchange, which, by Marx's meaning of exchange, was physical delivery of product without bargaining. In this physical delivery, equal values exchange for equal values, no matter how great the differences are in the quantity of hats, money, and shoes. Money has no use-value—it is solely the "form" of value in the process of exchange by physical delivery.

But this "substance" of value is shared between capitalists and laborers, and the sharing occurs in the process of production, not

[152] Marx, Karl, *The Poverty of Philosophy* (tr. 1847), 34, being Marx's reply to Proudhon's *Philosophy of Poverty*.
[153] This idea was taken over by Veblen as the "machine process." Below, p. 649.
[154] Marx, K., *The Poverty of Philosophy*, 34, 35.
[155] Above, p. 175, Chart 5.

in the bargaining process on the markets. Here is where "exploitation" occurs, because the capitalists own all the equipment and the output belongs to them, even before the laborer works upon the materials.

Thus it will be seen how it was that the share of the capitalists' exploitation, which was Marx's "surplus value," was augmented in two directions—greater efficiency and longer hours. Greater efficiency may come from new mechanization or from speeding up the laborers. This extends the vertical line of labor-power. But greater quantity may also come from longer hours. This extends the horizontal line. The multiple of the two enlarges the surplus value which goes solely to the capitalists, because the laborers have no bargaining power but can get only the minimum of existence. This was, indeed, the logical outcome of Ricardo's theory, and is none other than the modern problem, Who gets the gains from the improved mechanization of industry?

What we find, then, is that Marx was constructing a formula of efficiency and the mode of sharing the gains of efficiency between laborers as a class and all capitalists as a class. The amount of labor-power was not merely that of operating labor—it was also the amount of labor "embodied" in the fixed capital, owned by the capitalist. He thus avoided the fallacies of modern computations of efficiency which are based only on operating labor. He created a formula of efficiency by including both operating labor and the "overhead" of embodied labor in his meaning of social labor-power.

Thus the debate between Proudhon and Marx, like that between Malthus and Ricardo, turned on the distinction between efficiency and scarcity, and their correlated use-value and scarcity-value descended respectively from Smith's two meanings of labor-power and labor-pain. In the case of Ricardo and Marx, scarcity was presupposed as a constant factor and thus eliminated; but in the case of Malthus, the demand of consumers was made dominant; and in the case of Proudhon, efficiency and scarcity were made antithetical to each other.

Proudhon, by forcing Marx to bring into the open his concealed principle of scarcity, compelled him practically to abandon his theory of labor-power as the cause of value. "The difficulty of Proudhon," said Marx, "is simply that he has forgotten *demand*, and that a thing can only be scarce or abundant according as it is in demand. Demand once set aside, he assimilates exchange-value to *scarcity* and use-value to abundance." [156] Ricardo, he said, had explicitly assumed scarcity in his meaning of value. Consequently Proudhon,

[156] Marx, K., *The Poverty of Philosophy*, 40.

said Marx, after making exchange-value equivalent to scarcity, and utility (use-value) equivalent to abundance, "is astonished not to find utility value in scarcity and exchange-value, nor exchange-value in abundance and utility value." He never will find them together "while he excludes demand." Proudhon's "abundance" seemed to be "something spontaneous. He all at once forgets that there are people who produce and that it is to their interest never to lose sight of the demand." [157]

In other words, Marx's "producer" not only produces use-value, but he also produces it in limited quantities, so that the expected demand will give exchange-value to it. His use-value is already a scarcity-value by withholding supply in the process of production, including physical delivery as a part of the process.

This production in limited quantities, we take it, is what Marx meant by socially "necessary" labor-power. The word "necessary" means necessary to supply the demands of consumers. Herein Marx read into his concept of labor-power, whose principle is efficiency, the antithetic meaning of bargaining power, whose principle is scarcity. Our method is different. We separate each by a "virtual" elimination of the other, and then combine them on the principle of limiting and complementary factors. Hence, for us, the engineer as such increases production indefinitely, regardless of its price, but the business man restricts or regulates production in order to maintain its price. The two are limiting and complementary factors.[158]

The contradiction between Marx and Proudhon is again the contradiction between materials and ownership, brought out in more recent times by Veblen in distinguishing the engineer as the specialist in materials and efficiency, and the business man as the specialist in ownership and scarcity.

It turns on the historic double meaning of use-value. Marx said, twenty years after his debate with Proudhon, ". . . nothing can have value, without being an object of utility. If the thing is useless, so is that labor contained in it; the labor does not count as labor, and therefore creates no value." [159]

Here the question arises: Is it useless because its physical qualities are such that it cannot be used—like *rotten* apples—or is it useless because the quantity produced is greater than the quantity wanted—like *too many good* apples? Is it useless as depreciated use-value, or useless as diminishing scarcity-value?

The former was Proudhon's meaning of use-value—the latter his

[157] *Ibid.*, 41, 42.
[158] Below, p. 627, Strategic and Routine Transactions.
[159] Marx, K., *Capital* (1867, tr., Kerr ed., 1909), I, 48.

meaning of exchange-value. Marx had, as we have just now said, even a double meaning of use-value. When following Ricardo he excluded from use-value every meaning of scarcity-value. Use-value was measured by physical units such as "dozens of watches, yards of linen, tons of iron." In this respect he repeated Ricardo's distinction between value and riches, when he said, "it is through confounding the ideas of value and wealth (or riches) that it has been asserted that by diminishing the quantity of the necessaries, conveniences and enjoyments of human life, riches may be increased." [160]

This, again, was exactly what Proudhon had said when he distinguished use-value as abundance which increases the social wealth, and exchange-value as scarcity whose increase increases private wealth (assets).

But Marx had another meaning of use-value, which turned on physical units of measurement, such as tons and yards. Use-value is "independent of the amount of labor required to appropriate its useful qualities. The Use-values of commodities furnish the material for a special study, that of the commercial knowledge of commodities." "Exchange-value manifests itself as something totally independent of their use-value." "Use-values become a reality only by use or consumption." [161]

In other words, the meaning of use-value becomes here, not a product of labor or technology, but an attribute of physical measurement of commodities for further manufacturing or for consumption. But, if so, then the use-value is evidently a product of labor and of the engineer's knowledge of the physically useful attributes needed by manufacturers and consumers. Laborers and their managers do not make what is useless for the next producer in the chain of production. Labor simply adds usefulness (use-value) to the materials, whether it be the form, the time, or the place utilities (use-values) asked for by the next user. Marx here departed from the meaning of labor-power as laid down by Smith in his criticism of Quesnay. Labor does not produce bulk—it adds utilities (use-values) to the bulk of materials.

Yet Marx need not have separated use-values, physically measured, from his "labor-power." What labor produces *is* use-values physically measured. He needed only to construct a *ratio* between the quantity of use-values as output and the quantity of man-hours as input.

Use-value is indeed a technological concept, and in excluding

160 Marx, K., *The Poverty of Philosophy*, 38, 39.
161 Marx, K., *Capital*, I, 42, 45.

technology and use-value from political economy Marx was not alone. Practically all economists of the Nineteenth Century excluded technology and its output of use-value from political economy. Veblen brings it back under the name, "instinct of workmanship." We bring it back under the notion of *efficiency*, including output, input, use-value, managerial transactions, limiting and complementary factors, etc.

The basic reason, we take it, for this exclusion of technology was in the psychological and materialistic—instead of volitional— foundations for economics. Derived from psychology or materialism was the idea of building a whole system of economics, and even a whole social philosophy, upon a single principle, such as labor or wants; whereas the subject-matter is a complex of many principles. Modern economics is greatly concerned with investigations in the technology of all industries and agriculture. This does not mean that the economist, as such, is a chemist or a physicist. It means only that he includes the *activities* of scientists and engineers as the outstanding contributions to the production of use-values or wealth, and that he, in doing so, endeavors to give to them a proper setting in the complex whole. Historically, their contributions are cumulative. They begin with the physical sciences in the Eighteenth Century; then follow with the chemical sciences in the Nineteenth Century; then with the astonishing development of power producing and power transporting in the Twentieth Century; and they end with the psychological sciences of personnel management which furnish a foundation for managerial transactions. In the latter field, of managerial transactions, technology has forced its way into the field of economics, and the proponents of scientific management rightly criticized the economists who did not contribute anything to the solution of their problems of management.

When Marx had said, as above, that use-value lies outside the sphere of investigation of political economy and belongs to a special study of the "commercial knowledge of commodities," he stated, indeed, the view of Nineteenth Century economists. But if use-values are the output of managerial transactions, and if these are distinguished from bargaining transactions, then they are not merely a matter of commercial knowledge—they are the very real engineering process of controlling the forces of nature and human labor-power for the creation of use-values. This process may be thwarted by business, or financial, or labor interests; but it is this very conflict that requires managerial transactions, technology, and use-values to be included in the complexity of the entire subject-matter.

The same use-value, said Marx, may be utilized in various ways. But the extent of its possible applications is circumscribed by its distinct properties. Furthermore, it is thus limited not only qualitatively but also quantitatively.[162]

By "qualities" Marx can only mean the different kinds and grades of use-value; by "quantity" he apparently means, not the quantity of supply or quantity demanded, but the technological quantity—as, for example, whether a wagon can use five wheels or whether it needs only four wheels. Evidently in such a case there is an interdependent relation between the use-value of the wheels and their scarcity-value. But the two are always distinguished. The scarcity-value of the wheels is their *price* measured in money; but when measured in the quantity of labor-power embodied in them it is efficiency or inefficiency. But this use-value of the wheels is their civilization value—unmeasurable by Ricardo because subjective, but measured by Marx as three wheels, four wheels, or five wheels, depending on the number needed for that kind of wagon or automobile, at that stage of the art of transportation. This concept belongs to the theory of limiting and complementary factors.[163]

Marx, however, accomplished two improvements over Ricardo, thus furnishing a basis for the modern theory of efficiency. He displaced the subjective use-value of Smith and Ricardo, therefore unmeasurable, by an objective use-value, therefore measurable in bushels, yards, tons, and the number of watches or number of wheels. And he made clear the two dimensions of labor-power: the pressure, force, or energy; and the time during which it operates. His unit of labor-power was one labor-hour of simple unskilled labor, and he properly, therefore, means the same thing when he speaks of labor-power or labor-time.[164] But this output of use-values relative to input of labor-time is the measure of efficiency.

This must necessarily be the case, since efficiency and scarcity are limiting factors relative to each other. But, since exchange-value had the double meaning of bargaining and physical delivery, Marx had difficulty in excluding use-value from economics. He rightly said, as in the references cited above, that the exchange-value of commodities (bargaining) "manifests itself as something totally independent of their use-value." Use-value is "independent of the amount of labor required to appropriate its useful qualities" (by bargaining).

[162] Marx, K., *Capital*, I, 44.
[163] Below, p. 627, Strategic and Routine Transactions.
[164] Marx, K., *Capital*, I, 45.

It is evident, therefore, that Marx, in following Ricardo but by reducing metallic money to the labor-cost of production, had confused what in latter days is more clearly distinguished as efficiency and scarcity. He prepared all of the concepts needed to develop a theory of efficiency. But he gave to the term "productivity" a double meaning, the production of use-value (wealth) which he rejected as belonging to technology, and the production of value, measured by quantity of labor, which for him was the subject-matter of political economy. One is the production of use-value by increasing the supply; the other the antithetical "production" of scarcity-value by restricting the supply on account of the resistance of nature. We avoid this double meaning when we substitute the term efficiency for the term productivity, and when we distinguish, as above, bargaining transactions from managerial and rationing transactions.

But in order to convert Marx's terminology into terms applicable to efficiency we require, as above indicated, to distinguish the two terms output and input, from the two terms income and outgo. Output and input are the technological terms of use-value and labor-power, by which efficiency is measured. Income and outgo are the bargaining terms, equivalent to the legal terms acquisition and alienation and the pecuniary terms money-income and money-outgo, or their equivalent of income of commodities at their money value, or outgo of commodities also at their money value. This is the difference between wealth and assets.

IX. Menger, Wieser, Fisher, Fetter

The foregoing discussion has anticipated somewhat the school of psychological economists. Although Gossen, in 1854, Jevons in 1862, Menger in 1871, and Walras in 1874 originated independently the psychological or marginal utility theories of value, we select Menger's exposition, at the beginning of the Austrian school, because his psychological analysis is put in objective terms of quantity.[165]

Menger distinguished four prerequisites in order that a material thing may be an economic good in the sense that it has utility (*nützlichkeit*), namely,

(1) The knowledge or expectation of a human want (*Bedürfniss*);

(2)· Such physical qualities of the object (*güterqualitäten*) as make it fit to satisfy the want;

[165] Menger, Carl. *Grundsätze der Volkswirthschaftslehre* (1871). The second edition (1923), edited by his son, retains the original analysis, but incorporates Menger's answers to his critics.

(3) Knowledge, correct or erroneous, of this fitness;

(4) Such control over the thing, or of other things as instruments, that it can be obtained and used to satisfy the want (*die Verfügung über dieses Ding*).

The first and third of these prerequisites, we have already designated by the word, Meaning, since they indicate, not exact knowledge, but the emotional process of attaching importance to the object for human purposes. The second we designate use-value, since it is a physical attribute that does not diminish with abundance nor increase with scarcity, and is equivalent to Ricardo's and Marx's meaning of riches or wealth. The fourth we distinguish as the double meaning of either physical control, which Menger identifies with technology, or proprietary control, which he identifies with economy.[166]

Up to this point the concept of scarcity does not appear in Menger's prerequisites. He introduces this concept by his distinction between wants (*Bedürfnisse*) and quantity wanted (*Bedarf*).[167] Wants are strictly subjective, but quantity wanted is objective. Wants are mere feelings which differ in intensity. Quantity wanted is adaptation to circumstances. Quantity wanted is the quantity of a particular use-value (*Güterqualitäten*) wanted here and now. Hence it is always a limited quantity wanted at a particular time and place by a particular person or society. The error of preceding economists in holding that wants were unlimited, said Menger, was in their failure to distinguish kind, time, and place. All kinds of wants taken as a whole may be unlimited, but the quantity wanted of a particular kind here and now is a limited quantity.[168]

Menger devotes considerable space to showing that his newly formulated concept of "quantity wanted" is both a familiar concept and has an objective quantitative meaning. Wants in themselves (*Bedürfnisse*) are purely feelings of different degrees of intensity, and have no intellectual reference to the objective quantity wanted which is always a limited quantity at the time and place, for a particular person then and there circumstanced. The quantity wanted has reference to actually recognized needs (*Bedarfe*), which are not needs for an indefinite quantity, but for a limited quantity at the moment when larger and smaller quantities are being weighed in the balance relative to the larger or smaller quantities of other things wanted also, and in view of the limited power to obtain quantities of all things wanted, at the time and place. We do not

[166] *Ibid.*, 1st ed., 3; 2d ed., 11.
[167] *Ibid.*, 1st ed., 32; 2d ed., 32 n.
[168] *Ibid.*, 1st ed., 35 ff.; 2d ed., 32 ff.; especially 32 n.

want an unlimited quantity of beefsteak at a particular dinner—we want only just enough of the right kind, and we want several other eatables with it. The manufacturer does not want an unlimited quantity of pig iron here and now—he wants only the right amount to fit into the quantities of rolled steel products which customers will take off at profitable prices.

But Menger went further than the individual. His quantity wanted is wanted by society. His quantity available is made available by society. The relation between the two quantities is his "social relation" of scarcity. Put in mathematical terms this is the scarcity-ratio between quantity wanted by society and quantity made available by society. This ratio is Price. Each side of the social relation is independently variable. If the quantity wanted increases, the price rises; if it decreases, the price falls. If the quantity available increases, the price falls; if it decreases, the price rises.

This is, of course, none other than the familiar social relation of demand and supply. Menger holds that it is the *only* social relation with which economics is concerned, and he proceeds deductively to draw from it a complete theory of political economy. His originality consisted in connecting it up with subjective feelings of individuals.

These facts are commonplace and familiar enough, but the difference between Menger and Gossen, Jevons, or Walras, is that he stated the problem in these very terms of quantities from which he derived the subjective terms of feelings. The two are indeed inseparable and their statements were as familiar and commonplace as Menger's. But they had reached their conception through Bentham who conceived that feelings could be broken up into units and "lots" of happiness, but had not discovered all that was involved in the fact that these units of pleasure diminished in intensity with an increase in quantity of goods, or inversely, increased in intensity with a decrease in quantity of goods. They therefore started with the subjective feelings dependent on quantities, but Menger started with the quantities on which the feelings depended. Each is, indeed, a functional psychology of the interdependence of feelings and quantities, but theirs is the subjective side while Menger's is the objective.

Yet even Menger's quantities are not directly measurable. They are measurable indirectly by measuring their effects. Their effects are the social relation which constitutes his subject-matter of economics, namely, the relation between the quantity wanted (*Bedarf*) and the quantity available (*Verfügbar*) of a particular commodity.

It is evident that this relation is none other than the relation of Scarcity, or Price.

Thenceforth Scarcity rather than feelings is Menger's subject-matter of economics. The fact that he used the ambiguous term, utility (*Nützlichkeit*), which others interpreted in the Benthamite sense of pleasure, has concealed the real contribution of Menger, and has directed attention to the individualistic, diminishing intensity of feelings of want with increasing quantity of things wanted, whereas he was really developing the social idea of diminishing or increasing scarcity dependent upon the changing relations between the two variables, the quantity wanted by society and the quantity available for society. He was therefore merely giving to the old formula of Demand, Supply, and Price in terms of money, a more specific yet more universal meaning applicable to all goods, but without the use of money. His quantity wanted is Demand, his quantity available is Supply, his marginal utility is Price. Marginal utility (*Grenznutzen*) is the changing effects of the variable relation between quantity wanted and quantity available for society, which in a money economy is the Price that results from the changing relations between Demand and Supply. In a money economy, as in Menger's commodity economy, Demand and Supply cannot be measured directly, but the *effects* of their variations are measured. This measurement of effects is Price, so that price is the measure of the variable relations of Scarcity, and is the pecuniary equivalent of his marginal utility.

This was, indeed, a great and new insight. It changed psychology from Happiness to Scarcity.

It was Wieser who classified the functional relation between the hedonists' diminishing intensity of feelings and Menger's relation between the quantity wanted and quantity available. He acknowledged that his clarification was only what Menger had previously discovered, but he also misled the followers of the Austrian School by his use of the ambiguous term utility (*Nützlichkeit*). Had he and Menger used the term "diminishing scarcity" instead of "diminishing utility," and the term "price" instead of "marginal utility" (*Grenznutzen*), then it would have been plain that what he was doing was the formulating of a strictly objective and measurable theory of Scarcity.

Wieser's explanation of Menger's analysis turned on the distinction between Value and Price and his idea of their functional relation which he named the Paradox of Value.[169] There are two variable factors in the concept of Value, as we have already seen in Ricardo

---

[169] Wieser, F. von, *Natural Value* (1889, tr. 1893).

and Marx. However, with Wieser, the one is the diminishing intensity of feeling of want, named diminishing utility. The other is the increasing quantity of the thing wanted. Utility continues to diminish per unit with every increase of quantity available, so that, if utility alone were considered, it would diminish to zero and even would become a dis-utility—a nuisance. Thus he adopted the changed meaning of "utility" from use-value to scarcity-value.

But, on the other hand, the quantity available (utility) has its own independent variability. Combining the two variables, if the utility per unit does *not* diminish as rapidly as the quantity available increases, then the *value* of the increasing quantity rises. But if the utility per unit diminishes *more* rapidly than the increase in the quantity available, then the *value* of the increasing quantity diminishes.

This is the "paradox of value," since value is a multiple of the utility per unit and the quantity of units, each of which is independently variable.

If now we fall back on the double meaning of utility which we have previously discussed, we find that diminishing utility per unit is only a personification of price, and means none other than diminishing scarcity, that is, increasing abundance, whose measure is diminishing price. But the other meaning of utility is physical use-value which does not diminish per unit with abundance nor increase per unit with scarcity. Hence Wieser's "value" is the functional relation between scarcity-value, measured by money, and use-value measured by tons, bushels, etc. It is the familiar paradox of value in all occupations, industries, and agriculture.

Evidently this marginal utility can be converted to dollars and cents, and this use-value to bushels of wheat. The value of a crop of wheat is a function of the two variables, its scarcity-value measured by price (marginal utility) and its quantity of use-value measured by bushels. If there is no crop, its *price* rises symbolically to infinity but its *value* fa'ls to zero. If the quantity is a billion bushels and the price falls to $1.00, then the *value* of the crop rises to $1,000,000,000. If further the crop is 1,500,000,000 bushels and the price falls to 80¢, the value of the crop rises still further to $1,200,000,000. If, finally the crop is 2,500,000,000 bushels and the price falls to 40¢, the value of the crop falls to $1,000,000,000.

This is indeed a paradox, but a very familiar one since the days of Gregory King, two centuries ago.[170] Wieser himself points out that it is the same paradox as that which led Proudhon to his antin-

---

[170] See Palgrave's *Dictionary of Political Economy*, title: King, Gregory.

omy of value.[171] But whereas Proudhon set it forth as the Hegelian thesis, antithesis, and synthesis, Wieser sets it forth as the functional relation between utility and quantity, which however is the functional relation between price and quantity, and this in turn is the functional relation between scarcity-value and use-value, whose interdependent variable is Value.

This variability of the two factors may be pictured in another way, illustrated in Chart 3,[172] as is done by those who follow Gossen and Jevons, rather than Menger and Wieser.

The curve, in terms of utility, starts with an imaginary absence of any supply whatever—say water on a waterless desert—then proceeds with addition of units and their diminishing utility. Where there is no water whatever, each unit has indeed infinite utility, for it is a matter of life or death. But an increasing abundance of *use-value* of water is a diminishing *utility* per unit. At some point is the marginal utility. And at that point the value of the total quantity of water is the marginal utility *times* the quantity of water.

This, evidently, is merely a verbal formula for the obvious meanings of Scarcity and Abundance. An increase of abundance is the same thing as a decrease of scarcity. Put in terms of value, an increase of use-value is a decrease of scarcity-value per unit, and a decrease in abundance of use-value is an increase of scarcity-value per unit. The term utility here reveals its double meaning of scarcity-value and use-value. Scarcity-value is measurable as price, use-value is measurable as gallons, and value is measurable as the number of gallons at the price per gallon.

We can now see in terms of the multiple of marginal utility or price and of quantity of commodity or use-value, the same meaning of value which Ricardo and Marx pictured as the number of labor-hours times the resistance of nature for one hour. Value in terms of scarcity measured by money is price *times* quantity of commodity. Value in terms of diminishing utility is marginal utility *times* quantity of commodity, and value in terms of labor-power is number of man-hours *times* the resistance of nature. But the last is efficiency. The former are scarcity.

The more recent discussion of Wieser's Paradox of Value is the debate between Fisher and Fetter on the definition of price.[173] Fisher had distinguished price and value in the precise formula of Wieser, using "price," however, instead of marginal utility, and

---

[171] Wieser, F. von, *op. cit.*, 55, 237. Wieser says "antinomy of exchange value."
[172] Above, p. 175.
[173] Fisher, Irving, *The Nature of Capital and Income*, 11–16, 45–47; Fetter, F. A., "The Definition of Price," *Amer. Econ. Rev.*, II (1912), 783–813.

wealth instead of use-value. Price, with him, was used in the transactional sense of agreement upon a value per unit, and "value" as
"a given quantity of wealth [we should say assets] found by mul-
tiplying the quantity by the price." This "definition of value,"
he says, "applying, as it does, to an aggregate of wealth [assets]
instead of a unit, departs somewhat from economic usage; but it
follows closely the usage of business men and practical statisticians."
After commenting upon the various subjective and objective meanings given by economists, Fisher goes on:

> "It seems preferable to conform our definitions of value and
> price as closely as possible to business usage, which instinctively
> and consistently applies the term 'price' to the unit and value
> to the aggregate." [174]

He thus obtains the three magnitudes "quantity, price and value
of wealth," equivalent to Wieser's quantity, marginal utility, and
value, and our use-value, scarcity-value, and value.

Fetter, in criticizing Fisher from the psychological standpoint,
says:

> ". . . 'Value' is here turned to a use already filled. Any unit
> either of price or of quantity of goods, is arbitrary and must be
> always indicated either expressly or by implication, whenever a
> price is stated; as price in cents, ounces of bullion, per bushel,
> wagon-load, ton of grain, cotton, iron, etc. Conversely the term
> aggregate is an arbitrary one, and may be deemed a unit, if one
> please. Thus a bushel of wheat is but an aggregate of grains
> of wheat. Consequently the word price can be used without
> confusion either for the conventional unit or the aggregate of
> units, and nothing is gained by the innovation. On the other
> hand, the loss to terminology is great when the term value is
> taken from its subjective use in which it is indispensable, for
> thereby an understanding of recent value-discussion is made hope-
> less." [175]

Fetter's criticism turns on the *customary* as against the *individualistic* meaning of the words "arbitrary," "aggregate," and "conventional." Units of measurement are indeed "arbitrary," such as tons,
meters, yards, dollars. One nation has different units from other
nations. When, however, a *nation* is "arbitrary," or a practice is
"conventional" we name it custom, common law, or statute law.
Indeed, all institutions are conventional and even arbitrary, and, for
this reason Bentham dismissed them from economic theory and

[174] Quoted by Fetter, "The Definition of Price," *loc. cit.*, 797.
[175] *Ibid.*, 798.

Fetter from "recent value-discussion." But they are arbitrary and conventional, not in the individualistic sense, but in the collective sense that courts will use them in deciding conflicts of interest, and therefore no business man or working man can continue in business or get his wages if he "arbitrarily" sets his will against the collective legal units, and attempts to run his business or get paid according to his own subjective units of measurement. The economist may call them arbitrary if he forgets custom and law, and so separates himself from the usages that dominate individuals in their transactions. The word "conventional," for economics, means custom, the common law, and statute law.

Wieser's "paradox of value" satisfies Fetter's need of psychological explanation. It is a terminology where the term "value" is given "a subjective use" and is, in fact, an important contribution to "an understanding of recent value-discussion." Wieser's "diminishing utility" is subjective; his "marginal utility" is subjective; his functional dependence of utility on quantity is subjective; and his resulting "value" is subjective. The difficulty is that they are neither measurable nor enforceable at law, as is Fisher's magnitude of "quantity, price, and value." They do not conform to the legally enforceable units of measurement on which all transactions depend for accuracy and security. When "marginal utility" becomes price, most persons feel that it is the measure of the results of supply and demand on their particular transactions, which, for economic theory, is the principle of scarcity. When quantities of goods are produced or withheld, it is generally recognized that quantities of usefulness, or the economists' use-value, for society have been added or withheld. When a thousand tons of pig iron are sold at $20 per ton, it is generally stated that the *value* of that quantity is $20,000. This is the transactional, customary, and common-law way of looking at it.

Doubtless it was historically necessary for economic theory to pass through the psychological stage of hedonism in order to get away from the materialism of Ricardo and Marx. The discussion made revolutionary changes in the meanings of use-value and utility, and a better understanding of man's dependence on nature. But, in looking back upon it we see that it was the stage of "animism" through which every science has passed. Its quantities and forces were personified and therefore immeasurable. Alchemy became chemistry when Lavoisier dismissed spirits and measured quantities. Astrology became astronomy when the notions of spirits became Newton's laws of motion. So economic personification becomes economic science when Fetter's subjective utility or marginal utility becomes price, and Fisher's value becomes assets, measured by dollars, bushels, specifications of quality and enforced by custom and law.

X. FROM ABSOLUTISM TO RELATIVITY

Scarcity and efficiency are thus two changing ratios with which the science of economics begins. They are distinguishable but inseparable, and thus they require additional ratios to measure their changing relations to each other. The scarcity concepts descend from Smith and Malthus, the efficiency concepts from Ricardo and Marx. Their relativity was worked out deductively in the neoclassicism of Marshall.

By their method of operating with self-evident axioms, the classical, communist, and Austrian schools eliminated one or the other of the opposite terms of these ratios by assuming that its dimensions changed in proportion to changes in the other, and this became an absolutistic, instead of relativistic, scheme of concepts, somewhat analogous to the Euclidean, instead of non-Euclidean, concepts of space and time in the science of physics.

Smith and Ricardo eliminated the variability of *wants* of consumers (buyers) by assuming that they expanded or contracted equally with the supplies of materials or services offered by consumers in their function of producers (sellers). The decisive variables, therefore, in their conceptual schemes, were labor-pain with Smith, and labor-power with Ricardo and Marx.

The Austrian school (Menger, Wieser) eliminated both labor-pain and labor-power of producers (sellers) by their assumption of a "pleasure" economy, equivalent to Smith's assumption of abundance. But this pleasure, for them, kept pace with the diminishing intensity of wants of consumers (buyers), so that wants were the decisive variables in their scheme.

But Marshall coördinated the two schools by introducing the relativistic concept of changing ratios between two opposite changing quantities—the quantities wanted by consumers (buyers) and the quantities supplied by producers (sellers)—both of which were variable independently on their own account.

But there was another axiom common to all these schools which rendered absolutistic instead of relativistic all of the theories from Smith to Marshall. This was the assumption, derived from the popular concept of *corporeal* property, that everything valuable is owned, and *ownership*, therefore, was a constant factor varying exactly with the quantities of materials owned. Ownership, hence, like space or time in the science of physics, became an absolute "frame," or framework, unchangeable by its own initiative. Hence, for them, the decisive variables in the relation of ownership to materials were the changeable quantities of materials. This elimination of ownership is seen in their tacit (Austrian) or avowed (classical) assumption of the identity of production with selling and of consumption with buying. Everything produced is sold and everything consumed is bought. The assumption of identity is concealed in their double meaning of the word "exchange." If this word means selling and buying, then it means a legal process of alienating and acquiring ownership. If it means delivering and receiving materials or services, then it means a production process of adding "place utility" to the forces of nature. If, therefore, transfers of ownership (legal control) are themselves highly variable, independent of yet inseparable from the exchange of materials (or services) owned, then another relativistic concept must be constructed, which we name a transaction governed by working rules of collective action that transfer the *ownership*, whether with or without exchanging the materials.

Still another independent variable, money and credit, arising solely from the legal scheme of control, was eliminated from the classical and hedonic theories on the assumption of stability of prices, so that all changes in monetary and credit prices were equivalent to changes in labor-pain, labor-power, or pleasure or pain. Money became an absolutistic framework, itself unchangeable, while the changes occurred in the production, exchange, and consumption of products.

Scarcity and efficiency, from the relativistic standpoint, may be looked upon as variable social "forces" at work in determining the transactions of human beings. Scarcity is primarily distinguishable as power over others, and efficiency as power over nature. If they are forces, they differ in *degree* of force for each transaction, and it is the above-mentioned different *ratios* that measure differences in *degree*. Reduced to their simplest elements, these are the scarcity ratios of income to outgo in bargaining transactions, and the efficiency ratios of output to input in managerial transactions. So that two systems of measurement are used in economics, the measurement of *quantities* of materials, services, labor, money, debts, etc., and the measurement of *degrees* of force as ratios between the quantities. It is in the measurement of these *degrees* of social "force" that we shall find the problem of Reasonable Value.

Cohen, from a broader, philosophical point of view, has expressed the foregoing doctrines of relativity as the "principle of polarity." [176] He applies this principle to the several sciences and philosophies and especially to various "social philosophies." In general, it means that "opposite categories," such as individuality and universality, nominalism and realism, individualism and socialism, cosmopolitanism and nationalism, etc., "must always be kept together though never identified." They are not "incompatible alternatives," but are differences in *degree of emphasis* when applied to concrete cases, and, as such, are differences in *values* and not "real contradictions," as they are supposed to be in "the traditional controversies of philosophy." This principle of polarity, we take it, is a principle of relativity which rejects the earlier methods of elimination of factors as assumptions, or axioms, or things "taken for granted," and finds its economic concrete case in the concept of reasonable value, in a scheme where all things are continually changing by their own forces and relatively to each other.

We have suggested that the foregoing sketch of the history of economic science bears some resemblance to the history of physical science from Euclidean to non-Euclidean geometry. But there are important differences which make it misleading to speak of "Euclidean and non-Euclidean economics." The non-Euclidean physics is concerned, as shown by Reichenbach, with the "microscopic" and "macroscopic" relations of the universe, as affecting the basic concepts of space and time. But economics is concerned with the ordinary, everyday experiences of mankind in the world of "medium dimensions" midway between these extremes of the problems of physics. [177] Our analogy holds true only in so far as economic science is passing from what we name the absolutistic to the relativistic point of view. The customary ideas of space and time, employed in economics, are not dependent on microscopes or telescopes.

We do not mean that earlier schools of economists did not make *change* fundamental in their schemes. Indeed, what they were attempting was an explanation of the very changes brought about by the monetary, industrial, economic, and political revolutions since the discovery of America. Their absolutism consisted in carrying through their whole system of economics by making the changes occur in only *one* of many conflicting and simultaneous or successive changes.

An additional variable, conceived as something objective which can be measured by constructing appropriate units of measurement,

---

[176] Cohen, Morris R., *Reason and Nature* (1931).

[177] Distinctions made in popular form by Reichenbach, Hans, *Atom and Cosmos* (tr. 1933).

instead of something subjective and individualistic and therefore immeasurable and absolute, we summarize, in its most abstract form, as the principle of Futurity, separable in thought, but inseparable in fact, from the principles of Scarcity and Efficiency.

The concept of Time, in economic science distinguished from physical science, has shifted from the *past* time of classical and communistic theory, into the *present* time of hedonistic theory, until it is becoming the *future* time of waiting, risking, purpose, and planning. These are the problems of Futurity, another economic "force," not found in the physical sciences, but nevertheless approximately measurable in all the diversities of reasonable value. The transition from *posteriority* to *futurity* does not involve contradiction. It is another case of Cohen's "polarity," or differences in degree of emphasis among the various schools of economic philosophy.

CHAPTER IX

FUTURITY

I. THE NEGOTIABILITY OF DEBT

1. *Debts and Commodities*

When the science of Political Economy began to emerge in the Eighteenth Century, it fell in line with the theory, then dominant, of an original state of liberty and rationality of human beings. It was Rousseau, in his famous book *The Social Contract* (1762), who popularized the theory. Man was originally free but government had made him a slave. Man was also a rational being who would act according to reason if only he were free. This was the theory of the Declaration of Independence and the French Revolution. It remained the primary assumption of the classical, optimist, and psychological schools. They based their theories on an absolutely free individual who knows his own interest, and, if allowed freely to act, then the sum total of all acts would be a harmony of interests.

These theories of liberty and rationality accomplished extraordinary results in overthrowing absolute monarchies, abolishing slavery, and establishing universal education. But it was not because they were historically true—it was because they set up ideals for the future. Historically it is more accurate to say that the bulk of mankind lived in a state of unreleasable debts, and that liberty came by gradually substituting releasable debts. And historically it is more accurate to say, as Malthus said, that man is originally a being of passion and stupidity for whom liberty and reason are a matter of the slow evolution of moral character and the discipline enforced by government.

With the modern development of historical research, and especially with the aid of the modern sciences of sociology, anthropology, and historical jurisprudence, it is possible to reverse the Eighteenth Century illusion of an original state of liberty and reason, and to show the actual but resisted steps by which, out of the practices and aims of subordinate classes, releasable debts became the foundation of modern capitalism. Political economy becomes, not a science of individual liberty, but a science of the creation, negotiability, release, and scarcity of debt.

What we now know as the business classes who buy and sell, hire and fire, borrow and lend, and are now the "paymasters" of other classes, because they have legal control of industry, were originally slaves, serfs, or peddlers, who had no rights of citizenship, but depended upon the willingness and ability of feudal lords and kings to grant and enforce special privileges. The privilege most desired was self-government, that is, collective control of their own membership, free from the arbitrary violence of feudal lords. With this collective immunity they could set up their own courts and make their own rules for deciding disputes among themselves.

In this way originated the Merchant Guilds and the Law Merchant, and then the Craft Guilds; by means of which contracts and customs suitable to merchandising, manufacturing, and foreign trade were developed and enforced by their own courts, quite similar to those which we find nowadays in commercial arbitration and labor arbitration.

But the merchants and manufacturers needed more than immunity from aggression—they needed also the aid of courts created by the sovereign to enforce their contracts and customs, just as the movement for commercial arbitration is now going forward to obtain legislation requiring the law courts to enforce the awards made in their own arbitration courts. This latter movement is a curious repetition of what began to occur four hundred years ago in the courts of England, from which the common-law method of the American courts was derived.

Prior to the Sixteenth Century there was comparatively little buying and selling. It was limited to fairs and commercial boroughs. Only landlords and wealthy people could make contracts which the common-law courts would enforce. These people were distinguished above all others in that each had a seal which he could stamp in the wax on a lengthy document, as evidence of his promise to pay. It was named a "specialty." The transaction required time and solemn formality. It remains today in the sale and mortgage of real estate, though, under the Torrens system originating in Australia, even these formalities are done away with by a simple system of registration similar to the registration of ownership of automobiles.

But the merchants, who bought and sold commodities, did not have leisure, wealth, or political power. Their "parol" contracts could not always be enforced in court. But during the Sixteenth Century they became necessary and influential. The courts must now devise a way to enforce their hundreds and thousands of contracts. After several years of experiment the ingenuity of lawyers invented a simple assumption, which they read into the minds of the parties to a transaction. It was the assumption that merchants did not intend to rob, or steal, or misrepresent, but they intended to do what was right. This meant that if a merchant physically delivered a commodity to another person with the intention of making him the owner of it, then the other person intended to pay for it. Even if the price was not mentioned he intended to pay what was right. He assumed the duty to pay.

This is the "parol" contract, or rather, the behavior contract. Since the Statute of Frauds it is limited to contracts of small amounts. Yet it remains in the rules of the stock exchange where millions of dollars' worth of property is transferred in a few minutes by mere signs between frenzied brokers, the contracts to be enforced by the Stock Exchange itself, although they do not become enforceable in court until written. When a foreman accepts the product of a laborer, or the materials from a supplier, the corporation intends to pay for it. We take this intent for granted *now*, as a law of nature; but it was the invention of lawyers four hundred years ago. Mere acceptance of commodities creates a lawful debt, even though, psychologically, there may have been no intention to pay.

But this was not enough for the merchants. They needed also the legal power to buy and sell debts. It required the entire Seventeenth Century for lawyers to complete the invention of the negotiability of debts. What the merchants wanted was to convert their debts into money. In early history money had been a mere money of account, like the ox in Greece; then it became a metallic commodity. Then kings stamped the metal and made it the lawful means of paying taxes and paying private debts. Coined money then ceased to be a commodity. It became an institution, namely, Legal Tender, the collective means of paying public and private debts.

Two attributes had therefore to be given to coined money in order to distinguish it from commodities, and these again were the inventions of lawyers. One was negotiability, the other was release from debt.

If a merchant, in good faith, receives stolen coin from a thief in payment for goods, the money becomes his property, as against all the world, including the man from whom it was stolen. The thief acquired the amazing legal power to give good title to something he did not own. This is the meaning of negotiability. It had to be distinguished from assignability. A person cannot transfer to another a better title than he owns. He can assign only his "equity"

—the buyer is still liable for any liens upon the property. This is assignability. But the "buyer" of the so-called commodity, coined money, that is, the seller of goods, gets a complete title to the money, free from any obligation to prove his title. This is negotiability. Thus coined money differs from bullion, and even from foreign coins, not legal tender in the importing country. Bullion or foreign coins may be stolen and sold, and yet recovered by the lawful owner. Money may be stolen and, if received by the seller in good faith, "for value received," it cannot be recovered. The rightful owner can only sue somebody else for damages.

If the merchants' debts, therefore, were to be made like money they must also be made negotiable. Here another difficulty stood in the way. A promise had been considered a duty to fulfill the promise only to the person to whom the promise was made. It was a personal matter. A promise to work,[1] a promise to 'marry, cannot even yet be sold to a third party. It would be slavery, peonage, or concubinage, under the guise of freedom of contract. But why should not a promise to pay legal tender money, in specified amounts at specified dates, be sold to third parties in exchange for goods, even though the money is not yet in existence? It required not only the Seventeenth Century but all of the centuries following to invent ways of making this kind of promise negotiable. In the end, the law of "negotiable instruments" became a body of legal arrangements that converted the mere expectations of money into money itself.[2]

Parallel with this long period of developing the negotiability of debt was developing the idea of the natural right to private property. This right could not be made effective in England until Sovereignty was separated from property by the Revolution of 1689. As long as the sovereign could claim arbitrary authority over the lives and property of his subjects, there could not exist, as we have seen in the debate of Filmer and Locke, any inviolable right of property, however "natural" or "divine" it was claimed to be.

But this right of property contained in itself for another 150 years the two contradictory meanings of a commodity—the material thing and the ownership of the material. The brilliant work of the classical economists could be consistent only because they carried within themselves an unseen inconsistency. This did not stand out until the two decades of 1840 to 1860, when four schools of heterodox economists arose from this basic contradiction of the orthodox

---

[1] Exception has been made in cases of *irreplaceable* labor, such as actors and baseball players.

[2] Cf. Commons, John R., *Legal Foundations of Capitalism*, 235–261.

schools.   Proudhon converted this contradiction into anarchism, Marx into communism, Carey and Bastiat into optimism, but Mac-Leod took the ownership meaning of a commodity and left the physical meaning to production and consumption.

This double meaning of a commodity had always been both the popular and the economist's meaning.   The commodity was a useful thing that could be bought and sold, but while it was being used, either for production or consumption, it was not a commodity.   It was then only materials—including land, equipment, unfinished materials in process of production, or consumption materials in the hands of the ultimate consumer and no longer for sale.   Only on the markets was it a commodity.

What MacLeod did was to create the concept of "an economic quantity," saleable on the markets, and to substitute it for the physical materials of the classical economists.   This economic quantity he named a Debt, the economic equivalent of a legal Duty. This concept of an "economic quantity" was so strange to the economists that they could not understand it, but we find that it is the equivalent of the modern meaning of Capital.   This modern meaning is essentially a legal concept, since it is based solely on ownership.   Its strangeness to the classical economists consisted in that it contained Futurity as one of its dimensions, as well as the use-value and scarcity-value of the older schools.   Yet futurity is the essence of the ownership side of a commodity, which they had taken for granted.

Hence for the lawyer, MacLeod, it was not the materials, it was their *ownership* that was bought and sold by the legal process of alienation and acquisition.   Any ownership, therefore, and not the materials owned, was a "commodity."   One kind of ownership was the ownership of physical things—corporeal property.   The other was the ownership of debts—incorporeal property.   Both ownerships were therefore "commodities," since both could be alienated and acquired, the one on the commodity market, the other on the debt market.

Thus MacLeod, in 1856, the first lawyer-economist, was the first to develop the idea of a debt market.   He brought together in one generalization the exchange of ownership on the commodity market proper and exchange of ownership on the debt market.   For this reason he made "exchangeability" the only principle with which economics had to deal.   This exchangeability, he claimed quite correctly, had been actually the main principle of the classical economists.

MacLeod conceived, however, as he said, two classes of economic quantities exchanged against each other in that double transfer of ownership which we think has always been understood to be the meaning of a "transaction" as distinguished from an "exchange." Each economic quantity is indeed a debt created by a transaction. One is the debt of a seller to deliver a physical material, say 1,000 tons of steel, within a brief future, which we distinguish as a duty of *performance*. The other was a debt of the buyer to pay for the steel, in say 60 days, which we name a duty of *payment*. These debts are the economic equivalents of legal duties. Neither of these duties was a material thing, yet they had value in exchange. So here came in MacLeod's concept of an "economic quantity," a debt, equivalent to his concept of legal duty, which was, of course, not a physical quantity but which nevertheless was a saleable quantity, and therefore an economic quantity.

2. *Debt Market and Debt Pyramid*

It is upon MacLeod's distinction between the debt market and the commodity market that we are able to build the formula of a Debt Market and a Debt Pyramid, fitting his theory to the Federal Reserve System as of June 29, 1924. The debt market is usually known as the "money market," although it is only the market made possible by the negotiability of debts. Its daily record is the credits and debits of the Federal Reserve System, all the way from the 48 million buyers and sellers in gainful occupations, to the member and even non-member banks to whom these buyers and sellers transfer the ownership of their debts created by transactions, to be transferred again, if needed, to the 12 Reserve banks, themselves co ordinated by the Federal Reserve Board and the Treasury of the United States.

Non-member banks, and even Central banks of other countries on the "gold exchange" system, have access to the Reserve banks by selling their commercial debts to member banks, so that even the whole world is tied together by the negotiability of debts. This will appear at many points as we go along.

The amazing superstructure created by this system, through the impounding of gold in the central banks, has rightly been named "the Debt Pyramid," and the complexities are pictured in Charts 6 and 7. The interactions of this huge debt market based on a minimum of gold may be found in entire volumes published elsewhere, but we must pass on to a critical examination of the foundations laid by MacLeod.

There were several defects in MacLeod's reasoning, partly legal, partly economic, traceable mainly to the materialistic concepts of the classical economists by whom he was surrounded, and to the difficulties in his effort to construct the novel concept of an "economic quantity" which should not be materialistic. We shall trace

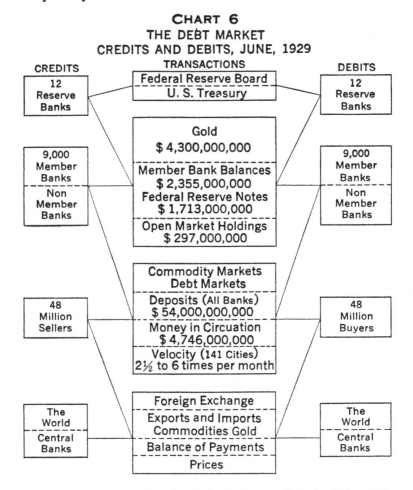

CHART 6
THE DEBT MARKET
CREDITS AND DEBITS, JUNE, 1929

CREDITS | TRANSACTIONS | DEBITS

| 12 Reserve Banks | Federal Reserve Board / U. S. Treasury | 12 Reserve Banks |

| 9,000 Member Banks / Non Member Banks | Gold $ 4,300,000,000 / Member Bank Balances $ 2,355,000,000 / Federal Reserve Notes $ 1,713,000,000 / Open Market Holdings $ 297,000,000 | 9,000 Member Banks / Non Member Banks |

| 48 Million Sellers | Commodity Markets / Debt Markets / Deposits (All Banks) $ 54,000,000,000 / Money in Circulation $ 4,746,000,000 / Velocity (141 Cities) 2½ to 6 times per month | 48 Million Buyers |

| The World / Central Banks | Foreign Exchange / Exports and Imports Commodities Gold / Balance of Payments / Prices | The World / Central Banks |

Compiled in part from data in *Federal Reserve Bulletin*, July, 1929, and December, 1929.

the solution of these difficulties from MacLeod's negotiability of debt (1856), through Sidgwick's distinction of the money market and capital market (1883); Wicksell's world debt-paying community (1898); Cassel's scarcity of waiting (1903); Knapp's release of debt (1905); Hawtrey's creation of debt (1919); and Fisher's over-indebtedness and depressions (1932). These were all developed out of MacLeod's writings beginning in 1856.

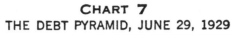

CHART 7
THE DEBT PYRAMID, JUNE 29, 1929

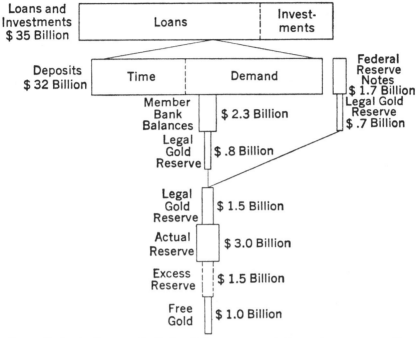

From *Federal Reserve Bulletin*, July, 1929, and December, 1929. "Free Gold" figure by courtesy of the Federal Reserve Board.

3. *Property and Property Rights*

"If it were asked," said MacLeod, "what discovery has most deeply affected the fortunes of the human race, it might probably be said with truth—*The discovery that a Debt is a Saleable Commodity. . . .* When Daniel Webster said that Credit has done more a thousand times to enrich nations than all the mines of all the world, he meant the discovery that a Debt is a Saleable Commodity or Chattel: and that it may be used like Money: and produce all the effects of Money." [3]

This saleable commodity, according to MacLeod, is "Wealth"! We name it "assets."

In fact, neither a debt nor ownership is wealth. They are institutions. We name them quantitatively as assets and liabilities, which we consider to be the business man's meaning of capital. By the legal invention of negotiability, gradually taken over from the custom of merchants during the Seventeenth Century, a debt

[3] MacLeod, Henry Dunning, *The Theory and Practice of Banking*, 2 vols. (1st ed., 1856; 6th ed. of 1923 cited), I, 200; *The Elements of Economics*, 2 vols. (1867; ed. of 1881 cited). Condensed statement in his *Economics for Beginners* (1884; 6th impression 1900, cited).

has been made saleable like the ownership of a commodity, and especially like the legal tender commodity, coined money. When a banker buys a debt, he is not buying a physical material, he is buying the institution called debt. And when a manufacturer buys physical material he is buying, not the material, but the ownership of the material.

MacLeod has been charged with counting the same thing twice, once as a physical thing, once as a property right. On this account his name has disappeared from the authoritative list of economists,[4] notwithstanding his great discovery of the principle of discount banking in regulating the inflow and outflow of gold, afterwards adopted by the Bank of England.

MacLeod did count something twice, but it was not the *thing* and the *right* to the thing, for he eliminated physical things altogether from economics and counted only the transferable right of ownership of debts and commodities. Yet he counted several other "things" twice—he counted two kinds of property rights—corporeal and incorporeal—as two existences during a year of time. He counted intangible property as a debt whereas it is the negation of debt.

Since he was the first, and indeed the only economist, to analyze the economics of legal rights on the basis of a lawyer's encyclopedic knowledge of the law,[5] and since his fallacies and the misunderstandings of his critics have confirmed economists in their adherence to Bentham's substitution of pain and pleasure for Blackstone's law and custom, we should discover wherein MacLeod's fallacies reside, and thereby discover how they may be corrected. For we conceive that, when once his physical metaphors and double-counting are eliminated, the way is clear for building economic theory on Property Rights, as he attempted to do.

The fundamental idea on which MacLeod's system is based, confused though it is by physical metaphors, is the principle of Futurity contained in the legal meaning of Rights and Duties. Futurity, for MacLeod, embodies itself objectively in a present "economic quantity," Credit, the equivalent of debt.

A proper assignment of MacLeod to his place may best begin with the criticism made by Böhm-Bawerk who himself did most of all economists to bring Futurity into subjective economics. Böhm-Bawerk, too, overlapped his subjective Futurity with technological concepts of Efficiency, much as MacLeod overlapped his legal

[4] His name did not appear in Palgrave's *Dictionary of Political Economy* until the edition of 1923.
[5] MacLeod was selected by a Royal Commission to prepare a digest of the law of bills, notes, etc., reproduced in *The Theory and Practice of Banking* and his *Elements of Economics.*

Futurity with physical metaphors. He eliminated MacLeod's "Rights and Relations" from economic theory, as MacLeod eliminated what afterwards was Böhm-Bawerk's psychology. With MacLeod, psychological desire, though fundamental, was immeasurable, and therefore furnished no basis for science. But, with Böhm-Bawerk, rights were social relations and involved double-counting.

Böhm-Bawerk observes [6] that economists have alternated between four independent concepts derived from a single physical object—fresh drinking water, for example. First is the physical thing, the water; second is its inherent objective quality, usefulness or utility; third is its useful service to man; fourth is the right to the water.

The first of these, the physical thing itself regardless of its qualities, Böhm-Bawerk rightly rejected because it could not be a subject-matter for economists, except as the bearer of its useful qualities. What they did was to select certain qualities, abstracted from other qualities. MacLeod's quality was exchangeability, which he identified with "wealth," and which was common to all of Böhm-Bawerk's four concepts.

If we examine the several meanings thus combined in the word "wealth" and distinguished by Böhm-Bawerk as his second, third, and fourth items, we shall find that they are really the starting points of three different sciences, each of which goes under the name of "Economics," but each of which is differentiated in modern research and instruction. Böhm-Bawerk's "inherent objective quality"—usefulness or utility, which we name technological use-value—is the subject-matter of Engineering and Home Economics. This is production of use-value without regard to MacLeod's test of exchangeability, or "bringing it into commerce." Böhm-Bawerk's "useful service to man" is the production and consumption of wealth, wherein the satisfaction of wants predominates, and this has become the subject-matter of Home Economics.[7] His "right to the water" is the subject-matter of legal control of persons through rights, duties, liberties, and exposures, and this is Institutional Economics, of which MacLeod was the originator.

The Physiocrats and Ricardo were agricultural and engineering economists; the Hedonists, including Böhm-Bawerk himself, were

[6] Böhm-Bawerk, E. von, *Rechte und Verhältnisse* (1881). His "relations" were what we call the intangible property of good-will, trade-marks, etc. Böhm-Bawerk's subsequent works cannot be understood except by reference to this earlier foundation which he laid in 1881.

[7] The "farm economists," who were originally home economists, have recently taken over markets and call themselves agricultural economists.

home economists; the institutionalists were proprietary economists. By double and treble meanings of words, by analogies, metaphors, and personifications, these different disciplines have historically been confused and overlapped. This is inevitable, because each "quality" operates within a "field" composed of the others, and the selection of any one is a mental operation of analysis, experiment, judgment, and purpose.

The predecessors of MacLeod, the Physiocratic and Classical economists, selected the second quality, namely, use-value, but mixed it with the others, and their "legitimate" offspring is engineering and agricultural economics. The psychological economists, like Böhm-Bawerk himself, selected the third, namely, useful service to man, and their offspring is home economics. But those whom we name the institutional economists selected the fourth, namely, rights of property.

The misunderstanding of MacLeod arises in part from the double meaning of "property." MacLeod cleared this up, but was not understood.

> "Most persons," he says, "when they speak or hear of Property, think of some material things, such as lands, houses, cattle, money, etc." But that is not the true meaning of Property. The word "Property, in its true and original sense, does not mean a material thing; but the absolute right to use and dispose of something. . . . Property . . . in its true sense means solely a Right, Interest, or Ownership; and, consequently, to call material goods Property is as absurd as to call them Right, Interest, Ownership." [8]

It is not "land, houses, cattle, corn," he goes on, but it is "property" in land, houses, cattle, and corn "and all other material things," that economics deals with. Property is the same as property rights; the material things have no value for economics except as they can lawfully be owned and their ownership lawfully transferred. Any other kind of holding or transferring is embezzlement, robbery, theft. Other sciences deal with things—economics deals with legal rights over things. Thus he shifted physical things to the future, and substituted his "economic quantity," the present rights to the future uses of the things.

Since MacLeod thus eliminated the double meaning of material things and ownership of the things, which came from his predecessors, and dealt therefore solely with property in the sense of rights to future things, the criticism upon his theory should be directed, not against his supposed double counting of *things* and *rights*, but

[8] MacLeod, H. D., *Economics for Beginners*, 23, 24.

against his double counting of *rights* themselves. This arose from his double meaning of the word Credit and from his inability to emancipate himself completely from the physical analogies of preceding lawyers and economists. It was his critics who did the double counting of property and things, and they overlook MacLeod's assertions that he does not count physical things at all as subject-matter of the science of economics.

He, however, left the misunderstanding for them in that he used their physical concepts to express his meanings. He counted the same thing only once, as the exchangeability of property-rights, which he called "property," and gave to all property rights the meaning of what he called an economic quantity, "credit." Economists had taken it for granted that a commodity was property. That was therefore a constant quality, and they could devote themselves to the physical production, transportation, exchange, distribution, and consumption of materials regardless of any variability in the assumed equivalent quality, property rights. But MacLeod eliminated the physical things as belonging to other sciences, and devoted himself to the exchangeability of rights to those things. Indeed, the fact that a certain species of property-rights, "saleable debts," was independently variable on its own debt market, was for him the starting-point of his system. But in this respect saleable debts were not different from property-rights in general—all property is credit and debt, he contended, since it is the expectation of receiving something valuable from others. And this mere expectation can be bought and sold.

4. *Corporeal, Incorporeal, Intangible Property*

(1) **Time and the Measure of Time.**—MacLeod had grave difficulty in distinguishing the present from the past and the future. In one place the present is a *zero* point of time; in the same connection it is *one year* into the future.[9] This is his distinction between "corporeal" and "incorporeal" property. Corporeal property extends into one year of the future. But incorporeal property extends solely into the future after corporeal property has ceased. Incorporeal property in one place begins at the present zero point of time, and at another place begins after one year of the future.

First, as to his zero point of time.

"Property, like Janus," he said, "has two faces placed back to back. It regards the *Past* and the *Future*," and is therefore "of Opposite qualities. . . . Now in all mathematical and physical

[9] MacLeod, H. D., *The Elements of Economics*, I, 154–159.

sciences it is invariably the custom to denote *Similar* Quantities but of *Opposite* qualities, by *Opposite* signs. Hence, as a matter of simple convenience, and following the invariable custom in Physical Science, if we denote one of these kinds of property as *Positive,* we may as a distinguishing mark denote the other as *Negative.* . . . If we denote property in a thing which *has been* acquired in time *past* as Positive, we may denote Property in a thing which is *to be* acquired in time *future* as *Negative.*" [10]

Now "mathematicians know," he says, "that we can perform the same operations with negative signs as with positive signs." And so MacLeod represented "property in the produce of the past," which he named corporeal property, by the positive sign *plus* ($+$), and "property in the produce of the future," named incorporeal property, by the negative sign *minus* ($-$). He showed them thus:

THE TOTALITY OF TRANSFERABLE PROPERTY [11]

PROPERTY IN THE PRODUCE OF THE PAST	PRESENT	PROPERTY IN THE PRODUCE OF THE FUTURE
Corporeal	o	Incorporeal Property
Positive ($+$)		Negative ($-$)
Lands, houses, etc...........	......	Annual income for ever
Money already earned by a merchant	......	His credit
Premises, stock of goods in a shop	......	The good-will
Money already earned by a professional man........	......	The practice
The printed copies of books, etc...	......	The copyright
Machines already made........	......	The patent
The capital of a commercial company............	......	The shares; annuities of all sorts; the funds; tolls; ferries; ground rent, etc.

Corporeal property, as seen in this tabular statement, is property rights in materials already produced. But in the same connection he says that corporeal property exists into one year of the future.

". . . though the yearly products of the land will only come into existence at future intervals of time, the Right or Property in them when they do come into existence is Present, and may be bought and sold like any material chattel, such as a table, a chair, or so much corn. That is to say, each of these annual products for ever has a *Present Value:* and the purchase money of the land is simply the Sum of the *Present Values* of this series

[10] *Ibid.,* I, 154–155.
[11] *Ibid.,* I, 159.

of future products for ever. Again, although this series of future products is infinite, a simple algebraical formula shows that it has a finite limit: and that finite limit depends chiefly upon the current average Rate of Interest. When the usual Rate of Interest is 3 per cent., the total Value of Land is about 33 times its annual value: consequently 32 parts of the 33 of the total Property in Land is Incorporeal: the remaining one part only being Corporeal." [12]

Here *corporeal* property is the expectation of one year, and *incorporeal* property does not begin until the end of that first year. This contradicts his tabular statement in which incorporeal property begins at a present zero point of time, but here his corporeal property seems to have no futurity, not even one year of futurity. The fact is, of course, that the *value* of his corporeal property includes all of his future "33 times its annual value." If so, then his corporeal property itself is also "incorporeal" property and should be transferred to the negative side of his tabular statement.[13]

The corporeal or positive side disappears altogether both *as property* and *as value*. It *may* have been property in the past and it *may* have had value in the past, but that is because the *past* was the *then present* and had the future before it. But now when that past is gone, at the present zero point of time, there has gone with it both property rights and the value of those rights.

In fact, the meaning of corporeal property is twofold, each looking towards the future. It means *holding* for one's own future use, and it means withholding from others what they need but do not own. The former is MacLeod's meaning when he speaks of the present right to the annual products forever. But they are not merely *annual* products. They are the right to have for one's own use *all* the future products immediately or remotely in the future.

The second meaning is "exchangeability," the right to withhold from others until a price is agreed upon. This right, as he correctly says, does not wait a year. It is a right which begins immediately at his present zero point of time. But this right of exchangeability is his meaning of the negotiability or assignability of both incorporeal and corporeal property.

He was brought to this double counting of future time by his rather crude confusion of Time with the measurement of time, namely, the year, or the "annual" income. He said,

"Debts or Credits are Commodities which are bought and sold like any material chattels: and for the convenience of Sale they

[12] *Ibid.*, 156–157.
[13] We name it, as below, "intangible" instead of "incorporeal."

must be divided into certain units: Coals are sold by the ton: corn by the quarter: sugar by the pound: and other things by the ounce. The *Unit of Debt* is the *Right to demand* £100 to be *paid one year hence*. The sum of money given to buy this Unit of Debt is its Price: and of course, the less the Price given to buy the fixed Unit of Debt, the greater is the Value of Money." [14]

Thus, if the debt is $100 payable at the end of one year, and the banker pays a price, $95, for it, the value of the banker's money is slightly over $5 per year. But if the price paid by the banker is reduced to $90, then the value of his money per year is slightly over $10.

This is, of course, only a *rate per year*, as he well understood, but it is the language of the money market which speaks of the "value" of money or the "price" of money as the rate of interest per year. Yet, treated as "discount" on the debt market this discount actually does occur at the present point of time, though the interval of future time may be one day or 90 days, converted for convenience to a unit of measurement, one year. Yet his notion of the "price of a debt," enabled MacLeod to make his important discovery of the proper discount policy of the Bank of England in controlling the outflow and inflow of gold.[15]

Consequently, MacLeod's concept of "the present," which starts in his tabular statement with a zero point of time between the past and the future, is shifted to an interval between two points of time —the beginning and ending of a year. It is on account of this curious overlapping during one year of future time that the criticism is plausible of double counting of a physical thing and the right to the thing. But he did not count the physical thing at all—he counted the ownership of the thing. His double counting was a double counting of future time, in the case only of corporeal property for one's own use, during one year of the future.

This overlapping of the future during MacLeod's first unfortunate year of the future must be looked upon as a trailing cloud of materialism from the commodity economists, and his own failure to distinguish consistently their corporeal *things*, coming up from the past, from his corporeal *property*, which looks only to the future as certainly as does his incorporeal property.

In fact, as suggested above, he did not use this double meaning in his system of economic theory, because his central idea was exchangeability. Economics, he says, deals only with exchange-values,

[14] MacLeod, H. D., *The Theory and Practice of Banking*, I, 57.
[15] Below, p. 429, Discount and Profit.

not with use-values which he held were psychological. Only exchange-values can be measured by money. Therefore the right of corporeal property, which he really intends, is the right, not to *use* the thing but is the right to *alienate the ownership* of the thing and to give a good title to the buyer.

This right of alienation does not wait a year, as he himself stated, and involves no overlapping of time or corporeal and incorporeal rights. The owner can give good title *now* if he has now the legal ownership. And he can *now* obtain the exchange-value of his right to the land or any other of his "corporeal" property, without waiting a year, though he may wait a year to get for himself the ownership of the crop which the land will produce. But the right of *alienation*, with which alone MacLeod deals, begins at the present point of time, and it is this that makes possible the present right to the exchange-value of the land, or to its future product, or to anything else. His "totality of transferable property" is assuredly his own more correct picture, wherein the present is a zero point of time instead of a future year of time.

That he does eliminate one year of the future from his meaning of corporeal property is seen in the same connection.

> We may have, he says, "a Property, or Right wholly severed and separated from any specific *corpus*, or matter in possession. It may not even be in existence at the present time. Thus those who possess lands, fruit trees, cattle, etc., have the Property in their future produce. Though the produce itself will only come into existence at a future time, the Property or Right to it when it does come into existence is Present, and may be bought and sold like any material chattel. Or the thing may be in existence, but it may be some one else's Property at the present time; and only come into our possession at some future time. Thus one may have the right to demand a sum of money from some person at some future time. That sum of money may, no doubt, be in existence, but it is not in our possession: it may not even be in the possession of the person who is bound to pay it. It may pass through any number of hands before it is paid to us. But yet our Right to demand it is present and existing, and we may sell and dispose of it as if it were a material chattel. Hence it is Property; but it is called *Incorporeal Property* in Roman and English law, because it is a mere abstract Right, wholly severed from any specific substance." [16]

Thus both corporeal and incorporeal property begin at the present point of time, and both are the present valuations that look forward to acquisitions in the future.

[16] MacLeod, H. D., *The Elements of Economics*, I, rearranged from pp. 152-156.

The commodity economists of the classical school ignored Time as a factor in economic theory, because, for them, time was only a mental abstraction and therefore had no economic value. And they were correct from their standpoint, because their units of investigation were material things (assuming that corporeal property was identical with the materials) and their method of investigation was an analogy to Newton's laws of motion of material bodies.

Time does not exist in the subject-matter of these physical sciences. It is placed there by human experience. Material things, and even animal life, have no idea of time. They just go on without thinking about it. But man, by his social activity of language and the making of tools for future use, constructs a sequence of future time which he gets out of himself and then reads into the world about him. Eventually, out of his own activity he constructs the abstract idea of time.

The first difficulty is the confusion of Time with the Measurement of Time. On this account no precise distinction could be made between the past, present, and future. With MacLeod, who first attempted to introduce time into economic theory, the idea of "the present" wavered between a point of time and a year of time. The present, for economists, like historians, had been the current events without any precise duration.

It required the whole of the Nineteenth Century, and even until the mathematical statistics of the Twentieth Century, for economists to find a place in economic theory, for Time and its Measurement. From these results we derive a distinction between a point of time and a duration of time, as well as a distinction between materials and ownership.

If we define "the present" as a moving zero *point* of time (MacLeod, mathematics), or as a moving *instant* of time without measurable dimensions (Peirce, Bergson), between the incoming future and the outgoing past, then there is no double counting of materials and ownership. The materials are mere physical accumulations from the past up to the present point of time. They do not exist as *ownership* or *value* for human beings until, from the present point of time, futurity is attributed to them. For ownership (corporeal and incorporeal property) is always a present right to a future use or sale of the materials immediately as well as in the remote future. The materials, as mere physical existences, are always in the past. They have, in themselves no futurity. But ownership and valuation of those materials always look to the future. The two are separated by a moving point of time, the present, when materials end, because in and of themselves they have no expectations; but their ownership and value begin at that moving point of time, the present, because these are human expectations regarding them.

This moving point of time which changes materials into ownership and value, has been pictured, during the past forty years, as a "flow" of time. A flow of time, in the physical sciences, is a succession of events. But, in economics, which is a science of human expectations, a "flow of time" is an *expected* succession of events.

But there is another quite different concept of future time, the *interval* between a present and a future point of time. This interval is usually distinguished as a "lapse" of time, but economists define it more precisely in human affairs as an *expected* interval between a present point of time and a future point of time. Böhm-Bawerk, in 1889, was the first to analyse the psychological foundations of this future *interval* of time. But its practical application is in the transactions which transfer titles of ownership. The transaction takes effect at a present point of time, say 12 o'clock September 1, 1932. It creates two debts (incorporeal property), a debt of future *performance* or delivery of materials, or services, whose ownership has been alienated by the transaction, and a debt of future *payment*, owed by him who has acquired ownership by the transaction. In other words, each transaction occurs at a point of time when ownership is alienated and acquired. But that transaction relates only to the future which alone gives *value* to the ownership.

It is this distinction between an expected "flow" of time, during which transactions successively occur, and an expected "lapse" of time during which waiting occurs, that finally permits the distinction between profits and interest, which had always previously been merged into one. Profit and loss occur in the repetition of transactions at successive points of time, but interest accrues during the interval between two points of time.[17]

(2) **Justification and Economics.**—If economics, as a science of human nature, deals only with the future which alone gives value to present ownership, what becomes of *past* materials, *past* ownership, and *past* valuations? They become merely *justifications* for what the individual does in the present or intends to do in the future.

We must place ourselves in the strictly human position of Peirce's notion of memory, activity, and expectation, at each successive instant of time. The past has gone, at that instant of time, but

[17] On the failure to distinguish a "flow" from a "lapse" of time see below, p. 649, Veblen

memory restores it in a double direction: the materials that have accrued up to the present, and the justification of the ownership now claimed in the present for the future. One is the accruals of past labor, the other is the vested rights claimed on account of lawful activities in the past. The latter were the "natural" rights of John Locke and the "property" of MacLeod.

If we look to the past, then all of the useful materials accumulated up to the present point of time were the social use-values of Marx's social labor-power acting in the past. Their *ownership* also has been historically divided into public and private property. Yet they are continually disappearing as property in the outgoing past which now has no longer any value, and are reappearing as property in the incoming future, which alone gives to them a present value. They reappear as value, assets, liabilities, ownership, transactions, and debts, for purposes of future production and consumption, future alienation and acquisition. They now, in the moving present, have no value accumulated from the past, as was imputed by the labor-theory of Ricardo and Marx, for value is only an expectation of future income and outgo.

They have, indeed, Marx's social *use-value*, his term for wealth, but that is a social concept, on which he built his justification of common ownership for the future. That kind of value will continue, if production and replacement continue, but it is not a value for the individual unless he can now expect to have a share of the social wealth for his private use. This expected share is private property.

Thus it is the same with property, or ownership, as with value. If the materials were property or value in the past, it was only because, at successive points of time, the past was the *then* present, looking towards the *then* future.

All that the present owner, therefore, can get out of his contemplation of the past is some kind of justification, argument, or pleading, for his present claim to rights of ownership. If a doubt or dispute arises he can justify himself in his argument before a court on his claims of present ownership, which is his present right either to pass a good title to others or to use the materials himself. His justifications are addressed to the court in such form as he expects the court will accept. These may be made on the general grounds of prevailing custom, combined with the specific grounds of what he has himself lawfully done in the past, such as his *past* labor and enterprise; or his *past* uncontested exercise of the rights of ownership; or his *past* lawful acquisition of ownership by inheritance; or his *past* lawful transactions in acquiring ownership by alienation of other lawful rights of ownership; or by any other effective method of pleading on the grounds of what happened in the past. This is justification of ownership, not the ownership itself; and is a justification of the present and intended economic activity which is the subject-matter of the science of economics.

This confusion of justification and economics is almost universal in popular, economic, and legal language, and is the prime difficulty at the threshold of economic science. As soon as an economic analysis reaches a disagreeable conclusion, the person who disagrees is prone to swing immediately from economics to justification or crimination. He appeals to a "natural right," a vested right, to what he has acquired in the past according to law and custom. But that is justification and not economics. Economics asks, What *is* that right to do as one pleases now and hereafter? What is the *value* of that right in the present? What *ought* to be the right or its value in view of conflicting rights of others, and of the social consequences of exercising that right?

Hence we conclude that MacLeod's *plus* sign for the past is justification; his *minus* sign for the future is corporeal, incorporeal, and intangible property. His *zero* sign for the moving present is transactions, valuations, and discounts of the future. This zero point of time separates justification from economics.

But MacLeod had two other defects in his analysis of Futurity: a lack of identity of credit and debt, and a double meaning of credit as debts and as sales.

(3) **Duty and Debt, Right and Credit.**—More serious than his overlapping of past and future time is MacLeod's failure to count the two opposing sides of the future as existing together in the present.

The negotiability of debts, by reason of a curious accident in the English common law, repeated in American law but not found in continental law, had separated the existence of a credit from the existence of the equivalent debt, holding that the *credit* comes into existence at the date of the transaction, whereas the *debt* does not come into existence until the later date when the *personal duty* to pay arrives. The "credit" can be bought and sold before the duty to pay the debt comes into existence.

This was a failure to identify a legal duty with what MacLeod had himself already named its "economic quantity," a debt. Of course, both legally the right and duty, and economically the credit and debt come into existence at the same time, and are extinguished at the same time. The right of the creditor to receive $1,000 in 60 days is the same as the duty of the debtor to pay $1,000 in 60 days.

Yet legally the duty of the sheriff to enforce the duty to pay does not yet exist and will not exist until the creditor gets the court to command the sheriff. But the credit exists as the identical quantity on the "asset" side of one firm and the "liability" side of another firm. And, from the standpoint of expectations the duty exists in a present status of Conformity, equal to the right which exists in the present status of Security.[18]

MacLeod faced this issue squarely and chose the fallacy. He, indeed, quoted eminent economists in opposition to himself.[19] Cernuschi had said: "The balance-sheet of every individual contains three accounts: existing goods, Credits, and Debts. But if we collected into one all the balance-sheets of everyone in the world, the Debts and the Credits mutually neutralize each other, and there remains but a single account: existing goods."

But MacLeod, as a common-law lawyer, replied by distinguishing a "duty" from a "debt." "A debt is not money owed by the Debtor, but the personal duty to pay money." The Roman lawyers, he said, had held that, when a merchant bought goods and gave his promise to pay in three months, that merchant was "in debt, but the remedy is deferred." But the English law "appears" to take a different view.

> "If an action be brought for the payment before the Credit has expired, it is a maxim of the English law that *Credit unexpired may be pleaded under the general issue:* that is, the defendant may reply that he is not in debt at all." And it appeared to MacLeod that this was "the correct view. When a merchant agrees to take a three months' bill in exchange for goods, and receives it, he is *paid* for the goods. . . . Consequently there is no Debt, or Duty to pay money, till the bill has matured. . . . The goods have become the actual property of the buyer, and his *Duty to pay* three months hence is no diminution of his present property. He has the absolute disposal of it in the meanwhile: and the Creditor has no Right to any portion of it; or to prevent him dealing with it in any way he pleases. Consequently, there are both the Right of Action, and the goods or the money, circulating in commerce at the same time."[20]

Evidently, herein, MacLeod relied upon the accident of a legal mistake in asserting that the credit and its right of action are in existence now, but that the debt and its duty to submit to the right of action are not in existence now. But each is in existence now for the same reason, namely, expectation and status.

[18] Above, p. 78, Formula of Economic and Social Relations.
[19] MacLeod, H. D., *The Elements of Economics*, I, 303.
[20] *Ibid.*, I, 290–291.

This mistake seems to be the origin of the popular and legal fallacy of American courts in the double taxation of land and mortgages as two economic quantities existing independently at the same time, the value of the debt and the value of the land. They do exist on two markets, but the personal duty of the landowner to pay does not yet exist. If the land is worth $10,000 on the real estate market and the mortgage-note is worth $5,000 on the money market, there are both the "right of action," $5,000, and the "goods or money," $10,000, "circulating in commerce at the same time," and the total taxable value is $15,000. Only the difficulty of administration and not recognition of the economic fallacy has begun to eliminate the taxation of mortgages.

We endeavor here to correct MacLeod's illusion by introducing *two* duties created by a transaction, and by an "economic status" occupied by the parties after the terms of the transaction take lawful effect. Each transaction, which exchanges rights of ownership, creates two legal duties, the duty of performance upon the seller and the duty of payment upon the buyer. The duty of performance is the duty of the seller to deliver, say, 1,000 tons of steel of a specified quality, shape, size, at a specified time and place. He has accepted the duty to deliver, and if his delivery does not come up to specifications, the buyer has MacLeod's "right of action" to compel the specified delivery or obtain damages. The contract which passes title to the tons of steel may have been made in New York, the delivery of the steel to be made in China. There has thus been created MacLeod's "economic quantity," a debt of future delivery by the seller and an equivalent "credit" or right to have the delivery on the part of the buyer. The title passed in New York but the delivery was due at a later date in Shanghai.[21]

Meanwhile the buyer can sell his right of performance against the seller, even on the high seas, to a third party, for it is a right to have future steel, worth more perhaps to him or somebody else when delivered in China or another part of the world than what he paid or promised to pay in New York.

What he paid in New York for transfer of title was a duty of payment, say $20 per ton, or $20,000 in 60 days. This was another economic quantity worth $19,800 to the seller as a creditor, which he could sell on the money market to another buyer, the banker, in exchange for the banker's demand debt, or deposit, to that amount. The many varieties of these credit instruments do not concern us here—only the general fact that every transaction creates two debts

[21] This, it will be seen, was a part of the issue in the Pittsburgh Plus case between a base price and a delivered price. Above, p. 52, From Corporations to Going Concerns.

and two credits, the economic equivalent of two rights and two duties, the right and duty of performance and the right and duty of payment.

But these rights and duties, credits and debts, are only expectations. They are "economic quantities" distinguished from material quantities, simply because they exist only in the future. But they do not exist only in the mind. They exist in the present activities and adjustments of plans. The adjustment of behavior to social expectations is historically known as a "status." [22] A status is an expectation of working rules within which the individual adjusts his present behavior. The status of the creditor is security of expectations. The status of the debtor is conformity to the security of the creditor. From the legal standpoint they are rights and duties; from the quantitative economic standpoint they are assets and liabilities; from the behavioristic standpoint of the rules that govern behavior they are security and conformity.

We endeavor to correct MacLeod's illusion by introducing the idea of an "economic status" and MacLeod's own idea of an economic quantity.

A status is an expectation within which the individual adjusts his present behavior. The status of the creditor is security of expectations, but the status of the debtor is expected conformity to the creditor's security. This is the two-sided economic status of assets and liabilities.

It is this two-sided status, instead of physical commodities and individualism, that makes economics proprietary and institutional. But nevertheless MacLeod, by accepting the separation of law and economics by the English and American courts, made the credit side of the transaction an independent economic quantity, bought and sold on the money markets until such time as it should be extinguished by enforcing the duty to pay the debt.

This led to the misinterpretation of MacLeod that he counted the same thing twice, once as a physical commodity and once as an expectation of a debt-payment secured by mortgage upon that physical commodity. But he did not count the physical thing at all. His fallacy was failure to count the liability side as existing at the same time as the asset side.

This was the failure that discredited MacLeod and caused his name to disappear from economic literature and his important discoveries to be attributed to others. Böhm-Bawerk has rightly said that MacLeod was the legitimate but disowned child of the classical

---

[22] Above, p. 78, Formula of Economic and Social Relations.

economists,[23] and this, we should say, was because the legal invention of negotiability converted the status of debt into what MacLeod said was a commodity. But a debt-credit is simply a negotiable institution, an economic status of security and conformity, an economic quantity with futurity as one of its dimensions, made saleable like a commodity; hence it fooled the economists from Smith to J. S. Mill, until MacLeod made them ridiculous by taking them seriously.

Adam Smith, for example, said MacLeod, "expressly includes Bank Notes, Bills of Exchange, and other securities," along with shoes and corn, under the term "circulating capital." "All modern writers call Bank Notes Capital." But, says MacLeod, "these are simply Rights or Credit."

And "when bank notes, mere Rights or Credit, are admitted to be Capital, the definition of the Science as the Production, Distribution and Consumption of Wealth becomes unintelligible. For who would understand the meaning of Production, Distribution and Consumption of Debts or Credits? Whereas everyone knows that Debts of all sorts are bought and sold like any material property. The most colossal branch of commerce in modern times —the system of Credit—consists exclusively in buying and selling Debts: and the exchangeable relations of Debts are governed by exactly the same general Law of Value as the exchangeable relations of material commodities."[24]

Yet his negotiable debts are the modern meaning of capital. The economists, said MacLeod, "never made the slightest attempt to bring the subject of Credit and Banking into the general body of the science: in fact, they have given up the whole subject of Banking in hopeless despair."[25] MacLeod resolves this difficulty by shifting the physical things to the future and by substituting mental acts and operation of law which give rise to property-rights. If property-rights are themselves credits, then banking is only a special case of the universal principle of buying and selling credits.

(4) **Exchangeability.**—There was a double meaning, says MacLeod, in Adam Smith's usage of the term Wealth. In the first half of his work wealth was defined as "the annual produce of land and labor"; in the second half it was anything exchangeable. Ricardo

[23] Böhm-Bawerk, E. von, *Rechte u. Verhältnisse*, 5 ff. See also Knies, K., *Geld u. Credit* (1876, 1895).

[24] MacLeod, H. D., *Economics for Beginners*, 13.

[25] This may be seen in John Stuart Mill's admirable chapter on Credit, which, however, has no relation whatever to the theoretical foundations of his explanation of Value as based on cost of production. His credit theory is based on psychology, something not admitted to his Ricardian theory of value and cost.

followed Smith but restricted his meaning to any product of labor designed to be sold.   John Stuart Mill had defined wealth as "everything which has the power of purchasing."   In this he followed Smith who had included bank notes, bills of exchange, and other securities as wealth.   These, said MacLeod, are rights of action, or credit, not different (except as to the "sources from which they spring") from funds, shares, good-will, the practice of professional men, etc., all of which are "exchangeable rights." [26]   Hence MacLeod followed what was included in all their meanings of wealth and made exchangeability the essence of wealth and value.   This, however, as we have said, confuses wealth and assets.

Furthermore, according to MacLeod and the other physical economists who made exchangeability the sole subject-matter of economics, an exact science can be developed only when, like the physical sciences, it can be reduced to mathematical equations.

"A physical science," he said, "is a definite body of phenomena all based upon a single idea, or quality, of the most general nature. . . .   Any quantity whatever in which that Quality is found is an element, or constituent, in that science, no matter what other Qualities may be found in it. . . .   Dynamics is the science of Force: and a force is defined to be 'Anything which causes, or tends to cause, motion or change of motion.' "   In Economics this Force is Demand.[27]

But the economist, as such, he goes on, does not investigate demand, for that "would introduce the whole of Psychology into Economics."

Value, indeed, "in its original sense is a quality, or desire, of the mind: it means esteem or estimation: as we speak of a highly valued friend.   But such Value is not an economical phenomenon. To bring value into Economics it must be manifested in some tangible form: as when a person manifests his desire, estimation, or *Value* for something by giving something in exchange for it to acquire possession of it. . . .   For an exchange to take place *requires the concurrence of two minds.* . . .   Hence it is clear that Value is a Ratio, or an Equation.   Like distance, . . . the Value of a thing is always something *external* to itself. . . .   A single object cannot have Value.   We cannot speak of absolute or intrinsic distance or equality. . . .   Any Economic Quantity may have Value in terms of any other." [28]

Thus MacLeod reduces economics to the then notion of a physical

[26] MacLeod, H. D., *The Elements of Economics*, I, 75–89.
[27] *Ibid.*, I, 3.
[28] *Ibid.*, 53, 54, 55.

science by reducing it to ratios of exchange, and it is these ratios that are Value. This science of exchange-ratios, he shows, was intended by all of the economists, ancient and modern. The term "production of wealth" meant, for the Physiocrats, for Smith and Ricardo, obtaining something from the earth or from labor for the sake of "*bringing it into Commerce.*" This was "productive labor"; and "unproductive labor" was that whose product did not come upon the market. "Consumption" was taking something off the market, and they did not include in economics the laws of consumption proper. MacLeod shows their inconsistencies, and how these can be avoided by dropping their ambiguous terms production, distribution, and consumption, and narrowing the science to what they really intended—the laws of exchange-value.

But what is it that is exchanged? Is it physical *things,* or is it the *rights* to the things? Is it the incorporeal property of debts or is it rights of *ownership* of the debts? Is it the intangible property of rights to buy and sell, or is it *ownership* of intangible property?

The economists, according to MacLeod, thought it was physical things that were exchanged, but the lawyer knew it was property rights in things or in debts that were exchanged. MacLeod resolved the difficulty by substituting for physical things an economic quantity, credit. This economic quantity can be owned, bought, and sold. Thus he began the modern meaning of Capital.

(5) **Double Meaning of Credit.**—But MacLeod had a contradictory meaning of credit. It meant a monetary income to be derived from the future payment of a debt, and it meant a monetary income to be derived from future sales of output. In short, it meant both debt-income and sales-income. The first we name, as he does, incorporeal property; to the second we give the more recent name, intangible property.

The contradictory meaning seems to have been derived by him from the creation of bankers' debts, or deposits, which have general purchasing power. A manufacturer alienates the ownership of his output and accepts in full payment the ownership of a commercial debt payable in 60 days. He sells the debt to a dealer in commercial paper or to a bank at a discount and accepts in full payment a banker's debt payable on demand and therefore payable without discount.

Both debts have purchasing power. The commercial debt, that is a "particular debt," is exchanged for a banker's demand debt. But the banker's demand debt, or deposit, is also a "particular" debt owed to the depositor by the bank. Yet the latter has general purchasing power, but the commercial debt for 60 days also has purchasing power, though at a discount on its face value. The banker's debt, therefore, accepted by third parties without discount in the sale of their commodities, is the same as metallic money. And metallic money, says MacLeod, is also a general credit, by which he means general purchasing power.

The so-called debtors in both cases of money and credit are the "whole world," that is, not debtors at all but sellers of anything who accept, without discount, the money or credit, in payment for the thing they sell. Money and credit are alike because both are negotiable and therefore carry no liens to be deducted from their face value. The bankers and business men themselves speak of their deposits as money or cash, though they are only negotiable debts past due, and therefore accepted without discount. MacLeod simply adopted their language.

So he had to distinguish between "general" credit and "particular" credit. General credit was the debts which any buyer might incur in the future when he bought a commodity. Particular credit was a debt actually incurred by an individual buyer picked out from the whole world of buyers. Yet the "particular" credit is the only debt, and the "general" credit is general purchasing power!

How he came about this contradictory meaning of credit when he changed economics from things to the negotiable ownership of things, may be seen from his account of the origin of money and credit: When I buy a horse or land, what I buy is not the physical thing, it is all the rights to the future uses of the horse or land, "against all the world." Those rights, he says, are "credits." By buying that bundle of "credits," a horse or land, I become a debtor to the seller. If I pay immediately by an assortment of cows and pigs, as in a barter economy, I also sell to him, not the animals, but my rights to future use and sale of the animals. This is another and similar credit, according to MacLeod, the one exchanged for the other.

If, now, this exchange of "credits," in the barter economy, is *equal*, then the transaction is closed. If it is *unequal*, then there remains a balance due on one side or the other. This balance may be paid immediately in money, or it may be deferred an interval of time. This is where money and credit originate.

With money or "general" credit the recipient can "collect his debt" from the rest of the world by *purchasing* other products or services. The rest of the world is therefore also his "debtor." Or, if the particular debtor of the transaction does not pay the balance immediately in money, then his duty to pay is shifted to a later time, and this again is a credit. But since this is saleable, then the rest of the world is also again his "debtor." Money and credit are each a "general" credit against all the world indifferently.

But there are two economic relations, quite the opposite, involved in the creation of debt. One is the creditor-debtor relation, the other is the seller-buyer relation. MacLeod was most concerned with the seller-buyer relation, that is, the negotiability, or exchangeability of debt, and he fitted his meanings of words to that fundamental fact which he took over from the economists. He was extraordinarily weak, as we have seen, on the creditor-debtor relation itself, on account of his acceptance of the mistake of the British courts. But, to make exchangeability of ownership, instead of exchangeability of things, the center of his system, was indeed a new insight. However, to name both the debt and its exchangeability a credit was similar to the mistake of the economists who made productive labor the labor whose product was designed for exchange, and unproductive labor the labor whose product was designed for home consumption, whereas both are productive. So MacLeod made a particular credit granted to an individual a private affair between the two, but its negotiability became a productive affair which, by increasing the velocity of transactions, increased the quantity of wealth "brought into commerce."

This was quite similar to Adam Smith's contradictory meaning of labor as the measure of value, namely, the quantity of labor that could be commanded in exchange, and the quantity of labor-power that increased the quantity of a commodity. The one meant scarcity, the other meant efficiency. These were not distinguished until Ricardo adopted labor-power as the measure of value and left the commanded labor to Malthus and other followers of Smith. So MacLeod did not distinguish the creditor-debtor relation created by a particular transaction between two persons from the exchange-value of that relation against "all the world," created by the device of negotiability.

MacLeod had also a double meaning of the word "command," an economic and a legal meaning. To command the services or commodities of producers, by offering them money or credit in exchange, was not distinguished from the command of performance or payment addressed to a debtor by the state. The one was economic power in bargaining, the other was legal power in enforcing a duty.

But it was further a confusion of two kinds of duties, quite readily derived from his lawyer's usage of the terms "act" and "omission." The duties of performance and payment are the duties that create the creditor-debtor relation, but the duty of avoidance creates exactly the opposite relation of liberty, the absence of duty. The buyer has no duty to buy and the seller has no duty to sell. But the duty of performance or payment could not be freely assumed or maintained unless "all the world" were subject to a duty of avoidance of interference. He made no use of this duty of avoidance, because that would be only a duty of omission, or the duty "not to act," which indeed it is, but not called for in his economic system of the positive acts of exchange made possible by negotiability of debts.

The creditor has indeed *two* rights, correlated with *two* duties in order to be secure that his debtor will pay. He has the positive right of payment against the debtor and the negative right of avoidance against "all the world." Duties of performance or payment are debts. But duties of avoidance are duties of all others not to interfere with the debtor's duty of performance or payment. MacLeod's so-called "general credit" against all the world was not a duty of performance, it was a duty of avoidance. And this duty of avoidance is also a duty of "all the world" not to interfere with the access of a seller to his customers.

It was the contradictory meaning of credit as future income from debt payments and future income from sales, as well as his overlapping meaning of corporeal property, that prevented his critics from understanding MacLeod's main point. Thus Böhm-Bawerk, his most painstaking critic,[29] who himself did most of all economists to bring Futurity into *subjective* economics, could not understand MacLeod who had preceded him thirty years by bringing Futurity into *objective* economics. If economics deals solely with property, that is, property rights, plainly it deals only with Expectations of Income. And if these expectations are to have a present existence as an economic quantity which can be measured, instead of a psychological feeling which can only be illustrated, then MacLeod found ready at hand, in the negotiability of credit and money, the objective existence of this economic quantity. He need only extend it to all property rights, whether commodities, money, or credit.

If the term credit was fancifully extended to purchasing power, it was because MacLeod had, in the idea of credit, a valid principle—Futurity, which united under one head all the special cases of ownership of commodities, of money, of credit, and of particular debts. It is this objective Futurity that Böhm-Bawerk could not understand when applied to physical materials, although he understood the subjective futurity of materials. It is plain enough when embodied in banking and investment, but how is it that rights of property in physical goods are also nothing else but Futurity in its

[29] Böhm-Bawerk, E. von, *op. cit.*

objective manifestation of property? He speaks correctly in naming MacLeod a legitimate but disowned child of the dominant theories of the time. He was disowned because he made debt the economic quantity of his science, instead of material things and labor, and created the mistaken impression of his critics that he counted *both* things and debts as "things."

Since debt is quantitative, measured on the markets by exchange-ratios, if the science of economics is made to rest on debt then we have a universal economic quantity on which to build. It is just as much quantitative when the present value of a debt is measured in dollars and cents as is a physical thing quantitative when wheat is measured by bushels or water by quarts.

Thus MacLeod, when he says that it is property rights that are exchanged, instead of things, means thereby, economically, that it is debts that are exchanged, measured in dollars. All property rights, for him, are ownership of debts. Not merely particular debts, like promissory notes, are debts, but all property rights, including corporeal property, bank notes and bank credit, are debts, in his double meaning of credit as debts and as purchasing power. It is not physical materials that are exchanged—it is total or partial rights to the future monetary or credit income to be derived by selling those materials. And those rights are ownership of particular or general debts.

It was not until the modern concept of "intangible" property began to be distinguished from MacLeod's "incorporeal" property that the meaning of exchangeability, or the right to buy and sell, including the right of access to markets without interference, could be separated in law from the incorporeal property of future enforcement of performance or payment of a debt. Here the future income from sales—namely, intangible property—is distinguished from the future income from debt-payments—namely, incorporeal property.

By means of this later concept of intangible property, we can see, by aid of the later analysis of Hohfeld, MacLeod is chargeable with using the term Rights with the double meaning of a Right and a "no-right," or Liberty. Or, in economic terms, he uses the term Credit with the double meaning of a Right to demand payment of a debt by a debtor and a Right to demand payment for a commodity by a buyer. The one we name the right-duty relation of creditor and debtor, the other the liberty-exposure relation of seller and buyer.

The explanation of the way in which MacLeod fell into this confusion of such opposite social relations will reveal a quite universal fallacy in both legal and economic meanings of words, having consequent disastrous social results. It will lead thereby to important distinctions that must be made in order to set forth a proper legal and economic analysis of transactions and going concerns.

MacLeod starts with the proposition that political economy is a science of the "laws of property," and not the laws of physical things or psychological feelings. Next, he narrows the subject to the Exchange-Value of these Rights of property, for otherwise it cannot be a "science" which always must deal with quantities and units of measurement. But, if he has eliminated physical things that come up from the past, and deals only with quantities that are expected to have a future existence, what can be the nature of those future quantities that have a present existence on the markets? They must be something that other persons are expected to do for the owner by way of furnishing to him "the produce of the future." The most general term for this expectation, which has a present existence on the present markets, he says, is Credit.

Credit, therefore, takes three forms. (1) The Present Value of all corporeal property rights. This is his "commodity credit." (2) The Present Value of future metallic money, which he names "metallic credit." (3) The Present Value of a particular credit running against a specified debtor. The last is the only true meaning of credit, which we distinguish as incorporeal property, a debt. The first two are intangible property—the right of avoidance, which is the right to be free in future bargaining transactions.

If we follow through MacLeod's line of reasoning upon this universal concept of credit as the quantitative dimensions of all property rights, we shall see how completely he was attempting to reverse the Time factor of the classical economists and of the Physiocrats. He substituted Future Time for Past Time throughout the entire subject-matter of the science (except in his unfortunate mistake in the matter of one year of corporeal property), but treated Future Time like a commodity brought backwards to present markets, as they had treated Past Time brought forward to present markets. It was thus that his theory was the "legitimate but disowned child" of the dominant theories of the period. But it was legitimate because rights to future income are exchangeable, like commodities. And it was disowned because the dominant theories did not separate ownership from materials owned.

(6) **Intangible Property.**—Examinations of MacLeod's "Totality of Transferable Property" [30] reveals that only two of his items of so-called "incorporeal property" are based on the meaning of debt, namely "annuities" and "funds." All the others are present owner-

[30] Above, p. 402, Totality of Transferable Property.

ships of future products, or of future money to be derived from the *sale* of future services or products.

The "annual income for ever" to be derived from his present corporeal property is either the expected products for one's own use or the money income from future sales of the products, or future "ground rent." "His credit" is not a particular credit against a debtor, but is the general "good credit" of a business man, that is, the good-will of investors and bankers who are expected to be willing to lend to him by buying his promises to pay. "The good-will" of his business is expected profitable transactions with customers. "The practice" is, again, the good-will of a lawyer's clients or a physician's patients, willing to pay for his services. Copyrights and patents are expectations of preferential or monopolistic sales-incomes. "The shares" of a commercial company are the present value of expected dividends or other opportunities to make a profit over and above all expenses. "Tolls" and "ferries," like patents, are expected preferential prices arising from franchises.

These, under modern decisions, should be named "intangible property." The only incorporeal properties, or credits in the economic sense of the duty of debtors to pay, are "annuities" and "funds," the latter being the present value of expected debt-payments.

These distinctions are not merely academic quibbles. They are of high social significance, for, as we have pointed out elsewhere, it has been the failure to distinguish the "industrial good-will" of workers from a "duty to work"—that is, to distinguish intangible property from incorporeal property—that has aroused resentment against the "yellow dog contracts" authorized by the United States Supreme Court.[31] It is this and similar problems that go back to the lawyer-economist MacLeod's double meaning of credit. His meaning of credit as an economic quantity is simply the present value of all expected incomes, whether the payment of debts or the payment of prices.

This double meaning is, however, the composite meaning of the modern going concern, which is the expectation that both debtors will pay their debts and "all the world" will pay profitable prices for materials or services. If I acquire title only to the physical equipment of a business but do not acquire title to it as a going concern, then I acquire title only to the scrap value which I might realize by dismantling the plant and selling the parts on the commodity markets in their then scrap condition. But if I buy it as a going concern, then I obtain title not to dismantled materials but to

---

[31] Hitchman Coal Co. *v.* Mitchell, 225 U. S. 229 (1917); Commons, John R., *Legal Foundations of Capitalism*, 294 ff.

a going plant turning out physical materials, as well as title to all debts owing the concern and rights of free access to markets. I obtain title to the expected total gross income indefinitely in the future, to be distributed to my employees, my creditors, my landlord, and myself.

Since, however, I am not an individual, but am an association of stockholders and bondholders, and not only that, but also am an association of all employees and agents as well as all who sell materials, and, since all of us expect to derive from that gross income of the concern our compensations for what we expect to contribute to the concern; then that gross income to be derived both from all purchasers of our joint product and all debtors to the concern is our joint income. It is apportioned among individuals by a variety of transactions, each of which creates, for the time, the creditor-debtor relation of incorporeal property, but each of which, for its continuance or repetition, depends upon a willingness of all to participate. This expected participation is intangible property.

The whole is a going concern. It is a joint willingness of all participants: the willingness of employees and managers to maintain and operate the plant; the willingness of customers to buy, of investors and bankers to lend, of material men to sell, and of others to participate. The so-called "right" of each to participate and to have compensation for participation is the intangible property of liberty and exposure. But the right of each individually to have compensation for his previous services is the incorporeal property of debt, wherein the concern is the debtor. MacLeod named it credit—it is a going-concern value. He looked upon it as a static economic quantity at a point of time. It is such, indeed, as a cross-section of a going concern at the point of time when an accountant makes his annual report, but it is a going process over an expected flow of time.

Technically, this going-concern value, for purposes of legislation and administration, has come to mean the present market value, at a point of time, of the stocks and bonds; or a calculation where the securities are not quoted. These signify the present value of the expected net operating income, less taxes. But, economically, going-concern value is the present value of all expected incomes of all participants, including the taxing authority, all of which account for the total gross income from sales.[32]

Three kinds of moral and legal duties arise which serve to keep the concern going by keeping up the attitude of willingness. The duties of performance and payment are taken upon themselves by

[32] Cf. Commons, John R., *Legal Foundations of Capitalism*, 182–213.

all who participate. These are the incorporeal properties of Debt. The duties of avoidance or non-interference are assumed by outsiders, including the state. The duties of forbearance are assumed where outside interference is unavoidable, especially in the case of monopolies, public utilities, or trade union rules. And the expectation of making all their contracts within these limits is intangible property. It is these expected rights and duties of performance, avoidance, and forbearance which constitute the intangible properties, and, in so far as the participants are free to participate or not participate, their willingness or unwillingness is the moral and legal meaning of the intangible property of liberty and exposure.

Thus the going concern is a succession of incorporeal and intangible properties, repeatedly created, continuing and lapsing. MacLeod named them particular credits and general credits. The particular credits are duties of performance and payment. The general credits are duties of avoidance and forbearance—not credits and debts at all, but liberties and exposures in the expected bargaining transactions. His particular credits are incorporeal property. His general credits are intangible property. And, considering the distinction between a Flow and a Lapse of Time, incorporeal property is an expected lapse of time, but intangible property is an expected flow of time.

(7) **From Corporeal to Intangible Property.**—Thus the institutional set-up gives us the idea of a going concern acting by means of inducements to participants in their forecasts of working, waiting, and risking, under rules that set limits to their bargaining, managerial, and rationing transactions. But the technological set-up gives us the idea of a going plant under the direction of the engineer, turning out a product of goods and services for ultimate consumers, under rules of technical efficiency. The two are inseparable, but they give us two different concepts of society ending in different social philosophies and concepts of government. One is the changing assets and liabilities of participants, the other is the changing ratios of input to output in the creation of the wealth of nations. One is the proprietary economics of transferable rights and liberties; the other is the engineering economics of input and output. The one is the scheme that not only distributes the shares, but, more important, keeps the concern agoing. The other is the resulting creation of an output that is to be shared.

The difficulty with the older physical and hedonic theories was in the fact that they could not avoid bringing in the proprietary economics by a back door while in the process of shutting it out from the front door. They had even defined wealth as materials and its ownership. But their concepts were static, instead of having the activity aspect of changing ownership by means of transactions. The proper methodology is first to distinguish the two factors of economics, each in its own right, then to bring them together in a concept of collective activity, which, by customary usage, seems to be satisfied by the idea of a going concern.

This signifies not so much the introduction of new concepts as the breaking up of the double meanings of older concepts. Thus the terms commodity and wealth had the proprietary meaning of ownership and the technological meaning of material things; the term "cost" had the proprietary meaning of outgo and the technological meaning of input, and the term value had the proprietary meaning of income received and the technological meaning of output furnished.

In the reconstruction of economic theory during the past few decades it has often required only a very slight change in a fundamental concept to make the transition from the static physical and hedonic concepts of a generation ago to the Twentieth Century institutional concepts of activity. Fetter's change, in 1907, from the Austrian concept of utility to the volitional concept of choice, although apparently a very slight change, because utility always had the double meaning of pleasure and choice between pleasures, nevertheless enabled him, by introducing the activity concepts, to change completely from Böhm-Bawerk's pleasure economy to modern institutionalism of activity, even though he insisted that he was holding fast to his psychology. He was really introducing the psychology of activity which is also the activity concept of intangible property.[33] So it is also with Fisher, America's leading mathematical economist. In 1907 he defined wealth, according to historical tradition, as material objects owned by human beings,[34] and this, when changed to the activity concepts, ended in the contradictory meanings of wealth as both increasing output and restricting output.

This contradictory meaning, as we have said, turns on failure to distinguish the institution of property from the technology of production. The puzzles are unnecessary if institutional economics is distinguished from engineering economics. Each is an economics of activity. Institutional economics is the activity of transactions in the relation of man to man, but engineering economics is the activity of increasing output in the relation of man to nature. The total man-power of the nation is its total active input, and the total control over nature's forces is the total output resulting from the

---

[33] See Fetter's latest work, *The Masquerade of Monopoly* (1931).
[34] Above, p. 251, Scarcity and Efficiency.

activity. But the institutional aspect is the activity of *sharing* and *forecasting* that output, which determines whether the concern itself shall go or stop.

Thus the institutional set-up of society is the changing assets and liabilities of individuals and concerns, which are, in turn, the economic inducements of the future that lead to working, waiting, and risking. It is the system of bargaining, rationing, managing, and forecasting, which expands, or restricts, or stops, or shifts input and output in different directions, or to different times of the near or remote future. It is the set-up of bargaining, rationing, and managing transactions in advance of production, which both determine the shares of the benefits and burdens and afford the inducements that keep the social concern agoing or not-going. But the engineering set-up of society is the march of the physical, biological, and psychological sciences, which give to mankind its command over nature to be used for happiness or destruction according to the collective action of the world's institutions. The two are very far from identical as was the case when the meaning of property was merely inactive corporeal property. Hence we substitute for the word "materials"[35] the *output* of materials and the *input* of labor; and for the words corporeal and incorporeal property, the expected physical *output* and money *income* of intangible property.

(8) **Commodity Market and Debt Market.**—In Fetter's important article on "The Definition of Price"[36] twenty years ago, Hadley was the only one of one hundred seventeen economists who defined price as the price of a "right." Hadley said, as quoted by Fetter, "A price, in the broadest sense of the word, is the quantity of one thing which is exchanged for another. A price, in the commercial sense of the word, may be defined as the quantity of money for which *the right* to an article or a service is exchanged."[37]

Fetter was examining only the physical and hedonic economists, not the institutional economists, such as Hadley, and was searching for a definition of price on which they might agree, regardless of their subjective or objective theories of value or monetary and non-monetary theories. The definition he arrived at was: "Price is the quantity of goods given or received in exchange for another good."

But evidently MacLeod's definition of price was the same as Hadley's. Price is the price paid for a right of ownership. It applies to both the commodity markets and the debt markets.

---

[35] Including "services."

[36] Fetter, Frank A., *Amer. Econ. Rev.*, II (1912), 783–813.

[37] Hadley, A. T., *Economics, an Account of the Relations between Private Property and Public Welfare* (1896), 70, 72. Italics mine.

On the commodity market I hand to you a book and you hand to me a dollar. That is a twofold physical act and has no meaning other than what animals might do in aiding each other. But, in human society, if I do not own that book I cannot lawfully hand it to you and receive payment for it. And even then I cannot make you the owner of that book against avoidance by all comers unless the law reads into my physical act another act—a mental "act of will"—my intention that you shall be the owner, as well as another mental act—your intention to become the owner. Then the law enforces, or is expected to enforce, that twofold act of will. Does economic science deal with that twofold physical act, or does it deal with that twofold mental act? Evidently the physical act is technological and is carried on by manual laborers under the command of owners. But the mental act is proprietary, and actually, by operation of law, transfers the ownership.

Again, I hand to you the book, and you take and keep the book but do not hand to me the dollar. The law now reads into the transfer of the book the same mental act of concurrence of two wills—my intention that you shall own the book and your intention to own it. But it reads also into the same physical transfer another physical transfer—this time an *expected* physical transfer of the dollar from you to me and my expected taking of the dollar with expected intention to make it my own. How will the economists deal with this pair of twofold physical acts? They are the same physical transfers as in the preceding illustration, but there has occurred a time-interval.

The economists give it up in despair, says MacLeod, and fall into hopeless confusion.[38]

The confusion arises from the fact that there are two markets, the "commodity" market and the "debt" market, and that the word "money" carries over the physical meaning of a commodity into the debt market, which then becomes, by analogy, a "commodity" market. Yet *coined* money, as we have said and shall see, is not a commodity. It is a debt-paying institution.[39] MacLeod himself did not effectively distinguish the commodity market from the debt market, on account of his double meaning of credit. In this he followed the materialistic illusion that prevails generally: A banker speaks of an increase in his "supply of money" for loan to customers, when he has merely received an increase in supply of debts owed to him by customers or other bankers. Customers and speculators ask what "money is worth," when they mean, what are debts worth?

---

[38] Knies afterwards treated it as an exchange with a time interval. Knies, K. E., *op. cit.*
[39] Above, p. 396, below, p. 457, Release of Debt.

This materialistic obsession might perhaps have been avoided by MacLeod and others, if, instead of the metaphor "money market," they had substituted the reality, debt market. Even the "commodity market," as MacLeod rightly describes it, is a market, not where commodities are exchanged, but where *ownership* of commodities is exchanged. And the "money market," is, also as MacLeod describes it, the market, not where money is exchanged, but where ownership of debts is exchanged.

The price, in each case, is a price given in "consideration" of a transfer of some form of legal control. It is "compensation" for services rendered, either immediate compensation or deferred compensation. This is the institutional meaning of alienation of rights and duties, not the physical meaning of exchange.

If MacLeod had effectively followed up his clue of a debt as a "saleable commodity," not by assimilating ownership of a debt to ownership of a commodity, but by consistently distinguishing a debt market from a commodity market, he would accurately have described modern business and would have avoided double counting. There would have been, simply, two markets instead of double counting on one market.

The stock exchange and the money market are the two wheels of the Debt Market: the large wheels, stocks and bonds, looking years into the future, and the small wheels, bank loans and deposits, looking hours and days into the future. Though stocks are not legally debts like bonds, yet they are becoming debts economically and even legally, and are thus conforming somewhat to MacLeod's description of a "saleable debt." Stocks are "liabilities" of the business to the stockholders, and even dividends are coming to be looked upon as customary debts owing to stockholders. This is even legally sanctioned in the case of public utilities regulated by law, where the total value of both stocks and bonds and the current rates of both interest and profit are used to compute the charges which the public must pay, as expected debtors, in order that bondholders may receive interest and stockholders dividends. The "public" is the debtor and the stockholders, as well as bondholders, are the creditors. And it is becoming, in special circumstances, a legal obligation upon the corporation to pay dividends to the stockholders, almost as much as the legal obligation to pay interest to bondholders.[40] The bondholders are simply preferred creditors, the stockholders are deferred creditors. Intermediate stages have been introduced, such as varieties of "preferred stocks" coming between bondholders as creditors and common stockholders as quasi-creditors.

[40] Dodge *et al. v.* Ford Motor Co. *et al.*, 204 Mich. 459, 170 N. W. 668 (1919).

Even where there is no legal sanction requiring payment of dividends on common stocks, there has arisen an economic sanction of the nature of good-will of investors. During the recurrent inflationary periods of American capitalism, boards of directors recognized no moral or economic, much less legal, obligation to pay dividends and maintain the market values of stocks. But with the incoming of thousands and millions of scattered investors, and the incoming of the banker period of corporations through the concentration of management in the hands of a mere fraction of the total ownership,[41] the economic necessity of maintaining the good-will of investors has required dummy boards of directors to adopt a policy of paying customary dividends. Evidently some kind of legal obligation is also required—it has begun in the so-called "blue sky" laws designed to protect investors in stocks and bonds.

Thus the stock exchange is the market for a graduation of long-time debts with legal and economic sanctions, from the extreme legally sanctioned bonds through the less sanctioned preferred stocks and many kinds of mere "rights," down to the lowest legally sanctioned but mainly economically sanctioned moral debts, historically known as common stocks.

In this limited respect MacLeod was prophetically correct for a few special cases but not generally when he represented *all* property rights as "debts" or "credits," and resolved economics into a set of creditor-debtor relations. They can become such only if the economic and moral sanctions to pay dividends become legal sanctions enforced by courts. But this is unlikely. The capitalistic system requires both the intangible property of stocks whose value depends on the Margin for Profit, and the incorporeal property of debts.[42]

But it does not follow that debts should be named commodities. If they are so described, then all that we can say is that MacLeod is talking metaphor and not science. He is confusing debts with purchasing power. The former is incorporeal, the latter is intangible property.

Yet what happens on a commodity market is similar to what happens on a debt market. Each is a market for a future money income, which MacLeod named a "credit." It is not physical things that are exchanged for physical money—it is titles of ownership of future money income, to be derived from ownership of present com-

---

[41] See Ripley, W. Z., *Main Street and Wall Street* (1927); Brookings, R. S., *Industrial Ownership, Its Economic and Social Significance* (1925); Bonbright, J. C., and Means, G. C., *The Holding Company, Its Public Significance and Its Regulation* (1932).

[42] Below, p. 526, Margin for Profit.

modities that are sold for titles to future money income. Each expectation is a credit, according to MacLeod, and commodity credits are sold for money credits. But they are not alike because one is a debt, the other is purchasing power. Yet each is the expectation of future money income.

This correctly explains Capitalism. The business man when he buys a commodity does not buy the physical thing—he buys the expectation of a future money income to be obtained by selling the commodity.[43] When the banker buys the business man's debt, he buys the expectation of a future money income to be obtained when the debtor sells his commodity and pays his debt. According to MacLeod, each is the purchase of a credit.

Hence a commodity market functions with a debt market. Here the two wheels are ownership of an output and ownership of short-time debts. On the commodity market short-time debts are created and immediately sold on the debt market in exchange for bankers' demand debts or deposits. The commercial debts are created for the purpose of sale, and because they can be sold to bankers. The only difference, then, between commodities and debts, is in the object that is owned and sold in exchange for bankers' demand debts. In the case of debts the object is future legal control of future money income to be paid by debtors on the debt market. In the case of commodities it is future legal control of physical things to be sold for future money. Both commodity and debt markets look forward to money income. Each is title to a future money income, one of which is a credit—incorporeal property—the other is future profit —intangible property.

The difference between the two is the difference between two kinds of price. One is a short-time price for the *use* of money on the debt market. The other is an exchange-price to be paid for ownership on the commodity market. This distinction underlies MacLeod's confusion of interest and profit, which we proceed to consider under his identification of discount and profit.

(9) Discount and Profit. *a. Two Kinds of Price.*

"The *Unit* of *Debt*," said MacLeod, "is the *Right* to demand £100 *to be paid one year hence*. The sum of Money given to purchase this unit of debt is its Price: and of course, the less the price given to buy the fixed unit of Debt the greater is the Value of Money. But in the Commerce of Debts it is not usual to estimate the Value of Money by the price paid for the Debt. As Money naturally produces a Profit, it is clear that the Price given

[43] Below, p. 555, Speculative Law of Supply and Demand.

for a debt payable one year hence must be less than the Debt. The Difference between the Price and the amount of the Debt is the profit made by buying it. This Difference, or Profit, is termed Discount. And it is clear that as the Price of the Debt decreases or increases, the Discount or Profit increases or decreases. In the Commerce of Debts it is always usual to estimate the Value of Money by the discount, or profit it yields. Hence, in the Commerce of Debts,—the *Value* of *Money* varies *Directly* as *Discount*. This rule embraces both branches of commerce— the *Value* of *Money* varies *Inversely* as *Price* and *Directly* as *Discount*. . . . In the Commerce of Commodities the Value of Money means the *Quantity* of the Commodity it can buy: in the Commerce of Debts it means the Profit, or Discount made by buying the Debt. . . . The *Rate* of *Interest* or *Discount* is the *Amount* of the *Profit* made in some given *Time*, as the year." [44]

These two kinds of price we distinguish as short-time price or discount, but not profit; and exchange-value, or purchasing power.

b. Two Kinds of Manufacture.

"A banker," says MacLeod, "never buys a Bill with Cash in the first instance. He buys the Bill, which is a Debt payable at a future time, by giving his customer a Credit in his books for the amount of the Debt, less the discount: which is a Right of action the customer has to demand the money if he chooses. That is, he buys a Right of action, payable at a future time, by creating or issuing a Right of action, payable on demand." [45]

From this it follows that bankers, according to MacLeod, are "not intermediaries between persons who want to lend and those who want to borrow. The fact is, that a banker is a trader, whose business is to buy Money and Debts, by creating other Debts."

Consequently the banker's profit does not consist in "the Difference between the interest he pays for the Money he borrows and the interest he charges for the money he lends. The fact is that a banker's profits consist exclusively in the profits he can make by creating and issuing credit in excess of the specie he holds in reserve. A bank which issues Credit only in exchange for Money, never made, and can by no possibility make, profits. It only begins to make profits when it creates and issues Credit in exchange for Debts payable at a future time. . . . The essential and distinctive feature of a Bank and a Banker is to *Create* and *Issue credit payable on Demand:* and this Credit is intended to

[44] MacLeod, H. D., *The Theory and Practice of Banking*, I, 57, 58, 59.
[45] *Ibid.*, I, 325.

be put into circulation and serve all the purposes of money. A bank, therefore, is not an office for *borrowing* and *lending* money: but it is a *Manufactory of Credit*." [46]

c. Commodity Price and Short-Time Price.—This discounted value, of the future debt-payment, is the price paid for the debt, but the discount itself is the short-time price paid to the banker for the use of his money. The banker "manufactures out of nothing" his own demand-debt, or deposit—a debt "past due"—to serve as money; with this he buys the time-debt of his customer, charging a short-time price for the use of his own debt past due. The time-debt afterwards increases in value as the short-time price decreases in amount towards maturity. This increase in value is MacLeod's "profit."

> "A trader," he says, "makes profits by buying goods at a lower price from one person, and selling them at a higher price to another. So a banker buys a commercial debt at a lower price from one person—namely, his own customer—and sells it at a higher price to another—namely, to the acceptor, or debtor. Thus the Debt the banker buys is increasing in Value every day from the time he buys it until it is paid off. It, therefore, produces a Profit, and is therefore Circulating Capital, just in the same way, and for the same reason, that the ordinary goods in any trader's shop are." [47]

Here, of course, there is a failure to distinguish an increase in value, due to the approach of a debt towards maturity, from an increase in value, due to buying in a cheap market and selling in a dear market. The latter is profit, derived from *two* transactions; the former is discount derived from *one* transaction. In the case of *two* transactions the term *price* means the *buying* price and the *selling* price. In the case of *one* transaction the term *price* means the rate of discount between the beginning and ending of the same transaction. It is this discount which, in order to bring out the contrast, we name "short-time price."

MacLeod's confusion of profit and discount is permitted by the negotiability of debts. A debt is bought from a creditor—the bank's customer—and, at maturity, seems to be sold to the customer's debtor—the acceptor. Apparently there are two transactions negotiated by the banker; actually there is only one.

The fallacy turns on the previously mentioned fallacy that the credit comes into existence *now* but the debt does not come into

[46] *Ibid.*, I, 326, 357, rearranged.
[47] *Ibid.*, I, 358, 359.

existence until the future date when the duty to pay matures. Both come into existence at the same time, and what the banker buys is the future *duty* of the debtor to pay. The banker does not again negotiate, this time with the debtor to pay. He merely enforces his right.

This circumstance requires us to render more precise our concept of a bargaining transaction, by distinguishing the "closing of the transaction" from the "closing of the negotiations." The negotiations are closed at the point of time when ownership is transferred by the transaction. But the transaction itself is not closed until, in the future, both the performance and the payment are completed.

In a cash transaction the negotiation and the transaction are closed together. On the commodity side, not merely the title to the commodity is transferred, but the commodity is delivered. On the money side, not only is the title transferred by closing the negotiation, but also the money is paid.

There thus arise two debts, created by the transaction: the duty of performance and the duty of payment. If both are performed immediately, then both the negotiation and the transaction are closed. But not until both of the *duties* are performed is the *transaction* closed. If a lapse of time intervenes the transaction is not closed until the *last* of the two duties is performed. If this is the duty of payment, then the transaction is not closed until the debtor pays. If it is the duty of performance, then the transaction is not closed until the service is performed or the materials delivered and accepted.

Hence a transaction, in the case of long-time debts of lands or peonage, may stretch out for years, but, in the case of short-time debts on the money market, it extends only for days. Thus a transaction is truly a creative process. It creates, not commodities, but an economic quantity and an economic status, and not until the transaction is closed by release of the debts of performance and payment is the status changed from debt to liberty.

Hence MacLeod's seemingly second negotiation, where the debt is sold to the debtor in exchange for the debtor's cash, is not a negotiation—it is the performance of the legal duty that closes the transaction by releasing the debt. The banker merely "collects" what is due, and gives evidence of full payment by transferring ownership of the debtor's debt back to the debtor.

It was failure to note this *interval* between the beginning and the closing of a transaction that permitted MacLeod to identify discount with profit. Discount is a "short-time price" charged for the expected service of *waiting* during the interval between the beginning and the ending of *one* transaction; but profit (or loss) is the *margin* between the *two* transactions of buying at one price and selling at another price.

Yet profit (or loss) can also be made between two transactions of *buying and selling debts* as well as two transactions of *buying and selling commodities*. A commercial bank which discounts its customers' paper at 6 per cent retail and then rediscounts at 4 per cent wholesale makes a profit. There are here really *two* markets and *two* negotiations, a retail market and a wholesale market, and therefore *two* transactions. The banker sells on the retail market at 6 per cent, that which he buys on the wholesale market at 4 per cent.[48]

MacLeod wrote at a time when the commodity economists had not yet distinguished interest from profit. It is the distinction which we have already noted as concealed in the double meaning of a "flow of time." Profits are made at different points in the flow of time when buying and selling occur, but interest is earned in the interval, or "lapse of time," between two points of time during which uncompensated waiting accrues.

MacLeod, of course, made the usual distinction between interest and discount. They mean the same thing but they differ as to the two dates of computing the same increasing interest as decreasing discount. By advancing the complete sum and waiting until the end of the year the "profit" is interest. By retaining the profit at the time of the advance, the "profit" is discount.[49]

But, while it is true, mathematically, that discount and interest are only two methods of computing the same rate of interest, there is a difference, which MacLeod himself noted, arising from the practice of discounting and rediscounting. If the price paid to the banker for the use of his money is paid in advance, that is, by deducting the interest in advance, it more nearly approaches MacLeod's idea of a price paid for a commodity. The banker charges one price for the use of *his* credit and pays a lower price to the bank that rediscounts for the use of *its* credit.

It is not strictly a "price"—it is a *rate*, extended over a period of time in the future. Future increments, or "rents," or interest expected for the use of money, are commuted into a present "capitalized" price, which is the amount of discount. We can preserve MacLeod's distinction by distinguishing commodity price from short-time price. Commodity price is the exchange price paid for commodities or securities. Short-time price, or discount, is the price paid in advance by deducting interest for the use of money.

[48] This distinction was not made until later by Sidgwick, below, p. 443.
[49] MacLeod, H. D., *The Theory and Practice of Banking*, I, 372.

They vary inversely, as MacLeod said, and they have a wider usage. The price, for example, of a bond varies inversely to the interest on the money which purchases it, but the bond-yield varies directly with the long-time price of money on that market. So with the short-time price of money. The price of short-time commercial paper varies inversely to the rate of discount, but the rate of discount is the short-time price charged by banks for the use of the money which purchases it.

Thus the price of the debt, or security, is like the price of a commodity. It is the money paid in exchange for the debt. But the discount is the price charged for the *use* of the money or credit which he buys. The two vary inversely. It was this meaning of short-time price that enabled MacLeod to make his discovery of the proper use of the discount rate in controlling the export and import of gold by the Bank of England.

d. The Bank of England.—Angell has said that "MacLeod was . . . the first writer to see that the discount rate is one of the *primary* determinants of the foreign exchange rates, and that it may be manipulated in such fashion as to correct the exchanges. Credit for the observation is usually given to Goschen, who did not bring out his study for another half-dozen years." [50]

Goschen wrote after the Bank of England had put into practice MacLeod's theory and was "not consciously trying to do anything new." But MacLeod had said that the major causes of a drain of specie are threefold, "the indebtedness of the country, a depreciated paper currency, and *a difference in the rate of discount,* between any two countries, more than great enough to pay the cost of transporting bullion." MacLeod also "came quite close" to "interpreting the short-run relations between money and prices in terms of changes in bank reserves and in discount rates," afterwards, in 1883, given its "complete and unequivocal form" by Sidgwick, and more completely by Marshall, in 1888.[51]

The way in which MacLeod came about his theory of manipulating the discount rate and thus regulating both the drain of specie and the level of domestic prices was through his theory of the "manufacture of debts" and the public purpose, rather than private profit, of the Bank of England. A private profit could be made by the "manufacture" of debts; but it was the public duty, as against private profit, of the Bank of England to counteract this profit when it caused a drain of gold.

[50] Angell, James W., *Theory of International Prices* (1926), 138.
[51] *Ibid.,* 117, 118, 138. It was not until Wicksell (1898) that this relation between discount and prices was fully explained. Below, p. 596, Wicksell.

In the first place MacLeod had to clear the ground of the confusion of ideas which looked upon bank notes as different from bank deposits. It was this confusion that underlay the Bank Act of 1844 which separated the Bank of England into two departments, the Issue Department for bank notes and the Banking Department for bank deposits. In the Issue Department, according to this Act, no issues of bank notes (beyond an original quantity authorized in the statute), could be made except upon deposit by the customer of an equal amount of gold. Bank notes had come to be looked upon as a matter of public importance but bank deposits were considered in the Act to be a purely private and even secret affair between the Bank and its customers, in which the government should not interfere.

But MacLeod contended that both bank notes and bank deposits were exactly of the same nature, legally and economically. Legally each was a demand-debt created by the Bank to serve as money. A bank deposit was as much an "issue" of money as a bank note, because each was the "manufacture" of a debt payable in gold on demand. And economically their effects were just the same, because each served the same purpose of drawing out gold on demand for export.

> Deposits, MacLeod said, are "merely so many bank notes in disguise. They are nothing but an enormous superstructure of Credit, reared upon a comparatively small basis of bullion: exactly like the Issues of Notes. . . . These apparent Deposits, instead of being so much cash, are nothing but the Credits, or *Rights of action,* the banks have created as the Price with which they have purchased the Cash and Bills which figure on the other side as *Assets.* A sudden increase in Banking Deposits is, in reality, nothing more than an inflation of Credit: exactly similar to a sudden increase of Bank Notes. . . . Hence this diminution of Deposits is *not a diminution of Deposits in Cash:* it is a contraction of Credit." [52]

The result of the Bank Act of 1844 turned out as MacLeod predicted. According to the Act, if gold is withdrawn from the Issue Department for export, then the Bank reduces its notes by just the amount of the withdrawal. The theory was that this reduction of notes would cause a reduction in the prices of home commodities so that it would be more profitable to export commodities than bullion, thus stopping the drain of gold.[53] But, behold, the Bank Act left a "gap" in the banking department. Gold could be with-

[52] MacLeod, H. D., *The Theory and Practice of Banking,* I, 329–330.
[53] *Ibid.,* I, 412.

drawn for export from the banking department merely by presenting checks and demanding gold, and there would be no reduction in the volume of bank notes although gold was leaving the country.[54] "There are, in reality," he said, "*two* leaks to the ship. The framers of the act could only perceive *one;* and they only provided against one: and were utterly astonished to find the ship rapidly sinking from the *other* leak, which they had forgotten."[55]   The Bank Act had to be "suspended" in the crisis of 1847 in order to permit the Bank to issue notes in excess of the gold which was being drawn off from the issue department to the banking department, and thus save business men and other bankers from "total destruction."[56]

The difficulty, according to MacLeod, was in the prevailing theory "that gold was only sent to pay a balance arising from the sale of goods, and that therefore it must cease of itself whenever these payments were made.   But this is a profound delusion."

". . . if the Rate of Discount in London is 3% and that in Paris is 6%, the simple meaning of that is that gold may be bought for 3% in London and sold at 6% in Paris.   But the expense of sending it from one to the other does not exceed ½%, consequently, it leaves 2¼ or 2½% profit on the operation. . . . When the Rates of Discount differ so much . . . *persons in London fabricate bills upon their correspondents in Paris* for the express purpose of selling them in London for cash, which they then remit to Paris, and which they can sell again for 6%. And it is quite evident that this drain will not cease so long as the difference in the Rates of Discount is maintained.   Moreover, merchants in Paris immediately send over their bills to be discounted in London, and, of course have the cash remitted them . . . the only way of arresting such a drain is to equalize the Rates of Discount at the two places."[57]

And he set forth this general principle, which has been adopted since that time: "When the Rates of Discount between any two places differ by more than sufficient to pay the cost of transmitting Bullion from one place to the other, Bullion will flow from where Discount is lower to where it is higher."[58]

Of this principle he said, "however it might be known among commercial men, had never yet, that we have seen, found its way into any commercial book whatever,[59] and most certainly had never been brought forward prominently before the public in Cur-

---

[54] *Ibid.*, II, 342–343.
[55] *Ibid.*, II, 343.
[56] *Ibid.*, II, 170.
[57] *Ibid.*, I, 418.
[58] *Ibid.*, II, 344.
[59] On the preceding knowledge by "commercial men" see Magee, James D., "The Correctives of the Exchanges," *Amer. Econ. Rev.*, XXII (1932), 429–434.

rency discussions, as a cause of an adverse Exchange, wholly irrespective of any indebtedness of the country, or of the State of the Paper Currency." [60]

How, then, is this Rate of Discount to be raised when gold is leaving the country and lowered when it is coming into the country? Can it be left to the private competition of bankers, each of them making private contracts with their customers for the profit of each? The Bank of England directors had contended that the rate of discount was a private affair between themselves and their business or banking customers who kept their reserves at the Bank, each in the pursuit of his own interest in seeking his own profit. But MacLeod showed that competition caused an "inordinate increase" in the number of bankers, leading to low rates of discount when the rates should be high to prevent the export of gold. [61] Moreover, "the interest of the merchants always is to get accommodation as cheap as possible." [62] Now that the Bank of England, by the custom that had grown up, had become the repository of the gold reserves of the country banks, its discount policy, in times of foreign drain of gold, must control the policy of other banks. Hence, he said, it becomes the duty of the directors of the Bank, *in advance of a crisis*, to act against, not only their own immediate interests, but also against the immediate interests of the business public and of the other banks, if the gold reserves of the nation are to be kept intact. The Bank's private interest must be subordinated to its public duty. "It is," says MacLeod, "the imperative duty of the Bank of England to keep a steady watch upon the Rates of Discount of neighboring countries, and to follow these variations so as to prevent its being profitable to export bullion from this country." [63]

In the following depression of 1857 the Bank directors, for the first time, acted upon this principle of public duty uttered previously by MacLeod, and checked the outflow of gold by early advances in the discount rate. John Stuart Mill afterwards could say that while the Bank prior to 1847 had acted on the principle that they had nothing whatever to consider but their interest as a bank, and that while in the Act of 1844 Sir Robert Peel, its author, had assured the Bank that "anything they did as mere bankers, in the management of their deposits, was no concern of the public, but only their own concern," yet since 1847 they had become aware

"that an establishment like the Bank is not like other bankers, who are at liberty to think that their single transactions cannot

[60] MacLeod, H. D., *op. cit.*, II, 344.
[61] *Ibid.*, II, 139.
[62] *Ibid.*, II, 366.
[63] *Ibid.*, I, 418.

affect the commercial world generally, and that they have only their own position to consider. The transactions of the Bank necessarily affect the whole transactions of the country, and it is incumbent upon them to do all that a bank can do to prevent or to mitigate a commercial crisis. This being the position of the Bank, and the Bank being much more aware of it since 1847 than they were before, they have not acted so entirely as before on the principle that they had nothing to consider but their own safety." [64]

Thus the Bank of England was the first great concerted action of private business men under modern capitalism to acknowledge, without legislation, their responsibility to the public—a responsibility arising out of the fact that national welfare had come to depend upon them by the very fact of their concerted action as a Central Bank of Issue and Discount, wholly apart from the acts of government which had expressly left them free to pursue their own interests in their own way. It required, indeed, the strong pressure of public opinion before the officers of the Bank of England were willing to accept the theories of economists like MacLeod, but MacLeod himself could say, in a later edition of his work on banking, "The necessity of passing the Act of 1844 was a deep discredit to the Directors of the Bank. It was a declaration that they were incompetent to manage their own business. But now that they have shown that they are perfectly able to do so, it is no longer necessary." [65]

The further duty of the Central banks to stabilize prices, as well as to correct the inflow and outflow of gold, was not expounded until Wicksell attempted it in 1898.[66]

(10) **From Psychological to Institutional Economics.**—It is significant that the formula of a transaction may be stated in terms of psychology. The producer sells 1,000 units of steel utility at a marginal utility of 20 per unit, or a total utility, or value, of 20,000 units minus the futurity discount or *agio* of 200 units, yielding the present utility of 19,800 units. All that is needed to shift it to institutional economics is to introduce rights of property; legal units of measurement; the creation, negotiability, and release of debt; the enforcement of the two duties of delivery and payment by the

---

[64] Quoted by Beckhart, B. H., *The Discount Policy of the Federal Reserve System* (1924), 29. This volume gives an excellent historical sketch of the bank-rate discussion in England and the resulting formula of discount policy based on the experience from 1797 to 1850.

[65] MacLeod, H. D., *The Theory and Practice of Banking* (4th ed.), II, 367. See also recent proposals in England on the necessity of changing the Bank Act so as to afford elasticity and greater discretionary power, similar to that authorized in the Federal Reserve Act.

[66] Below, p. 590, World Pay Community.

collective action of the state, or a board of trade, or chamber of commerce or similar body which sets up an organization for judicial decision or commercial arbitration. The formula would then read 1,000 tons of use-value, steel; $20 per ton marginal utility, or price; $20,000 future total utility or future value; $200 futurity discount; $19,800 present total utility, or value.

A study of the psychological economists from Jevons to Fetter shows that they have gradually developed their psychology almost to this ultimate identity, and now they might as well call themselves institutional economists as psychological economists. Fetter has made the transition from psychological to institutional economics, in his *Masquerade of Monopoly*.

The futurity discount shows itself differently according to different authors. Böhm-Bawerk's "agio" is *added* by adding more *labor* in the future in order to increase the future output. But Fetter's discount is *deducted* by reducing the amount of present labor and leaving the future output unincreased. Böhm-Bawerk described the former as "increasing the roundabout process," and, though he dealt mainly with the *agio,* it follows that the same relation between present and future is accomplished by *reducing* the "roundabout process." His "increase of the roundabout process" is sometimes misleading because the trend of modern invention is to *reduce* the length of the roundabout process, and thereby to reduce the amount of labor required to produce a machine of greater efficiency. But we draw our inferences in accordance with his apparent disregard of this fact. Our inference as to Böhm-Bawerk's meaning of roundabout process is correct wherever new machinery at less labor cost and greater efficiency is *not* substituted for old machinery at the same labor cost and the same efficiency.

This psychological valuation is undoubtedly what occurs in the case, for example, of the farmer, to the extent that he devotes his labor to the production of a future use-value for himself and family and *not for sale.* It applies also to Robinson Crusoe and to the field of consumption economics where nothing is produced for sale. The farmer knows, by experience with the economist's principle of "diminishing utility," that the value of his product for home use will decline too much if he produces too much. He knows also the useless sacrifice of working too much *now* with the result of producing more than he can use at home in the future, as well as the future sacrifice of family wants if he does not work enough now to produce as much as will be wanted at home.

Thus it is that this psychological economics, perfected by Böhm-Bawerk, is universal. It exists in the fundamental nature of human beings. It certainly has its place in all economics where production is not designed for sale. Therefore, while universal, it is not fitted to the business world. It deals only with labor, materials, and expectations, and rejects avowedly private property, the rights and duties relative to the ownership of those future products, and the transactions which both transfer *ownership* of physical materials and create the negotiable debts whose ownership also is transferred.

The basic reason for this disregard of ownership is in the starting point of *individual* psychology where there are no social conflicts of interest, instead of starting with the social psychology of negotiations and transactions, arising out of conflicts. Social psychology requires not only enforceable rights and duties; it requires also objective units of measurement such that all participants may know what to expect in the future, and such that a deciding authority may mete out judgment in quantitative terms.

As is often done in popular and economic language, the *measure* of a quantity is substituted for the *quantity* measured. We speak of weight, or the degrees of heat or cold on the thermometer, but these are measures of unseen physical forces operating quantitatively in our presence. So with an economic quantity. It is not a quantity of physical things, it is a quantity of Power or Force. It is a powerful unseen social force expected to operate in the unseen future, whose measurement by individuals in their present transactions is money value. Thus, though it may seem that MacLeod's concept, "economic quantity," is transcendental or imaginary, it is not so, for it is the unseen pressure of society in the unseen future which shows itself as a monetary measurement in present transactions.

When this system of measurement by means of money is introduced, then the economic quantity becomes the modern meaning of capital. Money *value* is the measure of an unseen economic quantity, capital. The distinction then is made between the "money market" and the "capital market," between "spot" and "futures," etc., etc., where the present cash or deposits at the banks constitute the "money market," and the bonds and stocks which are debts not yet due, or sales not yet realized, constitute the capital market.

The ownership of these economic quantities, the modern "capital," is transferred by transactions. Their transportation to all parts of the world is the credits and debits on bankers' and traders' books made or offset by telegraph, cable, wireless, telephone, or post office. The New York Federal Reserve Bank keeps up an hourly statement of the incoming and outgoing "money" on the New York money market. But this statement is merely a record of the credits and debits on that market. Only recently has the Reserve System published the item "ear-marked" gold, which is *physically* in the banks but is owned in other countries and therefore is *not* in the United States. The ownership is the economic quantity, not the materials.

This modern meaning of capital, as an economic quantity measured by money is both very powerful and very sensitive. Capital has solely a legal foundation and may disappear wholly if that foundation is revolutionized. The magnitude of capital reflects every change or fear of change in world economics. Yet this economic quantity is more powerful than governments. It sets labor to work or out of work. It pays debts and taxes. It makes wars.

But capital, an economic quantity existing in the future, is very sensitive. Our former illustration of a time-discount of $200 may be augmented by a risk discount of uncertainty. If this risk discount rises to 100 per cent, the present value of capital disappears entirely and industry stops long before that degree of risk occurs. But in times of prosperity the risk discount is less and may be counteracted in two ways, by raising the selling price or by raising the rate of interest or discount.

If the risk cannot be shifted to the buyer by raising the price, it may be absorbed by the seller by accepting a higher rate of discount. If there is no risk whatever, the rate of interest might fall to 3 per cent, or less; if it were 3 per cent as in our previous illustration, then the present value would be $19,900 instead of $19,800. We may assume that the ordinary risk discount is absorbed in the 6 per cent rate of interest in our illustration, and therefore the present value of the steel, including both interest and risk discount, is, as above, $19,800.

Here it is necessary to note an ambiguity that descends from the older meaning of the word "exchange." It is assumed by classical theory that each party gains by an exchange. Each transfers to the other what is of less value to himself and receives from the other what is of more value to himself. This is doubtless true, from the standpoint of the individual. He always chooses the better or the "less worse" under the existing alternatives open to him. He *always gains,* no matter how onerous the alternative rejected or avoided. But this confuses a personal psychology with an objective economic quantity.[67] The economic quantity which is sold in a transaction is exactly the same quantity, indeed the same thing, as that which is bought. The ownership of an economic quantity, say, a horse—or rather the expected useful services of a horse— is transferred in exchange for the ownership of cash or a bank

[67] As in the Austrian term "subjective exchange-value." Also above, pp. 307 ff., Opportunity.

deposit, say $100. The fact that one party *values* the horse more than the money or that the other party *values* the money more than the horse, is a subjective or personal matter. It is not objectively and measurably what happens in the transaction, where the ownership of a definite economic quantity is transferred, although the individuals concerned may value it differently.

So with the equivalence of credit and debt. Subjectively and individually the parties may value them as highly different magnitudes, the creditor for his purposes and the debtor for his purposes. But objectively the credit, say $19,800, is exactly the same economic quantity as the debt, $19,800. Each accrues equally towards maturity, but at any point of time they are the identical economic quantity.

Likewise with what we have said regarding the equivalence of Liberty and Exposure. Subjectively, the employer may feel, when his laborer quits, that he loses more than his laborer gains. Or the laborer may think he gains more by quitting than the employer loses by his quitting. Or the laborer may think he gains more by quitting than by remaining at work, while the employer may think he gains more by discharging him than by keeping him.

But objectively, when the laborer quits or the employer fires him, the employer loses a prospective economic quantity, say an expected day's work of the laborer—which is exactly the same economic quantity as that which the laborer now acquires and may dispose elsewhere. One of the two may know how to make a better use of that expected day's work than the other, but this is a personal matter and does not change objectively the economic quantity which, as such, is the same for each party. Since the ordinary laborer can quit at will the "economic quantity" is reduced by risk. But, in the case of "contract labor," or the professional contracts of actors, baseball players, *et al.*, the risk discount is greatly reduced.

Or, take the meaning of "good-will," or trade-marks—another relation of liberty and exposure which we have distinguished as intangible property, one of the largest assets of modern capitalism: Although the future income of "good-will" may be highly speculative, yet in a transaction its ownership as a present economic quantity may be transferred at a pecuniary valuation involving expected sales, prices, interest, and a high degree of risk, and therefore a high rate of risk discount. It may be deemed worth more by one party than by the other, yet objectively it is the same economic quantity, the modern meaning of capital as assets.

Even the meaning of a "going concern" is a similar economic

quantity whose present value may be the changing values of its stocks and bonds which measure the expectations of a pecuniary net income.

It is this transfer of ownership of an identical economic quantity which the court or arbiter considers—not the personal gains or losses, pains or pleasures, which individuals think they get or lose. The latter correspond to the psychological meaning of value, but we treat them merely as "talking points" in the negotiational psychology, which terminates in a transaction.[68]

Economists often use the term "goods," including such different concepts as physical goods, debts, stocks, bonds, good-will of a business, going concerns, where we, following MacLeod, use the term "economic quantities" of different dimensions which are bought, sold, or held for the future. This analysis is similar to that apparently intended by J. B. Clark, when he distinguishes "capital" from "capital goods."[69] His "capital" is a "fund of value"; his "capital goods" are the physical materials. Here the terms "production goods" and "consumption goods" are convenient terms and will be used, since they are evidently limited to the technology of producing and consuming physical materials. But if the term "goods" is extended to include stocks, bonds, bank deposits, credits, debts, or other forms of corporeal, incorporeal, and intangible property, they are a confusion (as MacLeod rightly said of Smith and Mill)[70] of production and consumption with credit and debt. In order to maintain this distinction we name material goods the technological capital of the classical economists, but ownership is the modern meaning of capital. Ownership is Clark's "fund of value," MacLeod's "economic quantity," and the assets and liabilities of corporation finance.[71]

(11) **Separation of Debt Markets.** *a. Money and Capital.*—Henry Sidgwick, in 1883,[72] was the first economist to make use of MacLeod's distinction of ownership and materials, but he corrected MacLeod by pointing out the difference between Wealth and Capital, which MacLeod had identified. Sidgwick's Wealth was "social utility," the result of labor; but Capital was private ownership of wealth.[73] Wealth was wealth; Capital was assets. The distinction turned on the meaning of interest.

---

[68] Above, p. 90, Closing the Negotiations and Closing the Transaction.

[69] Clark, J. B., *The Distribution of Wealth* (1899).

[70] Above, p. 413.

[71] Below, p. 487, Capital and Capitals.

[72] Sidgwick, Henry, *The Principles of Political Economy* (1883). Citations are made to the 2d ed., 1887, which, he says, was not altered on any point of fundamental importance.

[73] *Ibid.*, 83 ff.

"Interest," Sidgwick said, "is the share of produce that falls to the owner of Capital as such; meaning by 'capital' wealth employed so that it may yield the owner a surplus of new wealth. From the individual's point of view, such capital may reasonably be considered as still existing, even when the wealth has been spent without leaving material results, whenever it has been employed so as to secure the owner a reasonable expectation of having its equivalent returned to him along with interest, or even of receiving interest only in perpetuity." [74]

But Sidgwick distinguishes three kinds of capital—shares of stock, bonds, and land values.

". . . the dividends of such companies are to be regarded as merely interest on the Capital owned by the shareholders, no less than the money annually paid to the bondholders . . . and the yield of land is a species of interest." [75]

These three kinds of capital may greatly fluctuate after the original investment has been made. This depends on changes in the rate of interest (assuming a stable purchasing power of money).

"If the rent of a piece of land were to remain the same while the current rate of interest fell from 3 to 2 per cent the price of the land would *ceteris paribus* raise 50 per cent." [76]

Evidently the same can be said of his other forms of capital, namely, stocks and bonds. A fall of 33 per cent in the rate of interest would, if other things remain the same, produce a rise of 50 per cent in the magnitude of capital.

But this increase in the quantity of capital is not an increase in capital "from the point of view of the community."

An increase in their value "obviously does not constitute a real increase of wealth: since the command over the necessaries and conveniences of life possessed by the community is, speaking broadly, no greater because the exchange value of its instruments of production has risen in consequence of a fall in the rate of interest. But from the individual's point of view the increase of wealth is, in a certain sense, real and not merely nominal; for though the real income of the owner of the capital is not increased by the change, his power of purchasing consumable commodities has certainly increased, though he can only exercise it by spending his capital." [77]

[74] *Ibid.*, 256.
[75] *Ibid.*, 258.
[76] *Ibid.*, 259.
[77] *Ibid.*, 259.

But how shall this capital be expended and thus converted into consumable commodities? By converting it into bank deposits with general purchasing power.

Sidgwick proceeds to construct a definition of money which shall fit MacLeod's definition of a negotiable debt but shall avoid the physical analogy of a commodity. He faced the difficulty of defining a term "so fluctuating and uncertain" as money, by criticizing the objection raised by Jevons against attempting any definition at all. Jevons, says Sidgwick, had said it was a "logical blunder" to suppose that, by "settling the meaning of a single word [money or capital], we could avoid all the complex differences and various conditions of many things, requiring each its own definition." Jevons had referred to the contradictory objects which are or may be called money, such as "bullion, standard coin, token coin, convertible and inconvertible notes, legal tender and not legal tender, cheques of various kinds, mercantile bills, exchequer bills, stock certificates, etc.," each of which "requires its own definition." But Sidgwick replied that Jevons' position is "paradoxical" in maintaining that it is "logically correct to give definitions of a number of species, but logically erroneous to try to define their common genus." [78] The species themselves have the "same sort of difficulties, when one attempts to determine them precisely, as the wider notion 'money' does."

Then Sidgwick lays down an "essential and fundamental function of money," which shall serve him as the general function of the genus money. This is a function that will distinguish money from "goods," or "commodities," or "wealth," but will permit more detailed definitions of the differences which distinguish one species of money from another. This general function of money is that of being "used in exchanges, and other transfers of wealth where the object is to transfer not some particular commodity but command over commodities generally: it is as a medium of wealth-transfer that money is qualified for performing its other important function of measuring values." [79]

Sidgwick, on the basis of this fundamental function running through all the various kinds of money, explains how it is that business men, bankers, and even so distinguished an economist as Bagehot, define money at first as metallic money or bank notes, but in most of their reasoning speak of it as "bankers' obligations to pay money on demand, not even embodied in bank notes." The explanation is that "in ordinary times" a practical man is aware

[78] *Ibid.*, 217.
[79] *Ibid.*, 225, 226.

that "he can convert any portion of his bankers' liabilities into gold or notes [80] at will, and that he only leaves it in its immaterial condition for his own convenience. . . . Hence he naturally comes to think and speak of all the 'money at his bank' as 'ready cash.' So Bagehot conceives England to have 'more ready cash' than any other country," whereas what she has is more bank debts payable on demand.

Then, when it comes to a crisis and collapse of credit "the difference between bankers' liabilities and their means of meeting them becomes only too palpable; the same thing that he [Bagehot] has just called 'cash' appears to him in its opposite character of 'credit'; and he [Bagehot] views England's 'cash in hand' as being 'so exceedingly small that a bystander almost trembles at its minuteness compared with the immensity of the credit that rests upon it.' " [81]

With this double meaning of money in view, Sidgwick decides to follow MacLeod and adopt the term current in the money market, so as to denote by money the "whole" of the ordinary medium of exchange. He criticizes Mill who spoke "contemptuously" of MacLeod's "extention of credit being talked of . . . as if credit were actually capital," whereas, according to Mill, it is only a "permission to use the capital of another person." Sidgwick observes that, in a certain sense the same is true of gold coin.

". . . its only function is to 'permit' or enable its owner to obtain and use other wealth: and that it is only in this sense that Mill's statement is true of the credit or liabilities which a banker lends to his customers, whether in the form of notes, or under the rather misleading name of 'deposits.' This credit, no doubt, is a comparatively fragile and perishable instrument for transferring wealth; but that is no reason for ignoring the fact that, in a modern industrial community, it is the instrument mainly used for this important purpose." [82]

Sidgwick thereupon changes Walker's definition of money to conform to MacLeod's definition. Walker had defined money as "that which passes freely from hand to hand throughout the community in final discharge of debts and full payment for commodities." [83] But Sidgwick changes Walker's term, "from hand to hand," making it read, "from owner to owner," in order to include as money bank deposits which Walker had excluded from his definition of money, although he had included bank notes.

[80] Mainly Bank of England notes.
[81] Sidgwick, H., *op. cit.*, 223. See above, p. 397, The Debt Pyramid.
[82] *Ibid.*, 224 n-225 n.
[83] Walker, Francis A., *Money in Its Relation to Trade and Industry* (1st ed., 1879).

"It appears to be the difference between the two phrases which renders Mr. Walker unwilling to recognize deposits in banks as money; since they cannot 'pass from hand to hand,' as notes do. But surely when payment is made by means of notes (not being legal tender), the important fact is not the mere physical transmission of pieces of paper, but the transfer of claims on the banker: which is equally effected when payment is made by cheques." [84]

This criticism of Walker shows that Sidgwick had discarded the physical economists' notion of "exchange" and "circulation" as a physical delivery of commodities "from hand to hand," and had substituted MacLeod's institutional transfer "from owner to owner."

"No doubt," he said, "the receiver of the cheque *might* demand payment in notes: but similarly the receiver of notes might pay them in and have the sum added to his account. The former, again, might ask for payment in gold; but so equally might the latter. From neither point of view does there appear to be any essential distinction between the two. In saying this I do not mean to ignore the important practical difference that exists between payment by notes and payment by cheques. Cheques do not circulate as notes do: the receiver of a cheque commonly pays it without delay and thus selects the banker whose liabilities he consents to take as money, whereas the receiver of a note usually exercises no such choice; so that the transfer of bankers' liabilities is more complicated in the former case than in the latter; since . . . there is a change of bankers as well as a change of bankers' customers. But none the less is the essence of the transaction a transfer of bankers' obligations 'in final discharge of debts and full payment for commodities.' Accordingly a definition of money which includes bank notes generally and excludes the rest of bankers' liabilities is, I think, quite unacceptable." [85]

To find the definition of a "substitute for money" was Sidgwick's main difficulty in constructing a definition of money. An author's meaning of "substitute for money" must always be the residue of his meaning of "money." If money is only gold coin, then every other means of payment and purchase which transfers a title of ownership would be a substitute for money.

Sidgwick meets this difficulty under the heading of the "finality" of different kinds of money in the discharge of debts and full payment for commodities. He concludes that finality is a matter of degree, and that the "highest degree" of finality belongs to incon-

[84] Sidgwick, H., *op. cit.*, 226 n–227 n.
[85] *Ibid.*, 227 n.

vertible notes of a modern government as an internal medium of exchange, through the two legal devices of their acceptance by government at their nominal value in payment of taxes or other debts due to the public treasury, and their recognition as legal tender in the payment of private debts. This kind of money is even more "final" than gold. If gold is not legal tender, and if contracts to pay gold bullion in lieu of legal tender are conceivably not enforced in court,[86] then gold would have a lower degree of finality in payment of debts than legal tender notes.

Bank notes, *not* legal tender, says Sidgwick, have a lower degree of finality than inconvertible paper, not different materially, however, from that of bank deposits. This lower finality than legal tender is owing to the fact that the banks may be called upon to discharge their own debts in legal tender. But this liability is balanced by opposite transactions by which the banker receives gold or notes in exchange for his own liabilities. So that "in ordinary times bankers' liabilities are accepted in final discharge of ordinary debts."[87]

But, we hold, there is required an additional quality besides negotiability. In order that a debt may form a medium of exchange it must *not* be subject to any *time-discount* when it is tendered in payment or purchase. If subject to such discount it is not money but is—capital. Sidgwick does not seem to recognize this distinction. He centers his definition of money on "negotiability" but does not include also the absence or presence of time-discount as a basis of difference between money and capital. He says:

"... there are certain widely accepted securities—the bonds of some governments, of some railways, etc.,—which are so much more convenient for transmission than bullion that they are frequently used as substitutes for bullion in the payment of international debts. When such securities have come to be bought and sold with a view to the fulfillment of this function, to deny that they possess *pro tanto* the most essential characteristics of money, would be to make ourselves the slaves of language."[88]

True enough, we should say, these securities are negotiable, like money, and have a degree of "finality." But they should not be included in the definition of money because their value increases

[86] A modern device, designed to come within the constitutional prohibition against "impairing the obligations of contracts," is the agreement in a mortgage contract that the debt shall be paid in "gold coin of the United States of America of the present legal standard weight and fineness, with current rate of exchange on New York."

[87] Sidgwick, H., *op. cit.*, 227.

[88] *Ibid.*, 230.

as they approach maturity by reason of shortening the period of time-discount. But money, proper, carries no time-discount, and this is the reason why bank deposits may properly be defined as money. Bank deposits may be classified as money because they are bankers' debts *past due,* but "securities," whether short-time commercial debts or long-time bonds, etc., are debts *not yet due,* and are therefore to be classed under the heading of "capital."[89]

This conforms to the three kinds of markets, the "money market," including transfers of ownership of bankers' debts *past due;* the "short-term capital market" or transfers of ownership of debts *not yet due,* but due in a short time; the "long-term capital market," or transfers of ownership of debts *not yet due,* but due at the end of a longer future time, with interest-payments due annually or semi-annually. In short, the money market is the market for debts past due, and not subject to time-discount; the capital market is the market for debts not yet due and therefore subject to a time-discount. It is "capital" then, or debts *not yet due,* which are "substitutes" for money or *debts past due.*

The foregoing does not mean, of course, that the "value of money" in the sense of "purchasing power" does not change. That is another question. It means only that the value of money does not change by reason of future lapse of time. Debts *past due* have *no futurity* and are *not* capital, but are "cash," that is, a "deposit" account at the bank. Likewise the purchasing power of short-term or long-term securities may change, but this also is another matter. Debts *not yet due* have *futurity* as one of their dimensions and therefore *are* capital, and may be substitutes for "cash." They are "capital" because they signify a future appreciation of value, not as purchasing power, but as shortening a future lapse of time until the payments are due.[90]

Nevertheless, even with this distinction between money and capital (as a substitute for money), it was Sidgwick who, by means of MacLeod's negotiability, or transfer of ownership of debts, first eliminated the physical metaphor of "circulation" as well as MacLeod's physical metaphor of debts as "commodities." The modern bank check scarcely circulates at all. It is created, endorsed, deposited, and cancelled, in payment either of debts previously negotiated, or in payment of new debts currently created at current prices by the transfer of ownership of commodities. Only recently,

---

[89] They may be taken at a "risk discount," on account of insolvency or insecurity. But by "time discount" we mean an expected *interval* of time when waiting accrues.

[90] We are not here considering the other form of modern capital, "intangible property." We are considering only the negotiability of "incorporeal property."

in America, has the reality of what actually happens been made available for scientific measurement, in the statistics now reported and published of "debits to individual accounts." [91]   These debits are a record of the bulk of purchases by business men, and they are thereby a record of the transfer of bankers' demand debts from one creditor of the bank to another creditor.   The term "circulation" is not applicable to this process.   It is now, as it always was, a metaphor descended from the period of metallic money and drawn from the circulation of the blood.   Instead of metaphor the reality is debits on the banker's books and credits on the merchant's books arising out of transfers of ownership.   On this account we might name this kind of money by the act that gives it effect, and call it Debit Money, thereby retaining, for the rather small amount of paper money and coin, the name generally in use of "money in circulation."

It is this economizing of money by debits to accounts that Mac-Leod evidently had in mind when he spoke of Credit as "Productive Capital."   He meant, not that credit produces commodities, as labor does, but that credit increases the *velocity* of all transactions on which the production of wealth depends.   His idea was quite similar to that of Ricardo who distinguished machinery from capital —machinery increased the productivity of labor, but machinery was not capital.[92]   So with MacLeod, credit is productive, not that it *produces* something but that it increases the *velocity* of producing something.   In other words, what MacLeod did in fact was to change the meaning of production from "production" to "velocity of production," and this is the change from production to efficiency and from "circulation" to rate of repetition.

What MacLeod meant was that credit, by increasing the velocity of turnover in the sale and purchase of commodities, beyond what it would be with only metallic money, enormously increases, not production, but the *rate* of production of wealth.   That this was his meaning may be seen in his comparison of the use of metallic money as more "productive" than the practices of a barter economy. The technical purpose of metallic money compared with barter, and of bank credit compared with metallic money, is greatly to increase the marketing velocity of turnover of commodities, and this is a great increase in national productivity.   MacLeod's illustrations are in point.   In the ordinary course of business, he says, goods or commodities pass from grower or importer to manufacturer, then to wholesale dealer, then to retail dealer, then to customer or con-

---

[91] Above, p. 294, From Circulation to Repetition.
[92] Above, p. 348, Ricardo.

sumer. If the grower or importer gets ready money from the wholesaler he can immediately produce or import a further supply of commodities in the room of those he has disposed of. In a similar way, if the wholesaler receives ready money from the retailer he might immediately make further purchases from the manufacturer and so immediately supply the place of the goods he has sold. Likewise with retailer and consumer.

> "If everybody had always ready money at command, the stream of circulation or Production might go on uninterruptedly, as fast as Consumption or Demand might allow. . . . This, however, is not the case. Few or no persons have always ready money at command for what they require. . . . If the stream of Circulation, or Production, were to stop until the Consumers had paid for the goods in money, it would be vastly diminished. . . . But suppose that the merchant has confidence in the wholesale dealer's character and integrity, he sells the goods to the wholesale dealer on Credit. . . . That is, he sells the goods in exchange for a Credit or a Debt, instead of for money. . . . Hence we see that Credit has caused exactly the same Circulation or Production as money does." Hence, the next step is "to make the debts themselves saleable commodities; to sell them either for ready money, or for other debts for more convenient amounts, and immediately exchangeable for money on Demand, and therefore equivalent to money." Otherwise the mass of merchants' debts are "so much dead stock." It is the bankers who buy their "Dead stock" and, by giving "activity and circulation to it . . . convert it from dead stock into further Productive Power," and then the "whole mass of commercial debts is converted into Productive Capital." [93]

Evidently the same may be said of metallic money. It changes agriculture and industry from the slow process of barter to the rapid process of marketing. Says MacLeod, "Credit is Productive Capital exactly in the same way and in the same sense as money is." [94]

This suggests a double meaning of production, and indicates the failure of MacLeod's critics to comprehend MacLeod's accurate meaning of "productivity" distinguished from the then meaning of "production." Productivity is the *rate* of production. "Production" meant, for the classical economists, the production of use-values, without much reference to the *rate* of production. But machinery, money, and credit are alike in that they mean increasing the *velocity*

[93] MacLeod, H. D., *The Theory and Practice of Banking*, I, 303–305.
[94] *Ibid.*, I, 312.

of that production, thereby increasing that national productivity, or *rate* of production, which we name efficiency.

b. Capital-Yield and Bank-Rate.—In the foregoing discussion we have considered only the "incorporeal" property of short-term and long-term debts, as being the equivalent of short-term and long-term capital. But modern capital consists of intangible property as well as incorporeal property. Intangible property is the present value of expected net income from *future sales;* whereas incorporeal property is the present value of expected *payment of debts.* The two together constitute modern capital. The two were not distinguished by MacLeod, as we have seen, neither were they distinguished by Sidgwick. Sidgwick combines in the single concept of "savings," both the present values of bonds (incorporeal property) and the present values of shareholders' stocks and of land (intangible property). He treats them all, following the fallacy of Mac-Leod, as debts. He therefore does not distinguish the more modern "bond-yield" from "stock-yield," or, what is similar to stock-yield, the yield upon the present capitalized value of land. We shall name these and similar yields—upon the present capitalized values—the capital-yield.[95]

Sidgwick makes the distinctions turn on two kinds of interest, the capital-yield and the bank-rate.

Prior to Sidgwick economists were usually content to speak of the "average" rate of interest. But Sidgwick distinguished the rate of interest on short-term loans from the rate on long-term loans. Making an advance on MacLeod who had considered mainly the short-term loans of commercial bankers, Sidgwick said,

"Loans made for short periods by professional lenders of money must yield the latter some 'wages of management' as well as strict interest; on this ground, therefore, we might expect the rate of discount on bills of exchange to be higher than the rate of interest on capital generally. On the other hand, we have to consider that the banker to a great extent produces the money he lends, viz., his own obligations, which so long as his business flourishes he is practically never compelled to redeem; and that he may easily afford to sell the use of this commodity at a price materially less than the rate of interest on capital generally. Hence so far as he increases the extent and security of his business by lending his money chiefly to traders for short periods, competition may force him to make such loans at a rate not above—or even below—that of ordinary interest on capital permanently, though not less safely, invested. And this seems to be actually the case; partly, perhaps, because traders are specially

[95] Below, p. 598, From Marginal Productivity to Capital-Yield.

important customers of banks; but chiefly because it is convenient for bankers to lend money which the borrowers are bound to repay after definite short intervals, in order that they may at any time reduce easily the amount they have out on loan, if exceptionally large payments are required of them. Thus we have no ground for saying *a priori* that the rate of discount charged by bankers on mercantile bills will be—even on the average and after all allowance for differences of risk—the same as the rate of interest on capital generally; there is no economic reason why it should not be more than this, since the banker has to be remunerated for his trouble: and on the other hand there is no reason why it should not be materially less, if the value of the advantages above-mentioned is considerable; since a comparatively low rate of interest on the medium of exchange inexpensively produced by the banker himself would be sufficient to give him normal profit on his banking capital." [96]

This rate of interest received by bankers Sidgwick distinguishes as "value of the *use of money*," but the rate of interest received by those who are not "professional dealers in money" is "a price paid for the *use of savings*," or its equivalent, "the price obtained by the owner for the use of his capital."

Thus Sidgwick's distinction between money and capital turns on the distinction between a rate of interest paid to bankers *not* for their savings, and a rate of interest paid to others for the use of their savings. These savings, for him, are "capital" in the three forms of land values, stock values, and bond values at their present prices. In the case of the "professional dealers in money" interest is a bank rate, not paid for savings. In the case of other lenders interest is a capital-yield paid for savings.

But the two are not different, in this respect. A bank rate is as much a rate of interest paid for the use of savings, as is a capital-yield rate paid for the use of savings. Sidgwick's fallacy turns on two illusions, MacLeod's *manufactory* of credit instead of a *credit transaction,* and the *entity* of savings instead of the *market value* of savings.

(a) Manufacturer or Merchant?—Following MacLeod, Sidgwick pictures the banker as a "manufacturer of credit" *without cost* to himself, for the use of which credit he charges a price (discount).

But the banker is not a manufacturer. He buys the short-term or long-term debts of his customers by transferring to them, on his books, the so-called savings of others for which he has made himself responsible, on demand, by issuing his own debts past due (deposits).

[96] Sidgwick, H., *op. cit.*, 245–246.

Thus, if for a sixty day debt of $20,000 he pays, in the form of a deposit account, $19,800, then the latter is a transfer of that amount of liability, which he has incurred to others generally, to make their "savings" immediately available for them on demand. For assuming this liability he charges a price, the rate of discount, amounting, in this case, to $200, a rate of 6 per cent per year, or one per cent for two months.

Or, stating it inversely, the banker has *sold* to his customer the use of a part ($19,800) of his *general* "good credit," backed by his reputation, by his legal reserves, and by other legal requirements designed to strengthen his credit. For the use of this general credit he receives $200. But this "good credit" consists simply in his ability to pay depositors on demand. At the same time he has *bought*, in the legal sense of negotiation, the *particular* good credit of his customer ($20,000), so that his margin for profit on the one transaction is $200.

The same relation would hold true if the $20,000 were a long-term debt, or bond. But here the annual or semi-annual interest payments would be taken into account in arriving at the price, in terms of a deposit liability, which the banker would transfer, to this particular seller, from his liabilities to all other depositors for the return to them of their savings on demand, in terms of "cash" or general purchasing power.

Hence the banker is not a "manufacturer of credit." He is a merchant or middleman, buying and selling the "savings" of others in the form of their debts *not yet due* in exchange for his own debts *past due*. In such bargaining transactions it is not a manufacturers' "cost of production," as implied by MacLeod, that determines the price. It is the merchants' choice of opportunities, which we have previously analyzed as opportunity-cost, or disopportunity-value.[97]

In this respect, therefore, MacLeod confuses the manufacturer with the merchant. A manufacturer *without cost* is a merchant, meaning by cost the classical "positive" cost of production. He is, as we have seen in our analysis of the theories of Carey, Bastiat, and Böhm-Bawerk, a merchant, buying and selling the "savings" of the community. The merchants' costs are the "negative" costs of avoiding a lesser income by choosing a larger income, and his "values" are the "negative" values of avoiding a larger outgo by choosing a lesser outgo. These are "costless" in the positive sense of a manufacturer's cost of production, but nevertheless upon these

---

[97] Above, pp. 307, 310, Cost of Service and Value of Service.

costless choices of alternatives depends the solvency, liquidity, or bankruptcy of the banking concern.

(b) Savings and the Market Value of Savings.—This brings us to another illusion—the illusion regarding savings. The classical doctrine made savings equivalent to capital, having a "positive" cost of production—abstinence.[98] The degree of intensity of this abstinence from consumption was measured by the rate of interest. The pain of abstinence, or "cost of production" of savings, was severe if the rate of interest was high; less severe if the rate of interest was low.

But savings have a Capital-Value as well as a rate of interest. Sidgwick notes that savings are equivalent to capital only at the point of time when savings are used to purchase "capital" at the then market values of shares, bonds, or land. Thereafter they separate in value, if the rates of interest change.

But they do not "separate" at all. The savings disappear, as such, and something else reappears, namely, capital. The "capital" rises in value if the rate of interest falls, or falls in value if the rate of interest rises. "Capital" now becomes, not savings, but the increasing or decreasing market value of the savings.

But, we note, this market value of savings is not dependent only on rates of interest. It depends also upon the general conditions of prosperity, speculation, depression, bank liquidity, confidence, manipulations of values by insiders, fluctuations in the purchasing power of money, etc. The value of savings may be wiped out by a fall in the values of stocks, bonds, lands, or bankruptcy of banks. Or the value of savings may be enlarged by a rise in capital values.

The case is similar to the early classical doctrine of labor-cost of production of physical capital (materials). The original use-value output of labor, at the time of production, may be diminished afterwards by depreciation or obsolescence, or its use-value may be increased by new uses and fashions after it was originally produced.

So with savings when, theoretically, they are identified with capital. Savings occurred in the past, but capital is the discounted expectations of future income. There is no identity whatever between them. Indeed, savings, in Adam Smith's idea of thrift and parsimony, or Senior's idea of abstinence, disappear just as completely from the modern capitalistic system as did the labor theories of the early economists. The change has been from savings to the market value of savings, that is, from savings to capital. And when we say that the banker is a middleman, buying and selling "savings," what we mean is *not* savings, but present claims to future

[98] Below, p. 500, Scarcity of Waiting.

income. This is the modern meaning of capital divorced entirely from the obsolete meaning of savings. The word "savings" becomes only what may be named a propagandist catchword.[99]

This elimination of savings by substitution of capital-value seems to conform to the modern very colorless terms, bond-yield and stock-yield, and their union in the term capital-yield.[100] These terms are merely a statement of a *ratio* between capital-value and a rate of income claimed by the owners of the capital. All kinds of causation enter into the magnitude of this ratio, but in any case the ratios are standards of forecasting, not magnitudes of past savings.

This concept of a ratio is expressed in the every-day language of capitalists when comparing the valuations of their capital invested in any or all of the many varieties of short-term or long-term debts, or shares of corporations, or land values. The unit of measurement is the dollars per year of income. The amount of market value of capital required to obtain it varies inversely to the rate of interest, and directly with the expected net income. Thus, in our illustration, if the rate of interest is 6 per cent per year, then the amount of capital required to obtain it is approximately 17 to 1. Or if the rate of interest is 3 per cent, then the amount of capital required to obtain it is approximately 33 to 1; and so on for the great variety of rates of interest or discount.

Thus we arrive at a measurement of MacLeod's "economic quantity." It is a multiple *directly* of the annual expected monetary net income from sales or interest payments and *inversely* to the rate of interest. This idea began indeed long ago, in Europe, with land values calculated as the purchase price of so many years of the expected annual income.[101] If, as illustrated by Sidgwick, the interest falls from 6 to 3 per cent, then the years' purchase price rises from 17 to 33. In other words, *not* the savings, but the "capitalization" of income is doubled. It is these capitalizations of expected income that the bankers buy and sell in exchange for their own debts past due. And their demand liabilities are not their promises to restore savings on demand, but their promises to restore capital on demand, in terms of "cash," or general purchasing power.

c. From Single Causation to Multiple Causation.—Sidgwick states that his is a "statical" and not a "dynamical" analysis. By statics he means that the rate of interest is assumed to remain the same during the period of investigation, and that there is no appre-

[99] Below, p. 728, The Propagandist Ideal Types.
[100] Below, p. 598, From Marginal Productivity to Capital-Yield.
[101] Below, p. 487, Turgot.

ciable change in the purchasing power of money.[102] By dynamics he means all changes in money, institutions, and production. The two are what we mean by single causation and multiple causation. All sciences must make this distinction as an instrument of investigation. The foundations are necessarily laid in a single causation analysis. Each factor is successively reasoned out as though no change occurred in any of the others. But all are changing together. We shall reach a theory of multiple causation in the economic concept of limiting and complementary factors.[103] Meanwhile we proceed with various factors, the creation, scarcity, negotiability, and release of debt.

We have considered MacLeod's negotiability of debt. We now consider Knapp's release of debt, Hawtrey's creation of debt, and Cassel's scarcity of waiting.

II. Release of Debt

G. F. Knapp began a dynamic analysis in his concept of "a pay community." A pay community is concerted action of creditors and debtors in setting up a procedure for the release of debts. Knapp was the German MacLeod.[104] He founded his "State Theory of Money" on German and Austrian experience, as MacLeod had founded his common-law theory on British experience. Yet, unlike MacLeod, Knapp's money and debt were not commodities. They were institutions in the twofold meaning of negotiable debts and the concerted action of a debt-paying community for the purchase of debts and release of debtors. His "release of debt" is what we mean by "closing the transaction."

In his theory of money the "essential" attribute was the means of payment, and whether it were metal or paper was "accidental." Indeed, in order to safeguard himself from metaphors and to "replace the metallistic view" by an institutional view "founded on Political Science," he invented a Greek terminology, as do the biologists when they call an ape a hylobate. So metallic money is "hylogenic lytric"—a means of release from debt by weighing a material, but paper money is "autogenic lytric"—a means of release from debt by decree, legislation, or court decision.

What is this "essential" of the means of payment? It is to be found by a generalization that will include depreciated paper money,

---

[102] Sidgwick, H., op. cit., 259 passim. A more expanded static analysis was employed later by J. B. Clark, Distribution of Wealth (1899), whose "capital fund" was the psychological equivalent of Sidgwick's institutional capital value.

[103] Below, p. 627, Strategic and Routine Transactions.

[104] Knapp, Georg Friedrich, The State Theory of Money (translated and abridged, 1924, from the 4th German ed. of 1923; 1st German ed., 1905). Citations are to the translation.

like the Austrian State Notes of 1866, as well as metallic money. "For," says Knapp, "on close consideration it appears that in this dubious form of 'degenerate' money lies the clue to the nature of money, paradoxical as this may at first sound. The soul of currency is not in the material of the pieces, but in the legal ordinances which regulate their use." [105] The "metallist" or "numismatist," says Knapp, deals only with the "dead body" of money. He cannot explain either currency, circulation, or paper money. Paper money "may be a dubious and even dangerous sort of money, but even the worst sort must be included in the theory. Money it must be, in order to be bad money." [106] Knapp takes care to say that he does not recommend paper money pure and simple. "I know no reason why under normal circumstances we should depart from the gold standard."

Knapp's "essential" of a means of payment rests upon the distinctions between a releasable and a non-releasable debt, and the distinction between a commodity and a means of payment. A slave, we may say, is subject to a non-releasable debt, which is a life-long duty to serve his master, and this debt is imposed and sanctioned, not by the master, but by the administrative force of the community of which the master is a member and the slave an unwilling participant. But a freeman—the master himself—is subject mainly to releasable debts (lytric debts), from which, however, he can free himself by offering something (lytron) which the community deems acceptable as a ransom, emancipation, or payment.

Knapp does not enter upon this historical development of releasable debts out of non-releasable debts, which is the whole history of civilization. Hence he does not deal with debts of performance. He deals only with releasable debts of payment. A debt, as MacLeod maintained, is the economic quantity of which duty is the personal obligation. To release from debt is to release from duty, whether of performance or payment. Historically the stages are gradual, from the enforcement of formal and customary contracts of performance or payment, however onerous, to successive enlargements of the methods of release. The means and methods of release extend all the way from abolition of slavery and imprisonment for debt, from bankruptcy laws and wage exemption laws, down to the abolition of rent contracts in Ireland, the abolition of public utility contracts in America, the gradual abolition of term or life contracts for labor by substituting contracts "at will," the prohibition of truck payments and substitution of money payments,

[105] *Ibid.*, 2.
[106] *Ibid.*, 1.

and so on. In most cases that which is substituted for customary or contract debts is "reasonable" performance or reasonable payment, as may be determined by the public authorities. Debts and duties have thus been reduced by enlarging the methods and means of release from debt. Capitalism is the present status of releasable debts, and Knapp's definition of means of payment is a special case of the general principle of the changes in means and methods that have been going on through changes in the working rules of civilization for release from debt.

This is "the essential" of money, according to Knapp. Paper money is not in reality a "debt" of the State, although, for historical reasons, it carries a promise of the State to pay. It is, like metallic money, a means of release from debt.

"It frees us from our debts, and a man who gets rid of his debts does not need to spend time considering whether his means of payment were material or not. First and foremost it frees us from our debts towards the State, for the State, when emitting it, acknowledges that, in receiving, it will accept this means of payment. The greater the part played by the taxes, the more important is this fact to the tax-payer. . . . Payment with non-material money is for the country of its origin just as genuine a payment as any other. It is sufficient for the needs of domestic trade; in fact it makes such trade possible. It does not indeed satisfy certain other demands, but the phenomenon is not in itself abnormal." [107]

Knapp's subordinate distinction, the difference between a commodity and a means of payment, rests upon the first, the difference between a releasable and a non-releasable debt. He defines a commodity as an "exchange-commodity," starting from what he regards as "sufficiently elementary ideas." In this he states explicitly what all economists and lawyers imply in the word "commodity" itself. It means transferability of ownership, and the word "exchange" does not add to the meaning. An exchange-commodity is a commodity.

But is a commodity a means of payment? We cannot tell if we look only to "one transaction."

"When, however, in any society, for example, a State, it is a custom gradually recognized by law that all goods should be exchanged against definite quantities of a given commodity, e.g. silver, then in this instance, silver" is a *general* exchange-commodity "an institution of social intercourse; it is a commodity

[107] *Ibid.*, 52.

which has obtained a special use in society, first by custom, then by law." [108]

This socially recognized general exchange-commodity is always a "means of payment."

"It is untrue that every means of payment is a socially recognized exchange-commodity. . . . In order to be a commodity it must, in addition to its use in the manner provided by law, also be capable of a use in the world of art and industry. . . . The sheets of paper, which are all the eye of the craftsman sees in paper money, are an example of an object which has no other industrial use. They are therefore not an exchange-commodity, though they are a means of exchange." "A man who can employ the exchange-commodity he has received for some craft, but cannot pass it on in circulation, owns a commodity but not a means of payment." [109]

This metal, when used as means of payment, obtains a name, the "pound" or "dollar," which becomes in course of time, purely "nominal" so far as the original weight was concerned. And the name is even carried over to paper money, so that, from the standpoint of original weight it is not a reality—the meaning has been transferred to another purpose, a "unit of validity" for the payment of debts. It is now defined, not really, but historically.

Hence Knapp distinguishes money as a means of payment from both the "coins" and the paper which, for him, are mere "discs," "signs," "tokens," "tickets." "The [word] 'ticket' is then a good expression, which has long since been naturalized, for a movable, shaped object bearing signs, to which legal ordinance gives a use independent of its material. . . . The meaning is to be found out not by reading the signs, but by consulting the legal ordinances." [110] Formerly, before legal ordinances took effect, payment was made by weighing (pensatory); now payments are made by proclamation (chartality).

This legal significance arises from custom, and then is taken over by law which makes it universal within the jurisdiction of the State. In either case this significance is made clear by Knapp's concept of a "pay-community." A bank and its customers "form, so to speak, a private pay-community; the public pay-community is the State." [111] What happens in this "pay-community" is that the members pay their debts to each other in "units of validity," equivalent to "units of value." They are "valid" because accept-

[108] Ibid., 3.
[109] Ibid., 4, 6.
[110] Ibid., 32, 33.
[111] Ibid., 134; see below, p. 590, A World Pay-Community.

able to the community, by which is meant that the community, as a whole, makes them valid by releasing debtors from further duty to pay.

A means of payment, then, differs from a means of exchange in that the latter is a property of commodities in general which have exchange-value, but the former is a socially recognized ransom, or release from obligation otherwise imposed upon the individual by the community of which he is a member or participant. One is measured by a unit of exchange-value, the other by a unit of debt-paying validity. One is economic, the other is legal. This unit of validity is also a unit of value in so. far as it has exchange-value, though we know from history that it may have validity but not exchange-value.

It will at once be seen that this concept of "means of payment," or emancipation from debt, is a universal principle applying to all groups from primitive times to the most modern, in so far as they continue to be "going concerns," but with widely different rules respecting the instruments and performances that carry the signs of release from. debt. Herein Knapp advances beyond MacLeod, by means of his generalized concept of a "pay-community."

We need to go further and inquire, what are the sanctions by which Knapp's "pay-group" enforces upon participants the acceptance and use of that instrument of release. They are not only the "legal sanctions" of physical force, to which a purely "state theory" is limited, but they are also the moral and economic sanctions of what he designates "private pay-communities." The legal sanctions may be designated as legal tender or legal performance—the others are "extra-legal," for they are customary tender or customary performance. Take his instance of a commercial bank and its customers: What compels the customers to accept, in full payment of debts owing them, the demand-debts of a solvent bank evidenced by such a "ticket" as a depositor's check? These bank debts are not legal tender, either by statute law or common law, enforced by physical force—they are customary tender. Yet their acceptance by creditors, within customary limits, is economically, though not legally, compulsory, because anyone who wishes to do business or to continue in business in that community must accept these checks. If he persistently refuses them and always demands legal tender in payment, nobody within that pay-community will enter upon the ordinary business transactions with him. He is as effectively compelled to accept the customary tender of "good" bank checks in payment of debts owing him as he is compelled to accept legal tender. It is not only a matter of convenience with him, nor only a voluntary choice of alternatives, nor only the expectation that he in turn as a debtor can also pay his own debts with the same or equivalent bank checks, nor the expectation of redemption in legal tender—it is a matter of economic compulsion. It is the economic sanctions of competition, ending in profit or loss, success or bankruptcy, that enforce acceptance of the customary tender of bank checks. So that ultimately nine-tenths of the debt payments in the United States are accomplished, not by legal tender, but by customary tender.

The same is historically true of other "pay-groups." Means of payment originate as customary tender and may or may not afterwards become legal tender. For example—to transfer Knapp's Germanic history to Anglo-American pay-communities—at the Fair Court of St. Ives, in the year 1300,[112] Richard May complained that John Stanground had unjustly broken a covenant in that he had paid his debt for an ox and a pig in "crockards and pollards" instead of sterling. At the time when the covenant was made *one* crockard or pollard was customarily rated at *one* penny sterling, but between the beginning and the ending of the transaction the king issued a proclamation prohibiting crockards and pollards throughout England, "so that no one should receive them save only at the rate of *two* crockards or pollards for one penny sterling." The jurors of the Fair Court thereupon decided that the king's ordinance should prevail instead of their own custom and that John should pay to Richard an additional crockard for each penny sterling owed, with damages for "unjust detention" which later became known to economists as a subterfuge for interest.

The interpretation by Knapp, applicable to such a case as this, turns on the meanings of his terms "unit of value," and "unit of validity." He makes them identical, and uses the term "unit of value," not bothering about the difference between legal validity and economic value. His terms are void of economic or physical meaning and are purely legal terms with a "nominal" meaning. This "nominal" meaning is that of a unit of debt-paying validity, recognized, named, and enforced by the pay-community, whether it be the community of buyers and sellers at the Fair of St. Ives, or the community of banks and business customers of the Federal Reserve System, or the community governed by a medieval king, a modern legislature, or modern dictator. Individuals may greatly lose economic value, and others greatly gain that same economic value, in the transaction, as did Richard gain and John lose when

---

[112] *Select Cases concerning the Law Merchant, A.D. 1270–1638*, ed. by Chas. Gross, Selden Society Publications, XXIII (1908), 80, 81.

the physical or economic meaning intended by the words "sterling" or "crockard" was changed. But this is not the legal "essence" of the means of payment. The essence is that, when the payment is made in customary or legal tender, then the pay-community releases the debtor of any further obligation to pay.

This seems commonplace enough, and perhaps to be taken for granted without comment, as it was by the physical and hedonic economists. Its significance emerges, of course, when paper money or bank notes or bank deposits take the place of metallic money and are enforced upon nations and even the community of nations by the exigencies of war or the disappearance of gold from circulation, or by the impounding of gold.

Knapp places first importance, as the sanction which maintains a "means of payment," upon the need of paying compulsory debts owing to the State, such as taxes; and second importance upon the payment of voluntary debts owed between citizens or between the State and citizens and payable in legal tender. The first we shall name Taxes, as typical of all compulsory debts owing to governments, and the second we shall name Debts as typical of voluntary debts, including debts owed to the government when it treats itself as a private person buying and selling on the markets. Taxes are compulsory debts, such as dues, fees, assessments, customs, which the citizen owes, not by reason of bargaining transactions, but by reason of rationing by the State according to ideas of ability to pay or otherwise. They are more accurately named *authoritative* debts, since they are imposed by command and not invited by persuasion. But voluntary debts are debts proper, since they arise out of persuasion according to rules laid down by custom, common law, or statute, and are therefore more accurately named *authorized* debts. Authoritative debts are taxes, authorized debts are debts.[113]

The distinction holds likewise for private associations, such as trade unions, cartels, clubs, boards of trade. The dues, charges, assessments, payable by members to a private association, are authoritative debts, of the nature of taxes within that concern, while transactions between members according to rules of the association

---

[113] The Supreme Court of the United States, in interpreting the "legal tender acts," held that "upon a sound construction of the Acts of 1862 and 1863 which make United States notes a legal tender in payment of debts, public and private, neither taxes imposed by State legislation nor dues upon contracts for the payment or delivery of coin or bullion, are included, by legislative intent under the description 'debts, public and private.' " Lane County *v.* Oregon, 7 Wall. 71; Bronson *v.* Rodes, 7 Wall. 229; Butler *v.* Horwitz, 7 Wall. 258. This opinion of "legislative intent" applies to a particular act of Congress, and does not contradict the more general distinction between compulsory or authoritative debts and voluntary or authorized debts. On the terms "authoritative" and "authorized" see Commons, John R., *Legal Foundations of Capitalism*, 83-121.

give rise to authorized debts. Each kind of debt is equally enforced by the "pay-community," and the payment of each is equally compulsory, but the one originates *without* bargaining, the other *with* bargaining. The distinctions shade into each other, as shown by Seligman,[114] but they are clear enough to furnish a basis for what follows.

The question raised by Knapp is, Which is more important as the grounds for introducing the means of releasing individuals from their debts to other individuals? Is it taxes, or is it the authorized debts owed between citizens? Knapp answers that it is the former.

> "For," he says, "as soon as the State has elevated a kind of money (say the State notes) into the position of valuta [receivable and payable by the State], it cannot in its judicial capacity require that the private debtor should perform his lytric obligations [releasable debts] in one way and the State as debtor in another. So, if from political necessity the state announces that henceforth it will pay in State notes, as fountain of law it must equally allow the State notes to suffice for other payments. . . . When there is a dispute the State must decide as a judge that a payment in State notes is sufficient. If it did not, it would, as judge, be condemning its own course of action, and contradicting itself." [115]

While this, he contends, is logically true, yet historically we should consider the relative importance of the two factors, namely, the existing institutions and the urgencies of the State. When the institution of credit becomes dominant in the community against the older institution of metallic money, either by custom (commercial banks as above) or by law (Treasury notes, National Bank notes), the means of payment are dictated more by the need of paying debts than by that of paying taxes. At the same time if the needs or policy of the State are dominant for purposes other than the payment of private debts, then it is these peculiar public needs that dictate what shall be used as means of payment in private transactions.

Thus the two purposes of means of paying taxes and means of paying debts operate together, but historically they have been separated. The kings of England, prior to the year 1300, had dictated that only sterling should be accepted in paying all compulsory debts, or taxes, that were owing to the sovereign, except for payments in kind, but it was not until the king actually prohibited crockards and pollards in private transactions that the "pay-community" of

[114] Seligman, E. R. A., "Social Theory of Fiscal Science," *Pol. Sci. Quar.*, XLI (1926), 193 ff., 354 ff.

[115] Knapp, G. F., *op. cit.*, 110.

St. Ives eliminated payments in crockards. Means of paying private debts are separable from means of paying taxes. What the State decrees to be a means of paying taxes, need not even "logically" be decreed as a means of paying private debts. The merchants' court of St. Ives continued its own customary means of payment until the State actually prohibited them.

The more important distinction to be made, therefore, is not that between taxes and debts, as to which is predominant in designating the current means of payment, but is the distinction between public purpose and private purpose, as to which shall prevail in designating the means of payment of either taxes or debts. Shall the customs of business with their private purpose prevail, or shall it be the policy of government, whether legislative, administrative, or judicial, with its public purpose? These public purposes do not turn merely upon the collection of taxes, indeed they are not inconsistent with reduction of taxes, and therefore with their lessening importance in prescribing the means of private payment.

The procedure at the Court of St. Ives was repeated at the beginning of the Civil War in America. The Congress at first issued its "demand notes" for the purchase of war materials. These were usable as the means of payment of taxes, but were not legal tender in private payments. They were not accepted by the public in the payment of private debts, since they were at a premium for payment of customs dues, and so went out of general circulation. Hence, in the exigencies of war, the next step was taken to compel circulation by the issue of United States notes (greenbacks) with the legal tender quality of payment of both public and private debts. But these were not made legal tender in payment of customs dues. Further the Treasury was authorized to re-issue them in payment of government purchases on the commodity markets but not in payment of interest on the public debt.

The United States Supreme Court, interpreting the Constitution, at first denied the authority of Congress to give the legal tender quality to this paper money, but later reversed itself, and the legal tender greenback became a permanent means of payment of public and private debts. The grounds of this reversal were put, first, on the preservation of the Union in time of war, and afterwards on the supreme authority of Congress to declare public policy in times of peace. Thus public purpose was recognized as predominant over private purposes in determining the means of payment of private debts.[116]

[116] Hepburn v. Griswold, 8 Wall. 603 (1869); Knox v. Lee, 12 Wall. 457 (1870); Juilliard v. Greenman, 110 U. S. 421 (1884).

Again, when the change was made from bimetallism to the gold standard, in 1873, debtors were deprived of their former option of paying in the cheaper silver, but the public purpose prevailed, of establishing an equivalent to the gold standard of England and Germany, in order to facilitate foreign trade.

In 1910, when it was determined to establish the gold-exchange standard in the Phillipines, the insular government prohibited the export of silver coin. A merchant brought suit in the Federal court against the Philippine government on the ground that he was being deprived of his private property "without due process of law," a kind of deprivation prohibited by both the Constitution of the United States and the enabling act which set up the Philippine government. The merchant's silver coin was worth 8 cents per dollar more in Hong Kong than in Manila, and he was therefore being deprived, not of his coins, but of their value. This scarcity-value was conceded to be private property, but the United States Supreme Court held that "due process of law," in this case, meant the public purpose of establishing the exchange equivalent of a gold standard. Although the Philippine government may not have acted wisely, yet its act was a matter of predominant public policy and therefore the merchant was deprived of his property, *not without*, but *with* due process of law.[117]

These instances from Anglo-American history indicate the general principle, maintained by Knapp, that the State, as the supreme "pay-community," establishes the means of payment by mere fiat. But they indicate also that the general principle is not to be derived from the circumstance of payment of taxes, but from all the circumstances under which a public purpose is deemed by the governing authorities to be supreme over private purposes. In all of these cases private property—that is the scarcity-value of private property—was taken from one class of people, either creditors or debtors, either buyers or sellers, and transferred to another class, debtors or creditors, buyers or sellers, by the mere fiat of government in declaring what should be the lawful means of payment.

They indicate also, more clearly, what is Knapp's meaning of his term "unit of value." It is, indeed, a unit of legal validity, but not a unit of economic value. "Accessory kinds of money," he says, "with a positive *agio* [*e.g.*, gold and silver in the greenback cases, silver in the Philippine case] if their discs are used as a commodity, are worth more lytric units [debt-paying capacity] than they are valued as means of payment; 'to have value' (in exchange) is a property of commodities; to have validity is a legal

[117] Ling Su Fan *v.* U. S., 218 U. S. 302 (1910).

property of Chartal [authoritative] pieces." [118]   Legal validity releases the debtor from legal control by the creditor.   And if, in
economic terms, this is to be described as a unit of value, the
"value" is a new kind of use-value—the "use" of collective action,
which we name an institution.   A bushel of wheat or a dollar of
physical gold has a physical use-value of a technological character
in the arts and industry.   Out of them can be made flour and
jewelry.[119]   But the use-value of a human institution—in this special
case—is the usefulness to the creditor and debtor—to the creditor,
in that the pay-community relieves him of the burden of compelling
his debtor to pay; to the debtor, in that, after payment is made,
it releases him from further duty to pay.   This debt-paying usefulness is, indeed, the most important of all "social use-values," for
upon it is built Capitalism.

Here, however, comes into light the reciprocal side of every duty
to pay.   There is not only the duty of payment—there is, on the
reciprocal side, a duty of delivery of commodity or service which
we name a duty of performance.

This duty of performance is measured by units of use-value.
The duty to deliver a bushel of wheat on contract is reciprocal to
the duty to pay for the wheat.   Here the legal unit of validity is
the *bushel*, but the economic unit of value is the *price* of that
bushel of wheat.   By delivering the number of bushels which measures the quantity of commodity, he is released from further duty
of performance.   By delivering the number of dollars he is released
from further duty of payment.

Hence it is that Knapp's "pay-community" is also a performance-
community.   On the "pay" side it measures legal or customary
payment.   On the commodity or labor side it measures legal or
customary performance.   The one is legal tender, or customary
tender; the other is legal performance, or customary performance.
The one measurement releases the buyer from his duty to pay;
the other measurement releases the seller from his duty to deliver
a commodity or render a service.   In either case the thing that is
measured is anything that will serve as legal or customary means
of performance or as legal or customary means of payment.

Here we arrive at the complete meaning of Knapp's so-called
"unit of value."   It is a unit of legal, or customary, *measurement*
of the means of performance or payment.   As a unit of validity
it is only a unit of weights and measures, abstracted from the things
weighed and measured.   Hence the "nominality" and "chartality"

---

[118] Knapp, G. F., *op. cit.*, 164.
[119] *Ibid.*, 4.

(fiat) of his so-called unit of value, which is only a unit of validity. A "bushel" is also "nominal" and "chartal" (authoritative) in that our performance-community measures, by that unit, the amount of performance required in enforcing duties of performance. It is the legal unit of performance which the community enforces, like every other unit of measurement, in enforcing duties of performance. The dollar, too, is "nominal" in that the pay-community adopts it as a unit of measurement of the amount of payment to be required in enforcing duties of payment, no matter whether it consists of gold, silver, paper, or bank credit, which are the means of payment.

This is the only meaning that can be given to Knapp's so-called "unit of value." By being a "unit of validity" it is only a unit of measurement. It is the mere legal or customary system of weights and measures, abstracted from the things measured, and employed by the courts in order to apply the language of number to any kind of payment or performance. It is the unit of measurement in enforcing payments or performance and thereby liberating litigants from their duties of payment or performance. Units of measurement are, indeed, defined historically and not logically, for they are historical institutions developed from custom or law in order to make precise the administration of justice. All units of measurement are "nominal," just as language is nominal. Yet they have reality. Their reality is collective action, for they give precision to the working rules that determine how much or how little shall be paid or performed by individuals or corporations.

This brings us to the economic significance of these units of validity. Their institutional significance is the measurement, enforcement, and release of duty. They are the units used by the courts—therefore also in all private transactions liable to come before the courts—to measure, enforce, and release individuals in whatever may be determined to be, in conformity to public policy at the time, the reciprocal duties of performance and payment. Their economic significance is in the expected relative scarcity, at the time of negotiation in each transaction, of the means of performance and the means of payment.

This becomes the transactional meaning of value with its three measurable dimensions of use-value, scarcity-value, and future discount value. The first is measured by standard physical units, as bushels, or the physical weight of the dollar. The second is measured by the standard scarcity unit, the dollar. The third by a standard unit of time, the year. The first set of units measures the means of lawful performance; the second the means of lawful payment; the third the service of waiting and risking.

This leads us to a double meaning of Knapp's "ticket"—a bailment-ticket calling for the *use-value* of a commodity and a debt-ticket calling for the *value* of the commodity. A "ticket," he said, is a "sign" whose meaning must be found by consulting the law books. The common law has evolved legal instruments, or "tickets," corresponding to these two meanings of value as use-value and value.[120]

A claim upon a person for a commodity with regard only to its use-value, but regardless of changes in its scarcity-value or discount-value, is a "ticket" created by the law of bailment and may be distinguished as a "commodity ticket." It is the duty of the bailee (evidenced by a warehouse receipt, a bill of lading, a safety vault deposit, a gold or silver certificate) to deliver the commodity, and with it, of course, its use-value unimpaired, but without regard to changes in its price or any expected interval of time. But the offer to exchange one commodity-ticket, or legal claim, for another legal claim, is a matter of bargaining as to their scarcity and discount values; this, in law and economics, is its value. When the gold or silver certificates, which were the commodity tickets, or bailments, of primitive banking, were issued by the goldsmiths in excess of the gold or silver on hand, they had to be made, by law, bankers' debts instead of bailments, and were no longer a commodity ticket; they became value tickets. As a value ticket, or debt, they are a sign of the three-dimensional meaning of use-value, scarcity-value, and discount-value.[121] But as a commodity ticket, or bailment, they are a sign of only the use-value of the commodity.

This distinction between the use-value and the scarcity-discount-value of titles of legal control is not merely curious and metaphorical, it underlies all the historical paper money fallacies and disasters from John Law to Proudhon and Kellogg's American Greenbackism. Theirs was the failure to distinguish paper money as a bailment, or sign of use-value, from paper money as a sign of scarcity-value and discount-value. They therefore demanded enough paper money to "represent" all commodities, and did not provide precautions against inflation of prices. They confused the meaning of ticket as bailment, calling for a *commodity*, with the meaning of ticket as debt, calling for the *value* of the commodity.

A parallel confusion may often be found in the double meaning of the word "marketing." It may mean the mechanism of marketing or the bargaining on the market. In the mechanism of marketing a "ticket" like a warehouse receipt calls for the *physical*

---

[120] Cf. Commons, John R., *Legal Foundations of Capitalism*, 254.
[121] Below, p. 510, Transactional System of Money and Value.

delivery of the goods. But in the bargaining on the market the "ticket," like a commercial debt or a bank deposit, calls for payment of the *value* of the goods. If the bailment is negotiable it calls for the commodity. If the debt is negotiable it calls for the value of the commodity.

Thus it is that Knapp's means of payment become also means of purchase. If I physically receive a commodity from another person and become the owner of it, instead of a thief, burglar, or hold-up man, the law assumes that I have agreed to pay for it at a current price in the current legal tender, or its equivalent if acceptable to the previous owner, who is now assumed to be a seller instead of a victim.

So that the so-called "purchase" of a commodity or service is in law a debt, incurred by the so-called purchaser, for the commodity or service acquired, and the only difference between a sale on credit and a sale for cash is the difference in the lapse of time between the point of physical delivery of the commodity and the point of release from the debt. In a purchase "for cash," the payment of the debt occurs without a lapse of time worth measuring, but in the payment of a debt, in the popular meaning of debt, there is a lapse of time between the delivery of the commodity and the payment of the debt. Sale and purchase are as much credit and debt as are lending and borrowing, which, in law, as MacLeod showed, are also a sale and purchase of negotiable instruments. But in a sale the debt is paid without measurable lapse of time, while in a credit the debt is paid after a measured lapse of time. The time-differences may be distinguished as cash payment, short-time payment, and long-time payment of debts.

Hence Knapp, like MacLeod, is correct in considering all transfers of ownership of commodities as the creation of debts, and therefore correct in making no distinction between "means of payment" and "means of purchase." There is no distinction either in practice, custom, or law when once a "pay-community" takes the place of barter, and things are no longer merely physically exchanged without regard to ownership, as the physical economists really assumed, but the *ownership* of things is transferred in consideration of a means of debt-payment established and enforced by the pay-community.

It must be observed that Knapp's treatment of his problem turns on the distinction between legislation and administration. Legislation is what the State *promises* to do; administration is what it *does*. Of the Austrian State notes of 1866 (evidently applicable also to the American greenbacks of 1862), he asks "how these pieces stand in the eyes of the law."

". . . On their face they may admit that they are debts, but in point of fact they are not so if the debts are not meant to be paid. In the case of paper money proper the State offers no other means of payment; therefore it is not an acknowledgment of the State's indebtedness, even if this is expressly stated. The statement is only a political good intention, and it is not actually true that the State will convert it into some other means of payment. The decisive factor is not what the State would do if it could, but what the State does. It is therefore a complete mistake to see no actual payment in payment by inconvertible paper money. It is a true payment, though it is not material. . . . We keep most closely to the facts if we take as our test, that the money is accepted in payments made to the State's offices. . . . On this basis it is not the issue, but the *acceptation*, as we call it, which is decisive." [122]

To which we add, as above explained, compulsory acceptation by private persons as well as by State officers.

It is this distinction of legislation and administration that leads to Knapp's classification of means of payment as "genetic" and "functional." The genetic division gives account of their origin, and is twofold: pensatory, that is, payment by weight, and proclamatory, that is, payment by legal ordinance. And it is this distinction that gives rise to his idea of "nominality," because the same word, the dollar, the franc, the mark, is used in weighing and in proclamation.[123]

But the functional division is administrative, and leads to the distinction between "valuta" and "accessory." Valuta money is that which is valid in itself, in that the administration and courts employ it as means of payment. It may be specie or paper; its essential quality is the actual legal tender in use for paying debts and taxes. Accessory money is that which is valid in relation to the full legal tender (valuta) and may also be metal or paper. Valuta money (legal tender) does not function as a commodity and is never purchased. It is simply the "last resort" of the administration and the courts in payments, whether outgoing or incoming. But accessory money is a commodity, for it is purchased ultimately with legal tender money.[124]

Thus Knapp gets beneath the popular notion of money and into the more fundamental sociological notion. He substitutes nego-

[122] Knapp, G. F., *op. cit.*, 50, 51.
[123] Cf. Cannan, Edwin, *The Paper Pound of 1797–1821* (1919).
[124] Knapp. *op. cit.*, 158.

tiable institutions for physical commodities. The common man, he says, is by nature a "metallist." The banker, for example, says that he has received an increase in his supply of "money," and hence money is "easy," whereas what he has received is an increase in the volume of debts owed by him to his depositors. These debts are means of payment and it is, not money, but debts past due that are "easy." "Wall Street" is said to be the center of the "money market," whereas it is the center of the debt market. Economists speak of the "quantity of money," or the "quantity theory of money," whereas it is not a quantity of money but a quantity of debts, and this quantity of debts has somewhere an equal quantity of credits. The quantity of money is the quantity of debts, and the quantity of debts is the quantity of credits. The "real thing," the "reality," is not money—it is the present and expected repetition of debt transactions wherein the so-called "volume" of money is the "volume" of debts. Not a volume of things but a repetition of creditor and debtor transactions is the volume of money. The institutional reality of money is duty and debt, liberty and release from debt, by pay-and-performance communities; its physical reality is commodities; its economic reality is scarcity, usefulness, and discount.

Knapp especially avoided this economic reality and all "economic reflections" on his legal problem. We shall look to Hawtrey for these reflections on economic value suitable to Knapp's theory of legal validity.

III. Creation of Debt

Neither MacLeod nor Knapp connected their debt with a commodity, Knapp because he purposely avoided all "economic reflections," and MacLeod because he mistook a debt for a commodity. It remained for Hawtrey, in 1919, to distinguish a debt from a commodity, but to unite the two in a single transaction.

Hawtrey observes that the artificial things created by man, like money, teaspoons, umbrellas, are to be defined by the use or purpose which they serve, and are unlike the events and objects of nature, such as earthquakes and buttercups, wherein *purpose* does not enter into the definition.[125] The doctrines of the commodity economists made the primary purposes of money a store of value, a medium of exchange, a measure of value, and a standard of deferred payments. But Hawtrey, like MacLeod and Knapp, makes the primary

[125] Hawtrey, R. G., *Currency and Credit* (1919). Citations are made to 2nd ed. (1923), 1–16. See also Hawtrey, R. G., *The Art of Central Banking* (1932).

purpose of money the release of debts arising out of unequal trans-actions; its secondary purposes are the medium of exchange and the measure of value, so that its "store of value" is merely the market-value of a debt owed by other persons.

The commodity economists based their description of the four functions of money on a supposed historical development of money out of barter. But Hawtrey distinguishes what he calls the "logical" origin from the "historical" origin of money. The logical origin is that of serving as a "money of account" for the settlement of balances between traders, and as such it may be carried in the head or on the books without having physical existence.

Furthermore, there is a distinction between a debt and a promise to pay. A debt is "fundamentally an obligation to give not money but *wealth*." It arises out of the process of production itself, whereby "a service rendered creates a debt from the person to whom the product belongs to the person who renders the service." "Legally the use of money enables the debtor to close the transac-tion," or, as Knapp had said, to release the debtor from the obligation of his debt. But the debt itself is not *economically* paid until the creditor has gone into the market and drawn from it "so much wealth as is represented by the purchasing power he has re-ceived." Thus a debt is "wealth" owed to another, and money is the means of furnishing the wealth by paying the debt.

Here is where the "money of account" comes in. "If, instead of receiving money from the debtor, he assigns away his right in the debt to some one else in exchange for the appropriate amount of wealth, he has taken a short cut to the same end." This as-signment of a debt means that he is buying commodities from one class of people by means of debts owing him from other classes of people. But he could not do this continually unless all persons with whom he deals were also assigning to a middleman the debts owing to them. This middleman is the banker. And the bank credit which they receive in exchange from the banker is also merely a debt "differing from other debts only in the facilities allowed by the banker for transferring it to another creditor." They go to the banker, not for "money," but for "money of account," since he is the middleman who is keeping the accounts of indebtedness for the community, and is setting off their debts against each other and paying the balances by means of his own debts. It is Knapp's pay community.

Thus we start our economic theory, not with Adam Smith's as-sumption of individual liberty to produce and acquire wealth, but with Hawtrey's assumption of a duty to produce and deliver wealth. Although Hawtrey does not find it necessary to carry out the logical and historical implications of his starting point, the difference between his theory and that of the classical and hedonic economics is so great that we shall endeavor to bring out the contrast as we conceive it to be.

With Adam Smith the liberty of the individual was not only "natural," by which he meant logical, it was also historically the fancied original state of the individual. But with Hawtrey the logical is distinguished from the historical. The fundamental logical state of the individual, derived from his membership in society, is that of an obligation to deliver wealth to the producers who have rendered the service of producing and delivering wealth to him. This obligation to deliver wealth is debt, and debt is the economic equivalent of which duty is the legal equivalent. Wealth, with Smith, was commodities *freely* produced for the use of others who are expected freely to produce other commodities for exchange. Wealth with Hawtrey is commodities that *must* be produced for the use of others who have already rendered service but have not been paid. One is individual liberty, the other is social obligation. In the one case there is no duty to produce wealth, and the status is the liberty and exposure of the individual. In the other case there is the duty to produce wealth, and the status is the institution of debt. With Smith there was a complete divorce of the theory of credit from the theory of production, for production creates only an exchange-value, and credit has to be started on a different theory. But with Hawtrey the theory of production is, at one and the same time, a theory of both production and credit, for production creates a debt on the part of him who acquires the product, and the equivalent credit in behalf of him who delivers the product.

While Hawtrey does not enter upon an historical investigation designed to discover whether his "logical" analysis of what is "fundamental" was also historically fundamental (whereas Smith assumed that what he thought was logical was therefore historical), yet historical investigation, instead of romantic history, shows that Hawtrey's logical foundation, Debt, is also historically the fundamental starting point of an economic history which is not romance. Primitive societies have often the institution of "gift" which is their method of creating a debt, and they even are known to have set up a money of account. It needs only Knapp's distinction between unreleasable and releasable debts, and a consideration of such notable juristic inventions as assumpsit, negotiability, and legal tender, to bring about an economic theory which not only unifies production with credit but also unifies history with logic.

This will appear by noticing the way in which Hawtrey logically connects his leading concepts of money of account, medium of exchange, and standard of value, and then observing the way in which this logic correlates with historical process. He starts his logical origin of money by the supposition of a "completely organized and civilized society, with all the modern developments of commerce and industry" and then examines "to what extent such a society might have existed just as it is without the use of money." He starts with a cross-section of society. He finds that such a society, not having a commodity which serves as money, will adopt a "money of account." Interestingly enough, modern anthropologists have actually found primitive societies which do have, for transactions between members, exactly this money of account,[126] but which employ a commodity money for "foreign" trade with other communities. In other words, for their domestic trade, they create an economic equivalent of Knapp's pay-community and Hawtrey's money of account, so that Hawtrey's suppositious logic derived by abstraction from a modern credit society is substantially a picture of what has been historically found in primitive societies. This money of account is described by Hawtrey as follows:

"Goods are brought to market and exchanged. But even though there is no medium of exchange, it does not follow that they must be bartered directly for one another. If a man sells a ton of coals to another, this will create a *debt* from the buyer to the seller. But the buyer will have been himself a seller to some one else, and the seller will have been himself also a buyer. The dealers in the market can meet together and set off their debts and credits. But for this purpose the debts and credits which represent the purchase and sale of a variety of goods, must be reduced to some common measur*. In fact, a *unit* for the measurement of debts is indispensable. Where a commodity is used as money, it naturally supplies the unit for the measurement of debts. Where there is no money, the unit must be something wholly conventional and arbitrary. This is what is technically called a 'money of account.' Even when money is used, it may occasionally happen that the unit for the calculation of debts diverges in some degree from exact correspondence with the money in circulation. In that case the distinction between money and money of account immediately becomes a practical one. The value of the standard coin will be quoted in . . . the money of account, and varying amounts of the standard coin will be needed to pay a

---

[126] Turner, G., *Nineteen Years in Polynesia* (1861); Gordon-Cumming, C. F., *At Home in Fiji* (1885); Hoyt, E. E., *Primitive Trade: the Psychology of Economics* (1926). In Greece this money of account was the ox.

given debt. This is an approximation to the state of affairs which we are assuming." [127]

What, then, is the mechanism by which this money of account is stabilized, so that it will continue to be a uniform unit of measurement of debts from day to day, where there is no commodity nor legal tender used as money? A mechanism must take the place of a commodity. It is stabilized either by custom or by banks. In primitive communities, as we have noted, among the members of the community the account-money may be stabilized by custom whereas, in intertribal trade, commodity-money is used and is left to the forces of bargaining.

But in a modern community it is upon the bankers that is laid the burden of stabilizing the unit of money of account, if there is no commodity-money and no legal tender. The mechanism described by Hawtrey is not fanciful, he says, for it was the mechanism of the Bank of England during the fifteen years 1797 to 1812, when "the universal means of payment in England was the Bank of England note, which was not legal tender, and was merely the evidence of a debt due from the Bank, but a debt not payable in gold or any other medium." [128] It was merely a bank note, not different economically from a bank deposit, so that during that period commercial debts were paid, not in money nor even in a promise to pay money, but in the money of account managed by the Bank of England. It will thus be seen that Hawtrey's "money of account" is inconvertible paper money, and the unit of this money of account was the "paper pound." [129] So it is again after suspension of specie payments in 1931 by England and in 1933 by the United States.

The mechanism, without money or legal tender, is the same as Knapp's pay-community. Hawtrey says:

"The debts of the whole community can be settled by transfers in the banker's books or by the delivery of documents, such as bank notes, representative of the banker's obligations. So long as the bankers remain solvent, their obligations supply a perfectly adequate means for the discharge of debts, because [as MacLeod had said] a debt can be just as well cancelled against another debt as extinguished by a payment of money. Of course it is still true that if the banker himself is sued in a Court of Law, there is no legal tender in which he can be ordered to pay. But if he is solvent, he can obtain a credit from another banker. In fact, the

[127] Hawtrey, R. G., *Currency and Credit*, 2.
[128] *Ibid.*, 13, 14.
[129] Cf. Cannan, Edwin, *The Paper Pound of 1797–1821* (1919), xvii–xxix.

natural test of the solvency of a private trader would be his power of obtaining sufficient bank credits to meet his liabilities, and the test of the solvency of a banker would be the ready convertibility of his obligations into the obligations of other bankers." [130]

But here the question immediately arises, If we postulate a money-less society, without either gold or legal tender, and then find that the bank credits of solvent banks fulfill the same purpose as money, have we not contradicted our postulate by bringing in money under another name? No, because we have brought in something that is both legally and economically different from money.

". . . we are accustomed to think," says Hawtrey, "of bank credits as money. But this is only because for the practical purposes of every day the distinction between bank credits and money is rarely of any importance . . . a bank credit is *merely* a debt, differing from other debts only in the facilities allowed by the banker for transferring it to another creditor. No one imagines that a trade debt is money, though it may be as good an asset as a bank credit." [131]

Hence we get back to Hawtrey's original supposition of a society without a commodity-money and without legal tender, having only a voluntary money of account, and to his original question of whether the mechanism of banking can, without the commodity-money or legal tender, stabilize the unit of the money of account for the measurement and payment of debts.

It turns out that a debt is the same quantity as a price, or rather, the function of a price is "to determine the magnitude of a debt." Hence the unit for measurement of debts is identical with the unit for measurement of the prices which determine the magnitude of the debts. This is because a price is not looked upon by Hawtrey from the commodity point of view as the quantity of other goods obtained in exchange for a commodity, one of which goods is the commodity money, but price is looked upon from the transactional point of view as a legally recognized obligation created by the parties to a transaction. It is an outgrowth of the common-law doctrine of *assumpsit* as an element in the modern doctrine of contract originating in the Sixteenth Century. ". . . when a price of any commodity is quoted in a market, this constitutes an offer, the acceptance of which creates a debt from the purchaser of the commodity to the vendor. The function of the price is to determine the magnitude of this debt." [132]

[130] Hawtrey, R. G., *op. cit.*, 4.
[131] *Ibid.*, 5.
[132] *Ibid.*, 5. Of course Hawtrey is here speaking only of one dimension of the magnitude of a debt, the other dimensions being the other dimensions of Value.

Thus Hawtrey's supposition of a society without the commodity-money and without legal tender, but with only a money of account for the settlement of the balance of debts, is not merely a logical device for illustrating the difference between credit and money, it is also the "logic" of the historical situation which made it necessary for the courts, in interpreting and enforcing contracts, to have something more than an unstable money of account if economic security, distinguished from legal security, were to be obtained. How this necessity develops logically but not historically is explained by Hawtrey as follows.

Since the unit for the measurement of debts is the unit for the measurement of prices it is also "inevitably the unit for the measurement of values. The relative values of all commodities (in the economic sense of values) are measured by their relative prices. And the price of each commodity measures its value relative to the unit."

Here the term value is used in the economic sense of value-in-exchange. The price of a commodity is its value-in-exchange for money, that is, the amount of this money of account for which a unit of the commodity will exchange upon the market.

"So long as value means value in exchange, the value of anything, whether it be a commodity or the monetary unit of account, must always be a *proportion*—a value in terms of something else. Just as every commodity has a value in terms of the unit, so the unit of account has a value in terms of each commodity. It may be the equivalent, say, of a pair of trousers, or a ton of coals." [133]

Thus the "price" of a pair of trousers or a ton of coal, is, in the customary money unit, also the "value" of the trousers or coal.

Here it will be noted that value has the double meaning of value per unit, which is price, and of the value of a quantity of the commodity at the price. We have distinguished these meanings as price, and as quantity and value. From these two meanings a third meaning of value, the average of commodity prices, will be distinguished. This third meaning arises out of the fact that "the chief requirement of a unit of value is stability." Hence this third meaning of value is an average of all prices, which Hawtrey explains as follows. "It is all very well to say that the value of the unit must not vary, but there is no single interpretation of the value of the unit. Its value in coals may be stable, while its value in trousers may rise or fall." The same, however, is just as true of a commodity gold as of the supposed unit of account. "It is enough to

[133] *Ibid.*, 5–6.

say that if we can point to a tendency for *all* prices of commodities, reckoned in the unit, to rise together, that means that the value of the unit is falling; and a tendency for all prices to fall means that the value of the unit is rising." [134]   That is, if the average of all prices rises, then the value of the money unit is falling, and inversely, if the average of prices falls, the value of the unit rises. This is as true of the unit of account, without money, as it is of the unit of money.

If, then, without money, but with only a unit of account for the payment of debt balances, will the mere fact of "continuity in the use of the unit from day to day be of itself sufficient to prevent its value in commodities varying in either direction unduly, even though it be unrestrained by equivalence to any specified commodity"?

To answer this, see how the credit mechanism works. "When a banker lends, we say that he grants or creates credit, or 'a credit.' This is a loose way of describing a double transaction." What happens is that "two credits or debts are really created." One of them, the banker's debt, or "bank credit," payable on demand, is the property of the customer, owned by him as a "deposit," and used by him in the form of orders upon the banker to pay somebody else the amount of debt which the customer owes to that third party for commodities. The other debt, the customer's debt to the banker, "since it yields interest or discount for the period before it becomes due, supplies the banker's profit." [135]

How much of this bank debt owed to the customer will the customer buy from the banker by creating his own debt payable to the banker? He is guided, in the first place, "by the then prevailing market prices" if he is a buyer of goods, and by the prevailing prices which he must pay for materials and labor, if he is a manufacturer. He will buy as much bank debt, by creating his own debt, as will be needed to pay these prior producers during the interval between the time when they produce the goods and the time when he will receive payment from a purchaser of the commodity on the markets. But this purchaser and all succeeding purchasers of the commodity at wholesale and retail will also have to buy bankers' debts, by creating their own debts, in order to make these payments, and so on until the ultimate consumer has paid.

But this ultimate consumer, on the other hand, is continually receiving his purchasing power out of these same credits which the customers of the bank are borrowing at the bank. Their supply of purchasing power is regulated by the amount of these bank credits;

[134] *Ibid.*, 6.
[135] *Ibid.*, 10.

it is indeed actually paid to them in advance of the sale of their product by the very credit advances which bankers are making to the merchants and manufacturers. Although the ultimate consumers, such as wage earners, do not borrow at the bank, yet their employers do the borrowing for them, and thereby are able to pay them for their work several months, and even years, before they, as ultimate consumers, pay for the finished product.

Consequently all that is needed to finance the consumers' purchasing power at the prevailing market prices is the continuous creation every day by the banks of sufficient *new* credits to take the place of the *older* credits that their customers are continuously paying to the banks every day by means of these same new credits that the banks are creating every day. It goes in a circle, an endless circle of bankers buying their customers' trade debts by creating their own bank deposit debts, and enabling the same customers afterwards to discharge these trade debts by creating an equal amount of new bank debts with which to pay customers' trade debts, and so on in the continuous circle of paying the prices for goods on the commodity markets by creating and releasing debts on the money markets.

If this is done from day to day without a tendency of all prices to fall or rise together, then the principle of continuity is enough to maintain a stable value of the money unit of account. The "routine of the credit machinery . . . depends upon the new borrowing being on the whole sufficient and not more than sufficient to replace the advance paid off. . . . Granted this, the stability of every other part of the machine follows." [136]

But how about stability of value of the unit of account, with which we started?

> Suppose this routine is interrupted: "If we are to prove that the monetary unit will be a stable standard of value, we must show that if exposed to any disturbing cause the unit will tend to *return* to its former value, or, at any rate, that it will arrive at a new and relatively stable value not differing much from the old." [137]

On this point, consider first the disturbance caused by a curtailment of new borrowings, and then the disturbance caused by an expansion of new borrowings.

The curtailment of borrowing may occur if merchants give fewer orders to manufacturers, or if borrowers reduce their indebtedness instead of spending their credits for commodities and labor. In the

[136] *Ibid.*, 11.
[137] *Ibid.*, 11.

latter case consumers will purchase less commodities and, in either case, "a slackening in the creation of new credits means a diminution of orders to the manufacturers." [138]   This will spread in widening circles so that "the original restriction of credit will tend to repeat and reinforce itself."

But a corrective tendency soon begins to work.

"The restriction of credit means a restriction of the bankers' business.   The bankers will not willingly acquiesce in the consequent shrinkage of their profits, and they will try to tempt their customers to borrow.   They will, in fact, reduce their charge for interest." [139]

But it is not merely the bankers' willingness that reduces the rate of interest.   It is also economic compulsion.

"The curtailment of credit occasions a flagging of the demand for commodities.   This flagging of demand will produce a fall of prices.   The merchants will find that their stocks of goods lose value while they hold them, and this loss of value will diminish the profit out of which they pay interest on the loans with which these stocks are financed.   Falling prices of themselves therefore make borrowing less attractive and reduce the rate of interest which borrowers are willing to pay.   The bankers must reduce their charges of interest accordingly before they can even induce their customers to continue borrowing on the diminished scale which their turnover of goods will justify, and, if these customers are to be tempted to increase their borrowing, the rate of interest must be reduced even below this low level." [140]

But if these measures do not encourage borrowing, how far will the fall of prices go?   The credit operations will not dwindle to nothing, because disappointed merchants will be driven to borrow on any terms, "merely to keep their business alive."   Hence the old routine will revive, but on a lower level of prices—that is, a higher value of the unit—and there is no "tendency for it automatically to return to its former value."   It may continue to go still lower through a new disturbance which curtails new borrowings.

But take the contrary disturbance—something that causes an expansion of credit.

". . . This movement is even more unlimited in scope.   Self-interest prompts both the enterprising traders ever to borrow more, and the enterprising banker ever to lend more, for to each the

[138] *Ibid.*, 11.
[139] *Ibid.*, 12.
[140] *Ibid.*, 12.

increase in his credit operations means an increase in his business. . . . The general rise of prices will involve a proportional increase of borrowing to finance a given output of goods, over and above the increase necessitated by the increase of output. . . . Where will this process end? In the case of curtailment of credits the self-interest of the bankers and the distress of the merchants combined to restore the creation of credits, though not to its preexisting level. But in the case of expansion of credits there is no such corrective influence at work. An indefinite expansion or inflation of credit seems to be in the immediate interest of merchants and bankers alike." [141]

Again, the standard of value of the money of account is completely lost. Here is where money itself comes in. First, as a means for the legal discharge of debt by both the bankers and their customers. This is its primary purpose. "The bankers' obligation must be to pay money," because it is not of itself the legal means of discharging a debt.

Second as a medium of exchange, "because a purchase creates a debt, and money provides the means of paying the debt. When payment is made in ready money this merely means that the debt is *immediately* discharged." Thus a "medium of exchange" is, legally and economically, the creation and immediate discharge of a debt. It is discharged by voluntary acceptance if the medium is bank credit; by compulsory acceptance if the medium is money.

Third, a standard of value. "The value of a debt immediately due is necessarily equal to the value of the means by which it can be legally paid. Thus the problem of stabilizing credit is identified with the problem of stabilizing the value of money." [142]

Thus Hawtrey completes the economics of the legal problem started not only by MacLeod and Knapp, but also by Marx and Proudhon. It turns on the meaning of Property and Prices. With Marx and Proudhon the meaning of property was that of the classical and hedonic economists, namely, the exclusive holding of a physical object against all the world for one's own use. MacLeod added the legal meaning of "incorporeal property," namely a debt owed by one person to another, but he treated this debt like a commodity because, by the legal invention of negotiability it could be bought and sold like a commodity. Hence, misled by a mere technical accident of the English common law, he made this debt a duplicate commodity, additional to the physical commodity whose security or sale created the debt, not observing that the commodity market and the debt market were only two aspects of the same market.

[141] *Ibid.*, 12, 13.
[142] *Ibid.*, 16.

Then Knapp, by his concept of a pay-community, developed the principles, not of a commodity market, but of a debt market. Finally Hawtrey, by tracing each step in modern business transactions, on both the commodity markets and the debt markets, tied the two together by his twofold aspect of Price, a price on the commodity market determining the magnitude of a debt on the money market. On the legal side, where MacLeod had introduced only the legal device of negotiability, suitable to the transfer of ownership of a debt, Hawtrey added the early legal doctrine of *assumpsit*, suitable to the creation of the debt itself. This doctrine, in its modern development, has become the basis of almost all transactions on all markets, and is, in effect, the assumption that a mere offer and acceptance of a price on the commodity market creates, at that price, a debt, whose negotiability on the money market had attracted MacLeod, and whose release by bookkeeping in the office of a bank had attracted Knapp.

Thus a debt instead of a commodity becomes the subject-matter of a science that would unite in one functional relation of mutual dependence the production of wealth, the relative scarcities of wealth and of money, and the laws of property. Since Hawtrey's bankers' debts, or so-called "deposit currency" used as money, is a running account of credits and debits on the bankers' books, we may name it by the act that gives it effect and call it Debit Money. So that the three kinds of money are metallic money, paper money, and debit money.

Hawtrey, in 1919, dealt with those short-time debts of producers and the debts past due of bankers, which have changed the concept of money to the concept of "debits to accounts." For the historical transition itself we go back to Hume and Turgot, economists of the period of metallic money, then proceed to Cassel, Wicksell, Mises, Hyak, Keynes, and Fisher, economists of the period of debit money and central banks of money of account.

IV. Scarcity of Debt

1. *Scarcity of Metallic Money*

Parallel with the labor economics from Locke to Smith and Ricardo, Marx and Proudhon, and with the psychological economics from Bentham to Menger and Böhm-Bawerk which ended in the concepts of Efficiency and Scarcity, there was being developed a monetary economics from Hume, through Turgot, MacLeod, Sidgwick, Jevons, Cassel, Wicksell, Knapp, Hawtrey, and Fisher, which ended in the futurity concept of Debt.

David Hume, in 1752, introduced, in his attack on Mercantilism, three ideas which served to separate succeeding schools of economists into commodity theorists and monetary theorists. First was the distinction between Change and Stability; second, the distinction beween Scarcity and Custom; third, the equivalence of interest on money with interest on capital.

Hume's distinction between a *change* in the supply of money and *stability* of the supply of money relative to commodities and labor led the succeeding physical economists, not yet equipped mathematically to deal with relativity of change, to substitute labor for money as the unchanging measure of value throughout the ages and thus to confuse efficiency with scarcity. Afterwards, when John Stuart Mill quietly substituted metallic money for labor as the measure of value, the money had already changed from metallic money to debit-money, which for him, however, was something psychological, extraneous to his general theory of economics. Hume was dealing only with metallic money.

". . . in every kingdom," he said, "into which money begins to flow in greater abundance than formerly, everything takes a new face: labor and industry gain life; the merchant becomes more enterprising, the manufacturer more diligent and skillful, and even the farmer follows his plough with greater alacrity and attention. . . . Though the high price of commodities be a necessary consequence of the encrease of gold or silver, yet it follows not immediately upon that encrease; but some time is required before the money circulates through the whole state, and makes its effect felt on all ranks of people. At first, no alteration is perceived; by degrees the price rises, first of one commodity, then of another; till the whole at last reaches a just proportion with the new quantity of specie which is in the kingdom. In my opinion, it is only in this interval or intermediate situation, between the acquisition of money and rise of prices, that the encreasing quantity of gold and silver is favorable to industry." On the other hand, said Hume, "this interval is as pernicious to industry, when gold and silver are diminishing, as it is advantageous when these metals are encreasing. The workman has not the same employment from the manufacturer and merchant; though he pays the same price for everything in the market. The farmer cannot dispose of his corn and cattle; though he must pay the same rent to his landlord. The poverty, and beggary, and sloth, which must ensue, are easily foreseen." [143]

[143] *The Philosophical Works of David Hume* (ed. by Green, T. H., and Grose, T. H., new impression 1898), III, 313, 315 (in *Essays, Moral, Political, and Literary,* first published in 1752, "Of Money," "Of Interest," "Of Balance of Trade").

These changes in the scarcity of money exhausted their effect in the prices of commodities and labor. It was the "manners and customs" of the people that determined the quantity of commodities *saved* and the resulting rate of interest. "In a state where there is nothing but a landed interest, as there is little frugality, the borrowers must be very numerous and the rate of interest must hold proportion to it." This he contrasted with a land of commerce and manufacture.

"It is infallible consequence of all industrious professions, to beget frugality, and make the love of gain prevail over the love of pleasure. . . . In order to have a great number of lenders . . . it is not sufficient nor requisite that there be great abundance of the precious metals. It is only requisite, that the property or command of that quantity, which is in the state, whether great or small, should be collected in particular hands, so as to form considerable sums, or compose a great monied interest. This begets a number of lenders, and sinks the rate of usury; and this . . . depends not on the quantity of specie but on particular manners and customs, which make the specie gather into separate sums or masses of considerable value. . . . Those who have asserted, that plenty of money was the cause of low interest, seem to have taken a collateral effect for a cause; since the same industry, which sinks the interest, commonly requires great abundance of the precious metals. A variety of fine manufactures, with vigilant enterprising merchants, will soon draw money to a state, if it be anywhere to be found in the world. . . . Though both these effects, plenty of money and low interest, naturally arise from commerce and industry, they are altogether independent of each other." The greater or less quantity of money "has no influence on the interest. But the greater or less stock of labor and commodities must have a great influence; since we really and in effect borrow these, when we take money upon interest."[144]

This led to Hume's third idea of the equivalence of money with both the physical goods which are saved and with the physical goods which are the interest on the goods thus saved.

"If you lent me so much labor and so many commodities; by receiving 5 per cent you always receive proportional labor and commodities, however represented, whether by yellow or white coin, whether by a pound or an ounce."[145]

In other words, if higher or lower prices are paid for the commodities and labor that serve as *capital*, so also the same higher or

[144] *Ibid.*, III, 325–328.
[145] *Ibid.*, III, 322.

lower prices are paid for the commodities and labor that serve as *interest* on the capital. Hence, while a change in the scarcity or abundance of money causes a change in the prices of commodities and labor, it does not cause a change in the rate of interest. This is caused by a change in standards of living. Hume's analysis was directed towards exposing the errors and relieving the fears of mercantilism against an unfavorable balance of foreign trade. There need be no fear that a nation will lose its proper share of the world's gold and silver when the volume of commodity imports exceeds the volume of commodity exports. The correction will be made by the rise or fall respectively of domestic prices owing to the import or export of specie, until all "neighboring nations preserve money nearly proportionable to the industry and art of each." If the quantity of money in Great Britain is reduced by money exports in payment for commodity imports, then prices of labor and commodities will fall; other nations will "bring back the money which we had lost," and thus raise British prices to the international level. And prices could not permanently rise above that international level because "no neighboring nations could afford to buy from us; while their commodities, on the other hand, became comparatively so cheap, that, in spite of all the laws which could be formed, they would be run in upon us and our money flow out." [146]

Although Hume's argument was limited to its bearings on the international struggle of mercantilism for the precious metals, yet for nearly two hundred years his three new ideas served to divide the succeeding schools of economic thinking into the commodity theorists and the money theorists. On the commodity side, if money is only a changeable mirror of real capital and real interest, then money is nominal and should be eliminated altogether and attention be given only to physical nature, to labor and commodities. This school extended from Quesnay, Smith, Ricardo, and Marx to the managerial economists of recent times.

But, on the money side, if a *change* in the quantity of money has an effect in stimulating or depressing industry, then money is not nominal but is a causal factor in all transactions which determine production, accumulation, marketing, and consumption. The school of monetary theorists may be followed from Turgot's modification of Quesnay until they end in the disappearance of metallic money by the impounding of gold by central banks. The characteristic shift in these theories is the shift from the metallic money of Hume to the negotiable debts of MacLeod, and from ideas of occasional change to ideas of perpetual change.

[146] *Ibid.*, III, 333.

2. *Capital and Capitals*

Anne Robert Jacques Turgot, wisest of the Physiocrats, was to the French Revolution what John Locke was to the English Revolution. Friend and follower of Voltaire, Hume, and Quesnay, visited by Adam Smith during his sojourn in France, governor and reformer of a pauperized French province, Minister of Finance but dismissed for shifting the burden of public expenditures to the landed nobility, his reforms were reënacted fifteen years later by the Revolution which guillotined those whom he might have saved.

Turgot was executive of his own theories. While yet a provincial comptroller, twenty-five years before the Revolution, he had stated in manuscript the theoretical foundations [147] both for his reforms and for the modern monetary theories that succeed to the classical and hedonic commodity economists. Preceding the period of commercial banks, of stock exchanges and business corporations, at a time when money was silver, when landed property was "big business," when Feudalism was becoming Capitalism, he unravelled the tangle of money, value, capital, interest, the commodity market, and the money market.

"On the commodity market [*au marché*] a quantity of *wheat*," he says, "is estimated against a certain *weight* of *silver;* on the loan market [*commerce du prêt*] the object estimated is the *use* of a certain *quantity* of *values* during a certain *time*. In the first case it is a *mass of silver* compared with a *mass of wheat;* in the other case it is a *mass of values* compared with a certain fixed proportion of *itself*, which latter becomes the *price* of the *use* of this mass of value during a certain *time*." This time-price is interest.[148]

Cassel has said of this statement that, by rejecting the old idea of interest as a "price of money" and defining interest as "the price given for the use of a certain quantity of value for a certain time," Turgot had fashioned "a formula never afterwards surpassed in clearness and definiteness." [149] What, then, is this "object" which Turgot can call a "mass of values," for which a price, interest, is paid? It has two aspects which MacLeod distinguished as the incorporeal property of debt and the corporeal property of a landed estate. The former is a legal promise to pay silver for the use of

[147] Turgot, A. R. J., *Reflections on the Formation and Distribution of Riches* (tr. 1898). Citations are to the translation, changed, however, to my rendering of the French edition of 1788.
[148] *Ibid.*, Sec. 78.
[149] Cassel, G., *The Nature and Necessity of Interest* (1903), 20.

the value of silver. The latter is a right to have the yield of the land.

"A piece of land which produces an annual net income [*un revenu*] of *six sheep* can be sold for a certain value which can always be expressed by a number of sheep equivalent to this *value*. . . . The price of the landed property [*un fonds*] then will be simply a certain number of times its annual income; 20 times if the price is 120 sheep, 30 times if the price is 180 sheep. Thus the current price of lands [*des terres*] regulates itself by the ratio of its value of the property [*fonds*] to the value of the annual income, and the number of times which the price of the property contains the income is called the number of years' purchase [*le denier du prix des terres*]. Lands sell at twenty years' purchase [*le denier vingt*], thirty years' purchase, forty years' purchase, etc., when people pay for them 20, 30 or 40 times their annual income." [150]

Turgot named this purchase price of the landed property (*fonds*) also a "mass of values," and the six sheep per year a certain proportion of the mass received by the owner. This proportion between the number of sheep, which constitute the expected yearly income, and the number of sheep paid for the land, the latter constituting the "mass of value," is the "yearly price" which the owner receives for the use of the number of sheep originally required to purchase the landed estate.

What is it that determines this proportion between interest and capital? It is demand and supply. The proportion "must vary according as there are more or less people who wish to sell or buy lands, just as the price of all other articles of commerce varies according to the varying proportion between supply and demand." Thus, if the "mass of value" paid by the buyer of landed property is 120 sheep, and the annual income received by him is 6 sheep, then the price received by the buyer for the use of his 120 sheep in buying the land is 5 sheep per hundred per year, a ratio of 1 to 20. But if the competition of buyers of land runs the mass of value up to 180 sheep for an expectation of 6 sheep per year, then the price is 3 sheep per hundred per year. The seller of the land foregoes an expectation of 5 sheep per hundred per year when the buyer pays for the expectation a "mass of value" equal to 120 sheep; or the same seller foregoes an expectation of 3 sheep per hundred per year when competition forces the buyer to pay for the expectation a "mass of value" equal to 180 sheep.

[150] Turgot, A. R. J., *op. cit.*, Sec. 57.

Finally, Turgot, as did Hume, converts the loan, the land, and the yield per year into equivalent silver.

"Whether 20,000 ounces of silver on the commodity market are the equivalent of 20,000 measures of wheat or only of 10,000, the use of these 20,000 ounces of silver during the year will none the less, in the loan market, be worth the twentieth part of the principal sum, or 1,000 ounces of silver, if the interest is at twenty years' purchase [*au denier vingt*]." [151]

In other words, whether the price of wheat per bushel or of sheep per head is one ounce or two ounces of silver, makes no difference in the rate of interest, since this is a price paid in silver for the *use* of the silver, and the former is a price paid by the borrower in *using* the silver itself to buy commodities or land. If prices of commodities are doubled the interest remains the same, since it is a ratio between two quantities of money, but the changing prices are ratios between a quantity of money and a quantity of things not money. The one is the relation between capital and interest on the loan market; the other between buying and selling on the commodity markets.

The same principles hold true in manufactures of all kinds, and in all branches of commerce. It is Turgot's distinction between "capital" and "capitals." "Capital" is the "mass of values" advanced by entrepreneurs and lenders, but "capitals" are the "mass of accumulated riches" thus advanced. The distinction is similar to that made by J. B. Clark, a century and a quarter later, between a "fund of capital" and a "flow of capital goods." Capital, according to Turgot, is capital fund (*fonds*); but capitals are capital goods. What Clark measured as utility, Turgot measured as sheep or silver. They are, with Turgot, the identical mass of value, but capital is the value of money in purchasing goods, while capitals are the same value of the goods purchased with the money.

It is this distinction that gives to Turgot the "true idea" of Quesnay's "circulation of money," as well as his own distinction between saving and investment.

The circulation of money, he says, gives rise to "a mass of capitals, or of moveable accumulated riches, which having been at first advanced by the entrepreneurs in each of these different classes of labours, must return to them every year with a steady profit; but the capital is to be again invested and advanced anew in the continuation of the same enterprises and the profit is to provide for the more or less comfortable subsistence of the entre-

[151] *Ibid.*, Sec. 78.

preneurs. It is this advance and this continual return of capitals which constitute *what one must call the circulation of money;* that useful and fruitful circulation which gives life to all the labours of the society, which maintains movement and life in the body politic, and which is with great reason compared to the circulation of the blood in the animal body." [152]

This is the distinction between saving and investment. Saving is saving money. But investment is spending the money. The one accumulates *capital,* the other "forms" *capitals.* Says Turgot,

"Money plays scarcely any part in the sum total of existing capitals; but it plays a great part in the *formation* of capitals. In fact, almost all savings are made in nothing but money; it is in money that the revenues come to proprieters, that the advances and the profits return to entrepreneurs of every kind: it is therefore money that they save, and the annual increase of capitals takes place in money: but none of the entrepreneurs make any other use of it than to convert it *immediately* into the different kinds of effects upon which their enterprise depends; and thus this money returns to circulation, and the greater part of capitals exists only in effects of different kinds.[153] . . . Whoever, either from the revenue of his land, or from the wages of his labour or industry, receives each year more values than he needs to spend, may place this superfluity in reserve and accumulate it: these accumulated values are what is called *a capital.*" [154]

Turgot summarizes the different methods of employing "capitals" through investment and return of "capital," by means of money.

"The first is to buy a landed estate which brings in a definite net income (*revenu*).
"The second is to invest one's money in agricultural undertakings, by taking a lease of lands,—the produce of which ought to yield, over and above the price of the lease, the interest on the advances and the price of the labour of the man who devotes his riches and his toil to their cultivation.
"The third is to invest one's capital in industrial or manufacturing undertakings.
"The fourth is to invest it in commercial undertakings.
"And the fifth is to lend it to those who want it, in return for an annual interest." [155]

So much for investment. It is the active bargaining transaction of spending money. But saving is also active—it is the service of waiting.

152 *Ibid.*, Sec. 67.   154 *Ibid.*, Sec. 58.
153 *Ibid.*, Sec. 100.   155 *Ibid.*, Sec. 83.

"Whoever has seen the establishment of a tanner realizes the absolute impossibility of one poor man, or even of several poor men, providing themselves with hides, lime, tan, utensils . . . buildings . . . and living during several months until the leather is sold." Who, then, will make these advances? "It will be one of those possessors of *capitals,* or of moveable accumulated values. . . . It is he who will wait for the sale of the leather to return to him not only all his advances but a profit in addition, sufficient to make up to him for what his money would have been worth to him if he had employed it in the purchase of an estate, and, furthermore, for the wages due to his labours, his cares, his risks, and even his skill." [156]

Thus Turgot identified as one and the same mass of value the several concepts of capital and capitals, capital-fund and capital-goods, money-value and value of capital-goods, the negative act of saving, the active service of waiting, the bargaining transactions of spending the money saved and the investment of the savings in capital goods. Interest becomes the price paid for the service of waiting.

With these identifications Turgot proceeded to expose the errors of St. Thomas.

"The Scholastic theologians," he said, "have concluded from the fact that money produces nothing by itself that it was unjust to demand interest for money placed on loan.[157] . . . Money considered as a physical substance, as a mass of metal, does not produce anything; but money employed in advances for enterprises in Agriculture, Manufacture, and Commerce procures a definite profit. With money one can purchase an estate, and thereby procure a revenue. The person, therefore, who lends his money does not merely give up the barren possession of that money; he deprives himself of the profit or of the revenue which he would have been able to procure by it; and the interest which indemnifies him for this privation cannot be regarded as unjust." [158]

Thus Turgot's interest or profit is determined, not by positive cost but by alternative opportunities, named afterwards by Green and Davenport "opportunity-cost."

Turgot did not consistently distinguish between interest and profit; consequently he did not always distinguish between debt and purchasing power, or between saving and investment, which are the recent distinctions between incorporeal and intangible property. He used the word "pledge" (*gage*) where MacLeod used the word

[156] *Ibid.,* Sec. 60.
[157] *Ibid.,* Sec. 73.
[158] *Ibid.,* Sec. 73.

"debt," and he distinguished, as did MacLeod, between particular pledges, which are debts, and general pledges, which are purchasing power. "Every commodity," he said, "is a representative pledge [*un gage representif*] of all the objects of commerce." [159] Out of these particular pledges arises the universal pledge, money. They are pledges in the sense that commerce "gives to every commodity a current value relatively to every other commodity; whence it follows that every commodity is the equivalent of a certain quantity of every other commodity, and can be regarded as a pledge which represents it." [160]

Thus Turgot's "pledge," applied to money and all commodities, is the economic expected purchasing power equivalent to the juristic "intangible property." It is not a debt—it is expected power to agree upon prices of commodities in bargaining transactions. And it is property in the sense of a right of non-interference with one's liberty of access to markets and liberty in fixing by bargains the prices and values of things. His landed estate, or corporeal property, becomes intangible property when the expected corporeal income of sheep or wheat becomes the expected prices to be obtained by selling the sheep or wheat for money.

The most brilliant originality of Turgot was his concept of marginal productivity which, 160 years later, became Wicksell's concept of "natural interest," but was overlooked meanwhile on account of the prevalence of Ricardo's concept of marginal productivity. Ricardo's was a concept of labor-productivity; Turgot's a concept of "capitals" productivity. Turgot arrived at this concept in his effort to show the services rendered to society by increasing the supply of savings and thus reducing the compensation for waiting. He said,

"The current interest on money placed on loan can, then, be regarded as a kind of thermometer of the abundance or scarcity of capitals in a Nation, and of the extent of the undertakings of every sort on which it may embark. . . . The price of interest may be looked upon as a kind of level beneath which all labor, all agriculture, all industry, all commerce come to an end. It is like a sea spread over a vast area: the summits of the mountains rise above the waters, and form fertile and cultivated islands. If this sea happens to roll back, in proportion as it descends, first the slopes of the hills, then the plains and valleys, appear, and are covered with every kind of produce. It is enough that the water should rise or fall a foot to inundate immense tracts, or throw them open to agriculture. It is the abundance of capitals which

[159] *Ibid.*, Sec. 38.
[160] *Ibid.*, Sec. 33.

animates all undertakings; and the low interest of money is at once an effect and the indication of the abundance of capitals." [161]

Turgot extends this illustration, from industry and agriculture as a whole, to particular establishments. If, owing to *scarcity* of "capitals" the interest is 5 per cent, then the industries and agriculture are restricted to higher levels whose products sell at prices which yield 5 per cent for capital, and then the value of an estate yielding 50,000 livres is one million. But if, owing to *abundance* of "capitals," interest is 2½ per cent, then industry and agriculture expand to lower levels and the value of the same estate is two million.

Thus the "marginal productivity" of *capitals* is both the extensive and the intensive "marginal income" of *capital,* and these are two sides of the same abundance or scarcity of *capitals.* The output side is "every kind of produce"; the income side is silver obtained for the output on the commodity markets. They are of the same dimension, since the silver obtained is the exchange-value of the output. One side is *physical* productivity, the other side is *"value* productivity," a distinction often obliterated by a double meaning of "productivity." This value productivity, however, is income, not output. It is first a gross income. A net income of silver must remain for *capital* in order to pay interest, the price of the use of the mass of value advanced. Hence there are two dimensions of the same abundance or scarcity of *capitals*—the future and the present. The future is the net income of silver expected from the commodity markets; the present is the number of years' purchase price paid for that expectation on the *capital* market. For example, he says:

"A man who has a rent-roll of 50,000 livres has a property worth only a million if estates are sold at the twentieth penny [20 years' purchase]; he has two millions if estates are sold at the fortieth penny [40 years' purchase]. If interest is at 5%, all uncleared land whose produce would not bring 5% over and above the replacement of the advances and the recompense for the care of the Cultivator, would remain uncultivated. No manufacture, no commerce will maintain itself which will not bring in 5% over and above the wages of the undertaker's exertions and the risks. If there is a neighboring Nation in which the interest of money is only 2 per cent, not only will it carry on all the branches of commerce from which the nation where interest is 5% finds itself excluded, but, moreover, as its manufacturers and merchants can content themselves with a lower profit, they will place their commodities on all the markets at a much lower price." [162]

[161] *Ibid.* (Ashley ed.), Secs. 29, 90.
[162] *Ibid.,* Sec. 89.

Thus the abundance or scarcity of *capitals* operates in multiple fashion upon the mass of value which constitutes *capital*. It increases or diminishes the quantity of output of commodities along with the quantity of silver income for which the output is sold; and it, inversely, raises or lowers the present *value* of a landed estate, which is *capital*.

From this it follows that depreciation and interest of *capitals* are as much compulsory payments as wages of labor and compensation of tenants who cultivate the soil. The worn-out and used-up *capitals* must be replaced in order to maintain the *capital* unimpaired at its initial mass of value; and interest must be paid according to the existing state of abundance or scarcity of *capitals*. All of these payments are "indisposable," that is, economically compelled, in the sense that the State cannot, by physical compulsion, "appropriate without public injury a part of them for the public wants. . . . There exists no truly disposable revenue in a State except the net produce of lands." [163]

Hence the burdens of taxation must be removed, not only from manufacturers and merchants, but also from agriculture and money lending, and must be placed, not on agriculture, as Turgot's critics assume him to say, but on the landed proprietors and nobility to whom this rent was paid by these manufacturers, merchants, and agriculturists.

True, he says, the capitalist who is "possessor of a moveable *capital* has his choice whether he will employ it in acquiring landed property or put it to a profitable use in the undertakings of the agricultural or industrial class." But *after* he "has become an entrepreneur either in agriculture or in industry" he has no more a choice of alternatives than either the workers in industry or the peasant cultivators of the soil. Even if he lends to a "proprietor or an entrepreneur," while, unlike the workers and cultivators at that time, he can "dispose of his own person," yet he has no further choice respecting his capital itself, because it is "sunk in the advances of the enterprise, and cannot be withdrawn from it without injuring the enterprise, unless it is replaced by a capital of equal value." [164] The lender "belongs to the disposable class so far as his person is concerned, because he is engaged in no business, [but] he does not belong to it so far as the character of his wealth is concerned." [165]

On the other hand, the interest which the lender or capitalist receives on his money "is disposable" in the sense that he individ-

[163] *Ibid.* (French ed.), Sec. 95.
[164] *Ibid.* (Ashley ed.), Sec. 94.
[165] *Ibid.*, Sec. 96.

ually can use it as he pleases. But it is not disposable so far as agriculture, industry, or commerce is concerned, because they do not furnish interest to him gratuitously. Interest is determined by the general abundance or scarcity of capitals, and is therefore "the price and condition of that advance without which the enterprise could not be carried on. If this return is diminished, the capitalist will withdraw his money, and the undertaking will come to an end." This amount of interest, in so far as thus determined by the general abundance or scarcity of *capitals*, "ought to be inviolable and enjoy entire immunity, because it is the price of an advance, made to an enterprise, without which the enterprise could not go on. To touch it would be to augment the price paid for advances in all enterprises, and consequently to lessen the enterprises themselves, that is to say, agriculture, industry, and commerce."

It is different with the rents paid to landlords in so far as they do not work the land themselves for wages or profits, or do not make advances of capital on interest.

"All that the other classes of the Society receive is merely the wages and the profits that are paid either by the proprietor from his revenue [net income as rent], or by the agents of the productive class from the part which is set aside to satisfy their needs, for which they are obliged to purchase commodities from the industrial class. Whether these profits be distributed in wages to workmen, in profits to [*entrepreneurs*], or in interest upon advances, they do not change their nature, and do not increase the sum of the [net] revenue produced by the productive class over and above the price of its labor—in which sum the industrial class participates only to the extent of the price of its labor.

"The proposition then remains unshaken that there is no revenue [net income, or rent, for landlords] save the net produce of lands, and that all other annual profit is either paid by the revenue or forms part of the expenditure which serves to produce the revenue." [166]

How this comes about is explained by Turgot, not on Quesnay's doctrine of "natural rights," but on an historical analysis which will be seen to be an economic and institutional interpretation of history.[167] First is a territorial division of labor and exchange of products between the primitive cultivators of the soil.

Second, laborers are hired by these cultivators, or artisans are paid for their products by the cultivators, when once the "labour of the latter causes the land to produce beyond their personal wants."

Third, the wages of the laborer who has nothing but his toil to sell,

[166] *Ibid.*, Sec. 99.
[167] *Ibid.*, Secs. 1–26, 44, 63, 98.

"are fixed by contract [with the cultivator who] pays him as little as he can; and as he has the choice among a great number of workmen, he prefers the one who works cheapest. The workmen are therefore obliged to lower the price, in competition with one another. In every kind of work it cannot fail to happen, and as a matter of fact it does happen, that the wages of the workman are limited to what is necessary to procure him his subsistence."

Fourth, the position of the cultivator is different.

"The land pays him directly the price of his labour, independently of any other man or any labour contract. Nature does not bargain with him to oblige him to content himself with what is absolutely necessary. What she grants is proportioned neither to his wants, nor to a contractual valuation of the price of his days of labour. It is the physical result of the fertility of the soil, and of the wisdom, far more than of the laboriousness, of the means which he has employed to make it fertile. As soon as the labour of the cultivator produces more than his wants, he can, with this superfluity that nature accords him as a pure gift, over and above the wages of his toil, buy the labour of the other members of society. The latter, in selling to him, gain only their livelihood; but the cultivator gathers, beyond his subsistence, a wealth which is independent and disposable, which he has not bought and which he sells. He is, therefore, the sole source of the riches which, by their circulation, animate all the labours of the society; because he is the only one whose labour produces over and above the wages of his labour."

Finally, the cultivator himself becomes a tenant, first as peasant, then as capitalist, when population grows and land becomes scarce.

"The land filled up, and was more and more cleared. The best lands at length came to be all occupied. There remained for the last comers only the sterile soils rejected by the first. But in the end all land found its master. . . . Ownership could be separated from the labour of cultivation; and soon it was. . . . Landed properties as objects of commerce, [are now] bought and sold. . . . Many proprietors . . . have more than he can cultivate. . . . Instead of employing their whole time in toilsome labours he . . . prefers to give a part of his superfluity to people who will work for him. . . . The cultivator [is now] distinguished from the proprietor. By this new arrangement the produce of the land is divided into two parts. The one includes the subsistence and profits of the cultivator and the interest on his capital. What remains is that independent and disposable part which the land gives as a pure gift to him who cultivates it, over and above his advances and the wages of his trouble; and this is the portion of the proprietor, or the net income with which he can live without labour and which he carries where he will. Hence society is divided into three classes: the class of cultivators, for which we may keep the name of *productive class;* the class of artisans and others who *receive stipends* from the produce of the land. [Neither of these receive more than the recompense of their labor.] Third, the class of proprietors, the only one which, not being bound by the need of subsistence to a particular labour, can be employed for the general needs of the society, such as war and administration of justice, either by a personal service, or by the payment of a part of their revenue with which the State or the Society may engage men to discharge these functions. The name which, for this reason, suits it the best, is that of *disposable class.*" [168]

Whence, then, comes this net produce, this net output belonging to the disposable class of landlords over and above the amounts economically compelled to be paid to the industrious classes and to capitalists as interest on advances? It does not come from their savings. "Although the proprietors have a greater superfluity, they save less because, as they have more leisure, they have more desires and more passions; they regard themselves as more assured of their fortunes; they think more about enjoying it agreeably than about increasing it; luxury is their inheritance." But wage receivers and entrepreneurs of other classes, if they have "a superfluity beyond their subsistence, . . . are devoted to their enterprises; are occupied in increasing their fortunes; are removed by their labor from expensive amusements and passions; they save all their superfluity to invest it again in their business and so increase it." [169] Thus these other classes increase the abundance of capitals, reduce the rate of interest, extend cultivation to lower margins, and augment the mass of value belonging to landlords. [170] If, then, the landed proprietors' rents do not come from their own labor, or from their enterprise or interest on savings, but do come from the increased product of the labor, enterprise, and savings of others, they are partly a free gift arising from mere ownership of nature's resources, and partly a coerced income obtained by beating down the recompense of hired labor and peasant cultivators who do not own the land.

Hence these landlords should pay all the taxes. Capitalists would not suffer, though landlords would.

"If lands alone were burdened with contribution to the public charges, as soon as this contribution was regulated the capitalist

[168] *Ibid.*, Secs. 10–15.
[169] *Ibid.*, Sec. 100.
[170] *Ibid.*, Secs. 78, 81.

who purchased lands would not reckon in the interest of his money the part of the revenue which had to be set aside for this contribution: in the same way that a man who purchases a piece of land today does not buy the tithe the Parson receives, or even the tax so far as is known, but only the revenue which remains when tithe and taxes are deducted." [171]

No wonder the nobility dismissed Turgot for putting his theories into practice, and later brought on themselves the revolution of peasants, laborers, and capitalists. The French Revolution confiscated the lands of the nobility; Turgot would have increased their taxes.

Turgot's picture of marginal productivity should be compared with Ricardo's, made fifty years later. Turgot's was a monetary theory, Ricardo's was a labor theory. They reached similar conclusions regarding landlords, capitalists, and laborers. The value of landed property, for each of them, was a right of property for which the landlord, as mere owner, gave nothing to society, but the value of capitals represented an equivalent production of commodities and services for society. And, for each of them, the laborers without property obtained only the minimum of subsistence. But they reached their conclusions by opposite roads respecting the causes of rents upon which the capital-value of landed property depended. Ricardo's "rent" was the difference between the greater niggardliness of nature on the margin of cultivation and the lesser niggardliness on better agricultural land, in so far as the differences arose from "original and indestructible" qualities of the soil. Turgot's rent arose from a free gift of nature to landlords, over and above the revenue obtained by capitalists on the same margin of cultivation as that pictured by Ricardo. But, for each of them, rents also depended upon the level of wages, higher if wages were low, lower if wages were high.

Ricardo found the principle of diminishing returns and marginal productivity only in agriculture, but Turgot found it in all manufactures, commerce, and industry. Hence Ricardo gave to the marginal productivity of labor in agriculture a causal power which regulated the values of all commodities; but Turgot gave to the total abundance or scarcity of capitals in all occupations the causal power which determined how high or low marginal productivity should be in all occupations.

They reached their similar conclusions by monetary and non-monetary roads. Ricardo eliminated money and substituted the subsistence of laborers as "capital," so that capital became the amount of "embodied labour." Turgot retained the formation of capitals by the prices paid in the circulation of money, so that his capital became "embodied money."

Ricardo's *capitals* were the output of labor-power measured by man-hours, but Turgot's *capitals* were the outgo of investments measured by dollars.

On the other hand, Turgot's *capital* was the present value of future net income, but Ricardo's *capital* was the past share of the total product which the capitalist devoted to the subsistence of labor.

While it is evident that Turgot and Ricardo reached similar conclusions from monetary and non-monetary presuppositions, they were each reasoning for a period of metallic money, instead of bank credit; a period of individual enterprise instead of concerted action of going concerns; a period of tools instead of huge going plants operated by battalions; a period when Capitalism was only beginning or half begun, out of Feudalism or half-Feudalism. Yet they laid foundations later built upon.

If we carry over Turgot's analysis into equivalent terms of succeeding economists, his "mass of value" remains Capital, not as a mass of value but as a present valuation, or, as he named it, an "estimation," of expected net income. This "estimation" has many names, such as capital, capital-value, capitalization, invested capital, investment, advances, debts, credits. The estimation is made, not in sheep or wheat, not in silver or gold, but in bank debts. Instead of a flow of silver in circulation, we have the present and expected repetition of transactions on the commodity markets, the sale of the resulting debts to banks in exchange for deposit credits. These constitute the funds, the purchasing power, the measure of exchange-value, which are the equivalent of Turgot's value of silver in circulation. This repetition of credit transactions is conducted by agents of going concerns, and it is these going concerns that succeed to Turgot's landed estates. The ownership of the concern, or rather the ownership of the expected net income (*revenu*) of the concern, including both expected interest and expected profits, is represented by bonds and stocks of corporations, or by bonds and equity of landed property. The stock exchange becomes the market for Turgot's "mass of values"; the commercial banks become the debt market, which displaces his silver market; and on the commodity markets the prices and volume of his "capitals" are the repetition of debits to individual accounts. His marginal productivity of *capitals* and its equivalent marginal income for *capital* become the "bond-yield" and "stock-yield" of going concerns, around which commercial rates of interest fluctuate. His ratio of interest to the mass of value becomes the rise and fall of bond and stock prices inversely to the fall and rise of bond-yield and stock-yield.

3. *Scarcity of Waiting*

Cassel, in 1903, goes back to Turgot with his identification of the "mass of value" and the "quantity of waiting," and interest as the price paid for the service of waiting.[172]

Turgot had distinguished "capital" from "capitals." Capitals were the value of goods in money. Capital was the value of money in goods. The money paid as interest was paid for the "use of capital." Reduced to an "arithmetical quantity," said Cassel, "this use of capital is a quantity of two dimensions, the measure of it being a certain sum of value into the time of use."

But this, he continued, "is the same measure as that of waiting; and consequently we may infer that Waiting and Use of Capital denote the *same thing*. In fact, they signify one and the same productive service; 'waiting' is used to express what is done by him who supplies the service, and 'use of capital' to express what is obtained by him who buys the service." [173]

Thus waiting is a positive human service of furnishing the means of production, just as elementary, primary, and productive as is the service of working. "Coal," said Cassel, "is undoubtedly a factor of production, but not an independent one: it is produced by other factors, principally labor. But waiting cannot in this manner be resolved into more elementary factors; it is human exertion of quite a separate and particular character." [174]

Hence the elementary factors of production are working and waiting. The derived factors are physical goods, like coal, wheat, metals, buildings, even land, and finally consumption goods. They are effects along the process of the two elementary human services of working and waiting.

Senior (1834) had justified interest as a payment for abstinence,[175] the abstinence being a postponement of the use of consumption goods. But Senior's concept was only an ethical justification of interest and not an economic quantity. Cairnes later (1874) had attempted to give a quantitative meaning to abstinence. The measure of abstinence, he said, "will be . . . the quantity of wealth abstained from . . . multiplied by the duration of the ab-

[172] Cassel, G., *The Nature and Necessity of Interest* (1903), 20.
[173] *Ibid.*, 48.
[174] *Ibid.*, 89.
[175] Senior, Nassau, *Political Economy* (1834; citation to 6th ed. of 1872), 58.

stinence."[176] But Macvane (1887) had criticized Cairnes to the effect that "abstinence is not itself a primary fact of industry." It is merely a negative factor of "not-doing" anything. The more fundamental fact is the length of time that must elapse between the outlay of labor and the possession of the finished product."[177] Macvane then proposed Turgot's term "waiting" instead of abstinence.

Cassel criticized Macvane on two grounds, the quantity of waiting and the object waited for. He said,

Macvane's "term 'Waiting' does not contain more than one element—is a 'quantity of one dimension,' the dimension of time. This is, of course, inadmissible; 'waiting a certain time' means nothing, when it is not stated *what* is postponed. Perhaps it is Macvane's intention that 'waiting' should be taken to denote postponement of some *concrete* thing or enjoyment. But in that case we should have to give up the character of waiting as an arithmetical quantity, and this would make waiting a very useless conception. But there is a still graver objection to such a definition of waiting. There *is* very seldom a postponement of anything concrete; the man who saves does not as a rule know what he would have used his money for, if he had not saved it; he simply postpones the consumption of a certain sum of *value*. Hence 'waiting' is, *as a matter of fact*, measured by the product of such a sum of value and the time of waiting. This measure gives the ultimate definition of waiting; and waiting in this sense is one of the services which constitute the concrete costs of production."[178]

A similar treatment is accorded by Cassel to the two concepts invented by Jevons, the monetary "quantity of investment" and the psychological "quantity of abstinence."[179] Jevons had found that the "amount of investment" was a function of two variable quantities, M, the amount of money invested, and T, the duration of time during which the investment lasted, so that the dimension of investment is MT.

But Jevons had also constructed a quantitative dimension of "abstinence," out of his own original discovery of subjective utility as a diminishing intensity of pleasure equalized at the final utility. Hence his magnitude of abstinence was UT, the symbol U being the quantity of final utility, and the symbol T being the duration of time.

[176] Cairnes, J. E., *Some Leading Principles of Political Economy Newly Expounded* (1874), 87.

[177] Macvane, S. M., "Analysis of Cost of Production," *Quar. Jour. Econ.* (1887), I, 481, 483.

[178] Cassel, G., *op. cit.*, 41, 42.

[179] See Jevons, W. Stanley, *The Theory of Political Economy* (3rd ed., 1886), 232, 233.

But UT, or the magnitude of abstinence, was, according to Cassel, the same magnitude as MT, or magnitude of investment. Why not, therefore, name it also M or money, instead of U, or utility? Such was Cassel's interpretation.

"It does not seem . . . correct," he said, "to use such a term [as utility]. It cannot be anything but fictitious, so long as we have not really established a method of directly measuring intensities of feeling. The only measure of utility available for the economist seems to be the *price* offered for the commodity; and, if we accept this measure, we must replace U by M in the dimension for abstinence given by Jevons. This dimension becomes then identical with that of investment of capital." [180]

Thus Cassel builded on Turgot by reducing all subsequent theories to an arithmetic quantity equivalent to Turgot's "mass of value." We do not merely abstain, we participate in production by investment, and we do not wait for consumption goods, we wait for the "consumption of a certain sum of value."

But this waiting for the "consumption of value" is an inadvertence derived from Turgot. Value is not consumed, nor saved, nor waited for. Cassel afterwards proposed the terms "capital control" or "capital-disposal," as the equivalent of Turgot's "mass of value," and his "sum of value." These terms suggest more nearly the bargaining transactions of the debt and commodity markets. What they mean is legal control, a term which is equivalent to the incorporeal property of debt. He said, in 1918,

"The 'waiting' means that a man foregoes for a time the disposal of a certain sum of value. By this he enables another to dispose of capital for that period of time. The 'waiting' is thus, arithmetically considered, of the same magnitude as the control of capital, and is, like it, measured by the product of the capital and the time. It is, therefore, not generally necessary for the theory to use both expressions. We will in what follows use the word disposal of capital to indicate also the service which savers render to the capital market.

"In thus defining 'waiting,' we have at the same time defined the service for which interest is paid as an arithmetical quantity." [181]

Thus the meaning of the supposedly equivalent terms is clear. The one who foregoes a certain sum of value foregoes the alternative general purchasing power which he might have exercised at his

[180] Cassel, G., *op. cit.*, 49 n.
[181] Cassel, G., *The Theory of Social Economy* (1918; 1924. Citation from 1924 ed.), 184–185; *Theoretische Sozialökonomie*, 171 ff. (1926).

option on any of the present markets. He foregoes the purchase of both consumption goods and capital goods, which means that he foregoes both consumption and investment. By this he enables another to purchase consumption goods or capital goods, that is, enables the other to consume or invest.

But the two are not equivalent if we place ourselves at the point of negotiations looking towards the future.

There are, in fact, two persons who wait—the one who saves and the one who invests. This is the institutional distinction between incorporeal and intangible property. When we save we save money and wait for the debtor to pay. When we invest the money we buy commodities or labor and wait for customers to buy the output. In either case there is a volitional factor of assuming and transferring risks by planning for the future. The courts of law, when called upon to decide disputes arising out of transactions, have created the different kinds of property rights and liberties to fit the conflicting wills that participate in transactions. If, then, we picture ourselves, as do the courts, at the point of negotiations, and from that point look forward to the intentions and expectations of the participants, we can analyze the economic considerations taken into account in all transactions as waiting, risking, forecasting, and planning. Cassel, like others, distinguished this principle of futurity as "willingness"—the "willingness of people to wait" and their "willingness to run risks." While the two are inseparable, "nevertheless, in many transactions of modern society, the risk is reduced to such a minimum that it is practically not taken into account." [182]

That is to say, modern society has distinguished between the incorporeal property of security and debt, and the intangible property of liberty and exposure, arising out of transactions.

Each arises out of the same negotiations that determine transactions, and they are inseparable yet distinguishable. They are distinguished in the modern economic going concerns as services rendered to the concern for which the concern owes compensation. Interest is an obligation created for willingness to wait, wages for willingness to work, profits for willingness to run risks. Disputes may arise afterwards as to the degree of conformity between the subsequent performance and the expressed or implied willingness, but it is the volitions that create the legal relations for the particular individuals, which then take effect, tacitly if there is no dispute, or expressly by lawful decision if there is a dispute. This "operation of law," tacitly or expressly, is the release of duties of payment or

[182] Cassel, G., *The Nature and Necessity of Interest*, 135.

performance. The economic effects are the corresponding dimensions of the debts of payment and performance.

The monetary legal and volitional concept of capital as a quantity of "capital-disposal," which we name legal control, is quite the opposite, in relation to time, of the classical economist's concept of capital as an accumulation of physical goods stored up in the past for future production. Cassel expresses the change from the past to the future as follows:

> "The person who saves undoubtedly *abstains* from the consumption of certain commodities or services. From this fact a most curious conception of capital has arisen and caused much confusion in the science of political economy. Capital is regarded simply as an aggregate of these nonconsumed commodities, as 'a stock of goods of different kinds stored up somewhere,' as *Adam Smith* puts it; and accordingly, it is said, the function of capital is to serve as a fund stored up for the purpose of maintaining the laborers until the fruits of their labor ripen. This view of the matter is entirely erroneous. As a matter of fact, the commodities or services 'abstained from' are never produced; on the whole and broadly speaking, only that is produced which is required by the consumers. If the consumers decide to save and to invest their money in productive enterprises, it means that the industry of the society is diverted to some extent from the production of immediately useful things to the production of capital. Hence saving means diverting productive forces towards future ends." [183]

Thus the economic effects of the negotiational psychology of willingness are not the painful costs of abstinence nor even any painful "costs" of waiting. They are the volitional costs of foregoing available alternatives, either because the alternative buyer offers a lower income to the seller, or the alternative seller imposes a higher outgo on the buyer." [184]   But it is this choosing of alternatives that diverts production.

The same is true of the other aspects of human forecasting and planning. All of them, whether expected interest, expected profits, expected wages, etc., are alike in that the choices between present alternatives have the social effect of diverting production into the immediate or remote future.

But this choice of alternatives is simply a name for the economic situation which limits the choices, and this is merely the principle of scarcity, on account of which a price must be paid if the service is to be forthcoming.

[183] *Ibid.*, 134.
[184] Above, p. 307, on Opportunity-Cost and Dis-Opportunity-Value.

The service of waiting requires that a price must be paid, not on ethical grounds, but on account of scarcity.

"Interest," said Cassel, is "the price of waiting or of the use of capital. . . . But as the very service which is paid for is itself measured by a certain sum of money used during one year, the price of the service will be determined as a certain fraction of the sum. For this reason the price of waiting or the use of capital is quoted as a 'rate,' or so much 'per cent.' This circumstance should, however, not be allowed to obscure the fundamental fact that interest is a real price to be placed on the same footing as all other prices." [185]

This "same footing" for all prices is Cassel's idea of public policy. Under the ideal system of prices developed by the classical school, as their policy of free trade in opposition to the discriminations of mercantilism, the social function, or public purpose, of price requires that there shall be a uniform price paid for one and the same item of any commodity. The reason for this uniform price is scarcity of supply, and the price reduces demand by preventing satisfaction of the less essential wants. But a higher price also "causes a larger part of the productive services of society to be used in the production of that commodity. Thus a system of prices serves as a regulator, not only of the consumption but also of the whole production of the community." [186]

So it is with interest as a price. It must be high enough to bring out an adequate supply of waiting, but not so high as to cause a restriction of demand and ultimately an oversupply of waiting.

Since the demand for waiting is synonymous with the demand for disposal of capital, the quantity demanded "is measured by the product of a certain sum of money multiplied by a certain time." A company with a capital of $1,000,000 "uses yearly a quantity of waiting of one million units." The price paid for its use, or the rate of interest is the measure of its scarcity.

Thus, by the insight of Cassel, many concepts proposed by different schools of economists, since the time of David Hume, are reduced to the same arithmetic quantity of money *times* a future lapse of time, and to the universal principle of scarcity. Some of them are plainly subjective, as abstinence, impatience, time-preference, the saving instinct. Some are plainly objective, as money, capital, capitals, capital goods, physical capital. All are brought together in the volitional concepts of Futurity and Scarcity, such

[185] *Ibid.*, 92, 93.   [186] *Ibid.*, 73, 77.

as waiting and investment, which we distinguish in terms of activity as bargaining transactions, and, in terms of institutions as incorporeal and intangible property.

Cassel also distinguished between waiting for long periods and waiting for short periods.

". . . waiting for *long* periods is the real and principal form of waiting. Waiting for *short* periods is, in relation to this, a secondary form. The service performed by this kind of waiting corresponds only to small parts of a production process, and most generally to a special phase of distribution; and it is only by artificial means, particularly by the elaborate and ingenious mechanism of bills of exchange that this form of waiting has been made possible." [187]

It was Wicksell, in 1898, who constructed the idea of a functional relation between long periods and short periods of waiting.[188]

V. INTEREST AND PROFIT DISCOUNT

While interest and discount are usually contrasted as similar payments but looked at from the different time-standpoints of future and present, yet since all negotiations and transactions occur in the present, it is present discount rather than future interest that is the universal fact in all transactions. Mathematically, as we know, the same economic quantity, say 6 per cent per year, is larger when computed as discount than it is when computed as interest. And psychologically also the discount principle governs all transactions because the future interest is less certain than the present discount. Böhm-Bawerk based his theory on future interest which required therefore a future *agio* of consumption goods to be added to present valuation in order to equalize present and future values. But this assumes that the future is *now* known, whereas it is only guessed. In order to play safe the larger present discount motivates transactions, and this discount may rise to huge proportions according to the fear of risk. Consequently, if we start from the standpoint of the present, it is both interest discount and risk discount that dominate the negotiations made in all transactions. It is the difference between Böhm-Bawerk's pleasure economy which looks to greater abundance in the future, and MacLeod's discount economy which looks to the greater sacrifices of limited resources in the present and the doubtfulness of greater abundance in the future.

When the laborer goes to work he is not paid in advance. He

[187] *Ibid.*, 135.
[188] Below, p. 590, A World Pay Community.

waits till pay day. For the time being he is an investor in the
business. Each delivery of an added use-value to the employer's
materials creates an accrual of credits on his part and of debits on
his employer's part. It is a legal process of repeated offer and acceptance. Each accrual of use-value accepted by the foreman for
the employer is paralleled by an accrual of debt owed by the employer to the employee. The debt is liquidated on pay day, but
the use-value is merged into a joint product which the employer
expects will furnish him a credit against another debtor on a
commodity-market or debt-market. The principle here is the same
as when material men wait 30 days or 60 days for payments for
their materials.

The labor-debt is a short-time debt, and, by the custom of the
labor-market, the laborer's compensation for the service of waiting
is not computed separately, but is commuted into his compensation
for working. Likewise with any risks that he assumes. His forecast of risks, as Adam Smith asserted,[189] enters into his negotiational psychology before he goes to work, and it too is commuted
into his compensation for working. Custom, law, alternative opportunities, bargaining power, play their part, as they do in other
transactions, but nevertheless, when the laborer goes to work he
thereby has discounted in one transaction, as a creditor, a future
compensation for working, waiting, and risking. This process of
commutation by discounting may be named Forecasting. It yields
a present discounted valuation of a future compensation for working, waiting, and risking.

When it comes to the employer's markets, that which is implicit
on the labor market becomes explicit on the commodity and debt
markets. A manufacturer has a prospect that he will sell in 60
days a product which will be worth, at that time, $60,000. He
makes a loan at the bank, giving his note for $60,000 payable at
the end of 60 days. The bank discounts the note at 6 per cent
per year, or one per cent for 60 days. This means that the bank
becomes a debtor to the manufacturer on a deposit account of
$59,400, immediately available. With this amount the manufac-

---

[189] Above, p. 158, Adam Smith. I have added the laborer's *waiting* to Smith's *risking*.
This waiting by laborers is often more onerous than even their working or risking, as
may be noted in the case of the extraordinarily high rates of interest they are willing to
pay to "loan sharks" and "small-loan" companies, rising as high as 30, 40, or even 200
per cent per year. The commutation of "waiting" often appears also in the laborer's
willingness to work for *less* wages when he is paid daily or weekly than when he is paid
semi-monthly or monthly. I have seen, in the South, Negroes who consider *daily* payment
of wages more important than the *rate* of wages, and will choose employers who pay daily
in preference to those who pay weekly. Above, p. 307, Opportunity-Cost and Dis-Opportunity-Value.

turer buys materials for which he pays the material men by issuing to them his checks payable at the bank, on demand. Or if he pays cash, as wages and salaries, he draws a check payable to "cash," and draws from the bank the amount of currency which he then pays as wages in the envelopes of his wage-earners.

In either case, what happens is that the manufacturer has promised to pay the banker $600 for the 60-day use of bank credit in order that he, the manufacturer, may buy materials and pay wages and salaries 60 days in advance of the time when the product will be paid for.

This $600 must be paid by somebody. The way in which it is actually paid is this: the prices of materials and the wages of labor which the manufacturer is willing to pay now are $600 *less* than will be the expected total of the prices received for the product at the end of 60 days. In other words the *present value* of the materials and wages is the *discounted forecast value* of the product at the end of 60 days.

But the business man must also have profits for himself as well as his $600 interest which he pays to the banker. If he expects a margin of profit equal to an average of 6 per cent per year on all his sales, this margin will be one per cent for 60 days. He will get this profit by the same process of paying $600 *less* for materials and wages. In other words, in order to have a margin for both interest and profit, he will pay for materials and wages $1,200 less than he expects to receive for the finished product, making his payments for materials and wages $58,800 if he expects to be paid $60,000 for the product at the end of 60 days. This $58,800 is the present discount value or present worth of the commodity whose Forecast Value is $60,000.

Present value, therefore, results from a double discount of the forecast value, an interest-discount and a profit-discount. The interest-discount, in our calculation, is $600, the profit-discount is $600. The interest-profit-discount is $1,200. The accuracy of the double discount depends on the accuracy of the forecast. It may turn out to be a *loss* if the expected value, when it becomes a present value, turns out to be less than $60,000, or it may turn out to be a *profit* if the expected value turns out to be $60,000 or more.

These uncertainties concern us greatly in a dynamic analysis fitted to business cycles, for under such changing circumstances the interest-discount and profit-discount operate inversely. If the profit-discount is low on account of expected rising prices and larger sales, then the interest-discount may be high, as it was in

1919–1920. But if the profit-discount is high, as in 1932, on account of great risks of falling prices and reduced sales, then the interest-discount is low or disappears altogether because borrowing ceases.

These changes do not concern us now in our static analysis. If the interest-profit-discount is $2,000 instead of $1,200, then the present value or purchasing power is only $58,000 instead of $58,800. And so on for higher or lower forecast-discounts.

The same is true of long-term securities, as we have previously noted. If an issue of stocks and bonds at $1,000,000 par is sold for $900,000, in expectation that the stock-bond yield will be $100,000 per year, or 11 per cent, then the amount available for present construction purposes is $900,000. But if it is sold at $1,100,000 then that is the present purchasing power, and for the capitalists the capital-yield is 9 per cent.

Professor Fetter has admirably generalized these principles of discount and price, under the general principle of time-discount and capitalization. He thereby recognized the difference between Böhm-Bawerk's agio and the actual process of discount. He did so by reducing all future rents, profits, interest-payments, and even future prices of commodities to the single concept of *expected net income,* which he, like Böhm-Bawerk, named "rents," but he threw them into the future, unlike Böhm-Bawerk who retained them as present rents. Then these future "rents" are universally reduced by time-discount to a present valuation. This discounted valuation is the universal principle of capitalization, which is the modern meaning of Capital.[190]

But Fetter's time-discount is properly also a profit discount. One is the discount of waiting through an interval of time. The other is the discount of favorable or unfavorable events during the expected passage of time. The compensation for waiting is the expected interest payment. The compensation for risking is profit or loss. The risk-discount is a profit and loss discount.

Often profit and interest move together. If prospects of profit are favorable on account of less risk, the borrower can afford to pay a higher rate of interest, as in the year 1919. If the forecast of profit turns into a forecast of loss, new commitments will not be made to pay interest or even the principal of a loan, as in 1932. In short, the enterprise slows down or stops, because the risk-

---

[190] Fetter, Frank A., "Recent Discussion of the Capital Concept," *Quar. Jour. Econ.*, XV (1900–1901), 1–45; "The Passing of the Old Rent Concept," *Ibid.*, 416–455; *Principles of Economics*, Chaps. 8, 10, 15, 17 (1904); "Interest Theory and Price Movements," *Proceedings Amer. Econ. Assn.*, March, 1927, 62–122.

discount has greatly reduced or even eliminated present capital-value.

VI. THE TRANSACTIONAL SYSTEM OF MONEY AND VALUE

Our formula of a turnover of bargaining transactions has not hitherto included the banker. Yet all modern transactions require the participation of bankers. Even the "cash" payments, usually termed the "circulation of money," consist in drawing cash from the banks instead of transferring demand debts at the banks. This cash again "flows" into the banks in payment of debts owed to the banks. The banks themselves, if short on this "money in circulation," call upon the Reserve banks for "money," thus reducing their balances at the Reserve banks. Or, if long on circulation, they return their "cash" to the Reserve banks in order to pay debts to the Reserve bank and thus augment their Reserve balances.

Hence each of the two buyers and two sellers of a bargaining transaction, who make the whole of the debt-payments, must have not only an account at his bank, but also an understanding with the banker as to what he may expect towards obtaining the means of payment, which the banker will himself create as a deposit for carrying out transactions.

Thus our formula for a complete bargaining transaction must have four bankers, one for each of the two buyers and two sellers in the transaction. It matters not whether the four bankers are really only *one* banker, since no bank gives information to any customer of the accounts of any other customer. Even if four different bankers act in concert through clearing houses and the Federal Reserve System, their concerted action does not include the exchange of information as to the accounts of any of their customers, though bank examiners may obtain this information under their oath of secrecy. Consequently, as far as each of the four participants in the transaction is concerned, each has a separate private account and a private understanding with one of his own banks.

Out of each possible commercial transaction, therefore, arises the possibility of various types of short-time commercial debts, whether single name paper, trade acceptances, bankers' acceptances, or otherwise. All have the one fact in common that the sale of a commodity creates a business debt which the banker buys by selling to the business man his own deposit debt. The business debt lasts from one day to 90 days and the transaction is not closed until the debt is paid at the expiration of the time agreed upon. The bankers create, in exchange, debts "past due" and therefore payable on demand, to the extent of the discounted future value of the business debt, and these deposits are the checking accounts against which the customer immediately draws his check for the payment of other debts which he has contracted in his purchases of materials and labor.

Thus each loan transaction creates its own money. There is not a fund of money that "circulates," but there is a repetition of the creation, sale, and payment of short-time debts to the amount equivalent to the discounted values of the titles of ownership alienated. Two succeeding increases in value thus occur, based on forecasts of the prices of commodities: the increase in output of use-value of commodities to be added by the input of labor; and the increase in value of the discounted debt as it approaches maturity.

The first increase of value appears on the various commodity markets, as when the price of iron ore becomes the price of pig iron, then the price of rolled steel, of agricultural machinery, of knives and forks to be purchased by ultimate consumers. The second increase occurs on the money or debt markets, where each short-term debt increases in value by the reduced lapse of time until it is paid.

Each loan transaction thus creates its own money, for the banker is an active participant. The older controversy over quantity and commodity theories of money turned on theories of physical causation in which it was thought that the event first in order of time was the cause of the event subsequent, and the statistical proof or disproof turned on showing whether a change in the quantity of money preceded or followed a change in prices. But a transactional or forecast theory of money and prices is a theory of the transfer, not of goods, but of proprietary control of expected goods, since the goods come along later. The value agreed upon is the price of acquiring rights of ownership, and this price is always a forecast of the immediate or remote future. This kind of causation lies in the future, not in the past or present. Mitchell's investigations show that the changes in price usually come first, followed by deliveries, then by payments,[191] and this conforms to the principle that the "cause" of the price change is in the joint forecasts of the future, even a future extending beyond the date when the duty of payment is expected to arrive. Hence the appropriate doctrine of cause and effect is found in billions of transactions, where the banker who creates the money participates as a guide to the transac-

[191] Mitchell, Wesley C., *Business Cycles, the Problem and Its Setting* (1927), 137.

tion. While the engineer is the specialist in efficiency, and the business man is the specialist in scarcity, the banker is the specialist in futurity.

It is difficult to see how the older theories of quantity of money or quantity of commodities can apply to this process of valuation in the transactional process of transferring ownership of economic quantities, of transferring bank debts that serve as money, and of extinguishing the commercial debts in exchange for which the bank debts were created. These are, indeed, "magnitudes," but where are the physical quantities of money? The magnitudes are arithmetical statements of prices or values agreed upon in a repetition of bargaining transactions. Instead of a quantity of money we have a variable "turnover" of bank debts, the total volume of which is negotiated, created, cancelled, and renewed every 30 days or so, varying in magnitude, however, with the expected prices and quantities of commodities, of services and of debts whose valuations largely determine the magnitude of further debts created by further transfers of ownership. In such a case physical analogies do not apply—only statistical examination and experimentation on rates of turnover, on lags, forecasts, etc., can suffice. The transactional and forecast system of money proceeds from valuations of ownership wherein each banker's valuation creates its own money for the transfer of ownership.

This transactional theory of money seems to include and to go still further than Copeland's effort to disprove the quantity theory of money by showing that prices and volume of trade (PT) precede the quantity and velocity (MV) of money.[192] In his calculations of the "equation of exchange," he shows that "commodities" count for only two-thirds of the payments and the other third includes payments for "intangibles" such as interest, dividends, taxes, bonds, shares of stock, etc. By including these "intangibles" he reaches the conclusion that "most of the time PT is causally prior to MV."

But if we distinguish a commodity by its double meaning of materials and ownership, then the transfer of ownership always precedes the production of the materials. And this ownership is just as "intangible" as the other intangibles which he mentions, for all of them look to the future tangible materials which will be produced and obtained by present transfers of ownership. In the present transactions it is not materials that are transferred, it is present claims of ownership of future materials. This is just as true of the ownership of commodities as it is of the ownership of

[192] Copeland, M. A., "Money, Trade and Prices—A Test of Causal Primacy," *Quar. Jour. Econ.*, XLIII (1929), 648.

dividends, interest, taxes, shares, and bonds. All of them look forward to future ownership of materials, whether as production goods or consumption goods. The "equation of exchange," if we place it in the transactions at the present point of time, is always an equation of exchange of titles of ownership. And it is here, in the negotiations of transactions, that prices are made, for prices are paid for ownership and not for materials.

It happens that Copeland's "intangibles" look more usually into a long-distance future, or are intermediate transactions before the ultimate materials will be acquired, and that the ownership of commodities looks to a short-time future before the materials will be produced or consumed. This makes it more difficult but not less necessary to measure the time-distance between the transfer of ownership and the appearance of the materials. The *length* of future time is not good ground of distinction between ownership of commodities and ownership of the other intangibles. All are future, and the equation of exchange is always an exchange of ownerships which look to the future and not an exchange of materials whether at a present point of time or an immediate or remote future. Hence we should always expect PT to precede MV.

The foregoing indicates that money, in its modern meaning, is the social institution of the creation, negotiability, and release of debts arising out of transactions. If the payment is made without a lapse of time worth measuring, we name it a purchase or sale, and it differs from the short-time and long-time debts only in that the intervening stage of negotiability of the debt is omitted. Thus money is secondarily a medium of exchange—it is primarily a social means of creating, transferring, and extinguishing debts.

But if, as a social institution, each loan transaction creates its own money and the whole volume is created and extinguished every 30 days, then the definition of money should be converted from the static idea of a quantity to the dynamic idea of a process. The process is the billions of bargaining transactions, with the bankers as participants.

We take it that a process is more accurately described when verbs are substituted for nouns. Nouns are likely to be misleading because they give the impression of static quantities, but verbal nouns are fitted to the bargaining transactions which are none other than the process of pricing, valuing, and debiting, which create, transfer, extinguish, and recreate both economic quantities and the money which measures them as values. The price, the value, the debt, are each jointly determined, if not literally created, at the point of time when the agreement transfers the ownership of the economic quantity thus agreed upon, and all the variabilities, taken together in the sequence of time, are a process of pricing, valuing, and debiting by means of transactions.

We have indicated that money measures scarcity dimensions, and that this dimension, when measured by isolating a unit of an economic quantity, is its price. Price is the scarcity dimension of anything, whether commodities, stocks, bonds, services, or even waiting and risking.

But scarcity is only one of several dimensions of value functionally bound together, each of which must be measured in order to ascertain the variability of each and therefore the variable magnitude of the whole economic quantity which is valued. This magnitude of value and its equivalent debt, in the case of incorporeal property, is the magnitude, not of a single variable, price, as might be inferred from our inadequate notice of Hawtrey, but is a magnitude equal to the total value agreed upon in the transaction. This magnitude of value and debt, which is the modern magnitude of short-term and long-term "capital," requires analysis. We may resolve it into nine or ten, or perhaps more independently variable magnitudes, each reducible to, and yet concealed in, the total money measurement of every bargaining transaction and every debt. For, as Fisher has said, "one of the important functions of money is that it brings uniformity of measurement out of diversity." [193] Most of these variable magnitudes we may name, scarcity of the commodity or the securities dealt in, scarcity of means of payment, scarcity of waiting, expected lapse of time, risking, quantity of the commodity, kind and quality of the commodity, property rights, and bargaining ability. These we have reduced to the three variables of use, scarcity, and futurity.

It is therefore necessary to construct a transactional definition of value composed of these several independent variables, which, thus constructed, shall be of the same magnitude as the debt itself, to be created by the transfer of ownership at these valuations.

The classical economists eliminated "use-value" as incommensurable, and dealt only with exchange-value, abbreviated to "value." But if by "use-value" we mean, as they probably intended, the objective physical qualities of goods believed to be useful, then use-value is readily measured, and always is measured, by many different systems of physical measurement, such as the ton of steel, the pound of sugar, the loaf of bread, the kilowatt-hour, and so on. And it is also measured by increasingly minute systems of "grading" which standardize and classify differences in quality.

[193] Fisher, Irving, *The Nature of Capital and Income* (1906), 15.

The significance of these physical measurements is that the use-value *per unit* always remains exactly the same (minus depreciation or obsolescence), no matter what changes occur in its scarcity. This physical dimension is the volume of output of use-value which varies *directly* with changes in the number of physical units of the same quality, as a billion bushels of wheat have a billion times as much use-value as one bushel. Thus the three dimensions of use-value, always considered in bargaining transactions, are the kind, grade, quantity, depreciation, obsolescence, measured by physical units.

But scarcity-value varies in the opposite direction. It varies *inversely* to the quantity. As stated by Carl Menger, eliminating money and property, scarcity is the social relation between the quantity wanted and the quantity available,[194] which is, of course, one version of the social relation of supply and demand. Scarcity-value is thus a relation between two variable magnitudes, neither of which, however, can be measured objectively. The relation itself was formerly measured, by the classical economists, by units of nature's resistance to man, and by hedonic economists by units of nature's diminishing pleasure for man. But these were personifications. The proprietary measure of scarcity is price. Price is the "scarcity-tag," as suggested by one of my students. Here we measure—not demand nor supply directly, nor Menger's magnitude wanted or magnitude available—we measure the *effects* of the changing relation between the two as revealed in the prices agreed upon in each bargaining transaction. In a somewhat similar way we measure the magnitude of heat, not directly, but indirectly, by the expansion and contraction of mercury. The thermometer is an artificial contrivance for measuring certain of the effects of heat, as money is an artificial contrivance for measuring certain of the effects of scarcity. The one is a machine, the other is an institution. The machine measures a mechanical magnitude, the institution measures a proprietary magnitude.

Yet, as in all systems of measurement, the measuring instrument must have dimensions similar to those of the magnitude measured, whether we measure the magnitude directly or measure only its effects. A yard measures length directly. A pound measures weight indirectly, by comparison of similar effects. In any case an arbitrary unit is constructed so that differences and changes can be counted and compared in the language of number. So with scarcity. The artificial magnitude is the means of payment, whose scarcity is also a social relation between the quantity wanted and the quantity available. The quantity wanted is wanted for payments. The

[194] Above, p. 378, Menger.

quantity available is supplied by the joint activity of government, banking, and business concerns. Again, we cannot measure directly the quantity wanted nor the quantity available. We can only measure the effects of the changing relation between the two in the several bargaining, credit, and "capital" transactions. Thus price is a relation between two scarcity relations, one of which, money, is marked off in denominations for measuring the other.

In all of these measurements of relative change in magnitudes we can properly use, as we have done, the volitional terms cause and effect, because we are not concerned with the total complex of the universe, but are measuring specific changes of specific factors, picked out from the total universe, on the principle of limiting and complementary factors, for the immediate guidance and control of human conduct.

Price is indeed an effect, a cause, and a measure of scarcity, as can be seen in the process of bargaining. Here the volitional process is familiar and taken as matter of course. We use two systems of measurement, the measurement of scarcity and the measurement of quantity. One is the measure of scarcity-value, the other the measure of use-value. The price of wheat is one dollar per bushel. In order to measure scarcity we automatically suppose the quantity of use-value to be constant at one bushel. Then the scarcity of wheat, relative to money available for purchasing it, varies according to the number and fractions of dollars, which is its price. But, in order to measure the quantity of use-value, we in turn eliminate scarcity by automatically supposing the price to be constant, and the use-value then varies with the number and fractions of bushels. When we combine the two in one magnitude it is Value, with its two variables, scarcity-value, or price, and use-value, or quantity of materials.

This meaning of value, as noted above, is equivalent to the principles underlying what Fisher means by Value distinguished from Price.[195] Fetter's criticism of Fisher, at that point, regarding the meaning of a "unit," is inherent in the theory of measurement itself. Where a thing to be measured has two or more variable dimensions, the only way in which one of them can be measured separately is by supposing the others constant. The other variables do not disappear—they are still there but their variability is eliminated. In the bargaining process this is instinctively or explicitly done. The price is agreed upon, and, separately, the quantity to be taken at that price. The price is the price of a unit-quantity, the value is the aggregate number of unit-quantities taken at that price. Hence

[195] Above, p. 378, Fisher and Fetter.

in the case of the unit-quantity it is evident that value and price mean the same magnitude.

But in the case of an "aggregate of units" it is contrary to usage to speak of the *value* of the aggregate as the *price* of the aggregate. The "price" of one automobile is $1,000. This also is the "value" of the automobile as agreed upon. But if it is two automobiles then there are two prices, and the aggregate of two prices is the *value* of two automobiles. Similar usage applies to a farm or an entire going concern, taken as a unit. The "price" paid for the farm or the entire concern is also the "value" of the farm or concern. But if it is an aggregate of farms or concerns, then it is the "value," not the "price," of the aggregate.

This difference between value and price arises not merely because the only difference between market value and market price is a difference in quantity. It is because Value is a two-dimensional concept (omitting futurity)—with two different causations, the one being the scarcity-value, or price, determined by supply and demand, the other being the greater or smaller output of use-value which will be created in the labor process that follows the transaction.

The same reasoning applies to fungible goods where all the units are exactly alike. The "price" of wheat is the supply and demand, or scarcity-dimension of value, agreed upon by supposing the quantity of use-value constant at one bushel. Only for this one bushel, however, are price and value identical. But for more than one bushel or for a whole crop, the other dimension—use-value, a physical dimension—is variable, and for this aggregate of units the term is value.

Hence in all cases of pricing and valuing in the bargaining process, it may be said that the parties are explicitly, or perhaps automatically, on account of habit, measuring the two dimensions of value: the scarcity-dimension by price, on the assumption of a customary or legal unit of use-value, and the physical dimension by these physical units, on the assumption of an agreed price per unit. The combination of the two is valuing, and the result, including futurity discount, is value, "capital," and its equivalent debt.

This is one reason why money is different in kind from commodities. It is a standard of measurement. Each transaction involves two lawful units of measurement—a unit of payment and a unit of performance. The unit of performance measures the quantity of commodity that must be delivered as agreed upon in the transaction. The unit of payment measures the price per unit of commodity that must be paid. The multiple of the two is the value, equivalent to the two debts created by the transaction.

Without these lawful units of measurement modern business cannot be conducted; and it is not permissible, if one would interpret business since the days when kings arbitrarily changed the units, for economists to employ other than the lawful units of measurement. This may be done in home economics but not in business economics. This is one of the particulars where "institutional" economics, with its working rules, displaces the psychological and labor economics, for units of measurement are compulsory institutions and not the fancies of psychology or romantic history.

When Fisher illustrates his analysis of "quantity, price, and value" in terms of a bushel of wheat we understand that this is only illustrative of the need of having a common unit for measuring values, since for all of his actual measurements the money unit is used.[196]

Even the same is true of Wieser in the realm of psychology. Fisher might have cited Wieser as a "precedent" for his "novel suggestion" in answer to Fetter's challenge. Wieser's notable chapter on the Paradox of Value [197] is exactly Fisher's concept but in terms of diminishing marginal utility with increasing quantity of goods. Since, however, his "marginal utility" is only a personification of price, his "paradox of value" is only the familiar concept of value depending on the two variables, price and quantity. As price, or "marginal utility," diminishes with increasing quantity it follows that the *value* of the aggregate rises if the quantity is increasing more than the price is falling, and the value of the aggregate falls if price falls more rapidly than quantity increases. This is the "paradox of value" a formula worked out by Gregory King more than two centuries ago, in terms of money,[198] and is the well-understood relation between price, quantity, and value in all business and all statistics. It was a lapse from old Gregory's business sense when the labor and psychological theories of the Nineteenth Century diverted economists into fancy and magic, and forced Fisher to say, as late as 1907, that his formula "departs somewhat from economic usage." It did not depart from business or legal usage, or common sense, or Gregory King.

Yet there are other meanings of value. There is a meaning required by economists and popular usage on account of the instability of the general purchasing power of money. For money is not a stable unit for measuring scarcity, like a yard or bushel

---

[196] Fisher, I., *op. cit.*, 14.

[197] Above, p. 378, Wieser.

[198] King, Gregory, "The British Merchant," in his *Natural and Political Observations*, (reprinted 1802).

for measuring quantities. It is rather like a barometer whose index of atmospheric pressure must be corrected for each change in elevation above the sea level. The method of monetary correction is familiar. It consists in eliminating by computation the instability of the general purchasing power of money by converting all current prices to the level of a basing point, say the year 1860 or 1913. The inverse of this general purchasing power is conveniently named the "value of money," falling as the average of prices rises and rising as the average falls.

But this meaning of value is not Mill's meaning of "general power of purchasing" which includes money as one of the same kind of "purchasable commodities" over which the possession of a thing gives command. Nor is it the meaning implied in the statement, "value may be expressed in terms of any kind of wealth, property, or service, while the price of anything is always expressed in money." [199] Here the terms "wealth, property, or service" presumably include money, and price is not different in kind but is a special case of the value of wealth or property. As such the meaning of value is the same as Mill's, including money as one of the purchasable commodities. On the contrary, the term "value of money" is merely a brief name for the inverse of an aggregate of money-prices and indicating the degree to which money, as a unit of measurement, departs from stability. This we may name the purchasing-power meaning of value.

Closely connected but different from the transactional and purchasing-power meanings of value is the distinction usually expressed by the terms Nominal and Real Value, as when we speak of real income or real wages, contrasted with nominal income or wages. This meaning of real value comes nearest to Mill's meaning of value as exchange-value, and to the meaning of value in terms of "wealth, property, or service." But it differs essentially because those meanings included money itself as one of the purchasable commodities. But "real value" eliminates money entirely as something different in kind, and therefore "nominal," although in the transactional and purchasing-power meanings it is not nominal— it is as "real" as buying, selling, debts, and the modern meaning of capital. The farmer or wage-earner, however, wishes to know how much of the commodities which he buys can be obtained for the wheat or the labor which he sells. He can calculate the amount only by eliminating the money prices. This meaning of "nominal value" was what the classical and utility economists endeavored

[199] Fairchild, F. R., Furniss, E. S., and Buck, N. S., *Elementary Economics* (1926), I, 24.

actually to eliminate by substituting labor or pleasure for money. Modern statistics eliminates it virtually but not actually, and does so, not because money is nominal but because a different purpose is intended—measurement of the changes in the distribution of wealth, for which money is the instrument.

Other meanings of value and price, involving ethical or psychological elements such as "esteem value," belong to what we name negotiational psychology, because, if reduced to measurable dimensions in any negotiation they are money valuations. Taking these all into account, we have three different meanings of value, each based on the recognition of money as different in kind from the things whose ownership is bought and then sold for money. One is the transactional meaning of value as the multiple of price, quantity, and futurity discount, and therefore the equivalent of debt and "capital." Another is the purchasing-power meaning of value as an aggregate of prices. Third is the distributive meaning of value as real value, with money and prices as instruments for the distribution of wealth. Throughout these meanings are the several principles of scarcity measured by prices, quantity of use-values measured by physical units, and value as an aggregate of prices *times* quantities.

But there is the other variable dimension of value, implied in what precedes, and economics operates with this third dimension, the measurement of Time. But time, in the transactional process of valuing, is always Future Time. Futurity operates in the two dimensions of waiting and profiting (risking). Each of these is a dimension of discount, by virtue of which the present worth of a future quantity is less in its monetary magnitude than it would be if there were no interval between the present point of time when the transaction takes legal effect and the future point of time when the results are expected. We have distinguished the effects of futurity as the profit discount and the interest discount. Each is highly variable. If either of them reaches 100 per cent discount, then present value totally disappears and industry stops. It is the profit discount and not the interest discount that induced the curtailment of nearly all industry after July, 1929.

Risking and waiting operate by way of two different meanings of time which were not distinguished by the commodity economists, as seen by their failure to distinguish profit from interest. One is the repetition of points of time when events are expected to occur; the other is the interval between two points of time during which interest accrues. It is the distinction between a "flow" of time and a "lapse" of time, not always distinguished. Forecasting is expected risk, but waiting is expected postponement, and the two together create banks. The two dimensions of Futurity are inseparable in fact, for bankers, too, are forecasters, but the two are separable in measurement, and even in the division of labor between bankers and other business men.

In fact, all commodities which have value are more or less distant in space, and more or less future in time, as signified by the word "desire," or "want." When no longer desired they have moved across the present point of time into the past, as signified by "satisfaction."

In this futurity dimension of value there is evidently "action at a distance" and this is the occasion for psychological theories of value. Yet all of the psychology which economists need is of the dimension of futurity, when once they realize that "utility" and "disutility" were psychological personifications of scarcity. Hence the transactional definition of value becomes a purposeful definition, since it involves futurity. It is evident, indeed, that the entire concept of value is volitional instead of mechanistic, since value is a present estimate of something expected in the future, whether the immediate, the short-time, or long-time future. This psychological function is the unifying principle of the will, which somehow holds together all of the variable factors, and, since the will is itself highly variable, it might perhaps be named another variable of value. But this is superfluous because the psychological variability is immeasurable, and whatever influence it has has already been included in the negotiations aided by the various measurements of futurity.

Indeed, must futurity rest on subjective psychology? Is there an "objective" psychology on which it may rest? Without resorting to philosophical or rationalistic theories of objectivity, is there an economic object which is both psychological and objective, but is not a commodity? It must be an object which ties the future to the present in a way not dependent upon the feelings or wills of the individuals who do the valuing. If there is such an object, so constructed that it ties the future to the present independent of individual wills in each bargaining transaction, then that comes within the proper meaning of objectivity. A thing does not need to be physical in order to be "objective." It needs only to be independent of any individual will. With this understanding, then it is collective action which is the object, and which can be made a subject-matter of political economy.

It was MacLeod who first asserted that this subject-matter is not physical things but is property. MacLeod was speaking in the vocational language of lawyers who, for professional purposes, find it sufficient to identify property with property rights. The term property, however, on analysis to fit economics, involves three separable concepts, namely scarcity, futurity, and the rights, duties, liberties, and exposures created by collective action. Nothing is property that is not expected to be scarce, and everything expected to be scarce is quickly brought by collective action within the meaning of property rights. Even air is rationed to exclusive use by individuals when the expected scarcity of wave-lengths leads to conflicts over rights of use.

This scarcity-futurity dimension of property, as we have noted, has achieved a specific name of its own in the American valuation of public utilities, namely "intangible property" or "intangible value." Intangible property is the right to have the expected economic quantities measured as values to be derived from the expected sales of commodities or services; and an act of the legislature reducing "unreasonably" the prices to be charged in the future by public utility corporations is deemed by the courts to be confiscation of their property. It confiscates expected scarcity-values.

This "intangible property" differs decidedly from MacLeod's "incorporeal property." Incorporeal property must now be distinguished as a debt—the right of a creditor, including the State as a taxing power, to compel a debtor to pay a specified sum of money. But intangible property is the entirely different expectations, such as good-will, patent rights, railroad valuations, the right to continue in business, the right of access to a labor market, whose present valuation depends on the expectations of quantities and prices to be derived from future transactions under control of collective action. Hence even incorporeal property becomes "intangible property" by the device of negotiability, because the debt has now a market value, the "price" of the debt, which rises or falls according to the changing relative scarcities of long-time, short-time, and demand debts. This market value of a debt is its scarcity-value, or price, and it is this market price that is "intangible property" on the debt market just as the expected prices of commodities, services, or labor are both the intangible property and the intangible value of other sellers on the other markets. Their intangibility is their scarcity and their futurity, whose expectation is property, whose measure is price, and whose "objectivity" is both the modern meaning of capital and the collective action which, independent of individual wills, creates the rights of property.

Thus, whether it be corporeal property, incorporeal property, or intangible property, the meaning of property is the fourfold meaning of usefulness, scarcity, futurity, and the collective legal relations of rights, duties, liberties, and exposures. It means the right to hold, to withhold, to alienate, to acquire, and to be free from interference. This is the definition of bargaining transactions. When property is bought, then all or a part of these proprietary relations is transferred. It is not physical things which are exchanged—that is a labor process—it is rather rights, duties, liberties, and exposures that are transferred; and these, psychologically speaking, are a transfer of expectations of the future, which, however, possess a discount value in the bargaining transactions of the present.

MacLeod made the mistake of calling incorporeal property commodities, having independent existences apart from the future commodities or money to which the rights laid claim. And he did not distinguish, as lawyers usually do not, the intangible property of good-will and patents from the incorporeal property of debt, because each is saleable. Such intangible property was also a "commodity," in the sense that it is assignable. MacLeod's double failure arose from his incorrect concept of Time. If, however, property rights are, as MacLeod, the lawyer, and all lawyers know, merely an institutional device for making certain the expectations of the future and thereby tying future commodities, future prices, and future money to the present by compelling others, in the future, to deliver commodities or pay money, or to refrain from interfering with markets and prices—then property rights are as objective as commodities themselves, since even the latter refer only to future commodities, while the former refer to future acts of other persons in delivering commodities and making payments. These future acts of other persons are objective in the sense, not that they are physical commodities, but that they are independent of any individual will. Further, property rights, thus defined, do not count a commodity twice—once as the commodity and once as the right to the commodity—they count the future and the present of the same ownership of the commodity.

With these corrections respecting the function of time and the meaning of objectivity, MacLeod's basic proposition is correct. The subject-matter of institutional economy, distinguished from engineering and home economy, is not commodities, nor labor, nor any physical thing—it is collective action which sets the working rules for proprietary rights, duties, liberties, and exposures; and these are the present expectations of bargainers that the community will see to it that their bargaining valuations are carried out in the future by themselves and others, respecting commodities, labor, money, or anything now expected to have future usefulness and scarcity.

It is this that is another variable dimension of value—the expectations of what collective action will do through its customs, laws, rights, and liberties as administered by courts, executives, boards, and commissions, including central banks of issue. This variable dimension of value is usually taken as a constant, because value is a noun, and not the process of valuation. But not only Russia shows that it is variable, also American legal history shows that it is highly variable. We do not measure it directly—we measure it by its effects on pecuniary valuations made in present transactions.

Hence it is that we do not buy or sell commodities—we buy and sell their values, and these values are the pecuniary measurement of economic quantities, not of physical things but of expectations of legal control over future things. This legal control is expected collective action.

The economist naturally objects to these legal definitions of value and price as superficial. What he asks for is the reality underneath. But there is reality—it is the *future* reality of all "goods" that human beings desire. This expected reality follows the valuations of bargaining. Two further steps are needed, the legal process of requiring payment, performance, and non-interference; and the technological process of manufacture, transport, and delivery of the commodities under the commands of owners. Their valuation becomes that familiar negotiational psychology which now transacts business in the process of valuing and is formulated in the present transactions, whose participants are looking forward to the future acquisition of solid reality under the hoped-for stability of government, industry, and banking.

The buying and selling of legal control by value agreements is a highly psychological process, and only the language of psychology can interpret it, because its essence is Futurity. But the psychology needed is the negotiational psychology of persuasion, coercion, command, obedience, pleading, and argument, instead of the pleasure and pain of commodities. Each party to a transaction is confronted by his own competitors and by the competitors of the opposite party, and is driven by his needs and alternatives. This means preliminary negotiation, which legal analysis resolves into persuasion or coercion, fair or unfair competition, equal or unequal opportunity, reasonable or unreasonable price, all of them dominated by scarcity, expectation, and the customary and legal rules of the time and place. Then if these conditions of persuasion, fairness, equality and reasonableness are not met, or disregarded, the court, representing the collectivity, reads into the negotiations, by the historic doctrine of assumpsit, an offer and an acceptance, which creates a debt, determined and measured by the aforesaid dimensions of the value.

Thus the economic concept of value, and indeed of modern Capital, like the concepts of other sciences, passes through several historical stages until it reaches a doctrine of pure relativity expressed in numbers. It started with the popular primitive concept of something physically objective; then switched to something highly subjective; then added the dimension of future time; then took over the concept of property, which is the objective equivalent of scarcity, futurity, and the rights, duties, liberties, and exposures which are the collective effects and causes of scarcity. Then, with the incoming of mathematics based on previously accepted units of measurement, these variable dimensions, either directly or indirectly, by their causes or effects, began to be combined into numerical measurements of changing magnitudes of the changing economic relations of man to nature and man to man. Three systems of measurement are used in the process: the physical measure of use-value, the pecuniary measure of scarcity, and the pecuniary measure of expected risk and waiting. It is through these expectations that joint valuations are made.

These nine or ten factors of valuing and their equivalent debt are reducible to three, scarcity appearing in three aspects, the scarcity of commodities, the scarcity of means of payment, the scarcity of the service of waiting; quantity appearing in the kinds, qualities, and amounts of use-value; while future time appears in the discounts of waiting and risking, the latter subdivided into the risks of nature, of individuals, and of collective action.

Hence we make a transactional definition of value and its equivalent debt, and even of modern capital, composed of these variable dimensions of scarcity, use, and discount, whose combined variabilities are commuted into loans and debits to accounts.

Thus we pass from psychology to corporeal, incorporeal, and intangible property, which is modern Capital and Capitalism. At the very time when the American courts were constructing the concept of intangible property, the economic psychologists were constructing a parallel psychology. This reached its peak in Fetter. His psychological economics has many of the attributes of intangible property, but, because it is individualistic, it cannot have the institutional concepts of equal opportunity, fair competition, equality of bargaining power, or due process of law. All of these are involved in the transactional system of money, the monetary meaning of value, and the collective action of society.

VII. The Margin for Profit

There are two different problems relative to the part played by profit in the national or world economy. One is the dynamic problem, What makes the concern go? The other is the static problem, What share of the National Income do the profit-makers get for making it go? The former we name the *profit-margin*, the latter we name the *profit-share*.

Two derived and subordinate relations of profit we distinguish as *rate of profit* and *profit-yield*. The rate of profit is the rate on. the par value of stocks issued; the profit-yield is the stock-yield, or rate of dividends on the market value of the stocks. If the profit-rate is 6 per cent on the par value of the stock, then the profit-yield is 3 per cent on the market value if the stock is selling at 200, or is 12 per cent if the stock is selling at 50.[200]

These subordinate problems are quite interesting from the private standpoint of speculators and investors, but from the social standpoint the question is twofold—How does the margin for profit keep the nation agoing or stopping, and Does Society pay too much or too little for this service? One is a question of a process; the other of justification and crimination of the process. The two are not usually separated. Each is a question of social importance because the profit-makers are the paymasters of all other classes. Is it more important to keep the concern agoing or to distribute the output justly?

Running through the Nineteenth and Twentieth Centuries, from the time of Ricardo and Malthus who split on this issue, are distinguishable the two fundamental but opposing theories of the causes of alternations of prosperity and depression. One we name the *Profit-share* theories, the other the *Profit-margin* theories. Each is based on the ultimate fact that the business men, who have legal control of industry, are the ones who, by virtue of that control, determine whether production and employment shall continue, expand, or stop. The sole motive which dominates them is Profit. Corporations, which now control about 90 per cent of the

---

[200] On investment-yield, see Epstein, Ralph C., *Industrial Profits in the United States* (1934), investigation and publication by The National Bureau of Economic Research.

total production even in manufactures,[201] but control practically all production in other industries except agriculture, are created by law solely to accommodate the profit motive. Individuals may have other motives, but when they enter corporations all other motives are eliminated. Corporations are institutions for profit, as churches are institutions for worship, and homes are institutions for love.

Upon this ultimate fact of legal control the Profit-share theorists have argued that too much of the national income goes to the proprietary incomes, such as rent, interest, and profit, and too little to consumer's income, especially wages and salaries. Therefore consumers are not able to purchase back all of the products which they as laborers have produced. Hence overproduction, followed by business depression and unemployment. This was the Malthusian theory.

The Profit-margin theorists have argued that the cause of business depression and unemployment was the inability of business men to obtain a sufficient revenue over and above all expenses to enable them to make a profit and to continue in business without suffering loss and bankruptcy. This was the Ricardian theory.

Four stages of the Malthusian Profit-share argument we shall distinguish as the Consumption Stage, the Savings Stage, the Dividends-Lag, and the Sales-Lag stages of the argument.

On the other hand, the Profit-margin arguments have passed through two major stages. The first stage assumed that a margin for profit could be maintained only by cutting wages, while the later argument held that it was possible to maintain profits with increased wages if the price-level did not fall, but remained stable, or increased faster than wages. The former was the Ricardian theory, the latter is inferred from the theory of Wicksell.

The Profit-margin is the difference between the total of all liabilities incurred for all purposes and the gross income obtained from all sales of products. This margin is usually described as "profit on sales," or "net profit," while the total of all liabilities incurred in order to make the sales is usually described as the "cost of goods sold," or cost of production. Since, however, profit and loss are the balance of changing assets and liabilities, we use the institutional name "liabilities incurred" in place of the classical name "costs."

But, in this respect, we shall distinguish between the operating margin and the profit and loss margins. The operating margin is the operating net income out of which taxes, interest, and profit

[201] National Industrial Conference Board, *The Shifting and Effects of the Federal Corporation Income Tax* (1928), I, 24.

are to be derived, but the profit and loss margin is the net income of pure profit or loss remaining after operation, taxes, and interest have been paid. Hence we have several subordinate margins for profit to be considered, three of which we name the Taxable Margin (after interest is paid), the Financial Margin (after taxes are paid), and the Price-margin, or the effect of price changes on the margin for profit.[202]

The following percentage table of a typical income statement will indicate, so far as our present purpose is concerned, the relations between these various margins and will serve somewhat as an outline for what follows on the Margin for Profit. It is these variable margins for profit that are to be compared with the Share of Profit.

TYPICAL INCOME STATEMENT (PERCENTAGES)

Gross income			100
Gross sales	98		
Other income (Profit cushion)	2	100	
Cost of production			90
Operating expense	85		
Depreciation and obsolescence	5	90	
Net operating income (98 — 90)			8
Taxes			1
Taxable margin (for taxes and profit) 8 — 1 = 7			
Interest charges			1
Financial margin (for interest and profit) 8 — 1 = 7			
Profit and loss margin			6
(Profit on sales) 8 — 1 — 1 = 6			
Profit cushion (other income)			2

1. *The Share of Profit*

The Share of Profit depends upon what we mean by Profit. The communists and early economists did not distinguish profit from interest. But we now make the distinction. Interest is payment enforced by law and stipulated in contracts. The law guarantees that the debtor will pay, if he has the funds. Other-

[202] Other profit-margins will be considered below, p. 611, Automatic and Managed Recovery; p. 840, Accidents and Unemployment; p. 627, Strategic and Routine Transactions.

wise it declares him bankrupt. Interest is a legal relation between creditor and debtor. But profits are not guaranteed by law. They are a relation between buyer and seller, borrower and lender, employer and wage-earner, each of whom is at liberty to deal or not to deal, and each of whom is exposed to gain or loss on account of the liberty of the other to deal or not to deal. It is a liberty-exposure relation permitted and enforced by law. Profit is obtained by purchasing transactions at low prices, for materials, or low wages, or low interest rates, or rents, and by selling transactions at higher prices. If the procedure is reversed, the result is Loss.

Hence, those who have legal control of corporations and business generally are seeking for profit and are fearful of loss. Their business, then, is twofold: Forecasting and Planning, while those who get pure interest are merely Saving and Waiting.[203] Profit is the result of forecasting and planning, and this is the reason why, in a system of private property, those who can make a profit get legal control of industry, and if they cannot make a profit they lose legal control through bankruptcy. So, in asking what is the *share* of profit, we are asking how much does the nation pay for Forecasting and Planning. But in asking how much is the *margin* for profit we are asking how much do individual business men and corporations have after paying their debts.

M. A. Copeland, adopting the calculations made by W. I. King, has estimated that in the year 1925 the total national income of commodities and services could be valued at 82 billion dollars. But this included "non-cash" items not yet brought within the pecuniary system, such as the rental value of homes owned, the interest estimated but not paid in money, and the produce consumed at home. These non-cash items were valued at 8 billion dollars, so that the estimated money income was the remaining 74 billion dollars. This money income was shared as follows.[204]

On these calculations, therefore, it will be seen that while employees received, as salaries and wages, nearly two-thirds (63 per cent) of the national money income, and while 8 per cent was received as rents and royalties, and 5 per cent as interest, the share going to profits was about one-fourth of the national income (dividends 6 per cent, profits 18 per cent).

---

[203] As previously noted, stockholders are waiting as well as risking, just as bondholders are risking as well as waiting. If the statistics were fine enough we could make the distinction finer, but we have to be content with supposing that dividends are a part of pure profit and interest on loans are pure interest.

[204] Copeland, M. A., in *Recent Economic Changes*, National Bureau of Economic Research (1929), II, 767.

SHARES OF MONEY INCOME, 1925

ITEM	BILLIONS OF DOLLARS	PER CENT
1. Wages	30.8	42
2. Salaries	14.9	20
3. Pensions, benefits, compensations	1.1	1
4. Total share of employees	46.8	63
5. Rents and royalties	5.8	8
6. Interest	3.9	5
7. Dividends	4.1	6
8. Property income	13.8	19
9. Entrepreneurial profits withdrawn	13.7	18
10. Total	74.3	100

But this one-fourth of the national income includes estimates of what owners, who are not stockholders in corporations, such as farmers and unincorporated concerns, *would* have received as wages and salaries if they had been employees. King estimates that if their profits were divided into *pure profit*, as against the *labor income* which they would have received as wage-earners or lawyers, or doctors or stockbrokers, then the pure profit would have been only 4 billion dollars and their labor-income would have been 9½ billion dollars. Pure profit, including dividends, would then have been about 11 per cent (dividends 6 per cent, profit 5 per cent), while the labor-income of the profit-receivers would have been about 13 per cent of the total national income ($24 - 11 = 13$).

But this comparison of profits with wages and salaries is rightly disregarded. The business owner does not become indebted to himself for his own wage or salary. He takes the risk of getting no wage and no salary just as much as the risk of getting no profit. He may actually get, in the form of profit, an amount of income which would be no greater, and even much less, than the salaries or wages which he pays to others. But that is looking backward after the figures are compiled, and is not the way in which business is conducted. The business owner is looking forward, and what he might call his wage or salary, if he gets it, is merged into the expected margin of profit remaining after he pays all his debts. In other words, in order to conduct his business for the sake of profit, he becomes indebted to others for wages, salaries, rents, royalties, and interest, and then takes his chances, by foresight and planning, of getting in the future his own wage or salary, not as such, but as profit. The margin for profit is not only pure profit—it is also the margin for the business man's imputed wages and salaries in the guise of profits.

We may therefore return to King's calculations, and, without trying to be too exact, we may estimate that, in a year like 1925, labor received as wages and salaries 60 per cent of the national income, while property owners and entrepreneurs received 40 per cent. This 40 per cent, when subdivided, gives about 9 per cent for rent, 6 per cent for interest, and 25 per cent for profit. In other words, if the total national income, measured in dollars, was 75 billions, then labor's share was about 45 billions, and the share of property owners was 30 billions, divided into rent 7 billions, interest 4 billions, and profit 19 billions.

Evidently, if labor receives only 60 per cent of the product, then the *share* going to wages and salaries in the form of money will not purchase back the whole of the product.

Based on this evident fact, Matthew Woll, speaking for the American Federation of Labor, drew the following inferences.

> "Volume of production has, since the coming of mass production, gone steadily upward. . . . Total volume of wages has gone down. . . . The result of these trends has been a diminishing mass of purchasing power, more and more unable to satisfy its needs or to move by purchase the growing stream of output. . . . Labor's policy can be stated in a few words: mass consumption must be enabled to keep pace with mass production. . . . The first need of the nation is a higher and higher standard of living for the masses of the people, not solely to provide sufficient and increasing employment, but to advance social progress as a national policy." [205]

This line of argument originated with Rodbertus, after 1837, and we shall name the two stages of the argument the Socialist Stage and the trade-union stage of the Malthusian Sequence of Theories. The difference is that the socialists, following Rodbertus in this respect rather than Karl Marx, would accomplish the increase of purchasing power through action by government but the trade-unionists would accomplish it by voluntary organization of Labor.

Malthus had set up his theory as a means of *recovery* from the depression and unemployment following 1815, but Rodbertus, followed afterwards by Hobson, and others, set it up as a *cause* of

[205] Woll, Matthew, *Annals of the American Academy of Political and Social Sciences*, CLIV (March 1931), 85.

depression and unemployment.[206] The landlords and capitalists, according to Rodbertus, absorbed for savings and investment the increasing output of technological productivity, and the laborers were therefore unable to buy back for consumption what they had produced. The resulting overproduction, unemployment, and falling prices could be prevented only by establishing through government a normal working day and readjusting both hours of labor and wages, from time to time, so as to guarantee to laboring men a proportionate share in the increasing productivity of labor.

A more recent socialist writer, Alfred Baker Lewis,[207] has traced three stages of the socialist argument to the effect that, in order to prevent unemployment, the share going to labor should be increased at the expense of the share going to property. Modifying somewhat his terms, we name these stages of the argument the consumption stage, the savings stage, and the dividends-lag stage of the argument. We shall identify the first stage as the communist stage and the second and third stages as the socialist and trade-union stage of the argument. To these we shall add a fourth stage formulated by the collaborators, Foster, Catchings, and Hastings, which we name the sales-lag stage of the argument. The entire sequence of *profit-share* theories we designate the Malthus-Rodbertus sequence, to be distinguished from the *profit-margin* theories which we designate the Thornton-Wicksell sequence.[208]

(1) **Consumption and Savings.**—In the communist stage of the argument the conclusion reached was that all property-income, including rent, interest, and profit should be abolished by common ownership so that labor would receive as wages or salaries the total value of the product. This remedy, it was claimed, would abolish unemployment. Lewis says, regarding this communist stage of the argument:

"The explanation of periodic business depressions which has been urged most persistently is the one which traces these depressions to a general overproduction caused by the position and existence of profits in our industrial life. As crudely stated by the early Socialists, the theory was that the worker did not get the full value of what he produced owing to the fact that rent, interest, dividends, and profits as well as wages and salaries were paid out of the product, and consequently the workers could not

[206] Cf. Malthus, T. R., *Principles of Political Economy* (1821); *Letters of Ricardo to Malthus* (1813–23, ed. by Bonar, J.); Rodbertus, A. J. C., *Die Forderungen der arbeitenden Klassen* (1837 and subsequent publications); Hobson, J. A., *Economics of Unemployment* (1922).
[207] *The New Leader*, November 9, 1930.
[208] Below, p. 590, A World Pay Community.

buy back all that they produced. It is true enough that wages and salaries total less than the full value of what is produced because the owners of industry take a big chunk of the product in the form of property income. But the answer to the early Socialist argument was promptly given that those who got their income in the form of rent, interest, dividends, and profits, also consumed goods, and the spending of their incomes by the owners of industry would be sufficient to buy back that part of the total product which the wages and salaries of the workers were unable to buy." [209]

Faced with the foregoing argument that property owners were also consumers, the socialists, said Lewis, "replied that the owners of industry tended to spend a much smaller part and invest a much larger part of their income than did the workers, and it was their savings and investing which tended to cause a deficiency in the purchasing power of the consumer compared with the total product, or in other words, a general overproduction." Regarding this second stage of the argument, Lewis says:

"The fundamental difficulty with this theory is that saving is simply spending with a different object. Since spending money cannot very well cause overproduction, there does not seem therefore any good reason for holding saving responsible for overproduction, or underconsumption either. The man who saves and invests spends his money, although he spends it for capital equipment, or it may be for durable consumers' goods such as a home, just as truly as the man who spends his money for consumers' goods that will immediately, or at least very quickly be destroyed in the act of consumption. Even when a corporation saves by increasing its capital equipment, it is simply spending its money to pay wages to men working in the industries producing and erecting capital equipment, instead of paying out the money as dividends to stockholders who in turn would spend the money, indirectly of course, to pay the wages of men working in those industries producing the things which the stockholders decided to buy. Saving, in other words, is simply spending for producers' goods, of which capital equipment may be taken as the type, instead of spending for consumers' goods. The net effect of saving, therefore, is to create a tendency for labor to flow into industries producing capital equipment rather than industries producing consumers' goods.

"If a rich man, for example, decided to spend his money he might buy a yacht with part of his income, and this would cause labor to flow into the shipyards producing pleasure yachts. He might purchase the securities of the International Mercantile Ma-

209 Alfred Baker Lewis, in *The New Leader*, Nov. 9, 1930.

rine Company, and that would cause labor to flow into those shipyards producing freight or passenger vessels rather than pleasure yachts. The only essential difference between saving and spending is the difference in the direction given to the flow of the country's productive forces, and in any case there is no necessary reduction in the total demand for the output of these productive forces. So it seems clear that the act of increasing capital equipment does not in itself cause any general overproduction or general deficiency in consumers' purchasing power.

"If there were a marked increase in saving used to increase capital equipment in one year compared with another, the net effect probably would be to cause some slackening of activity in certain industries producing capital equipment, but that is not the characteristic of recurring periods of hard times. For the dominant characteristic of these periodic business depressions is the fact that all classes of industry suffer a depression below their normal activity, rather than some classes suffering from a slump while others are enjoying a boom." [210]

(2) Dividends-Lag.—Abandoning, then, the argument that a change in the shares going *simultaneously* to labor and capital would make a difference in the amount of employment or unemployment, Lewis states what we call the Dividends-Lag stage of the argument, as a difference in the *time* when profits are spent.

"Profits," he says, "could not be disbursed before the product from which they are derived has been sold, because they are not obtained nor even in existence until then. The same thing of course applies to dividends as well as to profits. For dividends are simply the method of disbursing the profits, and in part the rent and interest, obtained by corporations. This fact is important because it means that the profits derived from the business of a given year (or a given quarter) cannot be used to buy back that part of the product turned out during the year which the wages paid during the year cannot buy back. In other words, if the product produced in 1928 goes one half to wages and salaries and one half to profits and dividends, half of it, the profits half, cannot be used to buy the product of 1928 because it is not distributed till 1929."

The same principle would hold true if profits were distributed quarterly or semi-yearly. We may substitute a "given period of time" for his term "year" and not affect the validity of the argument.

But it may be objected, says Lewis, that "the profits earned in the previous year and distributed the year following that in which

[210] *Ibid.*

they were earned are used for that purpose. In other words the profits of 1927 are not paid out in 1927 but in 1928 and they are then used to buy back that part of the product of 1928 which the wages paid in 1928 are unable to buy back."

This objection, says Lewis, would be conclusive if the output of one year were the same as the output of the preceding year and if the shares were the same in the two years.

"Suppose that the product of 1928 is 50 billions divided ½, or 25 billions, to labor, and ½ as profits and dividends. The whole product will be sold, because, although the 25 billions of profits will not be paid out ready to act as effective demand in the market until 1929, 25 billion dollars earned as profits in 1927, but not paid out till 1928, will make up the difference."

But this equality of output in two successive years is not what happens. Lewis says,

"Let us suppose next that there is an increase of production in 1929 so that the product is 60 billions instead of 50 billions, divided as before, ½ to profits and ½ to wages and salaries. There will then be available to purchase the 60 billions of output in 1929, 30 billions of wages and 25 billions of profits earned in the previous year and distributed in 1929. This leaves unsold an amount of 5 billions." [211]

He carries the illustration further for a third year and shows a cumulation of unsold goods with each year's increase in output, and concludes:

"It is obvious that the amount of unsold goods will increase this way year by year as long as production keeps on increasing over the previous year. These goods are carried over in the form of increased stock in retailers' stores, and in the hands and warehouses of wholesalers, and increased stocks both of finished product and of raw material in the hands of manufacturers."

Lewis then goes on to show, quite accurately, how it is that unsold goods in retailers' hands work backward all along the line.

"Of course finally the result of an increase in the stocks of unsold goods on hand is that retailers cut down their orders to wholesalers, and wholesalers reduce their orders in turn to manufacturers, manufacturers shut down on production, throw their men out of work or put them on short time, and reduce severely their orders to the extractive industries for raw materials."

[211] *Ibid.*

And Lewis goes still further and shows why it is that business starts up again.

"It is true, of course," he says, "that the policy which manufacturers resort to, of throwing men out of a job or putting them on short time, intensifies and prolongs the depressions by reducing buying power as well as production. But even unemployed men eat. Even though out of a job they consume things. They draw on their savings bank accounts and borrow on their life insurance policies and so get money to move goods to some extent at any rate. To a considerable extent the workers get goods on credit from their neighborhood stores, so that the goods are moved, though no money passes the other way for a considerable time.

"Furthermore, some business is carried on during the depression without profit or even at an actual loss, so that the amount of purchasing power disbursed to consumers is greater than the price of that part of the product which is produced under such circumstances. In all these ways the stored-up stocks of goods are gradually reduced. Buying, at first in hand-to-mouth form, gains in volume, and industry starts once more to pick up." [212]

Finally, Lewis concludes with the *same remedies* which had been proposed in both the first and second stages of the socialist arguments, whose validity he had previously disproved.

"It is clear, therefore," he says, "that profits and other payments made in the same way as profits, such as dividends, are responsible for the periodic gluts which have been so characteristic of capitalism.

"The practical result from this line of reasoning is that any sort of political or industrial program which would tend to decrease the share of industry that goes to dividends and profits and increase the share that is paid as wages and salaries would tend to decrease the severity of our periodic industrial depressions, or lengthen the period of prosperity between them or both. A shift in our tax burden so as to cause more of the burden to fall on profits, or an increase of social services paid out of additional taxes on profits, or rate regulation directed toward decreasing profits, all will tend to reduce unemployment. The same desirable result would come from any strengthening of the powers of labor organizations so as to enable them, by favorable collective wage agreements, to increase somewhat the proportion of the product of industries that are paid in the form of wages, or from any extension of non-profit ways of carrying on industry, such as by producers' or consumers' cooperatives or by government ownership and operation."

[212] *Ibid.*

In the foregoing statement of the Dividends-Lag theory little or no account was taken of Undivided Profits and the disposition of Corporate Surplus. Evidently the profits *not yet* declared as dividends do not lie idle, like a hoard of money, in the vaults of the corporation. They are either used by the corporation in the purchase of commodities and labor for expansion of plant or restoration of depreciation, or are left on deposit at the banks to be loaned to other corporations for the purchase of commodities and labor, or are invested temporarily in the securities of other corporations which are purchasing commodities and labor. The only thing that happens when dividends are declared is the *transfer* of that much purchasing power from the corporation to the stockholders. The dividends-lag theory is fallacious because undivided profits are used to purchase as much commodities and labor as the same amount of profits when distributed as dividends.

(3) **Sales-Lag.**—Hence a second formula of the profits-lag theory, *i.e.*, the sales-lag theory, has been developed jointly by Messrs. Foster, Catchings, and Hastings.[213] The statement briefly runs, as published most fully by Hastings:

". . . business concerns as a whole do not disburse an amount of money equal to the value of the things which they produce, in addition to all money received from outside sources. . . . Even if producers of goods increase disbursements at the same time, and by the same amount, as the increase in the total sale price of their output, this increase in purchasing power may not reach the markets as soon as the goods; and, therefore, there may be an accumulation of unsold goods, until the new flow of money reaches its full volume on the retail markets. . . . Since producers of goods for a profit do not disburse this profit at the time the goods are produced, but only after the goods have been sold, they do not at the start of increased production disburse an amount equal to the sale price of the goods. . . . The temporary lag of the scale of profits behind the scale of production, and the readjustments in the relative value of goods . . . tend to cause an accumulation of unsold goods. . . . The cost of materials is not always paid currently. This fact sometimes prevents the creditor from making his current disbursements equal the full costs and profits of the goods which he is producing. . . . Organized Producers of Raw Materials, Producers of Semi-finished Products, Distributors, and Producers of Services and Intangible Goods also fail to make current disbursements equal to the value of the goods or services currently produced. . . . Thus . . . the

[213] Hastings, H. B., *Costs and Profits; Their Relation to Business Cycles* (1923); Foster, W. T., and Catchings, W., *Money* (1923); *Profits* (1925); *Business without a Buyer* (1927); *The Road to Plenty* (1928).

non-use of profits and the 'improper' use of profits, which together represent a considerable part of earned profits during a period of business revival and activity, are responsible for the accumulation of unsold goods at such times, with a commercial crisis as the inevitable, ultimate result, even if there were no other factors tending to produce the same outcome." [214]

The argument is expanded by Foster and Catchings:

"The discouraging result, which is usually called 'overproduction,' might better be called 'underconsumption.' Whatever it is called, it is due principally to two causes: first, the fact that industry does not pay out to consumers enough money to enable them to buy the increased output; second, the fact that consumers, under the necessity of saving, cannot spend even as much money as they receive from industry. And they have no other source of income." [215]

The conclusions reached from the sales-lag theory of profit are similar to those already noted from the consumption, savings, and dividend-lag theories of inadequate consumer purchasing power. The consuming power of wage-earners must be increased, in order that they may purchase the total product, *in advance* [216] of the business man's profits which will not be available for purchasing power until his product is sold.

But this sales-lag theory of profit may be shown to be equally fallacious with the dividends-lag theory and we substitute for it what may be named, in contrast, a *sales-forecast* theory of profit, or, what is its equivalent, a *risk discount* theory of profits.

2. Sales Forecast

Wages and salaries, it is evident, are paid in advance of the sale of the product, sometimes 30 days in advance, sometimes 30 years in advance. How, then, do the business men get their money with which to pay wages and salaries *in advance* of the sale of the product? Certainly wages and salaries cannot be paid until after the product is sold, any more than can profits be ascertained or dividends declared until after the product is sold.

It is the banking system that enables wages and salaries to be paid and used as purchasing power in advance of the sale of the product. It is this banking system also that enables profits to be

---

[214] Hastings, H. B., *op. cit.*, ix, 6, 9, 11, 14.

[215] Foster, W. T., and Catchings, W., *Business without a Buyer*, 167.

[216] It seems to be argued that consuming power consists in high *rates* of wages per day or hour, whereas it consists as much or more in steady employment. That is, consuming power consists in *annual income*, not in daily or hourly income. Below, p. 611, Automatic and Managed Recovery.

used as purchasing power in advance of the sale of the product from which the profits, as well as the wages, salaries, interest, and rent, will be derived. This banking system operates in two ways, commercial banking and investment banking. Commercial banking finances the *operation* of industries; investment banking finances the *capital equipment* of industries.

Commercial banking enables the business man to buy materials and pay wages *in advance* of the sale of the product. It is done by the forecast system of money which we have described. Not only future interest payments, but also future profits, taking into account the future risks, are *discounted* by the process of paying *less* in the present for materials and wages than the expected prices that will be received when the product is sold. Taking the simplified formula which we have used,[217] the present worth of a product expected to sell in 60 days for $60,000 is, by the double discount of interest and profit, $58,800 (interest $600, profit $600—total $1,200). There may be uncertainties, but for simplification we omit them, because we are concerned here only with the general principle of whether profits become purchasing power only *after* the goods are sold, or *before* the goods are sold. Is it only *realized* profit on each transaction, or is it *expected* profit on each transaction, that constitutes the purchasing power for present commodities and labor? If it is only *realized* profit on each transaction, which becomes purchasing power, then evidently the share going to profit lags behind production, and there is a gradual surplus of unsold goods accumulated. But if it is *expected* profit that determines the amount of *present* purchasing power, then there is no lag of profits as purchasing power behind production any more than there is a lag of wages as purchasing power.

In order, however, to understand the issue between the profits-lag and the profits-forecast theory of profit we need to examine again the mechanism of the banking system. We may ask: Is there not also an interest-lag? When does the banker get his $600 interest, and what does he do with it when he gets it? He evidently gets it 60 days in advance of the sale of the product, by the process of discount. He has loaned $60,000 to his customer payable by the latter in 60 days, but the banker has made himself liable on his books, to the seller of the commodity, for only $59,400 payable on demand.[218] The difference, $600, is just that much unused bank

[217] Above, p. 507.

[218] In addition, the borrower, by a custom of the banking business, is expected to maintain a balance, estimated by Philips at an average of 20% of his loans. In the illustration, this would amount to $12,000, leaving to the borrowers only $47,400, and to the banks $12,600 which the latter can loan to other manufacturers. In practice it might mean

credit,[219] which the banker can lend to any other manufacturer, and which the other manufacturer can then use, as a deposit account, immediately in purchasing materials and paying wages. By this process of discounting and transfer of bank deposits, the interest, $600, is paid out for *other* materials and *other* wages by *other* employers 60 days in advance of the sale of the particular product from whose sale the repayment of principal and interest will be made to the banker by the customer of the first manufacturer who bought the commodity for $60,000, payable in 60 days.

Hence there is no interest-lag if business is prosperous. The amount of interest is provided for in advance in the *lower prices* for materials and wages than the expected prices of the finished product. And the amount of this interest is actually used elsewhere by other manufacturers to create a demand for labor directly in their own factories, or indirectly by the demand for materials.

The same is true of profits. But here we must introduce the concept of a going concern. In the preceding illustration we picked out a single loan transaction of 60 days' duration. But this was only one of multitudes of similar transactions repeating themselves continuously, if all business is going on as usual, and transactions are occurring with other going concerns. Suppose this particular concern has a daily output and sale of $60,000 worth of finished product. Then each day of the year a profit of $600 is realized on a loan and commitment made 60 days previously. Each day this profit of $600 is realized because, 60 days previously, the manufacturer had paid in advance that much *less* for materials and wages than he now receives for his finished product, on account of the preceding profit-discount.

What does he do with this $600 daily margin of profit? He spends it or saves it. It has come to him in the form of checks drawn on a great number of banks which he has deposited in his own bank as a credit to his account. If he draws it out for personal consumption he spends it directly or indirectly in the employment of labor. But if he saves it he may do so in two or three ways. He leaves it as a credit-deposit to his account at the bank, in which case the bank can lend it to other business men for the employment of labor. If he is already in debt to the bank on account of loans, then his added credit-deposit reduces his net indebtedness to the bank. But it also reduces, by the same amount, the bank's demand liabilities,

that the manufacturer would borrow $72,000 in order to have a checking account of $59,400. See Philips, C. A., *Bank Credit* (1920). But these considerations do not apply to our simplified illustration.

[219] Equivalent to Hawtrey's "unspent margin." Hawtrey, R. G., *Currency and Credit*, 6 *passim*.

and, if the bank has not reached the lawful limit of reserves, then the bank has that much leeway in lending to other manufacturers the $600 by which the first manufacturer has reduced his net indebtedness. In either case the manufacturer has *saved* his profits and, through the commercial bank, has loaned it to other manufacturers with which they can immediately employ labor and buy materials.

Hastings, joining with Foster and Catchings, denies that this payment of a bank loan is equivalent to a disbursement of money for the purchase of goods and employment of labor. He says,

> "The money which the concern pays back to the banks may be *loaned* to *another manufacturer* (or even reloaned to the same manufacturer) to finance the production of goods. Thus, *ultimately, it may reach the hands of a consumer, but not until after it has paid for the production of additional goods.* The deficiency between the *value of goods produced* and the *purchasing power disbursed by producers* of goods would still exist. For this reason, we have not regarded the payment of a bank loan as a disbursement of money." [220]

Here is evidently a survival of the fallacy that consumption and not savings creates a demand for commodities and labor. The loan to another manufacturer by the bank is a "saving" of profit and is *immediately* used as purchasing power in buying materials and employing labor in the production of a commodity that will be sold later by that other manufacturer. It does not wait until it reaches the hands of a consumer.

Furthermore, the purchasing power thus disbursed is approximately *equal* (allowing for errors of forecast) to the *present* value of the discounted future sale value of the goods produced. For example, in our illustration the present value was $58,800 (deducting both the interest discount and the profit discount), which is the amount paid for materials and labor 60 days in advance of sale, so that, of course, the purchasing power disbursed is identical with the value of the material and labor purchased, *at the time when purchased.* It will be worth more in 60 days but the banking mechanism and the forecast discount take care of the difference.

Or the manufacturer, instead of letting the bank lend the equivalent of his profit to other manufacturers, may draw upon his account for the purpose of making payments in his own business, exactly as he did when he drew it out for personal consumption. He can

---

[220] Hastings, H. B., *op. cit.*, 95–96. Italics not in the original.

use it by "plowing" it back as "undivided profits" into his own business, in which case what is meant is that he uses it to employ labor in the construction of extensions or other enlargement of the plant. Or he can use it by paying directly the operating laborers in advance of the sale of their product, instead of borrowing at the bank in order to pay them in advance. In which case there will appear on the asset side of his books such items as "goods in process" or "inventory," presumably valued at what he had paid for them.

Or finally, if he has sold the finished goods to customers, on 30 or 60 days time, there may appear on the asset side of his books the item "accounts receivable," but there will not appear on the liability side a corresponding debt to the bank, because his $600 daily profit has been actually loaned to customers and his debt to the bank is reduced by that much. There appears however, on the liability side of his books, the item "accounts payable," on account of purchases of materials not yet paid for.

If his debtors reduce his "accounts receivable" by paying their debts to him, they do so by checks on their banks which he deposits at his bank and thus augments his own checking account available immediately for the purchase of materials and labor. On the other hand, if he reduces his "accounts payable," by paying his debts to other manufacturers, he also does so by a check on his own bank, which immediately the other manufacturer, by depositing it in his own bank, has available for the purchase of material and labor.

Hastings, again, denies that a reduction of "accounts payable" is a disbursement of money as purchasing power. He says,

> "Finally, we have the possibility that the $100 (increase in cash) might be used for the reduction of Accounts Payable. If the concern to whom the money is paid *has previously been disbursing money on account of costs and profits to the full extent of the goods produced,* it will not have to disburse this money in addition to full disbursements for the current period. It may even use this $100 to retire bank loans, without thereby upsetting the balance between the flow of purchasing power and the flow of goods. It is not unlikely, however, that the creditor concern *has failed to disburse the full amount required, on account of this purchasing power having been tied up in its Accounts Receivable;* and although it may now make up such deficiency, it will not be the same as if the money had been disbursed simultaneously with the production of goods." [221]

Here again is a remnant of the savings fallacy in support of the

[221] *Ibid.*, 96. Italics not in the original.

sales-lag fallacy, owing to failure to recognize the bank mechanism and the forecast discount. When the manufacturer uses his $100 to reduce accounts payable he transfers to his creditor a deposit of $100 by drawing a check on his own bank, and the creditor, by depositing it, augments his own account at his bank by $100. This is equivalent to reducing his bank loan $100 by increasing the bank's demand liability to him $100.

The error arises from the idea that the creditor concern failed previously to disburse the full amount required because its purchasing power had been tied up in accounts receivable. The only reason why accounts receivable should be "tied up" is because they are "bad debts." If they are good debts they are not tied up. They are then a part of his assets, on the strength of which his bank will advance purchasing power to him, at a discount, which he can use immediately to buy materials and labor.

This advance may be obtained usually in two ways, by a "customer's loan," or by selling the account receivable to the bank at a discount. In the case of customers' loans, which constitute the great bulk of American domestic banking, the accounts receivable are known to the bank, though not sold to the bank, and they constitute the customer's assets on the strength of which the bank "carries" the customer, by a loan and its corresponding checking account, to the amount deemed necessary until the accounts receivable are paid. Thus the accounts receivable do not "tie up" purchasing power until the goods are sold. They are the very foundation on which the banking mechanism advances purchasing power in advance of payment for goods sold.

The other method of bank advances is by way of actual sale of the account to the bank at an interest-risk discount, the bank creating a deposit to the account of the seller equal to the future face value of the account, less the discount. An instance of this is the Trade Acceptance or "two name paper" where both the seller and the buyer of the goods are liable for the payment of the bill when due. Here the "account receivable" disappears from the assets of the bank's customer, and in its place is merely a deposit of "cash at the bank," available immediately for purchases of materials and labor. Here again there is no profit-lag, nor interest-lag. The banking mechanism is created for the express purpose of preventing such a lag in purchasing power. It permits the creation of purchasing power during the process of production and before the goods are sold.

Furthermore, again, this purchasing power is approximately equal (allowing for forecast errors) to the *present value* or present worth of the goods produced, since their present value is none other than the amounts of purchasing power actually disbursed, at their current prices, for materials and labor in the process of production. It will "purchase back" all that is produced, *at their present values,* and when the future value becomes present value the same will be true. The forecast discount and the banking mechanism have provided the means of payment at present values of the products.

Thus, either through the commercial banks or through employment in one's own business, if business goes on as usual, all profits are immediately available as purchasing power for the employment of labor without waiting until the product is sold and not waiting until profits are converted into dividends. The change which we have made from the profit-lag theory is twofold; the *closing of a transaction* instead of the declaration of dividends; and the *repetition of transactions* in a going business instead of a single transaction isolated and treated by itself.

This substitution of transactions for the declaration of dividends enables us to re-enforce what we have previously said on the meaning of a transaction.[222] It has a beginning and an ending in time. The beginning we distinguish as Concluding the Negotiations. The ending we distinguish as Closing the Transaction.

The beginning is at the date and hour when the negotiations are deemed to take effect in the transfer of two ownerships. The ending of the transaction is at the date and hour when performance or payment, whichever is last, is completed. This last date is the date of closing the transaction, because the transaction creates two debts, the debt of performance which is released when the commodity is physically delivered and accepted; and the debt of payment which is released when the payment is accepted.

The transaction may be closed immediately, in which case both debts are paid immediately and this is a sale for "cash." Here the interval between performance and payment is so short that it is not usually looked upon as a debt, but it nevertheless is a debt wherein the interval is so short that it is not worth measuring for the purpose of calculating a discount or rate of interest. Or the transaction may not be closed until an interval of time has elapsed between performance and payment. Such a debt may be negotiable, and in our illustration the transaction was closed at the end of 60 days. The average turnover of such commercial transactions in the United States has been estimated at about 15 days, or a turnover of 26 times per year.[223] This means that, on the average, every 15 days

[222] Above, p. 432, Closing the Negotiations and Closing the Transaction.
[223] Above, p. 294, From Circulation to Repetition.

the margins of profit can be known on the intervening transactions. Meanwhile, these margins of profit are being converted into deposits for loans to other manufacturers or are being plowed back into extensions, or are being employed for operating expenses, including replacements. In any case they are "saved," and this saving is a continuous repetition of saving profits, and thereby is also created a continuous repetition of employing labor for production or construction out of profits.

The same is true of long-term bonds issued for construction purposes, and for the buying of machinery. Such a transaction is not closed until the end of ten, twenty, thirty years, as the case may be. Here, if properly calculated, it is expected that the duration of the loan will correspond somewhat to the duration of the equipment from whose operation the products are created, which, in turn, are to be financed by the short-term transactions of commercial loans. The new equipment depreciates, and if its life is expected to be, say ten years, then a ten-year bond bearing interest payable annually and backed by an annual sinking fund for the bonds, or depreciation fund for the equipment, equivalent to one-tenth of the principal, will close the loan transaction by the time the equipment is worn out or obsolete.

A large automobile organization is said to have the policy of "writing off" its machinery at the rate of 20 per cent annually, so that it is completely "charged off" at the end of five years. Obsolescence is the main reason. The company cannot compete, using machinery five years old, when competitors are installing new and more efficient machinery. If the company borrows the money on five-year bonds it would expect to set aside a sinking fund annually of 20 per cent of the principal.[224] But since it does not borrow the money it "writes off" the machinery from its assets 20 per cent per year, on account of depreciation and obsolescence. In either case the company must recoup itself by charging a price for the cars that will cover the total depreciation and obsolescence apportioned to each car, as overhead. If this is done by writing off 20 per cent of the original cost of machinery, then this amount will show itself in that much deduction from assets on the balance sheet and from profits on the income statement. If it is done by a sinking fund account, this account will appear as an asset which sets off that much from the liability incurred on account of the five-year bond. But the sinking fund asset is obtained by reducing the allowance for profit.

In either case what happens is that profits are retained instead of

[224] Compound interest would alter this somewhat.

being transferred as dividends to stockholders. The mere "writing off its machinery" is "saving" its profits to that amount. The process is not different from commercial loans or plowing back profits, except in the expected duration of the interval of time. It is the future prices and quantity of the cars or other product discounted to present value, along with the banking mechanism, that enables present profits to be "saved." In general it is the process of buying less material, constructing less machinery or buildings, employing less labor or paying lower prices and wages, and thus keeping down the present total debts or liabilities to an amount less than the expected future gross money income to be derived from the future sales of the finished product. Profits are "saved" as soon as they are earned, and, being saved, are expended for labor in advance of the sale of the finished product, and only the balance not saved is declared as dividends, to be in turn "spent" or "saved" by stockholders.

Hence we conclude, on account of the banking system for interest, and the forecast discount for profit, that there is no lag of profits as purchasing power, any more than there is a lag of wages as purchasing power. Profits are available and are used as purchasing power simultaneously with production, just as much as wages are available and used to purchase commodities simultaneously with production.

The sales-lag theory of profits is made plausible by a "circulation" theory of money. The theory, as we have seen, originated with Quesnay in France, where at the time, 1758, commercial banks were unknown and only metallic money constituted the "currency." Money was, for Quesnay, a commodity, like corn or wheat, and it "flowed" from buyer to seller in exchange for products. When paper money began to take the place of metallic money, it also "flowed" from hand to hand as a "circulating medium" enabling commodities to flow in the opposite direction.

The analogy is good enough. Quesnay took it from the circulation of the blood. Evidently, with only metallic or paper money in existence, the consumer cannot buy unless he actually has the physical coins or paper dollars in his pocketbook. Neither can the stockholder of a corporation employ his profits as purchasing power until dividends are declared in coin or paper. And the manufacturer cannot buy anything with his profits on sales until his product is actually sold and he gets the coin or paper.[225] With such a theory of money held over from the period of metallic money, if carried to

---

[225] This was the argument of Thomas Mun, in 1628, when he advocated negotiability of debts in order to obviate the need at that time of waiting until coin was obtained before

its limit, only wage-earners are purchasers of their product *at the time* when they produce it, and since they purchase the product only in the finished form of consumption goods, they cannot possibly purchase all of the material used in producing the consumption goods. Nor can their purchase of consumption goods possibly pay all the wages to the other laborers who produced only the materials, *at the time* when they were producing them.

The modern form of this physical concept of circulation—which has run through the centuries since Quesnay, and is the common-sense experience of all who do not grasp the mechanism of commercial and investment banking—appears in the following quotation from Foster and Catchings. After drawing a diagram of the "circuit flow of money" quite similar to the famous *Tableau économique* of Quesnay one hundred and seventy years before, these authors state:

"Some of the money completes the circuit quickly, some of it, slower. As shown in the diagram, a part of the consumer's income is spent directly for personal services and a part is paid to individuals for second-hand automobiles and other 'old commodities,' and is thus passed directly from one consumer to another. Most of the money spent by consumers, however, takes a longer course before it finds its way back to consumers. Part of the money that is spent for new commodities—a pair of shoes, for example—goes to the wholesaler; part of that money goes to the manufacturer; part of that money goes to the tanner; part of that money goes to the farmer who raised the stock; part of that money goes to the producer of harvesting machinery; part of that money goes to mechanics in the factory, and is thus returned to consumers. During the circuit from consumer back to consumer, some of the money spent for the pair of shoes passed through more hands than in our illustration; some of it passed through fewer hands. The part that the retail shoe dealer paid immediately in weekly wages to his clerks made the circuit quickly. The part that was set aside in cash as undivided profits of the shoe manufacturer may have taken a long time to make the circuit. It is the average time taken by all the money in the flow from one use in consumption to another use in consumption that we have called the circuit time of money." [226]

This physical analogy holds only for a period of metallic or paper money, but it does not fit commercial banking and its checking ac-

the merchant could avail himself of his sales to make additional purchases and thus increase the rate of turnover. See Mun, Thomas, *England's Treasure by Foreign Trade* (1664, probably written before 1628).

[226] Foster, W. T., and Catchings, W., *Money*, 306.

counts. It is the "cash and carry" plan of industry. It fits the pay envelope and the pocketbook. This "money in circulation" consists of an astonishing variety of coin and paper money, each of which is kept at par with gold by limiting its supply, and each of which is a special study and goes back to its own history which can be investigated in the statutes of the past seventy years.

All of this "money in circulation" passes physically from hand to hand in the purchase of commodities and payment of debts. But, strangely enough, this four to five billion dollars of money in circulation is disbursed for scarcely more than 10 to 20 per cent of all purchases. Over 80 or 90 per cent of the total values of all the buying and selling transactions of the country are made by means of bank checks against deposits.[227] Even so, all of this money in circulation comes from banks and is already included in debits to depositors' accounts. These "deposits" are bankers' debts past due, and therefore payable on demand, which have been created by the banks for the express purpose of buying the debts of business men *not yet due* but payable at a specified future time. A check drawn against these deposits does not circulate, except slightly by endorsement. It is an order on the banker to transfer on his books a demand debt of the banker (deposit) to the credit of another person. And this mere order is the purchasing power in practically all of the values of all transactions. Ordinarily the check exists only a day or two, but the loan or discount which made the check possible has an existence of one day, 30 days, 90 days, or more.

Hence each loan transaction creates its own money. Take, for example, a trade acceptance and a single bank dealing with a seller and buyer. A steel manufacturer sells to an agricultural implement manufacturer 1,000 tons of rolled steel at $40 per ton, payable in 60 days. The debt, "accepted" by the implement manufacturer, is $40,000. The banker buys the debt at 6 per cent discount, or 1 per cent for 60 days, and sets up a deposit on his books to the amount of $39,600 to the credit of the steel manufacturer. At the end of 60 days the implement manufacturer who has been building up a deposit account at the same bank, pays the debt by a check on his own account payable to the bank for $40,000 and the transaction is closed.

The transaction has created $39,600 purchasing power for the steel manufacturer, in advance of the time when the implement manufacturer is able to pay, besides the $400 which the banker can loan (provided he is within his legal reserve limit) to another manu-

[227] Snyder, Carl, in his *Business Cycles and Business Measurements* (1927), p. 134, estimates it at 80 per cent. Others have estimated it as high as 90 or 95 per cent.

facturer for immediate use. During the 60 days the deposit of the steel manufacturer is checked out as purchasing power but comes back to the bank, is credited, and can again be checked out; but at the end of 60 days the implement manufacturer has extinguished the loan of $40,000 by reducing his own deposits that much, and the bank has paid off its depositors. As far as that transaction goes it will show on the books of the bank at the beginning of the transaction, a loan of $40,000, a deposit $39,600, a surplus $400; and will show the same statement just before the loan is paid. But when it is paid by the implement manufacturer, both the loan and the deposit have been extinguished, leaving the bank its surplus $400. The transaction has created its own money. There is no "circulation." There is creation, duration, and extinction—in short, "turnover"— of purchasing power depending upon the expectations of prices and quantities.

Multiply this over-simplified transaction of a supposed single bank by a repetition of billions and even trillions of similar transactions during a year, add all the banks with their clearing houses, and we have, not a *circulation* system of money, but a *forecast* and *repetition* system of money. Each loan or discount transaction creates and extinguishes its own money in expectation of the increase in values which will be added by production and sale. Or, stating it inversely, the present value of its own product, in its unfinished condition at the *time of production,* is the discounted future value which it will have *at the time of sale.* The farmers, mine owners, lumbermen, in the basic industries expect to sell to the flour mills, blast furnaces, furniture manufacturers; these in turn expect to sell to the wholesalers, these to the retailers, and these at last to the ultimate consumers. All along the line they are furnishing materials to the next productive process until the final consumer is reached. And all along the line it is the *expected* prices and quantities of these materials to be bought by those next in the future line of production, which are discounted in the lower prices and wages paid in the preceding production of the unfinished goods.

The banking industry parallels this productive process and enables each producer, in addition to funds advanced by himself without borrowing, to obtain *in advance* the purchasing power needed, *at their present value in anticipation of their future value.* The consumer's money does not circulate—it is anticipated, discounted, and extinguished in each transaction back to its origins in the resources of nature, and it is each of these transactions, which, by the aid of the banking system, creates and extinguishes its own money.

Consequently there is no lack of purchasing power to purchase back all of the products that are produced, either because wage-earners do not get as wages the total value of what they produce, or because savings do not give as much employment as the same amount of money spent for consumption, or because dividends do not become purchasing power until paid, or because the profit on each sale does not become purchasing power until the goods are paid for. All of these arguments based on too large a *share* of the national income going to profit as the cause of accumulations of unsalable goods followed by unemployment are fallacious. We must look elsewhere for the causes of overproduction and unemployment, which we shall find, not in the *share* of profit but in the *margin* for profit and in the miscalculations of the forecast system of money.

3. *Employment-Lag*

We are now in position to consider what may be named the employment-lag theory of inadequate purchasing power. If laborers are out of work on account of technological unemployment, the share of labor in the national product is reduced by the amount of wages which they would have received, had they been employed. Consequently, improvements in efficiency not only displace laborers, but this displacement operates again to reduce their power, as a class, to purchase what the employed laborers are producing.

Paul H. Douglas has made the important distinction between Permanent Technological Unemployment and Temporary Technological Unemployment.[228] Regarding the first he concludes that "permanent technological unemployment is impossible." "In the long run," he says, "the improved machinery and greater efficiency of management do not throw workers permanently out of employment nor create permanent technological unemployment. Instead they raise the national income and enable the level of earnings and of individual incomes to rise."

If it be true that technological progress does not cause permanent unemployment, but rather raises the standards of living of all classes, yet, as has often been said, man does not live "in the long run." He lives from day to day, and temporary unemployment on account of improved technological efficiency, reduces the standards of living.

But the two questions must be separated. The one is the question, Are higher standards of living desirable on their own account? The other is the question, Do the higher wages needed to support higher standards of living furnish more employment for labor than

[228] Douglas, Paul H., "Technological Unemployment," *American Federationist* (August, 1930). See also his article "Technological Unemployment," *Bulletin of the Taylor Society*, December, 1930.

do lower wages with lower standards of living? We have answered these questions in the preceding discussion of the *shares* that go to capital and labor. Higher standards of living are desirable on their own account, for political and social reasons. But high wages do not furnish more employment for labor than low wages, because, in the latter case, the larger share going to rent, interest, and profit employs as much labor as the same share would employ if paid as wages. But we now consider these two questions from another standpoint, the increase in national efficiency.

The output per man, according to the calculations of the Federal Reserve Board, as cited by Douglas, was approximately 45 per cent greater in 1929 than it was in 1919, an average increase in efficiency of 4.5 per cent per year.

"This increase," says Douglas, "was accompanied by a decrease of 10 per cent in the number of wage-earners who were employed in manufacturing since instead of the 9.0 million who were so engaged in 1919, only an approximate 8.1 million were employed even before the depression of the end of 1929. . . . Nor was manufacturing alone. The output per person in mining increased between 40 and 45 per cent, . . . there was in addition a much greater amount of lost time within employment in the bituminous coal industry. The efficiency of the workers on our railways rose appreciably during those ten years if measured in terms of ton-miles per worker, and yet the number employed decreased by approximately 300,000, or by 15 per cent. Finally, due to the introduction of tractors, combines, and other types of agricultural machinery, and to the use of better methods of cultivation and stock feeding, the output per worker in agriculture increased by over 25 per cent; yet during these years, according to the estimates of the Department of Agriculture, not far from 3,800,000 persons left the farms for the cities, of whom at least 1,500,000 were men and women eligible for employment.

"The numbers employed in these four basic industries therefore declined by approximately 2,800,000 when, had they continued to employ the same proportion of the population as they had in 1919, there would have been over two million more workers employed in those lines." [229]

If three million laborers are laid off on account of greater efficiency of production, and if the laborers received an average wage of $4.00 per day or $1,200 per year, it is evident that the power of labor as a class to purchase what the employed laborers are producing has been reduced at the rate of $12,000,000 per day, or say 3.6 billion dollars per year. This deficiency in purchasing power

[229] Douglas, Paul H., *American Federationist* (Aug. 1930).

will continue until the laborers find jobs in expanding industries. But since it takes considerable time for new industries to spring up and new jobs to be created, there remains an employment-lag during which time the purchasing power of labor as a class is inadequate to purchase the increased output of those who retain employment.

Douglas gives four reasons for this employment-lag. (1) It takes time for the lower prices of goods at the factory to reach the consumer in the form of lower retail prices. (2) It takes time for newly expanding industries to create jobs enough to employ the numbers laid off by the contracting industries. (3) It takes time for workers to shift from contracting industries to expanding industries. (4) Workers are reluctant or unable to change to the different kinds of work in the expanding industries and are reluctant or unable to change their residence. And he adds a fifth which is a cause, not of unemployment but of lower standards of living: (5) Even if labor is ultimately transferred to an expanding industry it is frequently at a job which pays a lower wage and is less satisfactory than the one left.

Finally, Douglas suggests seven methods of reducing the losses from Temporary Technological Unemployment: (1) Better forecasting. (2) Better planning. (3) Less rapid displacement of labor. (4) Public employment offices. (5) Vocational training. (6) Dismissal wage. (7) Unemployment insurance, to which may be added Public Works. To these remedies much attention has rightly been given in recent years. Their purpose is to shorten the lag of employment and to get the laborers employed as soon as possible in new or expanding industries, where not only their standards of living may be restored but also their increased purchasing power will create a demand for commodities and labor.

But the *employment-lag* is also a *production-lag*. Reverting to our illustrations, if the purchasing power of labor is reduced 3.6 billion dollars per year by technological unemployment of 3,000,000 workers, and if we suppose that the share of labor in the new industries continues at 60 per cent and the share of property-owners continues at 40 per cent, then, in order to restore full employment a new product from these new or expanding industries must be created whose sale value is 6 billion dollars. If, as in 1925, for which year our calculations were made, the total sales value of all products was 75 billion dollars, this would mean an increase of sales to 81 billion dollars. But the *shares* would remain the same, 60 per cent for labor, now amounting to 48.6 billions instead of 45 billions, and 40 per cent for property-owners, now amounting to 32.4 billions instead of 30 billions. All of the new product would be purchased, as before, from the combined shares going to wages, rent, interest, and profits. But what would now happen would be that, on account of the increased efficiency and with the same number fully employed, the standards of living of all classes would be raised. Temporary unemployment of labor disappears because temporary unemployment of capital disappears, but it disappears on the basis of higher standards of living because national efficiency has increased.

Thus the "employment-lag" is entirely different from the "profits-lag." The profits-lag was a fallacious theory that profits are not available for purchasing back the product at the time when produced. But the employment-lag is a lag in the amount of product itself as well as a lag in wages paid. Here the fact is that laborers do not have purchasing power because they are not producing anything to be purchased. But, for the same reason there are no profits to be used as purchasing power. And there is no increase in commercial borrowing at the banks, so that there is a corresponding lag in commercial interest payments, which also would have purchasing power. In other words, the employment-lag, on account of technological improvements, is simply the failure of industry itself to expand rapidly enough. While there is unemployment there is also a falling off in profits.

Of course these temporary unemployments may come so fast on account of great waves of mechanical inventions, that what is really temporary looks like something permanent, because labor does not have time to get adjusted. The difficulty at such times is serious enough, but it is not because the *share* of labor is too small—it is because new industries do not expand fast enough. This is another question.[230]

The problem now again shifts to the margin for profit. Why does not industry as a whole keep on expanding, with the introduction of new products to take up not only the unemployed laid off from contracting industries but also to furnish new and expanding opportunities for profits, interest, and rent as well as wages? We consider first the double meaning of the so-called "law" of supply and demand.

4. *Supply and Demand*

In preceding sections we have considered industry and banking as a whole, but we now descend to particular industries and consider the supply of and demand for particular commodities, usually known as the "law of supply and demand," but more precisely known, in

[230] Below, p. 789, Prices; Reasonable Value.

the language of the functional relation between supply and demand as "elasticity of demand and supply." Stated in either terminology we shall distinguish the "business law of supply and demand," or "business elasticity of supply and demand" from the "consumers' law of supply and demand" or "consumers' elasticity of demand." [231] In order to make the distinction clear we shall summarize, from the article by Douglas already referred to, what we name the consumers' law of supply and demand, and then will notice how it is exactly reversed if changed over to the field of business where the speculative law dominates.

(1) **Consumers' Law of Supply and Demand.**—Douglas uses the Printing Industry for his illustration. He supposes that the man-hour efficiency of the workers doubles, and where 1,000 workers had produced 600,000 copies of a magazine, the same number of workers can now produce 1,200,000 copies in the same number of hours.

He then illustrates what would happen under three different supposed "elasticities of demand," that is, three different aspects of this consumers' law of supply and demand. If the elasticity of demand is "unity," the meaning is that a reduction of the price one-half (from 10 cents to 5 cents) will be followed by double the quantity demanded (from 600,000 copies to 1,200,000 copies) and the total weekly receipts will remain at $60,000. The same number of workers, 1,000, will continue to be employed at the same average $60 per week (barring the temporary unemployment previously disposed of). There will be no technological unemployment if elasticity of demand is unity, for unity means *the same gross sales*, $60,000.

But suppose, says Douglas, that the elasticity of demand is greater than unity. Suppose the sales are tripled (to 1,800,000) when the price is reduced to 5 cents per copy. Then the gross sales are *increased* from $60,000, where they stood when the price was 10 cents for each of 600,000 copies, to $90,000 when the price is 5 cents for 1,800,000 copies. The number of workers increases from 1,000 to 1,500 at $60, per worker. There is, of course, no technological unemployment in that industry if elasticity of demand is greater than unity. There is rather an increase in demand for labor.

But thirdly, suppose elasticity of demand is less than unity. Suppose the sales increase to only 900,000 copies when the price is reduced to 5 cents per copy. The gross sales now fall from $60,000 (when 600,000 copies were sold at 10 cents), to $45,000 (when

[231] Cf. Working, Holbrook, "The Statistical Determination of Demand Curves," *Quar. Jour. Econ.*, XXXIX (1925), 503, 519.

900,000 copies are sold at 5 cents), and the number of workers is reduced from 1,000 at $60 to 750 at $60.

But the readers of the magazine, the ultimate consumers, now have $15,000 remaining in their pocketbooks which were formerly spent on reading matter. These $15,000 will employ exactly the equivalent 250 unemployed workers (not the same individuals) at exactly the same $60 per week, no matter whether the former readers "spend" the money or "save" it. If they "spend" $15,000 they are employing the equivalent of the 250 unemployed workers at $60 per week in operating such "expanding" industries as automobiles, airplanes, chewing gum, movies, dance halls, and a myriad of other expanding enterprises. If they "save" the money then their savings bank invests it in $15,000 worth of new issues of bonds which will employ the same number, 250 workers, at $60 per week in industries which are also "expanding," such as laying down a double-track for a railroad, or building a blast furnace, or constructing a factory. Hence there is no technological unemployment even if elasticity of demand is less than unity, and no matter whether the consumers "spend" their money or "save" it.

Here, of course, Douglas' distinction between permanent and temporary unemployment must not be forgotten. His foregoing illustrations apply solely to permanent technological unemployment. They show, as already stated, that it is "impossible." But there remains temporary unemployment owing to these technological changes, simply because it takes time to change from "contracting" industries which employ less labor to "expanding" industries which employ more labor. Temporary unemployment is disregarded in order to illustrate the principle, and because the remedies are different.

(2) **The Business Law of Supply and Demand.**—Let us now change the illustrations from the ultimate consumers, who buy the magazines at retail prices, to the business men who are operating the printing industry for profit. It now appears that there are two laws of elasticity of demand, a consumers' law and a business law. They work in opposite directions.

If the prices of magazines rise, then consumers generally purchase *smaller* quantities of magazines (elasticity of demand is less than unity) and they purchase *larger* quantities of other things whose prices have not risen. Thus, in the illustration, if the price should rise from 10¢ to 15¢, the consumers would buy a *less* number of magazines and a larger number of newspapers whose prices had not risen. Or, if the price fell from 10¢ to 5¢, the consumers would buy *more* magazines, but, if their elasticity of demand is less than unity, as Douglas shows, they would have left a surplus $15,000 which they could spend or save for things other than magazines.

This is the consumers' law of elasticity of demand. It springs from the fact that ultimate consumers have only a *limited amount of purchasing power,* derived from what they have *previously* received as wages, rents, interest, or profits. In order to make their limited purchasing power go as far as possible they tend to buy *less* of those goods whose prices are rising and *more* of those whose prices are falling.

This tendency has been named the Principle of Substitution,[232] equivalent to choice of opportunities. It accounts for the interesting fact that prices of similar commodities tend to move in the same direction. If the price of magazines rises, then consumers reduce their demand for magazines and increase their demand for news-papers, so that the rise in price of magazines is checked by reduced demand, and a rise in price of newspapers is encouraged by increased demand. The principle of substitution tends to keep the two prices moving up together or moving down together.

This principle of substitution has universal application. If the prices of apples rise, the people generally purchase smaller quantities of apples and larger quantities of substitutes whose prices have not risen. The tendency thus is to check the rise of apple prices by reducing demand and to raise the prices of substitutes by increasing the demand. Or, if apples fall in price the tendency is to buy more apples and thus check the fall, but to buy less of substitutes and thus to intensify their fall. The result is that substitutes tend to rise and fall together as to their prices, and the universality of the principle of substitution makes it possible to speak of a general price level, either of consumers' goods or producers' goods, moving up or down, although this general level is only an average of several hundred prices each with its own peculiar elasticities of supply, demand, and substitution.

In this respect the speculative law of supply and demand is like the consumers' law. Prices of similar goods tend to rise and fall similarly, by the principle of substitution. But the speculative law is the opposite of the consumers' law in the *direction* of movement. If prices are *expected* to rise, the business man buys *more* instead of less, intending to make a profit by selling at the higher price. But if prices are *expected* to fall he buys *less* instead of more, and sells as quickly as possible, intending to avoid the expected loss at a lower price.

Thus when the consumer buys *less* instead of more, on a rising

[232] Above, p. 329, The Law of Substitution.

market, because prices *have* risen, the business man buys *more* instead of less, on a similar rising market, because prices are *expected* to rise. The consumer *does not expect to sell*. He only intends to make his limited purchasing power go further in satisfying his wants. The business man *does expect to sell*. He intends to make a profit, on a rising market.

The reverse happens on a falling market. The consumer buys *more* because the price *has* fallen, and his limited resources go further in satisfying his wants. But the business man *buys less* and *sells more* because prices are expected to fall. The more he buys the greater will be his loss when he sells. The more he sells *now* the less will be his loss afterwards.

Then, when all are competing to *buy first* on a rising market, in order to exclude others from buying what is expected to rise in price; or when all are competing to *sell first* in order to "get out from under" by "unloading" on buyers that which is expected to fall in price; then conflict of interests adds to self-interest in forcing the rise into a "boom" or the fall into a "slump."

This is the peculiarity of the capitalist system conducted on the basis of private property for profit. It is a perverse peculiarity which makes many people convinced that cycles of prosperity and depression cannot be prevented, as long as the system lasts. Hence the strength of the socialist and communist demand for abolition of private property and profit. The socialists would produce for consumption and not for profit. If, indeed, capitalism cannot accept "working rules" to prevent this inherent perversity, then perhaps communism would be preferable. But the alternative requires investigation and experiment.

In the first place, the consumers' "law" of supply and demand and the business or speculative "law" of supply and demand, in a capitalistic system, are two different aspects of the general principle of scarcity. Both are compulsory on individuals—the compulsion of scarcity and similarity of action. The ultimate consumer is *compelled* to economize his limited resources on the principle of marginal utility. His home depends upon the prices he pays out of the income he receives. The business man is *compelled* to buy early on a rising market, else others will buy what he must have; and he is compelled to sell early on a falling market to save himself from loss or bankruptcy. Hence it is not mere figure of speech to speak of a "law" of supply and demand. It is a law because individuals must obey or sink. This kind of a compulsory law we name a "custom."

It will be conceded, of course, that ultimate consumers are also to a limited degree influenced by *expected* price changes. If they expect the price of coal to rise they will lay up a stock of coal for the winter, if they have the purchasing power or credit. If they expect the price to fall they will not stock up. But, even so, their "speculation" is limited to their expected wants for consumption, not by the prospects of profit or loss through selling what they buy.

Where, then, does the business man get his money with which he can go beyond the consumers' law of demand and supply and build upon it the speculative law? He gets it from the banks. A merchant sells to another merchant a thousand tons of steel at $30 per ton. A debt of $30,000 is thereby created. It is created by two variable dimensions of the bargaining transaction. One is tons of steel, the other is the price per ton. The product of the two is Future Value. It is this Value that creates the equivalent debt, $30,000.

But the debt is not due until 30 days, and meanwhile it is negotiable. A banker buys it. If it is payable in 30 days at 6 per cent per year, it will be worth $30,000 at the end of 30 days, but is worth now only $29,850. The banker enters it on his books as a "loan" of $30,000, but a deposit of $29,850. The balance, $150, is an addition to the banker's assets. But the $30,000 is a debt of either the steel seller or the steel buyer or both (a trade acceptance) to the banker and can be sold to other bankers, in which case the other banker owes the first banker $29,850 plus accrued interest.

But the banker has given to the steel seller a credit of $29,850, which is his promise to pay the steel merchant, on demand, that amount of money. This bank debt is modern money. The merchant can draw checks upon it, which are also negotiable, and with these checks he can pay debts for materials, labor and interest.

But, suppose the steel business is prosperous. The merchants expect prices to rise and larger quantities to be demanded. They sell and buy 2,000 tons at $60 per ton. The value now is $120,000 instead of $30,000. It has increased fourfold, because both price and quantity have doubled. The corresponding debt has also quadrupled. The banker buys it. He can now charge, say 8 per cent, because the merchants are prosperous and his own reserves are running low. It will be worth $120,000 in 30 days—if the merchant is able to pay. The banker buys it at its present worth on an 8 per cent discount, namely $119,200, and creates a purchasing power for the merchant equal to that amount. The money created by the two transactions has increased fourfold. Every other industry feels the effect. The speculative law of supply and demand is at work. It is the hope of rising prices.

Then, for some reason, the price of steel drops to $25, and is expected to drop still further. The merchant will buy only 500 tons. The value and its equivalent debt is now only $12,500. The banker buys it at 4 per cent. It will be worth $12,500 in 30 days but its present worth is only $12,457.66. This is the amount of bank debt available as purchasing power for the merchant. The speculative law of supply and demand is again at work. It is the fear of falling prices and inability to pay.

Each loan or discount transaction has created its own money, and it has created a quantity of it dependent upon the expected prices and quantities of commodities that will be sold and will be paid for by other money similarly created. For payment on the exact date is compulsory, on the pain of bankruptcy. And the payment will be made, not in money, but by another check drawn by another merchant on the same or another banker. This other check extinguishes the original debt to the banker by a mere credit to his individual account on the books of the banker. But this other check itself becomes a debit to still another merchant's account on the books of the same or another banker. Thus debts are offset by debts, and the bank check becomes a tender in the payment of debts, not because the sovereign makes it so, but because business custom makes it so. We have named this customary tender, instead of legal tender.

Hence there are two kinds of "tender" which creditors are compelled to accept and thereby release their debtors from further obligation to pay. One is legal tender, the mere fiat of sovereignty. The other is extra-legal or customary tender, the customary action of business men. He who violates this custom of business cannot be a business man.

Thus there are two markets tied together by the credit system, from whose toils no business man and even no farmer or wage-earner can escape. They are the commodity markets and the debt markets. The commodity markets are the retail and wholesale stores, the produce exchanges, the real estate exchanges, and even the labor market, where people transfer the ownership of goods and services at prices agreed upon. The debt market, in part, is the commercial banks where the short-time debts thus created on the commodity markets are bought and sold. The debt market is also the security markets, such as the stock exchange, for long-time rights to future money; these are tied to the commercial banks by the negotiability of debts. Multiply our illustration of transactions on the steel market by millions and billions of transactions on all markets, all of them tied together by the credit system and many of them moving in similar directions by the principle of substitution, then correct our illustration by statistics, and we have the movements of stock prices, land values, and commodity prices.

Since the bank debt, or deposit, is equivalent to money, and moreover, is marvellously elastic at times, it serves as expansive purchasing power by which the business man can increase his demand for commodities and labor if prices are rising, and can decrease his demand if prices are falling. It works just the opposite of the consumers' law. The institution of credit is the biggest factor which enables the business man to buy *more* when prices are rising, whereas the consumer buys *less* when prices are rising; and the institution of credit is the biggest factor which *compels* the business man to buy *less* when prices are falling, whereas the consumer, since he does not do business on future sales, buys *more* when prices have fallen.

Thus while the consumer's elasticity of demand is limited by the quantity of purchasing power which he *has* acquired as wages, rent, interest, or profit, the business man's elasticity of demand is limited by the indefinite quantity of purchasing power which *may* be created for him outright, or transferred to him from the savings of others, by the banks, in expectation of the future profits to be made when he sells at future prices.

5. *Margins*

In the foregoing discussion of "shares," the total national income is divided into four shares; rent, interest, wages, profits. But this is not the way business is conducted. The business man—to whom we will give that name in so far as he gets profits and dividends—becomes first of all a debtor to all other classes. He becomes a debtor to wage-earners for wages, to bankers and bondholders for interest, to landlords for rent, to the government for taxes, to other business men for the materials to be worked over and sold to other business men as his finished product. That which is concealed in the calculation of shares is these bargains which create debts. The business man buys *materials* from other business men. Within the prices paid for these materials are concealed the wages, rents, interest, and profits of all preceding participants, back to the forests, the farmers, the railways, the manufacturers, the jobbers and bankers. The business man also pays *taxes*, and these taxes, when resolved into shares, are mainly the wages and salaries of government employees.

What the economist does for the whole nation, in these calculations of shares, is to take the whole nation, and then to divide the whole income into four shares. By doing this, all *materials* and all *taxes* disappear and are resolved into the shares which go into rent, interest, wages, and profits. And this is done *after* the statistics have been collected.

But let us look at it from the standpoint of the individual business man (or corporation) *before* the statistics are available: He becomes a debtor for wages, interest, rent, and *also* for *materials and taxes.* His profit will be the *margin,* between his debts for all these purposes and his gross earnings.

This analysis of the margin between his debts and his gross earnings will reveal how important is the distinction between strategic and routine transactions, which we shall consider below (p. 627). The relations between any of these various debts of the business man and the margin will change. In that change we shall see his problems. The factor which changes will be first one and then another of the various debts with which he deals. The one whose variation is most important at any point of time becomes, at that time, the strategic factor with which the business man must deal because of its own narrow margin for profit.

In order to get this distinction, we take an entirely different start. We must start with the income statement and balance sheet of a single concern: In the year 1927 Swift and Company, meat packers, reported gross earnings from all sales of products as $925,000,000. In order to get that gross income they paid, first of all, $470,000,000 for live stock. It was from this large amount paid for *materials* that all *preceding* profits, interest, rents, and wages were paid to those who had furnished the materials. The Swift Company then paid directly $4,250,755 interest to their creditors, the bondholders and bankers. Their statement does not show how much they paid to wage-earners. But this is immaterial for present purposes. Their total cost of production, which is their total indebtedness—including debts for wages, interest, taxes, materials, depreciation, and everything else—was $913,000,000, leaving only $12,000,000 as the amount available for profit.

But this amount of profit, $12,000,000, now appears in three directions as (1) a *rate* of profit, (2) a profit *yield,* and (3) a *margin* for profit.

As a *rate* of profit it is dividends compared with the *par* value of the stock, $200,000,000. Hence the *rate* of profit is 6 per cent. As a profit yield, or "stock yield," it is the rate on the *market* value of the stock, which, if the market value was $300,000,000, was 4 per cent, or, if the market value was $120,000,000, was 10 per cent.

But as a *margin* for profit the same $12,000,000 is compared with

the gross sales, $925,000,000.   Hence the margin for profit is only
1.3 per cent.[233]

The *rate* of profit and the *yield* of profit are not important for
our present purposes, but the margin for profit is important.   Stating this margin differently, for every dollar of gross income paid by
customers the company incurred and paid its debts of 98.7 cents in
order to get that dollar, leaving the margin for profit only 1.3 cents
per dollar of income, or 1.3 per cent of the gross sales.

This case may seem extreme, on account of the large amounts
paid for materials, and much depends upon the bookkeeping, the
turnover, concealed profits, etc.   In some years the margin is larger,
in other years there is loss instead of profit.   For some establishments the margin is very large, while for competing establishments
there is a *loss margin* instead of a profit margin.

No adequate investigation is available for estimating the average
margin of profit for all industries.   The best available source for
manufacturing corporations is the "Statistics of Income" compiled
by the Bureau of Internal Revenue of the Treasury Department for
the purpose of assessing the income tax on *net profits* (which is our
meaning of margin for profit).   On the basis of these statistics we
may make estimates of margins for manufacturing corporations,
which are estimated to produce and sell about 90 per cent of all
manufactured products, leaving only 10 per cent for individuals and
partnerships.[234]   We shall distinguish five types of margins which
we name the Operating Margin, the Profit and Loss Margin, the
Taxable Margin, the Financial Margin, and the Price Margin.

[233] In the Swift and Company *Yearbook* for 1925 (p. 17) the company estimates that
the profit per head of cattle and beef, *before* charging interest was $1.95.   The average
price paid for cattle was $60.08.   The total expenses, including freight, were $12.63; and
the net returns from by-products were $11.25 per head.   Consequently the margin for
both profit and interest in 1924 was 2.7 per cent of the operating cost of production and
2.6 per cent of the revenue per head.   If interest were deducted the margin for profit
alone would have been less.   The company also gives a comparative table from which we
take the following calculation of the financial margin, or margin for *both* profit and interest
per head of cattle and beef.

FISCAL YEAR	PROFIT AND LOSS BEFORE CHARGING INTEREST
1915	$1.64
1916	1.65
1917	1.29
1918	1.02
1919	0.70 (loss)
1920	0.06 (loss)
1921	1.13
1922	2.52
1923	1.10
1924	1.95

[234] National Industrial Conference Board, *The Shifting and Effects of the Federal Corporation Income Tax* (1928), I, 172.

TABLE I

Manufacturing Corporations, Amount of the Specified Items[235]

(In Million Dollars)

	1918	1919	1920	1921	1922	1923	1924	1925	1926	1927	1928	1929
1. Total receipts	44,167	52,290	56,649	38,442	44,763	56,309	53,995	60,921	62,584	63,816	67,368	72,224
2. Gross sales	44,167	52,290	56,082	37,645	42,576	53,889	51,436	57,084	59,863	60,932	64,361	69,236
3. Operating costs[a]	38,782	46,557	52,295	37,488	40,752	51,293	49,801	55,661	57,148	59,023	61,605	65,814
4. Depreciation	1,272	1,017	1,155	1,151	1,339	1,425	1,409	1,507	1,757	1,819	1,922	2,018
5. Operating margin[b]	5,385	5,733	3,787	157	1,824	2,596	1,635	1,423	2,715	1,909	2,756	3,422
6. Taxes	2,424	1,769	1,384	793	860	986	937	1,078	1,139	1,065	1,118	1,161
7. Interest	539	470	633	633	622	611	608	622	657	677	710	712
8. Total cost[c]	41,745	48,796	54,312	38,914	42,234	52,890	51,346	57,361	58,944	60,765	63,433	67,143
9. Margin for profit and loss[d]	2,422	3,494	1,770	−1,269	342	999	90	−277	919	167	928	2,093
10. Taxable margin[e]	4,846	5,263	3,154	−476	1,202	1,985	1,027	801	2,058	1,232	2,046	2,710
11. Financial margin[f]	2,961	3,964	2,403	−636	964	1,610	698	345	1,576	844	1,638	2,251
Number of manufacturing corporations reporting	67,274	67,852	78,171	79,748	82,485	85,199	86,803	88,674	93,244	93,415	95,777	96,525

[a] Includes depreciation. A deduction of 531 million dollars is made from this figure for 1925 as derived from the original source in order to allow for domestic taxes for that year. The 531 million is included in the tax figure for 1925.   [b] Line 2 less line 3.   [c] Sum of lines 3, 6, and 7.   [d] Line 2 less line 8.   [e] Line 5 less line 7.   [f] Line 5 less line 6.

[235] From *Statistics of Income* published by the U. S. Treasury Department. The figures may be taken as representative of the calendar year. A relatively small number of corporations reporting have a fiscal year other than the calendar year. This will not materially affect the use of the figures for our purposes.

TABLE II

MANUFACTURING CORPORATIONS, RATIOS OF THE SPECIFIED ITEMS[236]

RATIO	1918	1919	1920	1921	1922	1923	1924	1925	1926	1927	1928	1929
1. Gross sales to total receipts	100.0	100.0	99.0	97.9	95.1	95.7	95.3	93.7	95.2	95.5	95.5	95.9
2. Income other than gross sales to total receipts			1.0	2.1	4.9	4.3	4.7	6.3	4.8	4.5	4.5	4.1
3. Operating margin to gross sales	12.2	11.0	6.8	0.4	4.3	4.8	3.2	2.5	4.5	3.1	4.3	4.9
4. Depreciation to operating costs	3.3	2.2	2.2	3.1	3.3	2.8	2.8	2.7	3.1	3.1	3.1	3.1
5. Profit or loss to gross sales	5.5	6.7	3.2	3.4[a]	0.8	1.9	0.18	0.5[a]	1.5	0.27	1.4	3.0
6. Profit and loss on sales to total receipts	5.5	6.7	3.1	3.3[a]	0.76	1.77	0.166	0.45[a]	1.46	0.26	1.37	2.89
7. Final profit or loss to total receipts	5.5	6.7	4.1	1.2[a]	5.6	6.1	4.9	5.8	5.8	4.8	5.8	7.0
8. Taxes to taxable margin	50.0	33.6	43.9	∞[b]	71.5	49.7	91.2	134.6	55.3	86.4	54.6	42.8
9. Taxes to operating margin	45.0	30.9	36.5	505.1	47.1	38.0	57.3	75.8	42.0	55.8	40.6	33.9
10. Taxes to total costs	5.81	3.62	2.54	2.37	2.36	1.86	1.82	1.88	1.93	1.75	1.76	1.73
11. Interest to financial margin	18.2	11.8	26.3	∞[b]	64.6	37.9	87.1	180.3	41.6	80.2	43.3	31.5
12. Interest to operating margin	10.0	8.2	16.7	403.1	34.1	23.5	37.2	43.7	24.2	35.5	25.8	30.8
13. Interest to total costs	1.29	0.96	1.17	1.63	1.47	1.16	1.18	1.08	1.11	1.11	1.12	1.06

[a] Loss. [b] Infinity, assuming the taxable and financial margins to be zero.
[236] Computed from Table I.

Tables I and II present the statistical data from which our succeeding analysis of margins will be drawn.

(1) **Total Receipts and Gross Sales.**—The total receipts, or gross income, of corporations is derived mainly from the sales of their products and services. But during the past decade they have derived a noticeable share of their income from stocks and bonds of other corporations, and from government securities, time deposits, rents, and royalties, as well as from miscellaneous sources of non-operating income. The relation between the two sources of income is shown in Chart 8.

CHART 8

VOLUME OF GROSS SALES AND TOTAL RECEIPTS

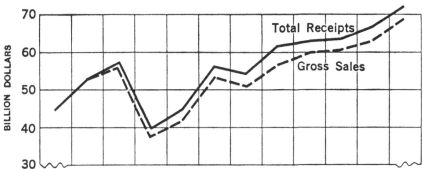

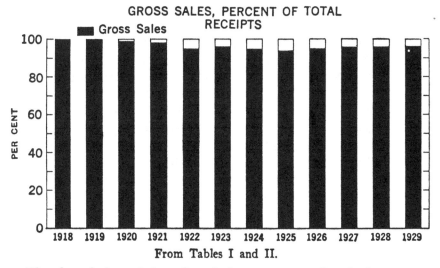

From Tables I and II.

The chart is intended to show in its upper part the absolute quantities, and in its lower part the ratio of sales to total receipts and the ratio of other income to the same base. Prior to the report of 1922, only figures for total receipts were given in the Treasury reports, no distinction being made between sales and other sources of income, but since that year as high as 6.3 per cent (1925) of the total receipts has been derived from the other sources of income, as distinct from sales. Before 1922 we follow the estimates of the National Industrial Conference Board as to the amount of the gross sales and other income.[237] This "other income" may be looked upon partly as a cushion designed to take care of unforeseen drops in sales income. Its influence will be seen in our analysis of the "profit cushion." We are concerned primarily with the income from sales.

(2) The Operating Margin.—Charts 9 and 10 are drawn to indicate the average operating margin of manufacturing corporations from the year 1918 to 1929, as derived from Tables I and II. By operating margin we mean the margin for Interest, Taxes, and Profit, after all operating expenses, including depreciation and obsolescence, are paid. It will be seen, from the upper part of Chart 9, that the gross sales of manufactured products varied greatly in money values, rising from 44 billion dollars in 1918 to 56 billion in 1920, then falling to 37 billion in 1921, then rising rapidly to 54 billion in 1923, with a sag in 1924, but culminating at 69 billion in 1929.

It is these gross sales that we name "value" or "value of product," since they are composed of the two variables, price and quantity sold. The term "value" thus includes in one pecuniary figure both the monetary and non-monetary factors of economics. In the language of business it is "gross sales." In the language of economics it is "Value."

On the other hand the gross operating costs include moneys expended for wages, salaries, materials, and also the maintenance, repairs, and depreciation of fixed capital. The margin between gross sales and operating costs is indicated by percentages of gross sales in the lower half of Chart 9. If gross sales are represented by 100 in each year, then the operating margin for interest, taxes, and profits was 12 per cent of the gross sales in 1918, but fell to four-tenths of one per cent in 1921, rose to 4.3 per cent in 1922, with a slightly additional rise to 4.8 per cent in 1923; fell to 2.5 per cent in 1925, rose again in 1926, and was 4.3 per cent in 1928 and 4.9 per cent in 1929, after a fall to 3.1 per cent in 1927.

Chart 10 is drawn in order to make further analysis of operating

[237] National Industrial Conference Board, *The Shifting and Effects of the Federal Corporation Income Tax* (1928), I, 173. "To give the greatest weight to the increasing proportion of income from sources other than gross sales, gross sales for 1919 were estimated as equal to gross income of that year. Gross sales for 1921 were interpolated by allowing a proportion of income from other sources half as great as in 1923." *Ibid.*, I, 173. For 1918 we take gross sales as equal to total receipts. For 1920, 1 per cent of the gross income is allowed for sources other than sales.

costs in so far as affected by Depreciation costs. Depreciation is usually described as an Overhead Cost, along with Taxes and Interest, because the three are fixed charges that do not vary with operating costs. But we distinguish Technological Overhead (depreciation), Government Overhead (taxes) and Financial Overhead (inter-

CHART 9
THE OPERATING MARGIN

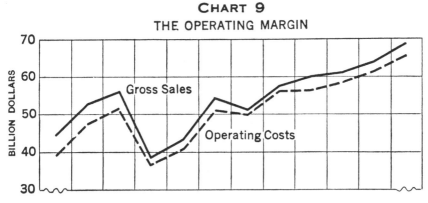

OPERATING MARGIN, PERCENTAGE OF GROSS SALES

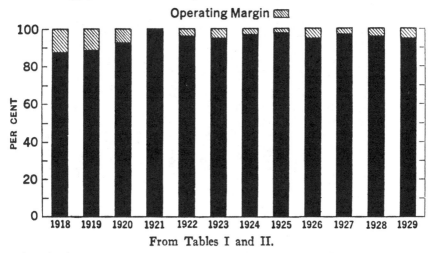

From Tables I and II.

est). And we distinguish True Depreciation (the technological overhead of wear and tear, depletion and obsolescence of the physical plant not cared for by maintenance and repairs), from False Depreciation which includes concealed profits or surplus over and above the actual costs of true depreciation. Since this distinction is a matter of investigation for each establishment, we assume that the allowances in the administration of the Federal Income Tax are "true," that is, technological depreciation, although they may turn out to be in part false depreciation.

True depreciation may be considered to be an overhead factor in operating costs. It is so considered in Charts 9 and 10. But it resolves itself into wages and materials for operation and hence is to be considered as a part of operating costs. It will be seen from

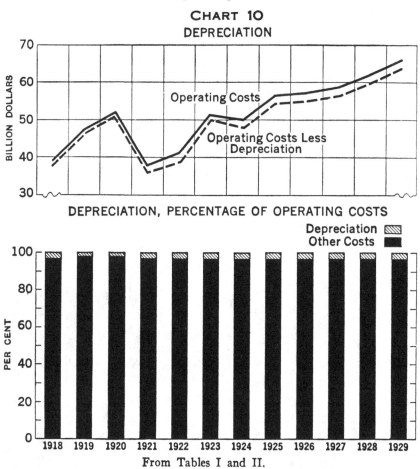

CHART 10
DEPRECIATION

DEPRECIATION, PERCENTAGE OF OPERATING COSTS

From Tables I and II.

Chart 10 that depreciation overhead is but a small proportion of the operating costs, the percentages ranging from 3.3 per cent in 1918 and 1922 to 2.2 per cent in 1919 and 1920.

(3) **Profit and Loss Margin.**—The foregoing has to do with operating costs, including depreciation, but not with total costs of doing business. By total costs we mean to include the three items: operating cost, taxes, and interest. And, since we have already considered depreciation to be the overhead in operating costs we shall consider taxes and interest as the overhead in Total Costs. We have seen in Chart 9 the relation between operating cost and gross sales. Chart 11 is intended to show the changing relations between Total

Costs and Gross Sales, and the resulting effect on the average Profit and Loss.

In Chart 11 the curve of gross sales is the same as previously shown in Chart 9. But the curve of Total Cost is the sum of operating costs plus the overhead of taxes and interest, as shown in line 8

CHART 11
THE PROFIT OR LOSS MARGIN

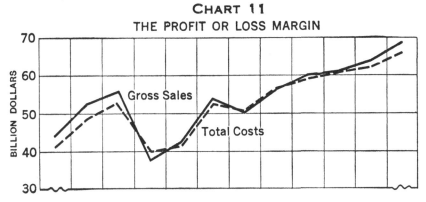

PROFIT OR LOSS MARGIN PERCENTAGE OF
GROSS SALES

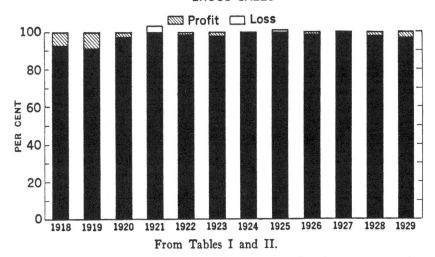

From Tables I and II.

of Table I. The result is the Profit or Loss Margin, represented as a percentage of the gross sales. Thus, in the year 1918, for each dollar of income from sales there remained an average profit of 5.5 per cent. In other words, during that year the manufacturing corporations paid, on the average, 94.5 cents in order to get a dollar of income, and their average margin for profit was 5.5 cents on every dollar of gross income from sales.

But in the poorest year, 1921, their net loss, on the average, was 3.4 cents for every dollar of income from sales. In that year these corporations paid, on the average, 103.4 cents in order to obtain 100 cents of sales income. Their profit and loss margin for other years may be seen from the charts, Tables I and II.

It is evident, from Chart 11, that there is no such thing as a "normal profit." Yet we may speak of a "yearly average profit on sales" equivalent to a "yearly average margin for profit." And we may speak of a "median" of the yearly average margins for profit on sales. Thus, the highest average margin of profit was 6.7 per cent on sales in 1919, and the highest average margin of loss was 3.4 per cent on sales in 1921 (Table II, line 6; Chart 11). The median is a profit margin of 1.7 per cent on sales, which is rather close to the average margins of 1923 (1.85 per cent) and 1926 (1.5 per cent). If a weighted average of the twelve years were calculated, it would be a profit margin of 1.6 per cent on sales.

We find that this comes rather close to the calculations of the margin for profit which we have previously made for Swift and Company. Thus the very narrow margin for profit on about one billion dollars of sales for that firm, which we suspected might be exceptional, turns out to be quite representative of the medium average margin for profit of 67,000 to 96,000 manufacturing corporations on sales of 37 to 64 billion dollars (Table II, line 9, Chart 11).

Yet, for various reasons and because fine precision is out of the question, we shall estimate the medium between the highest and lowest average margin for profits at 3 per cent of sales instead of the above 1.7 per cent calculated from the income tax returns. In other words, a medium average margin for profit of 3 per cent on sales for manufacturing corporations becomes a base line from which we can compare, not only the higher averages in prosperous times and the lower averages in times of depression, but also the high margins of prosperous firms and the low margins of "marginal" firms.

The meaning of this estimate is as follows: In medium times, between the peak of prosperity and the trough of depression, the average margin for profit in manufactures is about 3 per cent of the sales. But in exceptionally prosperous times, like 1918 and 1919, the margin for profit may have been more than twice as great.[238] Again, in depressed years, like 1921 or 1924, the average profit margin became a loss margin. In other years there was reason for speaking of "profitless prosperity."

[238] An example of marginal analysis may be found in Boris Emmet's *Department Stores* (1930). The terminology used is that of mercantile accounting but Emmet's analysis (which follows that of the Controllers' Congress of the National Retail Dry Goods Association) is similar to that which we use in our marginal analysis of the manufacturing corporations. Emmet's "Net Profit" is our margin for profit. For department stores with sales over $1,000,000, this figure, as a ratio to sales, ranges from a high of 3.6 per cent

We are next concerned with the taxable margin which pertains to problems of taxation, and with the financial margin which pertains to banking and bonds.

(4) The Taxable Margin.—Taxes of all kinds, whether income taxes or property taxes, whether shifted or not shifted by higher prices paid by customers, are rightly considered by each private business enterprise to be a fixed overhead cost of production enforced by government. Likewise with Interest. Interest is a relatively fixed charge, payable to bondholders and bankers, which we name the financial overhead. In order, then, to separate these two overhead charges for taxes and interest, and to estimate the effect of each on the preceding final margins for profit (Chart 11), we need to take each one separately. We shall then have the Taxable Margin for profit calculated *after interest is paid,* and the Financial Margin for profit calculated *after taxes are paid.*

Furthermore all taxes, like interest, must be paid out of current income, which, in this case, is gross sales. Consequently we have four different ratios to calculate (1) the ratio of taxes to gross sales, (2) the ratio of taxes to total costs of production (operation, interest and taxes), (3) the ratio of taxes to the operating margin (for interest, taxes and profits), and (4) the ratio of taxes to the taxable margin (taxes and profit). In Table I we have given the total amounts of taxes for the successive years. From this table we calculate in Chart 12 and Table II the different relations which taxes bear to total costs, to the operating margin, and to the taxable margin for profit and taxes (after interest).

We omit the ratio of taxes to gross sales, because (as seen in Chart 9) gross sales and total costs run so close together and even cross each other, that a curve of the ratio of taxes to sales could not be very different, on the chart, from the curve of ratio of taxes to total costs.

The curve of taxes as a percentage of total costs shows how very small indeed is the share of all taxes in the total costs of production. In the year 1918, with its high war taxes on surplus profits, the total tax (2.4 billion dollars) was 5.8 per cent of the total costs of production. But with the post-war reduction of taxes and the shift from profit to loss in 1921 (Chart 11) the total tax burden (793 million dollars) had fallen to only 2 per cent of the total costs of production. In 1926, with still lower income taxes and larger sales,

in 1923 to a low of 1.5 per cent in 1928. (See Table 16, p. 94, and Chart 2, p. 96.) Thus we find the margin for profit of department stores is lower than our estimated "medium" margin for manufacturing corporations. Emmet shows that the margin for profit of department stores depends largely on turnover, as faster turnovers decrease the ratio of expense to sales. See his Table 37, p. 135, *ibid.*

the taxes, although they increased to over a billion dollars, were yet only 1.9 per cent of total costs, and in 1928 only 1.8 per cent of total costs. On the whole, except in war time, internal taxes [239] were only about 2 per cent of either gross sales or total costs.

CHART 12

THE TAXABLE MARGIN

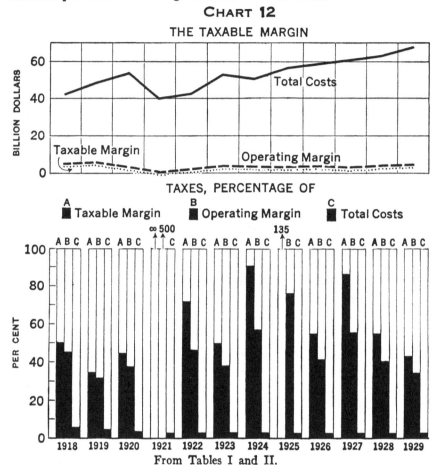

From Tables I and II.

But this 2 per cent does not measure the *burden* of taxes on industry and profits. The burden on industry must be measured by the relation of taxes to the operating margin, and the burden on profits must be measured by the relation to the taxable margin.

The operating margin is the *net operating income,* which, from Table I, will be seen to have ranged from 5,385 million dollars in 1918 down to 157 million dollars in 1921. This operating net income, or operating margin, is the source from which profits, interest, and taxes are to be derived. Chart 12 shows that in the war year

[239] The "external," or tariff taxes on imports, have been absorbed in the prices of materials and are concealed in the operating costs of production.

1918, the tax burden (2.4 billion dollars) was 45 per cent of the operating margin, but that in 1921 it was about 500 per cent of the operating margin. The reading, in the latter case, is that in 1921 the tax burden was five times greater than the average net operating income for taxes, interest and profit.

In 1925 as shown by Chart 12 and Tables I and II, the tax burden was 76 per cent of the average operating margin (for profit, interest, and taxes), whereas the lowest point of the tax burden during the ten years (1919) was about 30 per cent of the average net operating income. The intermediate burdens varied from 38 per cent in 1923 to 57 per cent in 1924; but the extreme range of the tax burden was 30 per cent of the average operating margin in 1919 and 500 per cent in 1921.

But this relation of taxes to the operating margin does not bring out fully the significance of the tax burden. We considerably enlarge this significance when we estimate the burden not only in its relation to the operating margin but also in its relation to the margin for profit and taxes, *after* we have deducted operating costs *plus* interest. This is not because interest is a prior charge to taxes, for it is not. The reason is that if a concern is a "going concern," it must pay both interest and taxes.

It is this margin after interest that we name the Taxable Margin, because it is the margin where only profit or loss and taxes stand face to face after both operating expenses and interest payments have been provided for.

Chart 12 shows that, in terms of the margin (or net income) for both profit and taxes, taxation at its lowest point of burden (1919) took, on the average, 34 per cent of this net income *after interest*. In 1921 there was a loss before taxes were paid. As the margin for profit and taxes had vanished, we may say that the burden of taxes on income available to pay them (interest having been previously paid) was in this year, on the average, infinitely great. Looked at from another standpoint, we may say that taxes accounted for 62 per cent of the loss on sales in this year of depression. This year was "abnormal." Taking the heaviest burden of the remaining years, we find the heaviest burden in 1925, when taxes were 134 per cent of the available margin for taxes and profits. In this year (1925) a loss on sales was incurred, partly because taxes on property are in no way adjusted to years of depression.

Thus, while *taxes* on manufacturing corporations, which produce 90 per cent of manufactured products, were usually less than an average of 2 per cent of the total cost of production, the tax burden on profits ranged from an average of 34 per cent to 134 per cent of the net income available to pay taxes and profits, after paying interest. And, in the worst year (1921), when, in place of a taxable margin, there was an average loss even before the tax overhead was met, taxes accounted, on the average, for 62 per cent of the loss— as previously shown in Chart 12.

(5) **The Financial Margin.**—We have seen the estimate made (above, p. 528) that the share of interest was about 6 per cent of the total of all incomes of the American people, amounting, in 1925, to about 3.9 billion dollars. It will have been noted from Table I that the interest payments made by manufacturing corporations to their bankers and bondholders, as reported for Federal Income Taxes, ranged between the narrow limits of 539 million dollars in 1918 to 710 million dollars in 1928. It is on account of this rather fixed charge on all industry regardless of prosperity and depression, that we name interest payments the Financial Overhead. When we shift our attention from the *share* of interest in the total income to the margin for profit *after* taxes are paid, which we name the Financial Margin, we must make calculations, as we did in the case of taxes, of the four ratios of interest (1) to gross sales, (2) to total costs of production, (3) to the operating margin (for interest, taxes, and profits), and (4) to the financial margin (for interest and profits). Chart 13, taken from Table II, line 11, indicates these ratios.

Again, as in the case of taxes, we omit the calculation of the ratio of interest to gross sales and attend only to what is nearly the equivalent, the ratio of interest to Total Operating Costs (Chart 9).

From Chart 13 it will be seen that interest payments are such a small part of the total cost of production (operation, taxes, and interest) that the curve which represents them is scarcely distinguishable on the scale needed to represent the financial burden of interest. Interest, as a cost of production, varies only, on the average, from the low point of one per cent of the average cost of production in 1919 to the high point of 1.6 per cent of the average cost of production in 1921. For the last four years for which data are available, the average ratio of interest to total costs of production has been 1.1 per cent.

As in the discussion of taxes, the relation of interest to the operating margin is taken as the burden of interest on industry, while the burden on profits is measured by the relation of interest to the financial margin.

The ratio of interest to the operating margin (for profits, interest, and taxes) we find on the average to have varied from a low point of 8 per cent in 1919 to a high point of 403 per cent in 1921. This means that interest in 1921 was over 4 times as great as the net income from sales available for profits, interest, and taxes. Chart 13 shows that the variation of this ratio in the more normal years, from 1921 to 1929, has been from 24 per cent to 37 per

CHART 13
THE FINANCIAL MARGIN

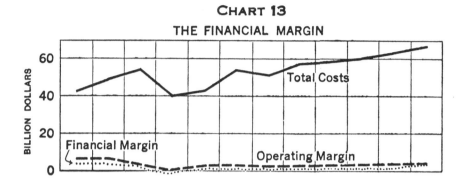

INTEREST, PERCENTAGE OF

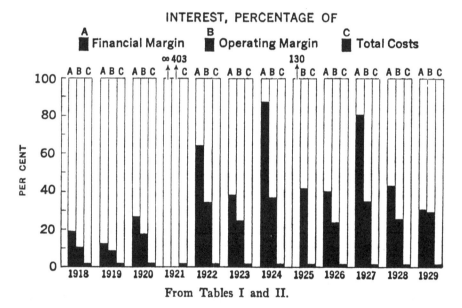

From Tables I and II.

cent. In a rough generalization interest takes, on the average, one-fourth to one-third of the operating margin.

When we ask the question, "What effect has interest on profits?" we must turn to the ratio of interest to the financial margin. To obtain the financial margin, we have subtracted taxes from the operating margin (or added it to operating costs), and we have remaining the dollar figures shown in Table I, line 11. We find that interest at its lowest point of burden, 1919, took 12 per cent of the net income after taxes. At its highest point, 1921, we find our margin for profit and interest has vanished, and we may say, as in the case of taxes, that the burden of interest on profits is infinitely great, there being on the average no net income for interest and profits but rather a loss (taxes being considered as previously paid). From the standpoint, however, of loss on sales for this year we may say that interest accounts approximately for 50 per cent of the loss. As this year (1921) was abnormal, let us turn to the year of the greatest burden, which we find in 1926 when interest was 180 per cent of the financial margin.

Thus we find the interest burden ranging from 12 per cent to 180 per cent of the income available for interest and profits (after taxes), namely our financial margin. In the worst year (1921) we find a loss in place of a net income.

Thus we see how the narrow margin between the business man's debts and his expected income intensifies the importance of any change in any of these debts. Even what would appear as a minor change in any one of them becomes of major importance when compared with its potential effects upon his profits.[240] It is this important effect which raises the rate of interest to a limiting factor at that point of time when the loans are negotiated.

(6) **The Price Margin.**—Far more important than the taxable margin and the financial margin is the Price Margin. For it is the changeable price margins that determine the changeable tax and financial margins. The preceding chart[241] shows the changing wholesale prices during 140 years. The chart shows the rising prices in England and America during the 25 years that followed the beginning of the French Révolution, then the sudden collapse, with slight recoveries, continuing to 1849. It was during the period from 1810 to 1820 that the debate occurred between Malthus and Ricardo on the issue of shares versus margins. Prices of commodities were falling as they have fallen since another world war. Falling prices were accompanied by unemployment. Malthus argued that the cause of unemployment was the fact that too much of everything had been produced, so that laborers could not consume what they produced. It was this that caused prices to fall. He proposed taxation for public works and large expenditures by landlords on their estates, so that laborers would be employed on work

---

[240] Of course the business man cannot know exactly what change in his profit margin will be occasioned by the change in the one factor with which he is then dealing. But he can be sufficiently sure that his profit margin will be very narrow so that he will know that any change will be highly important in reducing or increasing his profit margin.

[241] Above, p. 122.

that would not come upon the competitive markets and depress prices.

But Ricardo was alarmed by the proposition to increase taxes at the very time when business men were making little or no profit, and he contended rightly that just as much labor would be employed by taxpayers as would be employed by the taxes paid to laborers. The cause of unemployment, he contended, was the obstinacy of labor, which at that time was wholly unorganized, in refusing to work at lower wages.[242] If laborers would accept lower wages the employers would then have a margin for profit, even at the lower sales prices, and they would then employ the unemployed. And he argued against Malthus that there could be no such thing as general overproduction, because increased production of any one commodity would increase the demand for all other commodities. But there could be a general reduction in the margins for profit if wages were not reduced in the same proportion as prices were reduced.

Since Ricardo's time, more than a hundred years ago, the communists, socialists, and trade unionists have followed Malthus. They argued from the standpoint of shares; Ricardo and business men from the standpoint of margins. Rodbertus, in 1837, was the first to state the socialist argument in the subsequent form of an inadequate worker's share as the cause of industrial depression.[243] During the same period Karl Marx formulated his theory, beginning at the time of the Revolution of 1848 in the Communist Manifesto.

But, with the gold discoveries of 1849, world prices began again to rise. They continued, with slight recessions, until 1863, aided by the paper money inflation in the United States. Then began the world fall in prices, which continued, again with slight recoveries, until 1897. Then came another upturn until 1920, and another recession continuing with recoveries until the depression of 1929.

With these world-wide movements in the level of average wholesale prices we approach the problem of the Price Margin.

Let us recur to our previous illustration of one corporation in the printing industry. At 10 cents per copy, 600,000 copies are sold, yielding $60,000, or $60 per worker per week. But let this $60 now be broken up into all costs of production—all wages, interest, rents preceding profits of other business men embodied in the costs of materials, taxes, etc. Then allow, as the medium margin for profit of this individual corporation, 3 per cent of the

---

[242] *Letters of Ricardo to Malthus* (ed. by Bonar, J., 1887), 187–192.
[243] Rodbertus, K. J., *Die Forderungen der arbeitenden Klassen* (1837).

selling price. This amounts to $1,800, leaving $58,200 as the total cost of production per week. This total cost of production is the total new indebtedness incurred to get the gross income of $60,000 per week and to leave $1,800 as the margin for profit.

This 3 per cent margin for profit on the selling prices may be 10, 20, or 30 per cent *rate* of profit on the par value of the stockholders' shares, depending on how many par shares of stock were issued. That is a bookkeeping matter and does not here

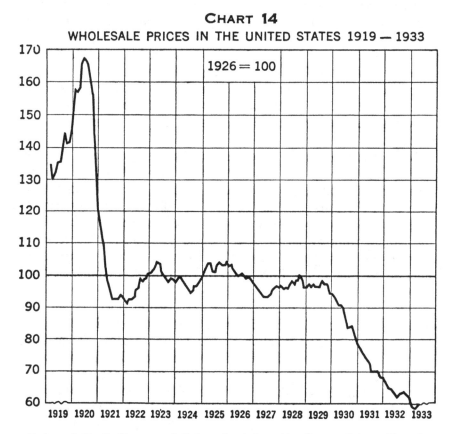

CHART 14
WHOLESALE PRICES IN THE UNITED STATES 1919 — 1933

1926 = 100

Index of U. S. Bureau of Labor Statistics, 550 Commodities. New 784 commodity index converted to 550 base by applying ratio of the respective averages for the year 1931. From the *Report of the Federal Reserve Board*, 1931; and *Federal Reserve Bulletin*, January 1932—May 1933.

concern us. But suppose a world-wide rise in the average purchasing power of money has taken place and the prices of all commodities are falling one per cent per month. This is about the rate at which they were falling after the summer of 1920, and again after 1929, as shown in Chart 14. To fit our illustration let us suppose that the debt of $58,200 was incurred at the beginning of the month and the product was sold at the end of the month. This fits the 30-day credit usually allowed to customers. Meanwhile the world-wide level of prices falls one per cent.

Hence, during the month of the illustration, apart from any technological increase in efficiency, the income from sales is reduced from $60,000 to $59,400. But this $600 is one-third, or 33 per cent, of the margin for profit ($1,800). Thus a general fall in prices, affecting all commodities substantially alike, reduces the margin for profit 33 per cent, through a fall of one per cent in the selling price.

If the margin had been 2 per cent for some other establishment, equal to only $1,200, then the margin would have been reduced 50 per cent through a fall of one per cent in the selling price, due to world-wide causes over which the individual business had no control. Or if, for a more prosperous establishment, the margin was 10 per cent, then a fall of one per cent in the selling price would reduce the margin for profit 10 per cent.

It might be argued that if the prices fall one per cent so that the gross sales fall from $60,000 to $59,400, the consumers would have that much more money ($600), which they could spend for other commodities, and thus could give that much additional employment to labor.

Here enters another side of the illusion above mentioned, that pays attention to *shares* of the national income instead of the *margins* for profit. Where did the magazine buyers get their $60,000, or their $59,400, which they could expend for other commodities? They got it from business men who became their debtors to those amounts. They got it, in part, *directly*, as wages, rents, and interest; or they got it, in part, *indirectly* as the wages, rents, interest, and profits embodied in the materials sold or the taxes paid. Consequently, these magazine buyers are not likely to get their purchasing power at all, if the margin for profit on all commodities is reduced 33 per cent by an average one per cent fall in the selling prices of all commodities. They cease to be magazine *consumers* because they are *unemployed*. And they are unemployed on account of what happened to the margin for profit.

This universal fact of *general* rise and fall in prices operates substantially alike on all margins for profit for all business men the world over. All of them, at substantially the same time, reduce employment. The universal cause operates substantially the same when elasticity of demand is unity, or greater than unity, or less than unity.

When we say "substantially alike," or "substantially at the same time," we mean to allow for variations in time or place in different establishments and different commodities. We need not here enter into details concerning these variations and lags. They are such that the effects in unemployment would not show themselves until several months after prices began to fall.[244]

The essential point, here, is not these variations from the average, nor the variations in the lags. The point is that our capitalistic system is conducted on amazingly narrow margins for profit, and if a change occurs in the average of all prices, that is merely a way of saying—no matter whether the causes may have been monetary or non-monetary—that the effect on the margin for profit the world over is substantially 33 times as powerful as it is on the wholesale prices of the commodities, if the average margin on sales happens to be 3 per cent. The *shares* going to profit drop out of consideration altogether. The *margins* for profit become the whole thing.

And this margin for profit is where the buyers of our magazines must look for their money to buy the magazines. All of them get their money from business men, who in turn get it from banks, and the business men, under modern conditions, are operating on narrow margins for profit. Whether business and employment shall go on, or shall expand, or slow down, or stop, depends on the expected margins for profit. It is not the *shares* which go to profits, nor to wages, that are important in keeping people employed. They are important enough for other purposes. But for the purpose of keeping capital and labor employed, in spite of technological improvements, it makes no difference, as Douglas shows, whether labor gets a half or two-thirds or four-fifths, or whether capitalists get a half or one-third or only one-fifth as their *shares*. Douglas is correct as to shares; but it is the *margins* and not the shares that count.

To state the issue squarely, Would the world-wide unemployment of 1930 to 1933 have been prevented if there had been an increase of wages corresponding to the increase in efficiency during the years 1923 to 1929? Would it have been prevented if the leading central banks of the world had coöperated after 1925 to stabilize the purchasing power of money at the 1926 level of wholesale prices? (We leave out of consideration, at this point, the question of practicability, but we shall assume that either method of prevention could have been put into effect.)

The answer to the first question was correctly made by Douglas.

[244] Below, p. 611, Automatic and Managed Recovery.

An increase in the *share* going to wages at the expense of the *shares* going to profits, rent, and interest would not have prevented the unemployment after 1929.

But it is to be noticed that Douglas' answer turns on the possibility that there will be *expanding* industries, to take over the unemployed who have been laid off by the *contracting* industries.

What is it that determines the possibility of expanding industries? It is the *speculative margin for profit*. If all prices are falling and expected to fall, then all margins for profit are reduced 10, 20, 25, 30 or more *times as much* as the fall in prices. Industries, therefore, do not expand. What seems to be technological unemployment is the consequence of their failure to expand.

On the other hand, if all prices are rising, then the margin for profit is increasing 20, 25 or more *times as much* as the rise in prices. With rising prices, industries expand, and there is no technological unemployment except that which Douglas describes as temporary.

But when the point is reached where all labor is fully employed, any further rise of prices is mere inflation, because the further increase in margins for profit by rising prices cannot put more laborers at work if they are already employed.

Hence, the proposed stabilization of the purchasing power of money permits particular industries to expand and to contract according to their different speculative elasticities of demand or supply. But it prevents general over-expansion, because it operates upon all speculative margins for profit. Whereas Ricardo would have maintained the customary margins for profit by reducing wages when prices were falling, the stabilization of general purchasing power would maintain the margins for profit with increasing wages as efficiency increased.

These are the other factors, not appreciated in early theories—higher standards of living and the increase in technological efficiency. Ricardo proposed that, in order to increase the margins for profit, wages should be reduced and therefore *lower* standards of living should be imposed on wage-earners. It turns out that his only reason for imposing lower standards of living was the general fall in prices of commodities after 1815. If he had considered the possibility of a stable level of prices he might have seen that his margins for profit could be maintained without reducing the standards of living.

Our illustration for the supposed printing industry may be converted into statistical averages for all industries by reference to Chart 14. These averages of wholesale prices are equivalent to the prices received by manufacturers, farmers, mine-owners, and others who control the industries from which their profits are derived. If we assume that, on the average, these commodities were sold on 30 days' time, and if we apply to these changes the marginal principle and the speculative principle, assuming also that the median margin for profit was 3 per cent of the selling price: then the sellers, in February 1919, at $130 had a total cost of production equal to $126.10 and their margin for profit was $3.90. But, since prices at that time were rising at the rate of 2 per cent per month, the expected price at the end of 30 days was $132.60, which, although it is an increase of only 2 per cent on the selling price ($130), is an increase of 66 per cent in the margin for profit.

Or, if the sales occurred at the peak when the average price was $168, and if the price began to fall at the rate of 3.6 per cent per month (as it did), then, in 30 days the price fell to $163, a decrease of $6. And if costs of production had risen to $158.01, leaving, as before, 3 per cent of the selling price as the margin for profit ($5), then the fall in price, although it was only 3.6 per cent of the selling price, was a fall of 120 per cent in the margin for profit.

These calculations, although they are illustrative only and are taken at an unusual period of rising and falling prices, nevertheless give us an idea of the high importance attached by business men to small increases or decreases in either costs or prices. This is because business men are "trading on the equity," and not on the total cost or price of commodities. An average change of 2 per cent either in the prices paid or in the prices received may mean a change of 30 per cent more or less in the margin for profit. If the change is upward, then profits are increased that much; but if the change is downward, then it may wipe out the profit altogether, leaving a deficit.[245]

(7) **The Profit Cushion.**—Thus far, we have been considering the margin for profit on *sales* of manufacturing corporations. We come now to the means developed by these corporations to ease the shock of adverse fluctuations in the margins for profit. In Chart 8 the relation between gross sales and gross income (total receipts) was shown. It was seen that sales never constituted less than 93.7 per cent of the total receipts, and that sales were usually between 95 and 96 per cent of the total receipts. The relatively small

---

[245] That a deficit may actually occur is due to the rule of overhead costs. A large part of the manufacturing costs may continue whether production goes on or not, in order to maintain the establishment as a going concern. In order to pay these, a limited amount of production will be carried on even though the profit margin has been wiped out and sales pay only the overhead costs.

amount of receipts derived from other sources we term the Profit Cushion, as portrayed in Chart 15.

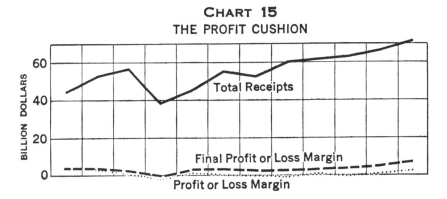

CHART 15
THE PROFIT CUSHION

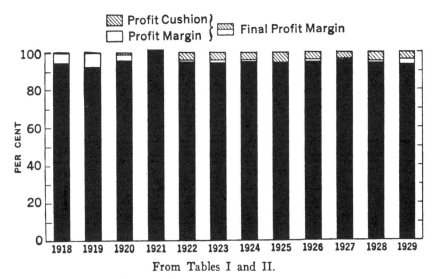

From Tables I and II.

Prior to 1919 it was the general practice of manufacturing corporations to depend on their operating income or sales as a means of making profit, to the practical exclusion of other sources.[246] About the year 1920 there began a rapidly growing practice, the development of other sources of income by investment of funds not paid out as dividends. We have mentioned these new income sources in the section on gross sales and total receipts (above, p. 565) as stocks and bonds of other corporations, government securities, time deposits, rents and royalties, etc. The first figures on these sources of income given in the reports of the United States Bureau of Internal Revenue are for the year 1922. In that year

[246] National Industrial Conference Board, *op. cit.*

4.9 per cent of the total receipts came from these sources other than sales. The margin for profit on sales shown by the lower curve in Chart 11 was, in 1922, as low as 0.8 per cent; but when the cushion provided by other income is added (shaded area in Chart 15) there is a final profit as shown by the upper curve of 5.7 per cent of the total receipts. The estimate of the cushion which we use for 1921 shows that the loss for that year was reduced from 3.2 per cent of the total receipts to about 1 per cent, a reduction of approximately 30 per cent of the loss on sales. The use of the cushion prevented a loss in 1925, and kept the average final profit, from 1922 through 1928, between 4.8 and 7.0 per cent of the total receipts, thus damping materially the fluctuations of our profit and loss margin on sales.

These relations are shown in Chart 15, where the profit and loss margin on sales and the final profit and loss are shown as percentages of the yearly total receipts. The profit cushion is shown as the area between these two curves, acting as a buffer for the fluctuations of sales.

This practice makes it possible for the corporations to maintain a flow of dividends going to the stockholders with some degree of steadiness in both good and bad business years. Hence our use of the term, *profit cushion,* to designate the practice.

This use of the profit cushion calls for no material change in our previous reasoning as to the effect of fluctuations of the profit and loss margin on employment and quantity of production. For when business men or manufacturing corporations become certain that their operations are resulting in a loss, their tendency will be, as we have shown, to curtail production and employment. Thus we find that the profit cushion benefits the stockholder, and makes business financially sounder, by preventing or lessening losses, but does comparatively little to prevent unemployment in periods of falling prices.

(8) **Vested Rights and Profit Margins.**—The foregoing makes a rather pitiful showing for profits, on the average. They are, indeed, a liberty-exposure relation. No wonder the business man, if he is smart, endeavors as soon as possible to convert his profits into a vested right, before they slip away. This he often does by "unloading" on others and "getting out from under," by selling to them, at the proper time, commodities or securities which he expects to fall in price and which they do not know about.

Many of the great successes in business are of this origin. The public generally does not distinguish between getting rich by efficiency and getting rich by unloading dead horses on others. Each is equally honorable according to the customs of business and the *caveat emptors* of legality.

The unloading usually consists in acquiring something that is free from the exposures of the narrow profit margins. The most certain of these are well-secured bonds and increasing land values in growing communities. The Vanderbilt estate is an instance of the former, the Astor estate an instance of the latter.

The one who can successfully convert his fragile profits into vested rights, before they break, accomplishes two things—he saves himself and his descendants for the future, and he compels future business men to exert themselves more keenly for their margins of profit because they are compelled to pay the fixed charges that have been passed on to them. The margins for profit do not increase—but the duties to pay interest on bonds and rents of land do increase, leaving the margins for profit widely fluctuating.

A corporation loaded up with balloon bonds may show a lower margin for profit than one without such burdens. A corporation earning fixed charges on the abuses of the past may have less margin for profit than a competitor that starts free. These are matters of grave social import, and they are even more grave because of the general failure to understand the difference between a margin and the vested rights handed down from the past. It is another instance of the failure to distinguish shares from margins. The shares may be wholly just or unjustified, but it is the margins that keep the concern going or stopping.

Thus the margin for profits has many social implications for a capitalistic civilization. Its significance and measurability have come to the front only with the recent rise of the scientific study of corporation finance.[247] It is none other than "trading on the equity," or "trading on margins," long since familiar in all forms of stock speculation. But it extends deeper to all the processes of production throughout the entire system of private property.

We have attempted to illustrate its computation by reference only to manufacturing corporations. And we have taken only averages, but the significance of the margin for profit is not fully revealed until applied to differentials. While the average margins on 50 to 60 billion dollars of sales may be only 3 per cent, yet there are included within this average individual corporations with margins at times perhaps as high as 50 per cent, and others obviously running below 3 per cent. These differentials suggest intricate problems of progressive taxation and the grave distinction between progressive

[247] See especially Lyons, W. H., *Corporation Finance* (1916), Gerstenberg, C. W., *Financial Organization and Management of Business* (1924).

taxes on individual incomes and on corporate incomes. Highly progressive taxes on individual incomes and vested incomes are justified under the modern inequalities of distribution, and these are derived from a variety of sources not in competition with each other. Yet a progressive tax on corporate net incomes derived from a single source in competition with similar enterprises may defeat the social purpose of a capitalistic civilization which uses the profit motive to increase the efficiency of production. Personal net incomes derived from dividends are a residuum for individuals after all corporate expenses have been paid; they are not the margin for profit exposed to competition. Equally important is the public policy respecting long-term bonds and the vested rights accumulated from the past, which place fixed charges on industry for generations to come, thereby reducing the margins for profit. It has been maintained that bonds should not be issued for terms longer than a single generation, which turns out to be even longer than the life of modern capital equipment reduced by depreciation and obsolescence. Also it has been maintained that these burdens imposed by the "dead hand" are increasing. However this may be, the margin for profit is the living hand, the brain, and the emotion that keeps capitalistic civilization agoing.

(9) **Margins and Costs of Production.**—The older theories of the classical economists, dominated by the idea of an automatic equilibrium which tends to bring fluctuating prices back to the normal costs, paid attention to the "cost of production." The modern institutional theories pay attention to the margin for profit which has no "normal" whatever, but girates pendulously from crag to crag. While the illusion of averages smooths out much of these predicaments yet it gives at least an idea of the order of magnitude that separates the theories of cost of production from the theories of margin for profit. Thus, the cost theorist would say that an accident or unemployment insurance premium of one or two per cent on the payroll could have little or no effect on employers in inducing them to prevent accidents or stabilize employment, because it amounts to less than one per cent of the costs of production; but the marginal analysis, which the employers themselves know too well, reveals that it reduces their margins for profit ten to thirty times as much as it increases their costs of production. The strategy of inducement to prevent accidents or to prevent unemployment is not the bulky costs of production but is the sensitive margins for profit.[248]

Similarly the cost theorist sees very little social effect in a one

[248] Below, p. 840, Accidents and Unemployment.

or two per cent change in the rediscount rates of central banks,[249] but if the narrow margins for profit of the most highly competitive of all transactions on the money and stock exchange markets are less than one per cent of the selling prices, then a change of one per cent in the costs of production may be 100 per cent of the margin for profit.

Likewise in a capitalistic civilization where keen competition is reducing the margins for profit as never known before, very slight discriminations or rebates in prices charged to competitors by a public utility corporation, or in taxes levied by governments, may throw one corporation into bankruptcy, not because its costs are slightly higher or because it is less efficient, but because its margin for profit is wiped out. It has only been within the past thirty years of narrowing margins for profit that the United States Supreme Court has recognized this new leverage of discrimination and has expanded the meaning of the common law to fit it.[250]

Evidently a different principle would apply in case of monopolistic corporations. The issue turns largely on whether the corporation is obtaining its profits by increasing its efficiency or by enjoying monopolistic and differentiated advantages not exposed to competition. It is the issue whether profits are "efficiency profits" or "scarcity profits."[251] This is the issue which arises on a world-wide scale on account of the changeable price margins.

(10) **Sequence and Elasticity.**—The foregoing kind of analysis, turning on narrow margins of profit, has often been attacked as illusory, because evidently you can wipe out the margins for profit, by very slightly changing any one of the factors. We have wiped it out by the fixed charges for interest, for taxes, and selling prices. The same might be done by changes in wages or in cost prices of materials purchased. If any one of the cost prices rises one or two per cent, the margin for profit may be reduced 10 to 30 times as much. Hence the whole analysis is said to be illusory and altogether circular in its reasoning.

This criticism overlooks sequence in time and the different elasticities of demand or supply. All of the factors do not change in the same direction at the same time, and, even if they do, some of them change at a higher or lower degree of elasticity of change.

All of these problems do not arise at one and the same time for the business man or statesman. They arise at different times, according to which factor is changing, or changing most or changing

[249] Lawrence, J. S., *Stabilization of Prices* (1928), Chap. XXII.
[250] Below, p. 773, Scarcity, Abundance, Stabilization.
[251] Foreman, C. J., *Efficiency and Scarcity Profits* (1930). See his Index.

least, or is most or least controllable at the time. They are the problem, not of all factors at once, but of limiting and complementary factors, the limiting factor alone being the one to which attention is paid when it is judged to be actually limiting on all the others at the time and place; and the complementary factors being in the future when one of them may become limiting and then another, as the case may be.[252]

The principle applies not only in private business but in public business. It is undoubtedly the greatest of all human gifts for men of action, which we name the gift of timeliness, and is the outstanding gift of the greatest warriors, the greatest statesmen, and the greatest business men, bringing under their control a nation of flutterbudgets. At one time, for the statesman, it may be taxes that are the limiting factor, at another time it may be prices, at another over-optimism, at another over-pessimism, at another foreign trade, at another domestic trade, at another health or credit, and so on in amazing variety. The point we now make is that each of these thousands of factors, at its own appropriate time, has its own compelling force, in modern capitalism, upon what is really a very delicate, strategic, and narrow margin for profit.

Economic theory, with its mathematics and statistics in this new transitional stage of collective action, is concentrating more and more upon the discovery of the changing limiting factors which create and release the recurring economic jams.

F. C. Mills, in coöperation with the National Bureau of Economic Research, has advanced this investigation of time-sequence materially.[253] He has classified the movement of prices, production, credit, and securities in so far as statistics are available, according to their proximity or remoteness from the ultimate consumer. This is equivalent to Böhm-Bawerk's stages of the roundabout process. But, instead of giving attention, as Böhm-Bawerk did, solely to the problem of interest, Mills takes into account all of the factors over a period of forty years and thus correlates them according to their changes in sequence of time and amplitude of variabilities in the ups and downs of the business cycles.

We have attempted, in our tables and charts, to follow the clue set by Mills and to bring together for the years 1919–1929, most of these changing factors. What he names "variability" of prices and production we name elasticity of supply, meaning thereby the

---

[252] Below, p. 627, Strategic and Routine Transactions; below, p. 840, Accidents and Unemployment.

[253] Mills, F. C., *The Behavior of Prices* (1927); *Economic Tendencies in the United States* (1932). The computations end with the year 1929.

degree to which a change in consumers' demand measured by retail prices and quantities consumed, is forecasted into prices and products in the more or less remote stages of production.

We distinguish between price and value, as previously indicated. The value of a producer's output is composed of the two factors, price and quantity of output sold at the price. It is from this combination that he derives the total value, or "gross sales," from which he is able to pay the several cost factors. If prices rise without an increase of product sold, or even with a reduction of output, or if product enlarges without an increase in price, his gross sales, or value of product, rise. And inversely. This we have seen in our charts where gross sales (value of product) are compared with total receipts and operating costs. And it is these *value* changes that we name elasticity of supply—elastic in two directions, prices and quantities, the combination always reduced to monetary terms.

Beginning with consumers' prices towards which all other prices even the most remote are directed, it is evident that the elasticity of output on the part of retailers corresponds exactly to, indeed is the same thing as, the elasticity of monetary demand on the part of consumers. Mills uses wholesale prices, instead of retail prices, as the index of consumers' demand, implying thereby the prices charged by wholesalers to retailers. We use wholesale prices as an index of manufacturers' prices charged to wholesalers.

(11) Summary.—We may then conclude that the fundamental reason why the *share* theories of the national monetary income do not account for the alternating booms and depressions is because increasing the share of one class reduces the shares of other classes and does not change the total purchasing power of all classes. The purchasing power of all classes, whether expended as savings or expended for consumption, furnishes the same employment for labor, barring temporary difficulties of adjustment. In order to increase the purchasing power of labor the unemployed must be put to work by *creation of new money,* and not by *transferring* the existing purchasing power of taxpayers to laborers, as Malthus proposed, nor by borrowing money by government which *transfers* investments but does not augment them.

This new money cannot be created and issued by bankers, either in commercial, investment, or central banks, because, in a period of depression, the margins for profit have disappeared, and there are no business borrowers willing to coöperate with bankers in creating the new money. In order to create the *consumer demand,* on which business depends for sales, the government itself must create the new money and go completely over the head of the entire banking system by paying it out directly to the unemployed, either as relief or for construction of public works, as it does in times of war. Besides, this new money must also go to the farmers, the business establishments, and practically all enterprises, as well as to wage-earners, for it is all of them together that make up the total of consumer demand.

It is this predicament of creating consumer demand by either inflation of bank credit or by issues of government paper money that requires us to take up the theories and practices of Central Bank policies which were newly formulated by Wicksell in 1898, and acted upon, more or less, in the post-war period by Central Banks of different countries throughout the world. We name this the Thornton-Wicksell sequence of Profit-margin theories.

VIII. A World Pay Community

The Thornton-Wicksell sequence of theories is a profit-margin sequence. It began with Henry Thornton in 1802, after the suspension of specie payments by the Bank of England (1797), and the sequence can be traced through Tooke, 1844, Wicksell, 1898, the post-war economists, Hawtrey, 1919, Keynes, 1930, Fisher, 1932, the policy of the Federal Reserve System after 1921, the policy of the Bank of England and the Bank of Sweden at the suspension of specie payments September 1931.

Thornton's theory was a central bank discount theory. He said, after the suspension of specie payments by the Bank of England in 1797,[254] that the upward limit to the quantity of paper credit (bank notes) turned principally on a comparison of the rate of interest taken at the Bank of England with the current rate of mercantile profit. If the bank rate was *below* this margin for profit, then merchants would increase their borrowings, and the Bank, no longer restricted by legal gold reserve requirements, but judging its creation of bank credit only by the solvency of borrowers, would continue to expand its issues of paper money to meet the "legitimate" demands of solvent business on the rising level of prices. But if the quantity of circulating medium ceases to increase, because the bank rate is raised, then the "extra profit is at an end." The theory reappeared with Tooke,[255] and received a new start at the hands of Wicksell, the Swedish economist, in 1898. Its sig-

---

[254] Thornton, Henry, *Paper Credit of Great Britain* (1802). Cf. article on "Price Stabilization" by John R. Commons, *Encyclopaedia of the Social Sciences.*

[255] Tooke, Thomas, *A History of Prices,* 1793–1856 (6 vols.), Comments and summaries at various points in the six volumes.

nificance will appear by recurring to Sidgwick's separation [256] of the short-term rates of interest on the money market from the long-term rates of interest on the securities and real estate markets. Low rates of interest on the latter markets were the basis of the American "greenback" theory, first set forth by Edward Kellogg, in 1849.

1. *Long-Term Rates of Interest and Prices*

In the year 1919 the Federal Reserve System acted upon the paper-money theory previously known as "greenbackism," whose originator had been Edward Kellogg, in 1849, and whose famous advocate was the eminent manufacturer, Peter Cooper, the "greenback" candidate for President in 1876. Kellogg was the American counterpart of the contemporary European Proudhon and Marx, all of whom proposed to reduce the rates of interest to the labor-cost of operating the banking business.

The theory of Kellogg and Cooper was known as the interconvertible bond system of money.[257] The purpose was both to reduce the usurious rates of interest charged by what they alleged was a banker's monopoly of gold and bank notes, and to restore the values of business concerns and landed property which, in the case of Kellogg, had been rapidly falling after 1837, and, in the case of Cooper, after 1865.

The theory overlooked the double meaning of the "value" of money, namely, the rate of interest or discount and the general purchasing power of money. Kellogg and his followers adopted the former meaning, and held that

"the value of money is determined by the interest that it will accumulate; and the value of all property is determined by the rent that can be obtained for it. . . . If the rent of any property be not sufficient to accumulate a sum equal to the estimated value of the property itself, in as short a period as money loaned, the property will fall in price until the rent bears the same proportion to the value of the property that the rate of interest bears to the principal. . . . The value of property depreciates in proportion to the increase of the value of the dollar that

[256] Above, p. 443, Money and Capital.

[257] Kellogg, Edward, *Labor and Other Capital: the Rights of Each Secured and the Wrongs of Both Eradicated; or, an Exposition of the Cause Why a Few Are Wealthy and Many Poor, and the Delineation of a System Which, without Infringing the Rights of Property, Will Give to Labor Its Just Reward* (1849, published originally in 1843. Reprinted, 1861, under the title, *A New Monetary System.* We cite the 8th ed., 1883); popularized in 1868 by A. Campbell, under the title, *The True Greenback.* Peter Cooper's writings, begun in 1867, and the Independent Party platform, are in his *Ideas for a Science of Good Government,* collected and published 1883.

measures it. Whenever the value of money increases by a rise of interest, there is a corresponding decrease in the value of property. . . . No man will invest his money in property unless he supposes that the property will yield as good an income as the money he pays for it. Therefore the price of property must fall whenever the interest on money increases, that the incomes from property and from money may be equal." [258]

Kellogg proposed that the rate of interest should be prevented from rising above one per cent, which he estimated to be the labor-cost of administering the banking system. This estimate was raised to three per cent by his followers of the National Labor Union in 1867 and the Greenback Party in 1876.[259] The government would print legal tender notes which would be loaned on mortgages at three per cent interest, to the amount of fifty per cent of the value of the land. The borrower then could use the legal tender notes in purchasing commodities and paying wages to labor, by which means the notes would get into general circulation. Any person receiving the legal tender could lend to others instead of purchasing commodities, or could invest the amount in Government Treasury Notes, not legal tender but bearing three per cent interest. In turn, a person owning the Treasury Notes, if he found an opportunity to make more than three per cent in industry or agriculture, could convert them, on demand at the Treasury, into legal tender money which he could then pay out for materials and labor.

In this way the rate of interest could not rise above three per cent, since, if a borrower were asked more than three per cent by a private lender, he could borrow from the government at three per cent, or borrow from someone else who in turn could borrow at three per cent. On the other hand, interest would not fall below three per cent, because a lender could always get three per cent by buying a Treasury Note, bearing that rate, with his legal tender money. In this way the rate of interest throughout the country would be stabilized at three per cent, instead of fluctuating, as it did, between one or two per cent in hard times and 10, 15, 100 or more per cent on real estate, commercial or call loans in prosperous times or in times of money stringency.

Kellogg's interconvertible money and bond scheme has reappeared frequently in Congress or in paper money proposals, often as a new discovery, without realizing its origin in 1849. Recently, since the fall of prices after 1929, it has reappeared as an agri-

---

[258] Kellogg, E., *op. cit.*, 153–154.
[259] See Commons, John R., and associates, *Documentary History of American Industrial Society*, IX, 180, 213 ff.

cultural relief program by means of non-interest bearing legal-tender United States notes (greenbacks) and the conversion of these notes into three per cent government bonds issued to take over mortgages on farm lands. If the market price of the bonds exceeds par, the Secretary of the Treasury is to be instructed to sell bonds and retire an equal amount of United States notes, and if the market price of the bonds falls below par, the Secretary is to buy the bonds in exchange for the legal tender notes. In this way it is expected, as in Kellogg's scheme, that the supply of bonds will be increased when their price is above par, thus bringing their price down to par, by issuing them for paper money and retiring temporarily the money; and the supply of bonds will be reduced when their price is below par, thus bringing their price up to par, by re-issuing the paper money in exchange for the bonds and retiring temporarily the bonds.

Kellogg contended that his paper money would not depreciate, as did the assignats of France, or the Continental money issued by the United States during the Revolution, because that money was "not representative of property," whereas his interconvertible money did represent property in the form of mortgages on real estate. If the government, he said, "had lent money for mortgages on productive land worth double the amount of the loan, and had provided notes bearing interest to fund the money, such paper money would have been representative of property, and invariably good." [260]

Yet Kellogg recognized that the values of lands or of any bonds, whose actual rent or interest was more than three per cent, would immediately rise if money could be borrowed freely and continuously at three per cent. But he did not follow it out to its inflationary results.

If a piece of land worth $1,000 yields $60 rent, or a bond at par yields $60 interest yearly, when the market rate of interest is 6 per cent per year, then that same land or bond would rise in value to $2,000 if interest is 3 per cent. The buyer of the land or bond would earn on one investment of $2,000 paper money the same $60 per year as he would earn on $2,000 paper money invested in Treasury notes, but it would be 3 per cent instead of 6 per cent.

If the land, therefore, rises to $2,000, then its value for mortgage purposes would be twice as great as before, and its owner could borrow, again at one-half the new value of the land, twice as much as before. Where he had borrowed $500 when the land was valued at $1,000, he now could borrow $1,000 when the land is valued at $2,000.

[260] *Ibid.*, 280, 281.

Meanwhile the commodity prices of the products of the land—its wheat, corn, livestock—would have risen also, as Kellogg also recognized, owing to the greater abundance of legal tender money. If it came about that these prices rose 100 per cent, as the land value had risen 100 per cent, then the $60 rent would now presumably be $120 rent in terms of the paper money. If the rent is $120, then the land could rise in value to $4,000 and still continue to pay a rent-yield of 3 per cent on its market value. Its mortgage-value, at one-half its market value, would now be $2,000, and the borrower could borrow $2,000 at 3 per cent. As long as there was no limit placed on the quantity of legal tender or the quantity of interconvertible Treasury Notes bearing 3 per cent interest, this spiral effect would continue, raising first the value of the land, then the prices of the products of the land, then the value of the land, then the prices, and so on to infinity.

The fallacy of Kellogg's reasoning was twofold: Confusion of the double meaning of the value of money as a rate of interest and as purchasing power; and the classic confusion of Producing power with Purchasing power. Producing power, as he interpreted it, is not merely the quantity of products, it is also the prices of the products. And stabilizing the value of money as a stable *rate of interest* operates exactly in the opposite direction by rendering unstable the value of money as *purchasing power*.

The Federal Reserve System, in 1919, acted upon Kellogg's theory. The Treasury was floating the Victory Loan at rates of interest equal to 4¼ per cent, at a time when the average of market rate was 5¾ to 6 per cent. The bonds were sold through member banks and the buyer was permitted ·to borrow the money to pay for the bonds and leave the bonds with the bank for security. In order to create a favorable market for the bonds at par, the rule was adopted by the System that on borrowings by member banks at the Reserve banks when secured by government bonds, the rediscount rate should be one-half of one per cent (4¼ per cent) below the rate when secured by commercial paper (4¾ per cent).[261] The result was that the member banks used government securities as collateral for 85 per cent of their borrowings, and commercial paper as collateral for only 15 per cent of their borrowings. The rate on government collateral became the effective rate.

The rediscount rate at New York on commercial paper as collateral had been 4 per cent in 1917, then raised to 4¾ per cent in 1918 and during 1919. During the same time the rate on government collateral, which was 3½ per cent in 1917, was raised to

[261] Below, p. 604, Chart 16.

4¼ per cent in 1918 and during 1919, maintaining the differential of one-half of one per cent in favor of government collateral until May 1921.[262]

The consequence was that if a banker deposited a government bond as collateral he could obtain a loan from the Federal Reserve bank at 4¼ per cent but could relend at 6 to 8 per cent on the general money market (open market commercial rate, Chart 16).

In this way the amount of borrowings secured by government obligations increased from almost nothing in 1917 to 1.7 billion dollars in May 1919, when the Victory Loan was being floated. As a result, during the period from March 1919 to May 1920 the total Reserve bank credit loaned to member banks increased from 2.5 billion dollars to 3.2 billion dollars; the Federal Reserve notes increased from 2.4 billion dollars to 3.2 billion dollars, and the demand deposits of all member banks increased from 12.7 billion dollars to 15.3 billion.[263]

The effect on prices was remarkable.[264] The wholesale price level rose 15 per cent by the end of 1919, and the impetus sent it up an additional 13 per cent by May 1920. Never before, in the history of wars, had there been a *post-war* inflation of prices. It resulted from the Kellogg theory of keeping the short-term rate of interest artificially below the market rates.

Finally, after the Victory Loans were sold, in November 1919, the Reserve bank in New York began its repeated increases in the discount rate, reaching the panicky 7 per cent in June 1920, on commercial paper, and 6 per cent on government collateral (Chart 16).

It is evident that if the Reserve banks had begun to raise their rates in April 1919, to 5 or 6 per cent, twelve months before they actually began to reach those rates, they could have prevented the post-war inflation of commodity prices and even have depressed prices in 1919, instead of 1921. But they were acting upon the Kellogg theory of interconvertible bonds and money, with the design of keeping the rate on Victory bonds below the market rate on commercial loans and capital generally, in order to sell the bonds at par. Had the rate not been thus artificially reduced, the market price of a 4½ per cent bond, as Kellogg had showed, would have fallen much below par, at a time when banks and lenders could obtain 6 per cent on their other loans. It was to avoid this that the inflationary low rate of interest was adopted.

---

[262] Not shown in Chart 16.
[263] Not shown in Chart 16.
[264] Above, p. 578, Chart 14.

2. *Short-Term Rates of Interest and Prices*

Quite the opposite of Kellogg's is the theory of Wicksell,[265] descended from Thornton. He took the other meaning of the value of money, not the rate of interest but the general purchasing power of money. He would stabilize the purchasing power of money instead of the rate of interest on money.

MacLeod, in 1856, had developed the theory of the effects of changes in the bank rate on the export and import of gold. Wicksell, in 1898, developed a theory of the effect of such changes on the general level of prices. Wicksell's theory was unnoticed until 1922 when the world's monetary gold had largely disappeared, and the Federal Reserve System, which now owned a surfeit of gold, had discovered that the Central bank rate, backed by open market sales of securities, might be used to prevent inflation of prices.

Wicksell occupies a transitional position between the individualistic physical theories and the post-war theories of concerted action by central banks. The influence of the older theories remained in his identification of "natural" interest with the marginal productivity of Ricardo, Turgot, and Böhm-Bawerk. This was his advance beyond the theory of Thornton in 1802. He endeavored to tie together the central bank rate with not only Thornton's commercial rates paid by *merchants* but also with the whole technological process and the financing of *production*. The modern theories appear in the threefold relation which he set up between changes in this natural interest based on productivity, changes in the average of commodity prices, and a world-wide concerted action of central banks in controlling changes in the rate of discount.

If the central bank rate is reduced, by world-wide action, below the marginal productivity of capital, that is, "natural" interest, then the bank customers are induced to increase their demand for bank credit by which they increase their demand for commodities and labor, and thereby raise the general level of prices.

In the opposite direction, if the central bank rate, by world-wide concerted action, is raised above the marginal productivity of physical capital, then the business customers, owing to narrow margins for profit, reduce their borrowings, reduce their demand for commodities and labor, and a fall in prices and employment is the result.

But if the central bank rate, by similar world-wide action, is kept approximately equal to the marginal productivity of physical capi-

[265] Wicksell, Knut, *Geldzins und Güterpreise* (1898).

tal, then the average of prices and the quantity of employment tend toward stabilization.

This theory was contrary to the official action of the Treasury and Reserve banks in 1919 and 1920, whose action, as we have noted, was conformable to the Kellogg theory. In 1919 the bank rate was much below the market rates and, according to Wicksell, this would cause the rise of prices that actually ensued. But in 1920 and the early part of 1921 the bank rate began to be above the market rates, and this, according to Wicksell, would cause the fall in prices that ensued.[266] The official theory, and the theory held generally, indicated that the bank rate should *follow* the market rates, because they had no theory of the relation of interest to prices. Wicksell held that the bank rate should *precede* the market rates in order to prevent a rise or fall of prices.

The need of world-wide concerted action, according to Wicksell, followed upon the well-recognized principle of MacLeod and the Bank of England after 1857, that a higher rate of discount in one country than in other countries would ordinarily extract gold from other countries, but if all countries acted together and all of them raised and lowered their discount rates together, then each country could raise or lower its individual rates slightly above or below the world-wide rate, according to the international balance of payments and the threatened export or import of gold.

This export and import of gold shows itself in the bank reserves, and Fisher has summarized the contribution of Wicksell in saying that his doctrine turned on keeping the discount rate "in tune with other rates." In this respect, he contended, Wicksell, "more than any one else" had made the valuable contribution "that, except for the gold reserve, the price level of a commodity where the deposit currency rules the price level, would be entirely at the mercy of the discount policy of banks."[267]

Thus the significance of Wicksell's contribution is in his proposed collective action of nations towards stabilizing the world-wide general level of commodity prices, at a stage of civilization when both metallic money and paper money have been subordinated to the debit money of commercial banks. How Wicksell came about this Utopian theory thirty-five years ago and how it awaited the post-war tragedies of capitalistic civilization for experimental investigation and testing, and how it must be modified to fit these experiments, are the outstanding economic, political, and diplomatic problems in a reconstruction of economic theory whose parallel is

[266] Charts 14 and 16.
[267] Fisher, Irving, *Proceedings Amer. Econ. Assn.*, March 1927, 108.

found only in the reconstruction of theory that followed the other world war of more than a hundred years before.

3. *From Marginal Productivity to Capital-Yield*

Three defects emerge in Wicksell's theory of forecast and central bank control—the measurability of marginal productivity, the divergence of open market and customer's rates, and the risk-discount.

There have been, historically, three versions of marginal productivity relative to the rate of interest, to which Wicksell added a fourth. Turgot's interpretation turned on the abundance and scarcity of savings, the greater abundance leading to lower rates of interest and therefore to the extension of production to lower margins. Causation was on the side of savings. Ricardo's interpretation started from the opposite point of view with the expansion of population which pushed labor and capital to lower levels of agricultural production, with a corresponding reduction in the rates of interest and profit. His causation was on the side of nature and population. Böhm-Bawerk's theory was that of the technological superiority of present goods, assuming that a given amount of labor now devoted to roundabout methods would produce an increasing output with the lengthening of the time after it was first employed.[268]

None of these theories took adequately into account the changes in the technological efficiency of capital through inventions and better organization. They were concerned mainly with the quantity of capital. Turgot measured the quantity of capital by his "thermometer," the rate of interest on long-time loans. Ricardo and Böhm-Bawerk measured the quantity of capital by the number of man-hours required to produce it. Wicksell rejected the man-hour measurement of quantity of capital and returned to Turgot's monetary measurement. But he introduced *changes* in the *efficiency* of capital instruments distinguished from the quantity of capital. Ricardo had, indeed, made a change in efficiency the base of his theory, but it was a declining rate of efficiency and therefore also of interest and profits, owing to pressure of population towards lower margins in agriculture. He had no effective theory of the inventions which have actually increased the efficiency of labor in all industries, overcoming the pressure of population towards lower agricultural margins. Karl Marx substituted increasing efficiency of labor for Ricardo's diminishing efficiency, but his was a trend upward of a surplus product belonging to owners instead of laborers.

[268] Above, p. 438, From Psychological to Institutional Economics.

But Wicksell noted that during a period of revolutionary inventions the marginal productivity of capital, that is, efficiency, is increased and thereby there is a greater demand for savings, and the natural rate of interest is increased. But during a period when technical improvements slow down and savings continue to increase, the marginal productivity tends to decline, and consequently there is a lesser demand for savings, and the natural rate of interest declines. Thus Wicksell, while measuring the quantity of capital by money, as did Turgot, measured the "natural interest" on capital by changes in technological efficiency of capital goods.

But Wicksell went further and identified the psychological interest of the subjective schools with both marginal productivity and interest on savings. We have noted this same identification by Cassel in his measurable quantity of "waiting," and the price paid for waiting. It comes out the same as Turgot's declining "price of interest," though modified by Wicksell's *changes* in efficiency. But Turgot's "price of interest" was pictured by him as either a low rate of interest causing the emergence of islands and then valleys of labor, in agriculture, industry, and commerce, above the level of the retreating sea, or a rise in the rate ("price") of interest causing their disappearance below the level of the rising sea.

The concept of marginal productivity, now converted by Wicksell to a concept of social efficiency, becomes a concept of two variables, the increase or decrease of the *rate* at which social output advances, and the increase or decrease of the *rate* at which new savings are accumulated. The natural rate of interest increases with increasing social output or decreases with diminishing social output; and also increases with a diminution in the supply of savings or decreases with an increase in the supply of savings.

One other variable was taken into account, namely fluctuations in the general level of prices. Such fluctuations would modify both the prices of commodities and the prices of all services, of commodities and labor, that entered into the technological process. Therefore, in order to work out his theoretical exposition, he, like Ricardo, Böhm-Bawerk, and all theorizers, eliminated this variable by assuming that the level of prices remained constant. With this assumption, then, we have four variables, social output, quantity of capital or savings, the market rates of interest, and the Central bank rate. The social output is supposed to be sold at invariable prices, regardless of changes in efficiency. The capital savings and the interest rates are therefore also measured by a constant purchasing power of money. So that, with these assumptions, no rise or fall in prices interferes with the equalization, at the rising or falling margins of production, of the social output and the monetary income of all participants in the production of that output. Marginal productivity becomes the equilibrium level where a surplus of physical productivity, measured by a stable price level, is equal to interest on savings, also unaffected by changes in the general price level.

Then Wicksell introduces *changes* in the price levels of consumers' goods (retail prices), changes in the price levels of producers' goods (wholesale prices and wages), changes in the marginal productivity of capital and labor, changes in the bank rate and the market rates of interest, and changes in the volume of money. These changes occur at different *rates of change,* and at different *times of change,* and it is in his observation and measurement of these lags and forerunners of the different changes that he derives his theory of the means by which the general level of prices may be stabilized by the concerted forecast action of central banks of issue and rediscount.

Wicksell's theory of marginal productivity occasioned a notable debate between Keynes, Hayek, and Hawtrey, in 1931 and 1932.[269] Hayek contended that Keynes left no place for profits in his theory of money and that his was purely a monetary theory not taking into account the non-monetary changes in the physical productivity of technological capital.

In the latter case Hayek fell back on Böhm-Bawerk's theory of the greater technical superiority of prolonging the period of production, that is, prolonging the roundabout process. If the roundabout process is prolonged by investment in larger quantities of technological capital, then the future marginal productivity of capital is increased. But if the process is shortened by investment in smaller quantities of technological capital, then the future marginal productivity of capital is decreased. These alternatives actually do occur in the business cycle, as Wicksell had shown, larger issues of bonds for new construction occurring in periods of depression when long-time interest rates (bond yield) are low, and smaller issues in periods of prosperity and high interest, or high bond-yield rates.

But it does not follow, as Böhm-Bawerk contended, that lengthening the roundabout process increases productivity, and shortening the process decreases productivity. The whole genius of modern invention is bent on *shortening* the roundabout process by building,

[269] Hayek, F. A., "Reflections on the Pure Theory of Money of Mr. J. M. Keynes," *Economica*, XI, 270; XII, 23; "Rejoinder" by Keynes, *Economica*, XI, 378. See also Hayek, *Prices and Production* (1931), and Hawtrey's review, *Economica*, XII (1932), 119, and his *Art of Central Banking* (1932). Keynes, J. M., *Treatise on Money* (1931), and *Essays in Persuasion* (1932).

say, a skyscraper in ten months when, according to obsolete methods, it might require several years, or would have been actually impossible. And the investment in this more efficient capital equipment is actually much less than in the obsolete equipment, relative to the expected output. It costs much less, and takes less time, per unit of expected output, to construct a huge dynamo and accompanying improved machinery which will turn out a product equal to the output of a whole battery of steam engines and obsolete machinery. From one point of view modern technology is shortening the roundabout process and from the other point of view it is requiring a less issue of bonds than formerly for new construction, if by roundabout process we mean *a given rate of output* in the future.

But these future rates of output or future marginal technological productivity, or future profits, are wholly immeasurable by any statistical device hitherto introduced. For these and other reasons Hawtrey eliminates the "production period" and rightly substitutes an explanation of the interval as depending mainly on the state of the producer's commitments, unfilled orders, inventories of stocks on hand, and facilities for putting additional capital and labor to work.

We must, therefore, look elsewhere for quantitative evidences of the actual forecasts of the business community which take into account all of the present circumstances as well as the expected changes emphasized by Wicksell and Hawtrey. If we station ourselves at a present point of time when negotiations are being conducted and commitments and purchases of materials and labor are being made, as contemplated by Hawtrey, for either the short distance or long distance future, we have for each establishment, as its guide in forecasting, its own experience and current operations, and the judgments which similar establishments and the general public are placing on the expectations of the future.

These forecasts involve two variables, the expected physical output and the expected prices at which it will be sold, in order to obtain a future margin for profit upon which the bankers may be willing to advance present purchasing power. For it is not physical output upon which the banking system is conducted. It is *expected* physical output *times* expected prices. In other words it is expected "gross sales." These forecasts of output *and* prices are continually changing, but the current run of long-distance forecasting can be ascertained by the current prices paid on the stock markets for stocks and bonds of corporations and on the real estate markets for land titles, each of them compared with the current net income of dividends, interest, and rent. These computations of "stock yield," "bond yield" and the "rent yield" on land values, are the nearest measurable approach to the *expected* output *times* expected prices. The stock and bond prices are highly speculative and changeable and often subject to manipulation and propaganda, but even so they indicate the extent to which, for the time being, and for any reason, those who invest and speculate are willing to extend future production to lower margins of output *times* price, or unwilling to be satisfied with the existing rates of return. If a 5 per cent bond whose par value is $100 is so thoroughly safeguarded that the market value is $200, then the investors buying the bonds are willing to permit the owners of that enterprise to enlarge equipment and extend production to a higher level of gross sales. This would be a bond-yield of only 2½ per cent and would be a lower margin of future physical productivity *times* a higher level of expected prices. If the market value, however, is only $50, then the bond-yield is 10 per cent and investors are unwilling to permit that establishment to enlarge equipment and extend expected output at expected prices beyond the 10 per cent limit.

The same principle applies to willingness to invest in shares of stock or in land values. But here the element of risk, which is far more variable than interest, and is indeed the factor of expected profit, becomes quite decisive. The discount on account of expected risk may rise to 100 per cent, in which case a share of stock whose par value is $100 sinks to a present market value of zero and disappears from the market though it may be "held" for its voting power. Or, if the expected risk is diminished by expected increase of output at expected increase of prices, then the price of the share of stock may rise well above par.

These principles are simple enough and well understood, but the point here noted is that they combine in one valuation (gross sales) both the expected output and the expected prices to be received for that output. They therefore subordinate the notion of a "natural" interest based only on technological capital or on lengthening or shortening the roundabout process. All of these variable physical outputs of the future, along with future variable prices, profits, and interest, have already been commuted on the capital markets in the present process of buying and selling stocks and bonds.

We name the yields from all of these long-term investments, following Sidgwick, the "capital-yield" instead of Wicksell's "marginal productivity." For they are the combined rate of yield for both profits and interest, ranging all the way from the most secure, where interest predominates, to the least secure, where profit predominates, in all the valuations made by present purchasers of titles to expected long-term incomes of both interest and dividends. If a weighted index could be constructed of the average capital-yield, then we should have an index, not of Wicksell's "natural interest," which is unmeasurable for banking and investment purposes, but of the entire institutional set-up which expands production or limits production according to the current wise or foolish, hopeful or panicky, judgments of all participants.

The nearest that we can approach, with existing statistical data, to this index of average capital-yield is the average yield, weighted according to new issues, of selected common and preferred stocks and bonds on the New York Stock Exchange. Such an index includes both expected supply and demand, or prices, as well as expected technological output to be sold at those prices. Our computation may be seen in the "Capital-yield" of Chart 16.

This calculation has many imperfections because incomplete, but, such as it is, it gives a rough clue in the present state of statistical research. If this index is compared as in Chart 16 with the open market commercial rates and with the rediscount rates of the New York Reserve bank, we begin to obtain a clue to the significance of Wicksell's analysis. The "capital-yield" does not eliminate non-monetary factors—it combines the technological output times the prices of that output, just as the capital market actually does.

Substituting, then, this formula of capital-yield for Wicksell's "natural" rate based on marginal productivity of technological capital, his theory would run as follows. He assumes, in the first place, a world-wide unity of action of central banks of issue and rediscount guided by the purpose of maintaining stability of the average purchasing power of money. By this unity of action, the interference of gold shipments to pay balances can be counteracted by transferring credits, or by ear-marking, from one nation to another, so that practically the gold reserves can be impounded and removed from both domestic and foreign exchange.

With this assumption, then, if the average world-wide capital-yield (his natural rate) is low, indicating an abundance of investment and speculative activity, the securities will sell at high prices; these high prices will be an inducement to increase the issues of new securities and thereby to increase the quantities of labor and materials that can be purchased, at existing wages and prices, for extensions and new construction. The total social investment and business activity, measured in quantities of labor and materials purchased, is thereby increased; and an increasing output will eventually ensue.

If, now, at the same time when the capital-yield (his natural rate) is low because the prices of securities are high, the bank rate is made yet lower than the capital-yield, the same tendencies

CHART 16
CAPITAL YIELD, OPEN MARKET RATE, AND REDISCOUNT RATE
1919 — 1933

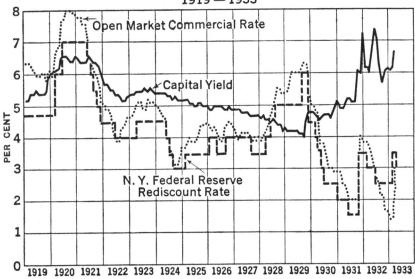

"Capital-Yield," average yield of 15 public utility bonds, 15 railway bonds, 15 industrial bonds, 20 industrial preferred stocks, and 90 industrial common stocks; weighted according to new issues of corporate bonds, preferred stocks, and common stocks as given in the *Commercial and Financial Chronicle,* 1919–1933; Yields of the different classes of securities as computed by Standard Statistics Company and quoted currently in the *Survey of Current Business.*

"Open Market Rate" average monthly rate on prime, 4–6 month commercial paper, from *Annual Report of Federal Reserve Board,* 1927–1928, 1931; and *Federal Reserve Bulletin,* Jan. 1932—May 1933.

"New York Federal Reserve Rediscount Rate" from *Annual Report of the Federal Reserve Board,* 1924 and 1931; and *Federal Reserve Bulletin,* Jan. 1931—May 1933; rate for period, 1919–1921 is that on 60–90 day paper; 1922–1933 rate, on all classes of paper.

will be transferred to current operation. Stimulated by this still lower bank rate, borrowers are induced to enlarge the amount of their short-time borrowings for immediate delivery of finished products, by shifting from purchases of long-time issues. These larger short-time borrowings have the same effect as the high prices of securities, for they enable the borrowers to increase their demand for labor and materials. This tends first to increase the quantity of operating labor and materials purchased for immediate production and thus to raise prices and wages even when all labor is fully employed, so that no addition can further be made to the quantity of output. This, we have seen, was the case in 1919.

But if, on the other hand, while the capital-yield (natural rate) is low, the bank rate is raised above the capital-yield, then the higher bank rate tends to counteract the low capital-yield. Borrowers are inclined to borrow less money at the banks for current operation and to put more money into long-time securities and thus, either prices do not tend to rise or quantities of output do not tend to enlarge, as they would have done when the bank rate was below the capital-yield.

Carrying the same reasoning throughout, it is not the *absolute* rise or fall of the bank rate that affects the average movement of output and prices, it is the *relative* rise or fall of the bank rate compared with the capital-yield. If the capital-yield is 6 per cent, then a bank rate of 4½ per cent, as in 1919,[270] is a low rate, and will initiate a tendency towards a rise of the average of commodity prices. If the capital-yield falls to 4 per cent, as in 1929, then the same bank rate of 5 per cent is a *high* rate and will initiate a tendency towards a fall in commodity prices.

Here will be seen the significance of Wicksell's use of the functional relation between borrowing money and buying goods, a relation quite familiar to all business concerns, but not made use of in the theories of the classical and hedonic economists. They had eliminated money as a mere "form," a "medium of exchange" having no effect on the exchange-values previously determined in the processes of production, pleasure and pain. But money, says Wicksell, is not a mere difference in "form," where it plays only a passive part, but in "reality," with money playing an active part.

The classical and communistic economists' supposition that money played a passive part, merely as a convenient means of exchange in transferring goods, not different from a highway as a means of transporting goods, and that therefore the rate of interest could be pictured as merely a "natural" rate payable in another universal commodity, money, might have been close to reality if their assumption was true that money was simply one form of a commodity, gold or silver, whose value was determined and measured by the same man-hours of labor-power that determined and measured the value of the other commodities. But with a bank debit system of money substituted for a metallic system of money, the bank rate of interest may and does, as Sidgwick had previously shown, change

[270] Chart 16.

differently from the changes in either their assumed "natural" rate as determined by the marginal productivity of capital or in the yield on the market value of capital. In other words, Wicksell here introduces a relation of multiple causation between Sidgwick's two static rates of interest, wherein the bank rate of interest does not always coincide with the capital-yield, and this lack of coincidence is reflected in the changes in quantities and prices of products.

Wicksell's doctrine of the relativity of the bank rate and the marginal productivity of capital makes inexplicable Fetter's criticism of what he calls "Wicksell's startling doctrine of discount policy." [271] Fetter rejects Wicksell's marginal productivity because it is a "value" productivity, which it certainly is, whereas marginal productivity is admittedly always a technological, or output, productivity. Wicksell's "marginal productivity" includes both output and the price received for the output. This is pecuniary value-productivity measurable as capital-yield. And it is so because the physical product is sold for money, and value is not psychic—it is money value.

Still more inexplicable is it that Fetter should have missed Wicksell's essential doctrine of the *relativity* of different interest rates. Fetter directs his attention solely to that half of Wicksell's doctrine where the bank rate is supposed to be *lower* than the "natural" rate, and agrees with Wicksell that this situation would cause a general rise of prices. Then he assumes that Wicksell intended that the money rate should *always* be kept lower than the natural rate, in which case there would ensue, as Fetter says, a "constant bank credit inflation and a constant rise of prices, in turn creating a motive for more commercial loans, *ad infinitum,* just as in the case of Russian and German paper money inflation." Fetter overlooks the other half of Wicksell's doctrine. The rise of prices can be stopped and even a fall in prices can be brought about by raising the bank rate above the "natural" rate.

A better understanding of Wicksell was shown by Fisher in his reply to Fetter,[272] where he approved of Wicksell's doctrine that reducing the bank rate below the natural rate would tend to cause an inflation of credit and a rise of prices, but pointed out that by raising the bank rate above the "natural" rate there would ensue a contraction of credit and a fall of prices; and, by keeping the discount rate "in tune with other rates" the tendency would be to maintain a stable level of the average of prices.[273]

[271] Fetter, Frank A., "Interest Theory and Price Movements," *Proceedings Amer. Econ. Assn.*, March 1927, 62, 98.

[272] *Ibid.*, 106, 107.

[273] *Ibid.*, 108.

4. *Open Market Rates and Customers' Rates*

Wicksell did not emphasize the distinction between short-term and long-term rates of interest, because he held that the two rates of interest tend to coincide on the markets. In this respect he was quite correct, if by short-term rates is meant "customers' rates." Indeed a comparison of our "capital-yield" with the average of "customers' rates," as developed in the notable work of Riefler,[274] shows that the two so nearly coincide that the differences cannot be distinguished in our Chart 16, and the customers' rate is therefore omitted from the chart. It is almost identical with our "capital-yield."

But it is different with the open market rate, as seen on the chart. The open market rate is a nation-wide rate yielded by marketing to thousands of banks through commission houses the short-term bills of great and well-known manufacturing establishments, which the banks buy out of their "surplus funds" not otherwise invested, and is therefore the most highly competitive market rate of interest. It is therefore directly affected by the central bank rate, as will be seen in Chart 16.

On the other hand, the customers' rate is practically a confidential rate agreed upon between a single bank and its individual customer, wherein the bank is expected to "carry" the customer, and the customer carries his balances at the bank. The bank is more directly guided by the alternative investment-yields on securities. And the customers' rates therefore more nearly coincide with the "capital-yield" than with the central bank rate. It is this difference between open market and customers' rates that largely explains Wicksell's merging of all short-term and long-term rates in an average *market* rate of interest which he contrasts with the *natural* rate of physical productivity; whereas others, like Hawtrey, lay more emphasis on the divergence of the short-term open-market rate compared with the long-term investment rate. It is the open-market rate that is most immediately and directly affected by central bank discount policy, whereas the customers' rate and its practical equivalent, the rate of capital-yield, are more slowly affected.

Thus we have to consider *two* margins of productivity, the operating margin and the construction margin. The operating margin corresponds roughly to the short-term loans on the "money" market, but the construction margin corresponds to the long-term bonds and stocks on the "capital" market. The two margins do not usually coincide, since, although the short-term interest and risk move up

[274] Riefler, W. W., *Money Rates and Money Markets in the United States* (1930), 62 ff.

and down sympathetically with the long-term interest and risk, yet their movements diverge and lag. If the short-term double discount of interest and risk is lower than the long-term discount, the inducement to manufacturers is to extend current production of commodities to lower margins of operating return on short-time commitments, and to withhold extension of plant and equipment from the still relatively higher margins on long-time commitments. The reverse occurs when the long-term rate is lower than the short-term rate. It is the familiar fact that at one time a plant is operating at less than capacity and borrowing less money *for operation;* at which time it is *enlarging its capacity* by issuing bonds and stocks when their prices are higher and the capital-yield is low.

5. The Risk Discount—Overindebtedness and Depression

But there are several other widely fluctuating factors which Wicksell eliminated by assuming them to be constant. These may be summarized as Risk. Wicksell was considering only the effects of changes in different rates of *interest* upon prices. He therefore eliminated changes in risk, which are changes in "confidence" and "lack of confidence." A "risk discount" of 100 per cent will stop business altogether. And this is because the risk operates upon, not the total cost of production, but the rather narrow, but greatly fluctuating, margin for profit.[275]

These risk discounts show themselves in the willingness or unwillingness of business men to incur debts, whether long-term or short-term debts. We turn to Irving Fisher's latest work for a vivid description of this relationship between risk and debt.

Irving Fisher has well portrayed the part played by the debt market to which he gives its proper setting in his nine main factors of booms and depressions.[276] Our interpretation agrees with Fisher's, to which the reader is referred, except that we begin, as does Hawtrey, with the *transactions that create the debts.* The other factors, says Fisher, not, however, in order of importance, are the currency volume, the price level, the net worth of business assets and liabilities, the profit margin, the production index, the psychological causes and effects of optimism and pessimism, the currency turnover including hoarding and the rates of interest.

Debts are more rapidly incurred on a rising market when the

[275] Below, p. 611, Automatic and Managed Recovery.
[276] Fisher, Irving, *Booms and Depressions* (1932), 82. This book is the most important yet published on the subject. It enables us greatly to reduce our discussion by referring the reader to it. He sets the total indebtedness of the United States, on compilation by Royal Meeker, at 234 billion dollars, equal to one-half of the national wealth.

risk is less. If debtors have borrowed too much—especially if they have misjudged the maturity dates—they are caught in a trap. The first symptom is "distress selling" by the weaker debtors, which forces a reduction in prices. This affects all competitive prices, and eventually the whole community may be involved in distress selling, the effect of which is to lower the general price level. "Distress selling perverts the law of supply and demand," because it is selling not to obtain a profit but to pay debts and maintain solvency.

This stampede liquidation actually reduces the volume of deposit currency at the banks, with which nine-tenths of modern business is conducted. When a debt to a commercial bank is paid by check out of a deposit balance, that amount of deposit currency disappears. In normal times a counter-tendency restores the bank deposits by new borrowings. But in a period of falling prices when the risk is great, this restoration does not occur, and the "credit currency" is contracted. Thus we have Fisher's "debt cycle," as the leading factor in changing both the volume of credit money and the general price level.

Expected risk is what is meant by fear, or confidence, on the part of those who control industry and make themselves responsible for payments to all other participants. The risk-discount is the most important factor in present valuation. If the time-discount in the form of *waiting* permeates all prices, as Fetter shows, the time-discount in the form of *profit-forecasting* more emphatically permeates all prices. The profit-forecast is most evident in the widely fluctuating prices of common stocks, and least evident in the prices of government bonds, but it affects all prices, securities, and commodities, as is too well known. Favorable prospects of rising prices reduce the risk-discount and enlarge thereby the demand for the services of all other participants. Unfavorable forecasts increase the profit-discount and reduce both the demand and the prices offered to other participants.

The relative weights assigned by the business world at different times and places to the interest-discount and the risk-discount is a matter of the gravest importance, and has given rise, especially since the war, to the new profession of forecasting. For the first time in the history of economic science, Futurity acquires a quantitative dimension in economic theory.[277] With the world-wide monopolistic concerted action of central banks, which Wicksell proposed, and with the wide possible range of the discount rate from

[277] See article "Forecasting" by Garfield V. Cox in *Encyclopaedia of the Social Sciences*, and references there given.

as low as one per cent up to as high as 6 to 10 or higher per cent, there can be no doubt that Wicksell's proposal could be made more powerful in causing a deflation than in causing an inflation of prices. With the modern very narrow margins for profit, very few industries could continue on a world-wide bank rate of 10 per cent, whereas it is obvious that a bank rate as low as one per cent could not, of itself, stimulate an inflation of prices, if risk is unfavorable. The criticism of Wicksell should turn, not on the assumption of a permanently low bank rate, but on the present infancy of the profession of forecasting and the political dangers of entrusting so great a power as control of the Bank rate to the concerted action of central banks.

6. *Experimental Tests*

The foregoing analysis of the Thornton-Wicksell theory is confirmed somewhat by the policy of England and other countries at the time of suspending gold payments in September 1931. The Bank of England went back to the Thornton theory of 1802, as it had not done when Thornton criticized its policy after 1797. The Bank of Sweden did the same, following more immediately the Swedish economist, Wicksell. But they exaggerated the Thornton-Wicksell theory in their determination to prevent inflation of prices. They raised the bank rates respectively to 6 and 8 per cent, at which rates business enterprise, on its narrow margins of profit, could not afford to borrow and expand. They succeeded, indeed, especially Sweden, in stabilizing prices for two years at their then level of September 1931,[278] but have not brought back full employment and production, whereas the gold prices in America continued to decline rapidly with decreasing employment and production, until checked by another suspension of gold payments in March 1933, this time by executive decree of the President.

7. *War Cycles*

It is to be noted, however, and is well recognized, that the deflation of prices since 1920, which is forcing practically all countries off the gold standard, is the result, not of any "natural" tendencies, but of war-time inflation and subsequent contraction.

Wicksell, indeed, in his theory of price stabilization had expressly eliminated war and the impounding of gold for war purposes, and he could not foresee the post-war impounding of gold

[278] Cf. monthly issues of *Skandinaviska Kreditaktiebolaget*, Gothenburg. The issue of October 1933 shows, for two years, a practical stabilization of wholesale and retail prices.

by central banks. We have considered his and other theories mainly with respect to their explanation of the short-term "credit cycles" that move up and down across the long trend, up or down, of prices.

But if these so-called long trends of prices are examined, they also are credit cycles of some thirty years' duration. They have depended not so much on the accidents of gold or silver mining as on the war financing that creates demand for commodities and labor for war purposes by means of paper money and the commercial credit of central banks. The trend downwards from 1815 to 1849 followed a twenty-five year world war financed by England with Thornton's "paper credit." [279] The trend downwards from 1865 to 1897 followed an American revolution, the Civil War, and the release of specie to other countries by the substitution of government credit in the United States. The trend downwards after 1920, after a war financed by credit, may similarly be expected to continue another thirty years, to 1950, unless arrested by world-wide concerted action. At this writing, in November 1933, the nations have definitely failed to get together on all questions of national and international conflicts of interest, whether economic, monetary, or military, and the future is unpredictable. The risk-discount is 100 per cent.

There is but one point that all theories practically agree upon since Wicksell's proposals—it is more difficult, by concerted action, to *start a recovery* from a long period of depression than it is, by similar action, to *stop an inflation* that causes the succeeding deflation.

8. *Automatic and Managed Recovery*

We close the writing of this book in November 1933. For the past eight months—the first time in history—a great nation has directed its leader to show them the way to a managed recovery instead of the automatic recoveries after all preceding depressions. Only twice before, at the conclusion of two great war cycles, 1847 and 1897, have similar depths been reached. But this time, in less than 13 years, instead of 30 or more years, after the war peak of decisive prosperity, have nations taken it into their hands to bring about a managed recovery instead of leaving it to natural law. Beginning with the Communism of Lenin, the Fascism of Mussolini, and extending to the Democracy of Roosevelt, the Nazism of Hitler, the Militarism of Japan, different nations, in their own way, have

[279] Above, p. 122, Chart 1.

sought a managed recovery from the wars of their capitalistic civilizations.

In America the President has been given temporary powers by Congress to preserve the capitalist system by means of one or both of the two great profit theories descended from the world war of the French Revolution—the profit-share theory and the profit-margin theory. Like any great leader, in time of crisis, he chooses whatever, at the time, seems to be the strategic factor, and then, having made a decision on that, he leaves its routine application to subordinates while he passes on immediately to the next strategic factor. But so many are they and so complex, that hostility arises at every turn. The capitalistic elements turn toward the Fascism that would preserve their margins for profit. Others turn towards communism or voluntary collective bargaining and codes that would re-distribute the shares against an increasing, or even abolished, margin for profit.

In the midst of the kaleidoscopic changes every day no *book* or succession of books can come out rapidly enough to keep up with the turnover of civilizations. The matter is one for daily, hourly, weekly publications. A book can only develop general principles and methods of investigation. The author and all others must turn, guided as they choose to be by principles and methods, to the immediate urgent problems which crowd upon all of them more or less alike. No one can foretell what either a great leader will do or what nations will do. We leave them at this point, and we watch and participate, each in his own little corner as opportunity may offer, from day to day, and week to week.

IX. SOCIETY

1. *From Costs to Shares*

The substitution of the institutional concept of capital-yield for the physical concept of marginal productivity rests upon a still deeper foundation of social philosophy than the pragmatic theories above discussed. It goes to the nature of society itself as a working concept of economic science. It requires us to ask the question, Who is Society? Is it the capitalists? Is it the landlords? Is it the laborers? Wicksell's theory, inherited from Ricardo, Jevons, and Böhm-Bawerk, personifies society as capitalists seeking interest and profits. Society therefore has a cost of production and its net income is this interest and profit.

All economists, indeed, take the social point of view, whether they be individualists, communists, fascists, capitalists, or otherwise. This requires them to get behind the institutional transactions of buying, borrowing, money, custom, law, capitalization, in order to arrive at the physical realities. The most important reality towards which all social production is directed is consumption goods. But these same consumption goods are also the necessary conditions of subsistence on which the population is able to produce more consumption goods. Consumption goods are the beginning and ending of the social process. It is these that constitute real wages, real profits, real interest, real rent, distinguished from the nominal or institutional wages, profits, interest, and rent.

Ricardo developed the idea that social capital was not tools or machinery, but was the quantity of consumption goods furnished to laborers by capitalists and landlords. This was society's cost of production. But profits, interest, and rent were the "net revenue" of consumption goods acquired by capitalists and landlords. Thus, for Ricardo, "society" was pictured as consisting of capitalists and landlords but not of laborers. The quantity of consumption goods furnished by capitalists to laborers was real capital, whereas machinery and fertility were human inventions by which the productivity of labor was increased, so that a net revenue of profit, rent, and interest, above labor's cost of living, might be acquired. He distinguished between "labor, capital, and machinery." Machinery was not capital, it was productivity, just as fertility was nature's productivity. And social capital was the goods furnished by capitalists and consumed by laborers.[280]

Karl Marx adopted the same view. His capitalists and landlords were the proprietors who owned the "gross revenue" of consumption goods, who paid in advance to laborers a minimum of consumption goods necessary to maintain their existence; the capitalists and landlords retaining for themselves, at the end of production, for rent, interest, and profit, the surplus of consumption goods, above what they originally furnished. Marx's "surplus" was Ricardo's "net revenue" of capitalists and landlords, but, with Marx, it was totally unearned.

Jevons followed Ricardo and Marx, but with money instead of man-hours as the unit of measurement. With Jevons, also, the social capital was the quantity of consumption goods furnished to laborers, equivalent to the "investment" of capitalists; but rent, interest, and profit were the money value of the social net income of consumption goods derived by capitalists and landlords over and above the money wages they paid to laborers to purchase consumption goods.

[280] McCulloch, J. R., *Works of David Ricardo* (1888), 5, Preface.

But Jevons, by using money instead of man-hours, substituted the new and important concepts of "free" and "invested" capital for the classical and communistic concepts of "fixed" and "circulating" capital. Free, or uninvested capital, according to the concept of Jevons, later adopted by Wicksell, should not be defined so as to include all of the miscellaneous circulating commodities which prior economists had included, such as raw materials, consumption goods, inventories, money—wherein the economists were misled by the analogies of anything physically movable—but should include only the quantity of consumption goods purchased by laborers with the money wages paid to them by capitalists. These money wages were the whole of the capitalist's investment,[281] but the quantity of consumption goods purchased therewith was, not only the *real* wages, but also the social cost of production, which therefore was social capital in the sense of "free" capital. Labor's consumption goods were free capital.

When once, however, the laborers had added their work to the natural materials owned by the capitalists and this added value had become the property of the capitalists, then that much of free capital, represented by that much of labor's consumption goods, disappeared, and its equivalent became the invested capital of all the capitalists. In the theories of Jevons and Wicksell, interest, profit, and rents now became, as with Ricardo and Marx, the additional quantity of consumption goods produced by laborers over and above their own previous consumption. These additional consumption goods are the capitalists' "surplus."

Böhm-Bawerk now appeared with two changes in the theory of Ricardo, Marx, and Jevons. Labor alone—including those who receive profits as "wages of management"—cannot produce wealth. Labor and management must be assisted by the "material services" rendered by the forces of nature. Hence, from the social point of view, which ostensibly eliminates property rights, not only must laborers and managers be furnished consumption goods in advance of production, but also those who furnish the uses of nature's material forces must be paid consumption goods before production can be started. These "uses" of material services Böhm-Bawerk named "rents," not in the narrow economic sense of Ricardo's unearned increment, but in the historical meaning of rent as a payment for the *use* of anything, such as the rent of a house, the rent of a machine, the rent of a farm, the hire of a horse, the hire of a laborer, but not the interest paid for the use of capital. But these rents were not money rents, for he had eliminated money. If so his

[281] Wicksell, K., *op. cit.*, 117 ff.

rents must be consumption goods which cannot be consumed in advance before the use of capital goods could begin.

This concept of Böhm-Bawerk was adopted by Wicksell. Consumption goods therefore are not only a wage-fund (including management fund), but also a land-rent fund.[282] Their significance is that they must be furnished in advance of production in order to set to work both the workers and the material forces of nature which labor requires for production. Capitalistic economy, Böhm-Bawerk had said, consists in employing, not only labor, including management, but also the uses of land and improvements for the purpose of creating the consumption goods of the future; and, inversely, the present consumption is derived, for the most part, from the labor and land uses of the past. The physical fixed and circulating capital are the products both of labor and nature's forces, and, just as the laborers who own their labor-power must be furnished their consumption goods in advance of production, so the owners of nature's productive powers must be paid their consumption goods in advance of production. One was a wage-fund of consumption goods, the other a rent-fund of consumption goods.[283]

The idea correlated by Böhm-Bawerk with these wage and rent funds, and adopted by Wicksell, was the underestimate in the present of consumption goods in the future, and consequently a lesser quantity of *present* consumption goods is equal to a larger quantity of *future* consumption goods. Since the wage-earners and the rent-earners value the present consumption goods higher than the future goods of like kind and quantity, the capitalist who furnishes them the present consumption goods, at their present valuation, in exchange for a larger quantity of future consumption goods, gains the *agio* as interest.

The test of the distinction is whether the consumption goods are received in advance or are received at the end of the period of production. If received in advance they are the social capital of consumption goods. If received at the end of the period of production they are the natural interest of consumption goods over and above the quantity of consumption goods consumed in advance of production. "Natural interest"—that is, consumption goods for the capitalist—is *not* received in advance. It is received *after* the productive process has yielded the necessary surplus. But the "natural" wages and rents—that is, consumption goods of wage and salary earners and rent-earners—are received in advance. They therefore are Jevons' "free" capital. But any consumption goods received as

---

[282] Wicksell, K., "Lohn-und Grundrentenfond," *op. cit.*, 114, 115.
[283] Böhm-Bawerk, E. von, *The Positive Theory of Capital* (tr. 1891), 420 ff.

interest are not received in advance and are not social capital.

This introduction of futurity marks Böhm-Bawerk as one of the greatest economists, without whose insight it would have been impossible to get a clue to the modern problems.

The result, however, is a materialistic concept of society in which, along with the theories of Ricardo, Marx, and Jevons, the laborers were power-machines stoked with consumption goods by capitalists in order to produce more consumption goods for the capitalists. But, with Böhm-Bawerk, who introduced futurity into the scheme, the "rents" or "material uses" must also somehow be provided in advance before production can go on. He thus distinguished landlords, wage-earners, and all others who furnish materials, from capitalists who get their income from future production.

Yet this was a most interesting *tour de force* in order to eliminate "rights and relations" from economic science and to build it solely on materials and pleasure.[284] On the material side Böhm-Bawerk returned to the pre-Ricardian productivity of nature's forces that labored along with man, and labor itself was a power-machine that had to be fed with coal and other consumption goods. On the psychological side he made those who wait for an *interval* of time for consumption goods the only beneficiaries of the future agio of consumption goods. Thus he left no effective place for those who make profits by transactions along the successive points of time. He shifted altogether from points of time when profits are made to intervals of time during which interest accrues.

By making nature productive, the same as productive labor, he returned to the beneficent nature ideas of Quesnay and Smith. This was perfectly consistent with his general philosophy that modern life had changed from the "pain economy" of Ricardo, Senior, and Marx, to a "pleasure economy," analogous to the divine beneficence, earthly abundance, and worldly happiness of the Eighteenth Century Age of Reason. But he substituted for divine beneficence the greater technological productivity of the roundabout process.

And he brought back by a side door the rights and relations of private property which he had elaborately excluded from economic science. For certainly consumption goods are not paid to "nature." They are paid to the *owners* of nature. Thus by eliminating property he eliminated scarcity from economic science. This again was consistent with his philosophy of pleasure and abundance, for only scarce things are owned.

It was from this same philosophy of technological abundance that Böhm-Bawerk derived his doctrine of choices, under the name of

[284] Cf. Böhm-Bawerk, E. von, *Rechte und Verhältnisse* (1881).

utility-cost, or the choice between the greater and lesser of two pleasures—in this case the pleasure of present consumption and the pleasure of future consumption. In this derivation he was unmindful of the Carey-Bastiat scarcity doctrine of choice between the greater and lesser of two pains.

The question arises, Why is not interest also paid in advance by society in the form of consumption goods in order to get the owners to wait? From the individual standpoint, indeed, the one who gets interest has to forego present consumption and wait for future consumption. He does not get his *real* interest of consumption goods until the future arrives. But is this true from the social standpoint?

There are also profits to be taken into account. The term "profits," in the earlier theories, was not clearly distinguished from either interest, on the one side, or wages of management, on the other side. As wages of management they were afterwards classified with labor as compensation for managerial labor; as such, they had to be paid in advance. This was the classification by Marx, Jevons, and Böhm-Bawerk. But, even yet, profits were not effectively distinguished from interest when the assumption continued to be made that profits bore an average relationship to interest, rising when interest rises, and falling when interest falls. This assumption is incorrect.

But profits, nevertheless, are *future* profits. From the individual standpoint they also, like interest, are not paid nor even known until the future arrives. Only then do they become the *real* profits of consumption goods. But, from the social standpoint, why are not profits also, like wages and rent, paid in advance of production in order to induce those who have business ability to take on the risks and responsibilities to others of future payments of wages, rents, and interest, as well as the future principal of the loans?

These questions, however trifling they may seem, go to the nature of society itself. If society is personified, then society has a cost of production in the shape of consumption goods that must be paid in advance of production, and society turns out to be the capitalists who wait for the consumption goods that constitute interest and profit. But if society is only a word whose meaning is the concerted action of all participants in a going concern, then its costs are not costs but are merely the *shares* of the total output which participants are able to command, individually and collectively, if the concern is to be kept agoing. And the laborers are no longer power-machines like the forces of nature. They are citizens with all the legal rights and duties of landlords and capitalists. Society, of course, knows nothing of pain, or cost, or waiting, or income, or value, or profit. It knows nothing at all. All that is known is known and acted upon by individuals. And what they know is how much of a *share* of the social output they can get if they are considered to be a part of the concern and if they participate to keep it agoing.

Hence, social cost is not a cost—it is a *share* of the social output acquired by individuals through the existing institutions of property. It is a share, not paid in advance, but *negotiated* in advance in order to induce all classes to refrain from withholding what they own and others need. It matters not whether the share is "earned" or "unearned." It is nevertheless a share which the institutions of property, liberty, and government require to be paid in the continuing future in order that the concern may continue to go. All participants, and not merely capitalists, are acting in expectation of the future. Hence all *expected* consumption goods, whether the most luxurious and extravagant living, or the meagerest consumption of the poorest laborers, or even the consumption of goods by children, beggars, and insane, are to be considered, not social costs, but social shares of production. Institutionally the last mentioned may appear as taxes. Socially they are consumption goods to be bought with the taxes. Consequently, all consumption goods are the social capital required to be consumed continuously, under existing institutions of property and government, in order that production may continue as it actually does or does not.

Thus there are revealed two contending views of society—the mechanistic and the institutional. The mechanistic eliminates private property but brings it back by the side door of ownership, in order to set up the inducements which lead people to work, to save, and to take risks for the production of future consumption goods. The institutional view is the ownership itself, which sets up the inducements which organized society holds out to keep the concern agoing. The mechanistic view has the tangible reality of physical things which can be handled, consumed, enjoyed, produced. It appeals to common sense and is the solid ground of the materialistic and psychological schools of economists. The institutional view is quite intangible because all of the physical things which it contemplates are in the immediate or remote future, and they exist only in the present expectations of stability of collective action. These present expectations we name negotiational psychology, which is collective forecasting.

Nevertheless, none of the participants can live on *future* consumption goods. Each of them must have the goods now. The modern institutional set-up, if it works smoothly, provides consumption goods *now* by means of both interest and risk discount. Böhm-Bawerk's futurity is property-rights.

2. *The Whole and Its Parts*

(1) **Mechanism, Organism, Concern.**—Whitehead has observed that the Eighteenth Century method of science had no notion of the organic unity of the whole in a changing relation of the parts to the whole. Hence, in formulating the method of modern science he constructs a formula of an "event" occurring at a moment of time and an "organic mechanism" as the changing time-succession of events. The "event" has the properties of retention, endurance, reiteration, and is, as it were, a cross-section of the moving mechanism at a moment of time. But the mechanism itself is "organic" in that it is a kind of prolonged interweaving of changing events, having, as Whitehead says, a past, a present realization, and a future life in its present events.[285]

Evidently when Whitehead injected the ideas "organic mechanism" and "future life" into the physical sciences, from the proton to the universe, he introduced metaphors transferred from living creatures and the human mind. We need, therefore, to distinguish a physical mechanism from a living organism, and an organism from the corresponding social institution, which we name a going concern. Whitehead's "organic mechanism" is, less metaphorically, a moving mechanism; but a living body, from microbe to man, is a going and dying organism; while a social institution is a purposeful going concern which lives in the future but acts in the present. If we seek to carry out the parallelism, then a mechanism is a succession of dead events; that which corresponds, in a living organism, to an event in physics is the metabolism which changes dead matter into living matter and back again; and the corresponding "events" in a social organization are the transactions whose expected repetition and working rules are a going concern.

If we seek for distinguishing marks by which these different types of the part-whole relation can be unified in their own field, we shall seek for principles which shall be peculiar to each. This analysis follows the methodological pattern set up in the foregoing discussion of ideal types. For this purpose the principle of nature's mechanism is blind pressure; the principle of organism is struggle for life; the principle of going concerns is concerted action for ends

[285] Whitehead, A. N., *Science and the Modern World* (1926); see also Smuts, J. C., *Holism and Evolution* (1926), and Akeley, L. E., "Wholes and Prehensive Unities for Physics and Philosophy," *Jour. of Phil.* XXIV (1927), 589, and "Knowing Something without Knowing Everything Else, as a Prerequisite in Electricity and Heat," *Jour. of Engineering Education*, XVIII (1928), 207.

foreseen in the future. In other words, the principle of Nature's Mechanism is Energy, that of Organism is Scarcity, that of Going Concerns is Willingness.

The reasons for seeking these unifying principles are found in the relations of the parts to the whole, and this is but another way of stating a doctrine of relativity. Each part performs a function in maintaining the existence of the whole, so that a change originating in one part is followed by changes in all of the others, and therefore followed by a change in the whole mechanism, organism, or concern. These functional changes, going on among the parts, are themselves respectively the events, metabolisms, or transactions; their repetition, under whatever may be their peculiar rules of action, is the mechanism, organism, or concern. Of course, by the terms Energy, Scarcity, and Willingness we mean not a substance nor entity, but a principle of similarity running through all the changing parts, actually constructed by the mind of the investigator to keep together the parts in a persistent form of unity.

But these going concerns have two parts, neither of which is mechanism or organism, because each represents two kinds of control by the human will. We name the one a Going Plant, or the expected technological control over nature. The other is a Going Business, or the expected succession of transactions, applicable to conflict of interests, mutual dependence, and the working rules which bring order out of conflict.

Thus, the term "going" has a different meaning from the "moving mechanism" which we suggested above as applicable to the physical sciences. A going concern exists only as long as there are expectations. It actually lives in the future and acts in the present, because it is the human will now acting towards future results. But there is no such principle in a moving mechanism applied to nature's physical forces. It simply "goes" and does not expect to go in one direction or another, nor to use instruments in the present which shall lead to anything in the future. But the going technological plant and the going business are constructed by the human will and are expected by the will to go somewhere. If the expectations cease they quit going.

Each of these parts, the Going Plant and the Going Business, may be treated as a whole in its own right, with its own "events" at a point of time, provided the two are not so conceived that each is independent of the Going Concern which is the larger whole of which they are parts.

With this precaution the term "mechanism," as applied to forces of nature under human control, is misleading. The proper term is an artificial mechanism culminating in such a term as the "machine age," which begins with stone tools and ends with wireless. Along with this is the other artificial mechanism, the going business. Each depends on the collective will. For these reasons we construct two types of economy, each dependent on the other, the engineering economy whose principle is efficiency, and the proprietary economy whose principle is scarcity.

The word "economy" itself means the whole activity of proportioning the parts so as to get the largest result or the minimum effort. Hence the term "economy" has always meant a part-whole relationship. But the more precise and measurable formula of this part-whole relation has been developing at the hands of economists during the past forty years as the two related formulae of Turnover and Limiting and Complementary Factors. The first marks the transition from older ideas of physical circulation to the modern ideas of velocity of repetition. The second marks the transition from mechanical theories of equilibrium to volitional control of the forces of nature and the activities of other people. Turnover is the velocity of repetition, but control of limiting factors is the extent to which advantage can be taken of these slow or rapid repetitions in directing future changes towards desired ends.

(2) **Velocity of Repetition.**—In the foregoing discussion of Turnover [286] we noted the estimate of an average period of production, introduced by Böhm-Bawerk, as five years from the consumption goods furnished to participants to the consumption goods produced by his "roundabout" method of production. Böhm-Bawerk stated this in terms of Ricardo's quantity of labor-power but Jevons stated it in terms of the investment of money paid to wage-earners for the use of labor-power. Wicksell adopted the concept of Jevons and constructed the idea of an average period of investment. This period is the average length of long-time bonds issued for the construction of capital.

It is this, then, that is Wicksell's average period of investment. For, what is it that remains to the capitalist after wages, profits, rent, and interest have been paid and the physical things thereby produced are immediately used up as raw material or gradually used up by depreciation? There does not remain for him the money payments which he has made, nor, of course, the consumption goods purchased and consumed by all who have been paid for their contributions. There remains only a book account of all expenditures made for the production of technological capital, at their then prices. This book account is Wicksell's individual "investment," but the

[286] Above, p. 294, From Circulation to Repetition.

average duration of all such investments is the average period both of production and of investment.

Wicksell was required by his concept of social turnover to compare the total quantity of consumption goods appearing as natural capital with the larger total quantity of consumption goods appearing as natural income during the period of turnover. The *excess* larger quantity at the end of the period was determined by the marginal productivity of capital. This was his natural interest. Hence is seen the significance of his introduction of a stable average of prices in order to obtain a concept of a stable magnitude of consumption goods as natural capital.[287] By assuming the average of prices to remain stable during the period of production, then money would be virtually eliminated and there would remain only changes in the quantity of consumption goods between the beginning and ending of the period. A greater or less enlargement would depend on the marginal productivity of the capital and would go to investors and entrepreneurs as interest and profit. Thus, taking Wicksell's illustration: suppose that investors pay $1,000,000 as wages and rent at the beginning of the period, and the laborers and landlords purchase therewith $1,000,000 worth of consumption goods, but that the goods sold to the laborers and landlords by the capitalists at the end of a year bring a return of only $1,000,000, assuming the average of prices to remain stable—in this case there will be nothing left for interest and profits. But if marginal productivity is such that the consumption goods sold at the end of the year to laborers and landlords yielded $1,100,000, then, assuming stability of prices, the marginal productivity has increased the quantity of consumption goods 10 per cent, and this 10 per cent increase goes to investors as "natural interest." If the marginal productivity has effected an increase of only 6 per cent in the quantity of consumption goods, the average of prices remaining stable, then natural interest will be 6 per cent, and so on.

It must, however, be noted that Ricardo, Marx, and Böhm-Bawerk accomplished by their "average labor-power" the same purpose of constructing the concept of a constant magnitude of capital that Wicksell accomplished by his stability of the average of prices. They did it by the same device of assuming a constant purchasing power of money, but they substituted average labor-power for average purchasing power.

It is therefore to be noticed that Wicksell's theory of natural interest does not confuse physical productivity with value productivity,

[287] Ricardo's assumption of stability of prices was that of particular prices and not the average of prices. The reason is that he used money-price as equivalent to man-hours.

as has been asserted.[288] He fully takes account of the two variable dimensions of value, namely, quantities and prices. Physical productivity is the production of quantities, but "value" productivity is the money income received by selling those quantities at current prices. In Wicksell's theory the prices are not eliminated—they are only assumed to remain constant by assuming a stable average of prices. With this assumption, then the variable quantity is the marginal productivity. By overlooking Wicksell's concept of a stable average of prices one may be misled into thinking that Wicksell confused value productivity with physical productivity. He did not confuse them, but by assuming a constant average of prices, his value productivity changed in proportion to his marginal productivity.

Ricardo's "natural capital" was the quantity of consumption goods destined for laborers and measured by the number of average man-hours required to produce it. He did not consider that either machinery or fertility were capital—they were only instruments which increased the productivity of labor employed in manufactures and agriculture above the quantity of goods consumed in the process, measured by the average man-hour. Capital, for Ricardo, was the quantity of consumption goods required by laborers, and its changing magnitude was measured by a constant unit—the average labor-power required to produce it. Any excess of consumption goods above this constant magnitude, created by the productivity of machines or fertility of soil, afforded rent, interest, and profit.[289]

But the physical meaning of Capital, like the orthodox meaning of wealth, had the double meaning of materials and ownership. Marx followed Ricardo but took the ownership meaning instead of the physical meaning. He had a similar constant unit of measurement, the average man-hour, which gave to him the similar labor-value of the output. But his "capital" was the value of the ownership, instead of Ricardo's value of the materials.

We endeavor in this book to correct these static double meanings, by substituting terms of activity. The activity terms that correspond to materials are input of labor and output of use-value. The activity terms that correspond to ownership are the outgo of money, which is investment, and the income of money which is sales of output.

For it is not materials, after all, that are created by the input of labor. It is the use-values of materials, and these use-values are the output which is sold. The total social output is the total creation

---

[288] Above, p. 378, Fetter and Fisher.
[289] Cf. *The Works of David Ricardo*, as cited above, p. 348.

of new use-values all the way from the earth to the retailer, to take the place of those worn out, obsolete, and consumed. If, then, the technological turnover occurs once in five years, the meaning is that the total of use-values created by all the manual, mental, and managerial labor is used up and recreated, on the average, once in five years, or at a rate of combined depreciation, obsolescence, and consumption equal to 20 per cent of the total per year. One fifth of the total use-values of all kinds, during the average period of production, must be created each year in order to replace depreciation, obsolescence, and consumption.

But the transfers of ownership proceed as we have suggested, at a rate perhaps 70 to 100 times as fast. For the nation as a whole it is enough to suppose that the proprietary turnover is 100 times as rapid as the turnover of material output. It may be 200 times as rapid in periods of speculation, or only 50 times as rapid in a period of extreme depression.

Three things must be observed regarding what we here name the proprietary or financial turnover distinguished from the technological turnover. One is the identity of money with the value of titles. Another is the turnover of debits. The third is the turnover of loans that authorize the debits.

The turnover of titles of ownership or legal control is identical with the turnover of the money value of the titles. One check for $1,000,000 on the securities market counts for velocity the same as one thousand checks of $1,000 each on the commodity and labor markets. Or $100,000 checked out for cash to be distributed in the pay envelopes of 5,000 employes counts no more than a check of $100,000 paid for securities. The so-called "money in circulation," which pays mainly laborers and retailers, is just so much debited to depositor's accounts. The subordinate "hand to hand" circulation is dominated by the debits to accounts.

Hence each debit is an "outgo" from the depositor's assets in exchange for a title of ownership of securities, commodities, or labor output, and, while the labor process is slowly adding use-values to materials, the same materials now become commodities on account of ownership, may change ownership ten to fifteen times at the hands of middlemen before any material change has been made in the materials themselves.

What happens on the money market is a quantity of deposits, say fifty billion dollars, which seems to be a quantity of money, but is a repetition of debt transactions, estimated to occur every 15 to 20 days, on the average. A quantity of debts is created by valuations of titles made in transactions and represented by checks drawn against banks for payment of other debts contracted in the purchase of other titles of ownership. If the average volume of deposit debts owed by bankers is fifty billion dollars and the turnover is 20 times per year, then the actual values of titles transferred in bargaining transactions are 1,000 millions of dollars per year.

Each sale of a title is a new credit at the bank and a new set of debits to accounts. These debits to accounts are only partly an outgo for commodities. Possibly a third or a half of them, as investigation might show, are payments for intangible or incorporeal properties. The stock exchanges require a huge quantity of credits and debits, with a rapid turnover. Payments of interest due represent no transfer of commodity values. Payments of taxes likewise. In fact all payments of all debts created by any kind of transaction may be condensed into the single term "transfers of titles of ownership at valuations equivalent to debits." The record of these transferred values, if complete, would be the total of all debits to accounts, the debits representing the creation, sale, and extinction of debts equivalent to the valuations of titles of ownership made at bargaining transactions.

The other part of the financial or property turnover is the turnover of the loans themselves, which create the deposits. We may estimate the rate of loan transactions at 12 times per year or once per month. Thus while the technological turnover is perhaps once in 1500 days, and the loan turnover is once in 30 days, the debit turnover is once in 15 days. Each is highly variable in time, place, and kind, but the figures are guesses at their ordinary relative velocities.

While the debits to accounts are reducible to transfers of ownership at the valuations indicated, they conceal the differences between the objects owned, and require further analysis on that account. An important difference is that existing between the creation of new commodities and the transfer of ownership of existing commodities. The creation of new commodities is the labor process merely adding the use-values of form, time, and place to the materials of nature. Its measurable equivalent is the man-hour input.

But these same workers are owners of their labor-power and must be paid, not for their output, but for their input of labor power. Their output goes off on the commodity markets. The title to their input of labor-power is specialized on the labor market, but in all such cases as self-employment it is concealed in the prices of their output. These may be named concealed or commuted wages.

This is the familiar distinction on the stock market between putting out "new issues" and refunding old issues: New issues mean new construction or expansion of equipment. Thus wages, explicit or concealed, are "new issues" for the creation of new use-values— but these are refunded by transfers of titles to the new use-values on the commodity markets, with allowances for profits, interest, and rents.

This is equivalent to the distinction made by Jevons and Wicksell, in their concept of investment. Investment was the wages, explicit or implied, paid for the labor-power, or input, which creates new use-values, but the sale of commodities is a transfer of investments, a kind of refunding of old issues.

Thus, by the concept of turnover, or velocity of repetition, we reach a solution of the apparent paradox that all the consumption goods of society are both social capital and social income. If we employ Böhm-Bawerk's average period of production as a usable economic concept, but add to it the institutional concept of owner-ship, then it is the period during which all fixed and circulating capital, which we name technological capital—the equivalent of investment when bought with money—is being converted from the consumption goods going to all participants as income, and is being reproduced as saleable output by the use of all the instruments which all participants have been induced by expected consumption goods to contribute.

During this average period of production, say five years, all the "savings" of society—which now we may name ownership of ma-terial goods—also disappear. But they reappear as ownership of new products. By taking the estimated five years, instead of one year, even all of the use-values in their technological form as well as their ownership form of investment, disappear and are renewed in possibly five years, on the average, while their change in ownership is renewed once in 15 days, on the average. Thus there is only a double process, at different rates of velocity—a process which has no beginning and no ending—of consuming, producing, and consum-ing; of investing, debt-paying, debt-renewing; of ownership and liquidation.

The concept of a rate of turnover, as we have said, like all human interpretations, is only a mental device for setting up a beginning and an ending of that which never begins nor ends, and thus enables us better to prepare for it. If, on the average, all human products are known to be created and to disappear within five years, then a better understanding is had of the large expenditures needed for depreciation and obsolescence, and of the evil of extending debts to future generations as well as increasing the burden of debts by cutting prices, instead of maintaining prices adequate to pay for depreciation and obsolescence as you go along. And, if money is created, and recreated 30 times a year by loan transactions, then it is not a circulation of physical things beyond human control, but is a continually disappearing quantity that can be made to reappear or not, according to collective human volitions.

We thus can see the significance of Wicksell's theory of the regulation of the general price level by concerted action of banks in changing the bank rate. It requires, say, only 30 days for the total volume of deposits to be changed by a raising or lowering of the bank rate. This change in quantity of deposits may reflect a change in the volume of transfers of ownership, or a change in the prices at which they are transferred, or a change in the quantity of short-term loans and discounts.

Thus the institutional set-up of society is the changing assets and liabilities of individuals and concerns, which are, in turn, the economic inducements that lead to working, waiting, and risking. It is the system of bargaining, taxing, and forecasting, made effective by collective action, which expands, or restricts, or shifts input and output in different directions or to different times of the near or remote future. It is the set-up of bargaining and rationing transactions, sanctioned by law, which both determine the shares of the social output and keep the social concern going or not-going. But the engineering set-up of society is the march of the physical, biological, and psychological sciences, which give to mankind its command over nature and human nature, to be used for happiness or destruction according to the collective action of the world's pay and performance communities.

3. *Strategic and Routine Transactions* [290]

While the formula of turnover has given us the statistical measurement of the part-whole relationship among economic transactions, it is the formula of Limiting and Complementary Factors, which, when changed to strategic and routine transactions, indicates the volitional process itself by which these results are attained. This formula of limiting and complementary factors has been gradually constructed since the time of Ricardo, until now it has become a highly important instrument of investigation, by means of which the older analogies of equilibrium give way to the actual process of human ability in controlling, through transactions, the physical and social environment. Hence the formula has two applications:

[290] Above, p. 52, Transactions and Concerns; below, p. 840, Accidents and Unemployment.

the control of physical forces through managerial transactions leading to greater or less efficiency measured by the ratio of output to input; and the control of other persons through bargaining transactions measured by the ratio of outgo to income. One is a going plant, the other is a going business. Hence we shall designate the one as the Efficiency meaning, the other as the Scarcity meaning, of Limiting and Complementary Factors. One is the Control of nature, the other the Control of other persons. The combination of the two, in the volitional meaning of strategic and routine transactions, is the meaning of going concern.

(1) Efficiency.—Man, of course, as has often been said, does not create something out of nothing. He merely controls the forces of nature so that they work for him. The results of this work are use-values. Hence use-value is not something passive attributed to external objects. It is the active energies of nature brought under control by man for his purposes. Their chemical, physical, and biological energies are nature's elements, or the "substance" of use-value, usually known as "elementary" utilities or, rather elementary use-values. But these elements are merely the activities of nature unutilized. They do not properly become use-values until they are used, and this means that they are not use-values until man puts his brains, hands, and management at work to control them. If there are 200,000 chemical compounds unknown to nature, it is these that are use-values. Nature's elements are useless to man unless his manual, mental, and managerial powers are used to make them work in the way he wants them to work. All that he does is to move them so as to change their form, time, or place, and to hold them without interference during the time needed to let them work out their own results. Through manual labor he moves them directly by his own physical power. Through mental labor he moves them indirectly by moving other things so that their own activities will work out results intended in wider space and future time. Through managerial labor he moves other people to move them.

This volitional process of controlling a strategic factor, through labor-power, in order that it, or its own energy, may control many other energies of nature is universal from the time when man first invented tools to the time when wave-lengths of the air do his bidding. Its universality is the principle of "limiting and complementary factors." The limiting factor is the one whose control, in the right form, at the right place and time, will set the complementary factors at work to bring about the results intended. A very little potash, if that is the limiting factor, will multiply the grain yield from perhaps five bushels to twenty bushels per acre. The sagacious mechanic is the one who busies himself with control of the limiting factor, knowing that the complementary factors will work out the results intended. The flutterbudget wastes his time on the complementary factors.

But the limiting and complementary factors are continually changing places. What was the limiting factor becomes complementary, when once it has come under control; then another factor is the limiting one. The limiting factor, in the operation of an automobile, at one time may be the electric spark, at another the gasoline, at another the man at the wheel. This is the meaning of efficiency— the control of the changeable limiting factors at the right time, right place, right amount, and right form in order to enlarge the total output by the expected operation of complementary factors.

We condense these changing factors of control into the volitional term, Timeliness. At its highest point of ideal efficiency it is the control of all complementary factors by controlling the changeable limiting factors at exactly the right time, place, form, and quantity.

It follows from this relation between limiting and complementary factors, since all are necessary to the whole operation of production, that the greatest efficiency is the best proportioning of all the factors in time and place. The intelligent manager of a farm or a factory is the one who knows promptly which is the limiting factor; when he controls it promptly, so that all factors are working smoothly together, he points with pride to what he calls his "good organization." What he means is that there is no limiting factor that holds back any or all of the others. The greatest efficiency has been obtained under the existing state of the sciences and the arts, because he has brought under control all of the limiting factors, which in turn are all the complementary factors.

Thus we can rightly say, regarding the operations of the human will, that the whole is more than the sum of its parts. The whole is not a total, it is a multiple. If a pile of coal is fed to the flames at the right time, right amount, right spread and quality, then the forces of nature multiply the puny effort of the stoker into a locomotive at sixty miles an hour. Nature knows nothing of limiting and complementary factors. Man reads them into Nature. They are wholly artificial. Nature's forces move on blindly and inevitably. But man interrupts them for his own purposes, and, if he knows which are the parts on which the whole depends, then he multiplies their effects into an output that they never intended. But if he would know how much he has multiplied he would measure the result not by dollars and cents, but by man-hours. The greatest efficiency is the greatest output per man-hour, or least man-hour input per given output. It multiplies the forces of labor and nature far more than they would be if merely added together. In a process of human activity the whole is greater than the sum of its parts.

(2) Scarcity.—But the scarcity meaning of limiting and complementary factors does not multiply the forces of nature—it merely transfers their ownership. The whole is no greater than the existing efficiency has made it. But some of the parts necessary to the whole may have a greater scarcity than the others, and since they are owned by different persons, their relative scarcities determine the prices at which they are bought. Since a multitude of limiting and complementary factors are necessary in any going concern, and since all of these are owned by somebody, a price must be paid for the legal right to own, use, and control them to the exclusion of other persons. The limiting factor now is the one which is relatively scarce and must be purchased in larger quantity or higher price, in order to keep the complementary factors agoing. We name its purchase the strategic transaction.

It follows that a variety of prices must be paid according to the relative scarcities of the several factors. The locomotive engineer, or the general manager, or the land site accessible to markets, is relatively scarce compared with the maintenance-of-way laborers, the errand boy, or the land used for agriculture. The universal principle, therefore derived from the scarcity meaning of limiting and complementary factors, is that the owners of the more slowly increasing and relatively irreplaceable factors of production absorb, as Professor Patten has said,[291] in their bargaining transactions, a larger share of the total money value of the product than the more rapidly increasing and readily replaceable factors. The limiting factors are those which are relatively scarce and irreplaceable, the complementary factors are those which are relatively abundant and replaceable. Their relative scarcities and abundance are measured, not by man-hours, but by dollars and cents.

Hence there is no constant or recognizable connection between the two meanings of the universal principle of limiting and complementary factors, or its volitional equivalent, strategic and routine transactions. In fact they belong to two different economies—the engineering economy of managerial transactions, and the proprietary economy of bargaining transactions. The fact that a small amount of potash multiplies greatly the *output* does not mean that the *price* of the potash shall be a monopolistic price or a cut-price. Engineering economy is the relation of man to nature. Here a little potash may play a great part. Proprietary economy is the relation of man

[291] Patten, S. N., *The Theory of Dynamic Economics* (1892), 18.

to man. Here a little potash may cost a little price, or a great price. The price of the limiting factor in engineering economy has nothing whatever to do with its efficiency. It has only to do with its scarcity. We cannot say that the labor of the engineer, the labor of the general manager, or the acre of urban land produces more wealth than that of the common laborer, the errand boy, or the acre of farm land, merely because the owners can get higher prices for their sale or use. All that we can say is that the engineer, the general manager, and the urban land are scarcer. The difference is preserved when we measure productivity by man-hours and scarcity by dollars.

Hence, the difference between the efficiency meaning and the scarcity meaning of limiting and complementary factors is that the control of limiting factors in the former case multiplies the output, but in the latter case it only transfers a larger share of the output at the expense of smaller shares of other people.

This question came to an issue between Menger and Wieser. Menger contended that control of the limiting factor multiplies the output. Wieser contended that it does not. The explanation is that neither of them distinguished efficiency from scarcity, although it is evident that Menger was speaking of efficiency and Wieser of scarcity. Neither of them uses the terms limiting and complementary factors. Both are speaking of "complementary factors." [292] But if we transfer their language to the volitional process, then the limiting factor is the one whose control is sought in order to control indirectly the complementary factors in its two meanings: efficiency which multiplies output; scarcity which transfers ownership.

Here again, in the bargaining transactions, the principle of Timeliness again appears, not as the augmentation of wealth in managerial transactions, but as the augmentation of assets for one person and the equivalent reduction of assets for other persons. The business man who buys when prices are low, who sells when prices are high, who withholds purchases until prices fall or withholds sales until they rise, who buys and sells at the right time and right quantity, augments his assets more than his competitor, who buys and sells at the wrong time. All of the factors which he needs are complementary to the business as a whole, but their prices are changeable. It is his judgment that decides the timeliness of his purchase of the limiting factors and his sale of the complementary or replaceable factors. But in doing this he does not enlarge the commonwealth—he only transfers the ownership.

[292] Menger, Carl, *Grundsätze der Volkswirthschaftslehre* (1871), 11 *passim;* Wieser, F. von, *Natural Value* (Malloch translation, 1930 ed.), 101 ff.

It is this distinction between efficiency and scarcity that enables us to see the double meaning of the word "marketing"—a labor process and a bargaining process. The labor-managerial process is the creation of place-utilities by delivery of the product to other laborers, but the bargaining process is the agreement on prices and values between owners of the product and owners of purchasing power. The distinction becomes important in the discussion of "coöperative marketing." Does coöperation mean more efficient marketing than that of the displaced middleman, measured by man-hours, or does it mean higher scarcity-values by greater power to withhold supply, measured by dollars? If it means the first, then coöperative marketing is coöperative production of wealth. If it means the second, then coöperative marketing is collective bargaining. If it means the former, then it is a managerial process which augments the use-values by adding place-utility (use-value). If it means the latter, then it is an ownership process which augments scarcity-values for one party and decreases them for the other party by relative bargaining ability.[293]

Thus the double meaning of the formula of limiting and complementary factors is its efficiency meaning and its scarcity meaning. The limiting factor in the production process is the one whose control sets the complementary factors in motion towards augmenting the output of use-values. The limiting factor in the bargaining process is the one whose ownership enables the owner to obtain, as income, a larger share of the total income, at the expense of a smaller share for others.

The part-whole relationship, in either case, appears in its two formulae of turnover and limiting factors, the one representing the statistical effects, the other the volitional control which uses or causes the effects. For, the terms "cause and effect" do not apply to the forces of nature. In nature, things merely "happen." But out of the complex happenings, man selects the limiting factors for his purposes. If he can control these, then the other factors work out the effects intended. The "cause" is volitional control of the limiting or strategic factors through managerial or bargaining transactions. The "effects" are the operations of the complementary factors and the repetition of routine transactions.

In either case volitional control depends on knowledge of the relations between the part and the whole. The whole is relatively constant though the parts are changing with greater or less velocity; and the whole is relatively constant only if the control of the changing limiting factors is judicious and timely. Stripped of what is

[293] Below, p. 749, Politics.

misleading in the analogies of equilibrium and turnover, we have the volitional process of repetition of managerial and bargaining transactions, creating, replacing, enlarging, or diminishing wealth by managing, and assets by bargaining, through strategic control of the respective changeable limiting factors.

(3) **Concerns.**—While the efficiency meaning and the scarcity meaning of limiting and complementary factors are entirely different, the meaning of going concerns is the whole of which both managerial and bargaining transactions are parts. Since the time of Ricardo with his diminishing efficiency of labor in agriculture, or of Turgot with his diminishing efficiency of capital-goods in all industries, economists have sensed, piecemeal, the doctrine of the part-whole relation implied in limiting and complementary factors. Carl Menger, in 1871,[294] advanced the doctrine decidedly by his formal theory of complementary goods wherein the missing factor in a total complement of land, labor, and capital, puts the other factors out of employment. This was the efficiency meaning of marginal productivity. But it is readily converted to the marginal utility theory of satisfactions. The marginal utility theory is the scarcity aspect of the doctrine of limiting and complementary factors. Each is the doctrine of proportioning the quantities of all the complementary factors needed to produce a desired result, in such a way that the maximum use-value or maximum scarcity-value shall be obtained, and this proportion, mathematically, is such that the marginal units are equal. Each factor diminishes in subjective utility as its supply increases. If the supply is too great, the additional subjective utility furnished by it is less than could be obtained if other factors (which now become limiting factors) were increased in quantity, and their subjective utility thereby diminished.

The doctrine evidently is true if prices are substituted for their subjective personification in terms of utility. If the price of one of the complementary factors declines, then the tendency is to purchase more of that factor, but if the greater quantity produced becomes thereby disproportioned to the others, then the total net income from all may be diminished. The remedy is either to restrict the purchase of this now complementary factor, or to increase the purchases of the now limiting factors. Thus the marginal increments obtained from each unit of money are made equal, thereby obtaining the maximum net income for the total expenditure. This is also a well-known and universal principle of technology, known as the "optimum" or the "best proportioning of the factors," or a "good organization" which, in more technical terms, is the process

[294] Menger, Carl, *Grundsätze der Volkswirthschaftslehre* (1871); 2d ed. (1923), 23.

of controlling the limiting factors in order that all the complementary factors may produce the maximum net output.

That meaning of efficiency-value, therefore, which is concrete in the actual transactions of a going plant, is the relative importance imputed to what is believed will turn out to be the limiting factor, the control of which at the present time and place is expected not only to obtain or retain control of the desired complementary factors, but also to produce the maximum net output from the whole operating concern. The factors themselves are continually changing their relations to each other. What is now a limiting factor becomes complementary when once it has been controlled. Then another factor becomes the limiting one in order to retain or expand the results from that which previously had been the limiting factor, but which is now complementary.

This doctrine of limiting and complementary factors in its objective meaning, or strategic and routine transactions in its volitional meaning, may be said to be the whole of the theory of political economy, just as it is the whole of the human will in its activity of seeking control of the environment, and is therefore an economic theory of the will. In this respect the doctrine may be distinguished as having three applications widely different in detail yet inseparable in fact, namely, scarcity, efficiency, and going concerns. The scarcity and efficiency applications we have already discussed as leading to confusion when the scarcity aspect and the efficiency aspect are not distinguished. It is the distinctions (which we have found also to be confused by the courts), between the going plant and the going business, which, working together in the larger range of limiting and complementary factors, constitute the going concern of a single enterprise or even of a whole nation.[295] The best going plant is one where the technological factors are rightly proportioned by managerial transactions; the best going business is one where the purchases and sales are rightly proportioned by bargaining transactions; the best going concern is one where technology and business are rightly proportioned. The best nation is that where rights, duties, liberties, and exposures are best rationed among individuals and classes. The technological economy is efficiency; the business economy is scarcity; the going concern economy is technology and business; the national economy is political economy. Each is a special case of strategic and routine transactions.

The technological economy is a "machine" distinguished from nature's mechanisms. For the doctrine of limiting and complementary factors is founded wholly on the principle of willingness

[295] Commons, John R., *Legal Foundations of Capitalism.*

and is even the whole of willingness in its concrete aspect of controlling the environment. The doctrine does not apply to nature's mechanisms where there are only centripetal and centrifugal forces, or conservation and dissipation of energy, without any purpose or planning for the future and therefore without any limiting factors on whose control the future events depend. A natural mechanism, such as an atom or a universe, knows no scarcity, no wants, no overpopulation, no limited resources, no economizing, no purpose, no futurity. It has therefore no limiting and complementary factors among which it chooses to perform, avoid, or forbear. It is mere energy as explained by Newton's laws of motion, or Einstein's relativity of time and space, or the laws of thermo-dynamics, or the conservation of energy, each of which, however, from the human point of view, is amazingly wasteful.

But when the mind of man constructs and operates a mechanism it is no longer Mechanism, it is Machine. A machine is the human will handed on from generation to generation by the institutions of language, number, custom, weights, measures, and so on. Here the factors—not of Whitehead's natural mechanism, but of artificial machine—become limiting and complementary, because futurity, purpose, economy, efficiency, have been put into them by the will of man. The limiting factor now is the one, such as a lever, or throttle, or wire, or gasoline, upon which, at the moment, depends the operation of the whole—made up, as it is, of all the complementary factors. If the operator physically controls the limiting factor at the right time, right place, and right amount, and if he controls one machine which is a limiting factor for other machines, then he has more than mechanism—he has a machine as a whole, or a going plant as a whole. In the agricultural plant, for example, at one time it may be that potash is the limiting factor, then nitrogen, then human labor, then managerial ability, and so on. Each of these is "input" and their best correlation yields the "optimum" which is the maximum output relative to total input, measurable as "efficiency." And, instead of the older doctrine of the Eighteenth Century that cause and effect are equal, we have a cause, the limiting factor, which when introduced by man, multiplies the effect desired far beyond anything known to nature. A very little potash added to the soil, when nature does not accidentally supply it, multiplies the combined output of all the factors from one or two bushels to twenty or thirty bushels per acre. But this is man's will, not nature's "economy."

In the biological mechanism, from amœba to man, that which corresponds to event in mechanisms and to transactions in going concerns is metabolism, the repetition and correlation of which is organism. Here is the entirely new science of Life and Death, and it is to the great credit of Darwin that he started the science of organism without borrowing any analogies from Newton's science of mechanism. There has, as yet, been discovered no scientific principle that can account for the origin of organism out of mechanism. Darwin's problem therefore was the Origin of Species, not the Origin of Life. His was a new concept, discontinuous from that of mechanism, the concept of Living Organism. And, if we examine the constituent details of Darwin's concept of organism we find that they are not "Life," of which we know nothing, but are the various ways in which Life acts. These ways in which Life acts are the variable motions conditioned upon that interaction between an organism, in which abilities are themselves limited, and that also limited environment of mechanisms and organisms which we name "limited natural resources." It is these actions and reactions between organism and environment which we name, not Life, but the Principle of Scarcity. They are Heredity, Overpopulation, Variation, Struggle, Death, and finally Survival of those organisms fitted, for the time, to obtain and use the limited natural resources. This concept of organism differs entirely from the concept of mechanism, whose underlying principle, Energy, may be expressed as a generalization of the three components, Pressure, Volume, and Time. Where Newton and his successors worked out the principle of Energy as the ways in which mechanism acts, Darwin worked out the principle of Scarcity as the ways in which organism acts.

But even so, Darwin distinguished between "natural selection" and "artificial selection." Artificial selection bears to Natural selection the relation that Machine bears to Mechanism. It is "artificial" simply because it is Purpose, Futurity, Planning, injected into and greatly controlling the struggle for life. Darwin admitted that his term "natural selection" was a misnomer, and regretted his resort to metaphor. It is more properly blind selection, while the artificial kind is purposeful selection. Natural selection, which is natural survival of the "fit," produces wolves, snakes, poisons, destructive microbes; but artificial selection converts wolves into dogs, nature's poisons into medicines, eliminates the wicked microbes, and multiplies the good microbes. A Holstein cow could not survive if left to natural selection—she is a monstrosity created by artificial selection for the sake of the good she can do for man in the future. She is truly, not Whitehead's organic mechanism, but man's organic machine, relieved from nature's principle of scarcity and converted into man's institution of private property.

Yet, so powerful was Darwin's achievement of natural selection that when economists and sociologists came to the problem of society and civilization, Darwin's concept of natural organism became, by analogy again, the foundation of their concepts of society, which reached their peak of absurdity at the hands of Herbert Spencer. Society was a "social organism," and the energy that kept it going was the food, the feelings, instincts, emotions, physiology, and latterly the glands, all operating on the principle of natural selection; overlooking the rhetorical precept that a more proper analogy would be, not any natural organism including wolves and snakes, but the highly artificial dog or cow transformed by human purpose.

Here it is, when introducing purpose, as brought out clearly by Judd [296] in criticizing and summarizing the work of predecessors in the various social sciences, that another concept, Institutionism, also discontinuous from Darwin's organism, makes its appearance with its own principle, distinct from either Newton's Energy or Darwin's Scarcity—the principle which we name Willingness. For, on examination of the constituents which go to make up the concept of Institutionism, we find that their dominant character is the expectations of the future, distinguishable, for economic purposes, as Futurity, Custom, Sovereignty, Scarcity, and Efficiency. These are entirely different from, yet founded upon, the Pressure, Volume, and Time which make up Newton's mechanism with its principle of Energy. And they are different from, but founded upon, the heredity, variability, overpopulation, struggle, death, and survival which make up Darwin's principle of Scarcity.

Hence it is more than poetic metaphor that has led economic theory through the stages of mechanism and organism to the stage of going concerns. These metaphorical theories have been even a correct use of analogy in the scientific sense of similarity arising out of similar functional relations. But the analogies were too narrow. They did not include the artificiality introduced by human purpose. Hence they became metaphors. Modern economics is subordinating, in a practical way, these principles of energy and scarcity under the larger principle of willingness, and its major problem is to bring them together again as parts of a functioning whole.

Thus a going plant is, not a "mechanism," but a machine, from the standpoint of producing use-values by overcoming the resistances of nature, and the ratio of input of human energy to the output of use-value is calculated in the same way as the ratio of input of water-power to the output of electric energy. This is the efficiency

[296] Judd, C. H., chapter on "Social Institutions and the Individual" in *The Psychology of Social Institutions* (1926), 56–77.

dimension of a going concern, and the one which engineering economists assume to be the whole. It is machinism, not mechanism.

Likewise a going business is similar to an organism in that the principle of scarcity runs through all of its transactions. This principle takes the form of conflict, variability, competition, survival, but also, as Hume pointed out, it takes the form of ethics, property, and justice. Hence it is artificial selection, not natural selection.

This is because the peculiar way in which the going concern takes up the principles of efficiency and scarcity is through the principle of Futurity in its many aspects, which, taken together, are none other than the principle of Willingness. The separation in fact of these separate fields is impossible. Yet they must be separated in thought by their own terminology, as Darwin did for organism and Newton for mechanism; and they are separated in fact by Smith's division of labor, before they can be brought together, in thought and fact, in the functional processes of going concerns. All organisms are mechanisms, but with scarcity added. All concerns are organisms and mechanisms, but with purpose added. It is this added purpose that becomes the general principle requiring to be worked out within its own field and its own terminology, so that the principles of mechanism and organism to which it is added become themselves subordinate and greatly changed, yet necessary in their revised form.

This separation in thought and fact and then reunion in the concept of a whole applies, in detail, to the transactions whose expected orderly repetition is the going concern. Managerial transactions pertain to the mechanism and efficiency of the concern; bargaining transactions to the principle of scarcity throughout the concern; executive, legislative, and judicial procedure to the unity and continuity of the concern through subordination of members to the whole by the rationing of benefits and burdens. And these transactions, since the principle of scarcity runs through them, have curious analogies to the factors which Darwin discovered in organisms. Custom, the repetition of transactions, is analogous to heredity; the duplication and multiplication of transactions arise from pressure of population; their variability is evident, and out of the variabilities come changes in customs and survival. But here the survival is the "artificial selection" of good customs and punishment of bad customs, and it is this artificiality, which is merely the human will in action, that converts mechanisms into machines, living organisms into institutionalized minds, and unorganized custom or habit into orderly transactions and going concerns.

For man's mind is more than a living organism. As organism it is only a highly developed brain. This brain is a mere part of an animal organism until it has become "institutionalized."[297] Thereupon it acquires a widened scope of activity which we call mind and will. Its first institution is signs, words, numbers, speech, writing, which we call the language of words and numbers. This is a habit for the individual and a compulsory custom handed down from generations of individuals—in short, an institution. Man's other institutions are fire, tools, machinery, family, government, and so on,[298] whose enduring repetition, upon the artificial principle of proportioning the limiting and complementary factors, we name going concerns.

Hence man is more than organism—he is institutionism, and it is only the institutionalized mind that evolves that remarkable time-dimension of economic activity to which we give the name, Futurity. Futurity is institutional—the isolated infant and man, like an animal, would know little or nothing about it. This institutional extension of the organism's brain into remote future time is inseparable from its extension into remote space. And it is these two institutionalized extensions of brain activity that make possible the highly developed modern going concerns in industry and government which give orders around the world and to generations unborn.

As to Time, the energy of mechanisms operates without any reference whatever to its passage, and the Time factor which is introduced into the measurement of output is solely an external operation of the human mind, not internal for the mechanism itself. The concept of Time is constructed only by the institutionalized mind.

But scarcity is essentially a matter of the passage of time for the organism itself, since, even in the lowest organisms, there is always an interval between the effort to obtain a share of the limited food supply and the satisfaction of wants derived from that share. This is the germ of Futurity. In animal life this interval of time is so short that the response to the stimuli of want is properly described as instinctive. Instinctive effort is provided by heredity and scarcity but the interval of time between effort and satisfaction is so short that the response, by analogy to mechanics, is said to be automatic or direct. But a strictly automatic or direct response, without an interval of time, is true only of mechanisms, for they experience no wants or efforts and no interval between effort and satisfaction. Their energy flows on regardless of the necessity of distinguishing

[297] See the illuminating discussion of the "institutionalized mind" in Jordan, E., *Forms of Individuality, an Inquiry into the Grounds of Order in Human Relations* (1927), 133–187.

[298] See Sumner, W. G., and Keller, A. S., for an exhaustive study of institutions in *The Science of Society*, 4 vols. (1927–28).

between external objects that satisfy wants and those that do not, or that must be avoided.

Hence in the organism is also the germ of choice of alternatives, whereas mechanisms do not choose. Moreover, this interval of time is, of course, an interval between present and future—present action which is the response and future satisfaction from which proceeds the stimulus. But the interval is short enough so that it can be bridged by heredity and instinct without the aid of reason and social institutions. It is instinctive time, not institutional time.

Thus it is that in the principle of scarcity, which came into the world with living organisms, is found the germs of all that which afterwards we characterize as the principle of Willingness. And it may be that here the science of institutions can be made continuous with the science of organisms, which has not yet been understood in the case of the metabolism that converts dead matter into living flesh. Yet in the futurity-dimensions of present activity, afforded by the expectations of institutions, the human organism converts future happenings into present action. How this happens physiologically we do not know. What we say of Time holds of Space. It is only institutionalized brains that compass the world, and they do it through the going concerns and machines that serve as instruments.

In these two extensions into future time and distant space, with almost immortality and ubiquity, the going concern is more than mechanism and more than organism. It is just what the language of everyday man says it is and the courts have taken over—a very precious going concern that embodies his expectations of beneficial transactions and calls on him for loyalty, patriotism, and personification.

We have previously indicated the feasible position which so-called "behavioristic psychology" should occupy in economic theory, when once behavior is analyzed as performance, avoidance, forbearance. These latter are dimensions of the will-in-action that unite law and economics. The word "behaviorism" has been appropriated by those who treat the individual in purely individualistic fashion as a physiological and anatomical mechanism.[299] But, in economics, the individual is a participant in transactions and a member of going concerns. Here it is not so much his physiology, his "glands" and "brain patterns" that interest us—it is whether he performs, forbears or avoids, as a whole personality. The recent "behaviorism" has done much in child psychology and advertising, but not much in the behaviorism of going concerns. Here it is that the will means

[299] E. g., Watson, J. B., Behaviorism (1924).

individual and collective action in three physical and economic dimensions—performance, avoidance, forbearance—a kind of behavior unknown to any physical science and only incipient in the biological sciences, but capable of being analyzed and measured like electricity or gravity, in terms peculiar to itself.

Physical sciences got away from metaphorical entities such as "force," or "energy," not by rejecting the idea, but by changing it from unanalyzed souls, spirits, and entities into variable dimensions of motion. So with the will. We get away from it, not by rejecting it but by analyzing and measuring its motions. In getting away from the will because it is "metaphysical," the "behaviorists" jump over from the external behavior of the will to the internal behavior of metabolism, thinking that they have left no metaphysical gap between the will as one kind of behavior and physiology as a supposed similar kind of behavior. But there is an impassable gap. They are not continuous. Only by metaphysics—or rather by metaphor—is the gap filled. The lesson of other sciences would say that this metaphorical jump should not be made. Treat the individual will, we should say, as a whole in its own behavioristic dimensions, and let physiologists and anatomists treat the insides of the organism as another whole.

But let us, for our present purposes, forget physiology and anatomy—or rather, forget how it is that one kind of subjectivity, the mind, gets into or out of another kind of subjectivity, the physiological body—and let us analyze what the resultant whole, which is none other than the will, actually does. It performs, avoids, forbears, as a whole organism, and it does so in association with other wills, through transactions and going concerns, in expectation of joint results. Acting as a whole concern, through performance, forbearance, avoidance, the individual will is thus the behavioristic nexus of individuals that connects all the specific applications which we name the transactions and working rules of going concerns— expressed as opportunity, competition, power, rights, duties, liberties, exposures, uses, efficiencies, scarcities, expectancies—with the general principle that unites them all, which we name the principle of willingness.

In this analysis of human behavior, the concepts of time and motion differ entirely from the concepts of time and motion in all other sciences. We have traced all of MacLeod's fallacies to one fundamental defect—his concept of Time. We shall trace Veblen's fallacies to his failure to analyze Time. Paradoxically enough, while MacLeod had the concept of Future Time, he did not have the concept of Motion. We picture motion, by physical analogy, as a

Flow of Time. A flow of time, mathematically, is a zero point of time, the Present, moving forward without dimensions and therefore non-existent, between the incoming Future and the outgoing Past. This concept MacLeod did not have, though, in one connection, he represented the Present by zero. But psychologically the Present is an instant of time, as Peirce portrayed it, shading off less vividly in two directions, towards the Past and towards the Future. The Past is Memory, the Present is Sensation, the Future is Expectation. They all exist together in the mind, like the notes of a tune, at that present point of Time which is, not zero, but the present event, which is the present transaction. In this way Peirce converted Hume's skepticism into Pragmatism, and mathematics into willingness.

It is this pragmatic concept of time that enables us to make distinctions between different measurable dimensions of future time conforming to usage. The "present" is the Immediate Future, measurable institutionally in seconds. minutes, and perhaps an hour or two, but so short an interval of time that it practically involves no feeling of waiting or risking. The short-time future ranges from the "over-night" rate on the stock market to the 30, 40, or 90 days' period of the usual commercial loans, where the waiting is appreciable and therefore is measured. The long-time future is any duration in excess of short-time future. These distinctions are not so much arbitrary as they are customary, and are therefore all the more useful in a practical analysis of behavior. MacLeod assumed that Time somehow is objective, embodied as one of the dimensions of his saleable commodity, a debt, and that it therefore came in time-chunks, variable according to the period of the debt, like use-value or scarcity-value. But Time is wholly institutional. Mechanism and organism know nothing of Time. It comes in the expectations which dominate present behavior according to the customs of different classes of people, and the same classes in different transactions. The most accurate measurements of future time are made on the debt markets for short-time and long-time futurities. But in the processes of consumption, of play, exercise, work, and other familiar situations, it is the expectations of the instant future, so brief as not to be worth measuring, that dominate activity.

Thus the "flow of time," objectively, is the Motion of the Instant; while subjectively it is the stream of memory, sensation, expectation of the Instant, as well as the physiological metabolism of the living body. Since we can know these subjective motions only by the motions of the living creature which experiences them, the flow of time is the behavior of the individual in its dimensions of performance, avoidance, forbearance. Hence we have one kind of motion—individual performance, avoidance, forbearance—lying between and connecting two other kinds of motion—the external motions of the universe, including other human beings, and the internal physiological motions which somehow accompany memory, sensation, and expectation. It is this flow of human behavior as a whole, lying between the flow of external motion of the universe and other people and internal motions of physiology, accompanied mysteriously somehow by Memory, Sensation, and Expectation, that, in economics, we name Transactions and Going Concerns motivated by the principle of Willingness. It is the Human Flow of Time directed towards the future, and an economic theory based upon it is neither a materialistic theory of commodities, nor a subjective theory of sensations or physiology, but is a volitional theory of economic activity directed towards purposes in the future.

As to the classical and hedonic economists similar observations are called for. Our analysis of the will-in-action as performance, avoidance, forbearance, in view of the future, is superficial enough, but always the things nearest are the last investigated. The analysis gets away from the undue simplification which picks out only one quality of the will—that which is tied metaphorically to commodities by pain, pleasure, or diminishing utility, and which builds upon that metaphor a mathematical system of economic theory. But the individual will is a whole, in its own personality, operating through transactions and within concerns, which, in turn, are other wholes of concerted action.

Thus the transactional analysis of the will makes possible an economic theory which avoids that dualism of ethics and law on the one side, and economics on the other, which started with Smith and Bentham, because it combines in one concept, Willingness, the ethical and legal relations of rights, duties, liberties, and exposures of performance, avoidance, and forbearance with the economic analysis of Value and Valuation as Future discounted risk-value and scarcity-value.

These preliminaries make it possible to apply to transactions and going concerns the principle of limiting and complementary factors as both legal and economic factors. The two principles of scarcity and futurity explain the application. For the individual who would obtain advantages for self, the limiting factors are the particular behavior of self or others, at the time and place, upon which depends the complementary behavior of others. In a suit at law the limiting factor may be, at one time, the judge, at another the jury, at another the sheriff. In a manufacturing concern the limiting factor may be the mechanic, the foreman, the superintendent, even the scrub-woman, upon whose control, by means of the managerial transactions of command and obedience, the totality of transactions depends. The result of this control is a "going plant" as a whole with its measurable result—efficiency. It is out of these social relations of control over individual behavior, backed by the sanctions of collective control, that a right to command obedience may become the limiting factor in the sense of an immediate "right of action."

The foregoing "efficiency" relations are inseparable from "scarcity" relations, since here the question is as to the abundance or scarcity of the limiting and complementary factors when needed, and consequently as to the prices or taxes that must be paid to obtain them. Efficiency and scarcity are separable in analysis but not in reality, since they operate functionally upon each other in making up the going concern. The quantity of gasoline needed to operate a car, or number of mechanics or foremen needed to operate a plant, or number of judges to operate a bench, is separable in thought but not in fact from the price, or wage, or salary.

Thus the universality of the principle of limiting and complementary factors appears in all sciences in so far as the human will endeavors to operate the subject-matter for a purpose. Those factors are deemed important which are limited in amount relative to other factors. All of them must be present in expectation but only the supposed limiting ones are present in action. The complementary ones are in the future so far as action is concerned. If they are secure so as to be available when needed, then no attention is paid to them. They become the routine transactions of a status in the concern. Thus a person's "rights" exist now, and he "has rights," but in billions of transactions they are routine and not strategic. If they are secure, then only in one case out of billions do they become the limiting factor. If insecure, then everything else is dropped and armies go out to control the limiting factor.

This doctrine of limiting or strategic, and complementary or routine, factors and transactions measurable as efficiency, scarcity, and futurity, seem to be all that there is in the metaphysical problems of "essences" and "existences." Essences are the secure expectations of complementary factors, but existences are the insecurities of limiting factors upon whose present control the security of the others depends. Plato's "essences," however, were far remote from even these expectations, for they were eternal entities never expected to be realized, and they stood to reality in the relation of an eternal whole entirely separated from its changing parts. But in the modern meaning of "essences" they are an external existing something, even an "absolute," that awaits a time when it shall come down and be embodied in actual behavior. If this is what is meant, then "essences" are merely the expectations of complementary factors. This substitution of "essences" for mere expectations, seems to have been done in the case of Kant's Pure Reason, Santayana's Pure Essence, and the neo-Kantian distinction between Essences and Existences. MacLeod's and the lawyers' "natural rights" seem also to be a similar preëxisting essence waiting to be discovered as an existence in actual transactions.

But if we examine the meanings which these non-existences have in the actual process of transactions, we find that an essence or abstraction is simply an expected similarity of repetition when needed. It is not an idea of an eternal absolute or external nothing previously existing that comes down and gets embodied. It is futurity embodying itself in present values and valuations, and constituting a present expectancy. It is, indeed, a very real expectation, not attended to, however, because it is secure, much as air is a real expectation not attended to unless it gets too hot, too cold, or too scarce.

Thus Kelsen rightly holds that the "essence" of legal relations is found in the two items of an "operative fact" and an "enforcement" by an official, and he denies that the terms right, duty, power, liability, etc., are "legal" terms in the sense of pure law. They indicate social or ethical relations, not legal relations.[300] Much illumination and accuracy are contributed by Kelsen in this analysis, but we reach a similar result by way of the pragmatic doctrine of Futurity and the economic doctrine of Limiting and Complementary Factors. MacLeod's abstract right now existing becomes an expectation of Kelsen's legal compulsion indicated by a "right of action" in case such is necessary in order to obtain the commodity, service, or money claimed from another person. Assuming that an established system of law may be expected to continue, the "essence" of legal relations is merely the expectations of similarity of repetition by officials in the compulsory transactions of compelling obedience on the part of citizens. If so expected, it is not, in the many billions of transactions, the limiting factor to which value is now imputed. The limiting factor is the immediate behavior of the private parties—their promises, the kind, quality, amount of economic goods, etc., as the case may be. The expected similarity of official behavior is highly decisive in any estimate of present value, but it is not the limiting factor at the time of action, if its expectation is

300 Voegelin, Erich, "Kelsen's Pure Theory of Law," *Political Science Quarterly*, Vol. XLII, June 1927, 276; Kelsen, Hans, *Allgemeine Staatslehre* (1925).

secure. The decisions of courts effect great changes in values and great transfers of value from individuals and classes to other individuals and classes. It is the expectations thus created that are designated rights, duties, liberties, exposures. These are, indeed, the social and economic expectations based upon the expected political power of citizens, collectively or individually, in controlling the behavior of legislators, courts, and executives. This is not Platonism, or neo-Kantism, or Absolutism—it is Analytic Pragmatism.

The reconciliation between essences and existences is in the pragmatic doctrine of Futurity. Rights and Values *now* exist, at the instant of action, but they exist as futurities. They make up a status of expectation. Legal Power does not now exist in action, if it is not exercised, but it does exist in the status of security of expectations, which is just as good and even better. It is the future behavior of which rights is the name of the present expectation. Legal Power is the future itself, Right is its futurity. Value is the present expectation of future limited supply of goods to be obtained by means of rights.

These are not abstractions—they are expectations—the expectations of collective action. These rights, values, and powers exist, all of them, at the present time, but they exist only as the present status of expectations, ready to be "embodied" when needed in transactions, at which time they will be limiting factors in the then present. These mental expectations are Locke's "ideas" and Plato's and Kant's "essences," regardless of time, and therefore they are Whitehead's "eternal," "timeless" principles and concepts. But concretely, pragmatically, and timefully, they exist as limiting or complementary factors at the moment of action. Even then the complementary factors exist only as futurities—yet futurities are the only "objects" on which mankind acts. They are Peirce's "realities," their "essence" is Future Time, their present "existence" is Expectation or Status, and their present external reality is the flow of transactions and going concerns.

It is these doctrines of futurity and of limiting and complementary factors that are the economists' answer to the metaphysical problem of philosophers since the time of David Hume. Hume, enlarging on Berkeley, had held that we know only the sensations of objects at the moment, and that we do not know, by our physical senses, either the relations between our sensations or the relations between things of the external world from which our sensations arise. During the century and a half since Hume, the constant theme of all philosophy has been nothing else but giving a decent status to relations, the most outstanding solution having been Kant's transcendentalism. But his solution separated a world of the absolute, which consisted only of relations, from the world of empiricism which consisted only of experiences. Then in James' Radical Empiricism, an extension of Peirce's pragmatism, the preceding doctrines of empiricism from Stewart, Hodgson, and Peirce were developed into a psychology wherein the internal "known" and the external "known" are two sides of the same functional process, such that not only sensations are identical with objects sensed, but also the reactions between the objects were identical with sensations of the relation. Further developments have been made in the recent Gestalt psychology, which is the German rendering of American pragmatism. However these various philosophies and psychologies of empiricism, rationalism, realism, pragmatism, Gestaltism, etc., may turn out as to the ultimate nature of the will,[301] the economic doctrine of the will is frankly an environmental or institutional will wherein the changing relations between the limiting and complementary factors are directly known or expected through the lessons of experience. Herein it is Dewey's psychology that most nearly fits the case. The human will experiences the *relations* between factors, as well as the factors themselves, else it could not know how to get remote results by controlling the strategic factors which in turn modify other factors; and a result far greater than the individual could accomplish is actually accomplished by machines and institutions.

It is indeed from the relation between limiting and complementary factors that the mind derives the ideas of cause and effect. By controlling the limiting factor at the right time, right amount, right place, it controls the other factors and the result is a going machine, a going business, a going concern. This control has one comprehensive name, Timeliness. Timeliness is, indeed, learned by experience, and is a part of that feeling of fitness which cannot be imparted by mere intellect. It furnishes the difference between Art and Science, between the abstract concepts of Willingness and of the Concrete Will in action at a particular time, place, and environment. The scientist or philosopher may devote himself to the abstract concepts, regardless of Time, but the man of affairs must attend to

[301] Cf. Stewart, Dugald, *Collected Works* (1854–1860); Hodgson, Shadworth H., *The Theory of Practice*, 2 vols. (1870); Peirce, C. S., *op. cit.*; James, Wm., *Essays in Radical Empiricism* (1912); Dewey, John, *Human Nature and Conduct* (1922); Bradley, F. H., *The Principles of Logic*, 2 vols. (1883, 1922); Evans, D. L., *New Realism and Old Realism* (1928); Smuts, J. C., *Holism and Evolution* (1926); Köhler, W., *The Mentality of Apes* (translated by Ella Winter, 1927), and *Gestalt Psychology* (1929); Koffka, K., *Growth of the Mind* (translated by R. M. Ogden, 1924); Peterman, Bruno, *The Gestalt Theory and the Problem of Configuration* (translated 1932).

their timeliness.   Cause and Effect have properly been eliminated from physical sciences, and equations have been substituted.   Mathematical economists incline also to eliminate cause and effect from economics.   But cause and effect are of the essence of economics and of its principle of willingness, which accomplishes future ends by timely control of the present limiting factors.

Thus we have an economic concept of the Will—the Will-in-action, guided by purpose and expectation.   Both the empirical theory of cause and effect set forth by J. S. Mill and the absolutist theory set forth by Bradley [302] are realized in the economic theory of the Will controlling the limiting factors in order to multiply the future output for all, or to acquire a larger income for self by diminishing the income of others, or of extending the Will to distant space or distant future by control of corporations or other concerns, each of which, in its own field, depends upon the best proportioning, by means of transactions, of all limiting and complementary factors in view of what may be intended.

[302] Mill, J. S., *A System of Logic* (1st ed. 1848; citation to 8th ed., 1925), 211–241; Bradley, F. H., *The Principles of Logic* (2d ed. 1922), 583 ff.

Printed in the United States
by Baker & Taylor Publisher Services